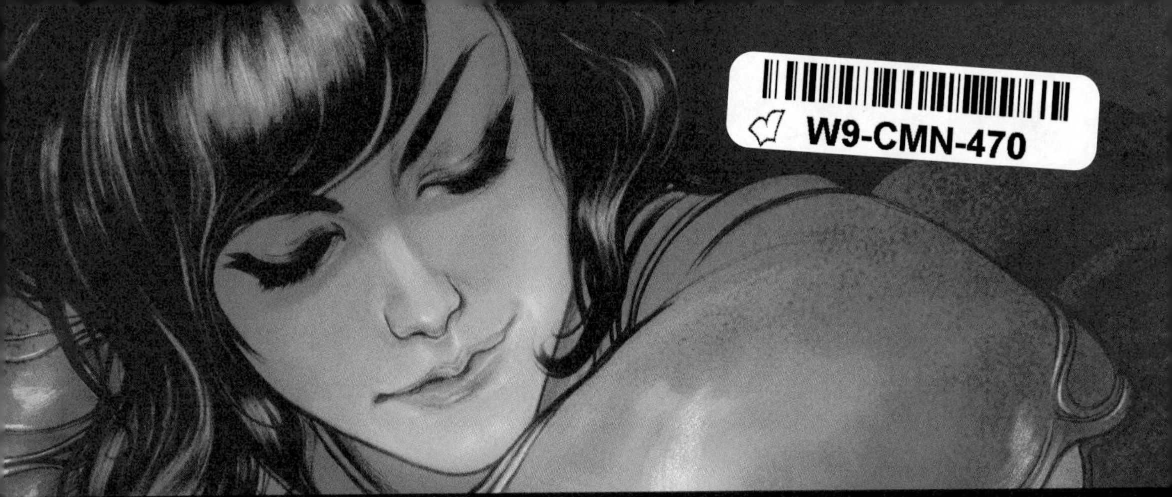

FABLES: CAMELOT

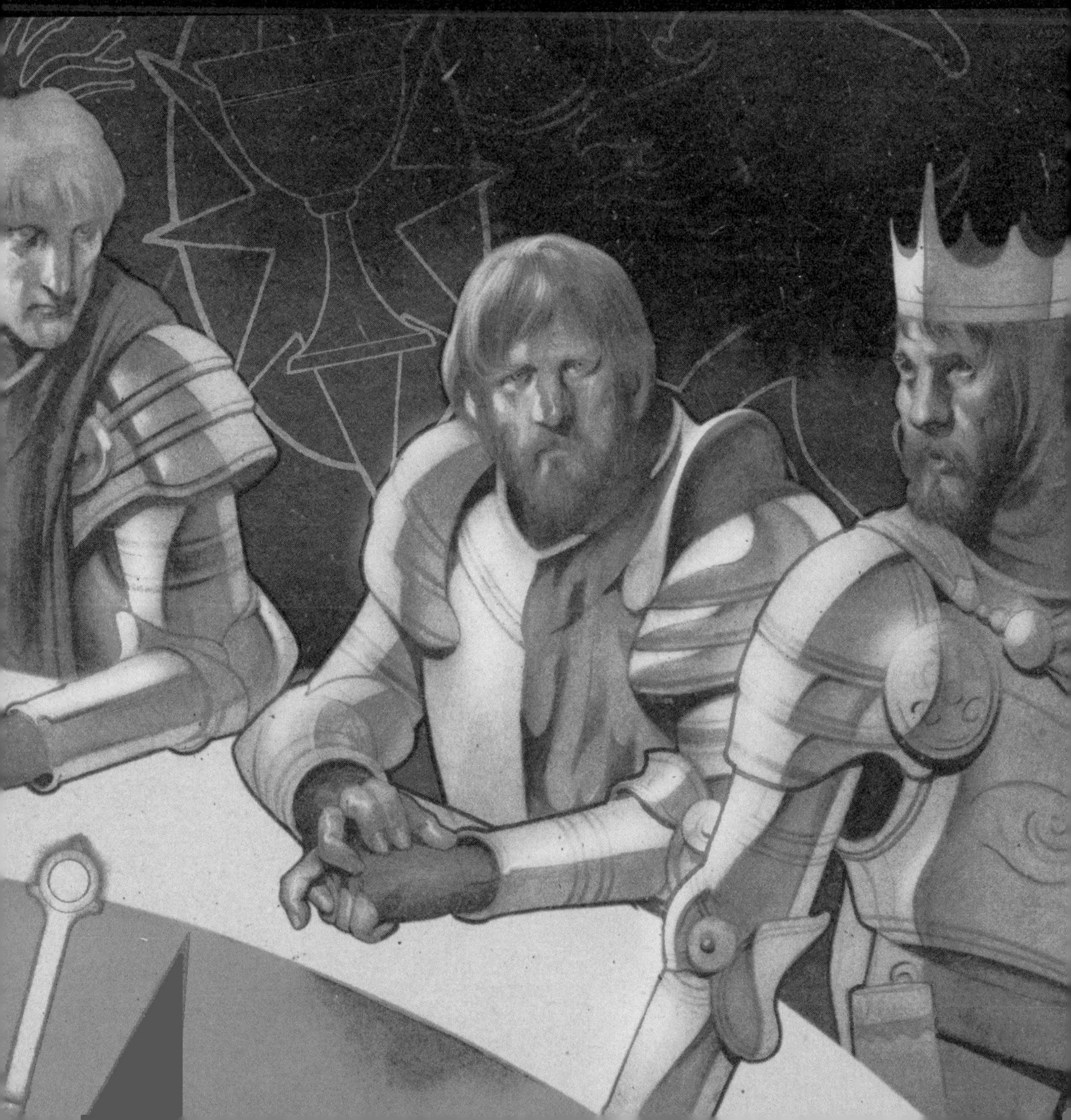

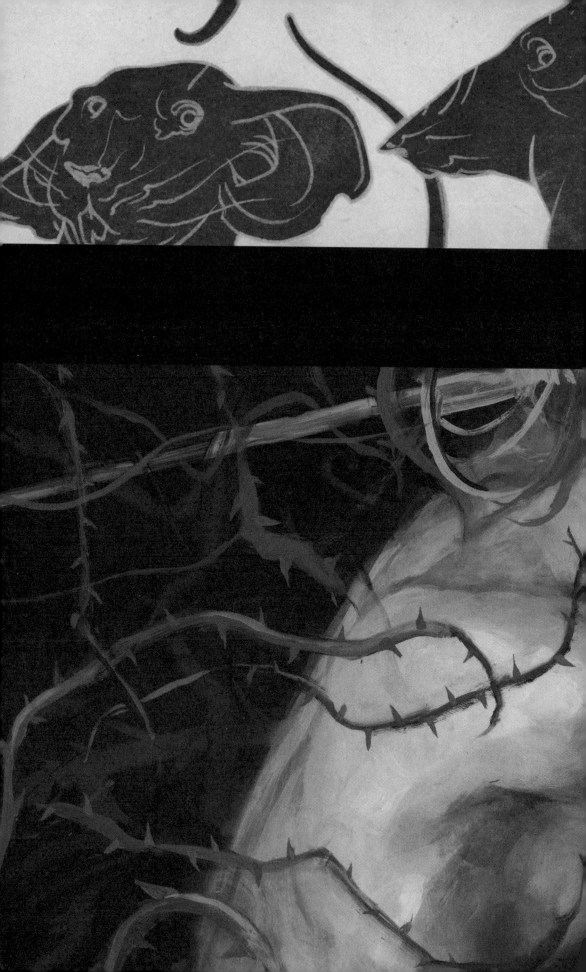

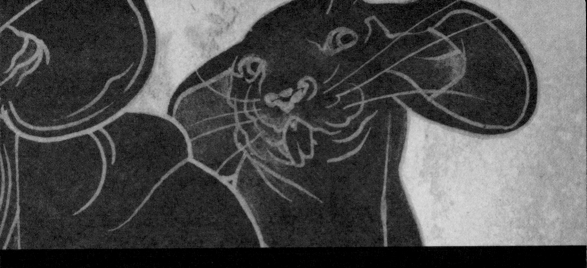

FABLES: CAMELOT

FABLES CREATED BY BILL WILLINGHAM

Bill Willingham
Writer

Mark Buckingham
Steve Leialoha
Russ Braun
Barry Kitson
Andrew Pepoy
Gary Erskine
Artists

Lee Loughridge
Colorist

Todd Klein
Letterer

Daniel Dos Santos
Cover Art

Joao Ruas
John Van Fleet
Mark Buckingham
Greg Ruth
Daniel Dos Santos
George Pratt
Christopher Moeller
Nimit Malavia
Original Series Covers

SHELLY BOND
Executive Editor – Vertigo and Editor – Original Series

GREGORY LOCKARD
Associate Editor – Original Series

SARA MILLER
Assistant Editor – Original Series

SCOTT NYBAKKEN
Editor

ROBBIN BROSTERMAN
Design Director – Books

HANK KANALZ
Senior VP – Vertigo and Integrated Publishing

DIANE NELSON
President

DAN DIDIO and **JIM LEE**
Co-Publishers

GEOFF JOHNS
Chief Creative Officer

AMIT DESAI
Senior VP – Marketing and Franchise Management

AMY GENKINS
Senior VP – Business and Legal Affairs

NAIRI GARDINER
Senior VP – Finance

JEFF BOISON
VP – Publishing Planning

MARK CHIARELLO
VP – Art Direction and Design

JOHN CUNNINGHAM
VP – Marketing

TERRI CUNNINGHAM
VP – Editorial Administration

LARRY GANEM
VP – Talent Relations and Services

ALISON GILL
Senior VP – Manufacturing and Operations

JAY KOGAN
VP – Business and Legal Affairs, Publishing

JACK MAHAN
VP – Business Affairs, Talent

NICK NAPOLITANO
VP – Manufacturing Administration

SUE POHJA
VP – Book Sales

FRED RUIZ
VP – Manufacturing Operations

COURTNEY SIMMONS
Senior VP – Publicity

BOB WAYNE
Senior VP – Sales

To Ken, with continuing gratitude.
— Bill Willingham

To the soundtrack of my average working day:
BBC Radio 4, keeping me educated, informed, and
entertained, and to the many bands and artists
whose music sets the rhythm to which I work
and inspire me to draw, including The Tangent,
Frost*, Transatlantic, Yes, King Crimson, Genesis,
Stackridge, The Albion Band, Fairport Convention,
Pendragon, Arena, IQ, Spock's Beard, The Flower
Kings, Jethro Tull, XTC, Ben Folds, Kate Bush, It
Bites, Magenta, Gentle Giant, Amanda Palmer,
Chris Opperman, The Jane Austen Argument, The
Divine Comedy, Tori Amos... and many, many more.
— Mark Buckingham

Logo design by Brainchild Studios/NYC

FABLES: CAMELOT

Published by DC Comics. Copyright © 2014 Bill Willingham
and DC Comics. All Rights Reserved.

Originally published in single magazine form as FABLES
130-140. Copyright © 2013, 2014 Bill Willingham and
DC Comics. All Rights Reserved. All characters, their
distinctive likenesses and related elements featured in this
publication are trademarks of Bill Willingham. VERTIGO
is a trademark of DC Comics. The stories, characters and
incidents featured in this publication are entirely fictional.
DC Comics does not read or accept unsolicited submissions
of ideas, stories or artwork.

DC Comics, 1700 Broadway, New York, NY 10019
A Warner Bros. Entertainment Company.
Printed in the USA. First Printing.
ISBN: 978-1-4012-4516-0

Library of Congress Cataloging-in-Publication Data

Willingham, Bill, author.
  Fables. Volume 20, Camelot / Bill Willingham, Mark
Buckingham.
    pages cm
  ISBN 978-1-4012-4516-0 (paperback)
  1. Fairy tales — Comic books, strips, etc. 2. Legends
— Comic books, strips, etc. 3. Graphic novels. I.
Buckingham, Mark, illustrator. II. Title. III. Title: Camelot.
  PN6727.W52F434 2014
  741.5'973—dc23
                              2014010271

SUSTAINABLE FORESTRY INITIATIVE
Certified Chain of Custody
Promoting Sustainable Forestry
www.sfiprogram.org
SFI-01042
APPLIES TO TEXT STOCK ONLY

Table of Contents

WHO'S WHO IN FABLETOWN

RODNEY AND JUNE

Transformed from carved wood into flesh and blood to serve as spies for the Adversary, this husband and wife switched sides to serve Fabletown instead.

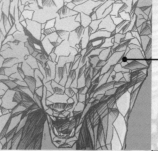

BIGBY

The celebrated Big Bad Wolf, now reduced to a pile of broken glass.

HOPE

Rose Red's patron, the divine embodiment of this most necessary of human attributes.

OZMA

The misleadingly youthful-looking leader of Fabletown's wizards and witches.

DOCTOR SWINEHEART

The greatest surgeon of this or any other world.

LAKE

A powerful servant of the Fates, she both collects and assigns destinies.

LEIGH DUGLAS

Jack Sprat's newly lean widow, groomed for revenge by her recently deceased patron, Mister Dark.

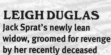

RED RIDING HOOD

Flycatcher's best gal.

WINTER WOLF

Another child of Snow and Bigby, she has taken up the mantle of her late grandfather to become the new North Wind.

AMBROSE WOLF

The most cautious of Snow and Bigby's cubs, he is destined to record their tragic story for the ages.

THE STORY SO FAR

As Bigby set off to search the known worlds for his missing children, his beloved Snow White stayed in the mundane world to care for their remaining cubs. But almost immediately a new and unexpected threat presented itself, in the form of an important figure from Snow's past — so far in her past, in fact

SNOW WHITE

Fabletown's former deputy mayor, wife of Bigby, and mother to their seven cubs.

ROSE RED

Snow White's sister and the leader of the non-human Fable community.

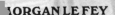

MORGAN LE FEY

The onetime antagonist of King Arthur and a valuable member of Fabletown's magical community.

KING COLE

The once and future mayor of Fabletown.

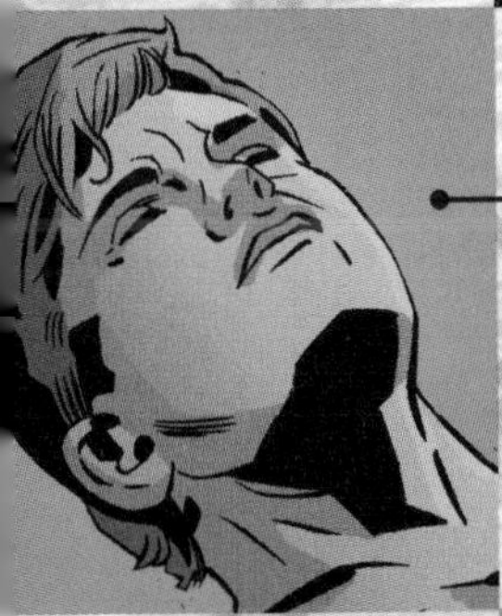

PRINCE BRANDISH

Snow White's first husband, and a stickler for marital fidelity.

FLYCATCHER

The former Frog Prince and Fabletown janitor, now the ruler of the Kingdom of Haven in the liberated Homelands.

WEYLAND SMITH

A blacksmith and craftsman of great renown, and one of Haven's founding citizens.

THERESE WOLF

Snow and Bigby's wayward daughter, newly returned from a life-altering trial.

MADDY

Also known as the Invisible Walker, this Fable is stealthier than an owl covered in coal dust.

GEPPETTO

Fabletown's former Adversary, now a much-reviled fellow citizen.

But Prince Brandish of Castle Lancedore, Protector of the Golden Realm and Marshal of the West, was very real indeed, and so was his claim on his long-lost bride. As Snow White's first husband, Brandish was protected by sacred oaths as well as some obscenely powerful magic, and he wasted no time in asserting his rights. After imprisoning Snow in Castle Dark, he faced off against Bigby in a duel to the death — a fate that proceeded to claim them both. Or so it seemed.

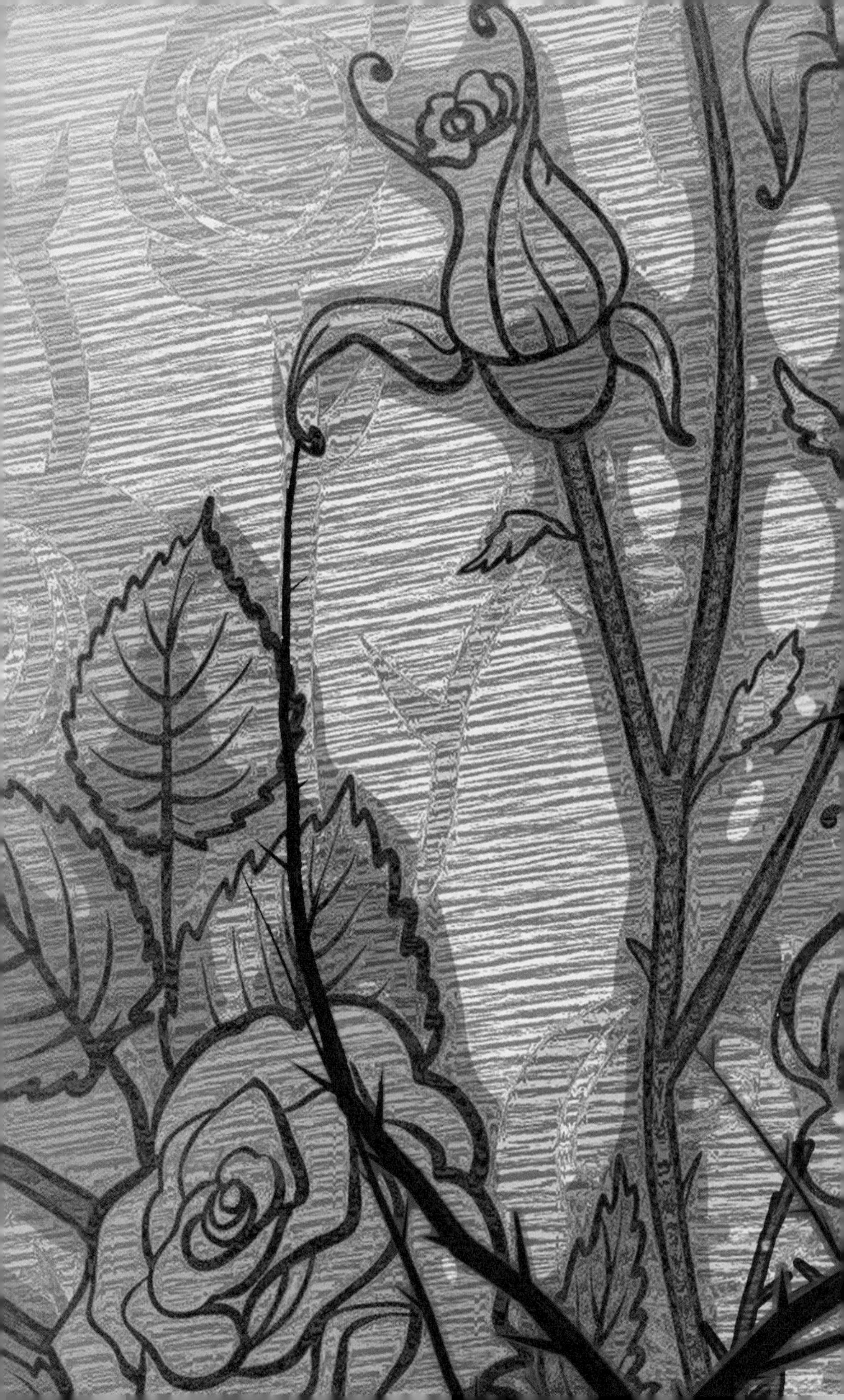

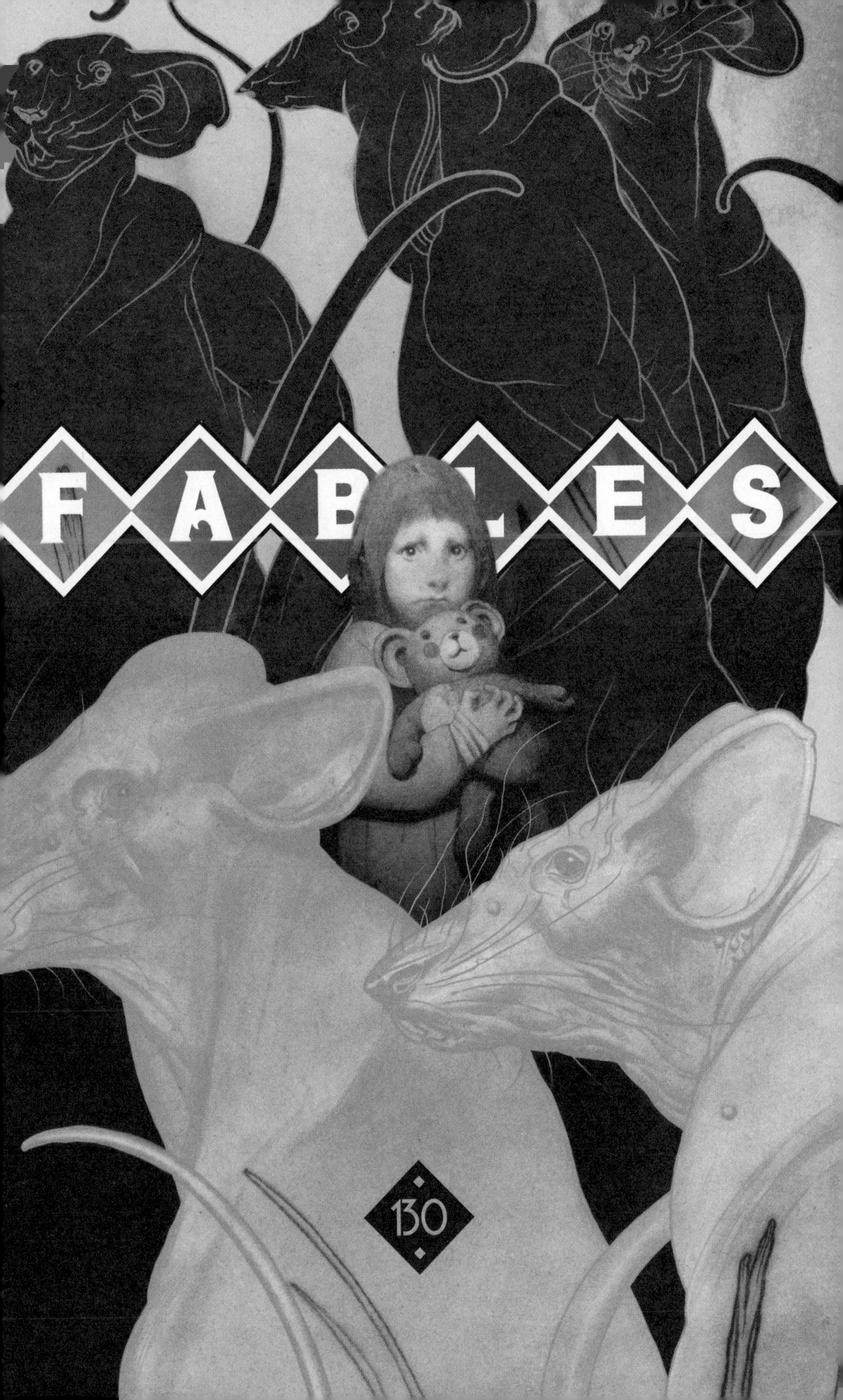
FABLES
130

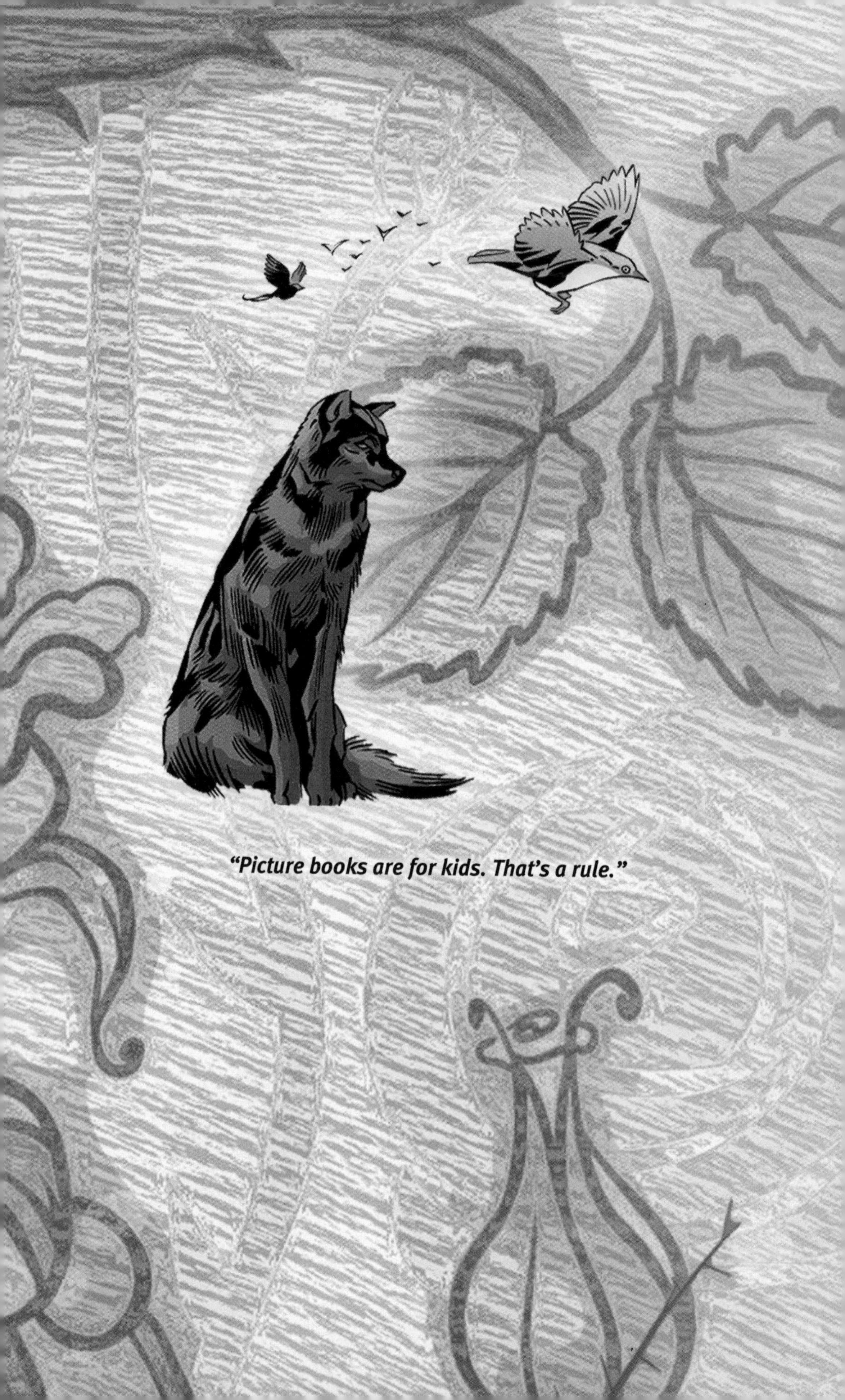

"Picture books are for kids. That's a rule."

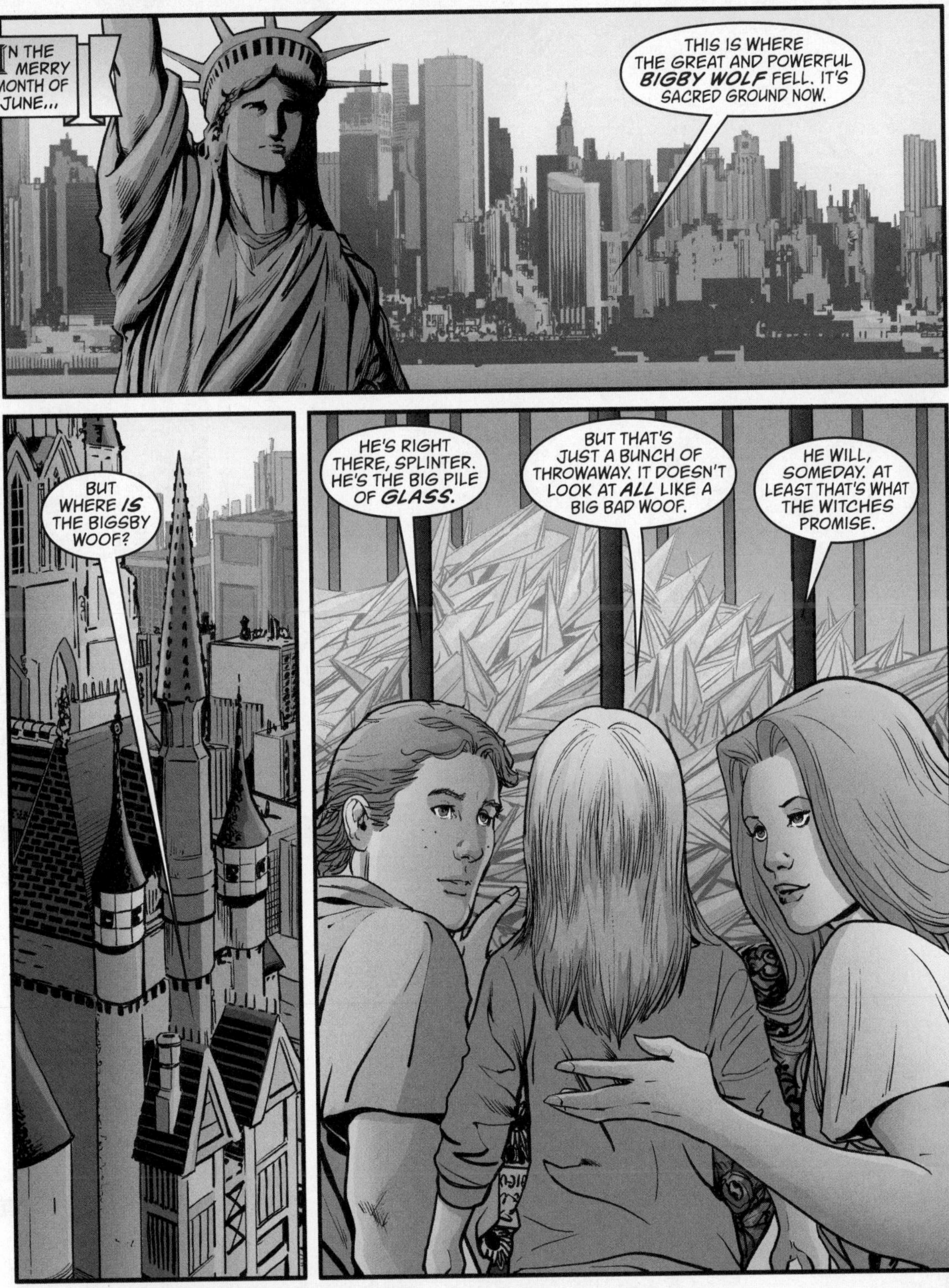
IN THE MERRY MONTH OF JUNE...
THIS IS WHERE THE GREAT AND POWERFUL BIGBY WOLF FELL. IT'S SACRED GROUND NOW.
BUT WHERE IS THE BIGSBY WOOF?
HE'S RIGHT THERE, SPLINTER. HE'S THE BIG PILE OF GLASS.
BUT THAT'S JUST A BUNCH OF THROWAWAY. IT DOESN'T LOOK AT ALL LIKE A BIG BAD WOOF.
HE WILL, SOMEDAY. AT LEAST THAT'S WHAT THE WITCHES PROMISE.

JUNEBUG

In the merry month of June, the young daughter of two former wooden children of Geppetto gets a story all her own, if only by virtue of her name.

BILL WILLINGHAM writer/creator **BARRY KITSON** artist **GARY ERSKINE** finishes pp 4-11 **LEE LOUGHRIDGE** colors **TODD KLEIN** letters

JOÃO RUAS cover **GREGORY LOCKARD** associate editor **SHELLY BOND** editor

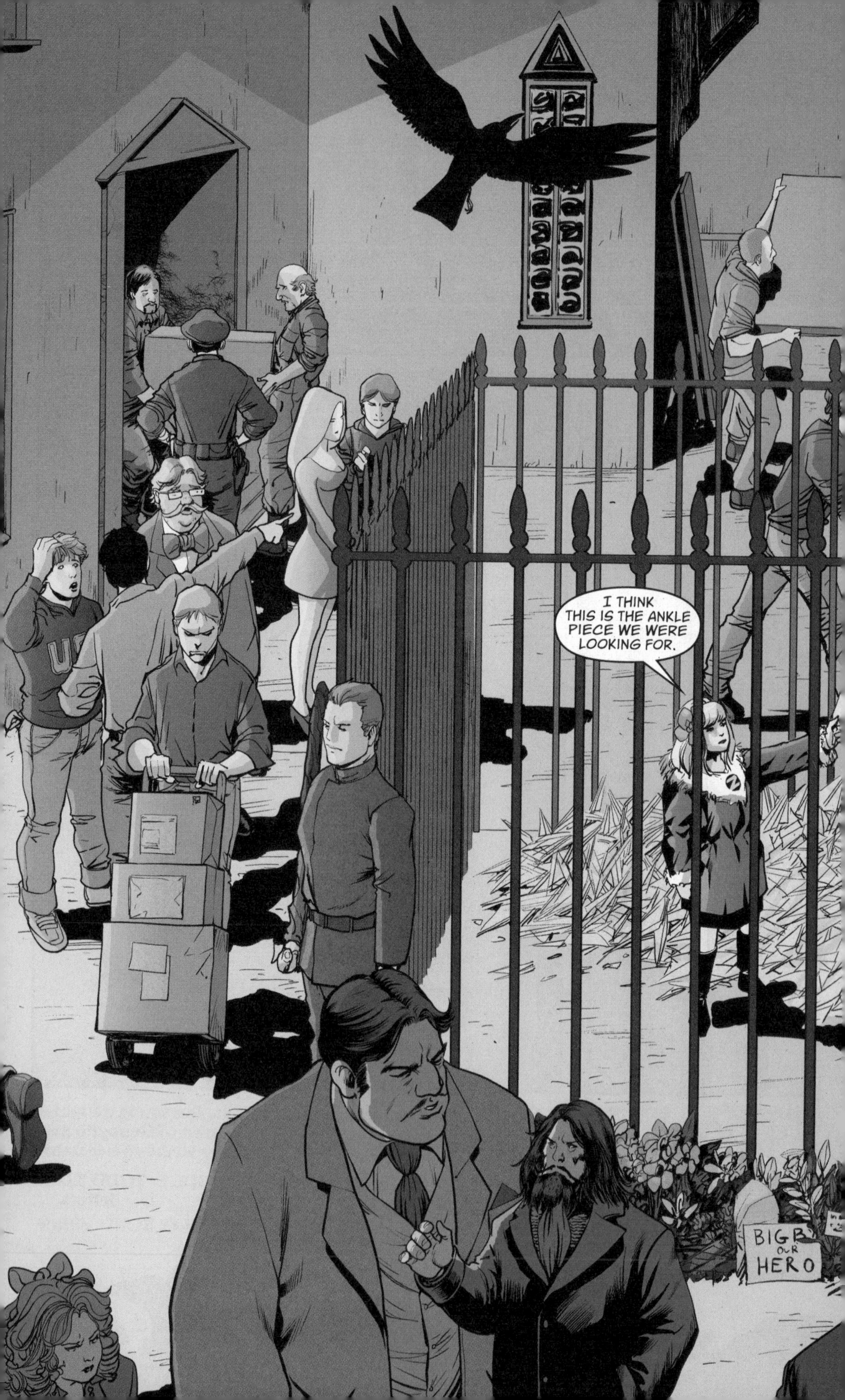
I THINK THIS IS THE ANKLE PIECE WE WERE LOOKING FOR.
BIGB OUR HERO

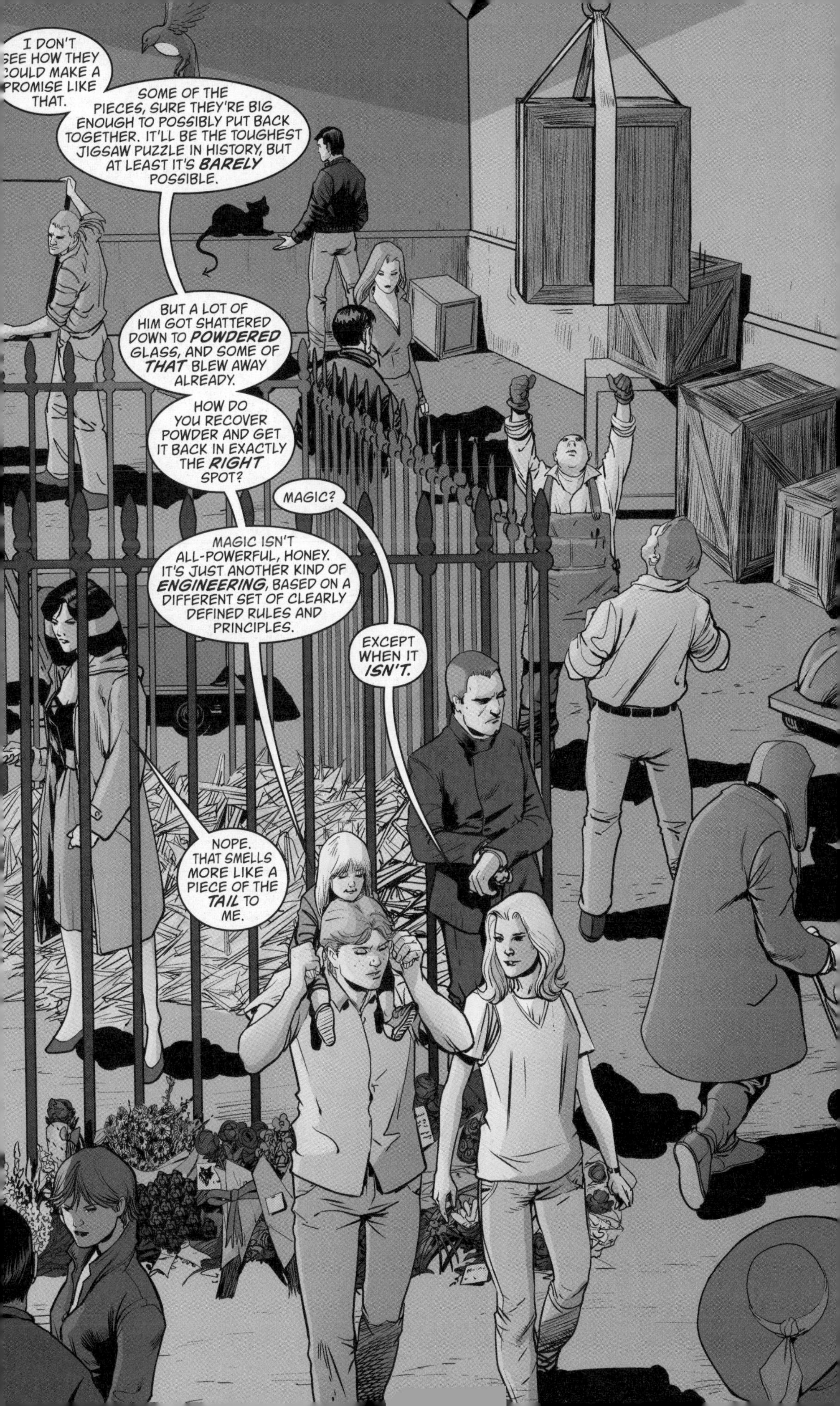

I DON'T SEE HOW THEY COULD MAKE A PROMISE LIKE THAT.
SOME OF THE PIECES, SURE THEY'RE BIG ENOUGH TO POSSIBLY PUT BACK TOGETHER. IT'LL BE THE TOUGHEST JIGSAW PUZZLE IN HISTORY, BUT AT LEAST IT'S ***BARELY*** POSSIBLE.
BUT A LOT OF HIM GOT SHATTERED DOWN TO ***POWDERED*** GLASS, AND SOME OF ***THAT*** BLEW AWAY ALREADY.
HOW DO YOU RECOVER POWDER AND GET IT BACK IN EXACTLY THE ***RIGHT*** SPOT?
MAGIC?
MAGIC ISN'T ALL-POWERFUL, HONEY. IT'S JUST ANOTHER KIND OF ***ENGINEERING***, BASED ON A DIFFERENT SET OF CLEARLY DEFINED RULES AND PRINCIPLES.
EXCEPT WHEN IT ***ISN'T.***
NOPE. THAT SMELLS MORE LIKE A PIECE OF THE ***TAIL*** TO ME.

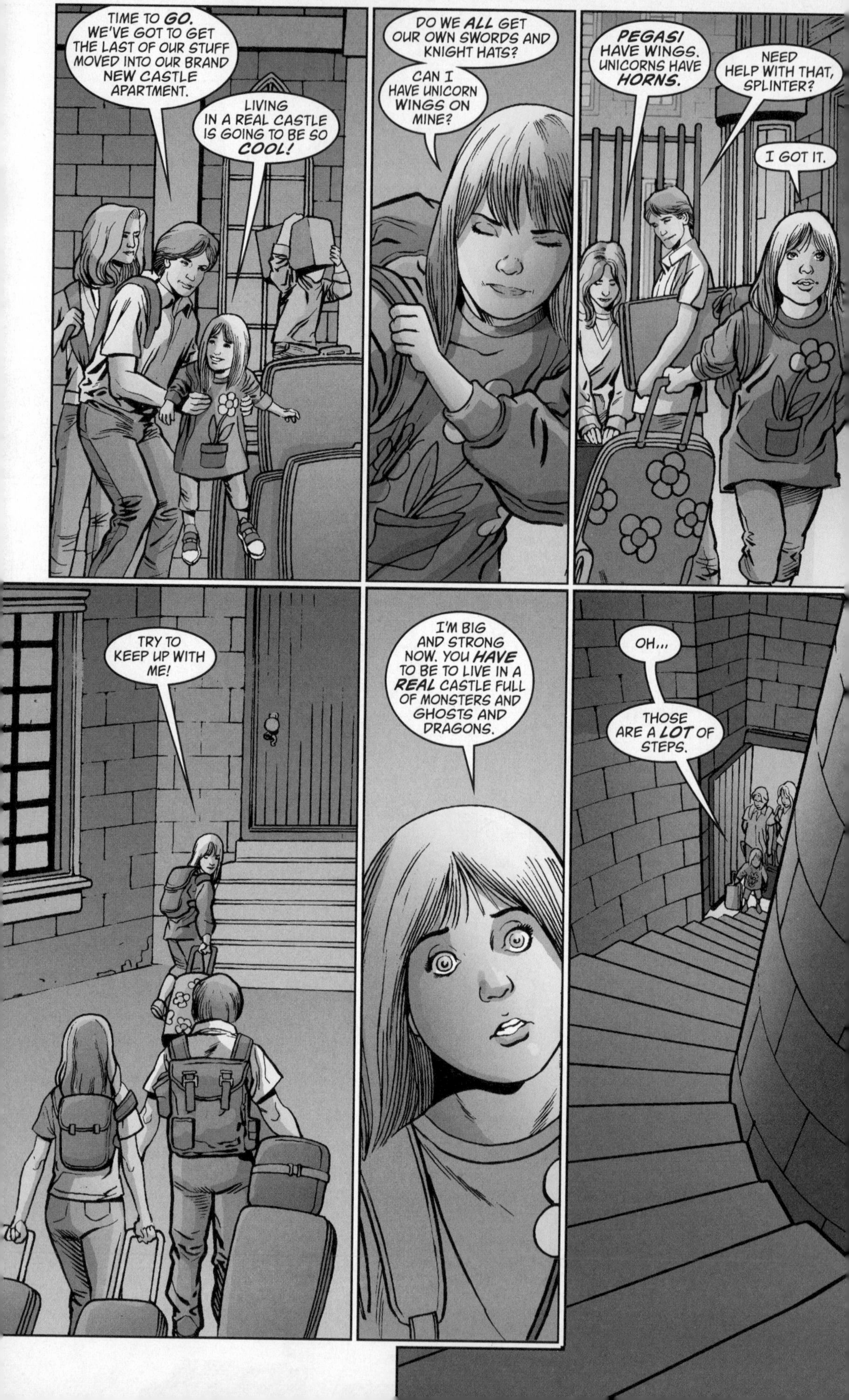
TIME TO GO. WE'VE GOT TO GET THE LAST OF OUR STUFF MOVED INTO OUR BRAND NEW CASTLE APARTMENT.
LIVING IN A REAL CASTLE IS GOING TO BE SO COOL!
DO WE ALL GET OUR OWN SWORDS AND KNIGHT HATS?
CAN I HAVE UNICORN WINGS ON MINE?
PEGASI HAVE WINGS. UNICORNS HAVE HORNS.
NEED HELP WITH THAT, SPLINTER?
I GOT IT.
TRY TO KEEP UP WITH ME!
I'M BIG AND STRONG NOW. YOU HAVE TO BE TO LIVE IN A REAL CASTLE FULL OF MONSTERS AND GHOSTS AND DRAGONS.
OH...
THOSE ARE A LOT OF STEPS.

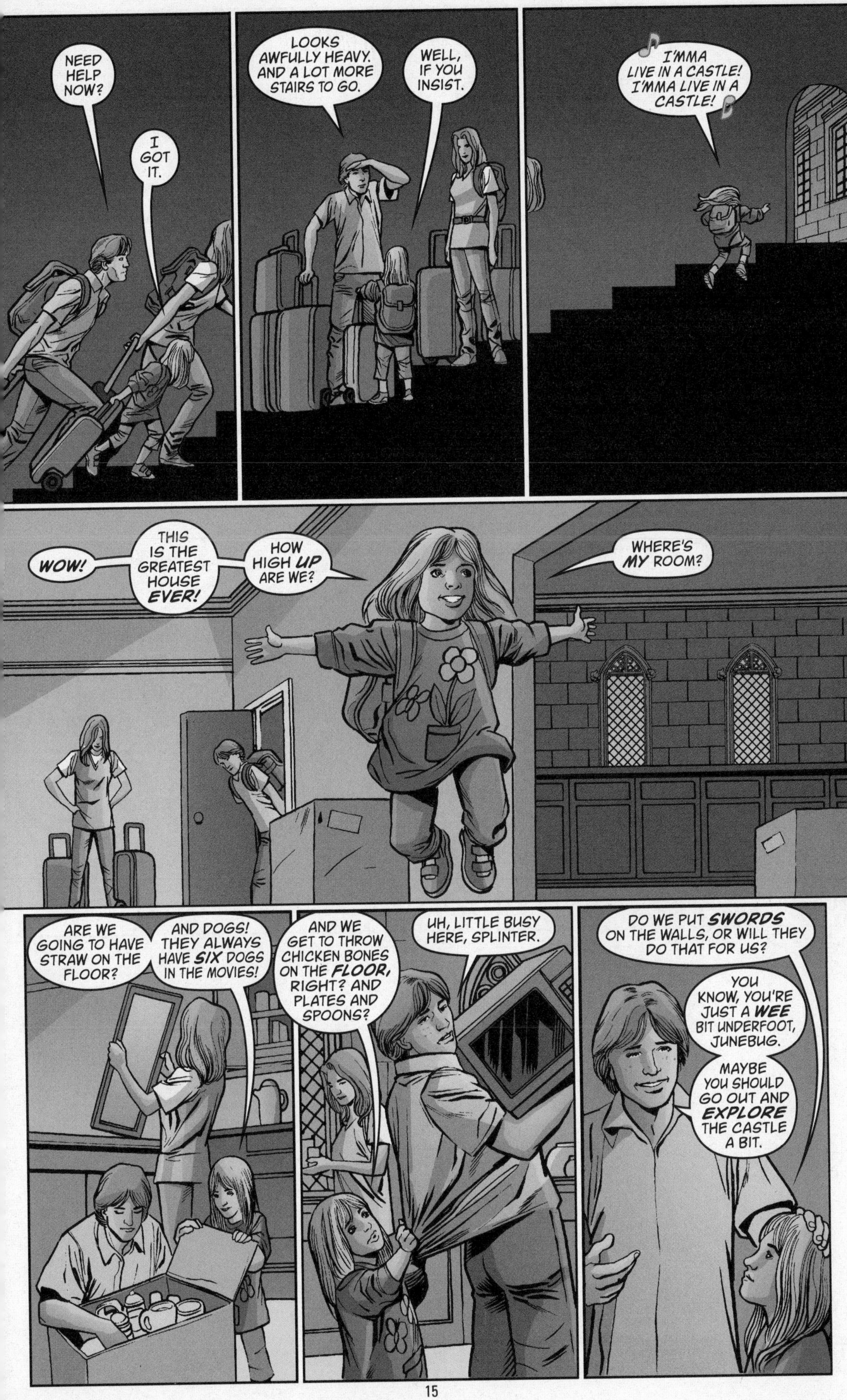
NEED HELP NOW?
I GOT IT.
LOOKS AWFULLY HEAVY. AND A LOT MORE STAIRS TO GO.
WELL, IF YOU INSIST.
I'MMA LIVE IN A CASTLE! I'MMA LIVE IN A CASTLE!
WOW!
THIS IS THE GREATEST HOUSE EVER!
HOW HIGH UP ARE WE?
WHERE'S MY ROOM?
ARE WE GOING TO HAVE STRAW ON THE FLOOR?
AND DOGS! THEY ALWAYS HAVE SIX DOGS IN THE MOVIES!
AND WE GET TO THROW CHICKEN BONES ON THE FLOOR, RIGHT? AND PLATES AND SPOONS?
UH, LITTLE BUSY HERE, SPLINTER.
DO WE PUT SWORDS ON THE WALLS, OR WILL THEY DO THAT FOR US?
YOU KNOW, YOU'RE JUST A WEE BIT UNDERFOOT, JUNEBUG.
MAYBE YOU SHOULD GO OUT AND EXPLORE THE CASTLE A BIT.

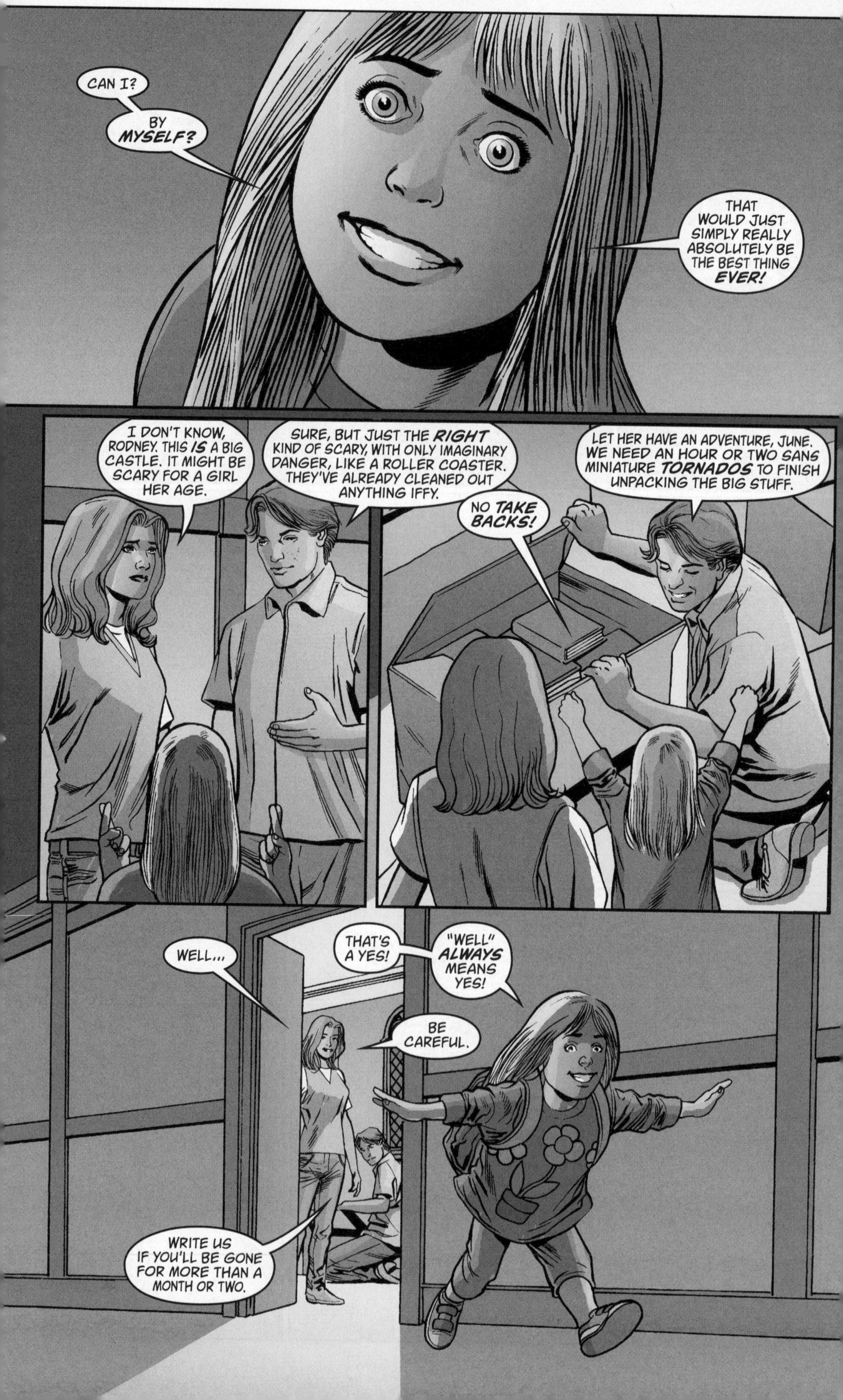
CAN I?
BY MYSELF?
THAT WOULD JUST SIMPLY REALLY ABSOLUTELY BE THE BEST THING EVER!
I DON'T KNOW, RODNEY. THIS IS A BIG CASTLE. IT MIGHT BE SCARY FOR A GIRL HER AGE.
SURE, BUT JUST THE RIGHT KIND OF SCARY, WITH ONLY IMAGINARY DANGER, LIKE A ROLLER COASTER. THEY'VE ALREADY CLEANED OUT ANYTHING IFFY.
LET HER HAVE AN ADVENTURE, JUNE. WE NEED AN HOUR OR TWO SANS MINIATURE TORNADOS TO FINISH UNPACKING THE BIG STUFF.
NO TAKE BACKS!
WELL...
THAT'S A YES!
"WELL" ALWAYS MEANS YES!
BE CAREFUL.
WRITE US IF YOU'LL BE GONE FOR MORE THAN A MONTH OR TWO.

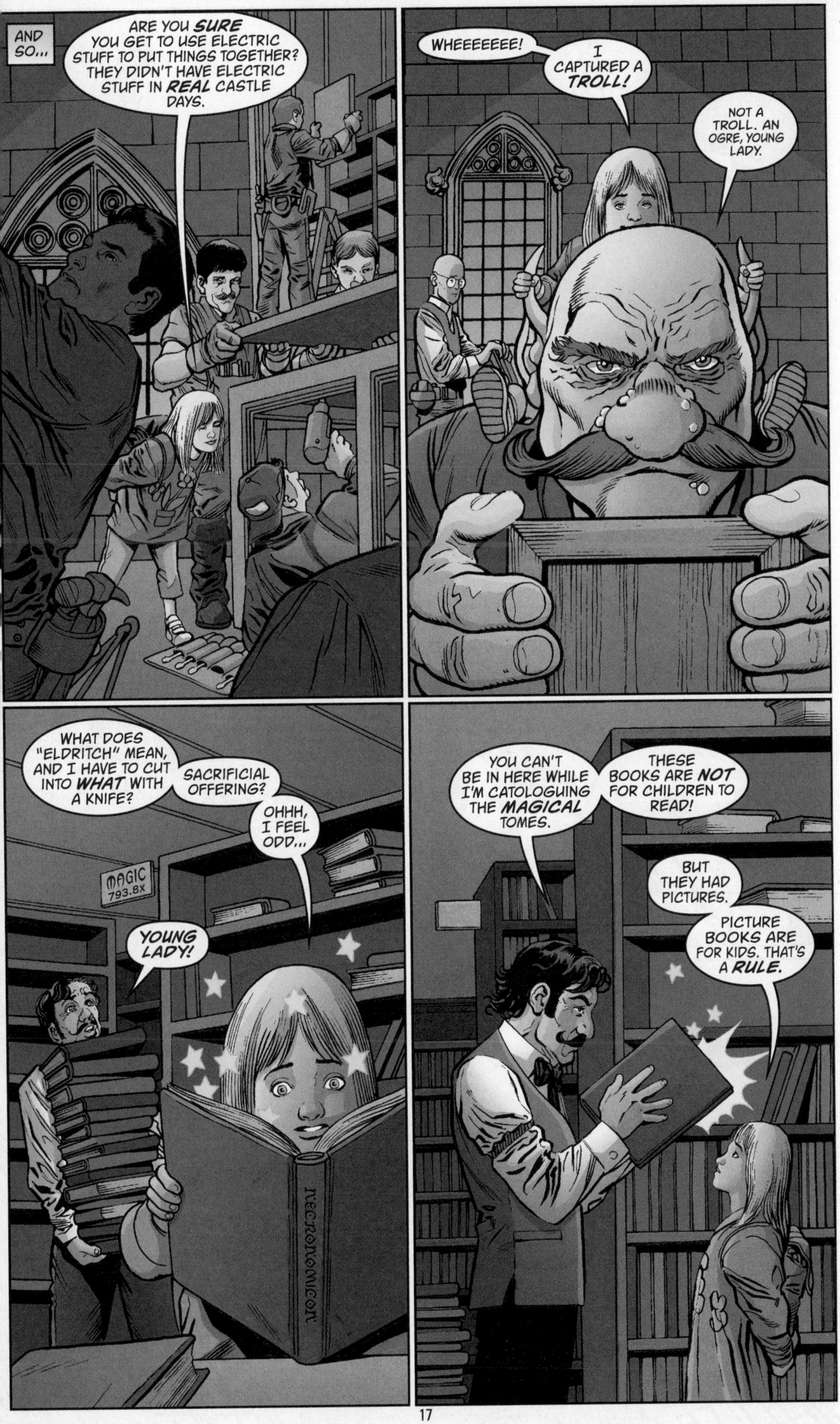
AND SO...
ARE YOU SURE YOU GET TO USE ELECTRIC STUFF TO PUT THINGS TOGETHER? THEY DIDN'T HAVE ELECTRIC STUFF IN REAL CASTLE DAYS.
WHEEEEEEE!
I CAPTURED A TROLL!
NOT A TROLL. AN OGRE, YOUNG LADY.
WHAT DOES "ELDRITCH" MEAN, AND I HAVE TO CUT INTO WHAT WITH A KNIFE?
SACRIFICIAL OFFERING?
OHHH, I FEEL ODD...
MAGIC 793.8X
YOUNG LADY!
NECRONOMICON
YOU CAN'T BE IN HERE WHILE I'M CATOLOGUING THE MAGICAL TOMES.
THESE BOOKS ARE NOT FOR CHILDREN TO READ!
BUT THEY HAD PICTURES.
PICTURE BOOKS ARE FOR KIDS. THAT'S A RULE.

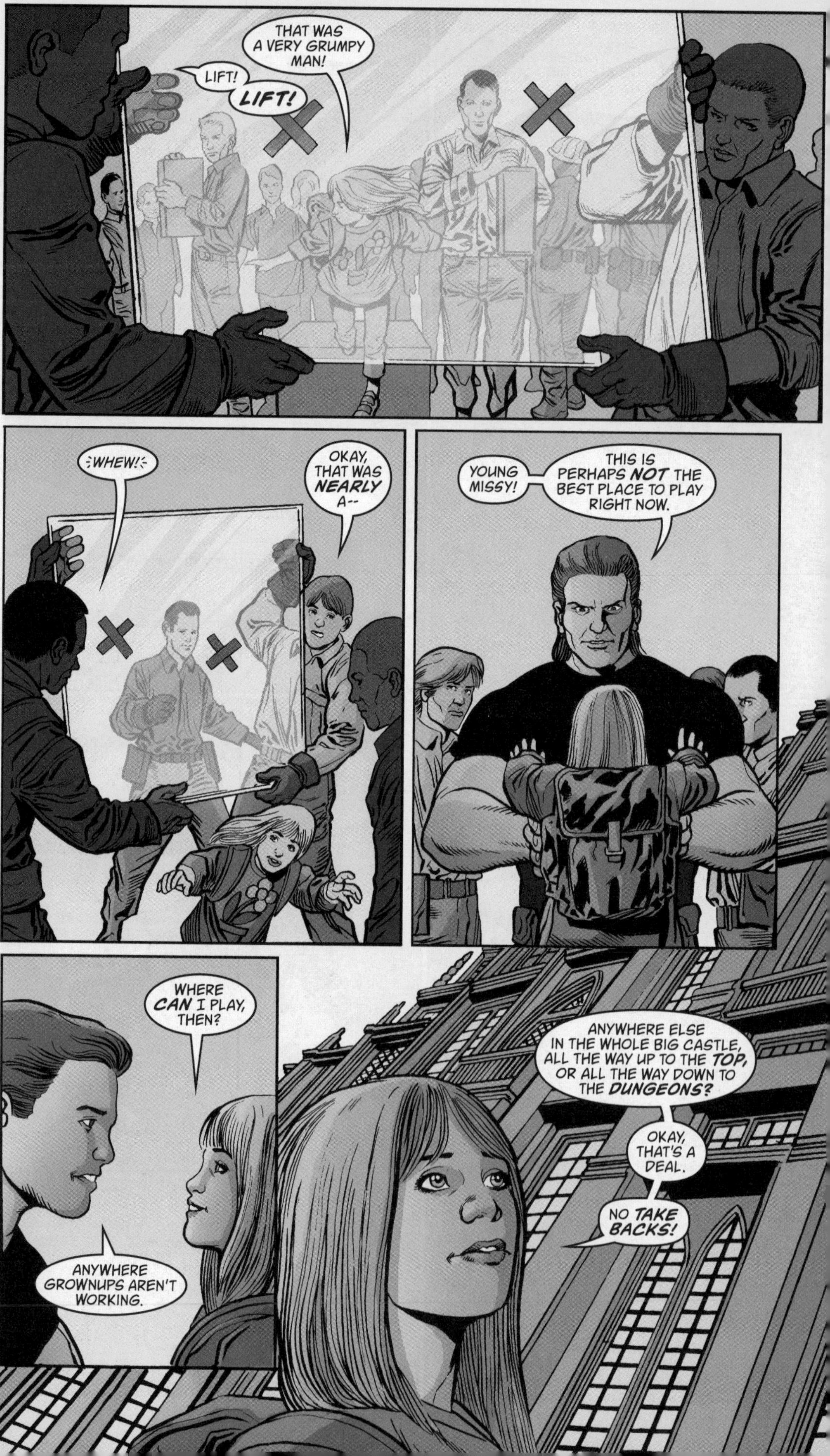
THAT WAS A VERY GRUMPY MAN!
LIFT! LIFT!
:WHEW!:
OKAY, THAT WAS NEARLY A--
YOUNG MISSY!
THIS IS PERHAPS NOT THE BEST PLACE TO PLAY RIGHT NOW.
WHERE CAN I PLAY, THEN?
ANYWHERE GROWNUPS AREN'T WORKING.
ANYWHERE ELSE IN THE WHOLE BIG CASTLE, ALL THE WAY UP TO THE TOP, OR ALL THE WAY DOWN TO THE DUNGEONS?
OKAY, THAT'S A DEAL.
NO TAKE BACKS!

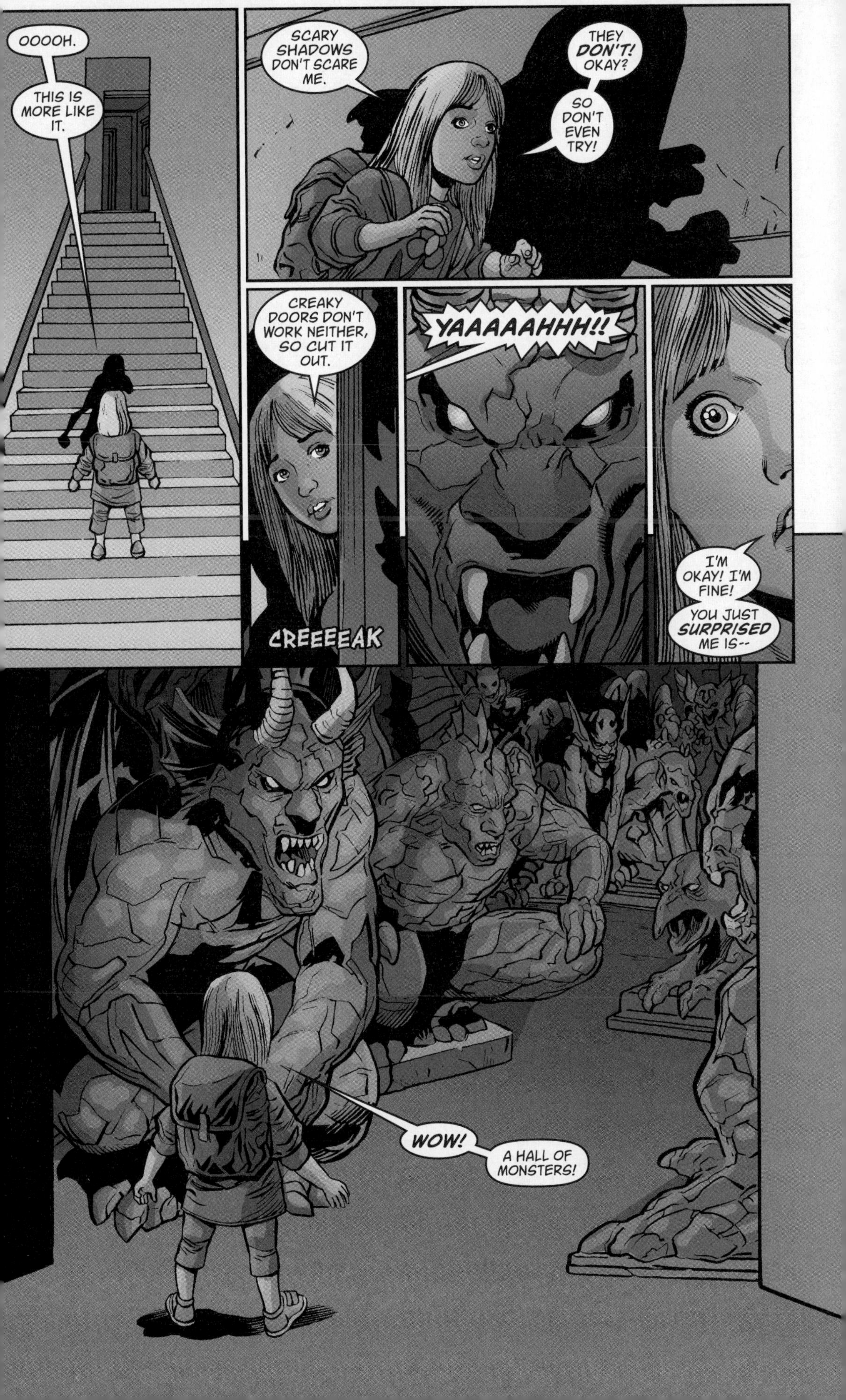
OOOOH.
THIS IS MORE LIKE IT.
SCARY SHADOWS DON'T SCARE ME.
THEY DON'T! OKAY?
SO DON'T EVEN TRY!
CREAKY DOORS DON'T WORK NEITHER, SO CUT IT OUT.
CREEEEAK
YAAAAAHHH!!
I'M OKAY! I'M FINE!
YOU JUST SURPRISED ME IS--
WOW!
A HALL OF MONSTERS!

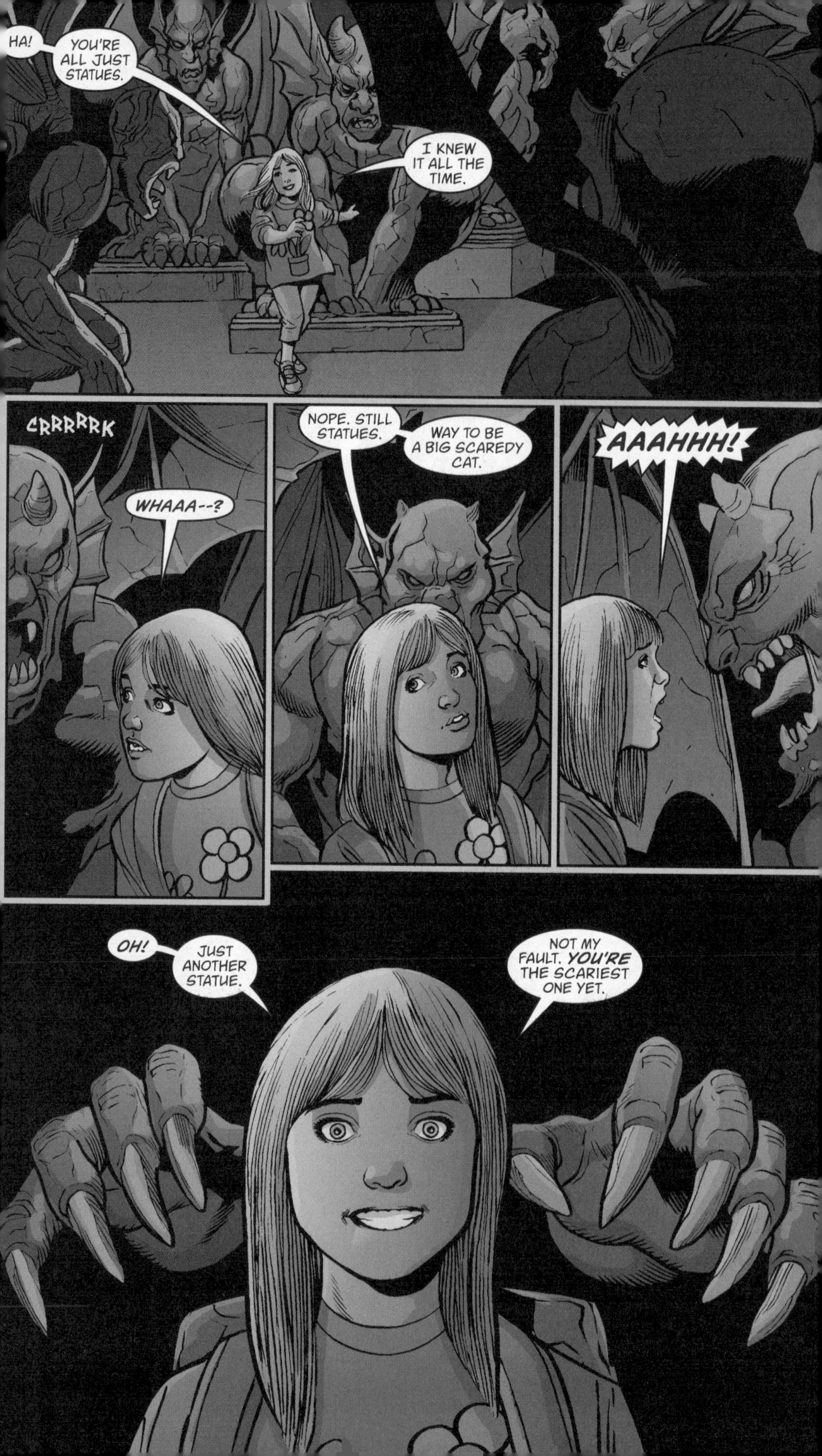
HA!
YOU'RE ALL JUST STATUES.
I KNEW IT ALL THE TIME.
CRRRRRK
WHAAA--?
NOPE. STILL STATUES.
WAY TO BE A BIG SCAREDY CAT.
AAAHHH!
OH!
JUST ANOTHER STATUE.
NOT MY FAULT. YOU'RE THE SCARIEST ONE YET.

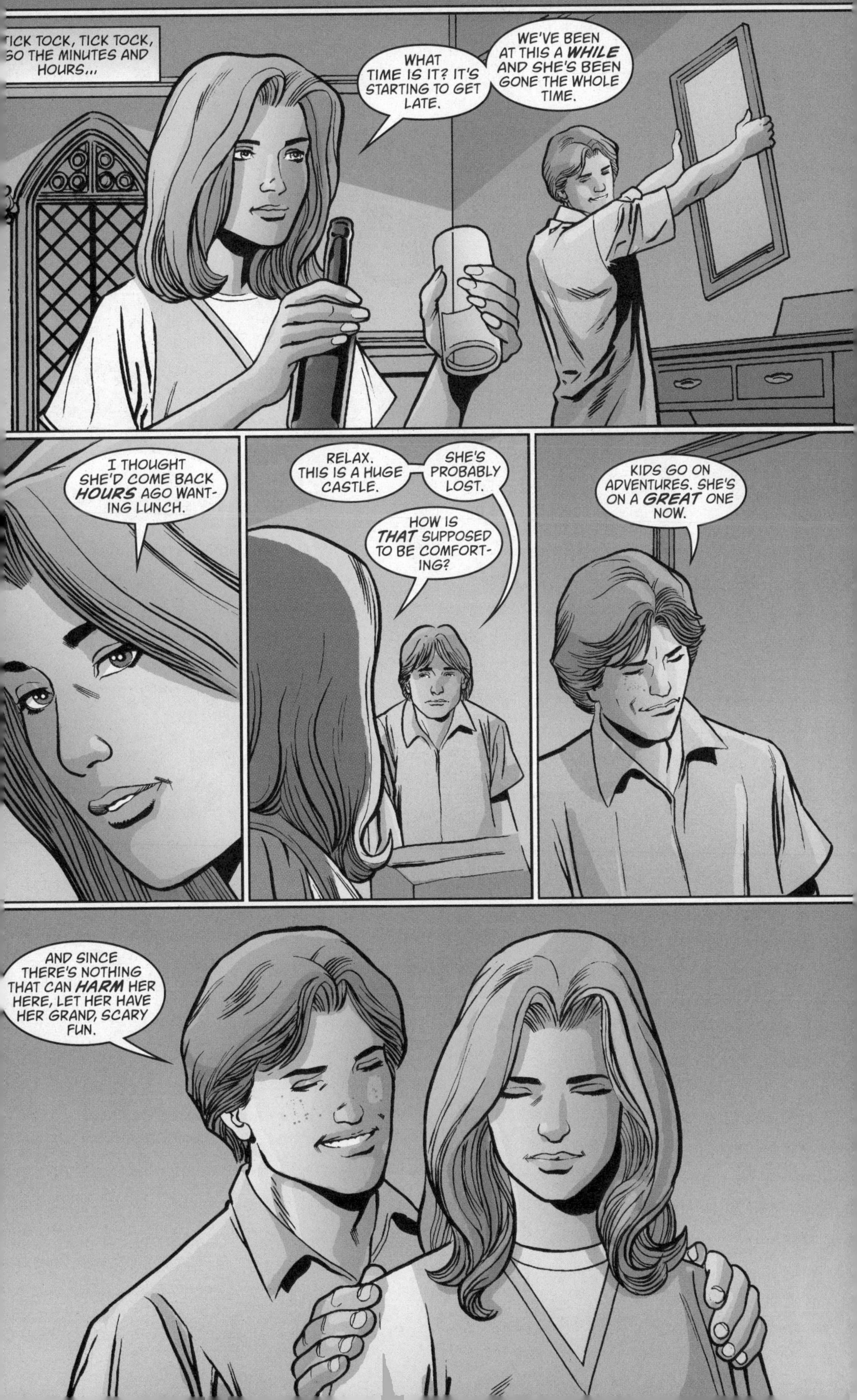
TICK TOCK, TICK TOCK, GO THE MINUTES AND HOURS...
WHAT TIME IS IT? IT'S STARTING TO GET LATE.
WE'VE BEEN AT THIS A WHILE AND SHE'S BEEN GONE THE WHOLE TIME.
I THOUGHT SHE'D COME BACK HOURS AGO WANTING LUNCH.
RELAX. THIS IS A HUGE CASTLE.
SHE'S PROBABLY LOST.
HOW IS THAT SUPPOSED TO BE COMFORTING?
KIDS GO ON ADVENTURES. SHE'S ON A GREAT ONE NOW.
AND SINCE THERE'S NOTHING THAT CAN HARM HER HERE, LET HER HAVE HER GRAND, SCARY FUN.

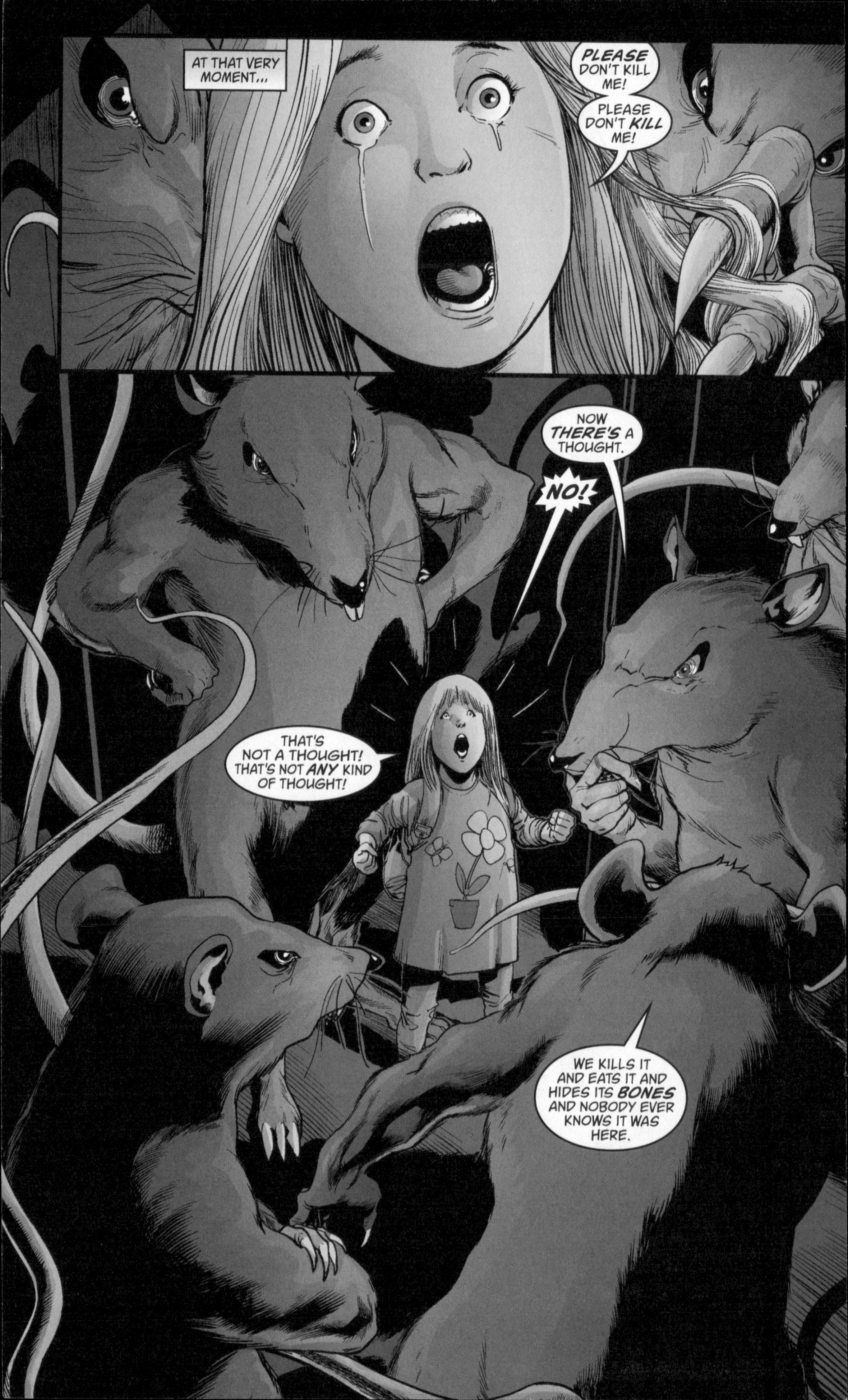
AT THAT VERY MOMENT...
PLEASE DON'T KILL ME!
PLEASE DON'T KILL ME!
NOW THERE'S A THOUGHT.
NO!
THAT'S NOT A THOUGHT! THAT'S NOT ANY KIND OF THOUGHT!
WE KILLS IT AND EATS IT AND HIDES ITS BONES AND NOBODY EVER KNOWS IT WAS HERE.

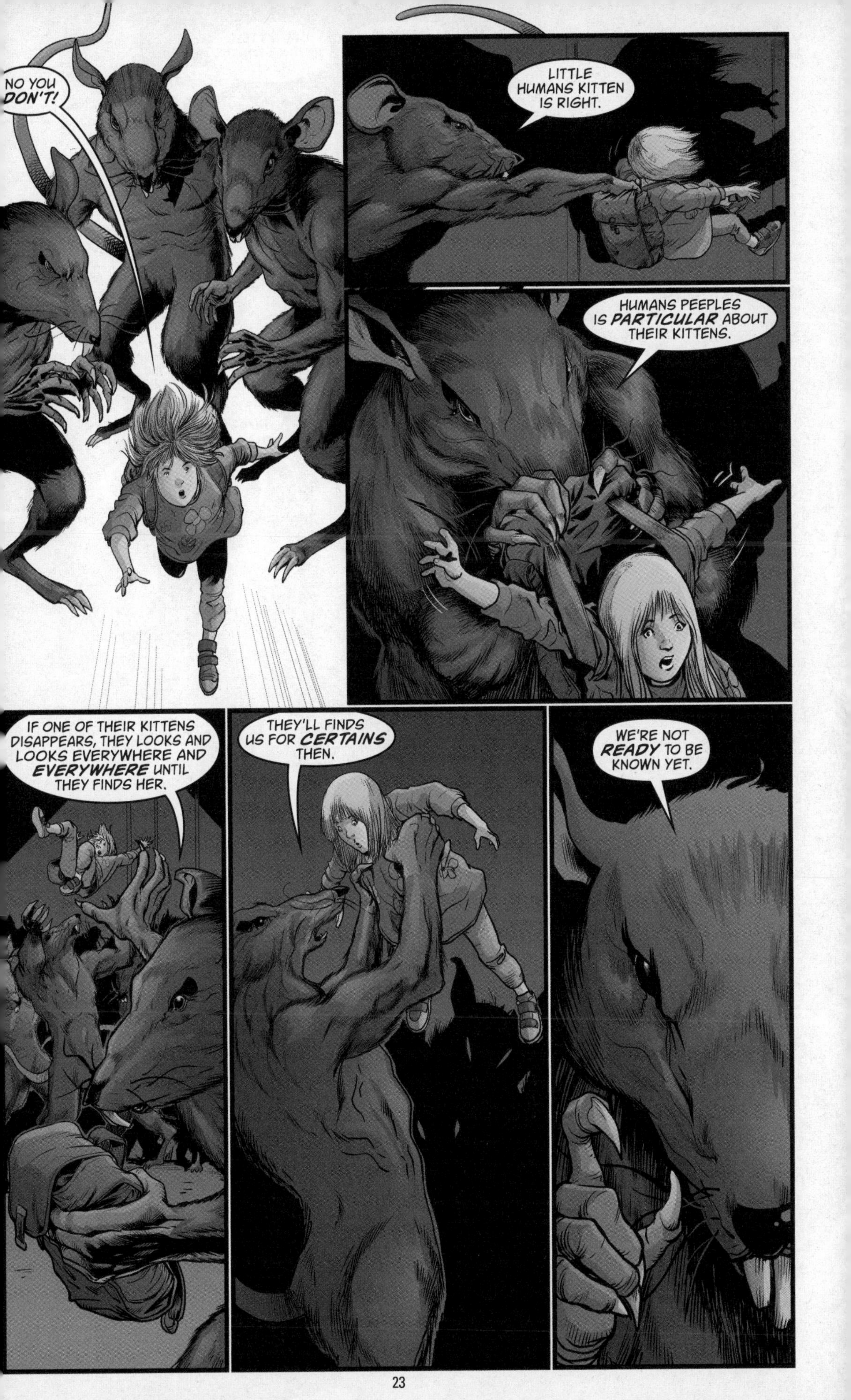
NO YOU DON'T!
LITTLE HUMANS KITTEN IS RIGHT.
HUMANS PEEPLES IS PARTICULAR ABOUT THEIR KITTENS.
IF ONE OF THEIR KITTENS DISAPPEARS, THEY LOOKS AND LOOKS EVERYWHERE AND EVERYWHERE UNTIL THEY FINDS HER.
THEY'LL FINDS US FOR CERTAINS THEN.
WE'RE NOT READY TO BE KNOWN YET.

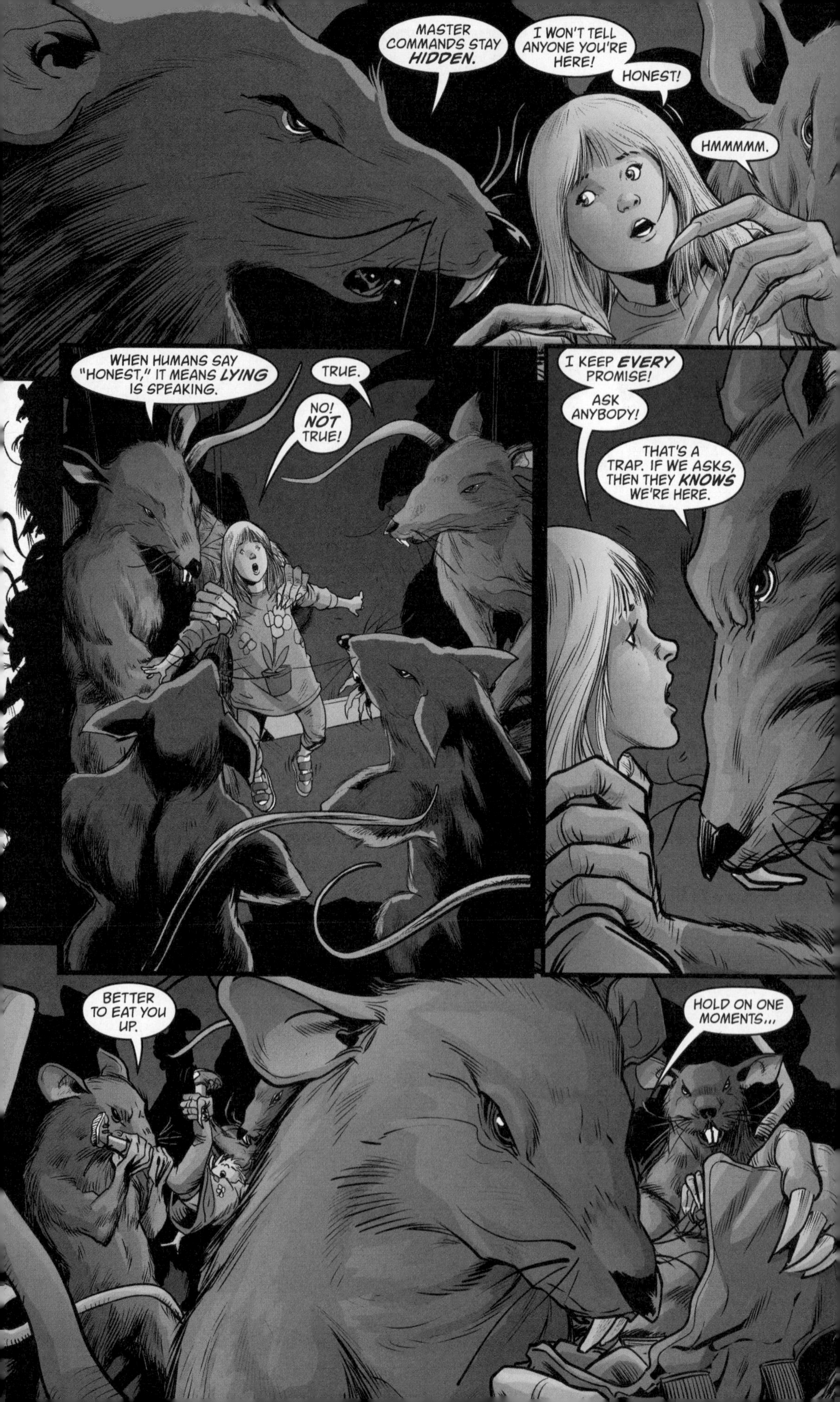
MASTER COMMANDS STAY HIDDEN.
I WON'T TELL ANYONE YOU'RE HERE!
HONEST!
HMMMMM.
WHEN HUMANS SAY "HONEST," IT MEANS LYING IS SPEAKING.
TRUE.
NO! NOT TRUE!
I KEEP EVERY PROMISE!
ASK ANYBODY!
THAT'S A TRAP. IF WE ASKS, THEN THEY KNOWS WE'RE HERE.
BETTER TO EAT YOU UP.
HOLD ON ONE MOMENTS...

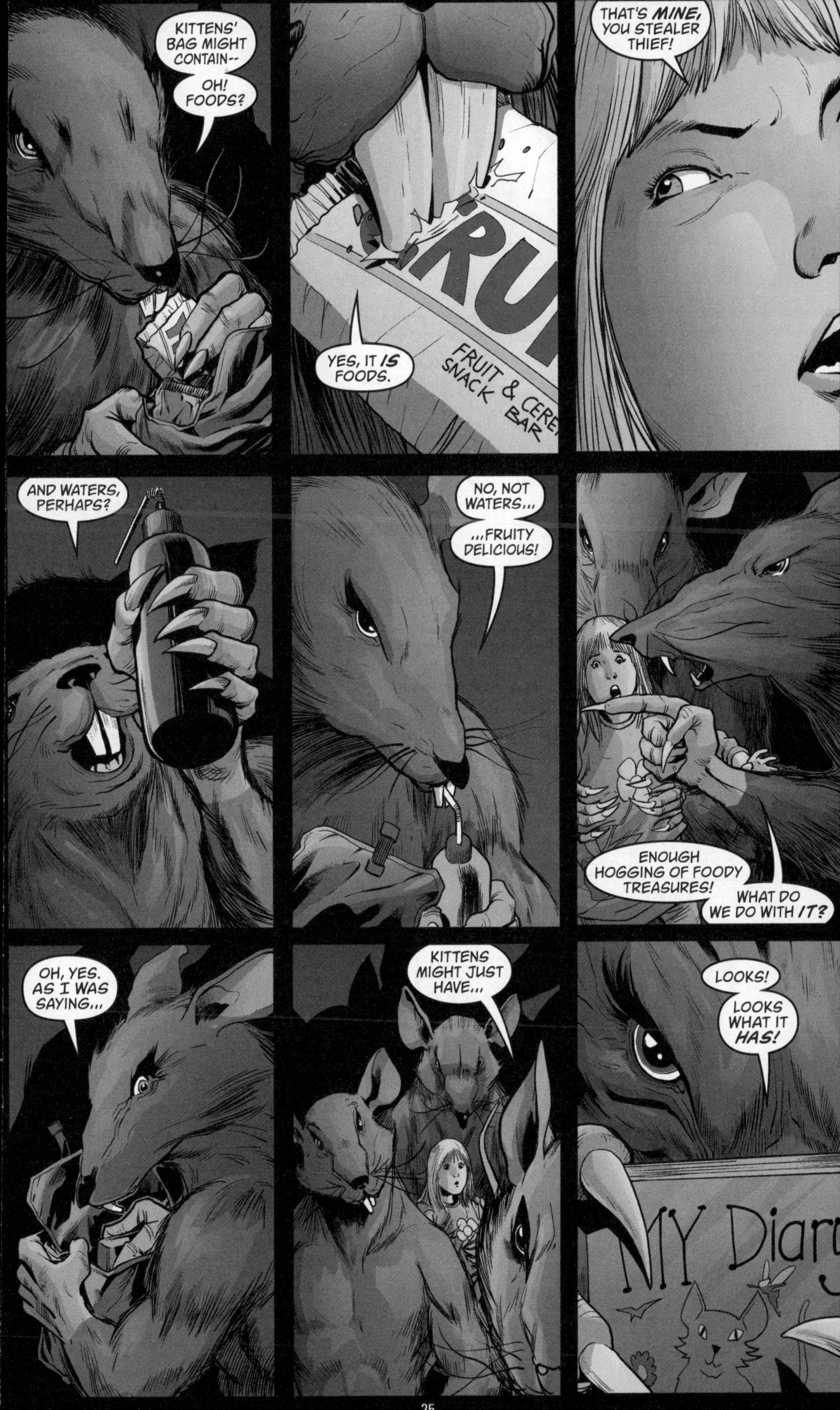
KITTENS' BAG MIGHT CONTAIN--
OH! FOODS?
YES, IT IS FOODS.
RU
FRUIT & CERE
SNACK BAR
THAT'S MINE, YOU STEALER THIEF!
AND WATERS, PERHAPS?
NO, NOT WATERS...
...FRUITY DELICIOUS!
ENOUGH HOGGING OF FOODY TREASURES!
WHAT DO WE DO WITH IT?
OH, YES. AS I WAS SAYING...
KITTENS MIGHT JUST HAVE...
LOOKS!
LOOKS WHAT IT HAS!
MY Diar

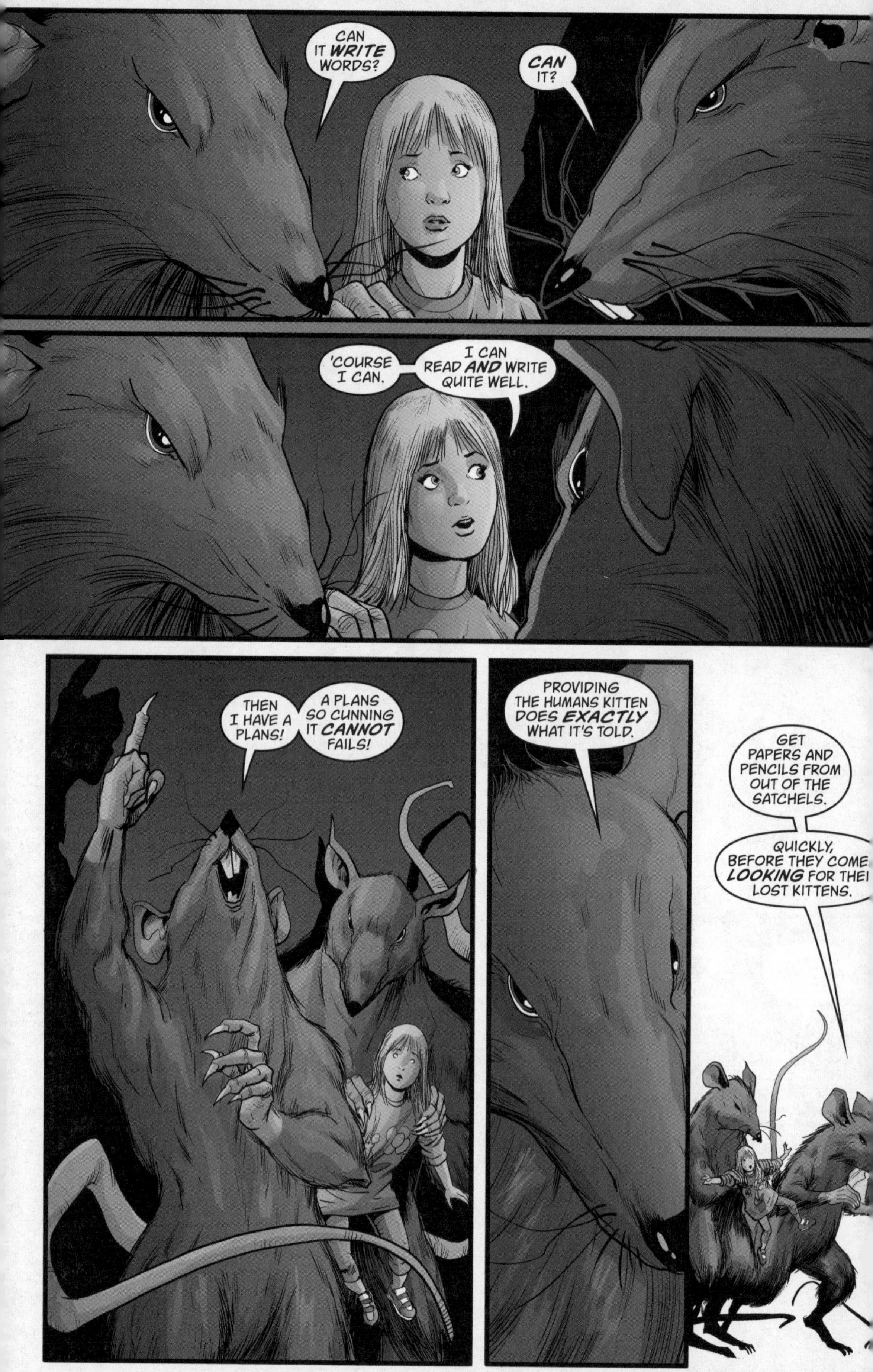
CAN IT WRITE WORDS?
CAN IT?
'COURSE I CAN.
I CAN READ AND WRITE QUITE WELL.
THEN I HAVE A PLANS!
A PLANS SO CUNNING IT CANNOT FAILS!
PROVIDING THE HUMANS KITTEN DOES EXACTLY WHAT IT'S TOLD.
GET PAPERS AND PENCILS FROM OUT OF THE SATCHELS.
QUICKLY, BEFORE THEY COME LOOKING FOR THEI LOST KITTENS.

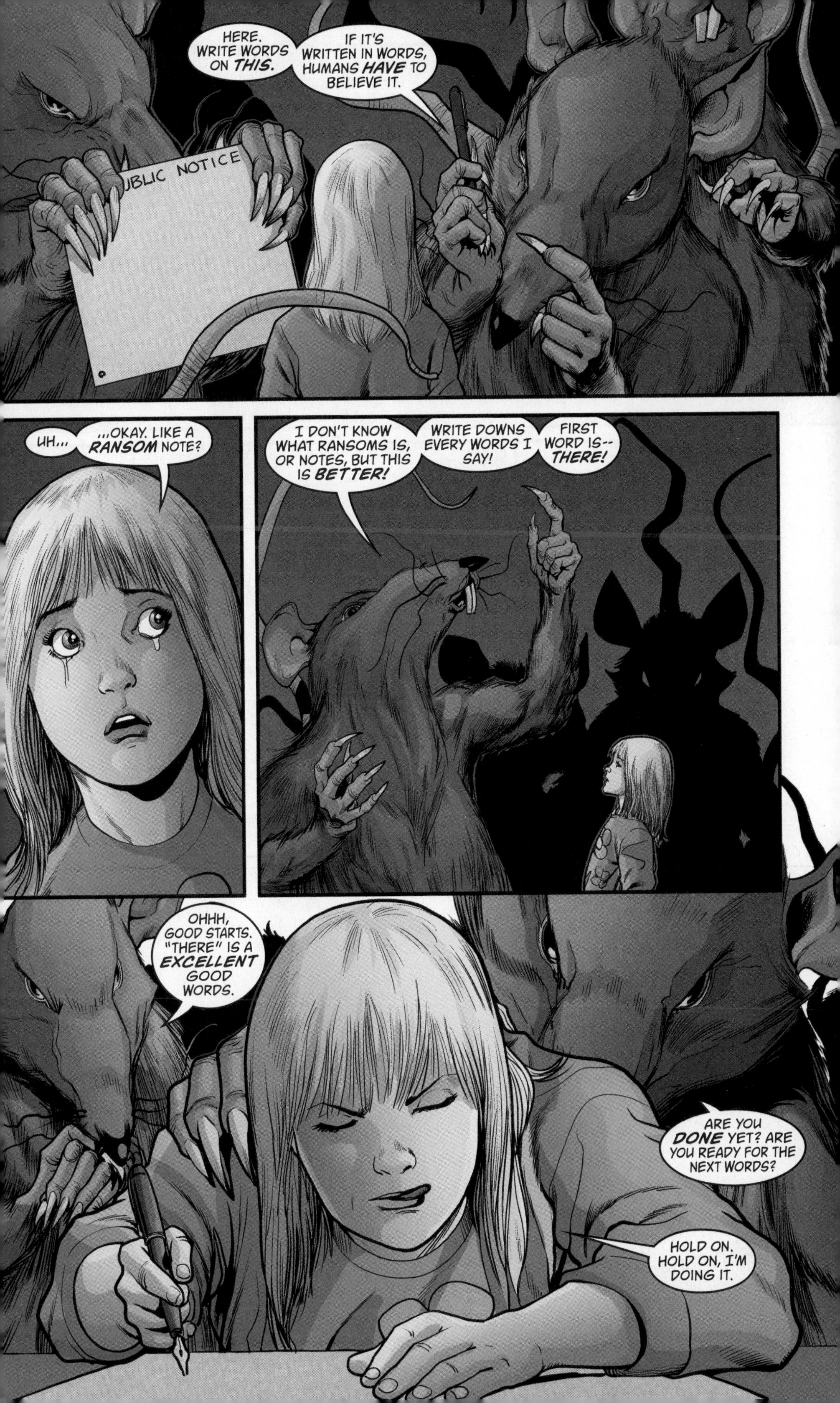
HERE. WRITE WORDS ON THIS.
IF IT'S WRITTEN IN WORDS, HUMANS HAVE TO BELIEVE IT.
UBLIC NOTICE
UH...
...OKAY. LIKE A RANSOM NOTE?
I DON'T KNOW WHAT RANSOMS IS, OR NOTES, BUT THIS IS BETTER!
WRITE DOWNS EVERY WORDS I SAY!
FIRST WORD IS-- THERE!
OHHH, GOOD STARTS. "THERE" IS A EXCELLENT GOOD WORDS.
ARE YOU DONE YET? ARE YOU READY FOR THE NEXT WORDS?
HOLD ON. HOLD ON, I'M DOING IT.

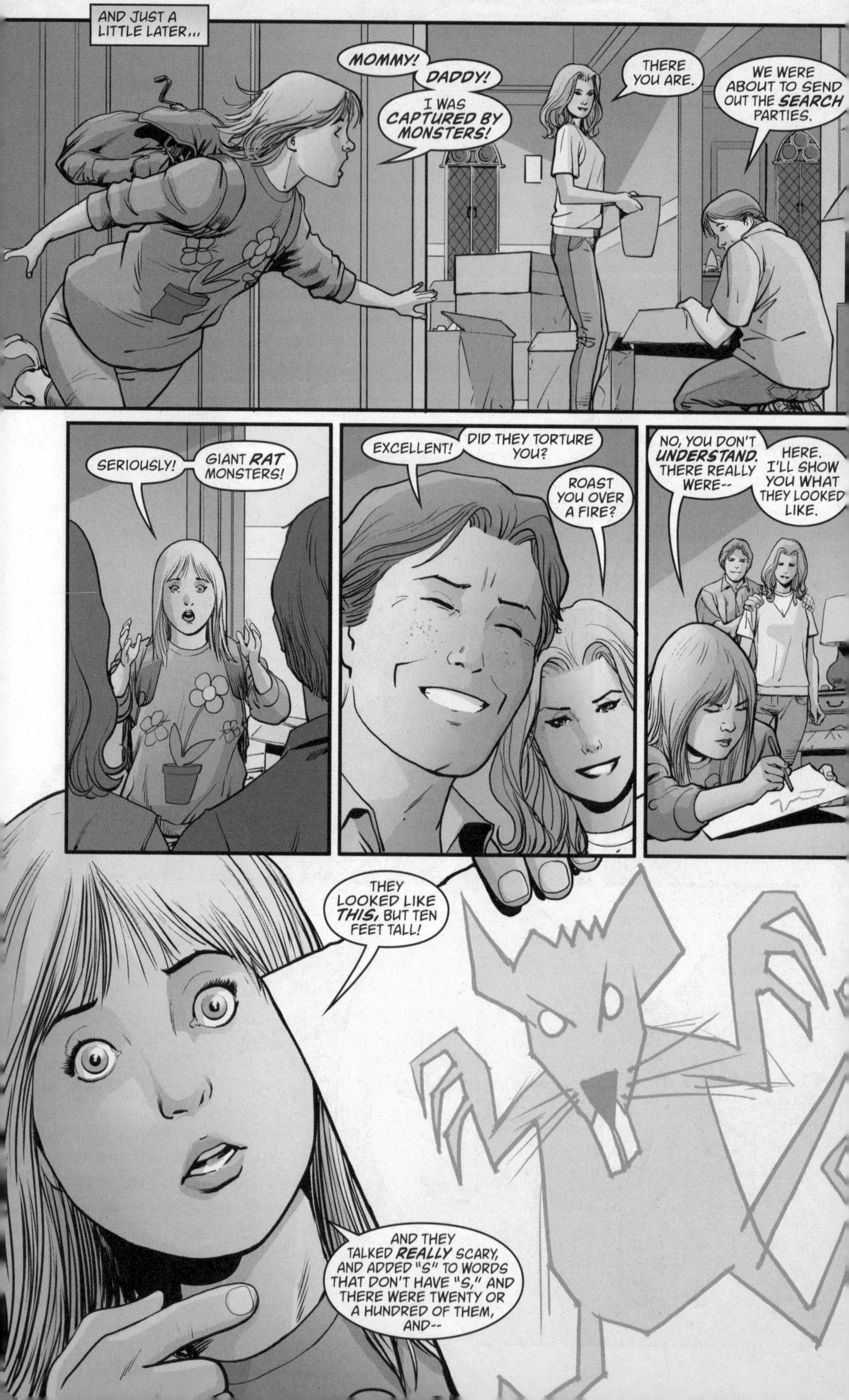
AND JUST A LITTLE LATER...
MOMMY!
DADDY!
I WAS CAPTURED BY MONSTERS!
THERE YOU ARE.
WE WERE ABOUT TO SEND OUT THE SEARCH PARTIES.
SERIOUSLY!
GIANT RAT MONSTERS!
EXCELLENT!
DID THEY TORTURE YOU?
ROAST YOU OVER A FIRE?
NO, YOU DON'T UNDERSTAND. THERE REALLY WERE--
HERE. I'LL SHOW YOU WHAT THEY LOOKED LIKE.
THEY LOOKED LIKE THIS, BUT TEN FEET TALL!
AND THEY TALKED REALLY SCARY, AND ADDED "S" TO WORDS THAT DON'T HAVE "S," AND THERE WERE TWENTY OR A HUNDRED OF THEM, AND--

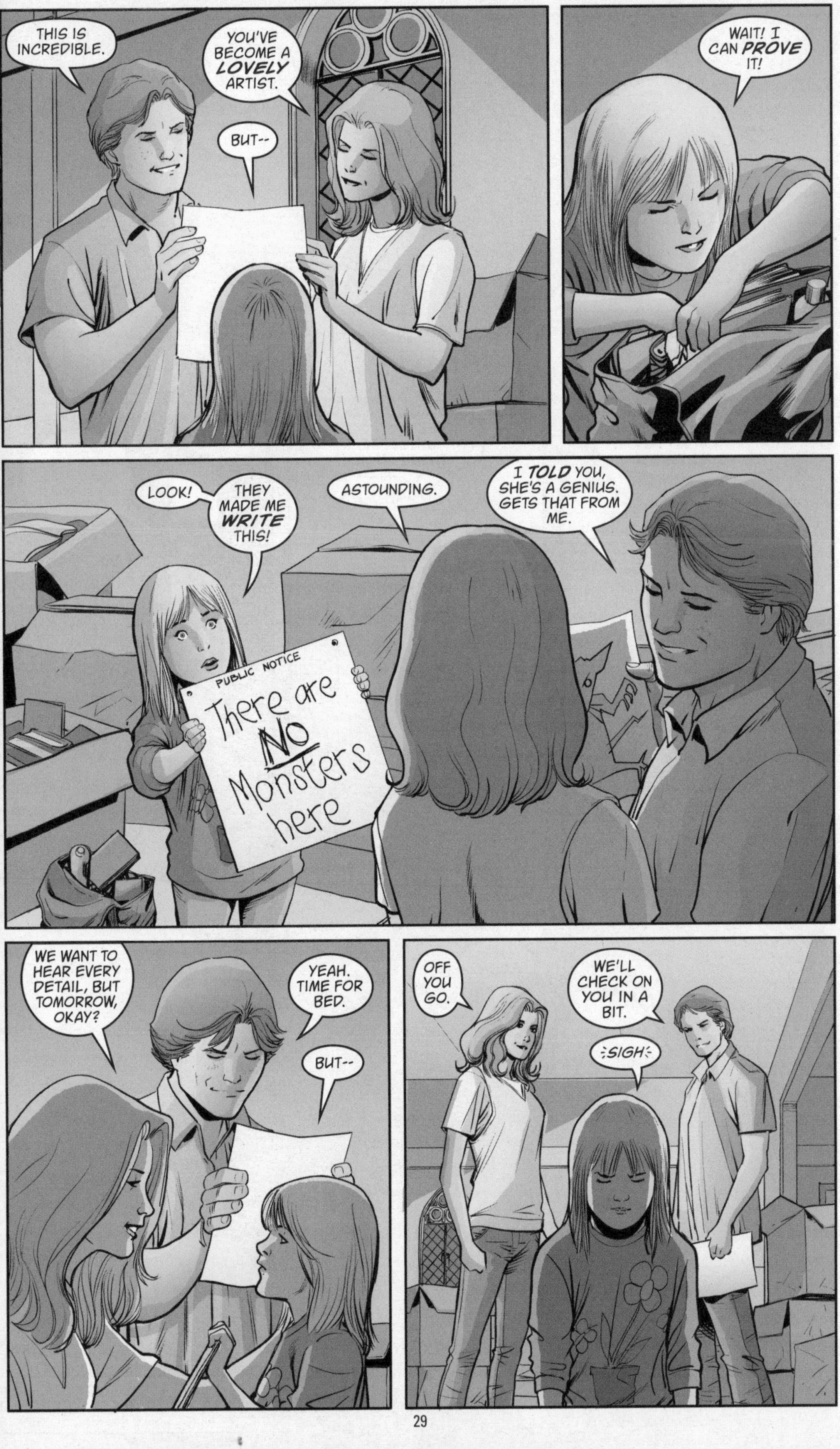

THIS IS INCREDIBLE.
YOU'VE BECOME A LOVELY ARTIST.
BUT--
WAIT! I CAN PROVE IT!
LOOK!
THEY MADE ME WRITE THIS!
ASTOUNDING.
I TOLD YOU, SHE'S A GENIUS. GETS THAT FROM ME.
PUBLIC NOTICE
There are NO Monsters here
WE WANT TO HEAR EVERY DETAIL, BUT TOMORROW, OKAY?
YEAH. TIME FOR BED.
BUT--
OFF YOU GO.
WE'LL CHECK ON YOU IN A BIT.
SIGH

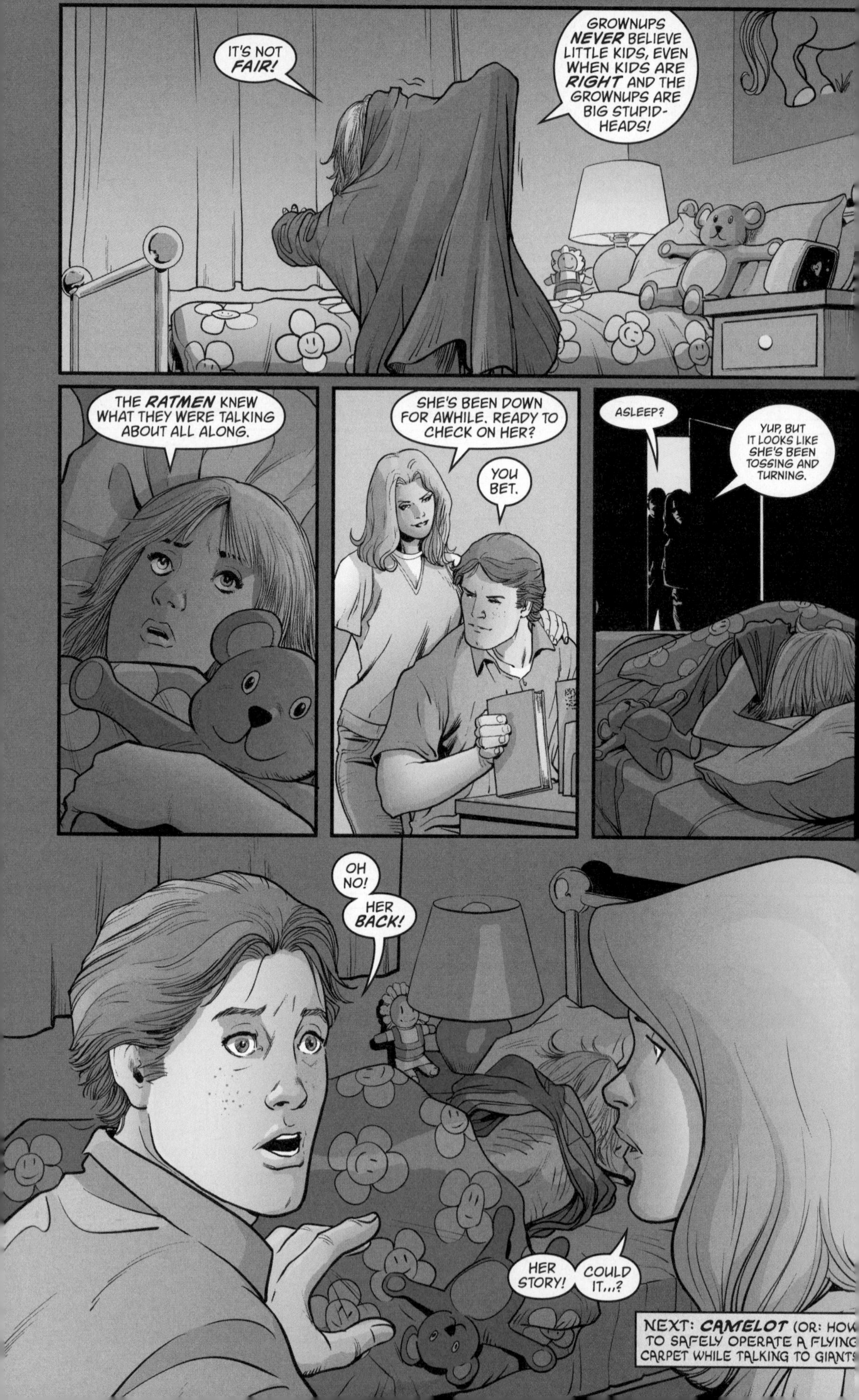
IT'S NOT **FAIR!**
GROWNUPS **NEVER** BELIEVE LITTLE KIDS, EVEN WHEN KIDS ARE **RIGHT** AND THE GROWNUPS ARE BIG STUPID-HEADS!
THE **RATMEN** KNEW WHAT THEY WERE TALKING ABOUT ALL ALONG.
SHE'S BEEN DOWN FOR AWHILE. READY TO CHECK ON HER?
YOU BET.
ASLEEP?
YUP, BUT IT LOOKS LIKE SHE'S BEEN TOSSING AND TURNING.
OH NO!
HER **BACK!**
HER STORY!
COULD IT...?
NEXT: **CAMELOT** (OR: HOW TO SAFELY OPERATE A FLYING CARPET WHILE TALKING TO GIANTS

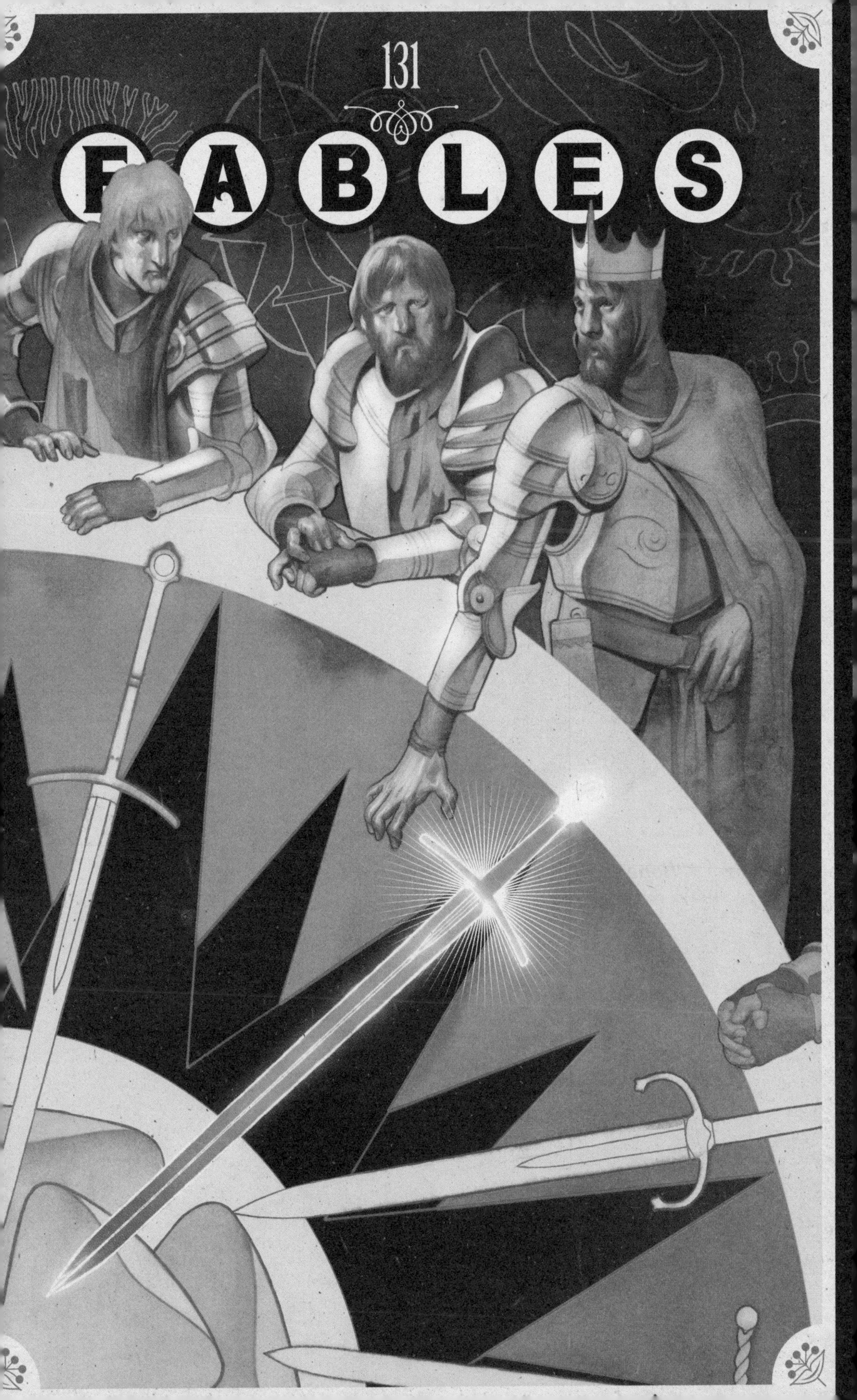
131
FABLES

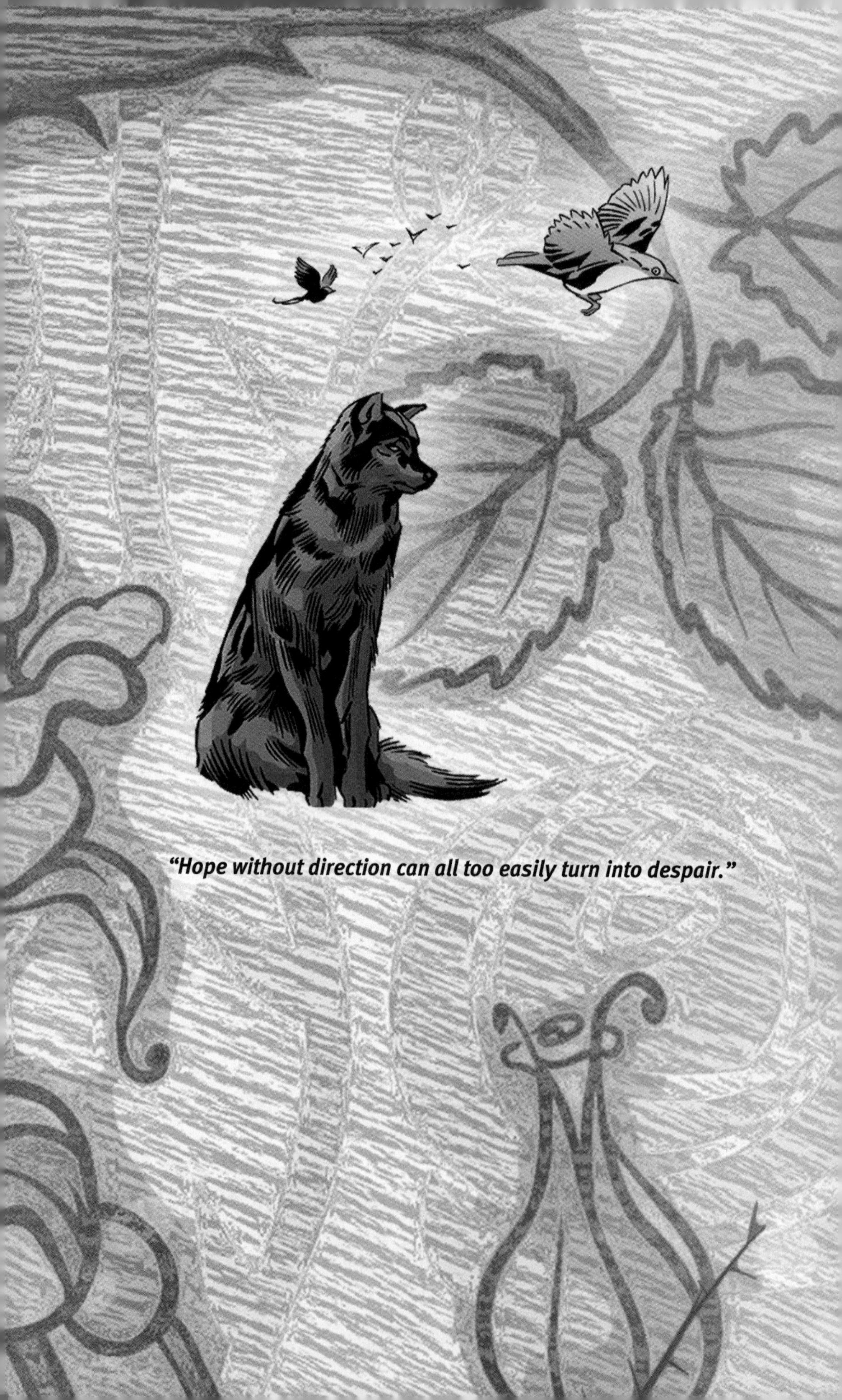
"Hope without direction can all too easily turn into despair."

FABLETOWN.

IT'S SIMPLE, BUT THAT'S NOT AT ALL THE SAME AS BEING *EASY*.

A Heart Remote and Unyielding

⊹ Part One of ⊹

Camelot

Bill Willingham
writer/creator

Mark Buckingham
pencils

Steve Leialoha
inks

Lee Loughridge
colors

Todd Klein
letters

João Ruas
cover

Gregory Lockard
associate editor

Shelly Bond
editor

BIGBY IS A NATURAL SHAPECHANGER, EVEN THOUGH HE'S NEVER WORKED TO *DEVELOP* THAT ABILITY.

NO NEED, THEN, FOR US TO TRY TO REINVENT THE WHEEL, CRAFTING A *NEW* SPELL TO TURN GLASS INTO A LIVING WOLF. HE CAN DO ALL THE HEAVY LIFTING THERE.

OUR JOB IS TO *DIRECT* THE OPERATION--TO HELP SHOW HIM THE WAY. NUDGE HIM ALONG, IF YOU WILL.

IT HASN'T BEEN MY EXPERIENCE THAT BIGBY *NUDGES* ALL THAT WELL.

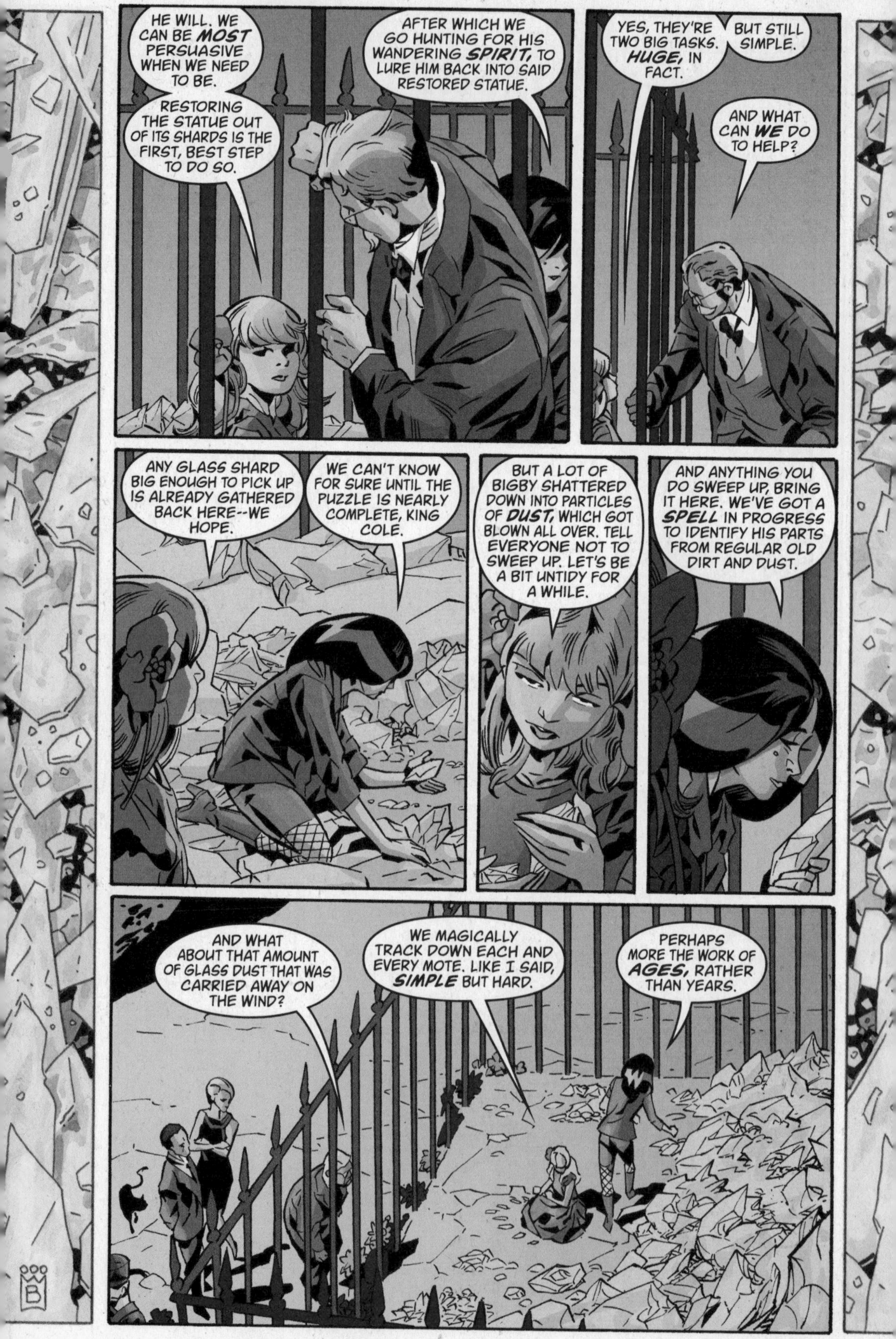
HE WILL. WE CAN BE MOST PERSUASIVE WHEN WE NEED TO BE.
RESTORING THE STATUE OUT OF ITS SHARDS IS THE FIRST, BEST STEP TO DO SO.
AFTER WHICH WE GO HUNTING FOR HIS WANDERING SPIRIT, TO LURE HIM BACK INTO SAID RESTORED STATUE.
YES, THEY'RE TWO BIG TASKS. HUGE, IN FACT.
BUT STILL SIMPLE.
AND WHAT CAN WE DO TO HELP?
ANY GLASS SHARD BIG ENOUGH TO PICK UP IS ALREADY GATHERED BACK HERE--WE HOPE.
WE CAN'T KNOW FOR SURE UNTIL THE PUZZLE IS NEARLY COMPLETE, KING COLE.
BUT A LOT OF BIGBY SHATTERED DOWN INTO PARTICLES OF DUST, WHICH GOT BLOWN ALL OVER. TELL EVERYONE NOT TO SWEEP UP. LET'S BE A BIT UNTIDY FOR A WHILE.
AND ANYTHING YOU DO SWEEP UP, BRING IT HERE. WE'VE GOT A SPELL IN PROGRESS TO IDENTIFY HIS PARTS FROM REGULAR OLD DIRT AND DUST.
AND WHAT ABOUT THAT AMOUNT OF GLASS DUST THAT WAS CARRIED AWAY ON THE WIND?
WE MAGICALLY TRACK DOWN EACH AND EVERY MOTE. LIKE I SAID, SIMPLE BUT HARD.
PERHAPS MORE THE WORK OF AGES, RATHER THAN YEARS.

SO EVEN IF IT TURNS OUT FOR THE BEST, THOSE CHILDREN ARE *DOOMED* TO GROW UP WITHOUT A FATHER?

WHAT CAN I SAY, YOUR HONOR? LIFE IS NEITHER FAIR NOR EASY.

THIS IS A COMPLEX AND INTERESTING PROJECT AHEAD OF YOU, BUT NOT A *MEDICAL* ONE. ART, RATHER THAN SCIENCE, IS NEEDED. I'VE NO COMPELLING BUSINESS HERE.

I SHOULD RETURN TO AFFAIRS THAT ACTUALLY FALL *WITHIN* MY SPHERE OF RESPONSIBILITY.

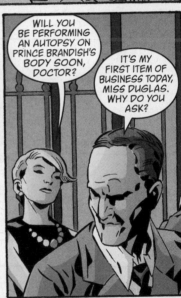

WILL YOU BE PERFORMING AN AUTOPSY ON PRINCE BRANDISH'S BODY SOON, DOCTOR?

IT'S MY FIRST ITEM OF BUSINESS TODAY, MISS DUGLAS. WHY DO YOU ASK?

I THOUGHT I'D OFFER MY HELP. AFTER ALL, I WAS YOUR *NURSE* FOR MORE YEARS THAN I CARE TO COUNT.

TIME TO START EARNING YOUR KEEP AGAIN?

GOOD FOR YOU.

WE'LL WANT TO EXAMINE *HIS* BODY TOO, DOCTOR. IN CASE MORE THAN HIS SWORD WAS MAGICAL.

WHEN I'M DONE, YOUNG LADY. *DIBS*, AS THE MUNDYS SAY.

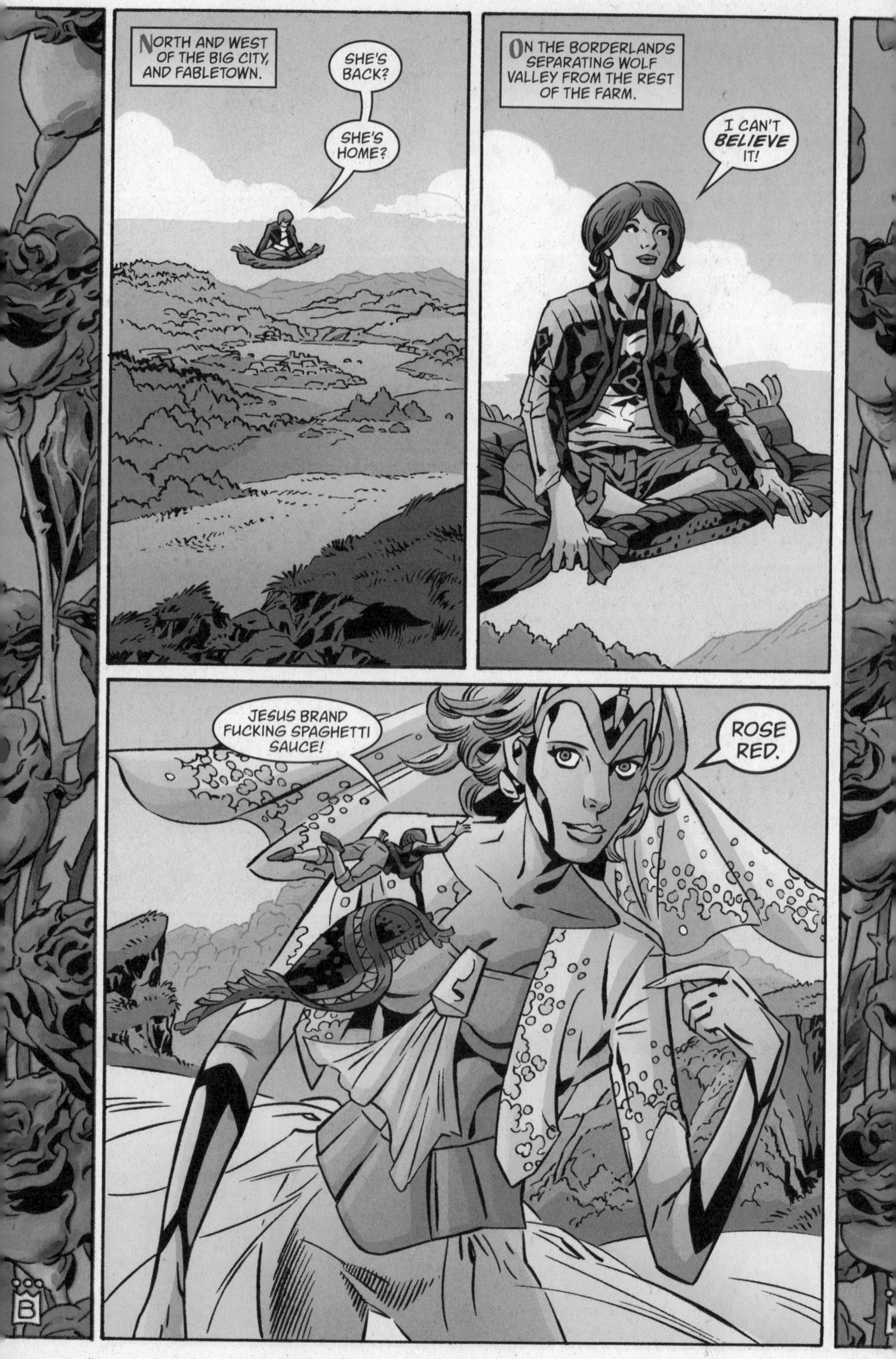
NORTH AND WEST OF THE BIG CITY, AND FABLETOWN.
SHE'S BACK?
SHE'S HOME?
ON THE BORDERLANDS SEPARATING WOLF VALLEY FROM THE REST OF THE FARM.
I CAN'T BELIEVE IT!
JESUS BRAND FUCKING SPAGHETTI SAUCE!
ROSE RED.

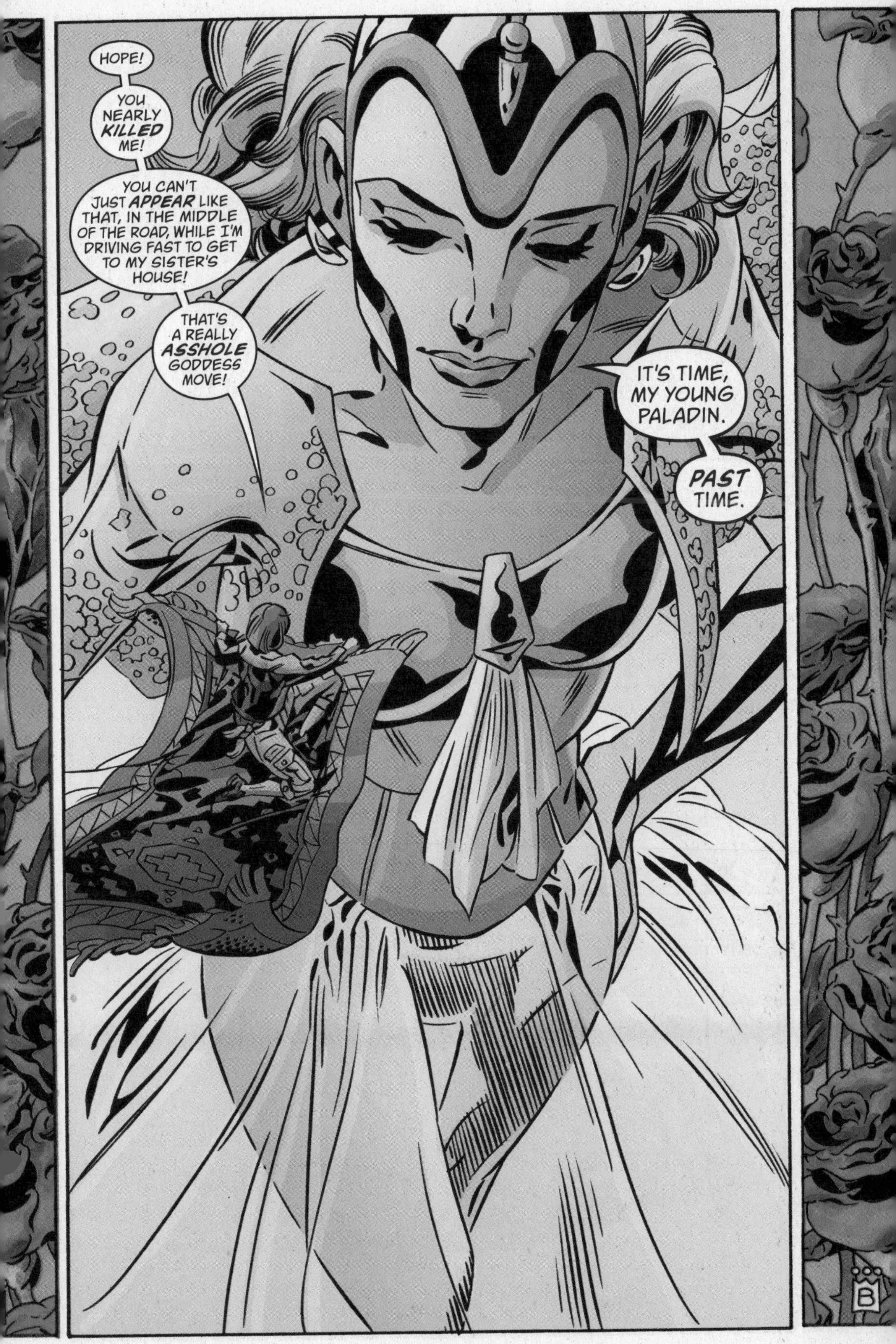
HOPE!
YOU NEARLY KILLED ME!
YOU CAN'T JUST APPEAR LIKE THAT, IN THE MIDDLE OF THE ROAD, WHILE I'M DRIVING FAST TO GET TO MY SISTER'S HOUSE!
THAT'S A REALLY ASSHOLE GODDESS MOVE!
IT'S TIME, MY YOUNG PALADIN.
PAST TIME.

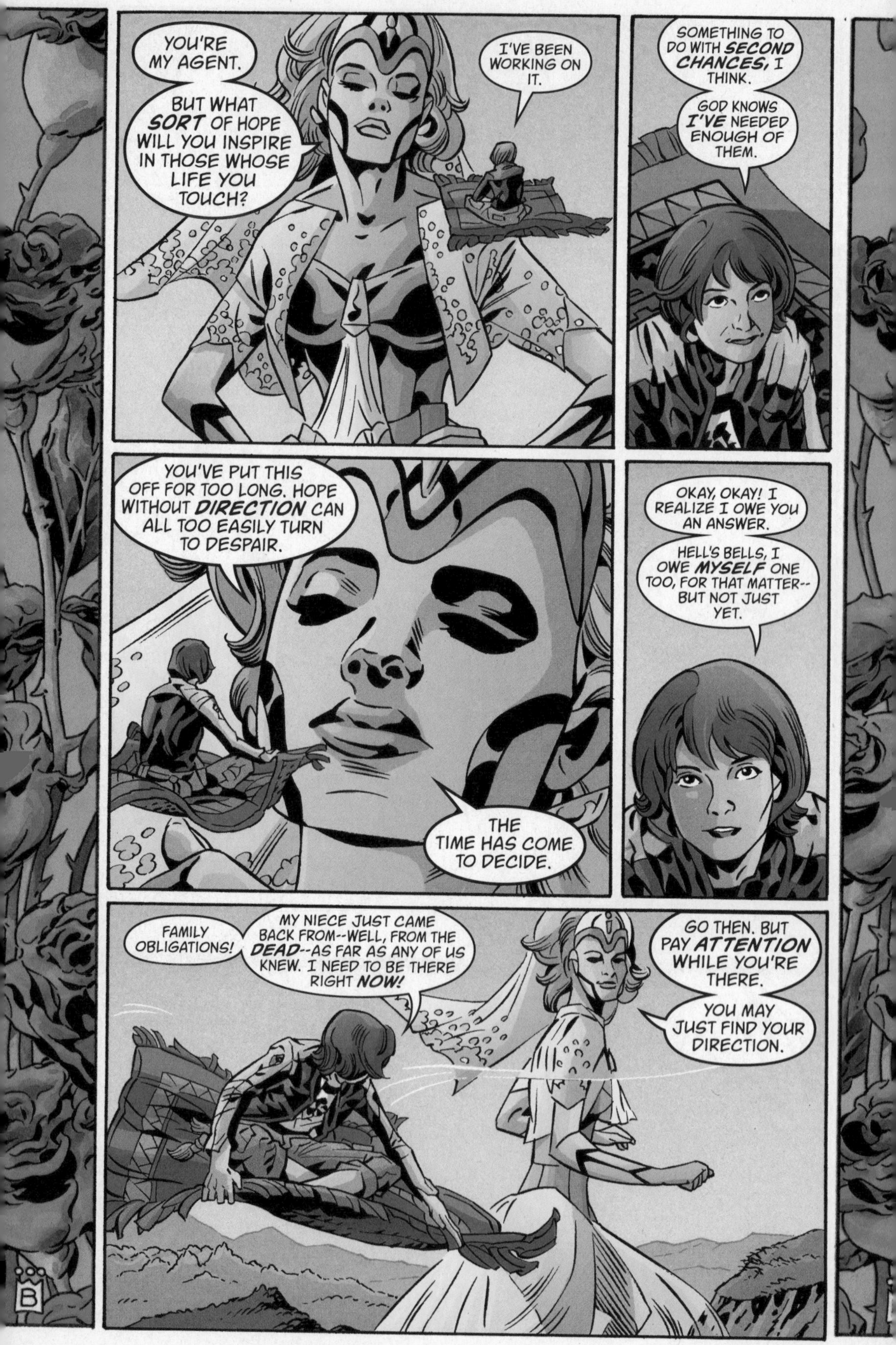
YOU'RE MY AGENT.
BUT WHAT SORT OF HOPE WILL YOU INSPIRE IN THOSE WHOSE LIFE YOU TOUCH?
I'VE BEEN WORKING ON IT.
SOMETHING TO DO WITH SECOND CHANCES, I THINK.
GOD KNOWS I'VE NEEDED ENOUGH OF THEM.
YOU'VE PUT THIS OFF FOR TOO LONG. HOPE WITHOUT DIRECTION CAN ALL TOO EASILY TURN TO DESPAIR.
THE TIME HAS COME TO DECIDE.
OKAY, OKAY! I REALIZE I OWE YOU AN ANSWER.
HELL'S BELLS, I OWE MYSELF ONE TOO, FOR THAT MATTER-- BUT NOT JUST YET.
FAMILY OBLIGATIONS!
MY NIECE JUST CAME BACK FROM--WELL, FROM THE DEAD--AS FAR AS ANY OF US KNEW. I NEED TO BE THERE RIGHT NOW!
GO THEN. BUT PAY ATTENTION WHILE YOU'RE THERE.
YOU MAY JUST FIND YOUR DIRECTION.

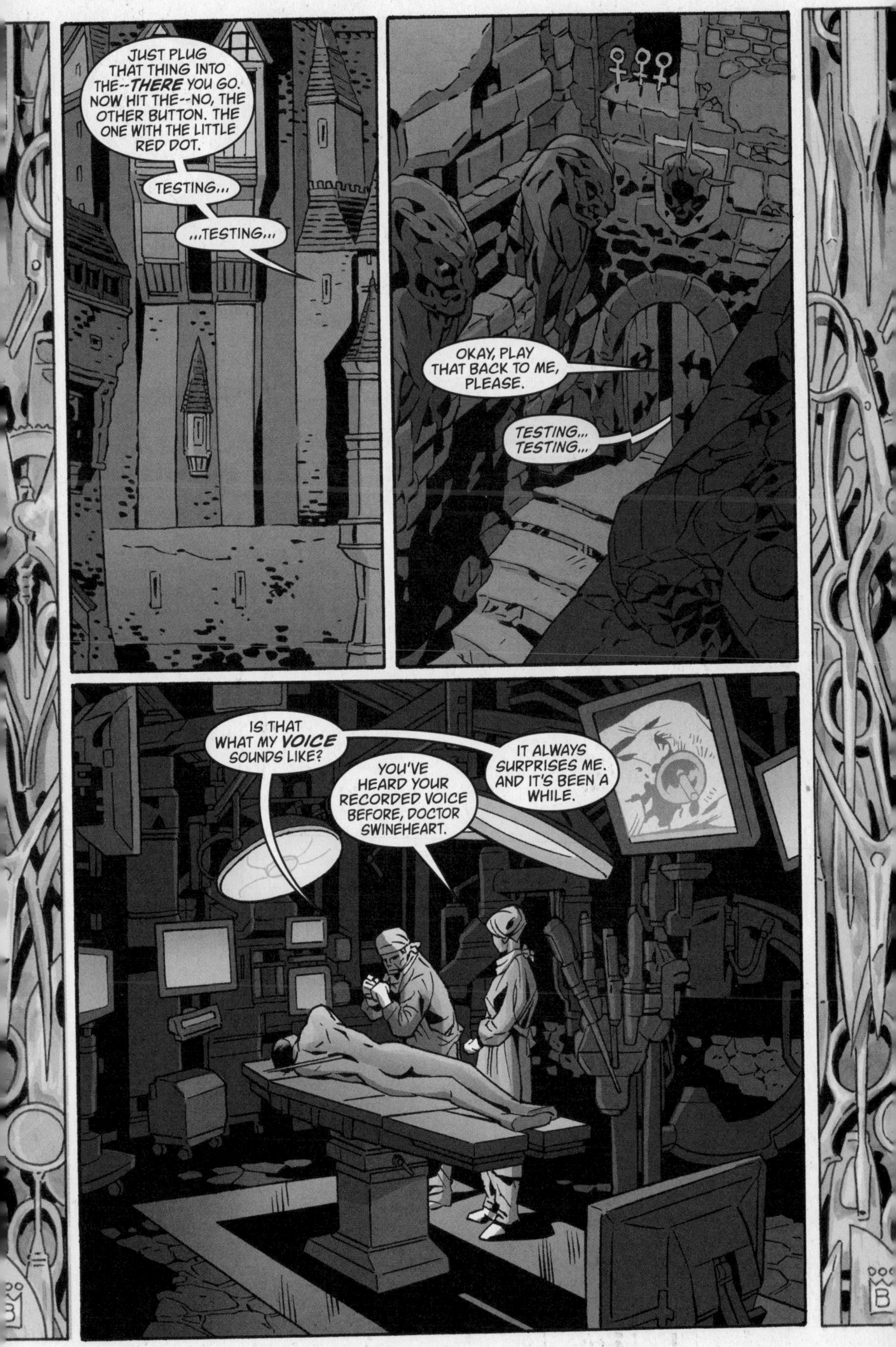
JUST PLUG THAT THING INTO THE--THERE YOU GO. NOW HIT THE--NO, THE OTHER BUTTON. THE ONE WITH THE LITTLE RED DOT.
TESTING...
...TESTING...
OKAY, PLAY THAT BACK TO ME, PLEASE.
TESTING... TESTING...
IS THAT WHAT MY VOICE SOUNDS LIKE?
YOU'VE HEARD YOUR RECORDED VOICE BEFORE, DOCTOR SWINEHEART.
IT ALWAYS SURPRISES ME. AND IT'S BEEN A WHILE.

OF COURSE. NOT SINCE BOY BLUE.

ARE WE RECORDING AGAIN?

WE BEGIN THE POST MORTEM EXAMINATION OF A CADAVER IDENTIFIED AS *PRINCE BRANDISH.* NO OTHER NAMES.

ACTUALLY, *WERIAN HOLT* WAS THE NAME BY WHICH I KNEW HIM.

NOW, NOW, LEIGH. YOU CAN'T HAVE FORGOTTEN SO SOON. I DON'T DO *DUETS.* THE GOOD DOCTOR IS STRICTLY A *SOLO* ACT.

IF YOU'VE COMMENTS TO ADD, YOU CAN INCLUDE THEM WHEN YOU TYPE UP MY NOTES.

SUBJECT IS MALE, HUMAN. APPROXIMATELY TWELVE STONE. APPEARS TO BE THIRTY YEARS OF AGE, PLUS OR MINUS. GINGER HAIR. NO NOTICEABLE SCARS OR TATTOOS.

THERE ARE SIX INJURIES ON THE BODY. FIVE ARE MINOR. ONE IS MAJOR AND THE PUTATIVE CAUSE OF DEATH.

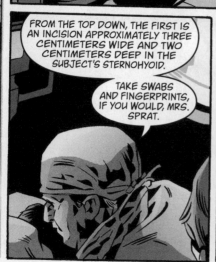

FROM THE TOP DOWN, THE FIRST IS AN INCISION APPROXIMATELY THREE CENTIMETERS WIDE AND TWO CENTIMETERS DEEP IN THE SUBJECT'S STERNOHYOID.

TAKE SWABS AND FINGERPRINTS, IF YOU WOULD, MRS. SPRAT.

SORRY--MISS DUGLAS.

THE SECOND CUT IS LOCATED...OH, BY THE WAY, I'VE BEEN MEANING TO TELL YOU. I'M WILLING TO *SLEEP* WITH YOU NOW, NURSE, IF YOU'RE STILL INTERESTED.

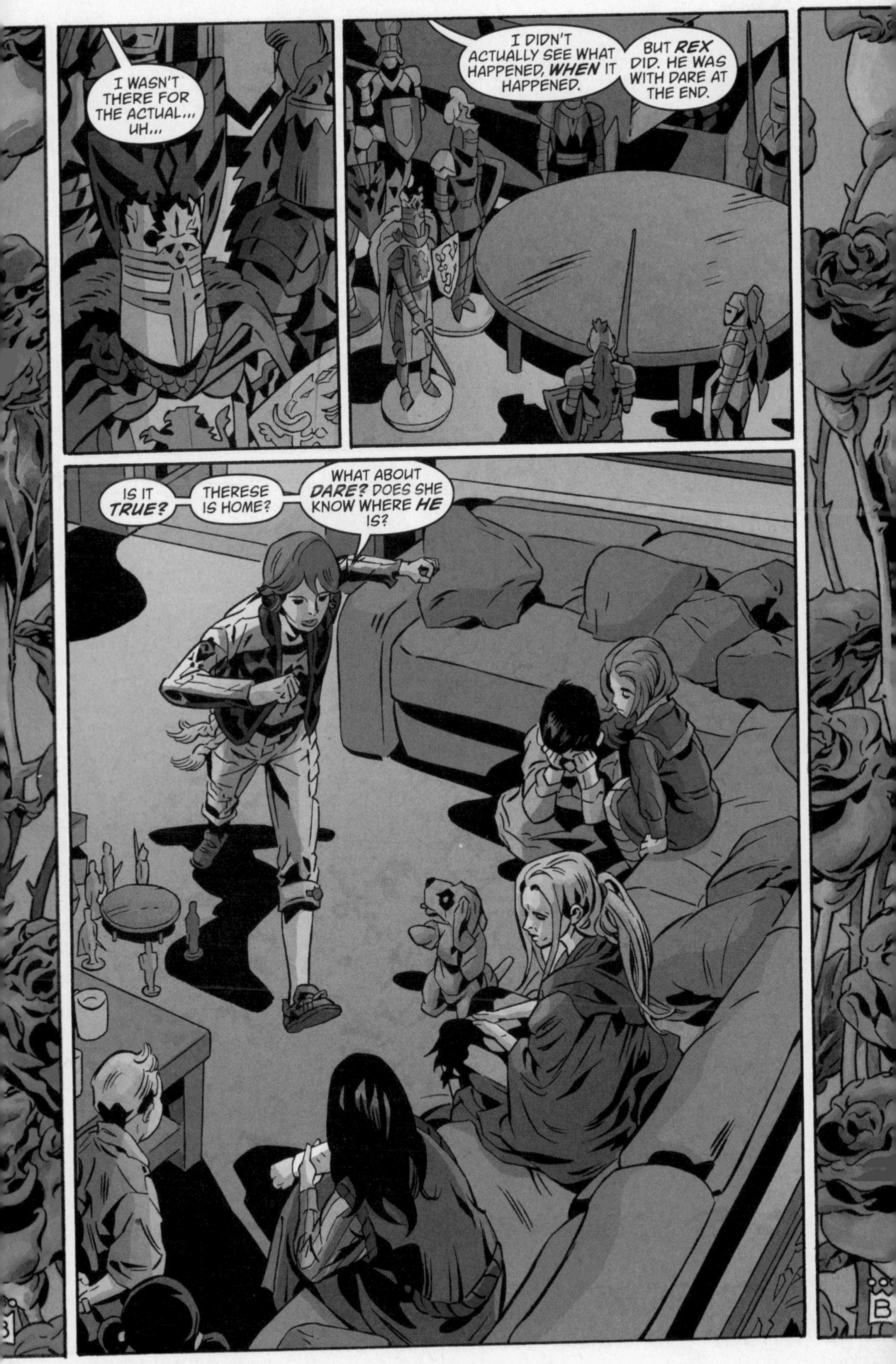
I WASN'T THERE FOR THE ACTUAL... UH...
I DIDN'T ACTUALLY SEE WHAT HAPPENED, WHEN IT HAPPENED.
BUT REX DID. HE WAS WITH DARE AT THE END.
IS IT TRUE?
THERESE IS HOME?
WHAT ABOUT DARE? DOES SHE KNOW WHERE HE IS?

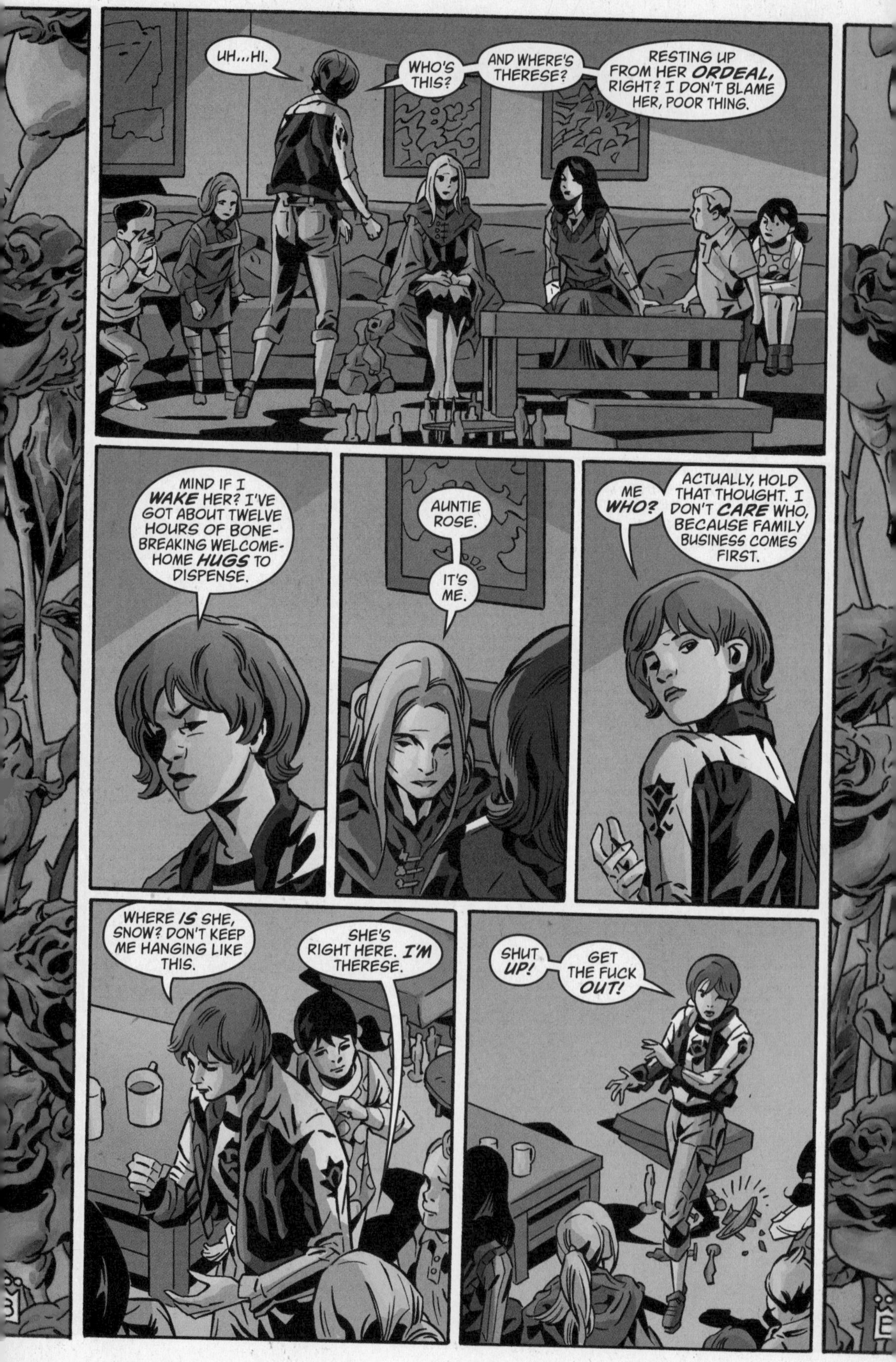

UH...HI.
WHO'S THIS?
AND WHERE'S THERESE?
RESTING UP FROM HER ORDEAL, RIGHT? I DON'T BLAME HER, POOR THING.
MIND IF I WAKE HER? I'VE GOT ABOUT TWELVE HOURS OF BONE-BREAKING WELCOME-HOME HUGS TO DISPENSE.
AUNTIE ROSE.
IT'S ME.
ME WHO?
ACTUALLY, HOLD THAT THOUGHT. I DON'T CARE WHO, BECAUSE FAMILY BUSINESS COMES FIRST.
WHERE IS SHE, SNOW? DON'T KEEP ME HANGING LIKE THIS.
SHE'S RIGHT HERE. I'M THERESE.
SHUT UP!
GET THE FUCK OUT!

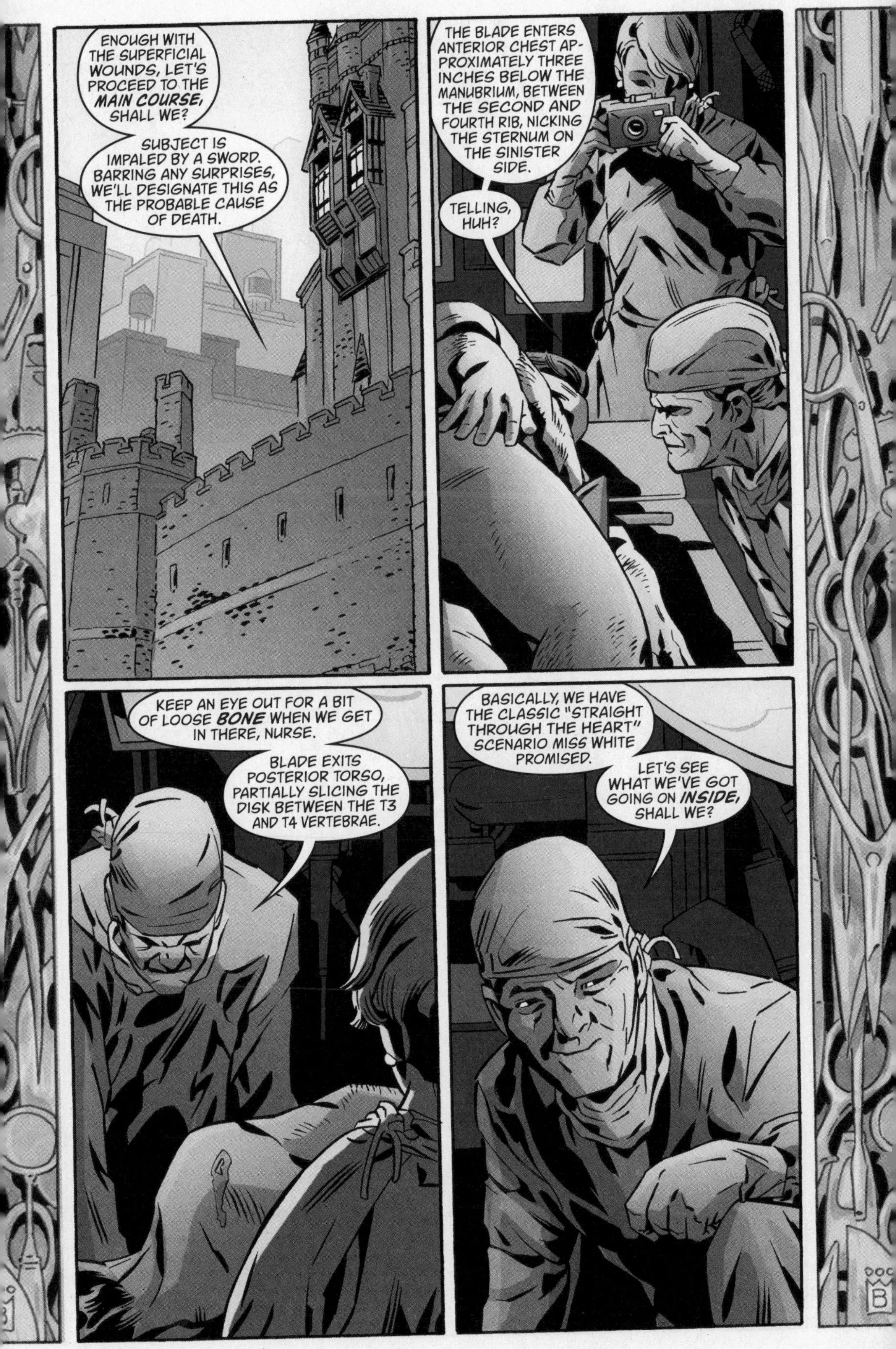
ENOUGH WITH THE SUPERFICIAL WOUNDS, LET'S PROCEED TO THE MAIN COURSE, SHALL WE?
SUBJECT IS IMPALED BY A SWORD. BARRING ANY SURPRISES, WE'LL DESIGNATE THIS AS THE PROBABLE CAUSE OF DEATH.
THE BLADE ENTERS ANTERIOR CHEST APPROXIMATELY THREE INCHES BELOW THE MANUBRIUM, BETWEEN THE SECOND AND FOURTH RIB, NICKING THE STERNUM ON THE SINISTER SIDE.
TELLING, HUH?
KEEP AN EYE OUT FOR A BIT OF LOOSE BONE WHEN WE GET IN THERE, NURSE.
BLADE EXITS POSTERIOR TORSO, PARTIALLY SLICING THE DISK BETWEEN THE T3 AND T4 VERTEBRAE.
BASICALLY, WE HAVE THE CLASSIC "STRAIGHT THROUGH THE HEART" SCENARIO MISS WHITE PROMISED.
LET'S SEE WHAT WE'VE GOT GOING ON INSIDE, SHALL WE?

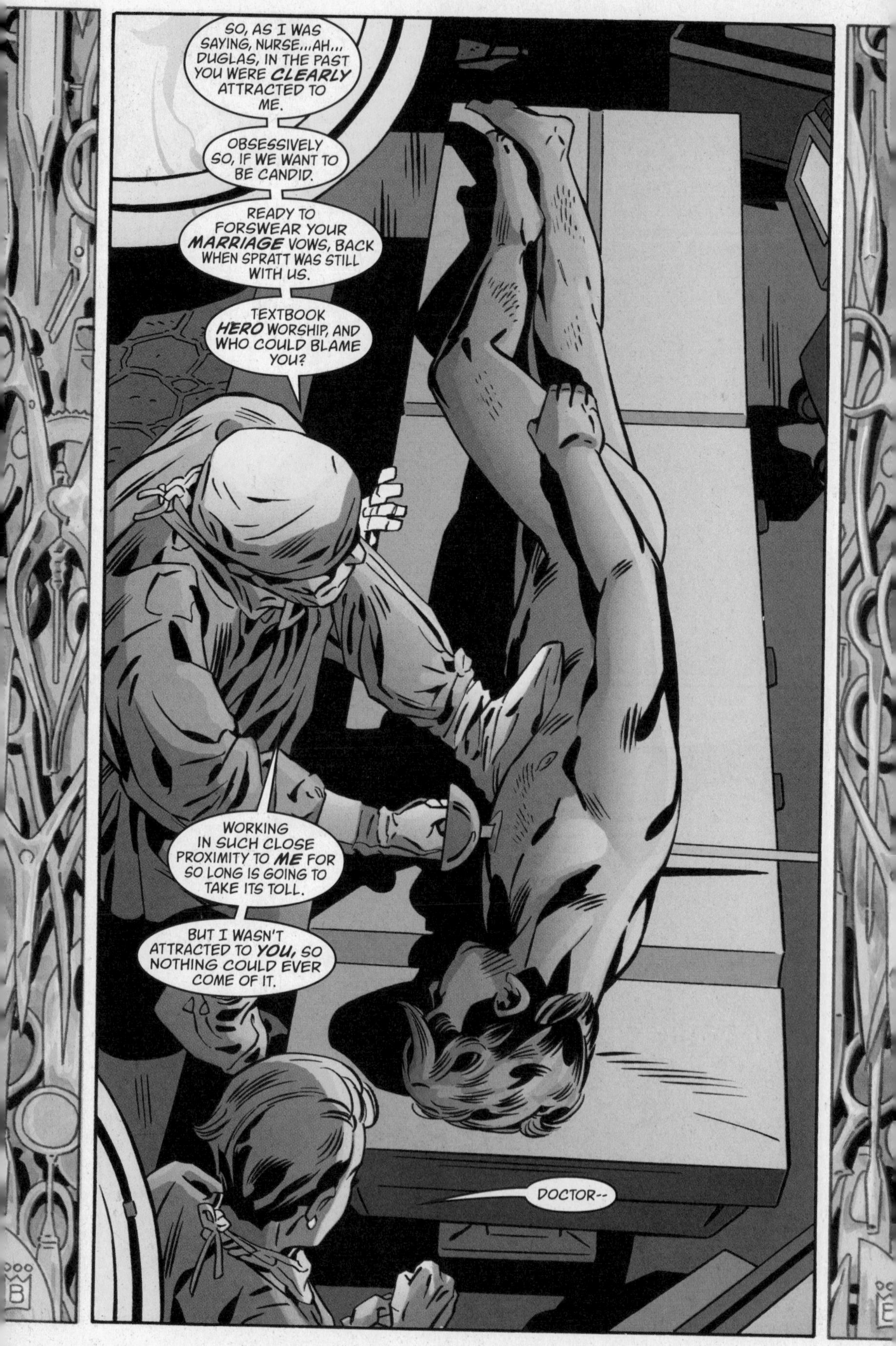
SO, AS I WAS SAYING, NURSE...AH... DUGLAS, IN THE PAST YOU WERE CLEARLY ATTRACTED TO ME.
OBSESSIVELY SO, IF WE WANT TO BE CANDID.
READY TO FORSWEAR YOUR MARRIAGE VOWS, BACK WHEN SPRATT WAS STILL WITH US.
TEXTBOOK HERO WORSHIP, AND WHO COULD BLAME YOU?
WORKING IN SUCH CLOSE PROXIMITY TO ME FOR SO LONG IS GOING TO TAKE ITS TOLL.
BUT I WASN'T ATTRACTED TO YOU, SO NOTHING COULD EVER COME OF IT.
DOCTOR--

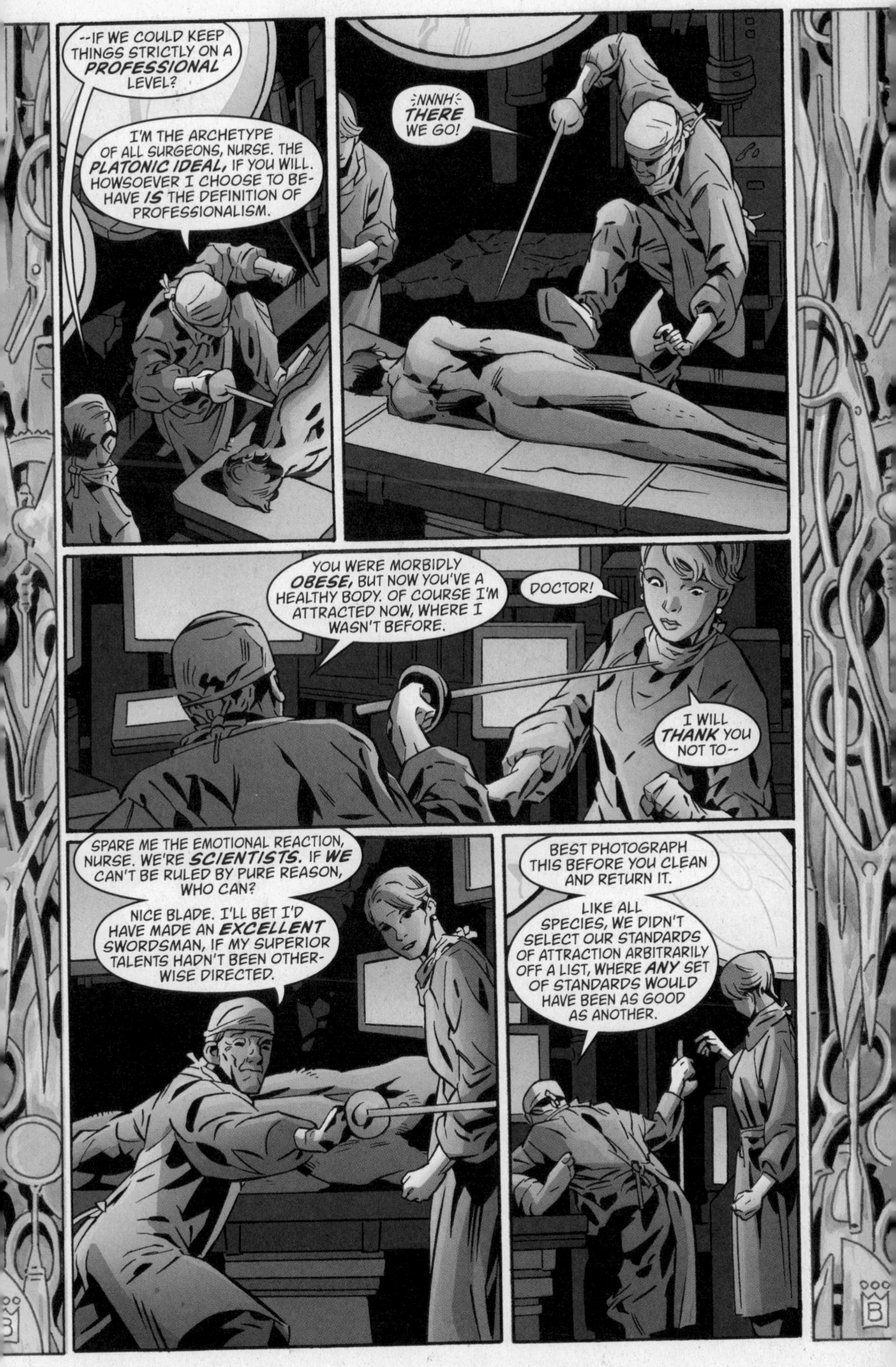
--IF WE COULD KEEP THINGS STRICTLY ON A PROFESSIONAL LEVEL?
I'M THE ARCHETYPE OF ALL SURGEONS, NURSE. THE PLATONIC IDEAL, IF YOU WILL. HOWSOEVER I CHOOSE TO BEHAVE IS THE DEFINITION OF PROFESSIONALISM.
NNNH THERE WE GO!
YOU WERE MORBIDLY OBESE, BUT NOW YOU'VE A HEALTHY BODY. OF COURSE I'M ATTRACTED NOW, WHERE I WASN'T BEFORE.
DOCTOR!
I WILL THANK YOU NOT TO--
SPARE ME THE EMOTIONAL REACTION, NURSE. WE'RE SCIENTISTS. IF WE CAN'T BE RULED BY PURE REASON, WHO CAN?
NICE BLADE. I'LL BET I'D HAVE MADE AN EXCELLENT SWORDSMAN, IF MY SUPERIOR TALENTS HADN'T BEEN OTHERWISE DIRECTED.
BEST PHOTOGRAPH THIS BEFORE YOU CLEAN AND RETURN IT.
LIKE ALL SPECIES, WE DIDN'T SELECT OUR STANDARDS OF ATTRACTION ARBITRARILY OFF A LIST, WHERE ANY SET OF STANDARDS WOULD HAVE BEEN AS GOOD AS ANOTHER.

WE'RE GENERALLY ATTRACTED TO WHAT'S HEALTHY, AND WHAT WILL CREATE MORE VIABLE OFFSPRING.

BEGINNING MY *Y* INCISION. INTO THE BODY CAVITY WE GO.

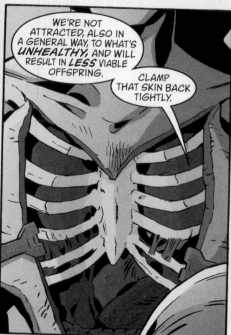

WE'RE NOT ATTRACTED, ALSO IN A GENERAL WAY, TO WHAT'S *UNHEALTHY*, AND WILL RESULT IN *LESS* VIABLE OFFSPRING.

CLAMP THAT SKIN BACK TIGHTLY.

NO BROKEN RIBS, BUT THERE'S THAT NICK OUT OF THE STERNUM, *EXACTLY* WHERE I CALLED IT.

SO YOU WANT TO MAKE *BABIES* WITH ME?

NO, OF COURSE NOT. HAND ME THE SAW, PLEASE.

BUT THAT'S THE ENGINE *DRIVING* THE DESIRE. QUIT PRETENDING TO BE INSULTED. YOU KNOW THIS AS WELL AS I.

SPREADERS.

HELLO, WHAT'S THIS?

NOW *THAT'S* ONE FOR THE RECORD BOOKS.

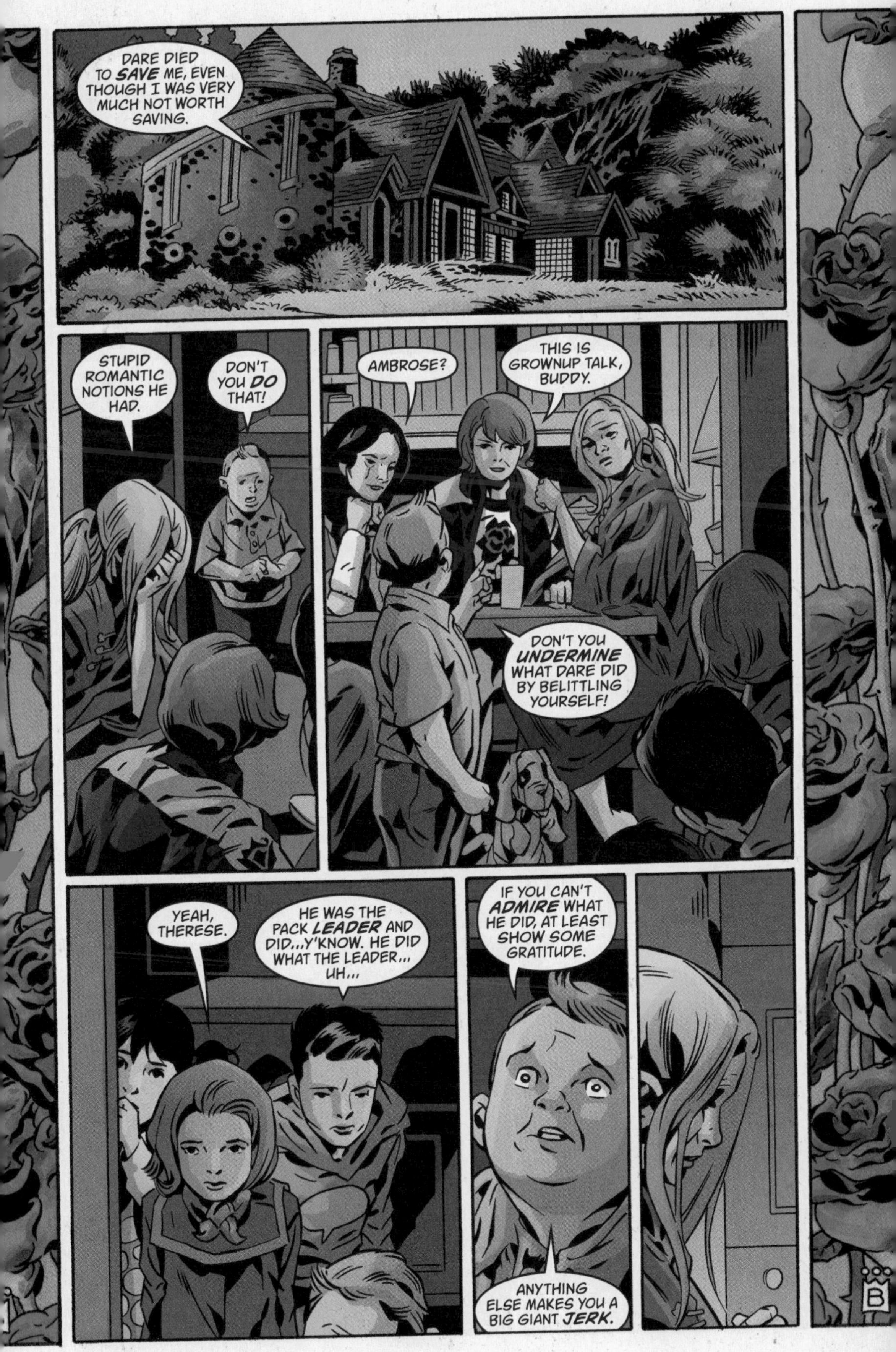
DARE DIED TO SAVE ME, EVEN THOUGH I WAS VERY MUCH NOT WORTH SAVING.
STUPID ROMANTIC NOTIONS HE HAD.
DON'T YOU DO THAT!
AMBROSE?
THIS IS GROWNUP TALK, BUDDY.
DON'T YOU UNDERMINE WHAT DARE DID BY BELITTLING YOURSELF!
YEAH, THERESE.
HE WAS THE PACK LEADER AND DID...Y'KNOW. HE DID WHAT THE LEADER... UH...
IF YOU CAN'T ADMIRE WHAT HE DID, AT LEAST SHOW SOME GRATITUDE.
ANYTHING ELSE MAKES YOU A BIG GIANT JERK.

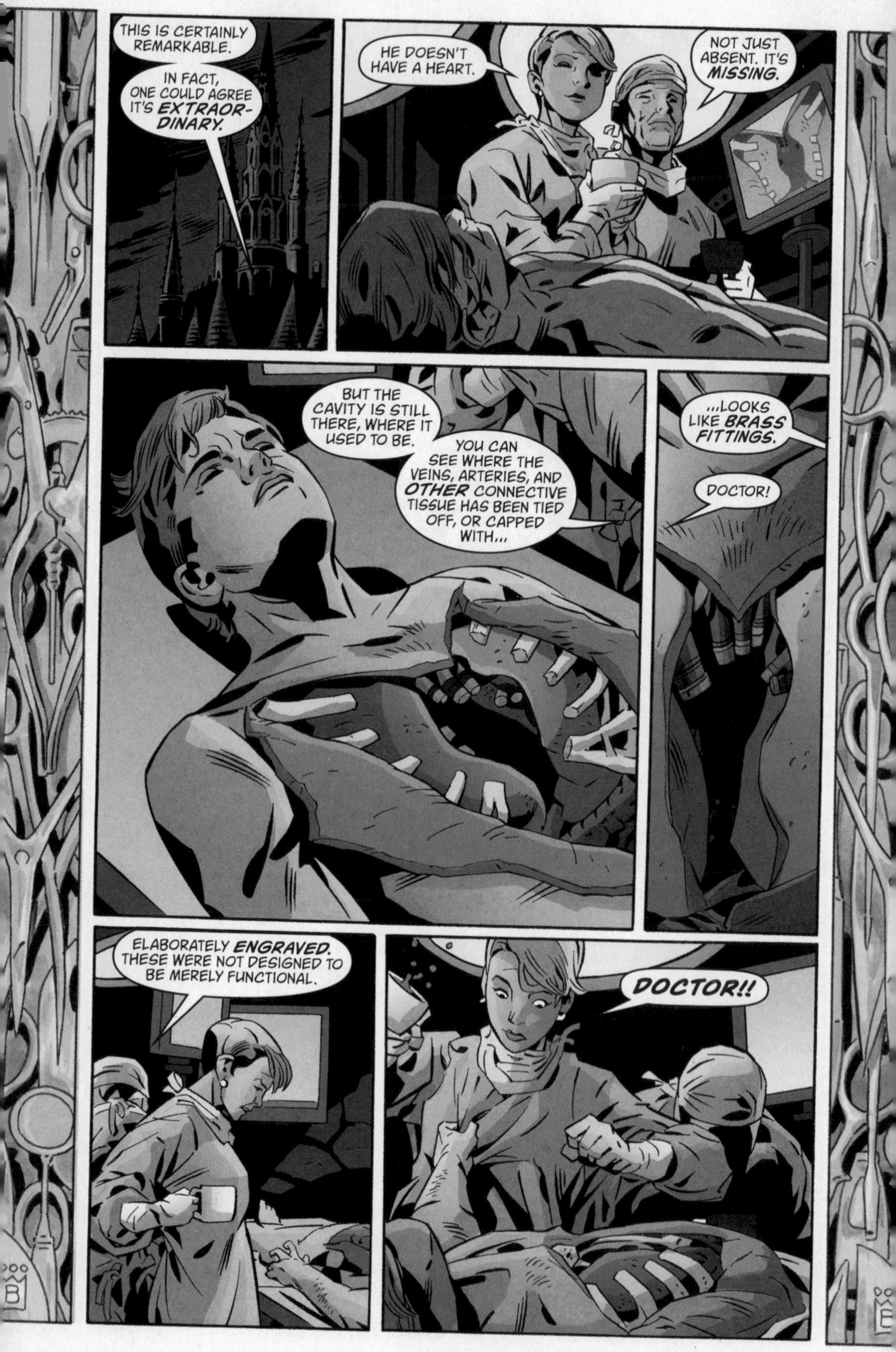
THIS IS CERTAINLY REMARKABLE.
IN FACT, ONE COULD AGREE IT'S EXTRAOR-DINARY.
HE DOESN'T HAVE A HEART.
NOT JUST ABSENT. IT'S MISSING.
BUT THE CAVITY IS STILL THERE, WHERE IT USED TO BE.
YOU CAN SEE WHERE THE VEINS, ARTERIES, AND OTHER CONNECTIVE TISSUE HAS BEEN TIED OFF, OR CAPPED WITH...
...LOOKS LIKE BRASS FITTINGS.
DOCTOR!
ELABORATELY ENGRAVED. THESE WERE NOT DESIGNED TO BE MERELY FUNCTIONAL.
DOCTOR!!

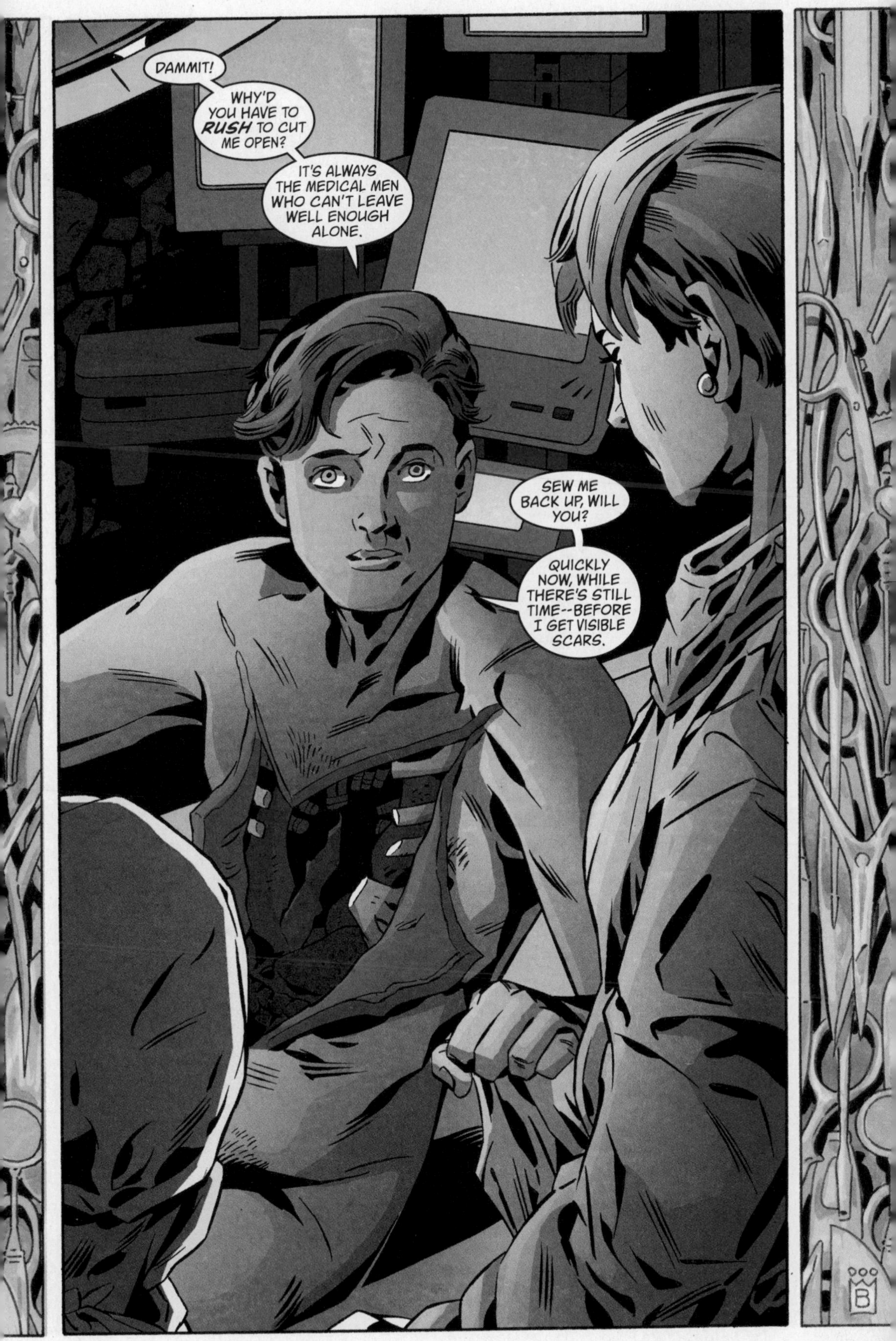
DAMMIT!
WHY'D YOU HAVE TO RUSH TO CUT ME OPEN?
IT'S ALWAYS THE MEDICAL MEN WHO CAN'T LEAVE WELL ENOUGH ALONE.
SEW ME BACK UP, WILL YOU?
QUICKLY NOW, WHILE THERE'S STILL TIME--BEFORE I GET VISIBLE SCARS.

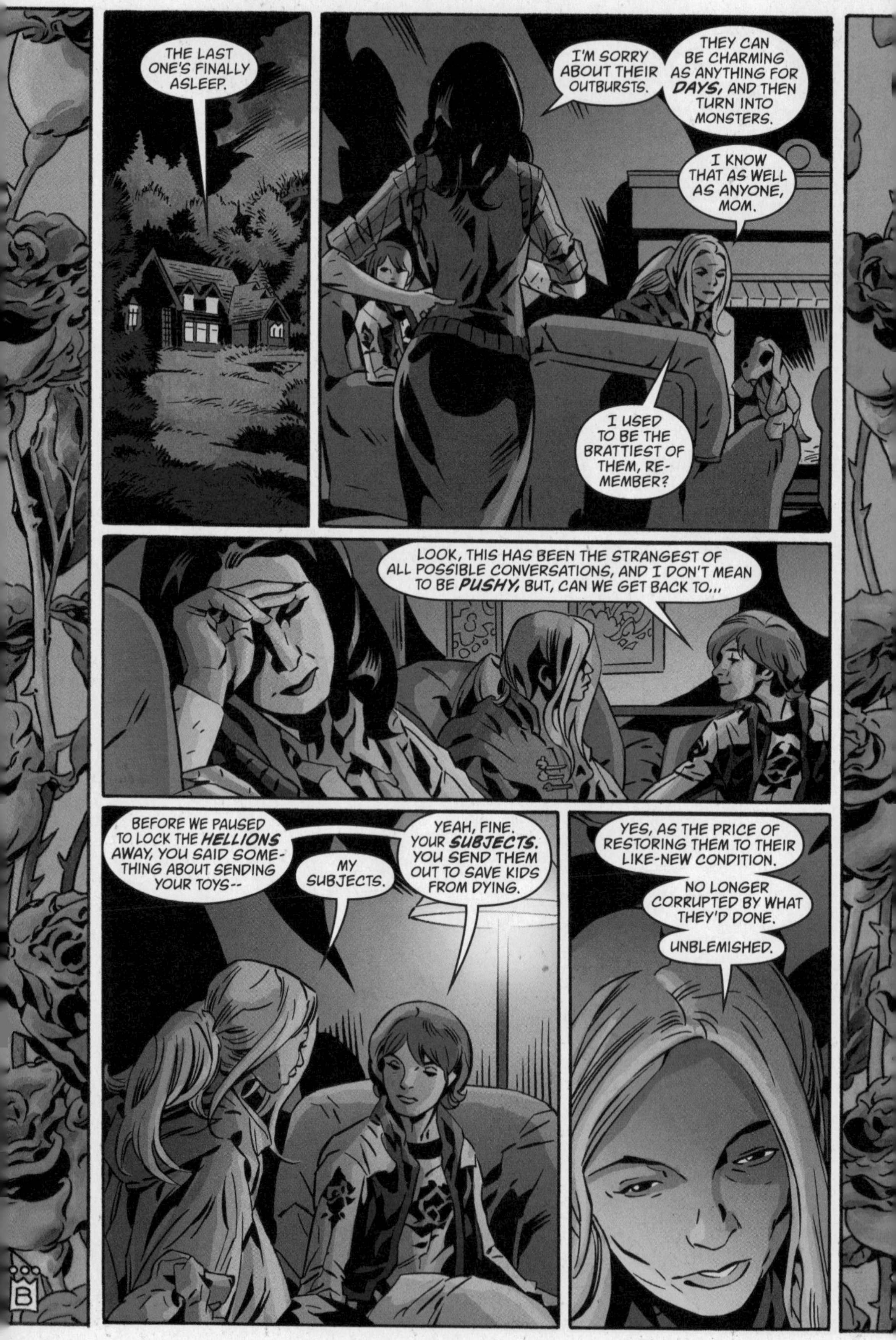
THE LAST ONE'S FINALLY ASLEEP.
I'M SORRY ABOUT THEIR OUTBURSTS.
THEY CAN BE CHARMING AS ANYTHING FOR DAYS, AND THEN TURN INTO MONSTERS.
I KNOW THAT AS WELL AS ANYONE, MOM.
I USED TO BE THE BRATTIEST OF THEM, RE- MEMBER?
LOOK, THIS HAS BEEN THE STRANGEST OF ALL POSSIBLE CONVERSATIONS, AND I DON'T MEAN TO BE PUSHY, BUT, CAN WE GET BACK TO...
BEFORE WE PAUSED TO LOCK THE HELLIONS AWAY, YOU SAID SOME- THING ABOUT SENDING YOUR TOYS--
MY SUBJECTS.
YEAH, FINE. YOUR SUBJECTS. YOU SEND THEM OUT TO SAVE KIDS FROM DYING.
YES, AS THE PRICE OF RESTORING THEM TO THEIR LIKE-NEW CONDITION.
NO LONGER CORRUPTED BY WHAT THEY'D DONE.
UNBLEMISHED.

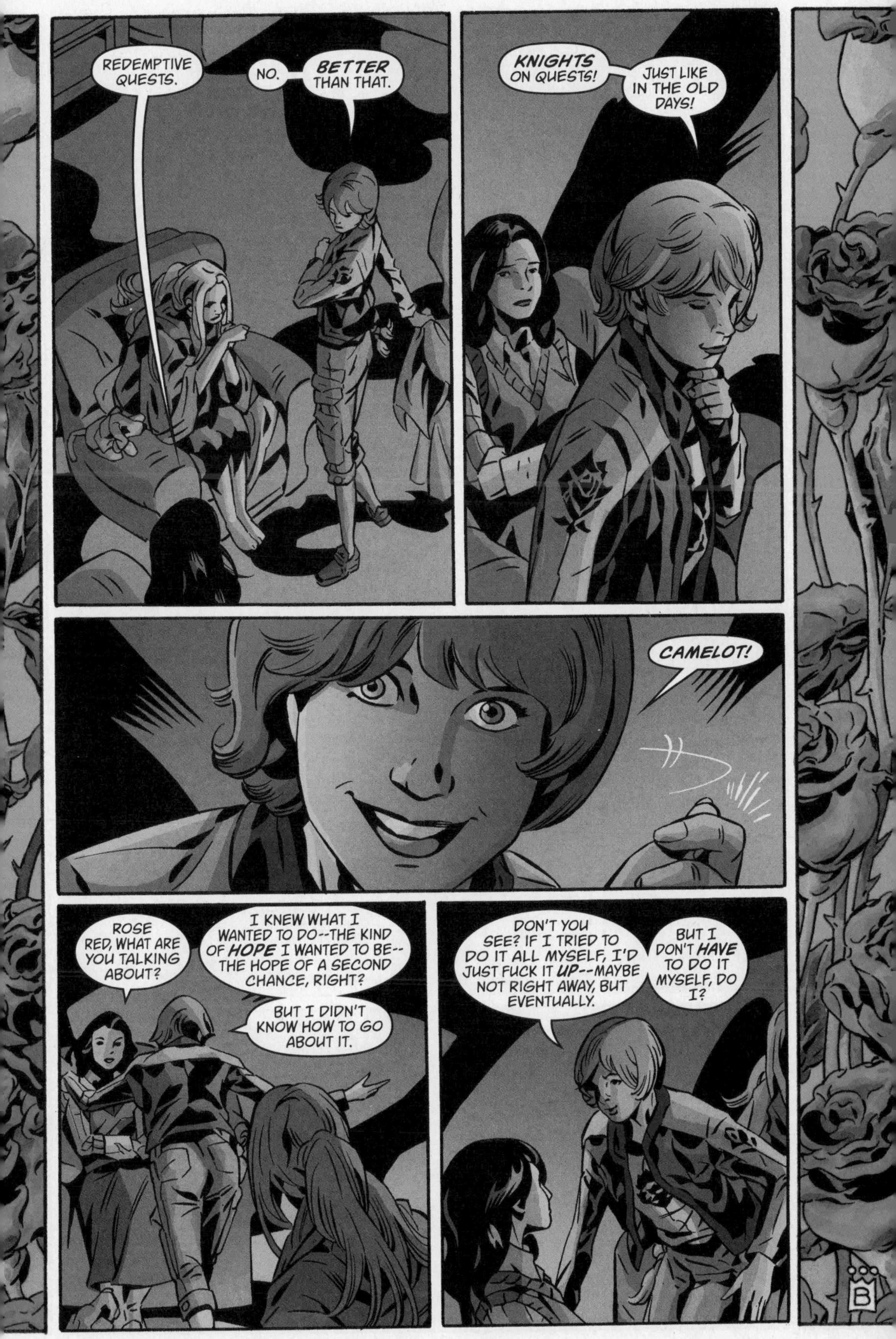

REDEMPTIVE QUESTS.
NO.
BETTER THAN THAT.
KNIGHTS ON QUESTS!
JUST LIKE IN THE OLD DAYS!
CAMELOT!
ROSE RED, WHAT ARE YOU TALKING ABOUT?
I KNEW WHAT I WANTED TO DO--THE KIND OF HOPE I WANTED TO BE--THE HOPE OF A SECOND CHANCE, RIGHT?
BUT I DIDN'T KNOW HOW TO GO ABOUT IT.
DON'T YOU SEE? IF I TRIED TO DO IT ALL MYSELF, I'D JUST FUCK IT UP--MAYBE NOT RIGHT AWAY, BUT EVENTUALLY.
BUT I DON'T HAVE TO DO IT MYSELF, DO I?

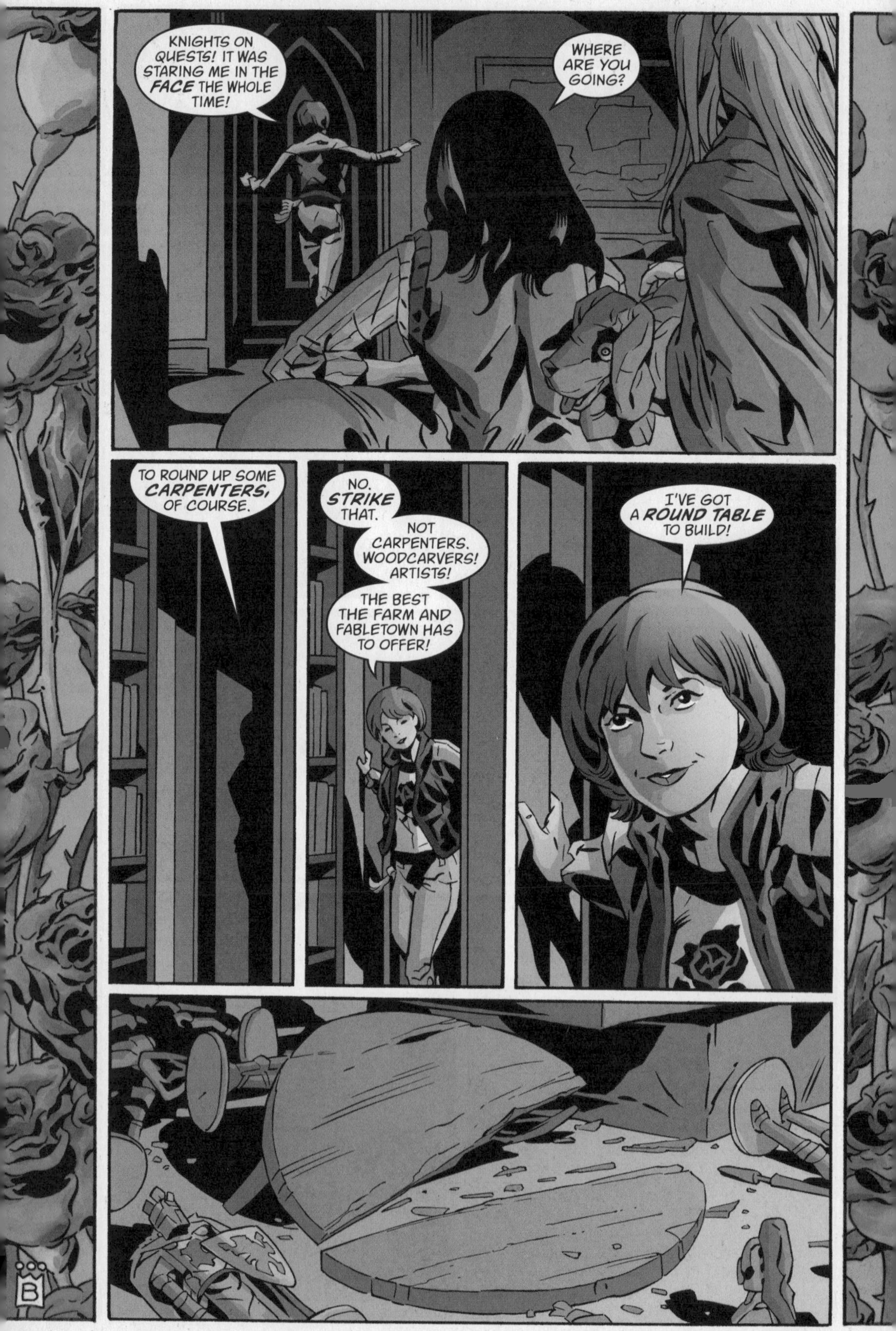
KNIGHTS ON QUESTS! IT WAS STARING ME IN THE *FACE* THE WHOLE TIME!
WHERE ARE YOU GOING?
TO ROUND UP SOME *CARPENTERS,* OF COURSE.
NO. *STRIKE* THAT.
NOT CARPENTERS. WOODCARVERS! ARTISTS!
THE BEST THE FARM AND FABLETOWN HAS TO OFFER!
I'VE GOT A *ROUND TABLE* TO BUILD!

NEXT: A BRIEF SHINING MOMENT.

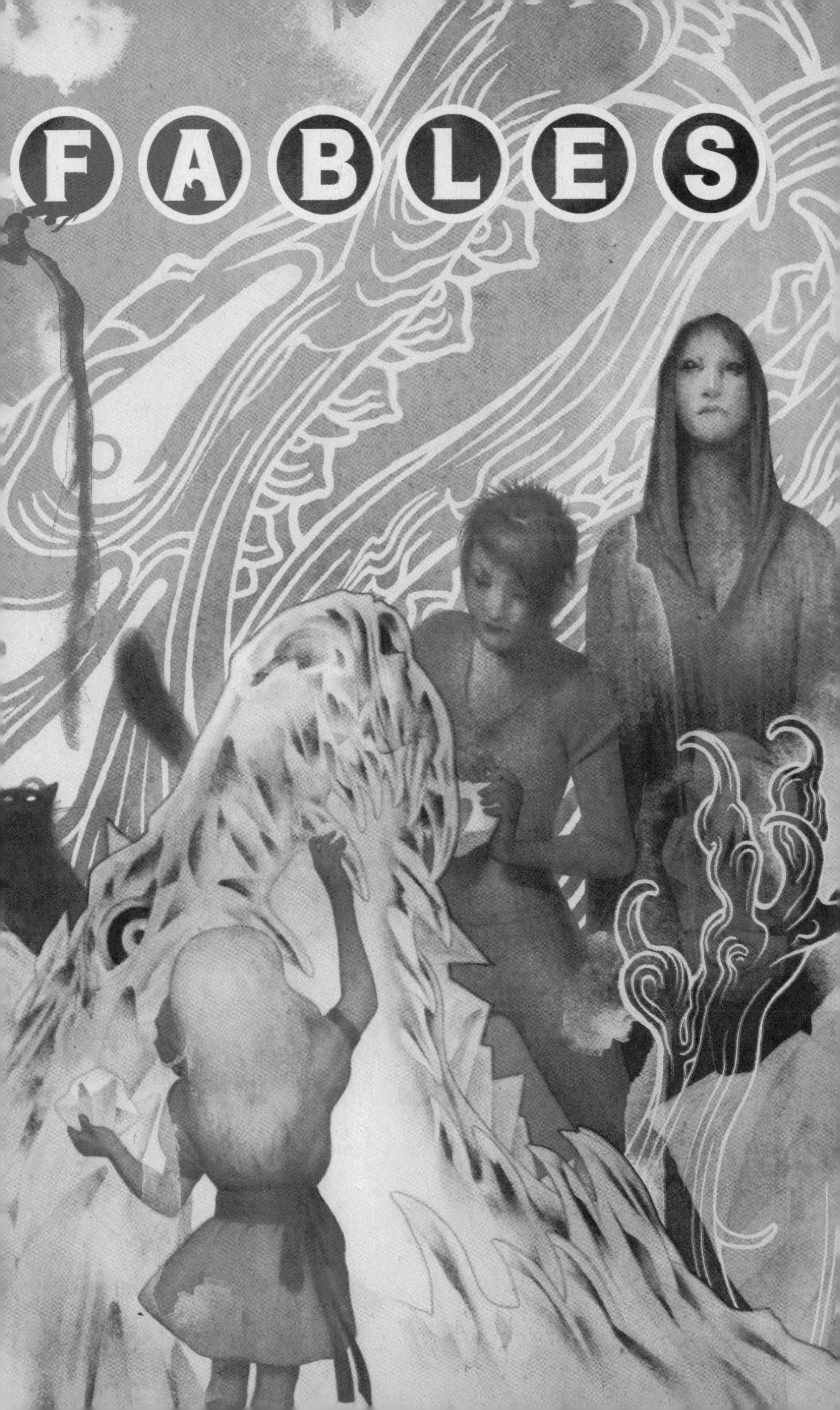
FABLES

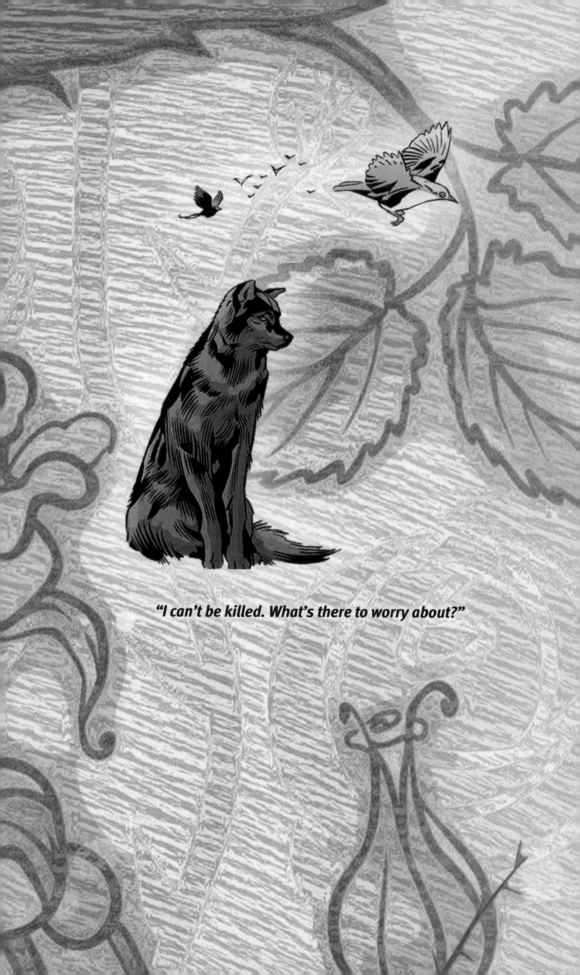

"I can't be killed. What's there to worry about?"

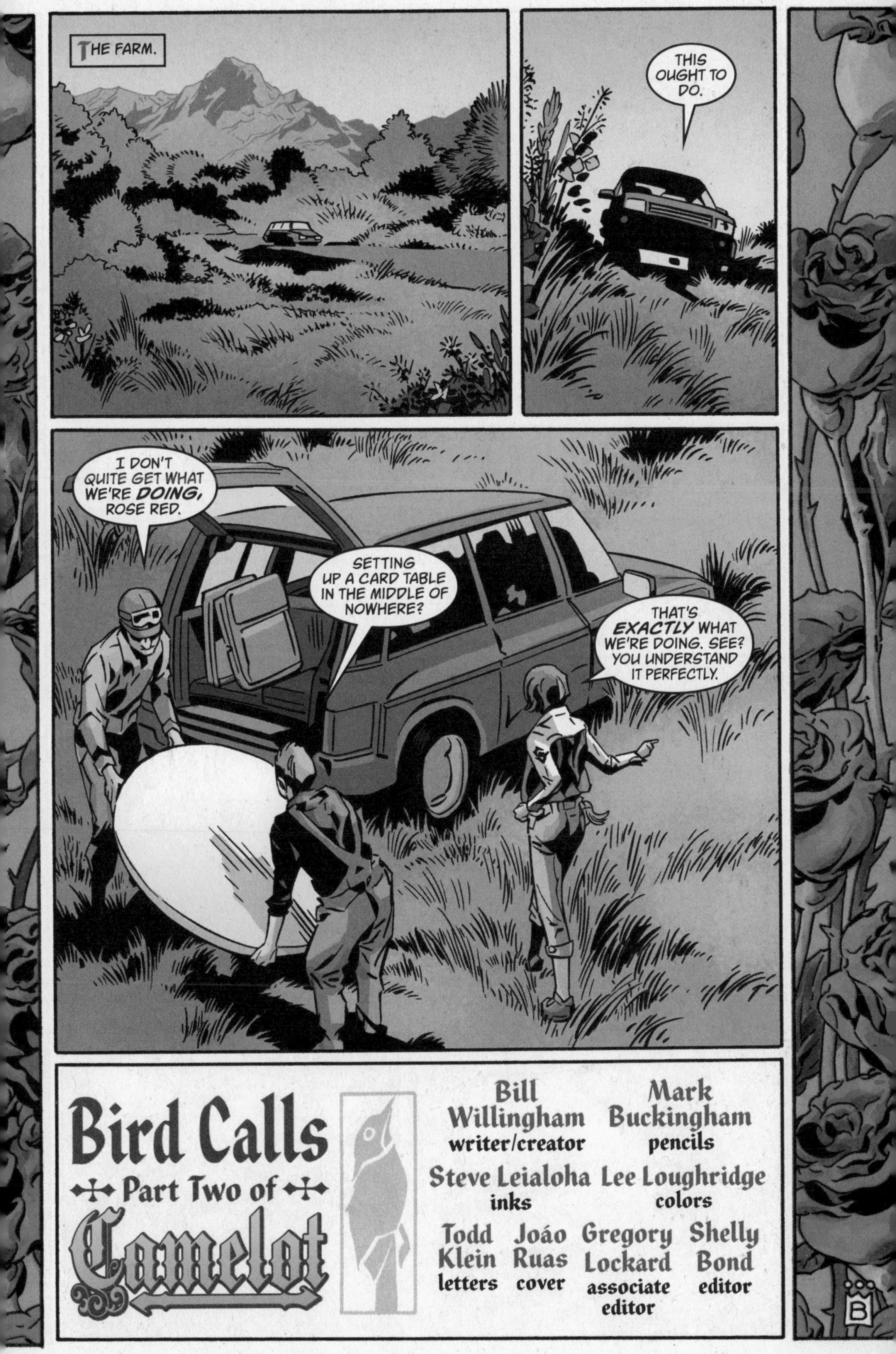

THE FARM.
THIS OUGHT TO DO.
I DON'T QUITE GET WHAT WE'RE DOING, ROSE RED.
SETTING UP A CARD TABLE IN THE MIDDLE OF NOWHERE?
THAT'S EXACTLY WHAT WE'RE DOING. SEE? YOU UNDERSTAND IT PERFECTLY.
Bird Calls
Part Two of
Camelot
Bill Willingham writer/creator
Mark Buckingham pencils
Steve Leialoha inks
Lee Loughridge colors
Todd Klein letters
Joáo Ruas cover
Gregory Lockard associate editor
Shelly Bond editor

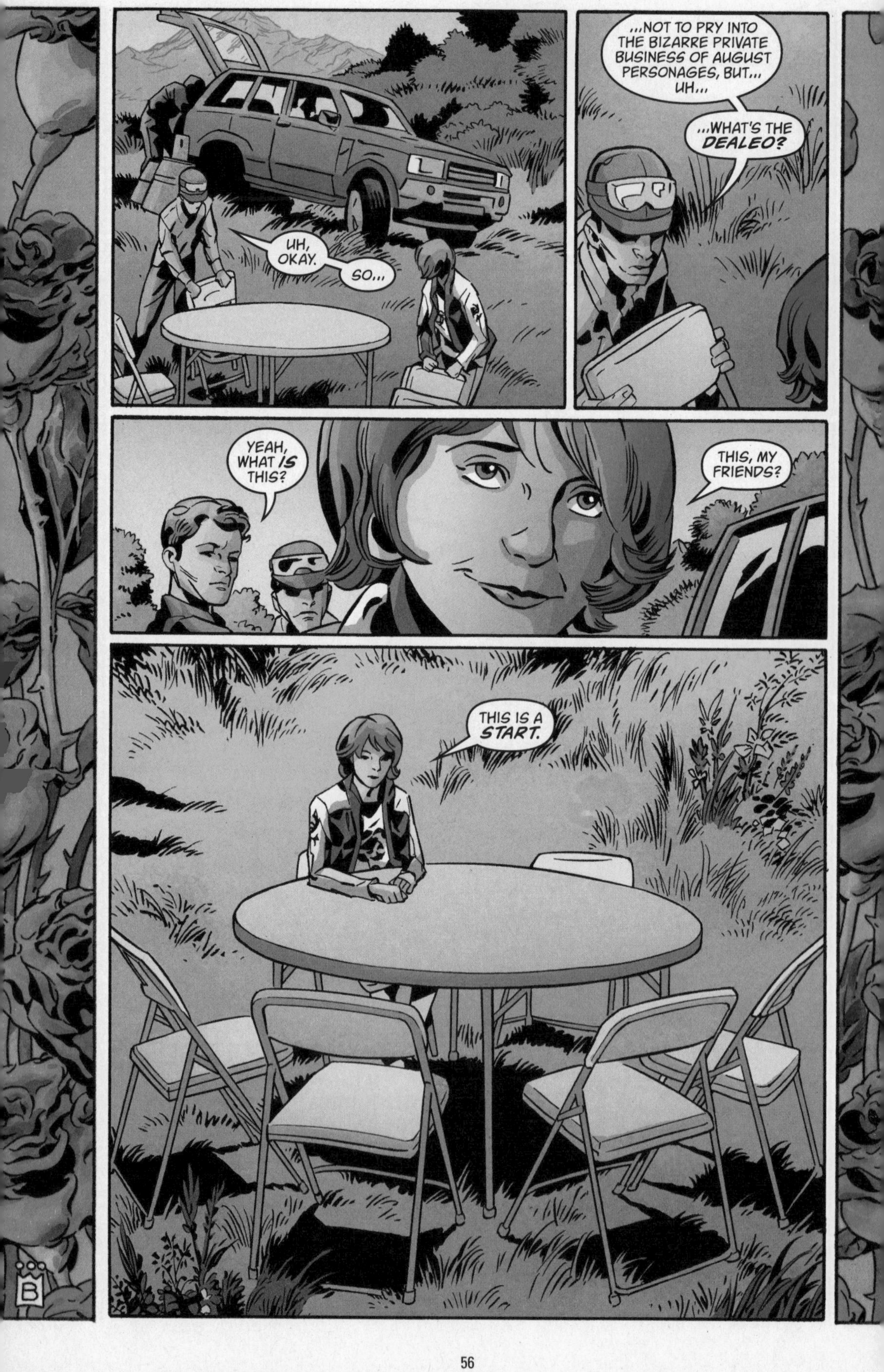
UH, OKAY.
SO...
...NOT TO PRY INTO THE BIZARRE PRIVATE BUSINESS OF AUGUST PERSONAGES, BUT... UH...
...WHAT'S THE DEALEO?
YEAH, WHAT IS THIS?
THIS, MY FRIENDS?
THIS IS A START.

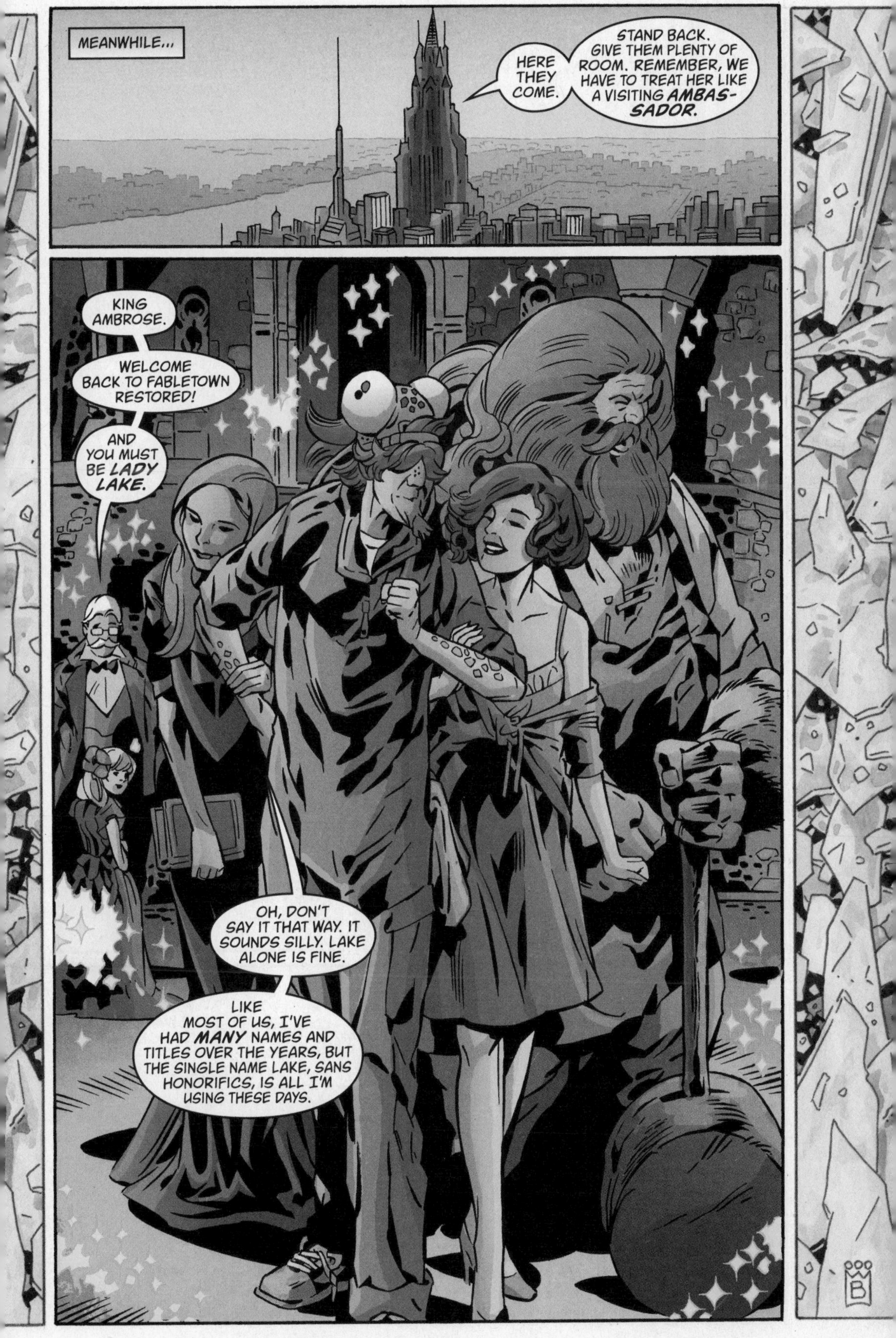
MEANWHILE...
HERE THEY COME.
STAND BACK. GIVE THEM PLENTY OF ROOM. REMEMBER, WE HAVE TO TREAT HER LIKE A VISITING AMBASSADOR.
KING AMBROSE.
WELCOME BACK TO FABLETOWN RESTORED!
AND YOU MUST BE LADY LAKE.
OH, DON'T SAY IT THAT WAY. IT SOUNDS SILLY. LAKE ALONE IS FINE.
LIKE MOST OF US, I'VE HAD MANY NAMES AND TITLES OVER THE YEARS, BUT THE SINGLE NAME LAKE, SANS HONORIFICS, IS ALL I'M USING THESE DAYS.

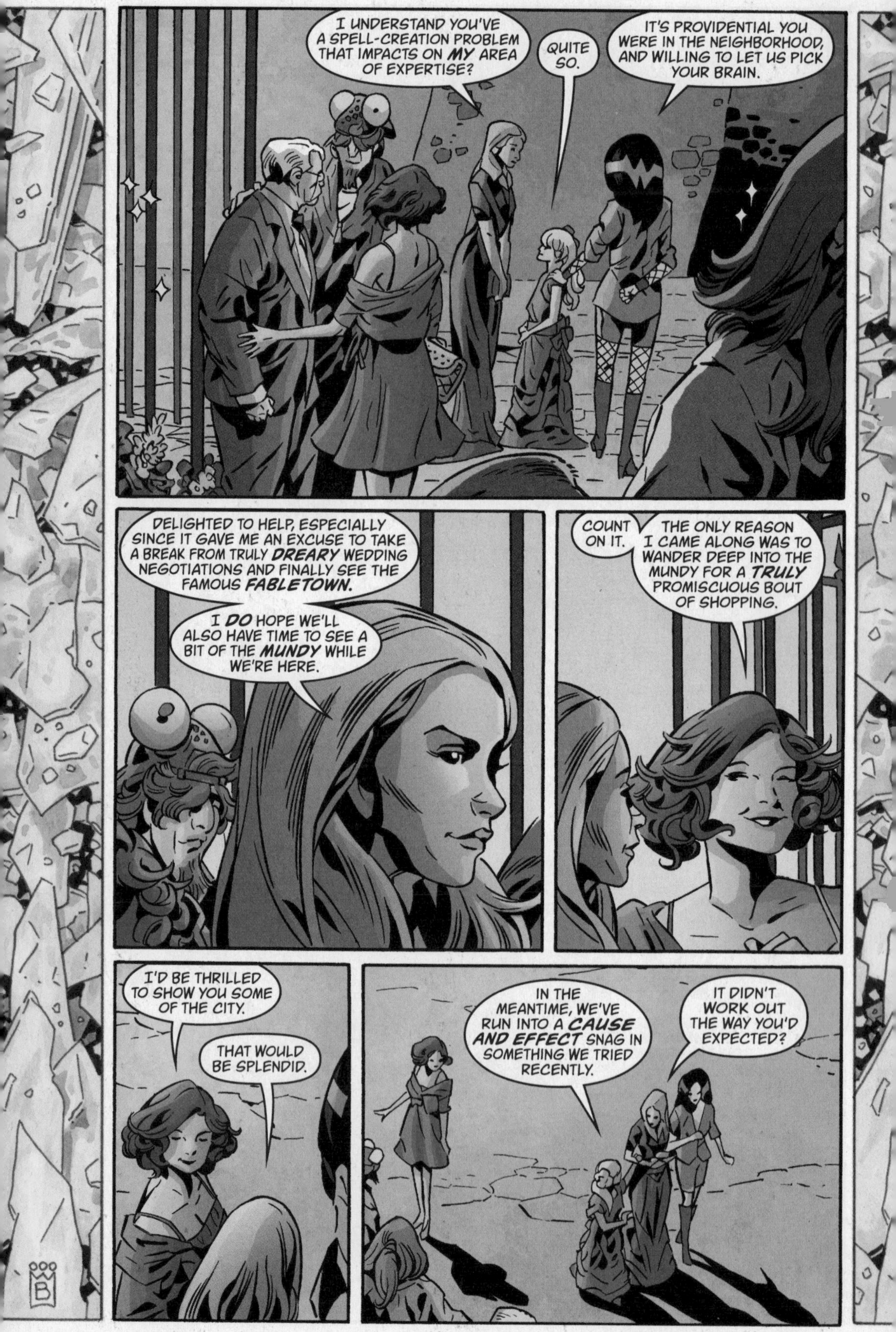
I UNDERSTAND YOU'VE A SPELL-CREATION PROBLEM THAT IMPACTS ON *MY* AREA OF EXPERTISE?
QUITE SO.
IT'S PROVIDENTIAL YOU WERE IN THE NEIGHBORHOOD, AND WILLING TO LET US PICK YOUR BRAIN.
DELIGHTED TO HELP, ESPECIALLY SINCE IT GAVE ME AN EXCUSE TO TAKE A BREAK FROM TRULY *DREARY* WEDDING NEGOTIATIONS AND FINALLY SEE THE FAMOUS *FABLETOWN.*
I *DO* HOPE WE'LL ALSO HAVE TIME TO SEE A BIT OF THE *MUNDY* WHILE WE'RE HERE.
COUNT ON IT.
THE ONLY REASON I CAME ALONG WAS TO WANDER DEEP INTO THE MUNDY FOR A *TRULY* PROMISCUOUS BOUT OF SHOPPING.
I'D BE THRILLED TO SHOW YOU SOME OF THE CITY.
THAT WOULD BE SPLENDID.
IN THE MEANTIME, WE'VE RUN INTO A *CAUSE AND EFFECT* SNAG IN SOMETHING WE TRIED RECENTLY.
IT DIDN'T WORK OUT THE WAY YOU'D EXPECTED?

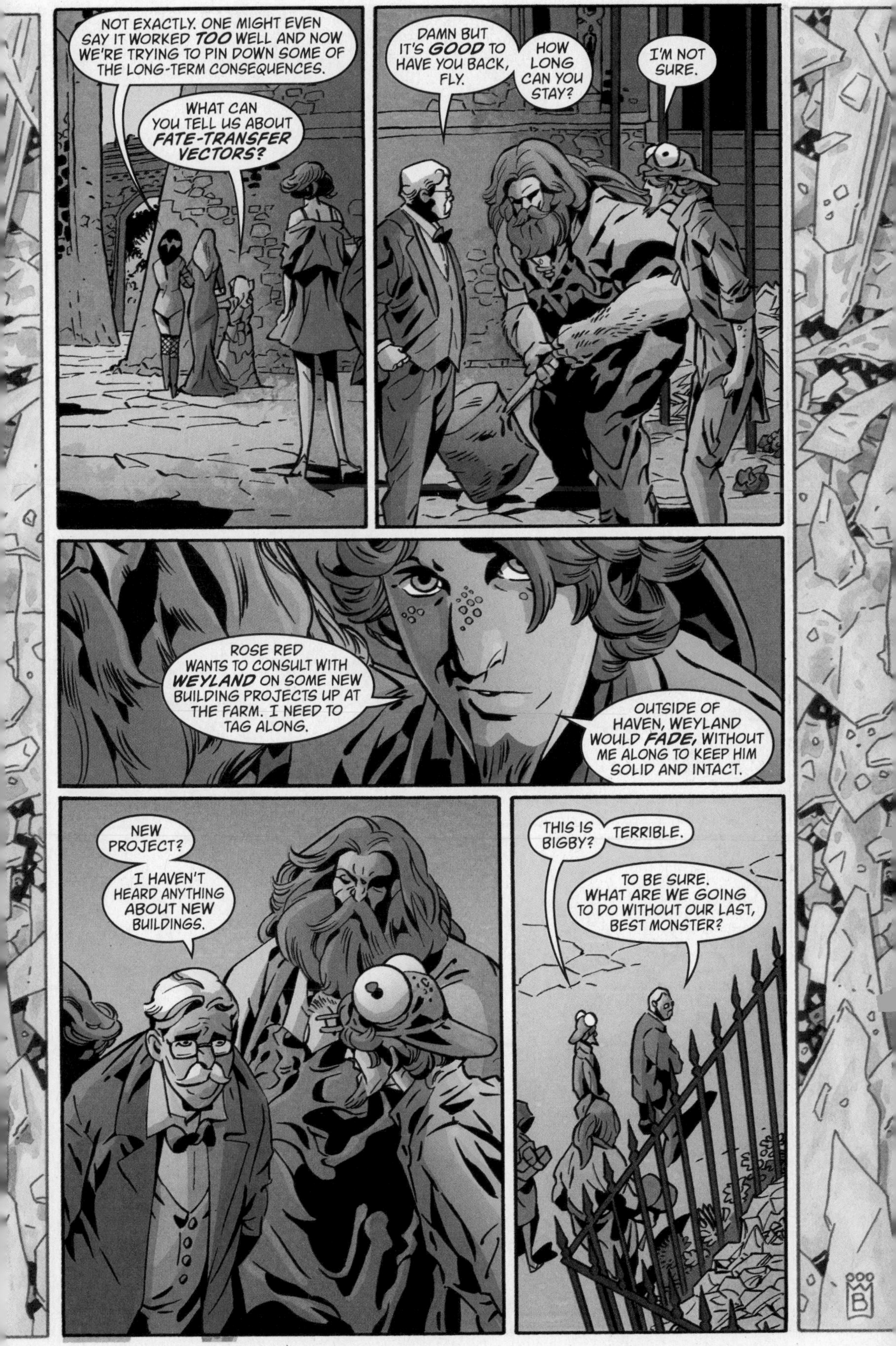
NOT EXACTLY. ONE MIGHT EVEN SAY IT WORKED TOO WELL AND NOW WE'RE TRYING TO PIN DOWN SOME OF THE LONG-TERM CONSEQUENCES.
WHAT CAN YOU TELL US ABOUT FATE-TRANSFER VECTORS?
DAMN BUT IT'S GOOD TO HAVE YOU BACK, FLY.
HOW LONG CAN YOU STAY?
I'M NOT SURE.
ROSE RED WANTS TO CONSULT WITH WEYLAND ON SOME NEW BUILDING PROJECTS UP AT THE FARM. I NEED TO TAG ALONG.
OUTSIDE OF HAVEN, WEYLAND WOULD FADE, WITHOUT ME ALONG TO KEEP HIM SOLID AND INTACT.
NEW PROJECT?
I HAVEN'T HEARD ANYTHING ABOUT NEW BUILDINGS.
THIS IS BIGBY?
TERRIBLE.
TO BE SURE. WHAT ARE WE GOING TO DO WITHOUT OUR LAST, BEST MONSTER?

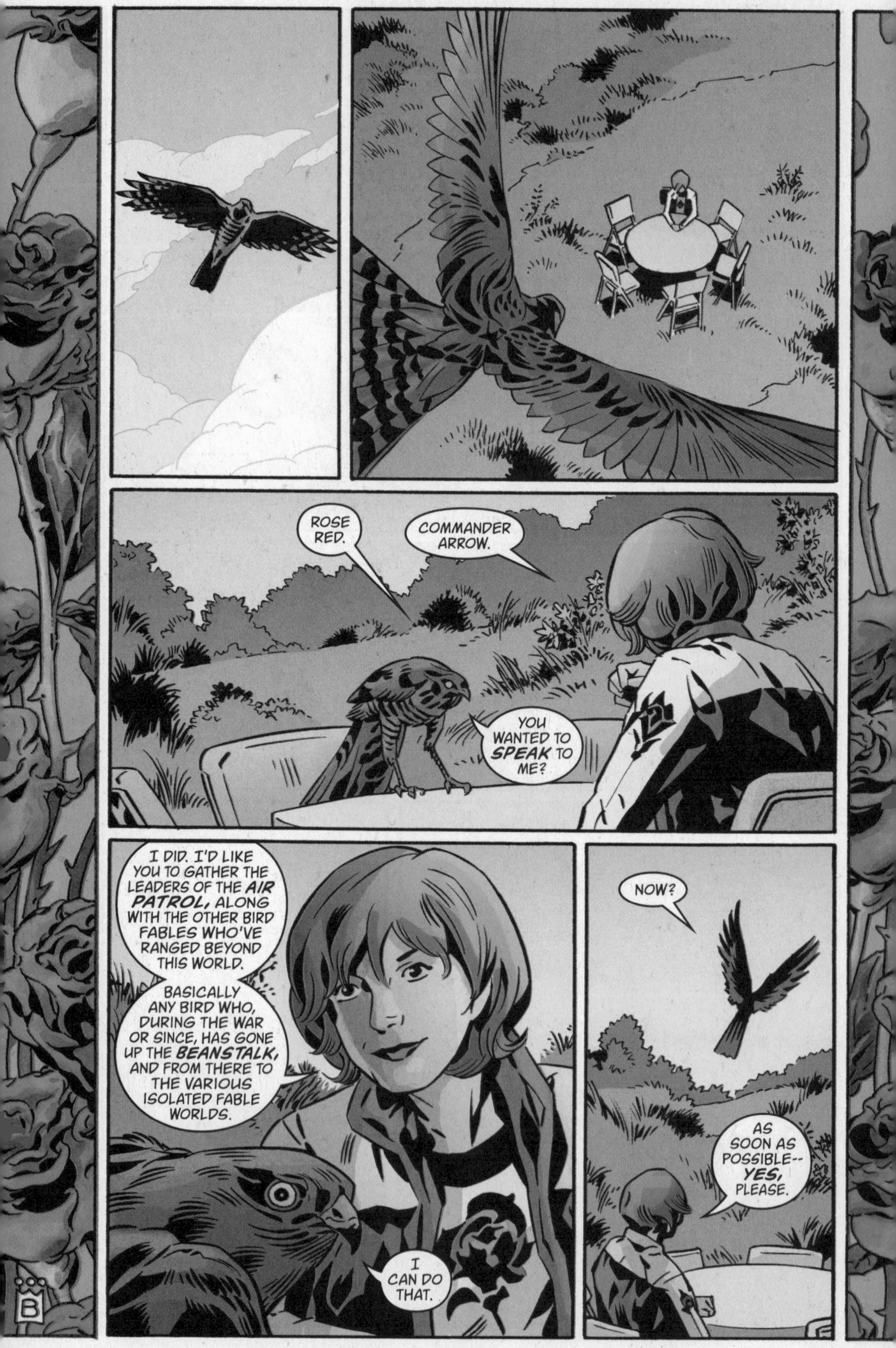
ROSE RED.
COMMANDER ARROW.
YOU WANTED TO SPEAK TO ME?
I DID. I'D LIKE YOU TO GATHER THE LEADERS OF THE AIR PATROL, ALONG WITH THE OTHER BIRD FABLES WHO'VE RANGED BEYOND THIS WORLD.
BASICALLY ANY BIRD WHO, DURING THE WAR OR SINCE, HAS GONE UP THE BEANSTALK, AND FROM THERE TO THE VARIOUS ISOLATED FABLE WORLDS.
I CAN DO THAT.
NOW?
AS SOON AS POSSIBLE--YES, PLEASE.

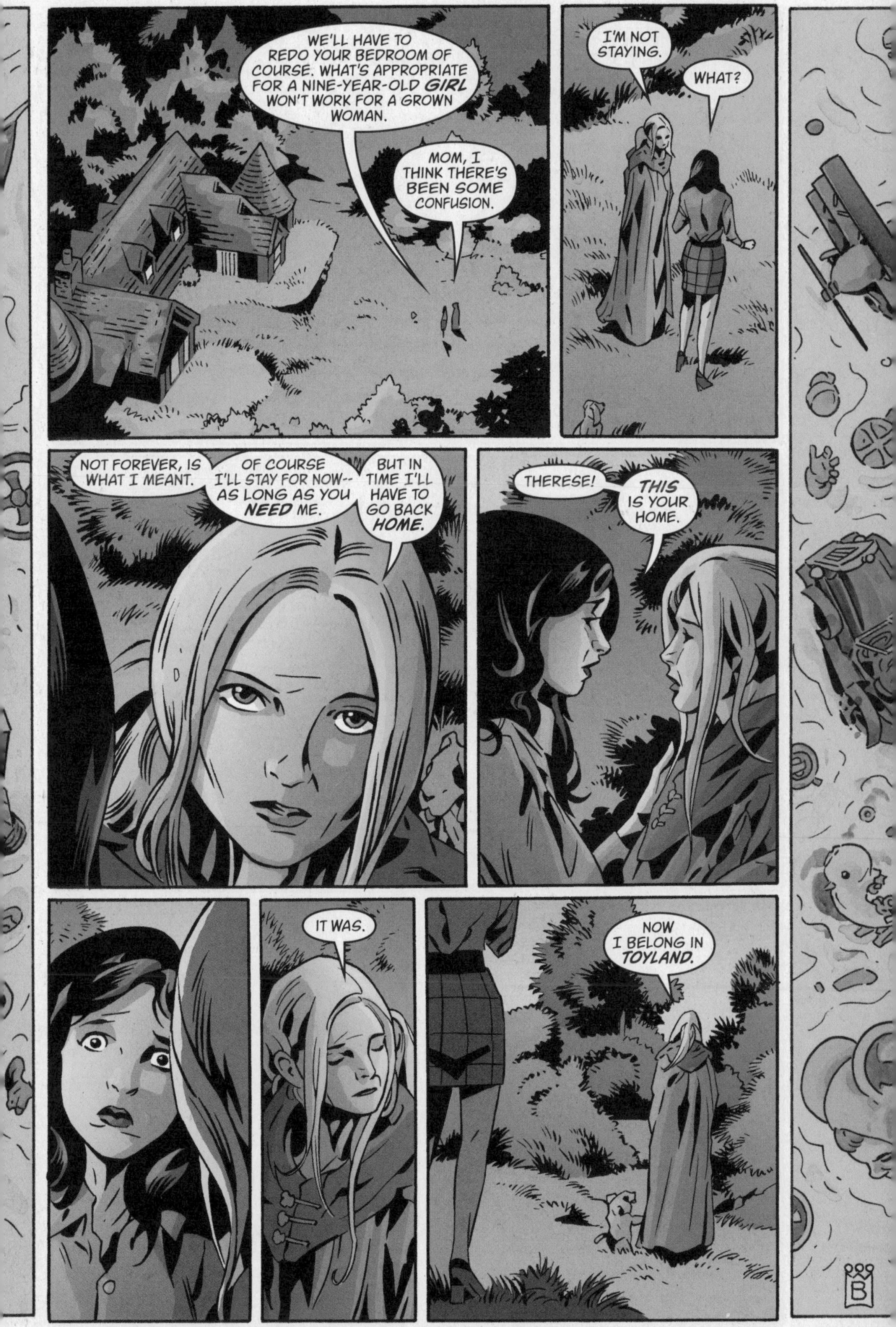
WE'LL HAVE TO REDO YOUR BEDROOM OF COURSE. WHAT'S APPROPRIATE FOR A NINE-YEAR-OLD GIRL WON'T WORK FOR A GROWN WOMAN.
MOM, I THINK THERE'S BEEN SOME CONFUSION.
I'M NOT STAYING.
WHAT?
NOT FOREVER, IS WHAT I MEANT.
OF COURSE I'LL STAY FOR NOW-- AS LONG AS YOU NEED ME.
BUT IN TIME I'LL HAVE TO GO BACK HOME.
THERESE!
THIS IS YOUR HOME.
IT WAS.
NOW I BELONG IN TOYLAND.

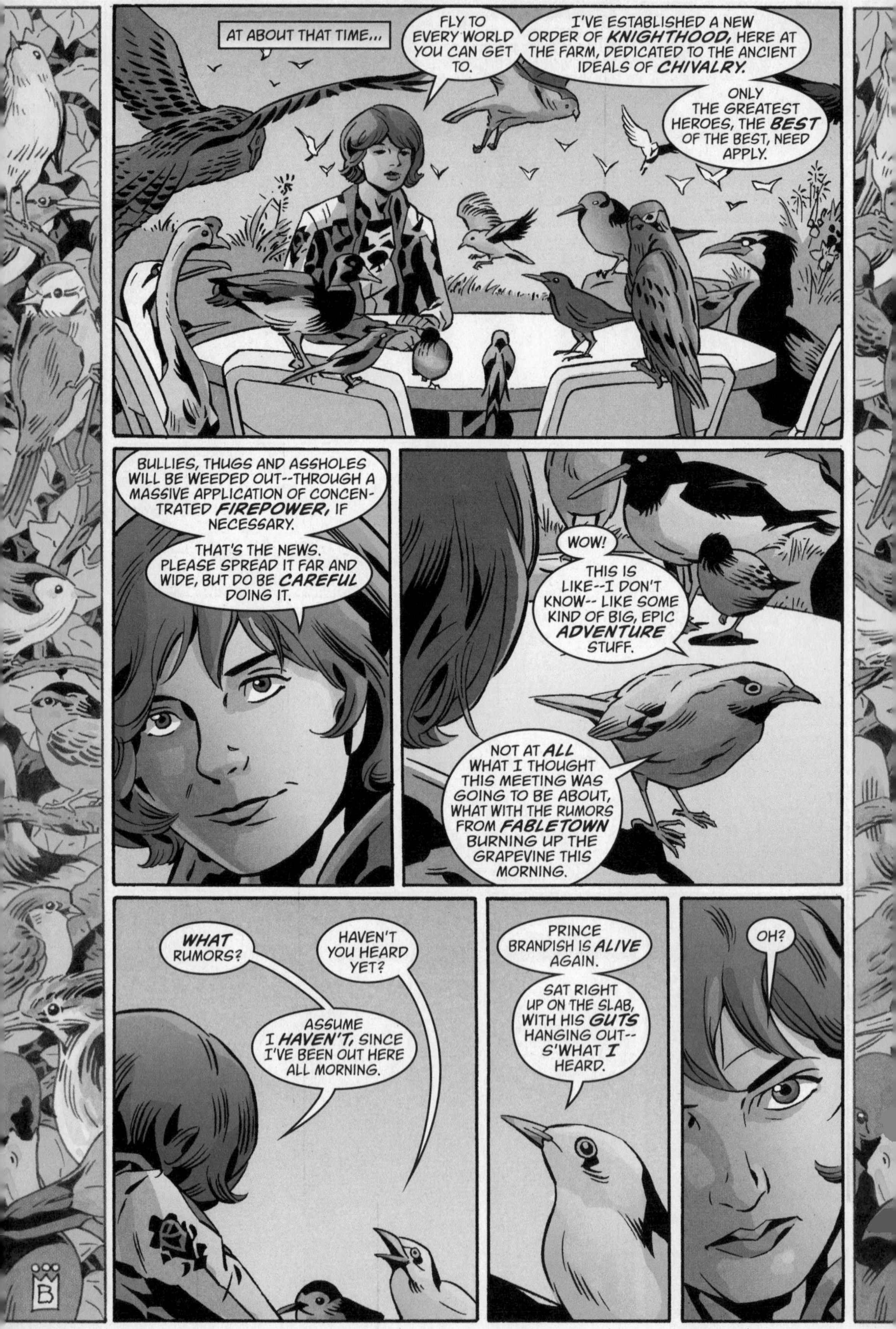
AT ABOUT THAT TIME...
FLY TO EVERY WORLD YOU CAN GET TO.
I'VE ESTABLISHED A NEW ORDER OF KNIGHTHOOD, HERE AT THE FARM, DEDICATED TO THE ANCIENT IDEALS OF CHIVALRY.
ONLY THE GREATEST HEROES, THE BEST OF THE BEST, NEED APPLY.
BULLIES, THUGS AND ASSHOLES WILL BE WEEDED OUT--THROUGH A MASSIVE APPLICATION OF CONCENTRATED FIREPOWER, IF NECESSARY.
THAT'S THE NEWS. PLEASE SPREAD IT FAR AND WIDE, BUT DO BE CAREFUL DOING IT.
WOW!
THIS IS LIKE--I DON'T KNOW-- LIKE SOME KIND OF BIG, EPIC ADVENTURE STUFF.
NOT AT ALL WHAT I THOUGHT THIS MEETING WAS GOING TO BE ABOUT, WHAT WITH THE RUMORS FROM FABLETOWN BURNING UP THE GRAPEVINE THIS MORNING.
WHAT RUMORS?
HAVEN'T YOU HEARD YET?
ASSUME I HAVEN'T, SINCE I'VE BEEN OUT HERE ALL MORNING.
PRINCE BRANDISH IS ALIVE AGAIN.
SAT RIGHT UP ON THE SLAB, WITH HIS GUTS HANGING OUT-- S'WHAT I HEARD.
OH?

SO, YOU'RE *LITERALLY* A HEARTLESS BASTARD.

NOT SO, MISS DUGLAS. I *HAVE* A HEART, BUT I DON'T KEEP IT IN ITS ORIGINAL CONTAINER.

I HAVE IT TUCKED AWAY SOMEWHERE DISTANT AND *SAFE.*

OH, LORDS ABOVE AND BELOW!

AND AS LONG AS *IT* REMAINS UN-HARMED, I CAN'T BE EITHER.

YOU *DID* IT!

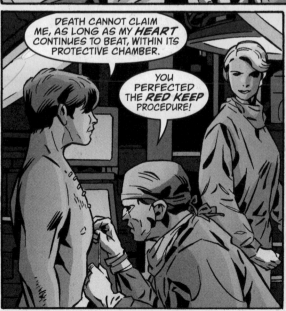

DEATH CANNOT CLAIM ME, AS LONG AS MY *HEART* CONTINUES TO BEAT, WITHIN ITS PROTECTIVE CHAMBER.

YOU PERFECTED THE *RED KEEP* PROCEDURE!

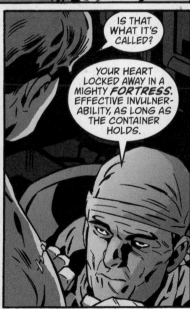

IS THAT WHAT IT'S CALLED?

YOUR HEART LOCKED AWAY IN A MIGHTY *FORTRESS.* EFFECTIVE INVULNER-ABILITY, AS LONG AS THE CONTAINER HOLDS.

THE TRICK IS KEEPING ITS LOCATION SECRET.

I WAS ONLY ABLE TO REMOVE *MINE* FOR SIX DAYS BEFORE IT BEGAN TO PETER OUT.

AND EVEN THEN I HAD TO REPLACE IT WITH A *PIG'S* HEART IN MY OWN CHEST, WHILE IT WAS REMOVED.

I *MUST* MEET THE PRACTITIONER WHO SOLVED IT!

GOOD LUCK WITH THAT. YOU MIGHT BE ABLE TO FIND HIS *GHOST* WHIMPERING IN SOME DARK AFTER-REALM.

NO!

POOR FELLOW DIED ON THE END OF MY DINNER KNIFE, WHEN I *FEASTED* HIM FOR HIS GRAND ACHIEVEMENT.

AFTER ALL, I COULDN'T HAVE HIM REPEATING HIS MASTERWORK ON *LESSER* SUBJECTS.

MUCH MORE VALUE IN *EXCLUSIVITY.*

AND FOR THE RECORD, MISS DUGLAS, THE *"BASTARD"* PART ISN'T ACCURATE EITHER. MY PARENTS WERE BOTH MARRIED AND DEVOTED.

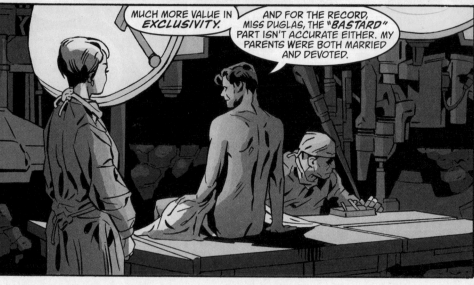

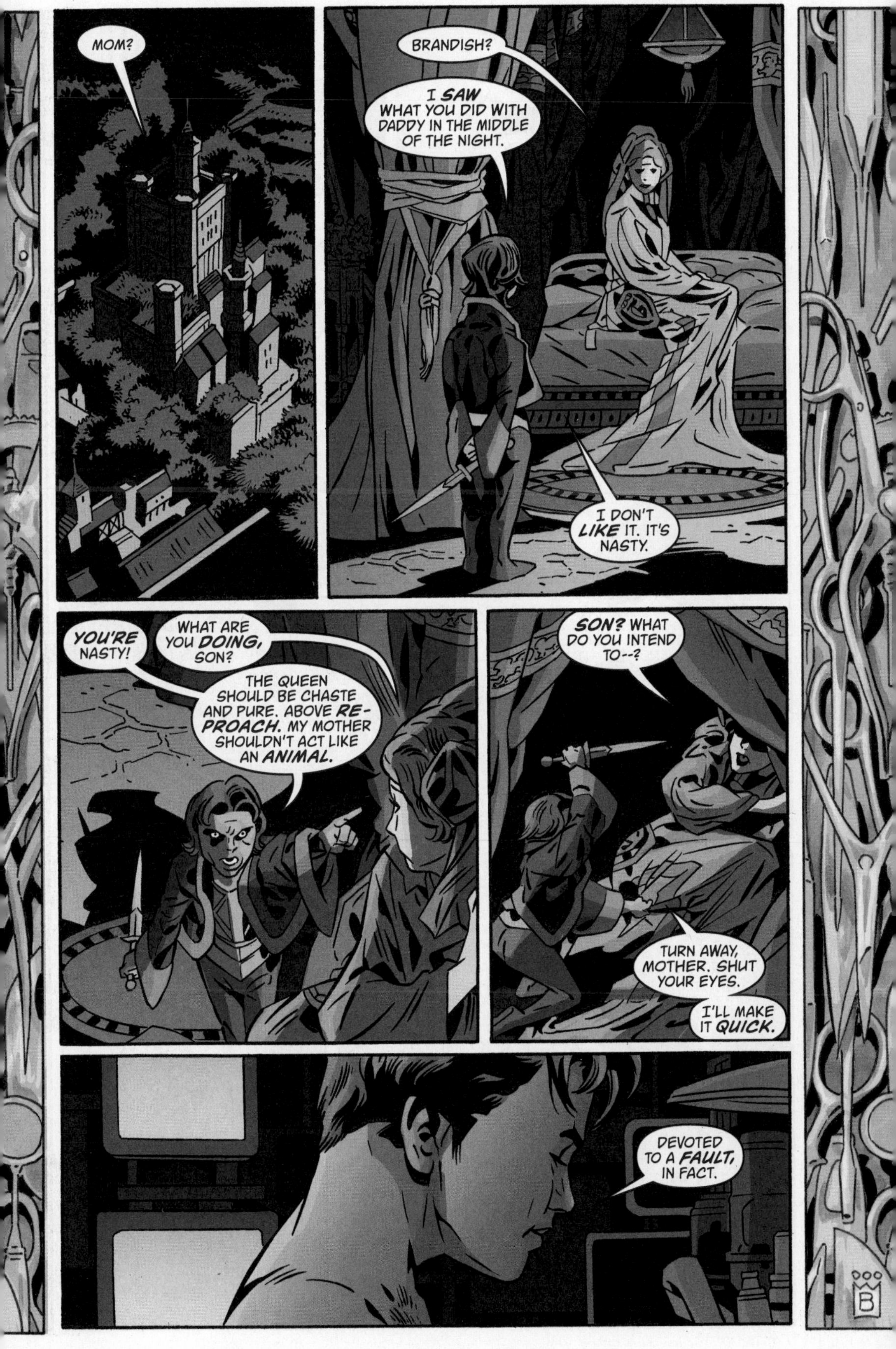
MOM?
BRANDISH?
I SAW WHAT YOU DID WITH DADDY IN THE MIDDLE OF THE NIGHT.
I DON'T LIKE IT. IT'S NASTY.
WHAT ARE YOU DOING, SON?
YOU'RE NASTY!
THE QUEEN SHOULD BE CHASTE AND PURE. ABOVE RE-PROACH. MY MOTHER SHOULDN'T ACT LIKE AN ANIMAL.
SON? WHAT DO YOU INTEND TO--?
TURN AWAY, MOTHER. SHUT YOUR EYES.
I'LL MAKE IT QUICK.
DEVOTED TO A FAULT, IN FACT.

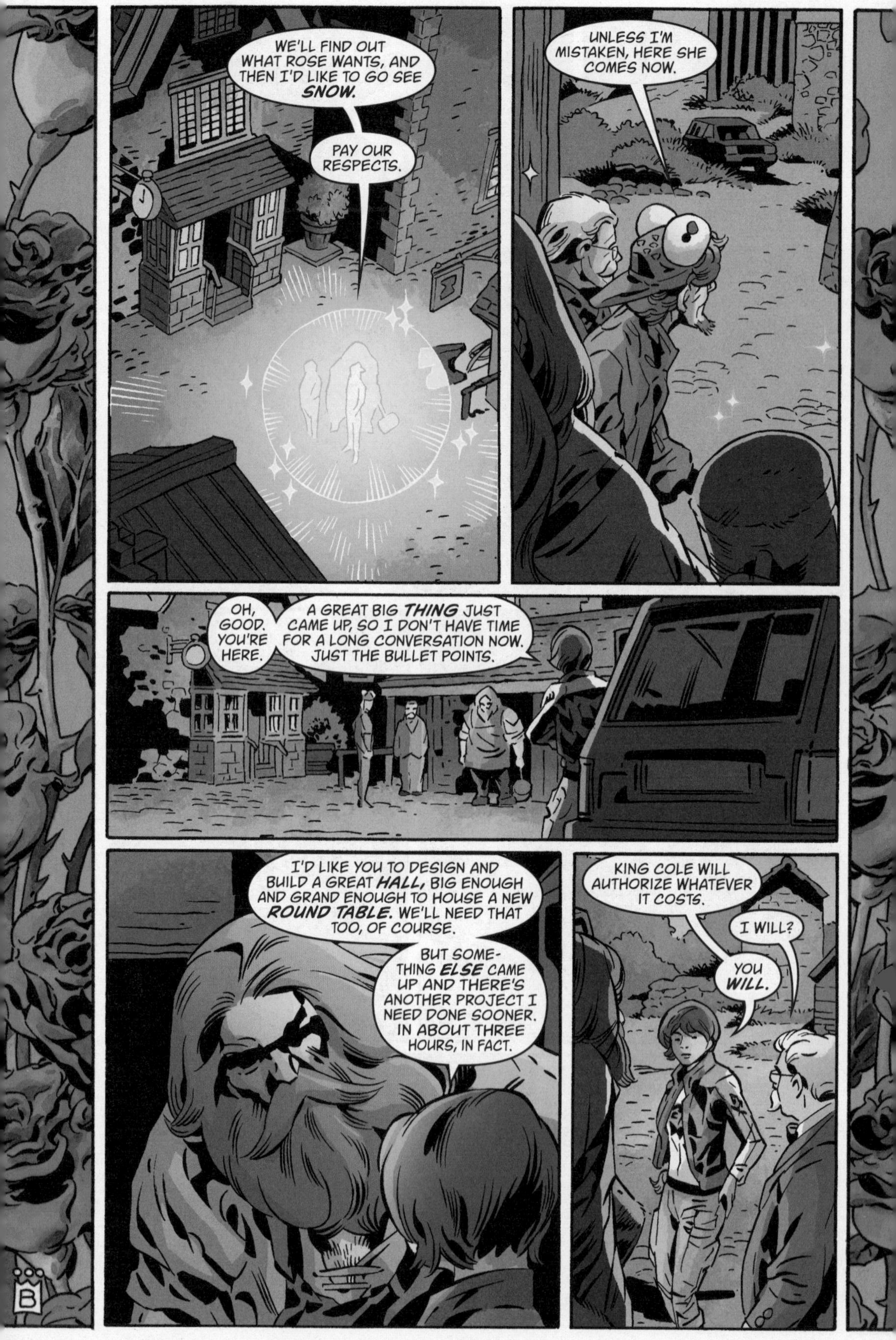

WE'LL FIND OUT WHAT ROSE WANTS, AND THEN I'D LIKE TO GO SEE SNOW.
PAY OUR RESPECTS.
UNLESS I'M MISTAKEN, HERE SHE COMES NOW.
OH, GOOD. YOU'RE HERE.
A GREAT BIG THING JUST CAME UP, SO I DON'T HAVE TIME FOR A LONG CONVERSATION NOW. JUST THE BULLET POINTS.
I'D LIKE YOU TO DESIGN AND BUILD A GREAT HALL, BIG ENOUGH AND GRAND ENOUGH TO HOUSE A NEW ROUND TABLE. WE'LL NEED THAT TOO, OF COURSE.
BUT SOMETHING ELSE CAME UP AND THERE'S ANOTHER PROJECT I NEED DONE SOONER. IN ABOUT THREE HOURS, IN FACT.
KING COLE WILL AUTHORIZE WHATEVER IT COSTS.
I WILL?
YOU WILL.

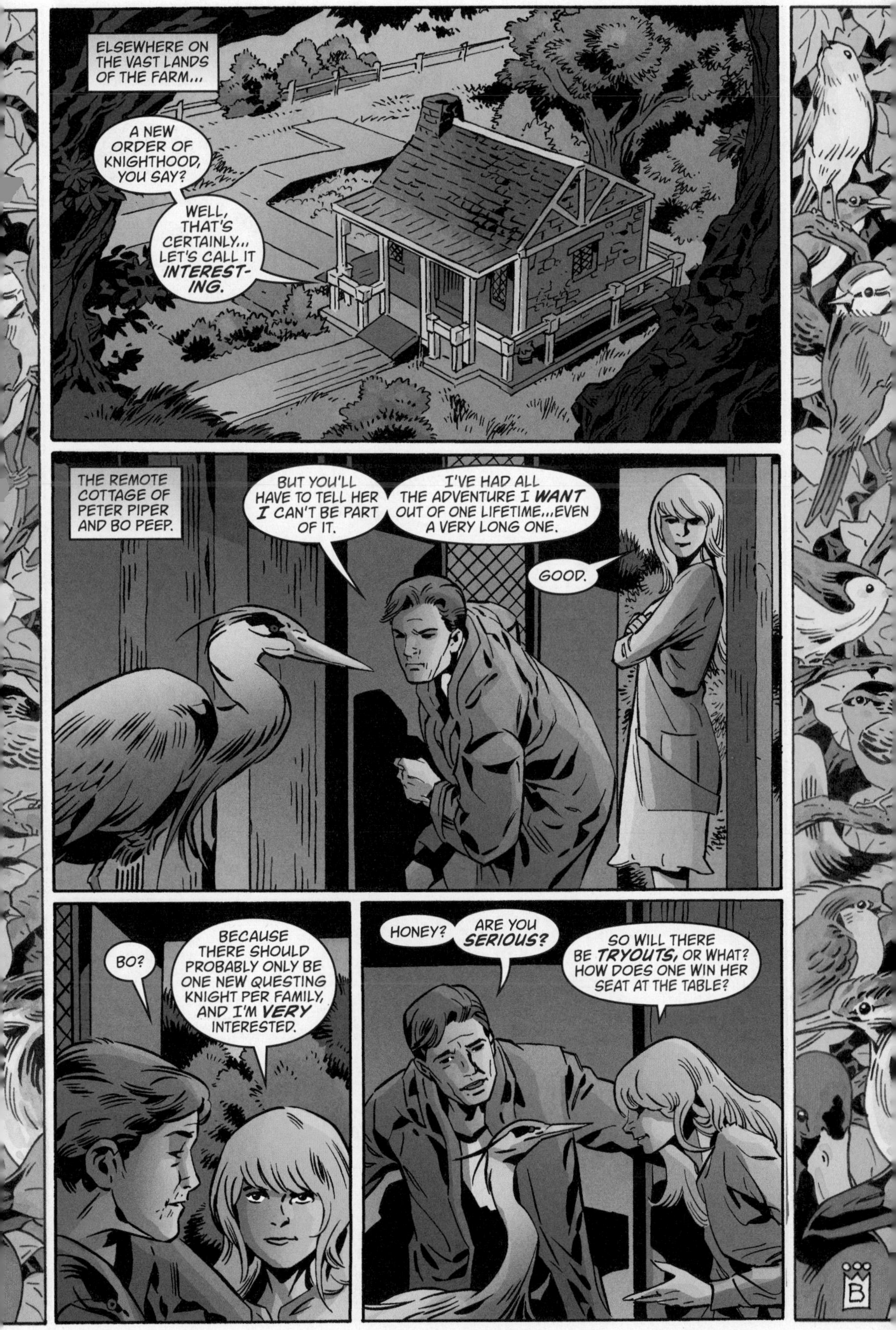

ELSEWHERE ON THE VAST LANDS OF THE FARM...
A NEW ORDER OF KNIGHTHOOD, YOU SAY?
WELL, THAT'S CERTAINLY... LET'S CALL IT INTERESTING.
THE REMOTE COTTAGE OF PETER PIPER AND BO PEEP.
BUT YOU'LL HAVE TO TELL HER I CAN'T BE PART OF IT.
I'VE HAD ALL THE ADVENTURE I WANT OUT OF ONE LIFETIME...EVEN A VERY LONG ONE.
GOOD.
BO?
BECAUSE THERE SHOULD PROBABLY ONLY BE ONE NEW QUESTING KNIGHT PER FAMILY, AND I'M VERY INTERESTED.
HONEY?
ARE YOU SERIOUS?
SO WILL THERE BE TRYOUTS, OR WHAT? HOW DOES ONE WIN HER SEAT AT THE TABLE?

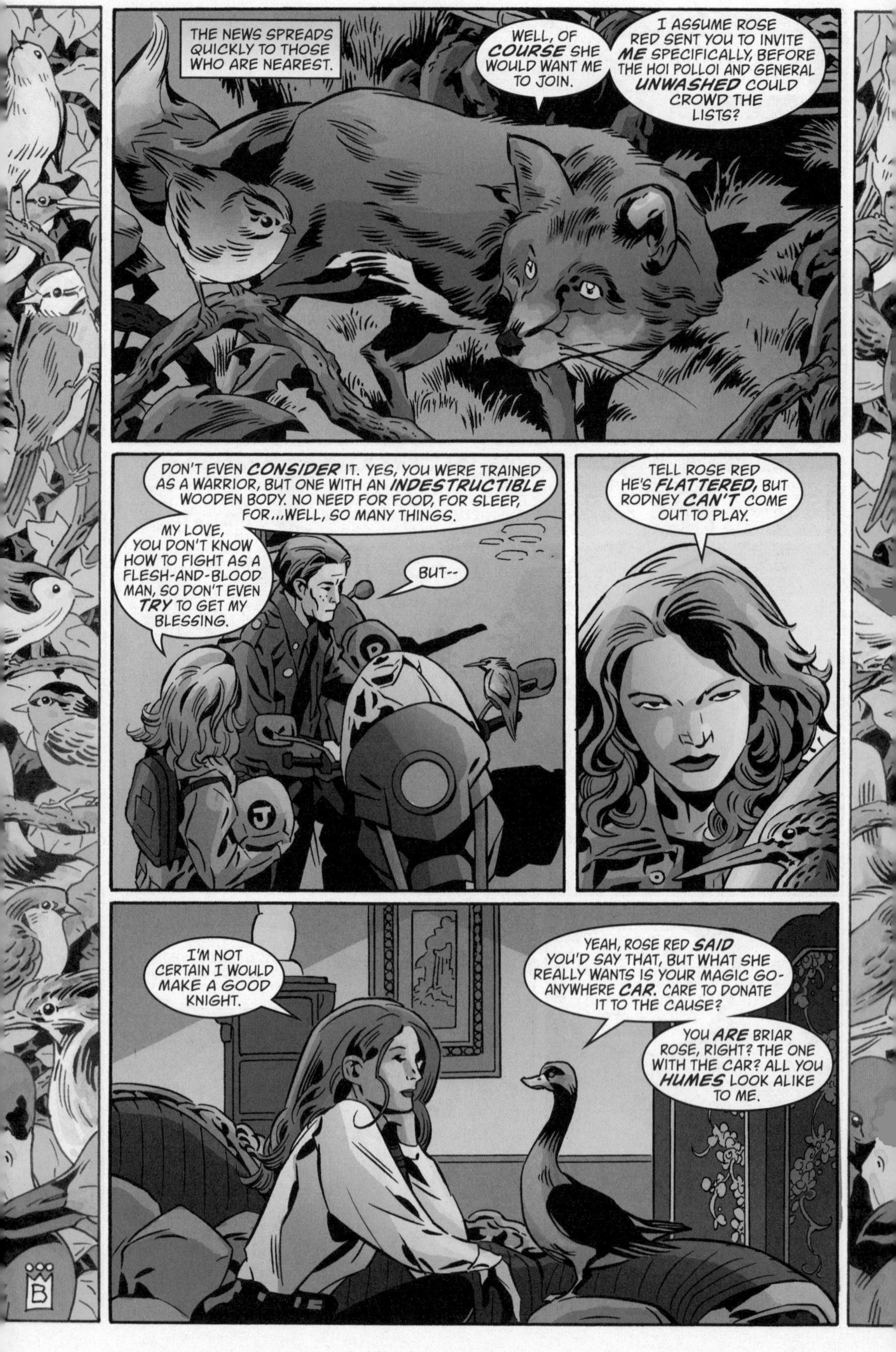
THE NEWS SPREADS QUICKLY TO THOSE WHO ARE NEAREST.
WELL, OF COURSE SHE WOULD WANT ME TO JOIN.
I ASSUME ROSE RED SENT YOU TO INVITE ME SPECIFICALLY, BEFORE THE HOI POLLOI AND GENERAL UNWASHED COULD CROWD THE LISTS?
DON'T EVEN CONSIDER IT. YES, YOU WERE TRAINED AS A WARRIOR, BUT ONE WITH AN INDESTRUCTIBLE WOODEN BODY. NO NEED FOR FOOD, FOR SLEEP, FOR...WELL, SO MANY THINGS.
MY LOVE, YOU DON'T KNOW HOW TO FIGHT AS A FLESH-AND-BLOOD MAN, SO DON'T EVEN TRY TO GET MY BLESSING.
BUT--
TELL ROSE RED HE'S FLATTERED, BUT RODNEY CAN'T COME OUT TO PLAY.
I'M NOT CERTAIN I WOULD MAKE A GOOD KNIGHT.
YEAH, ROSE RED SAID YOU'D SAY THAT, BUT WHAT SHE REALLY WANTS IS YOUR MAGIC GO-ANYWHERE CAR. CARE TO DONATE IT TO THE CAUSE?
YOU ARE BRIAR ROSE, RIGHT? THE ONE WITH THE CAR? ALL YOU HUMES LOOK ALIKE TO ME.

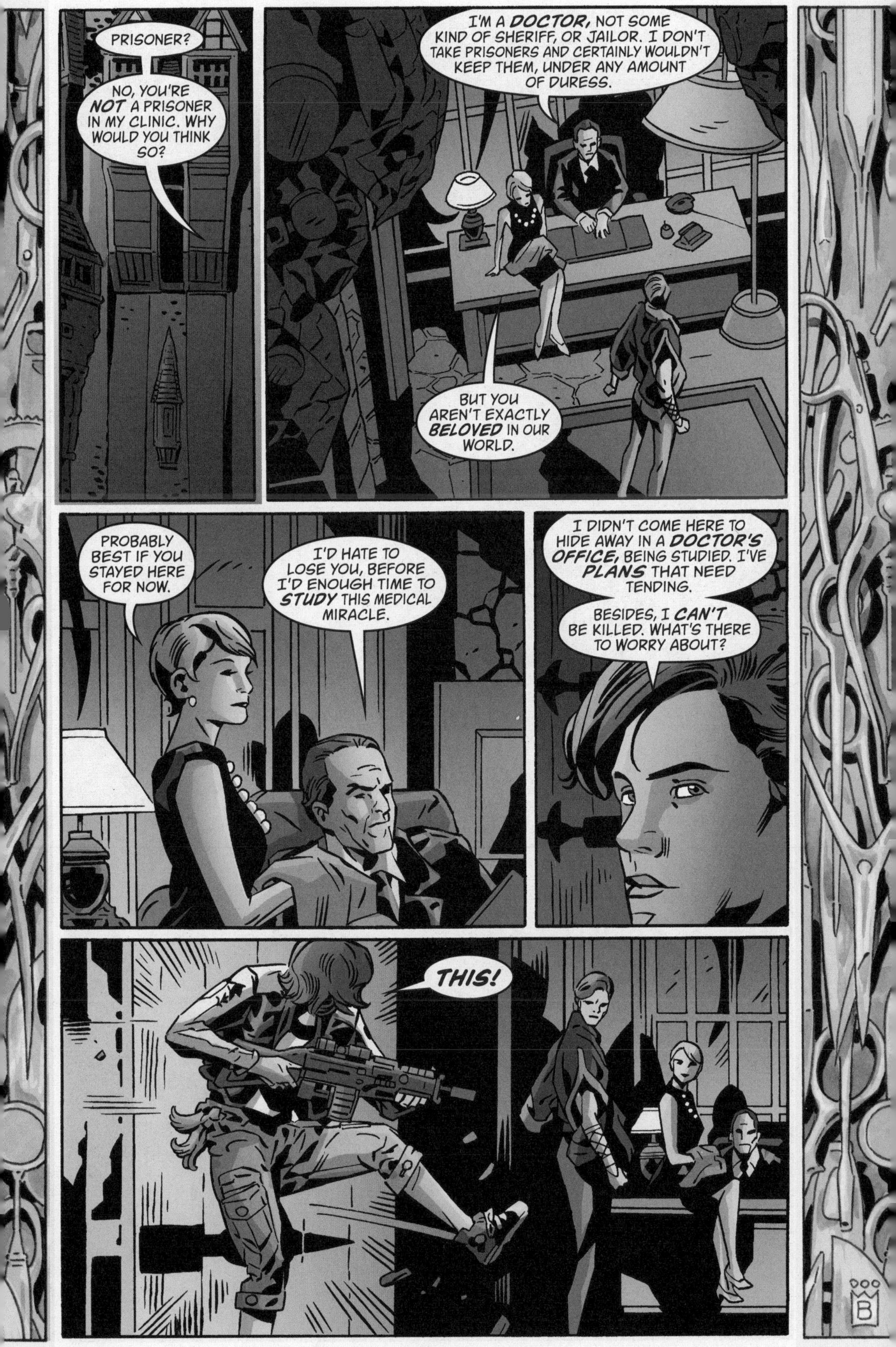
PRISONER?
NO, YOU'RE NOT A PRISONER IN MY CLINIC. WHY WOULD YOU THINK SO?
I'M A DOCTOR, NOT SOME KIND OF SHERIFF, OR JAILOR. I DON'T TAKE PRISONERS AND CERTAINLY WOULDN'T KEEP THEM, UNDER ANY AMOUNT OF DURESS.
BUT YOU AREN'T EXACTLY BELOVED IN OUR WORLD.
PROBABLY BEST IF YOU STAYED HERE FOR NOW.
I'D HATE TO LOSE YOU, BEFORE I'D ENOUGH TIME TO STUDY THIS MEDICAL MIRACLE.
I DIDN'T COME HERE TO HIDE AWAY IN A DOCTOR'S OFFICE, BEING STUDIED. I'VE PLANS THAT NEED TENDING.
BESIDES, I CAN'T BE KILLED. WHAT'S THERE TO WORRY ABOUT?
THIS!

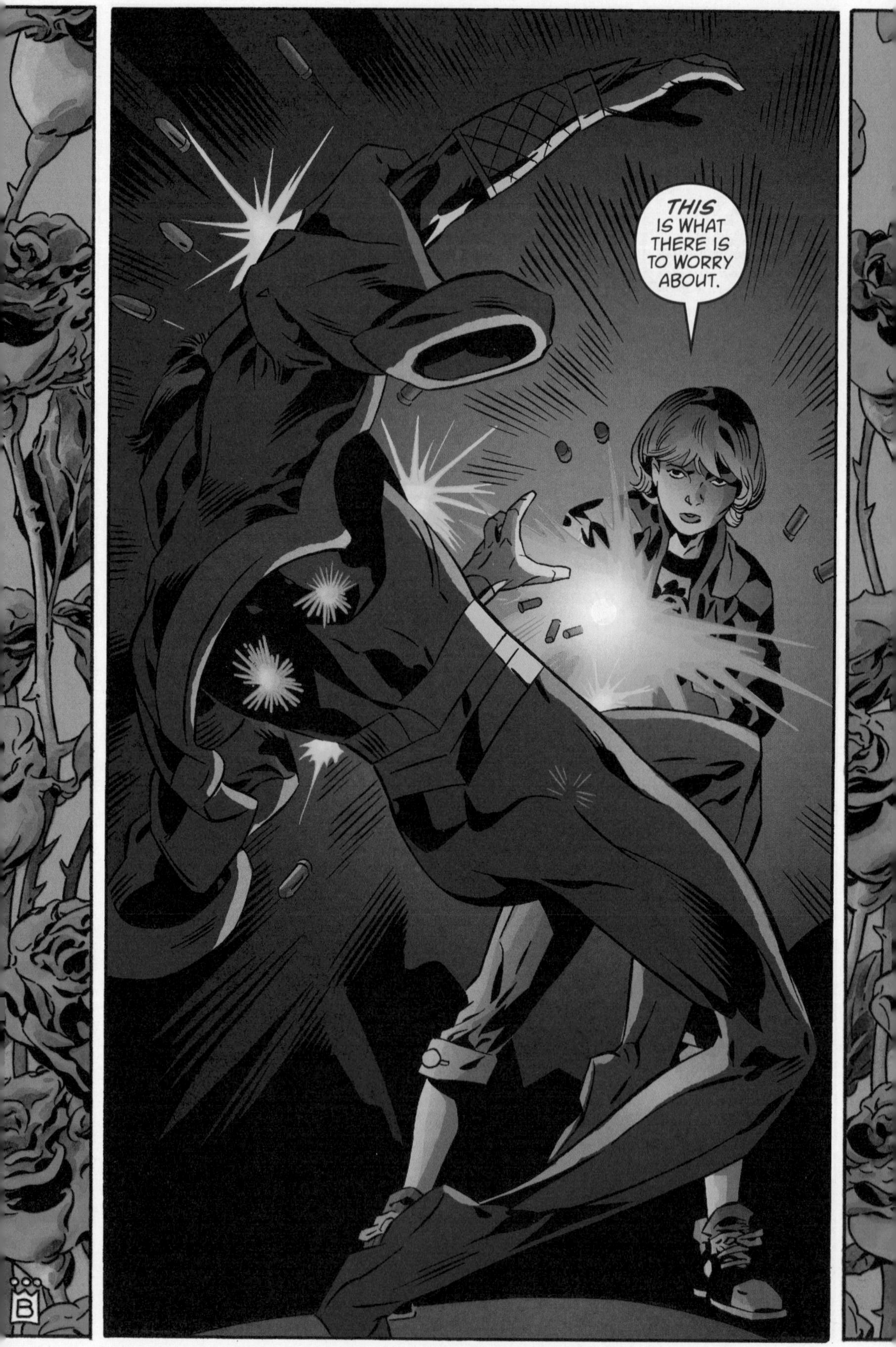
THIS IS WHAT THERE IS TO WORRY ABOUT.

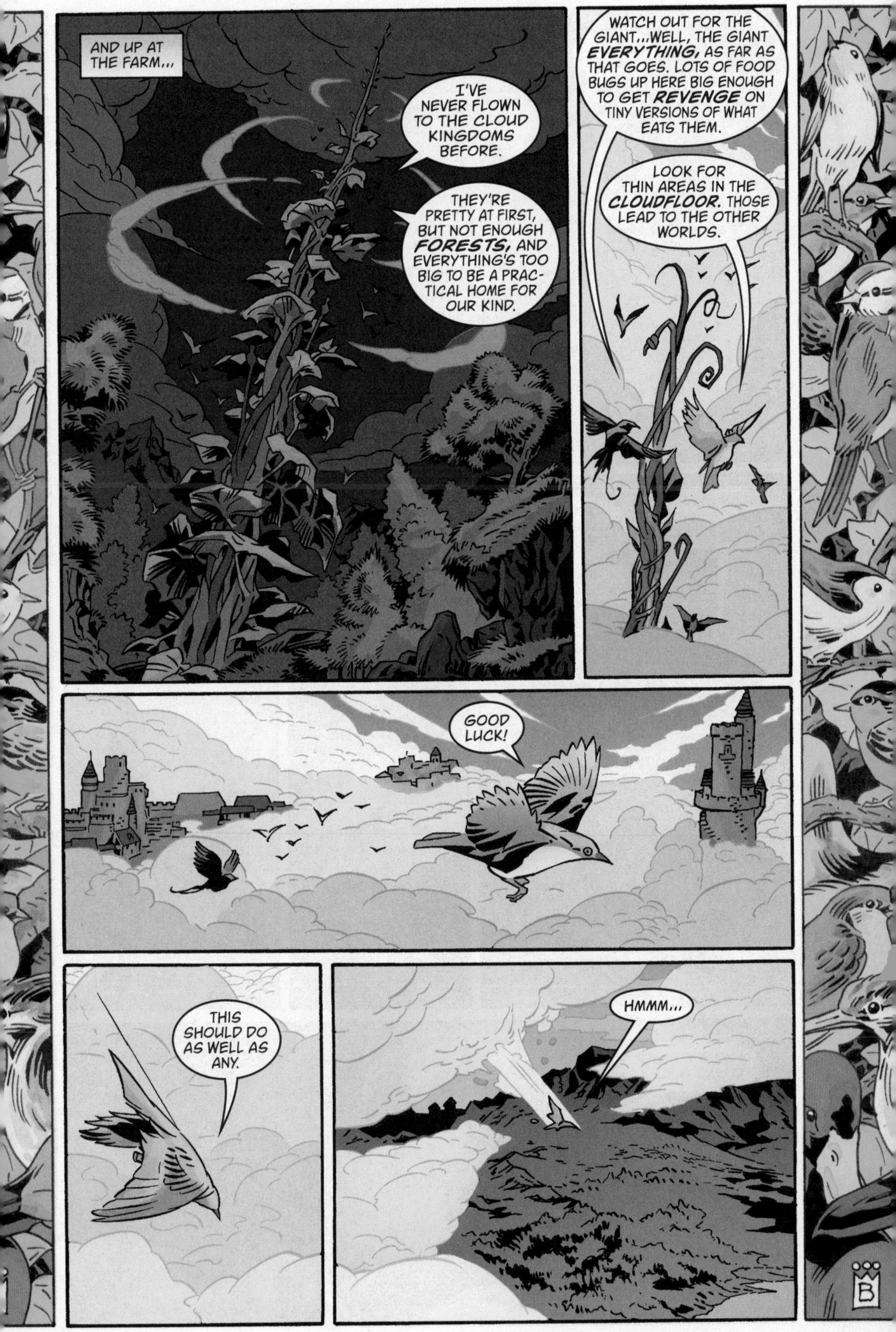

AND UP AT THE FARM...
I'VE NEVER FLOWN TO THE CLOUD KINGDOMS BEFORE.
THEY'RE PRETTY AT FIRST, BUT NOT ENOUGH FORESTS, AND EVERYTHING'S TOO BIG TO BE A PRACTICAL HOME FOR OUR KIND.
WATCH OUT FOR THE GIANT...WELL, THE GIANT EVERYTHING, AS FAR AS THAT GOES. LOTS OF FOOD BUGS UP HERE BIG ENOUGH TO GET REVENGE ON TINY VERSIONS OF WHAT EATS THEM.
LOOK FOR THIN AREAS IN THE CLOUDFLOOR. THOSE LEAD TO THE OTHER WORLDS.
GOOD LUCK!
THIS SHOULD DO AS WELL AS ANY.
HMMM...

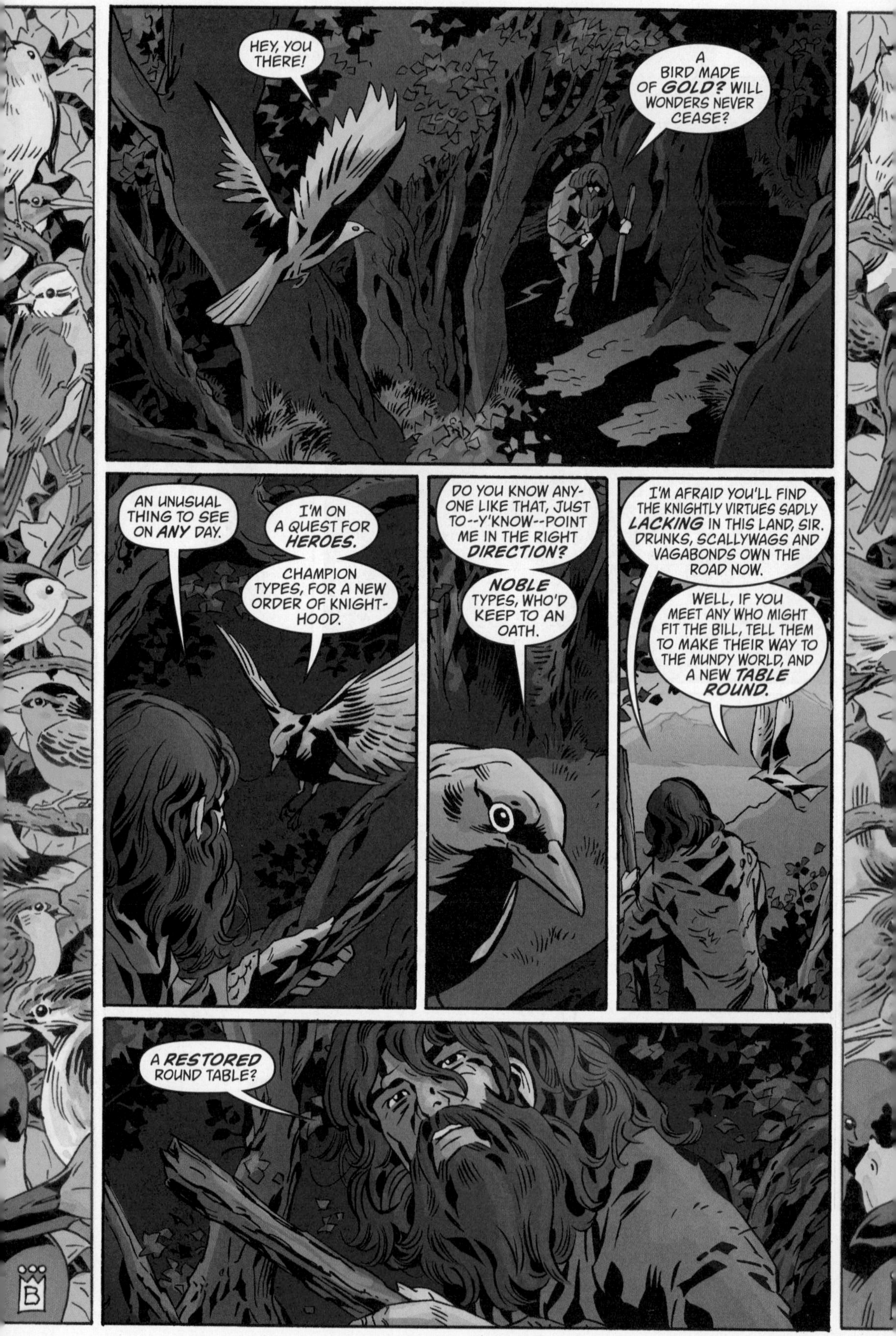
HEY, YOU THERE!
A BIRD MADE OF GOLD? WILL WONDERS NEVER CEASE?
AN UNUSUAL THING TO SEE ON ANY DAY.
I'M ON A QUEST FOR HEROES.
CHAMPION TYPES, FOR A NEW ORDER OF KNIGHT-HOOD.
DO YOU KNOW ANY-ONE LIKE THAT, JUST TO--Y'KNOW--POINT ME IN THE RIGHT DIRECTION?
NOBLE TYPES, WHO'D KEEP TO AN OATH.
I'M AFRAID YOU'LL FIND THE KNIGHTLY VIRTUES SADLY LACKING IN THIS LAND, SIR. DRUNKS, SCALLYWAGS AND VAGABONDS OWN THE ROAD NOW.
WELL, IF YOU MEET ANY WHO MIGHT FIT THE BILL, TELL THEM TO MAKE THEIR WAY TO THE MUNDY WORLD, AND A NEW TABLE ROUND.
A RESTORED ROUND TABLE?

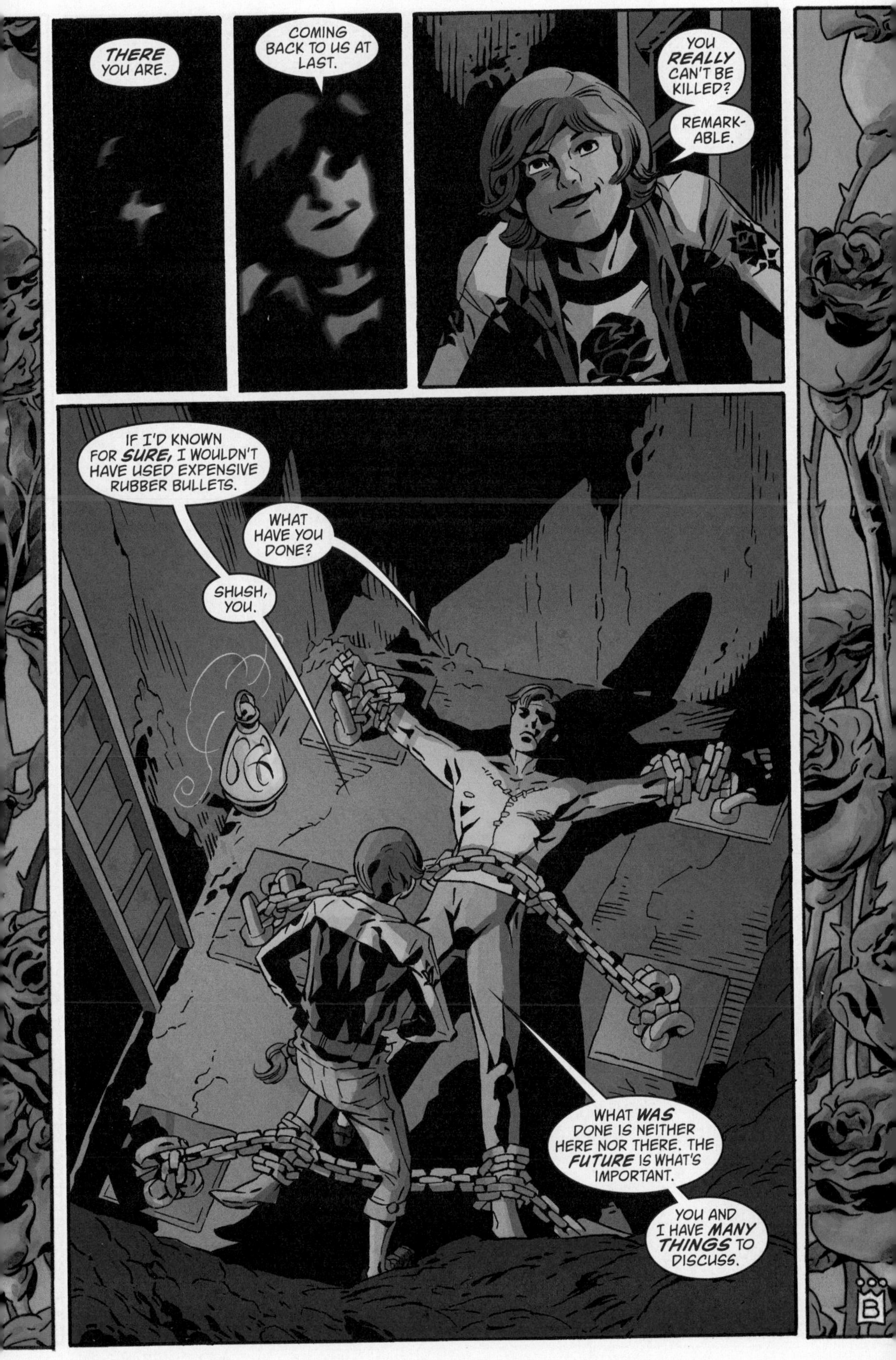
THERE YOU ARE.
COMING BACK TO US AT LAST.
YOU REALLY CAN'T BE KILLED?
REMARK-ABLE.
IF I'D KNOWN FOR SURE, I WOULDN'T HAVE USED EXPENSIVE RUBBER BULLETS.
WHAT HAVE YOU DONE?
SHUSH, YOU.
WHAT WAS DONE IS NEITHER HERE NOR THERE. THE FUTURE IS WHAT'S IMPORTANT.
YOU AND I HAVE MANY THINGS TO DISCUSS.

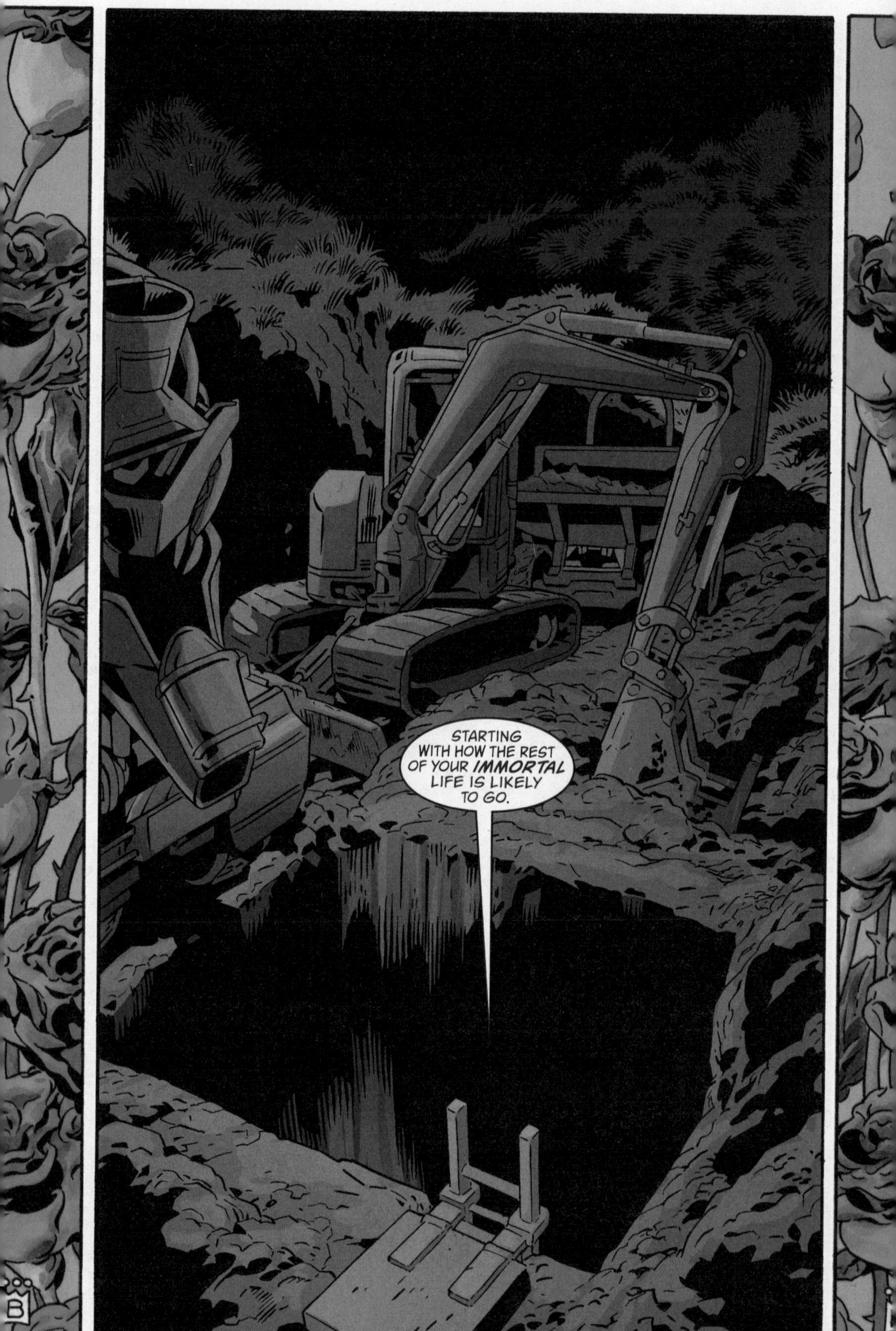
STARTING WITH HOW THE REST OF YOUR IMMORTAL LIFE IS LIKELY TO GO.

NEXT: LIFE IN A PIT

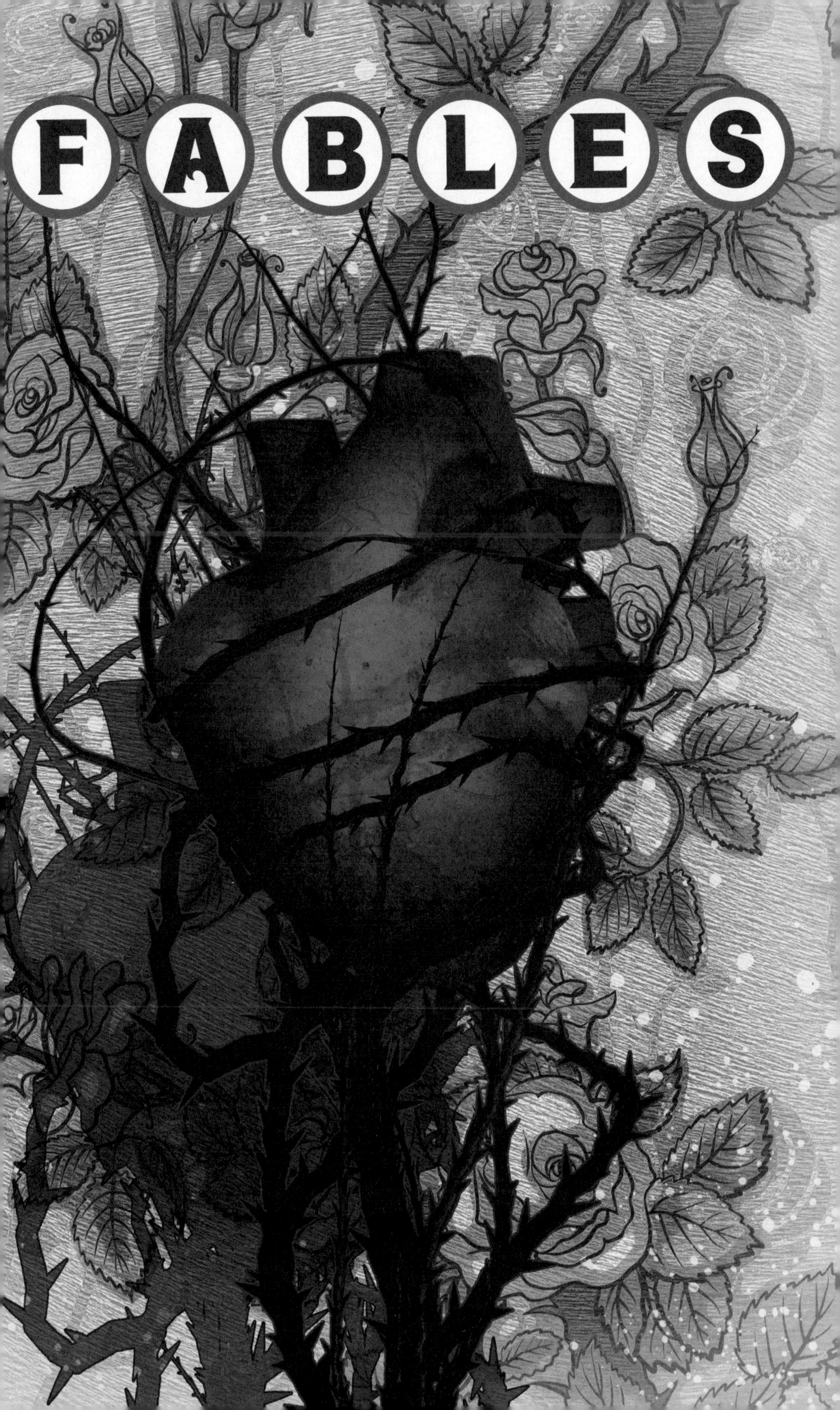
FABLES

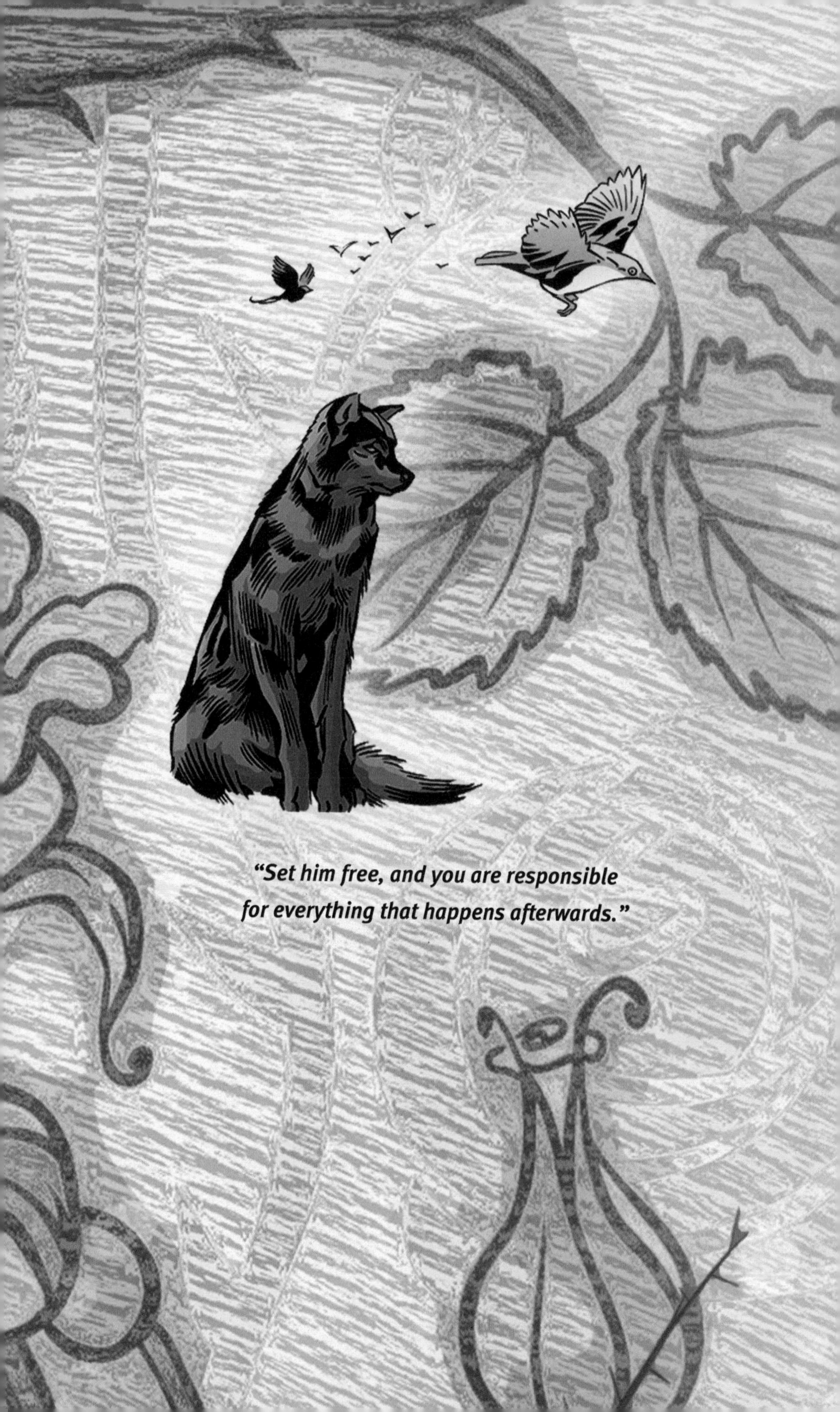
"Set him free, and you are responsible
for everything that happens afterwards."

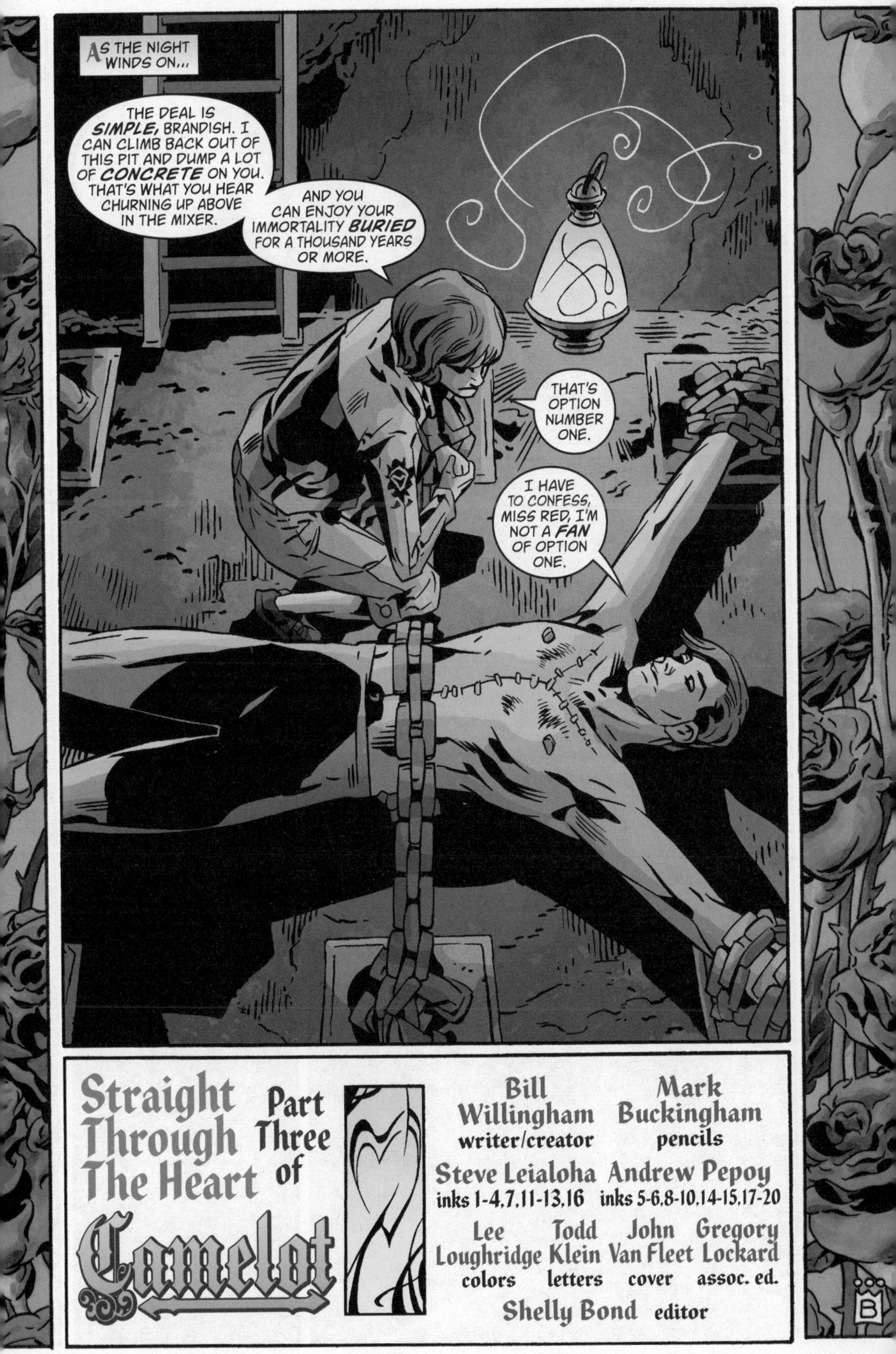
AS THE NIGHT WINDS ON...
THE DEAL IS SIMPLE, BRANDISH. I CAN CLIMB BACK OUT OF THIS PIT AND DUMP A LOT OF CONCRETE ON YOU. THAT'S WHAT YOU HEAR CHURNING UP ABOVE IN THE MIXER.
AND YOU CAN ENJOY YOUR IMMORTALITY BURIED FOR A THOUSAND YEARS OR MORE.
THAT'S OPTION NUMBER ONE.
I HAVE TO CONFESS, MISS RED, I'M NOT A FAN OF OPTION ONE.
Straight Through The Heart
Part Three of Camelot
Bill Willingham writer/creator
Mark Buckingham pencils
Steve Leialoha inks 1-4,7,11-13,16
Andrew Pepoy inks 5-6,8-10,14-15,17-20
Lee Loughridge colors
Todd Klein letters
John Van Fleet cover
Gregory Lockard assoc. ed.
Shelly Bond editor

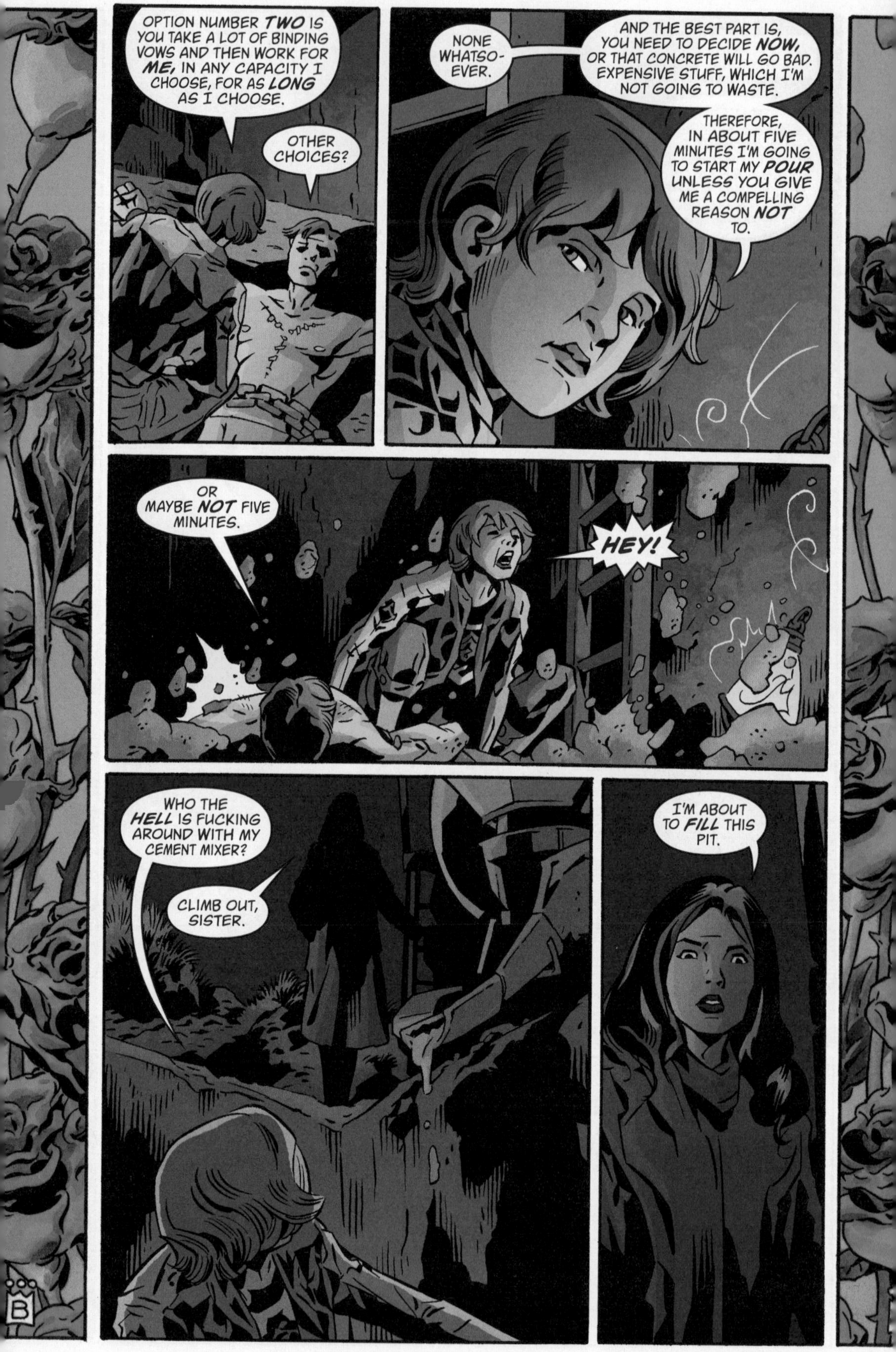
OPTION NUMBER TWO IS YOU TAKE A LOT OF BINDING VOWS AND THEN WORK FOR ME, IN ANY CAPACITY I CHOOSE, FOR AS LONG AS I CHOOSE.
OTHER CHOICES?
NONE WHATSO-EVER.
AND THE BEST PART IS, YOU NEED TO DECIDE NOW, OR THAT CONCRETE WILL GO BAD. EXPENSIVE STUFF, WHICH I'M NOT GOING TO WASTE.
THEREFORE, IN ABOUT FIVE MINUTES I'M GOING TO START MY POUR UNLESS YOU GIVE ME A COMPELLING REASON NOT TO.
OR MAYBE NOT FIVE MINUTES.
HEY!
WHO THE HELL IS FUCKING AROUND WITH MY CEMENT MIXER?
CLIMB OUT, SISTER.
I'M ABOUT TO FILL THIS PIT.

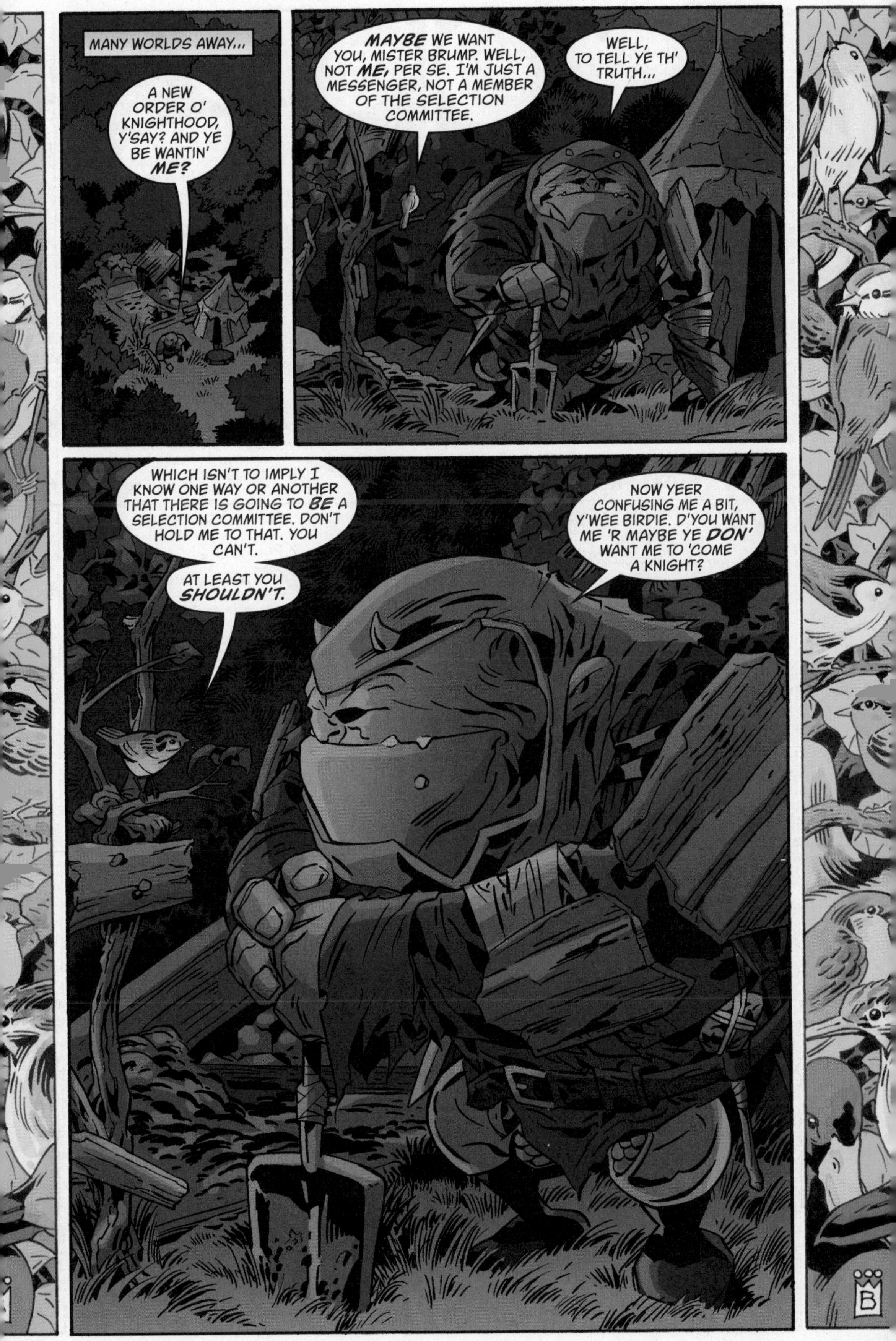
MANY WORLDS AWAY...
A NEW ORDER O' KNIGHTHOOD, Y'SAY? AND YE BE WANTIN' ME?
MAYBE WE WANT YOU, MISTER BRUMP. WELL, NOT ME, PER SE. I'M JUST A MESSENGER, NOT A MEMBER OF THE SELECTION COMMITTEE.
WELL, TO TELL YE TH' TRUTH...
WHICH ISN'T TO IMPLY I KNOW ONE WAY OR ANOTHER THAT THERE IS GOING TO BE A SELECTION COMMITTEE. DON'T HOLD ME TO THAT. YOU CAN'T.
AT LEAST YOU SHOULDN'T.
NOW YEER CONFUSING ME A BIT, Y'WEE BIRDIE. D'YOU WANT ME 'R MAYBE YE DON' WANT ME TO 'COME A KNIGHT?

I HA' T' CONFESS, I DON' KNOW'F TIS A GOOD THING. **NOT** THE NEW ORDER OF KNIGHTHOOD, MIND YE. I'M NOT EQUIPPED T' JUDGE IT GOOD OR NOT.

BUT I MEAN, I DON' KNOW IF TIS A PROPER THING THA' **I** BECOME A KNIGHT. **FOLLOW** ME, Y' FEATHERED LADDIE?

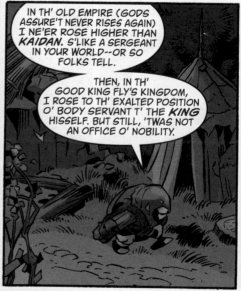

IN TH' OLD EMPIRE (GODS ASSURE'T NEVER RISES AGAIN) I NE'ER ROSE HIGHER THAN **KAIDAN.** S'LIKE A SERGEANT IN YOUR WORLD--OR SO FOLKS TELL.

THEN, IN TH' GOOD KING FLY'S KINGDOM, I ROSE TO TH' EXALTED POSITION O' BODY SERVANT T' THE **KING** HISSELF. BUT STILL, 'TWAS NOT AN OFFICE O' NOBILITY.

AN' THEN, SHAME E'ERLASTING, I COMMITTED A MURDER MOST FOUL N' WAS RIGHTLY **CONVICTED** BY TH' KING HISSELF. SENTENCED T' DIE, WUST I.

M'DOOM MOST MERCIFULLY SUSPENDED, MIND YOU, ELSE WHA' AM I DOIN' **HERE,** STILL FLESH AN' BLOOD, AN' NOT A WANDERIN' GHOST?

BUT A **KNIGHT?** THA'S A TITLE O' NOBILITY AN' RESPECT, RESERVED FOR THOSE O' PROVEN MILITARY PROWESS AN' GOOD JUDGMENT.

ME, A CRIMINAL UNDER BANISHMENT. IS **THAT** TH' PROPER CLAY FROM WHICH T' SCULPT SOMEONE AUTHORIZED T' BEAR ARMS AN' METE OUT JUSTICE?

I THINK THAT'S THE **POINT.** ROSE RED'S NEW ORDER IS ALL ABOUT CHAMPIONING SECOND CHANCES. I THINK THAT'S WHY THE QUESTING SPELL LED ME TO YOU.

IT LOOKS LIKE **YOU'RE** IN NEED OF A SECOND CHANCE.

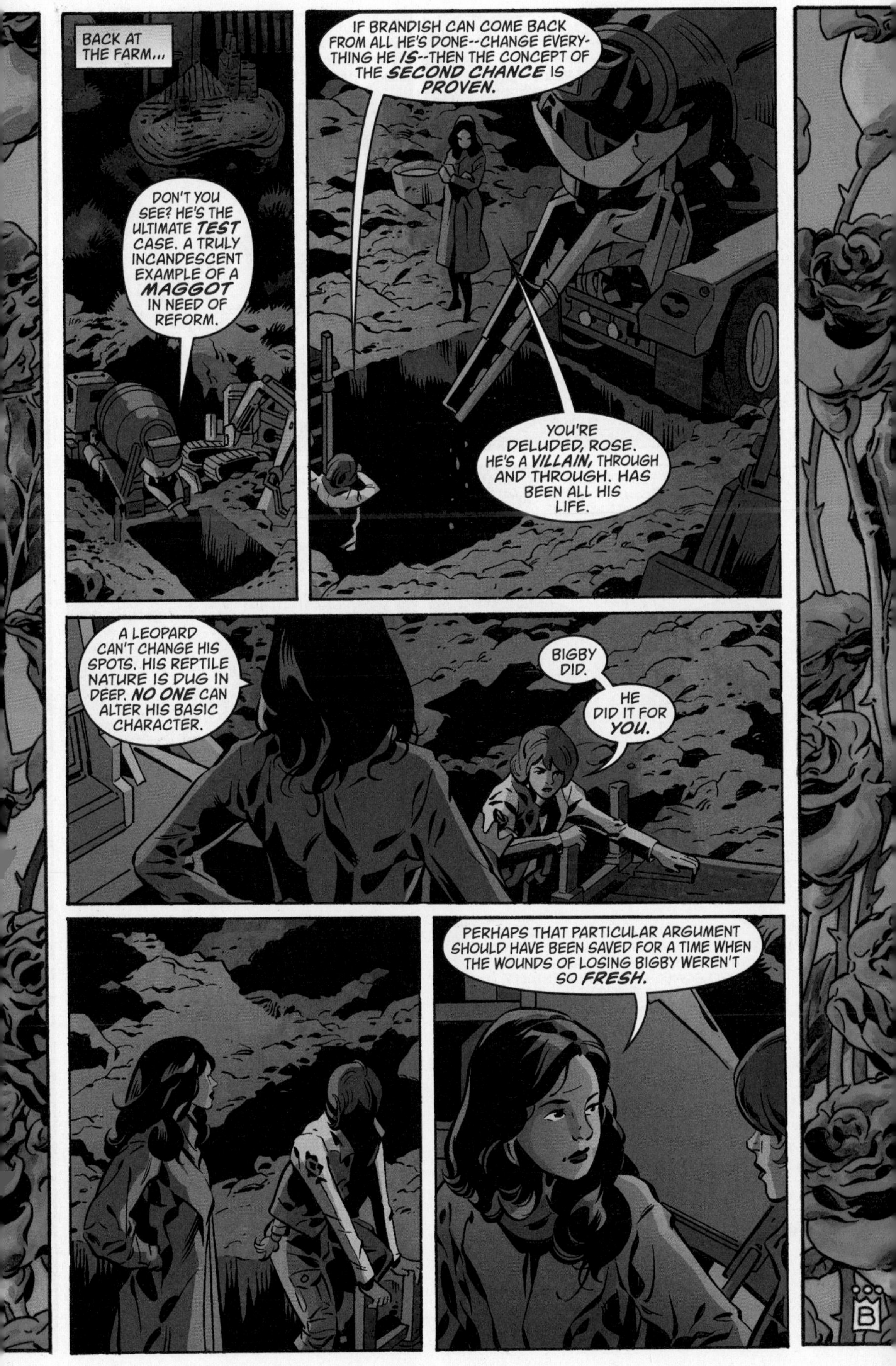

BACK AT THE FARM...
DON'T YOU SEE? HE'S THE ULTIMATE TEST CASE. A TRULY INCANDESCENT EXAMPLE OF A MAGGOT IN NEED OF REFORM.
IF BRANDISH CAN COME BACK FROM ALL HE'S DONE--CHANGE EVERYTHING HE IS--THEN THE CONCEPT OF THE SECOND CHANCE IS PROVEN.
YOU'RE DELUDED, ROSE. HE'S A VILLAIN, THROUGH AND THROUGH. HAS BEEN ALL HIS LIFE.
A LEOPARD CAN'T CHANGE HIS SPOTS. HIS REPTILE NATURE IS DUG IN DEEP. NO ONE CAN ALTER HIS BASIC CHARACTER.
BIGBY DID.
HE DID IT FOR YOU.
PERHAPS THAT PARTICULAR ARGUMENT SHOULD HAVE BEEN SAVED FOR A TIME WHEN THE WOUNDS OF LOSING BIGBY WEREN'T SO FRESH.

AND THE MAN WHO *TOOK* HIM FROM ME IS THE SAME ONE LYING DOWN THERE, WAITING ON A WIFE'S RIGHTFUL *VENGEANCE*.

OKAY, YOU'RE *RIGHT*, SNOW. MY TIMING SUCKS. ALWAYS HAS.

BUT IF THIS IS GOING TO *WORK*, IF I'M TRULY GOING TO BE A PALADIN OF HOPE, THEN THERE WILL BE *POWER* BEHIND MY MAD AND DARING SCHEME.

MAYBE POWER TO ALTER EVEN THE *DARKEST* HEART.

HAVEN'T YOU HEARD? BRANDISH DOESN'T *HAVE* A HEART. AT LEAST NOT ONE WITHIN OUR REACH.

AND HOPE IS A *LIAR*. IT'S NOTHING MORE THAN DISAPPOINTMENT DEFERRED.

TRUST ME. THIS WILL TURN TO *SHIT* IN THE END.

JUST LIKE ALL OF MY UNDERTAKINGS DO?

I DIDN'T SAY THAT, BUT IF THE SHOE FITS...

REMEMBER ALL THOSE TIMES YOU WISHED THERE WAS SOMEONE TO WARN YOU JUST BEFORE YOU WERE ABOUT TO DO SOMETHING MONUMENTALLY *STUPID*?

WELL, *THIS* IS ONE OF THOSE MOMENTS, AND I'M THE ONE APPEARING JUST IN TIME TO WARN YOU.

DON'T *DO* THIS, ROSE. DON'T DRIVE THIS NEW WEDGE BETWEEN US, AFTER WE TOOK SO LONG FINDING OUR WAY BACK TO EACH OTHER.

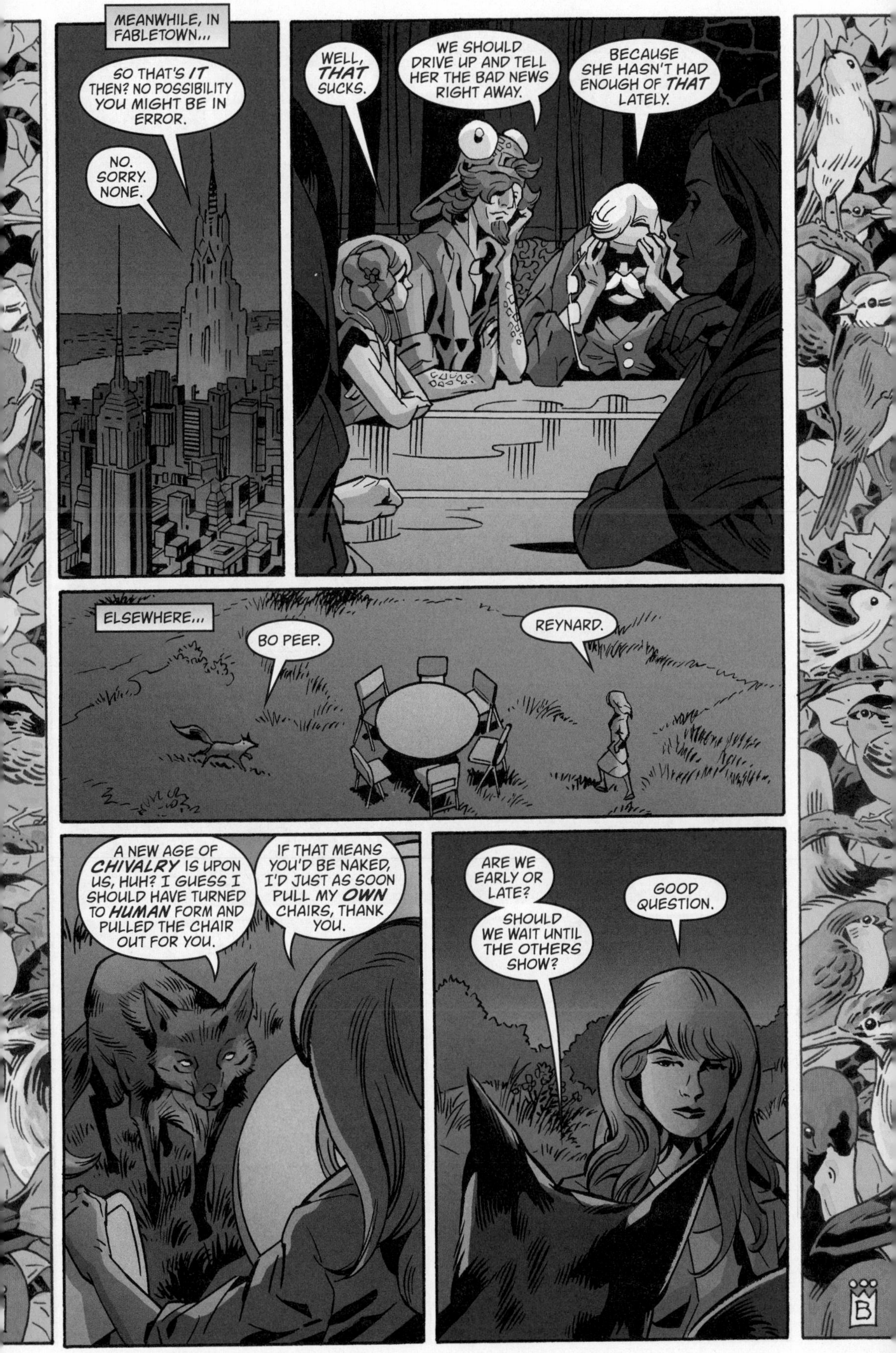
MEANWHILE, IN FABLETOWN...
SO THAT'S IT THEN? NO POSSIBILITY YOU MIGHT BE IN ERROR.
NO. SORRY. NONE.
WELL, THAT SUCKS.
WE SHOULD DRIVE UP AND TELL HER THE BAD NEWS RIGHT AWAY.
BECAUSE SHE HASN'T HAD ENOUGH OF THAT LATELY.
ELSEWHERE...
BO PEEP.
REYNARD.
A NEW AGE OF CHIVALRY IS UPON US, HUH? I GUESS I SHOULD HAVE TURNED TO HUMAN FORM AND PULLED THE CHAIR OUT FOR YOU.
IF THAT MEANS YOU'D BE NAKED, I'D JUST AS SOON PULL MY OWN CHAIRS, THANK YOU.
ARE WE EARLY OR LATE?
SHOULD WE WAIT UNTIL THE OTHERS SHOW?
GOOD QUESTION.

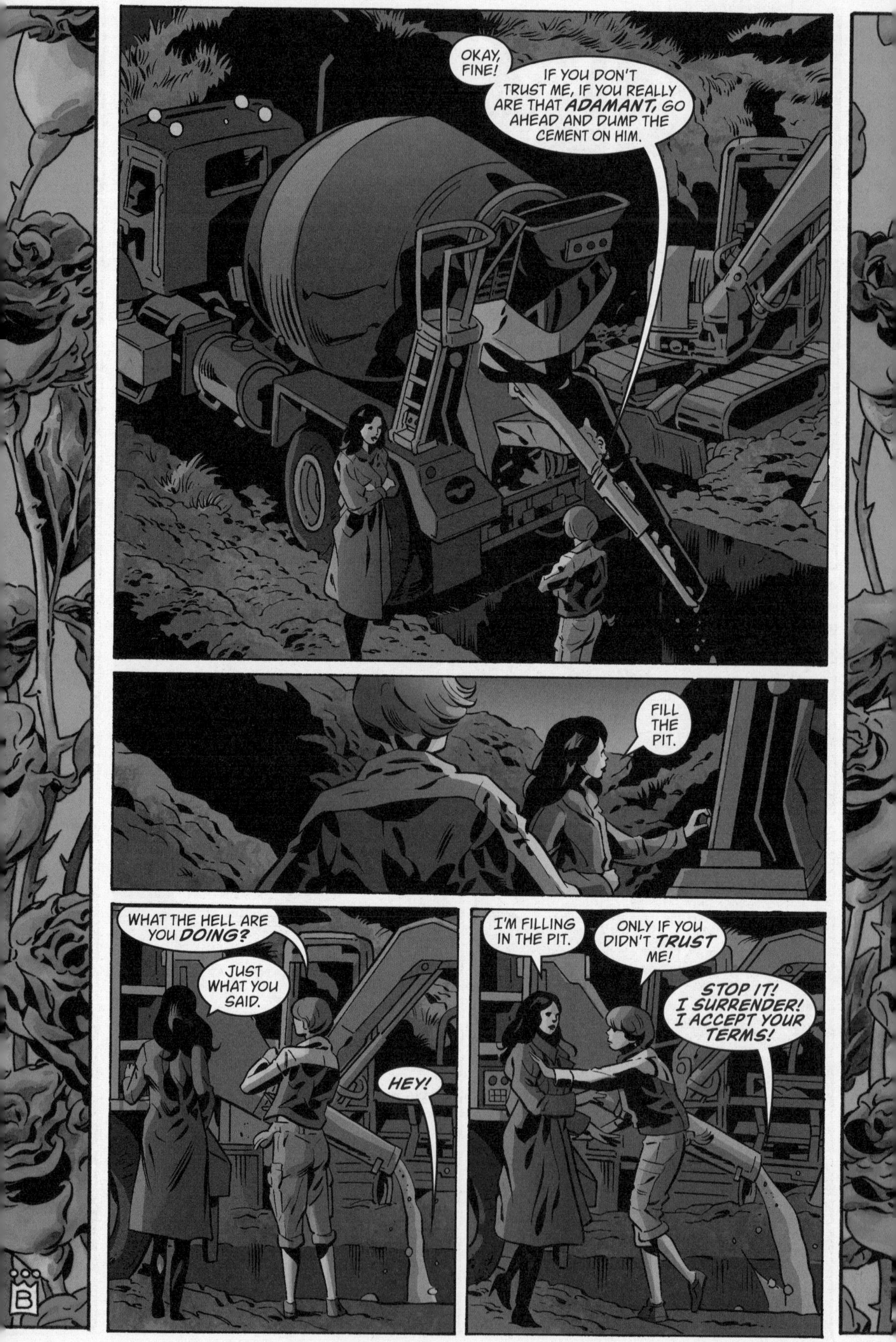
OKAY, FINE!
IF YOU DON'T TRUST ME, IF YOU REALLY ARE THAT ADAMANT, GO AHEAD AND DUMP THE CEMENT ON HIM.
FILL THE PIT.
WHAT THE HELL ARE YOU DOING?
JUST WHAT YOU SAID.
HEY!
I'M FILLING IN THE PIT.
ONLY IF YOU DIDN'T TRUST ME!
STOP IT! I SURRENDER! I ACCEPT YOUR TERMS!

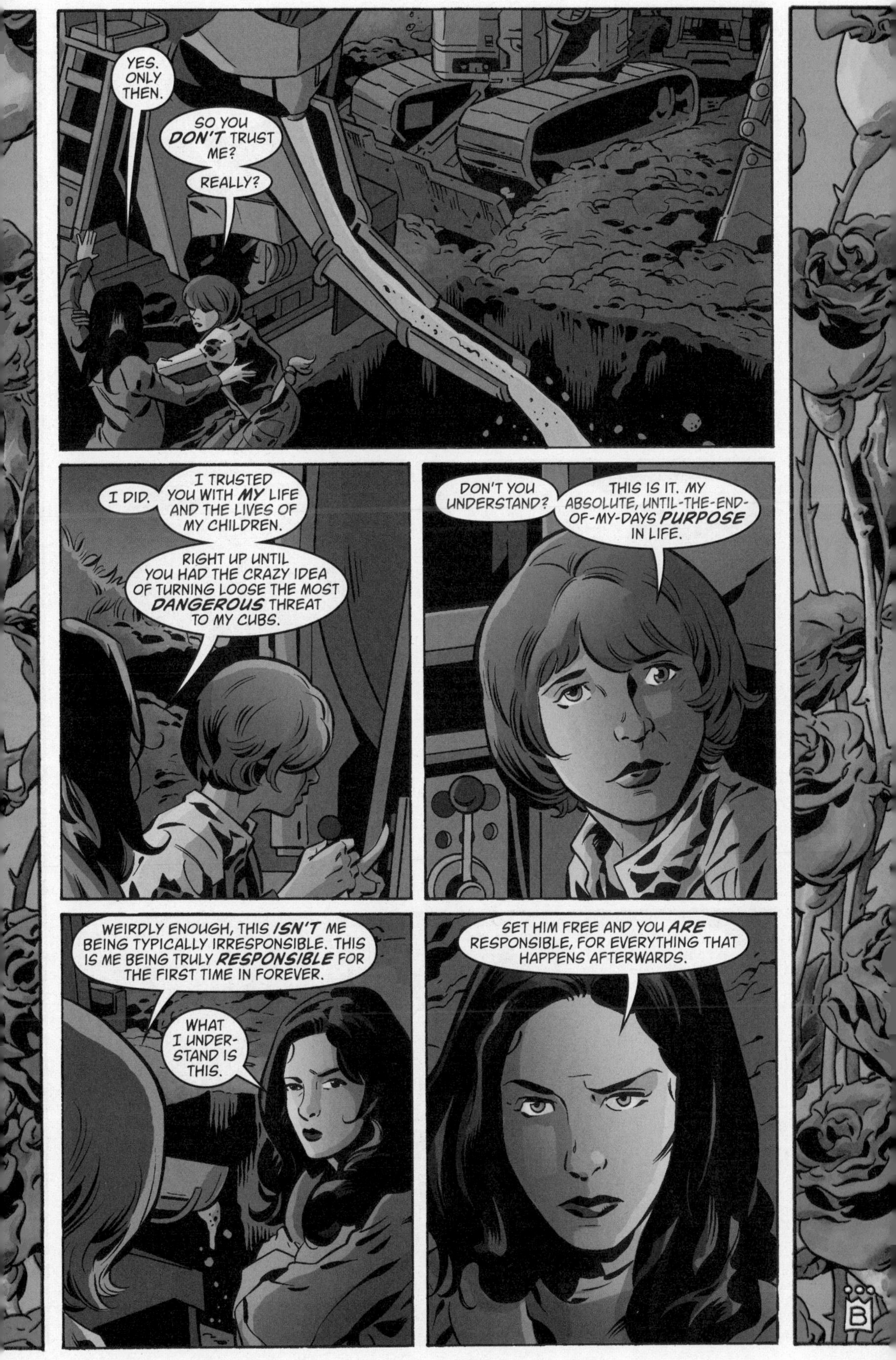
YES. ONLY THEN.
SO YOU DON'T TRUST ME?
REALLY?
I DID.
I TRUSTED YOU WITH MY LIFE AND THE LIVES OF MY CHILDREN.
RIGHT UP UNTIL YOU HAD THE CRAZY IDEA OF TURNING LOOSE THE MOST DANGEROUS THREAT TO MY CUBS.
DON'T YOU UNDERSTAND?
THIS IS IT. MY ABSOLUTE, UNTIL-THE-END-OF-MY-DAYS PURPOSE IN LIFE.
WEIRDLY ENOUGH, THIS ISN'T ME BEING TYPICALLY IRRESPONSIBLE. THIS IS ME BEING TRULY RESPONSIBLE FOR THE FIRST TIME IN FOREVER.
WHAT I UNDERSTAND IS THIS.
SET HIM FREE AND YOU ARE RESPONSIBLE, FOR EVERYTHING THAT HAPPENS AFTERWARDS.

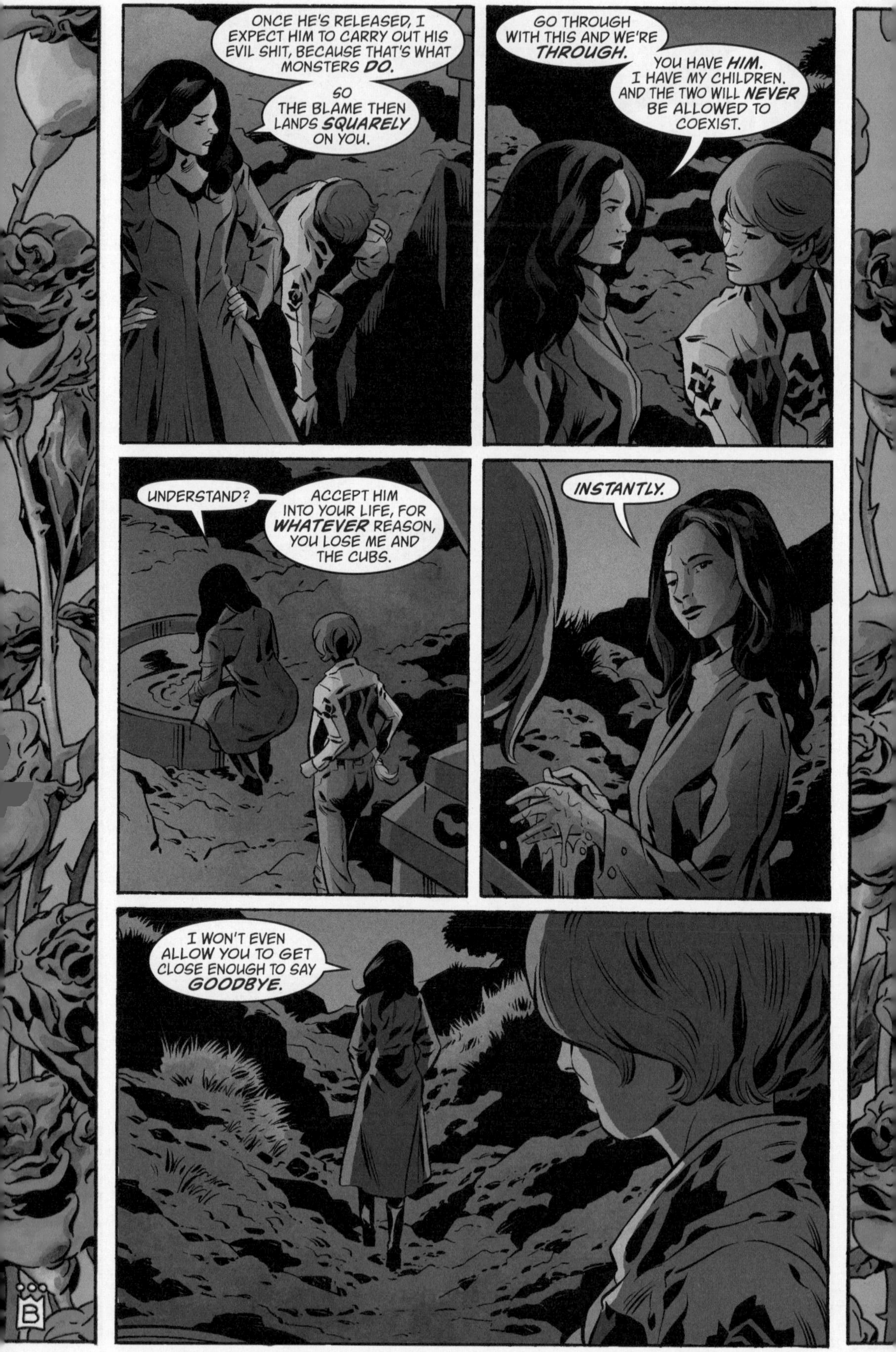
ONCE HE'S RELEASED, I EXPECT HIM TO CARRY OUT HIS EVIL SHIT, BECAUSE THAT'S WHAT MONSTERS DO.
SO THE BLAME THEN LANDS SQUARELY ON YOU.
GO THROUGH WITH THIS AND WE'RE THROUGH.
YOU HAVE HIM. I HAVE MY CHILDREN. AND THE TWO WILL NEVER BE ALLOWED TO COEXIST.
UNDERSTAND?
ACCEPT HIM INTO YOUR LIFE, FOR WHATEVER REASON, YOU LOSE ME AND THE CUBS.
INSTANTLY.
I WON'T EVEN ALLOW YOU TO GET CLOSE ENOUGH TO SAY GOODBYE.

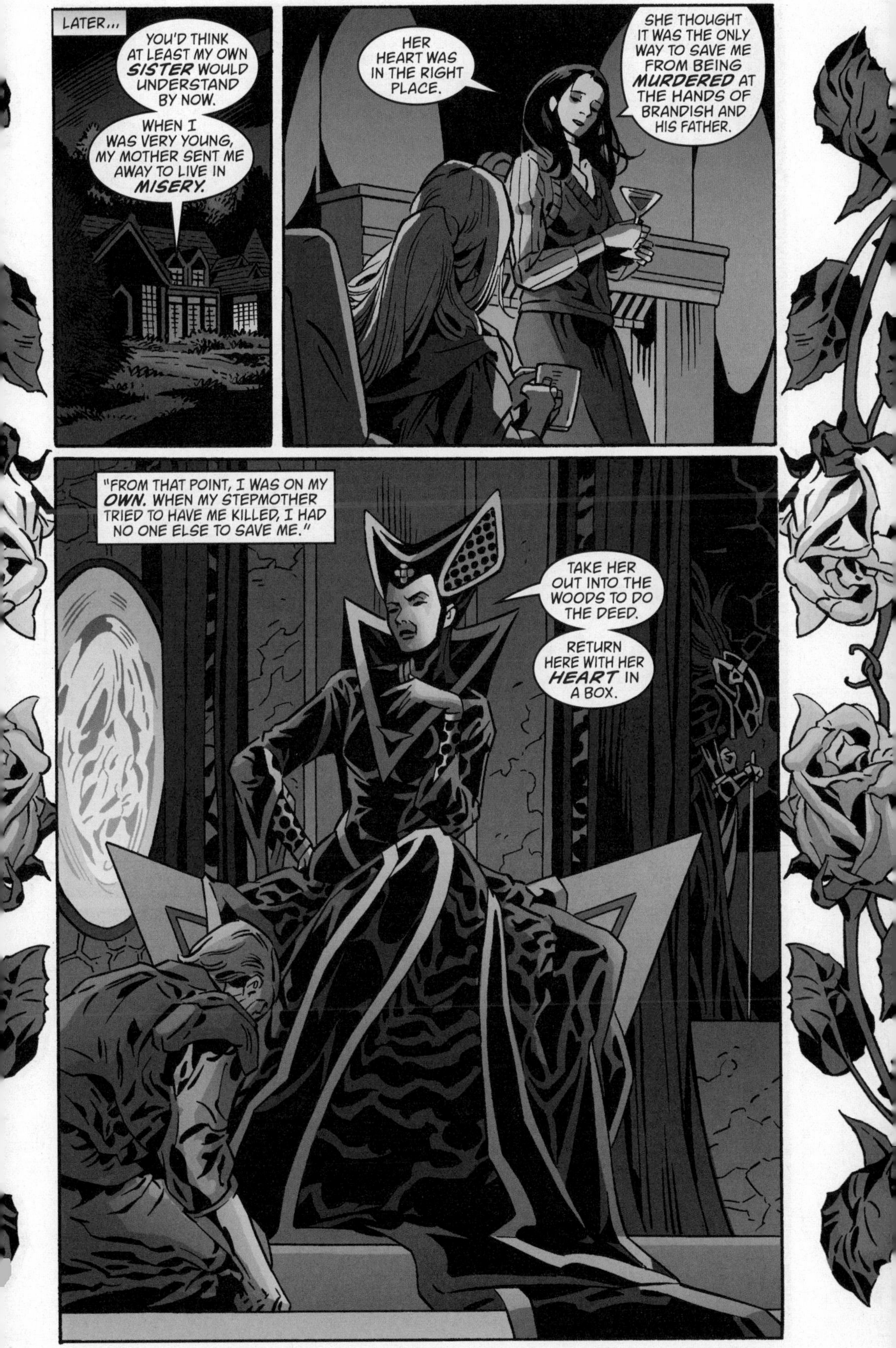

LATER...
YOU'D THINK AT LEAST MY OWN SISTER WOULD UNDERSTAND BY NOW.
WHEN I WAS VERY YOUNG, MY MOTHER SENT ME AWAY TO LIVE IN MISERY.
HER HEART WAS IN THE RIGHT PLACE.
SHE THOUGHT IT WAS THE ONLY WAY TO SAVE ME FROM BEING MURDERED AT THE HANDS OF BRANDISH AND HIS FATHER.
"FROM THAT POINT, I WAS ON MY OWN. WHEN MY STEPMOTHER TRIED TO HAVE ME KILLED, I HAD NO ONE ELSE TO SAVE ME."
TAKE HER OUT INTO THE WOODS TO DO THE DEED.
RETURN HERE WITH HER HEART IN A BOX.

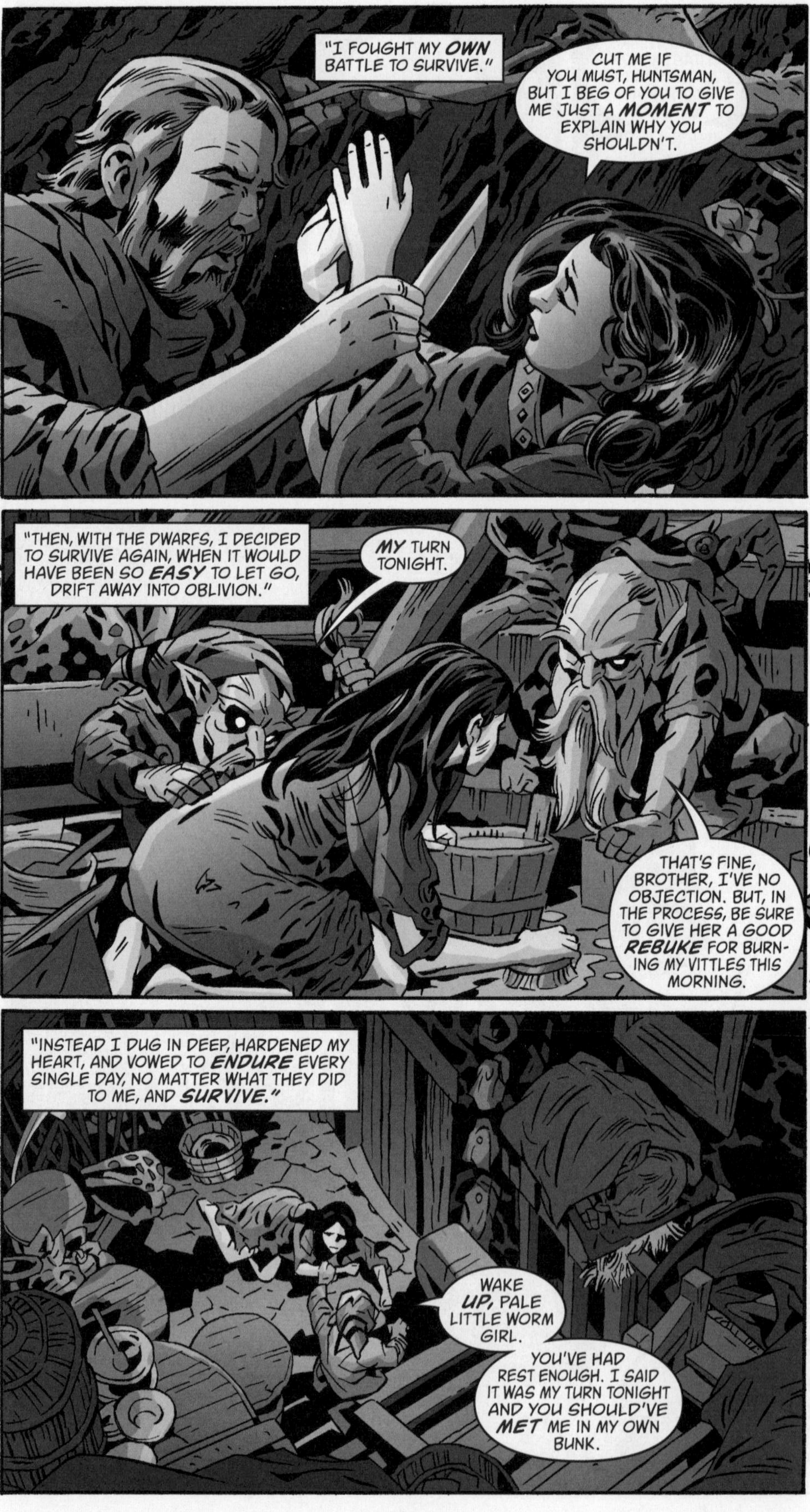
"I FOUGHT MY OWN BATTLE TO SURVIVE."
CUT ME IF YOU MUST, HUNTSMAN, BUT I BEG OF YOU TO GIVE ME JUST A MOMENT TO EXPLAIN WHY YOU SHOULDN'T.
"THEN, WITH THE DWARFS, I DECIDED TO SURVIVE AGAIN, WHEN IT WOULD HAVE BEEN SO EASY TO LET GO, DRIFT AWAY INTO OBLIVION."
MY TURN TONIGHT.
THAT'S FINE, BROTHER, I'VE NO OBJECTION. BUT, IN THE PROCESS, BE SURE TO GIVE HER A GOOD REBUKE FOR BURNING MY VITTLES THIS MORNING.
"INSTEAD I DUG IN DEEP, HARDENED MY HEART, AND VOWED TO ENDURE EVERY SINGLE DAY, NO MATTER WHAT THEY DID TO ME, AND SURVIVE."
WAKE UP, PALE LITTLE WORM GIRL.
YOU'VE HAD REST ENOUGH. I SAID IT WAS MY TURN TONIGHT AND YOU SHOULD'VE MET ME IN MY OWN BUNK.

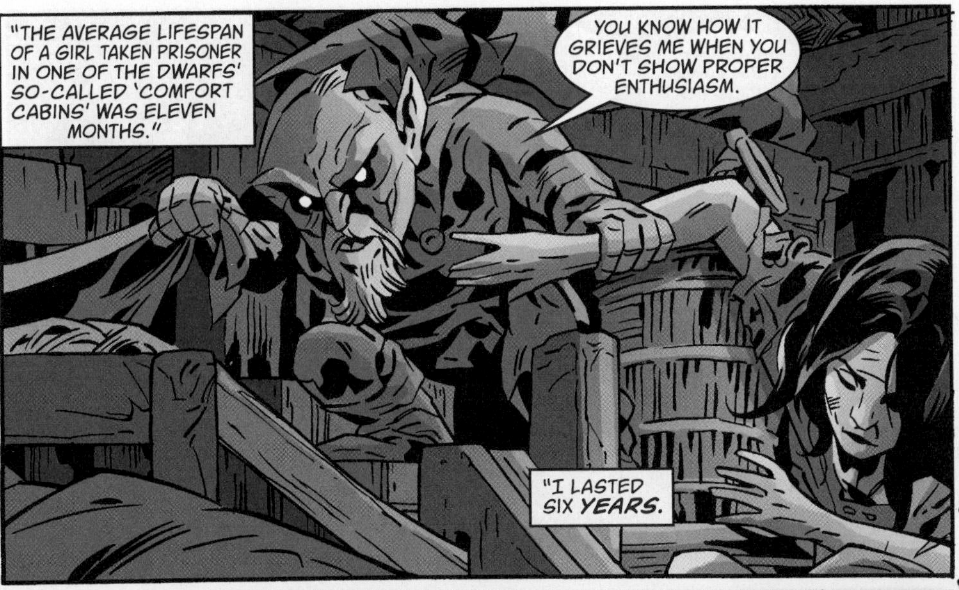
"THE AVERAGE LIFESPAN OF A GIRL TAKEN PRISONER IN ONE OF THE DWARFS' SO-CALLED 'COMFORT CABINS' WAS ELEVEN MONTHS."
YOU KNOW HOW IT GRIEVES ME WHEN YOU DON'T SHOW PROPER ENTHUSIASM.
"I LASTED SIX *YEARS.*

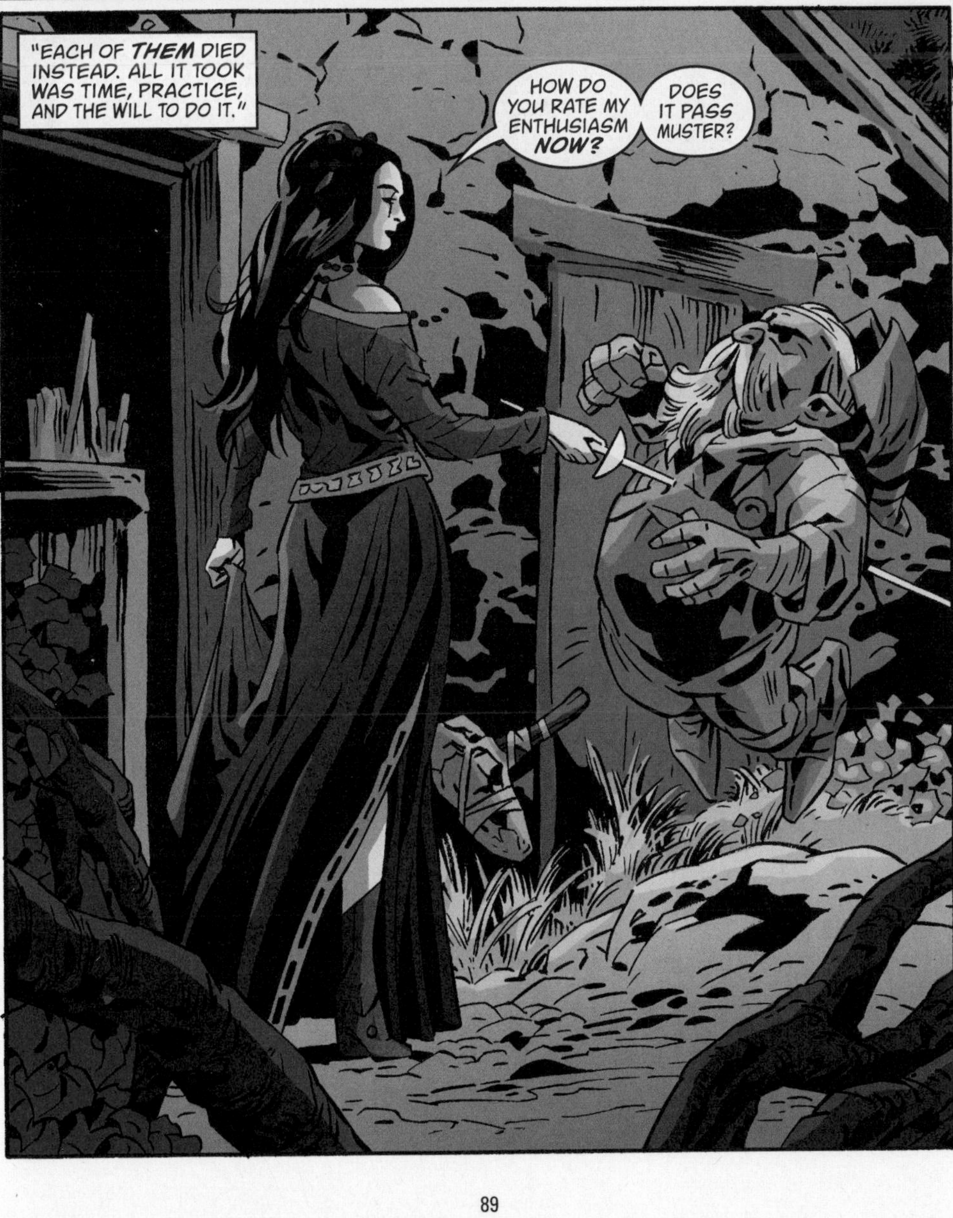
"EACH OF *THEM* DIED INSTEAD. ALL IT TOOK WAS TIME, PRACTICE, AND THE WILL TO DO IT."
HOW DO YOU RATE MY ENTHUSIASM *NOW?*
DOES IT PASS MUSTER?

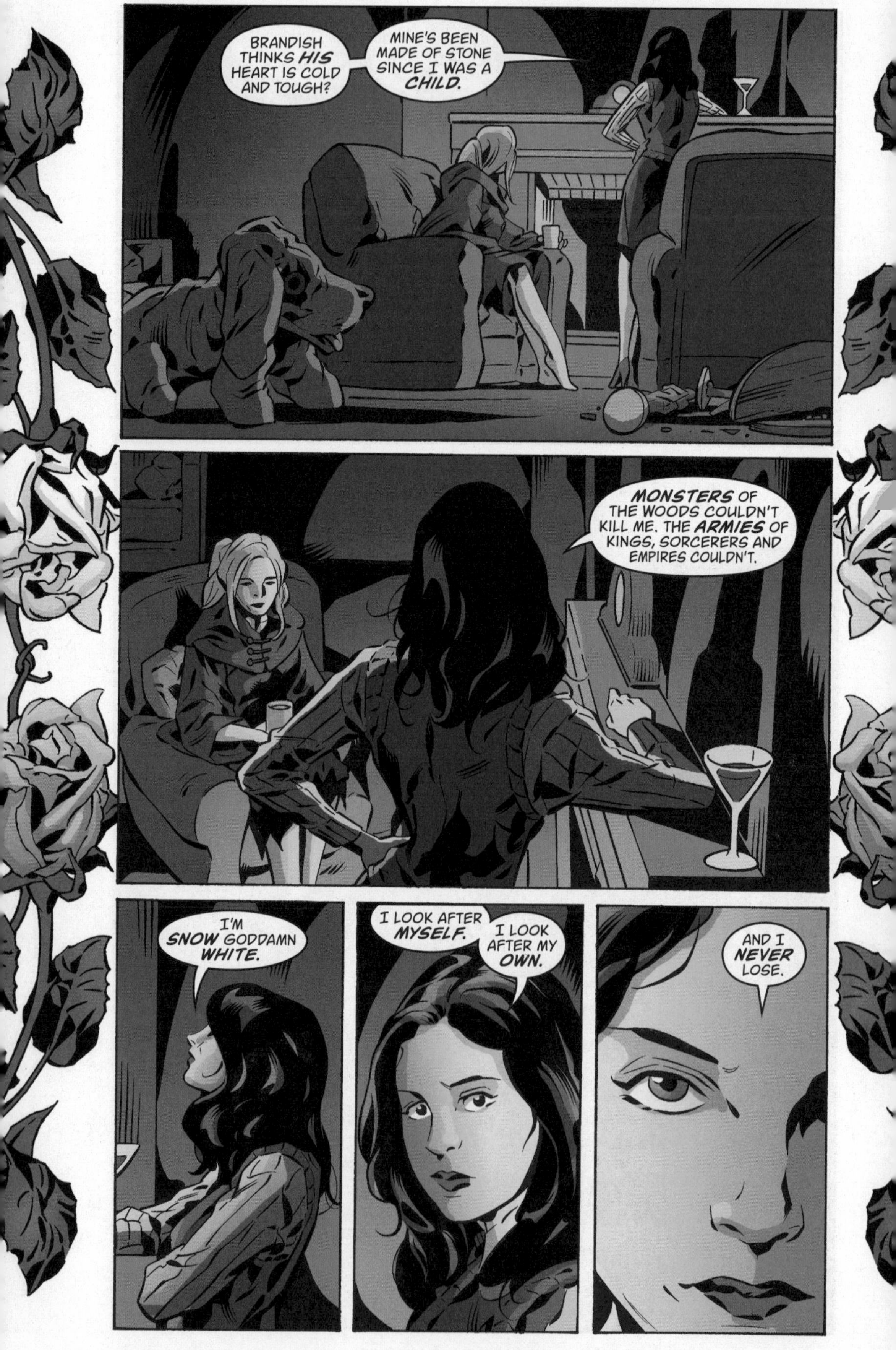
BRANDISH THINKS HIS HEART IS COLD AND TOUGH?
MINE'S BEEN MADE OF STONE SINCE I WAS A CHILD.
MONSTERS OF THE WOODS COULDN'T KILL ME. THE ARMIES OF KINGS, SORCERERS AND EMPIRES COULDN'T.
I'M SNOW GODDAMN WHITE.
I LOOK AFTER MYSELF.
I LOOK AFTER MY OWN.
AND I NEVER LOSE.

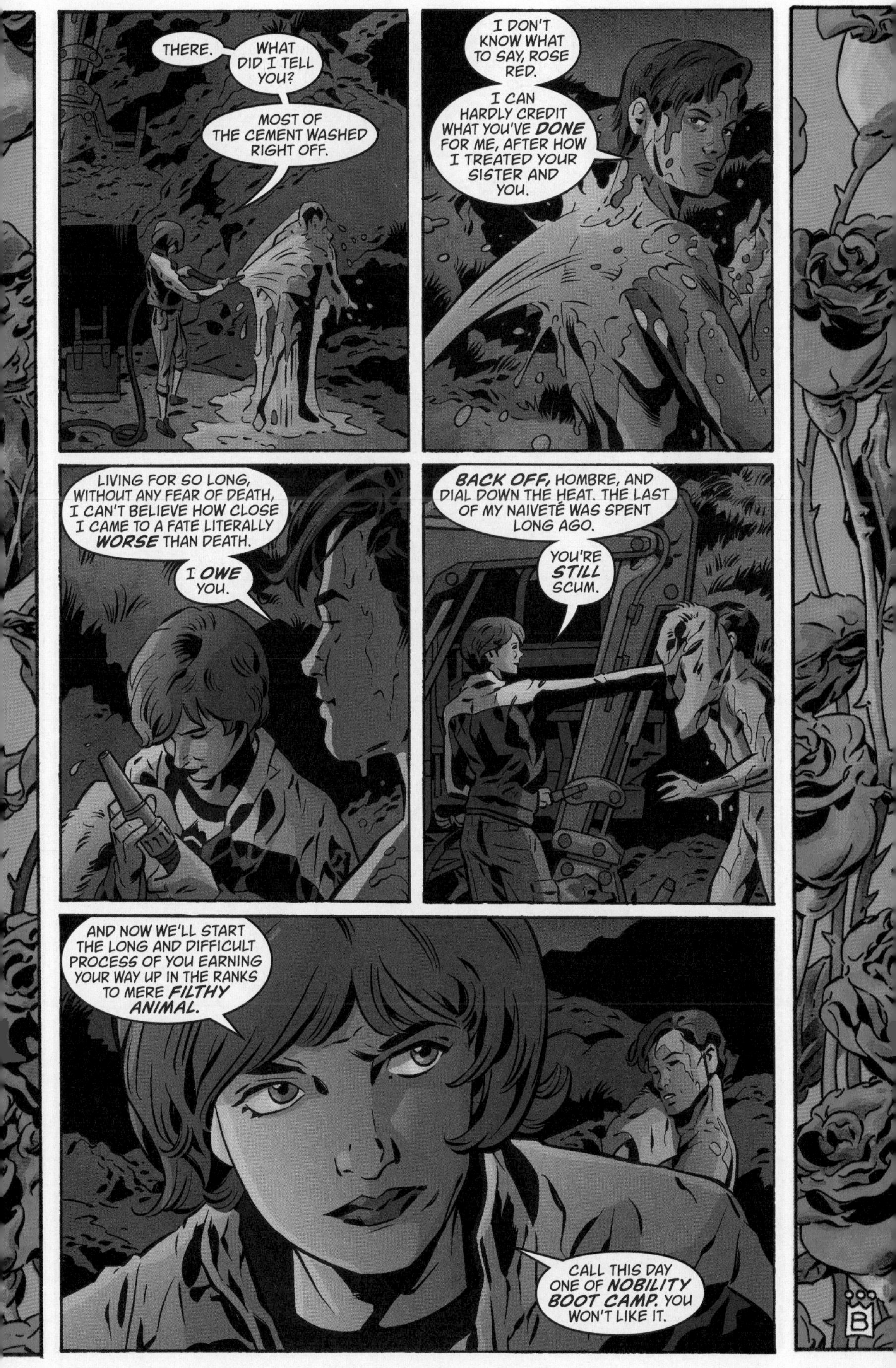
THERE.
WHAT DID I TELL YOU?
MOST OF THE CEMENT WASHED RIGHT OFF.
I DON'T KNOW WHAT TO SAY, ROSE RED.
I CAN HARDLY CREDIT WHAT YOU'VE DONE FOR ME, AFTER HOW I TREATED YOUR SISTER AND YOU.
LIVING FOR SO LONG, WITHOUT ANY FEAR OF DEATH, I CAN'T BELIEVE HOW CLOSE I CAME TO A FATE LITERALLY WORSE THAN DEATH.
I OWE YOU.
BACK OFF, HOMBRE, AND DIAL DOWN THE HEAT. THE LAST OF MY NAIVETÉ WAS SPENT LONG AGO.
YOU'RE STILL SCUM.
AND NOW WE'LL START THE LONG AND DIFFICULT PROCESS OF YOU EARNING YOUR WAY UP IN THE RANKS TO MERE FILTHY ANIMAL.
CALL THIS DAY ONE OF NOBILITY BOOT CAMP. YOU WON'T LIKE IT.

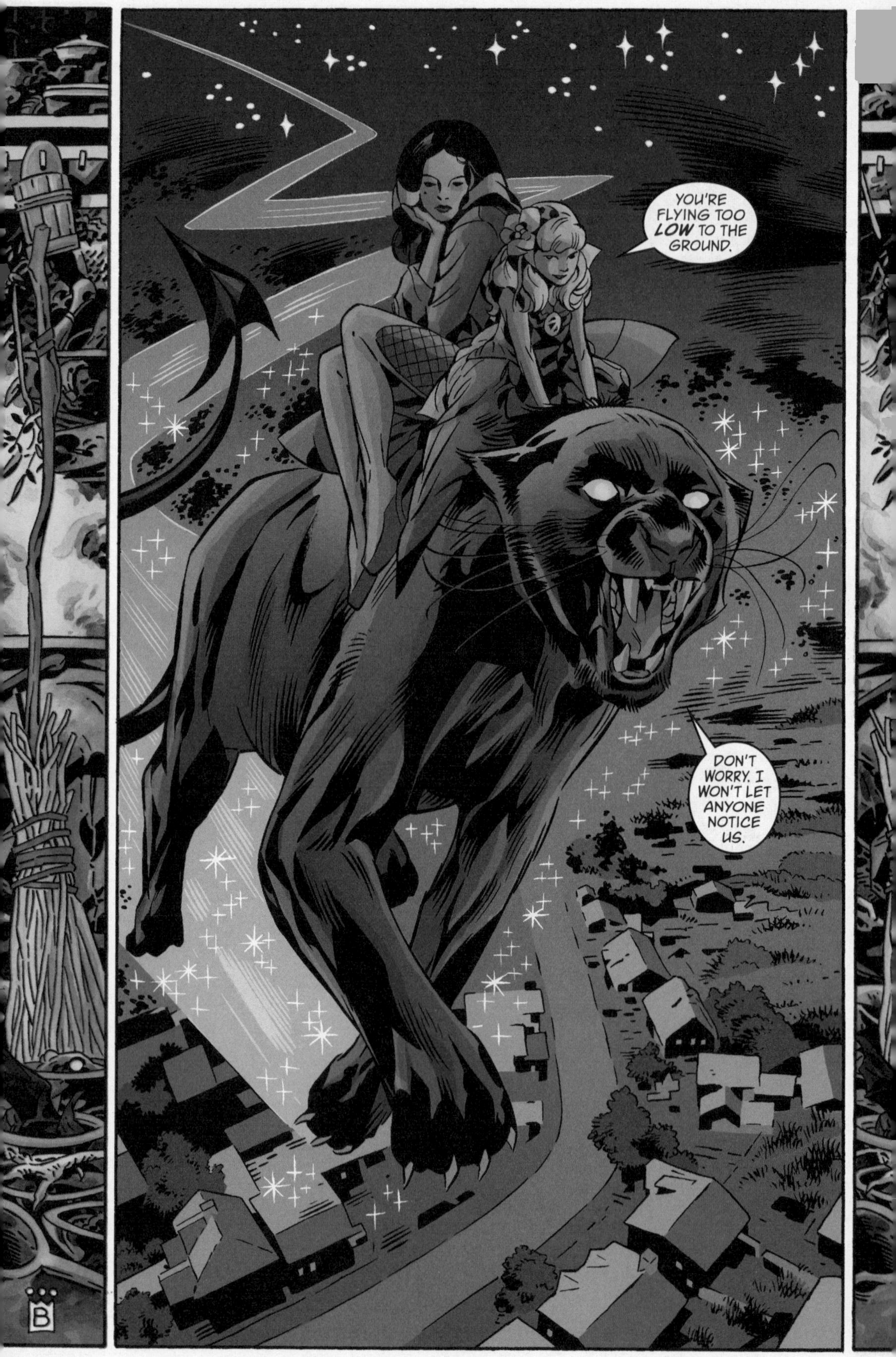
YOU'RE FLYING TOO LOW TO THE GROUND.
DON'T WORRY. I WON'T LET ANYONE NOTICE US.

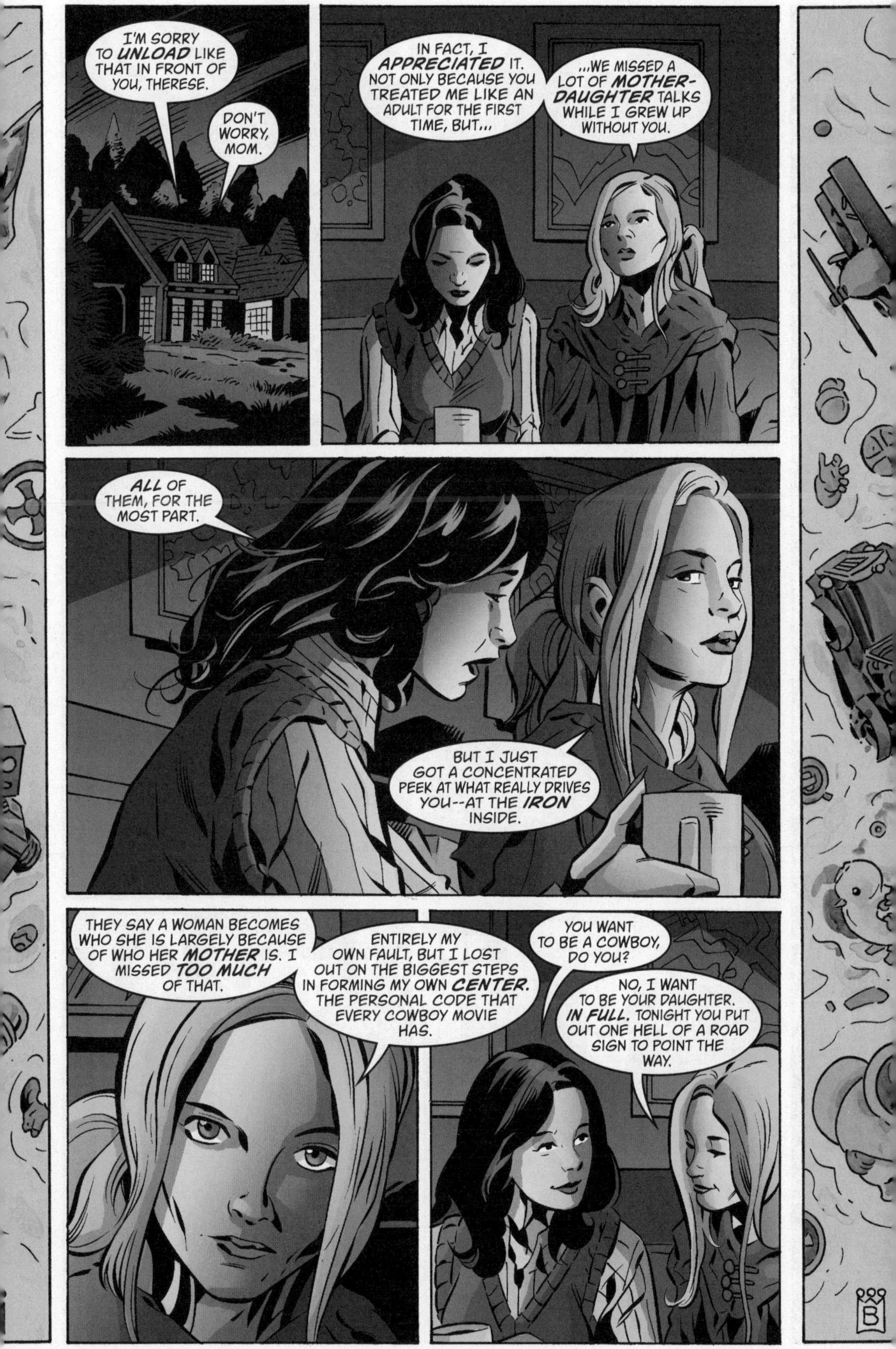
I'M SORRY TO UNLOAD LIKE THAT IN FRONT OF YOU, THERESE.
DON'T WORRY, MOM.
IN FACT, I APPRECIATED IT. NOT ONLY BECAUSE YOU TREATED ME LIKE AN ADULT FOR THE FIRST TIME, BUT...
...WE MISSED A LOT OF MOTHER-DAUGHTER TALKS WHILE I GREW UP WITHOUT YOU.
ALL OF THEM, FOR THE MOST PART.
BUT I JUST GOT A CONCENTRATED PEEK AT WHAT REALLY DRIVES YOU--AT THE IRON INSIDE.
THEY SAY A WOMAN BECOMES WHO SHE IS LARGELY BECAUSE OF WHO HER MOTHER IS. I MISSED TOO MUCH OF THAT.
ENTIRELY MY OWN FAULT, BUT I LOST OUT ON THE BIGGEST STEPS IN FORMING MY OWN CENTER. THE PERSONAL CODE THAT EVERY COWBOY MOVIE HAS.
YOU WANT TO BE A COWBOY, DO YOU?
NO, I WANT TO BE YOUR DAUGHTER. IN FULL. TONIGHT YOU PUT OUT ONE HELL OF A ROAD SIGN TO POINT THE WAY.

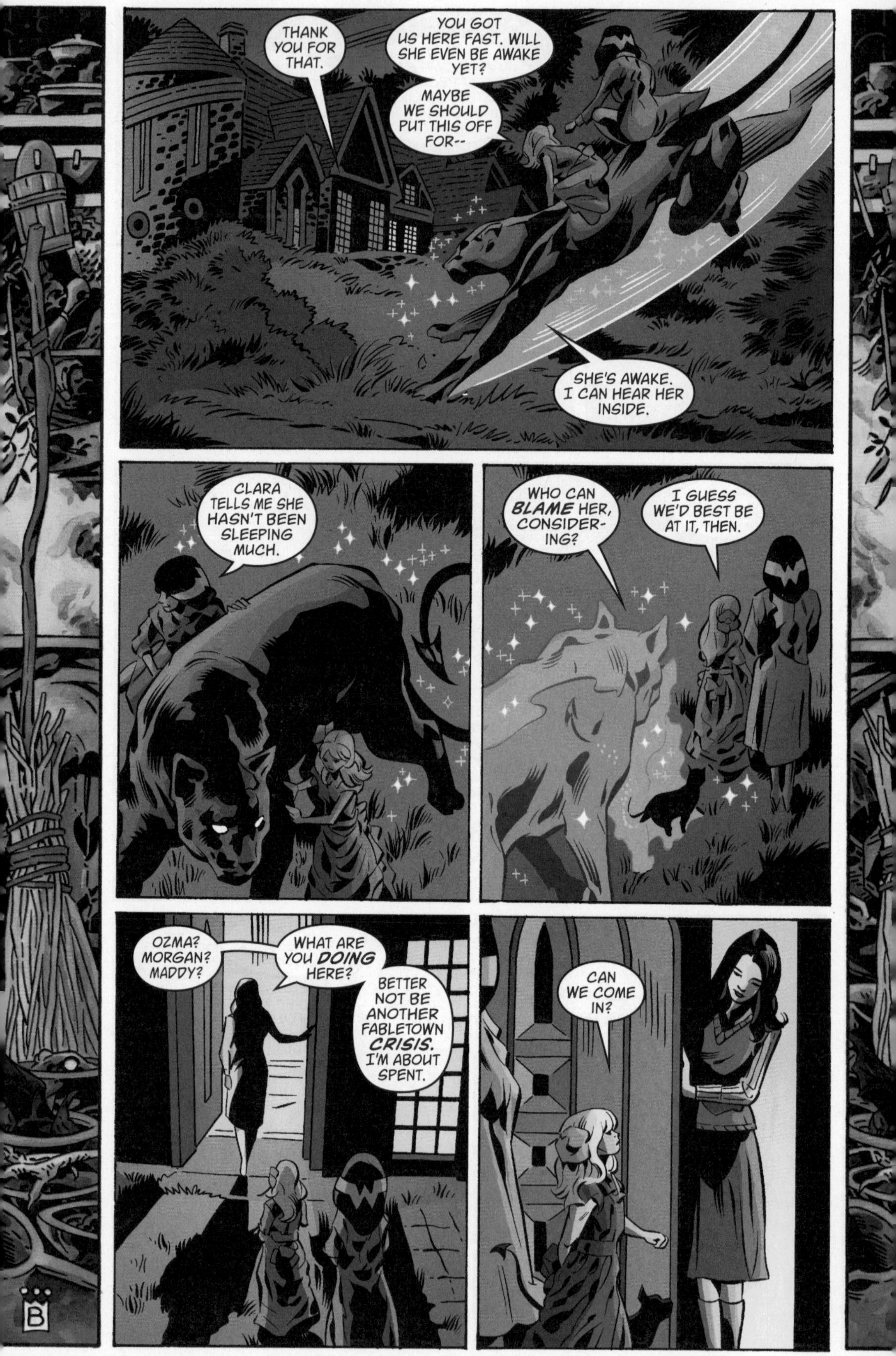
THANK YOU FOR THAT.
YOU GOT US HERE FAST. WILL SHE EVEN BE AWAKE YET?
MAYBE WE SHOULD PUT THIS OFF FOR--
SHE'S AWAKE. I CAN HEAR HER INSIDE.
CLARA TELLS ME SHE HASN'T BEEN SLEEPING MUCH.
WHO CAN BLAME HER, CONSIDER-ING?
I GUESS WE'D BEST BE AT IT, THEN.
OZMA? MORGAN? MADDY?
WHAT ARE YOU DOING HERE?
BETTER NOT BE ANOTHER FABLETOWN CRISIS. I'M ABOUT SPENT.
CAN WE COME IN?

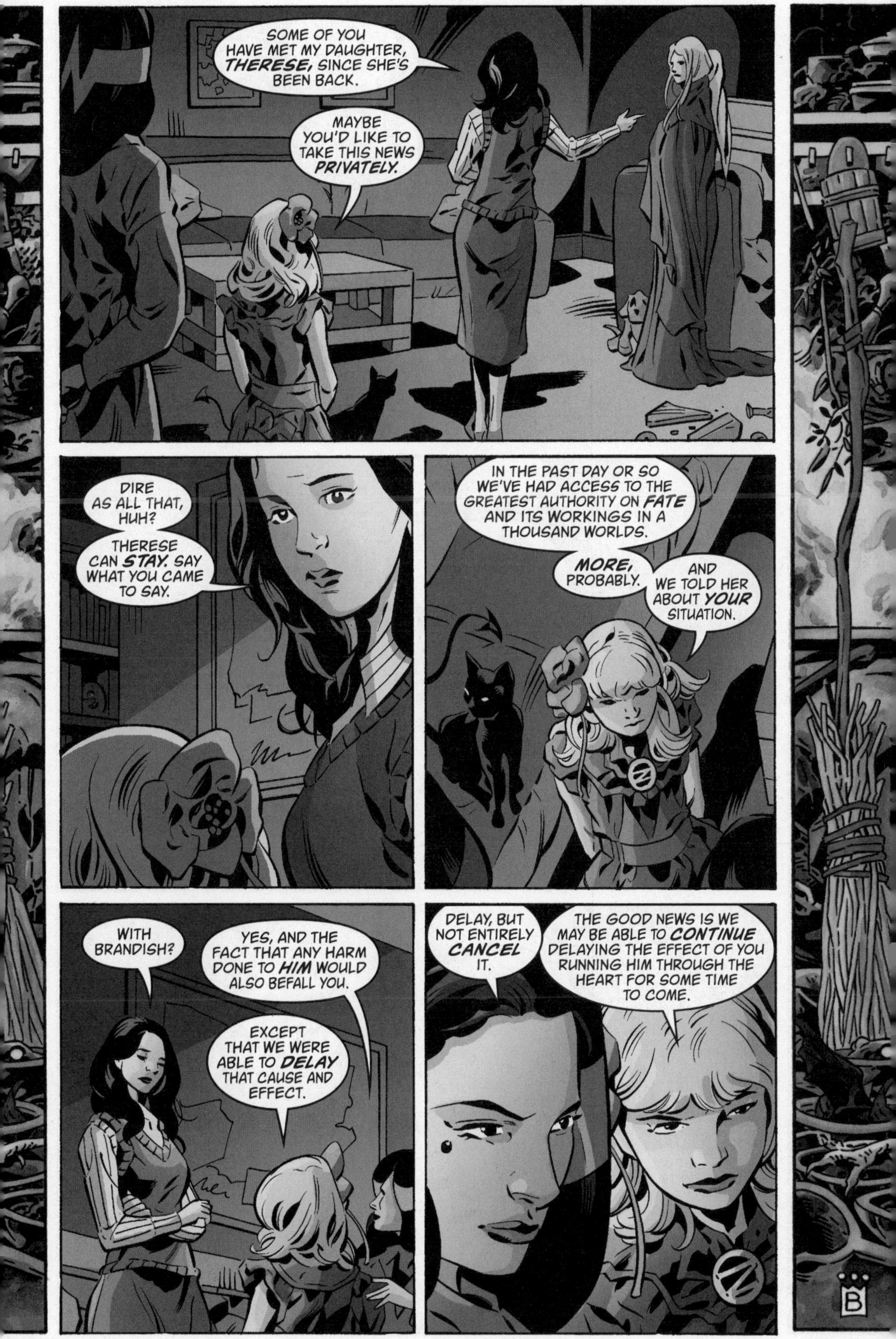
SOME OF YOU HAVE MET MY DAUGHTER, THERESE, SINCE SHE'S BEEN BACK.
MAYBE YOU'D LIKE TO TAKE THIS NEWS PRIVATELY.
DIRE AS ALL THAT, HUH?
THERESE CAN STAY. SAY WHAT YOU CAME TO SAY.
IN THE PAST DAY OR SO WE'VE HAD ACCESS TO THE GREATEST AUTHORITY ON FATE AND ITS WORKINGS IN A THOUSAND WORLDS.
MORE, PROBABLY.
AND WE TOLD HER ABOUT YOUR SITUATION.
WITH BRANDISH?
YES, AND THE FACT THAT ANY HARM DONE TO HIM WOULD ALSO BEFALL YOU.
EXCEPT THAT WE WERE ABLE TO DELAY THAT CAUSE AND EFFECT.
DELAY, BUT NOT ENTIRELY CANCEL IT.
THE GOOD NEWS IS WE MAY BE ABLE TO CONTINUE DELAYING THE EFFECT OF YOU RUNNING HIM THROUGH THE HEART FOR SOME TIME TO COME.

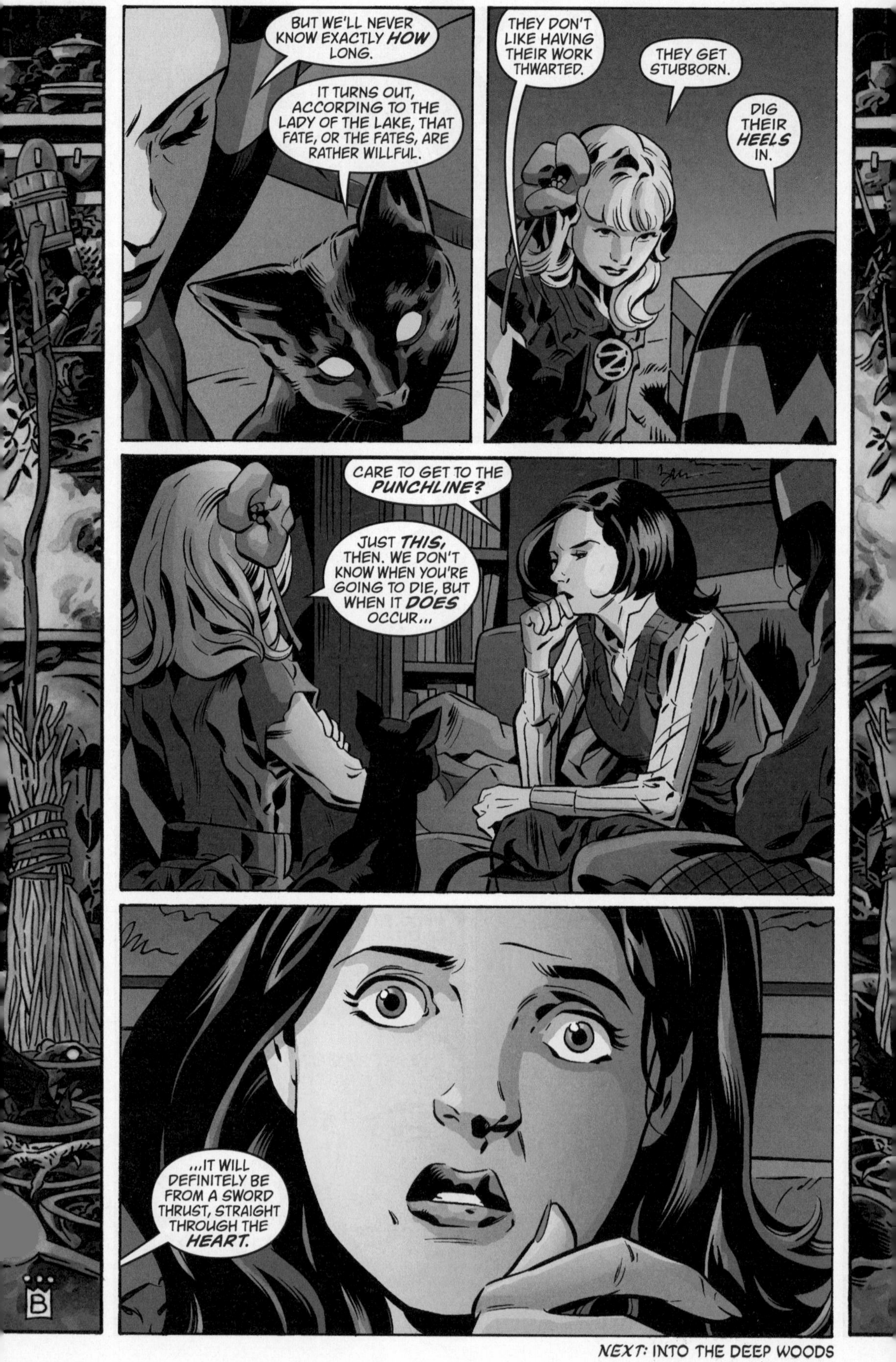
BUT WE'LL NEVER KNOW EXACTLY HOW LONG.
IT TURNS OUT, ACCORDING TO THE LADY OF THE LAKE, THAT FATE, OR THE FATES, ARE RATHER WILLFUL.
THEY DON'T LIKE HAVING THEIR WORK THWARTED.
THEY GET STUBBORN.
DIG THEIR HEELS IN.
CARE TO GET TO THE PUNCHLINE?
JUST THIS, THEN. WE DON'T KNOW WHEN YOU'RE GOING TO DIE, BUT WHEN IT DOES OCCUR...
...IT WILL DEFINITELY BE FROM A SWORD THRUST, STRAIGHT THROUGH THE HEART.

NEXT: INTO THE DEEP WOODS

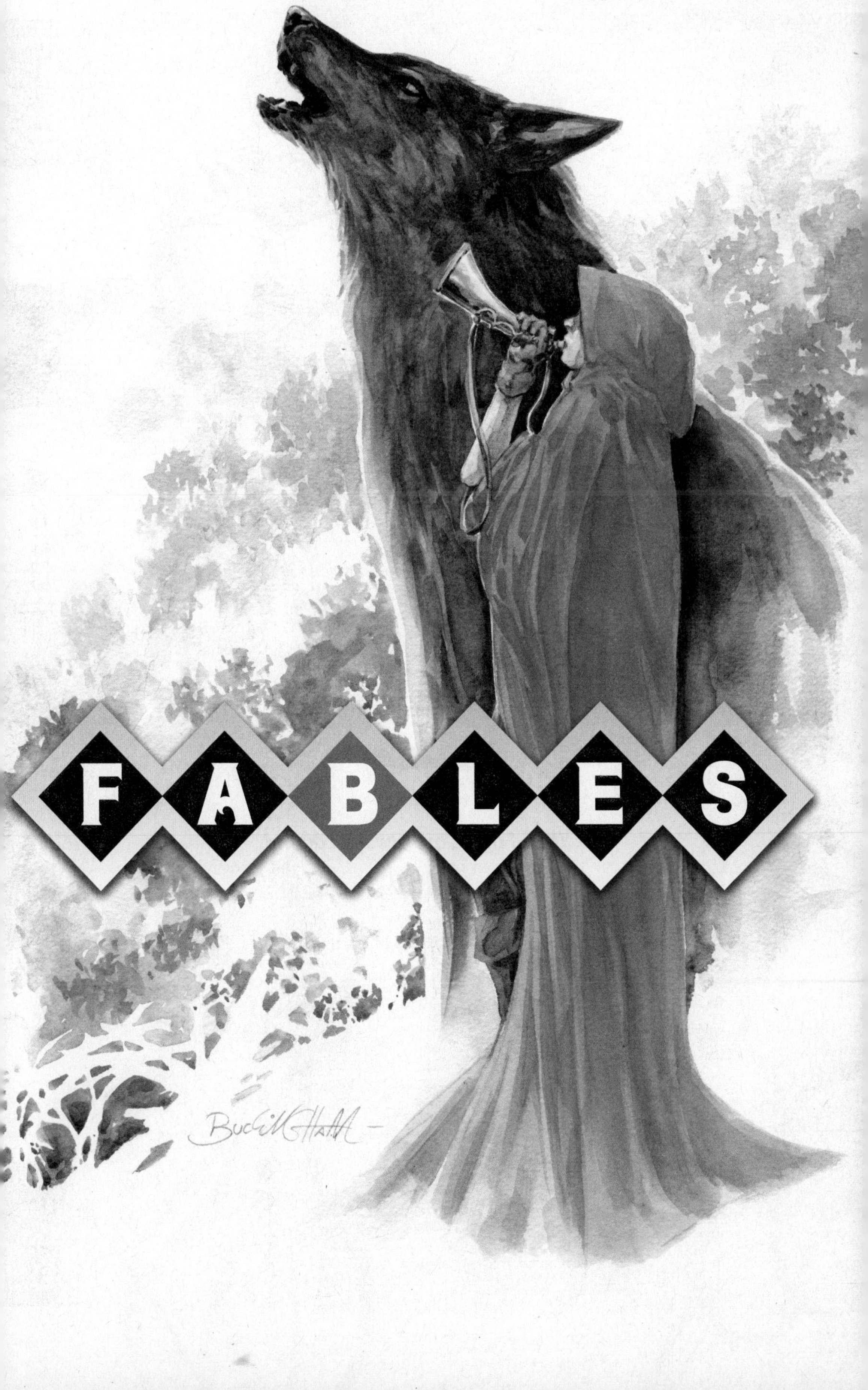
FABLES

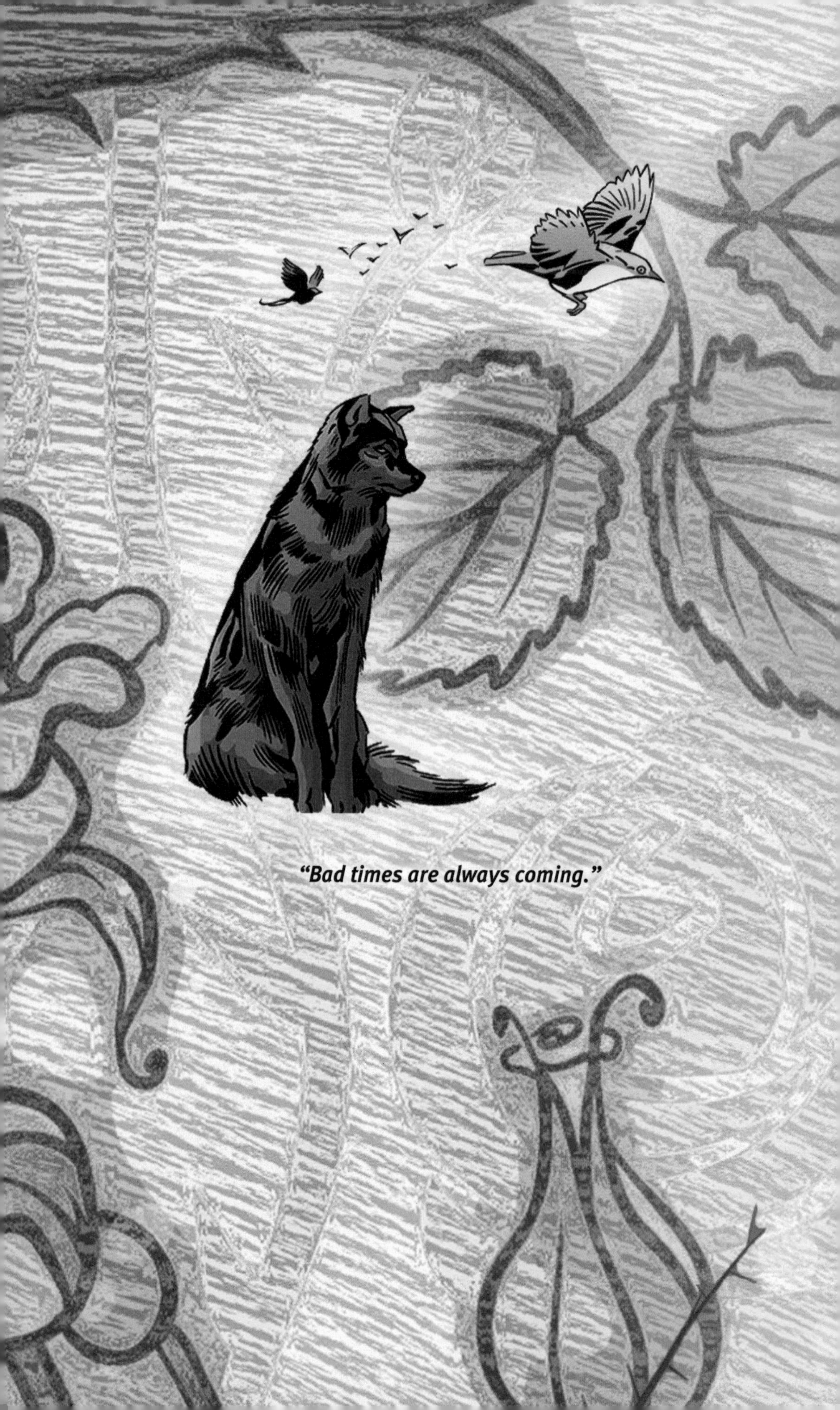
"Bad times are always coming."

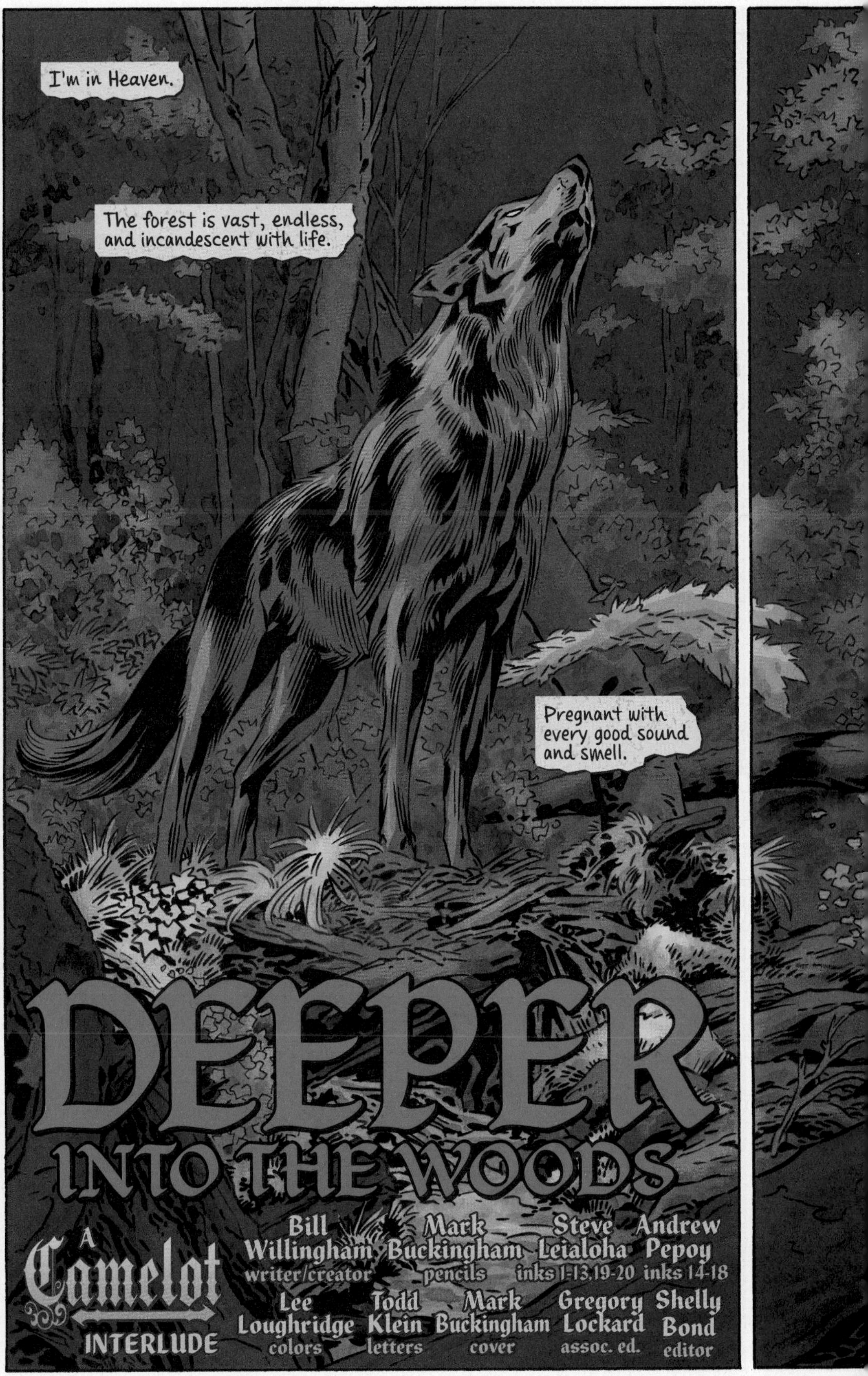

I'm in Heaven.
The forest is vast, endless, and incandescent with life.
Pregnant with every good sound and smell.
DEEPER INTO THE WOODS
A Camelot INTERLUDE
Bill Willingham writer/creator
Mark Buckingham pencils
Steve Leialoha inks 1-13,19-20
Andrew Pepoy inks 14-18
Lee Loughridge colors
Todd Klein letters
Mark Buckingham cover
Gregory Lockard assoc. ed.
Shelly Bond editor

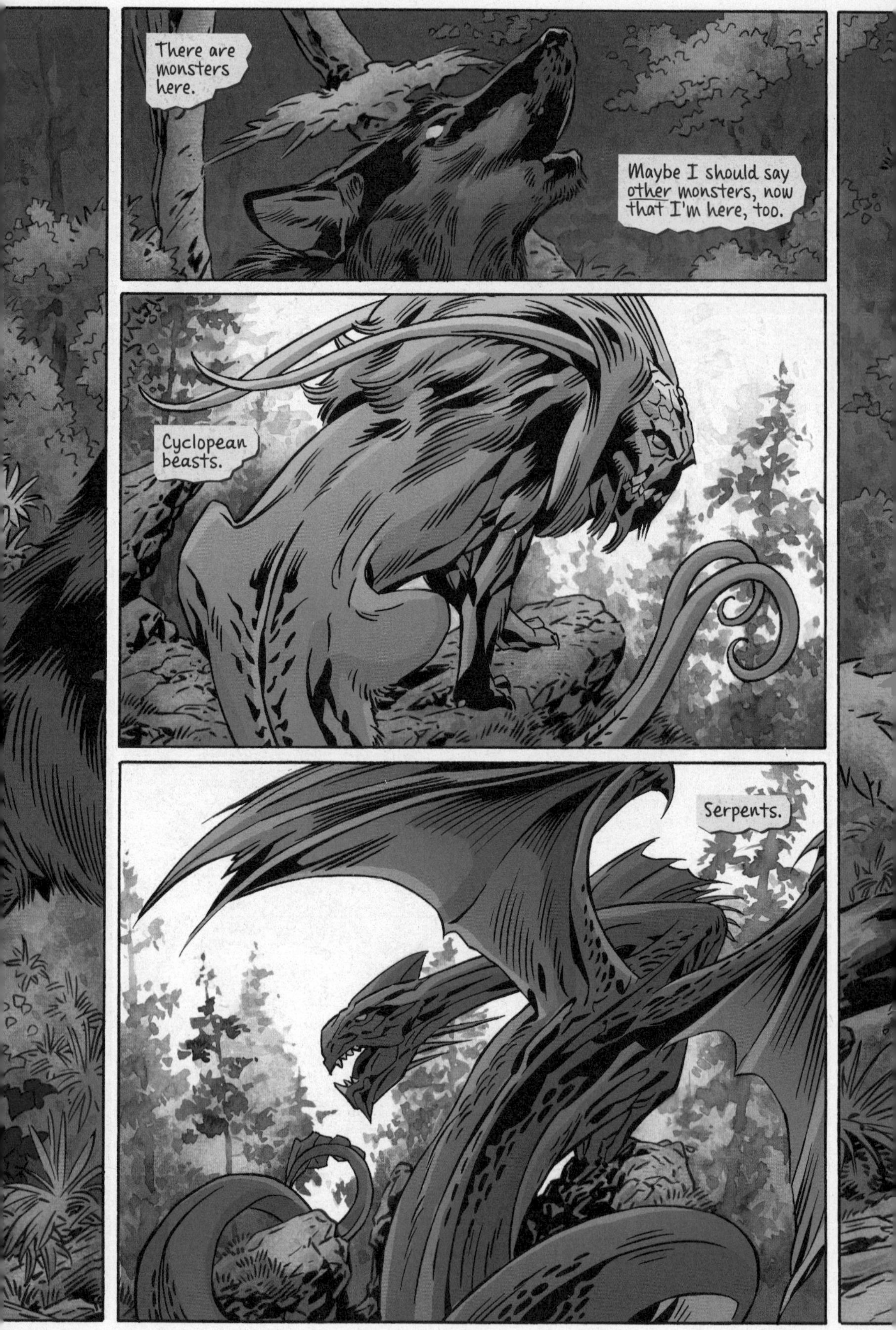

There are monsters here.
Maybe I should say other monsters, now that I'm here, too.
Cyclopean beasts.
Serpents.

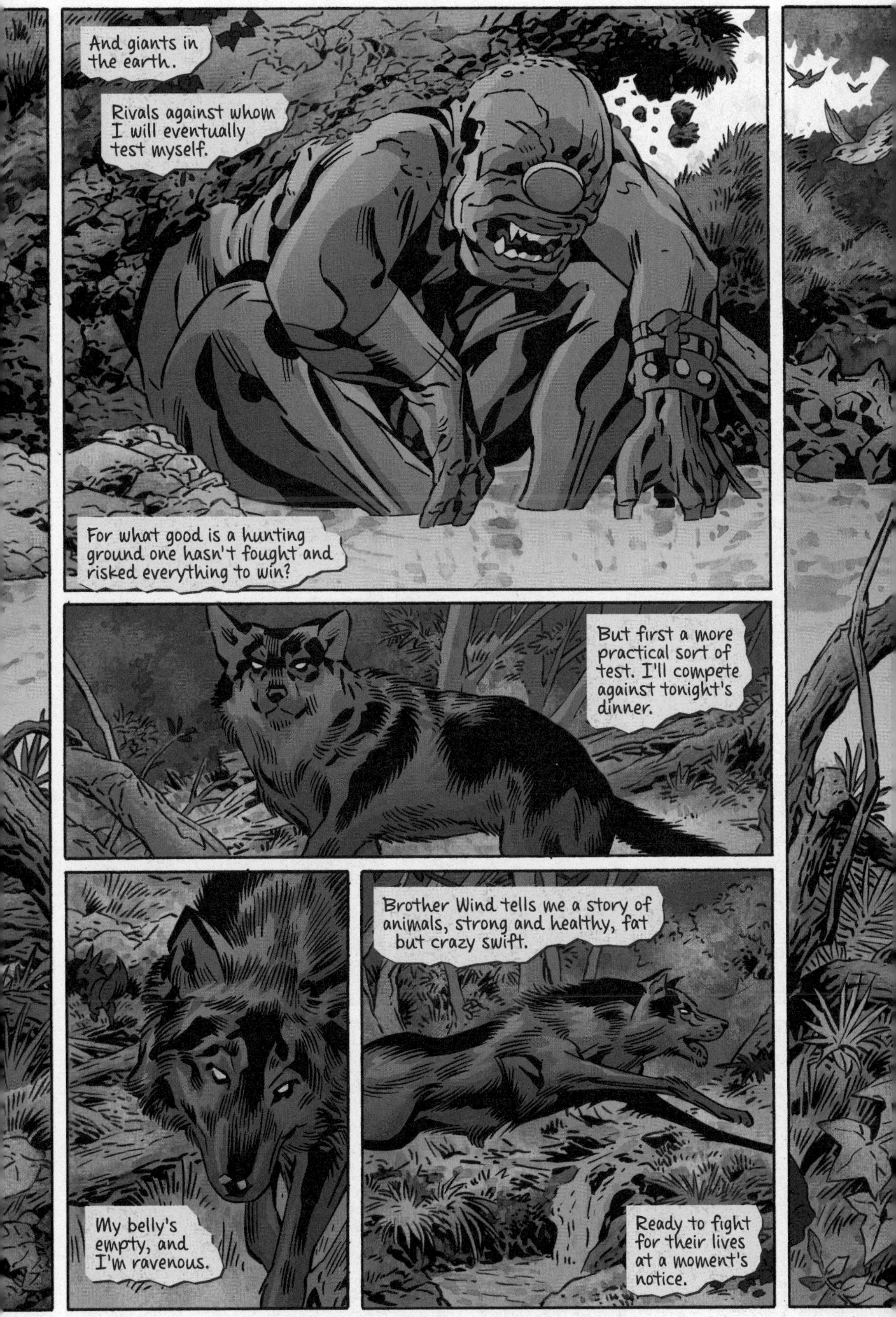
And giants in the earth.
Rivals against whom I will eventually test myself.
For what good is a hunting ground one hasn't fought and risked everything to win?
But first a more practical sort of test. I'll compete against tonight's dinner.
My belly's empty, and I'm ravenous.
Brother Wind tells me a story of animals, strong and healthy, fat but crazy swift.
Ready to fight for their lives at a moment's notice.

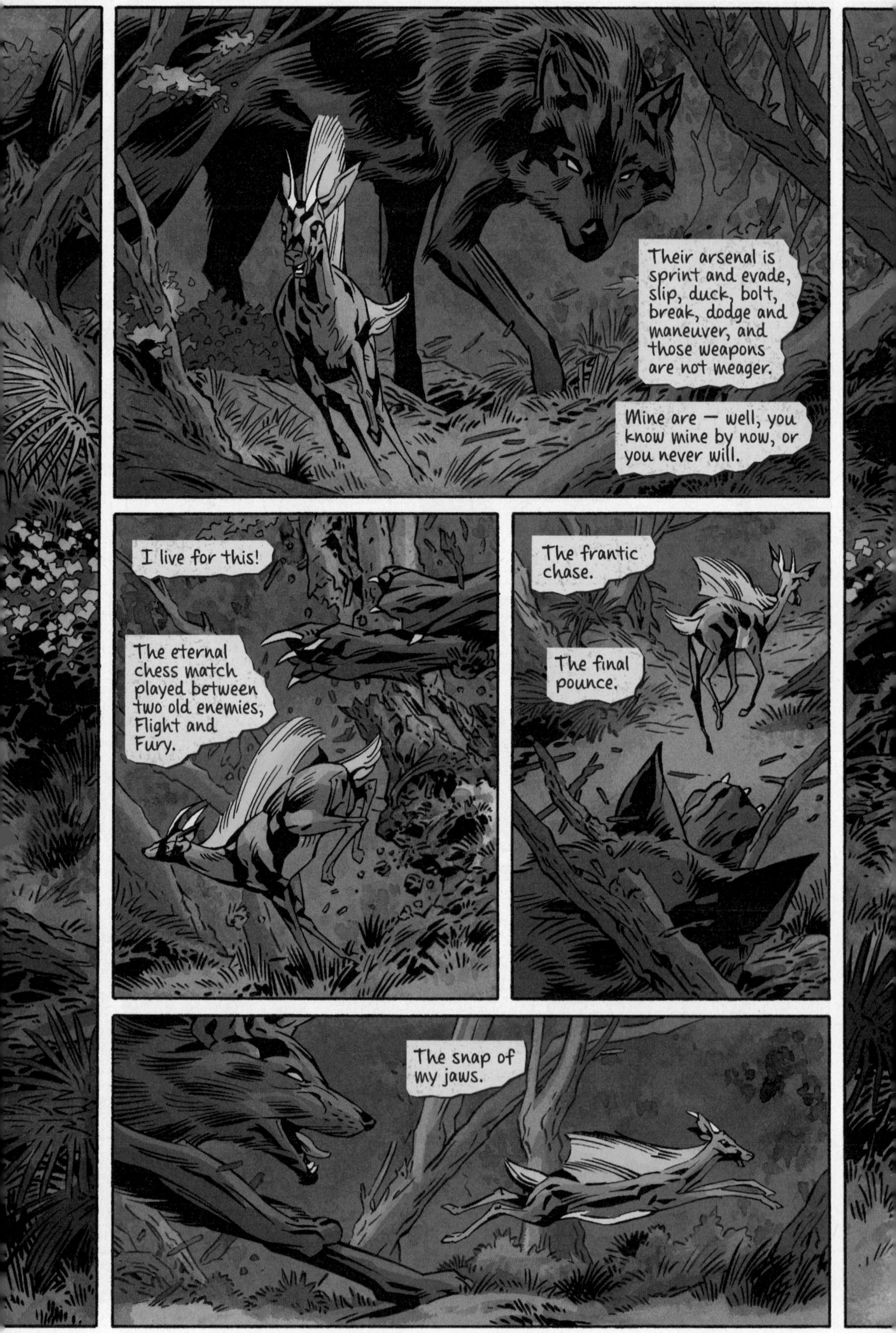

Their arsenal is sprint and evade, slip, duck, bolt, break, dodge and maneuver, and those weapons are not meager.
Mine are — well, you know mine by now, or you never will.
I live for this!
The eternal chess match played between two old enemies, Flight and Fury.
The frantic chase.
The final pounce.
The snap of my jaws.

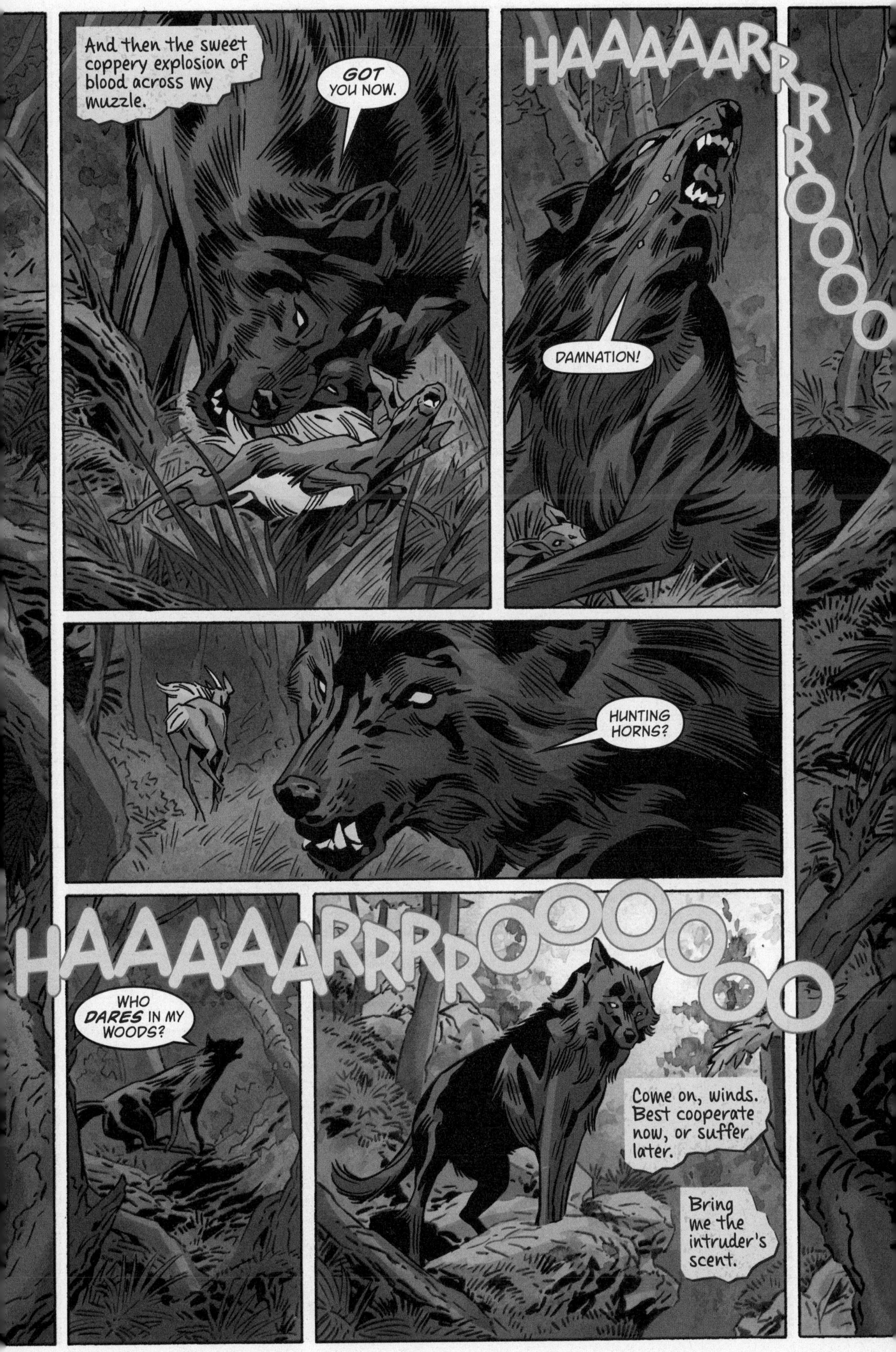
And then the sweet coppery explosion of blood across my muzzle.
GOT YOU NOW.
HAAAAARRRROOOOO
DAMNATION!
HUNTING HORNS?
HAAAAARRRROOOOOOO
WHO DARES IN MY WOODS?
Come on, winds. Best cooperate now, or suffer later.
Bring me the intruder's scent.

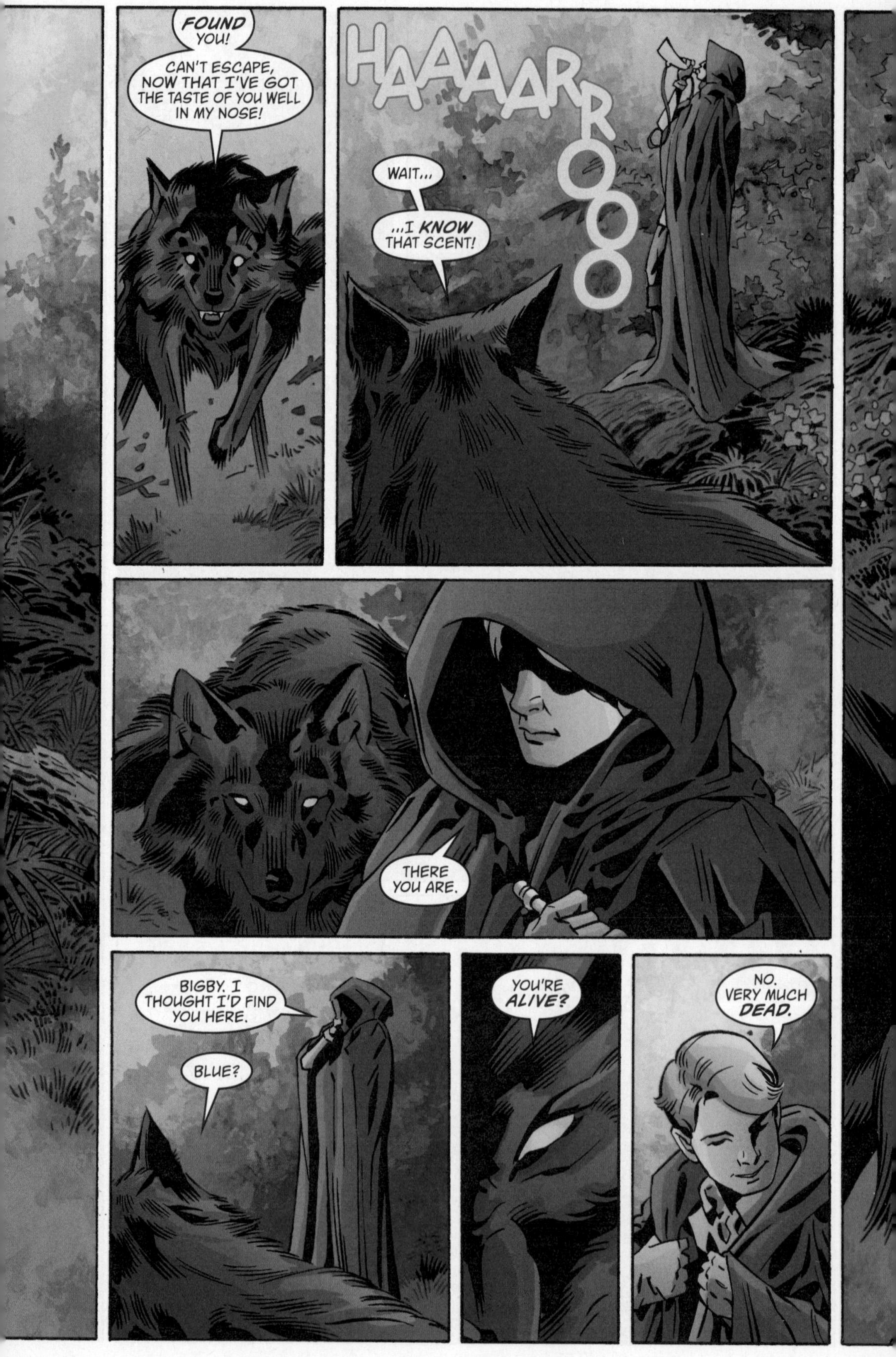
FOUND YOU!
CAN'T ESCAPE, NOW THAT I'VE GOT THE TASTE OF YOU WELL IN MY NOSE!
HAAAARROOO
WAIT...
...I KNOW THAT SCENT!
THERE YOU ARE.
BIGBY. I THOUGHT I'D FIND YOU HERE.
BLUE?
YOU'RE ALIVE?
NO. VERY MUCH DEAD.

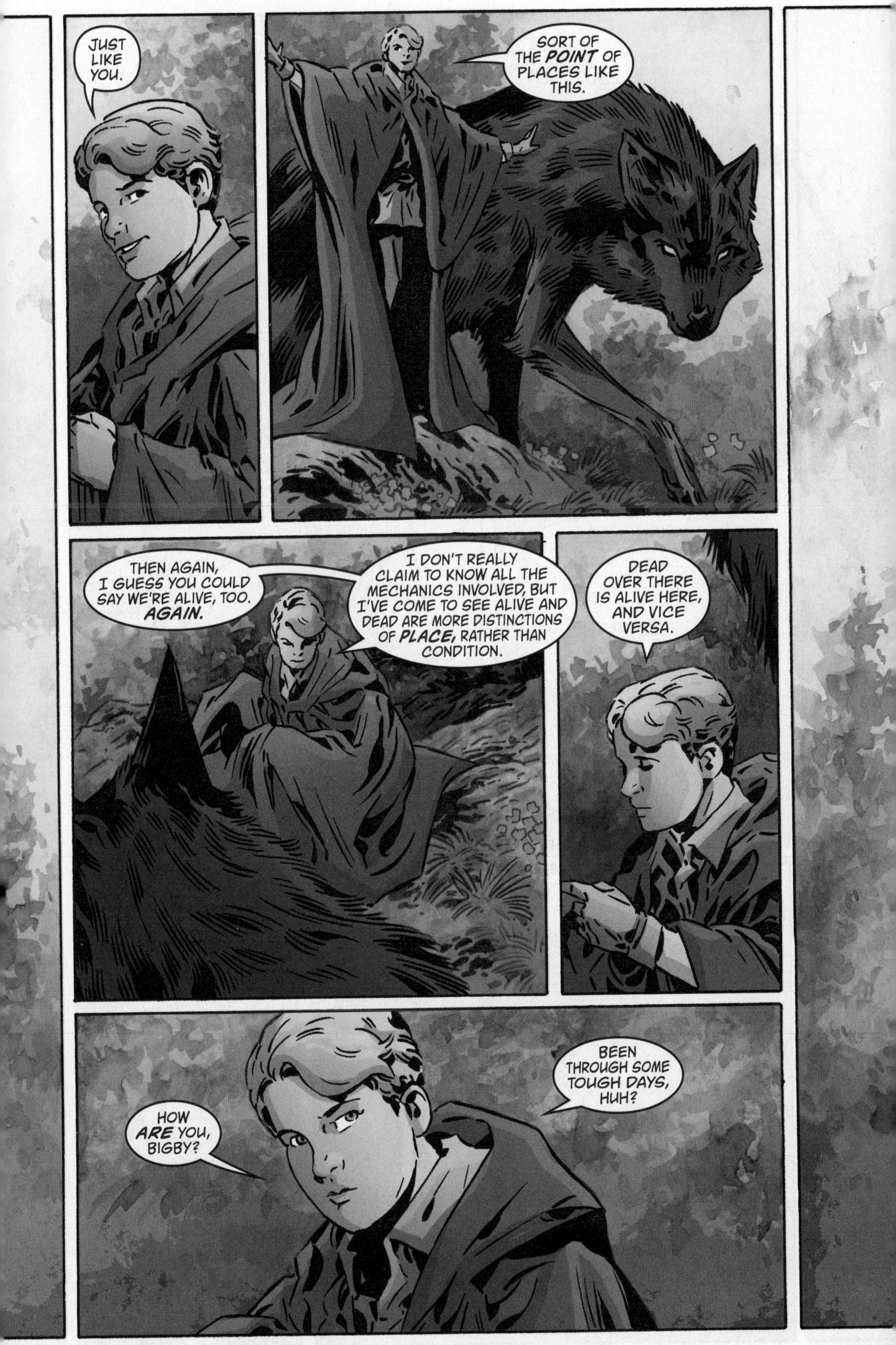
JUST LIKE YOU.
SORT OF THE POINT OF PLACES LIKE THIS.
THEN AGAIN, I GUESS YOU COULD SAY WE'RE ALIVE, TOO. AGAIN.
I DON'T REALLY CLAIM TO KNOW ALL THE MECHANICS INVOLVED, BUT I'VE COME TO SEE ALIVE AND DEAD ARE MORE DISTINCTIONS OF PLACE, RATHER THAN CONDITION.
DEAD OVER THERE IS ALIVE HERE, AND VICE VERSA.
HOW ARE YOU, BIGBY?
BEEN THROUGH SOME TOUGH DAYS, HUH?

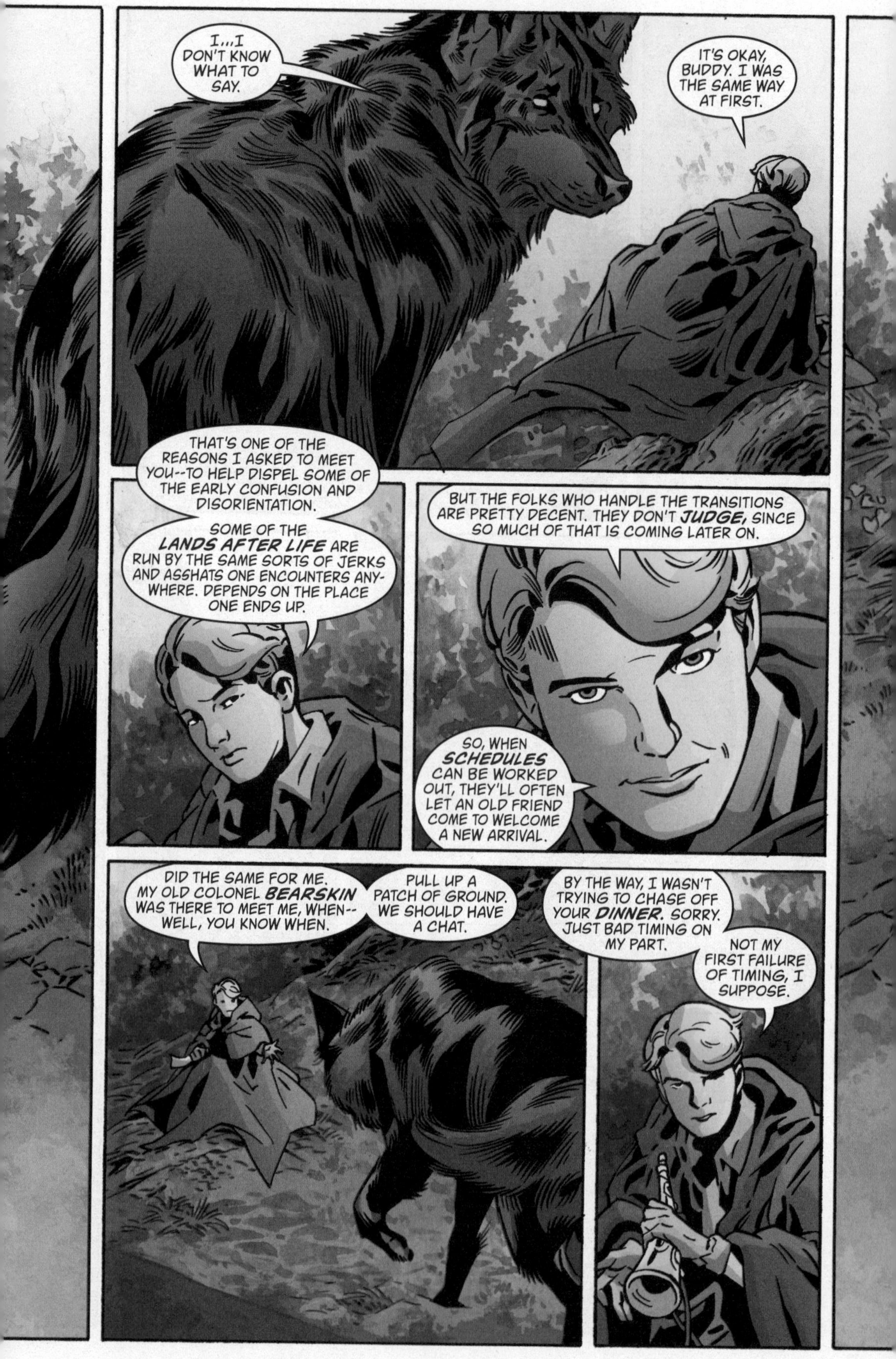
I...I DON'T KNOW WHAT TO SAY.
IT'S OKAY, BUDDY. I WAS THE SAME WAY AT FIRST.
THAT'S ONE OF THE REASONS I ASKED TO MEET YOU--TO HELP DISPEL SOME OF THE EARLY CONFUSION AND DISORIENTATION.
SOME OF THE LANDS AFTER LIFE ARE RUN BY THE SAME SORTS OF JERKS AND ASSHATS ONE ENCOUNTERS ANYWHERE. DEPENDS ON THE PLACE ONE ENDS UP.
BUT THE FOLKS WHO HANDLE THE TRANSITIONS ARE PRETTY DECENT. THEY DON'T JUDGE, SINCE SO MUCH OF THAT IS COMING LATER ON.
SO, WHEN SCHEDULES CAN BE WORKED OUT, THEY'LL OFTEN LET AN OLD FRIEND COME TO WELCOME A NEW ARRIVAL.
DID THE SAME FOR ME. MY OLD COLONEL BEARSKIN WAS THERE TO MEET ME, WHEN--WELL, YOU KNOW WHEN.
PULL UP A PATCH OF GROUND. WE SHOULD HAVE A CHAT.
BY THE WAY, I WASN'T TRYING TO CHASE OFF YOUR DINNER. SORRY. JUST BAD TIMING ON MY PART.
NOT MY FIRST FAILURE OF TIMING, I SUPPOSE.

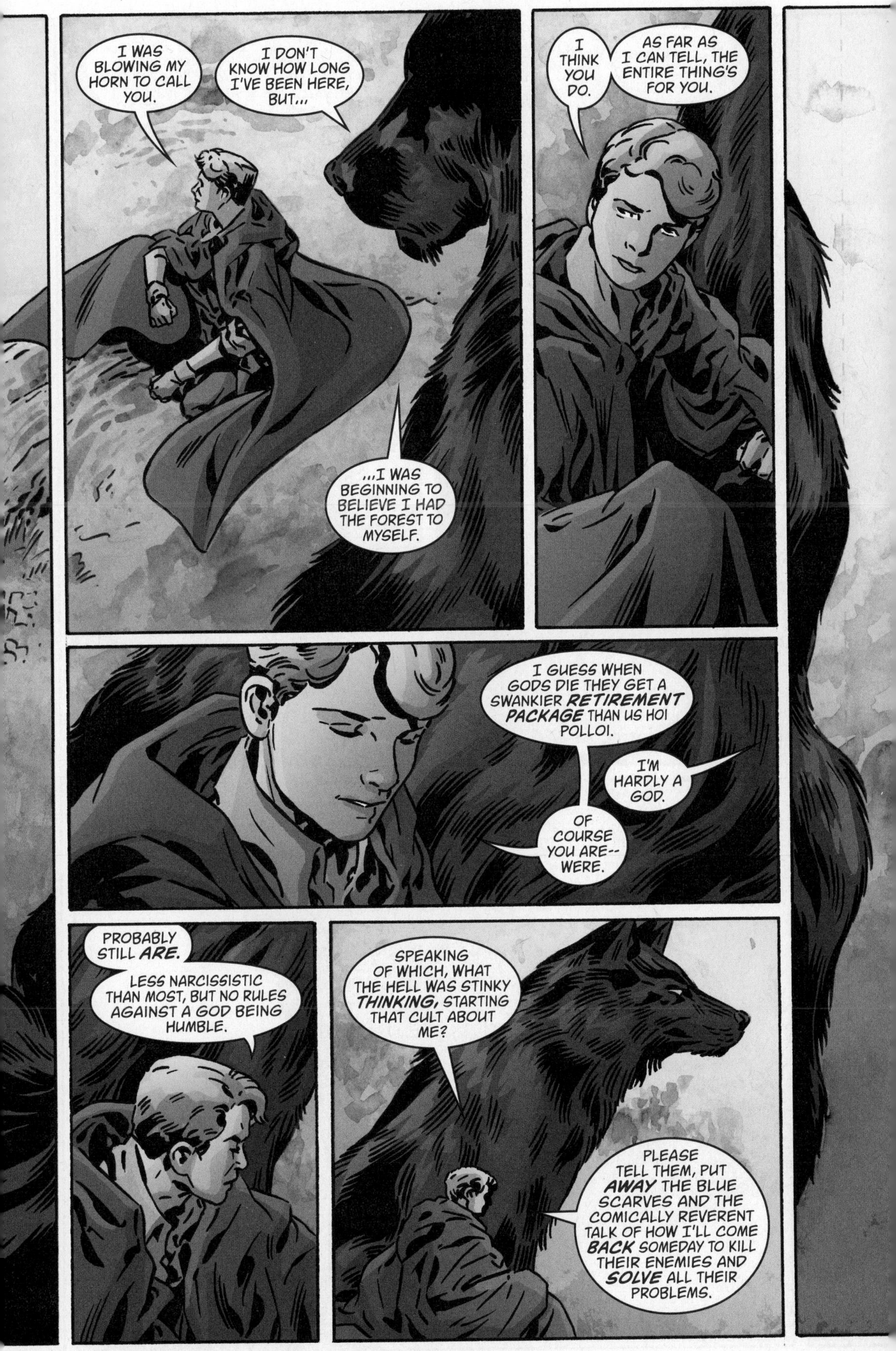
I WAS BLOWING MY HORN TO CALL YOU.
I DON'T KNOW HOW LONG I'VE BEEN HERE, BUT...
...I WAS BEGINNING TO BELIEVE I HAD THE FOREST TO MYSELF.
I THINK YOU DO.
AS FAR AS I CAN TELL, THE ENTIRE THING'S FOR YOU.
I GUESS WHEN GODS DIE THEY GET A SWANKIER **RETIREMENT PACKAGE** THAN US HOI POLLOI.
I'M HARDLY A GOD.
OF COURSE YOU ARE-- WERE.
PROBABLY STILL **ARE.**
LESS NARCISSISTIC THAN MOST, BUT NO RULES AGAINST A GOD BEING HUMBLE.
SPEAKING OF WHICH, WHAT THE HELL WAS STINKY **THINKING,** STARTING THAT CULT ABOUT ME?
PLEASE TELL THEM, PUT **AWAY** THE BLUE SCARVES AND THE COMICALLY REVERENT TALK OF HOW I'LL COME **BACK** SOMEDAY TO KILL THEIR ENEMIES AND **SOLVE** ALL THEIR PROBLEMS.

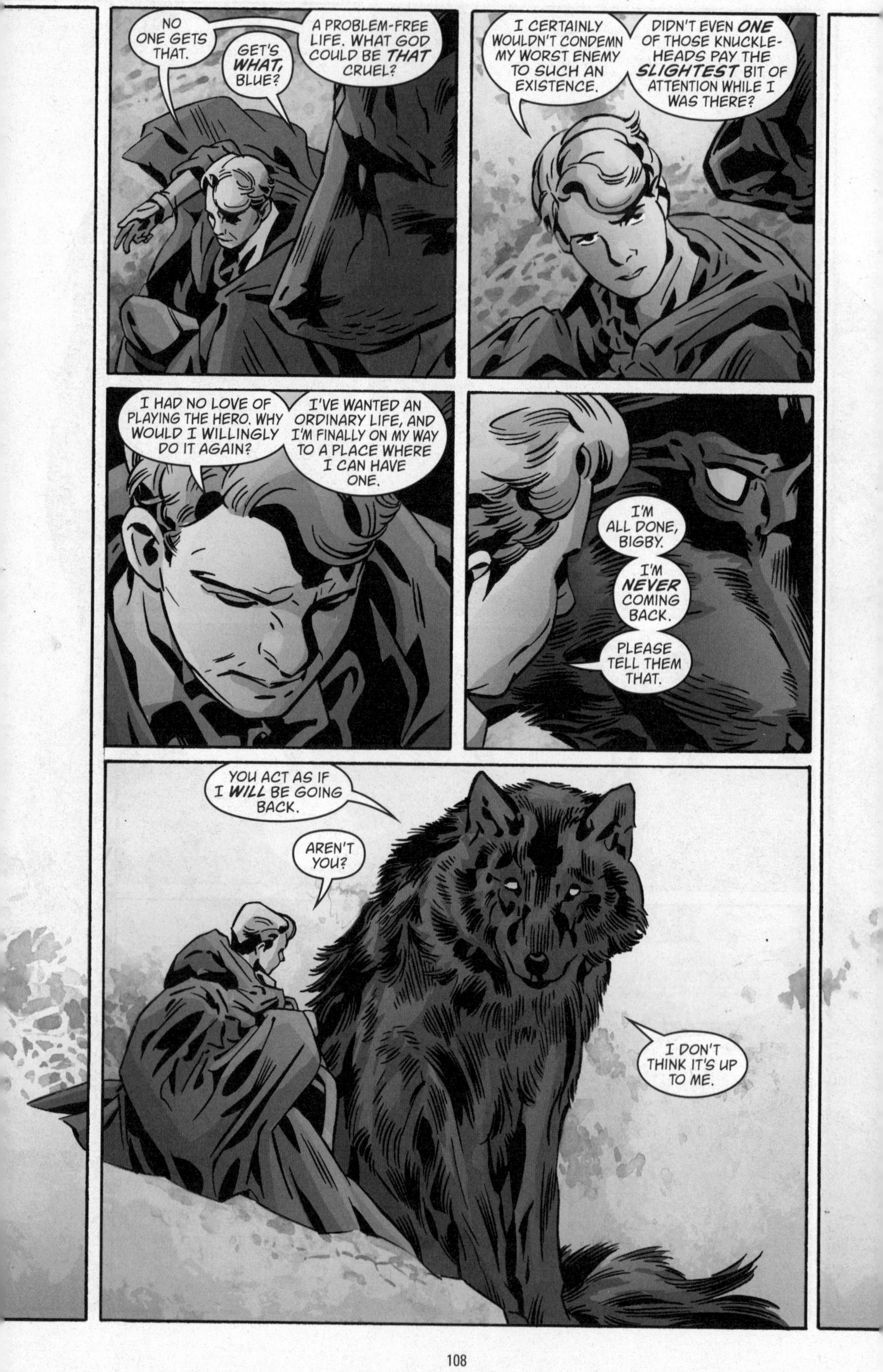
NO ONE GETS THAT.
GET'S WHAT, BLUE?
A PROBLEM-FREE LIFE. WHAT GOD COULD BE THAT CRUEL?
I CERTAINLY WOULDN'T CONDEMN MY WORST ENEMY TO SUCH AN EXISTENCE.
DIDN'T EVEN ONE OF THOSE KNUCKLE-HEADS PAY THE SLIGHTEST BIT OF ATTENTION WHILE I WAS THERE?
I HAD NO LOVE OF PLAYING THE HERO. WHY WOULD I WILLINGLY DO IT AGAIN?
I'VE WANTED AN ORDINARY LIFE, AND I'M FINALLY ON MY WAY TO A PLACE WHERE I CAN HAVE ONE.
I'M ALL DONE, BIGBY.
I'M NEVER COMING BACK.
PLEASE TELL THEM THAT.
YOU ACT AS IF I WILL BE GOING BACK.
AREN'T YOU?
I DON'T THINK IT'S UP TO ME.

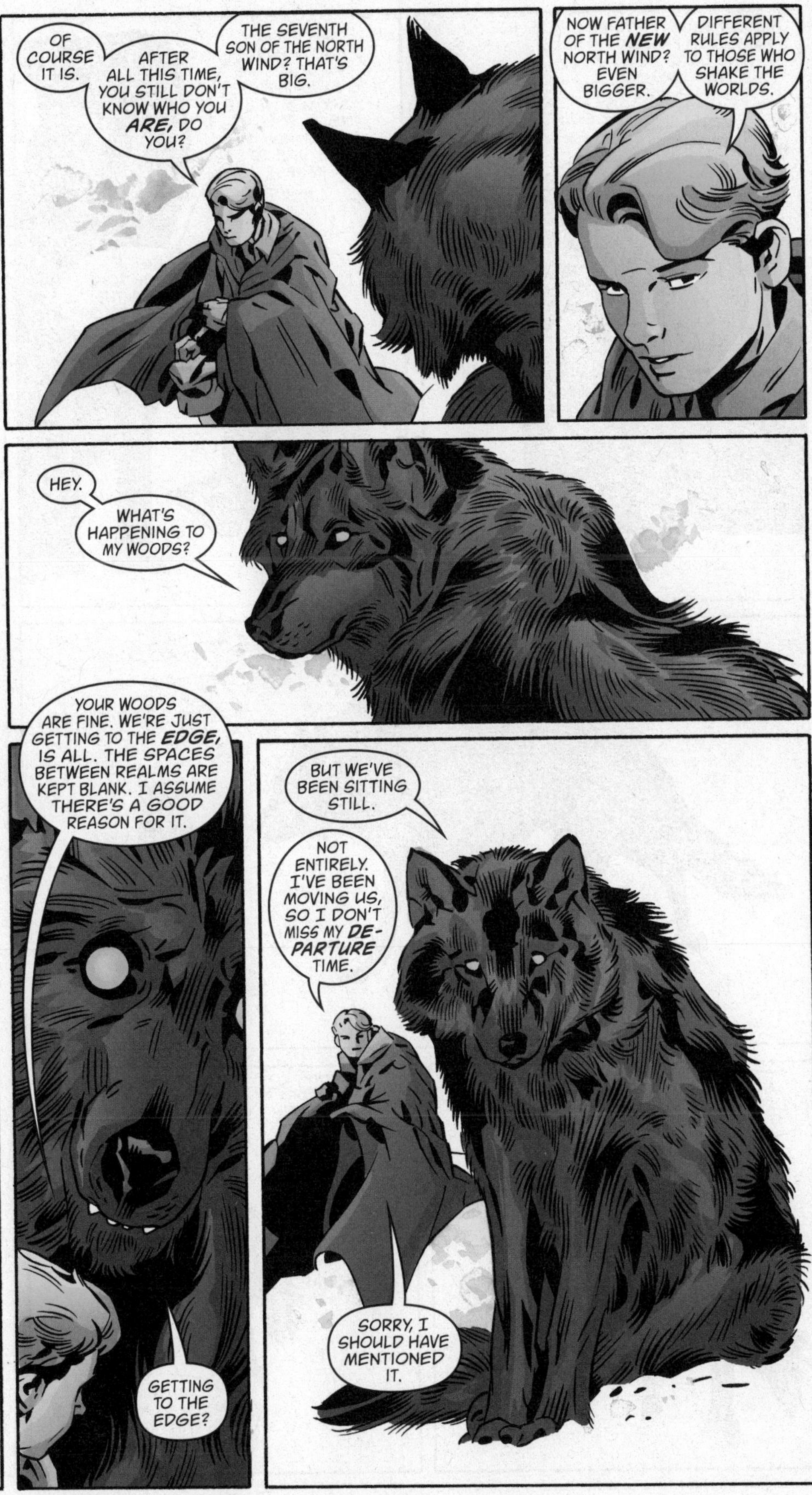

OF COURSE IT IS.
AFTER ALL THIS TIME, YOU STILL DON'T KNOW WHO YOU ARE, DO YOU?
THE SEVENTH SON OF THE NORTH WIND? THAT'S BIG.
NOW FATHER OF THE NEW NORTH WIND? EVEN BIGGER.
DIFFERENT RULES APPLY TO THOSE WHO SHAKE THE WORLDS.
HEY.
WHAT'S HAPPENING TO MY WOODS?
YOUR WOODS ARE FINE. WE'RE JUST GETTING TO THE EDGE, IS ALL. THE SPACES BETWEEN REALMS ARE KEPT BLANK. I ASSUME THERE'S A GOOD REASON FOR IT.
GETTING TO THE EDGE?
BUT WE'VE BEEN SITTING STILL.
NOT ENTIRELY. I'VE BEEN MOVING US, SO I DON'T MISS MY DE-PARTURE TIME.
SORRY, I SHOULD HAVE MENTIONED IT.

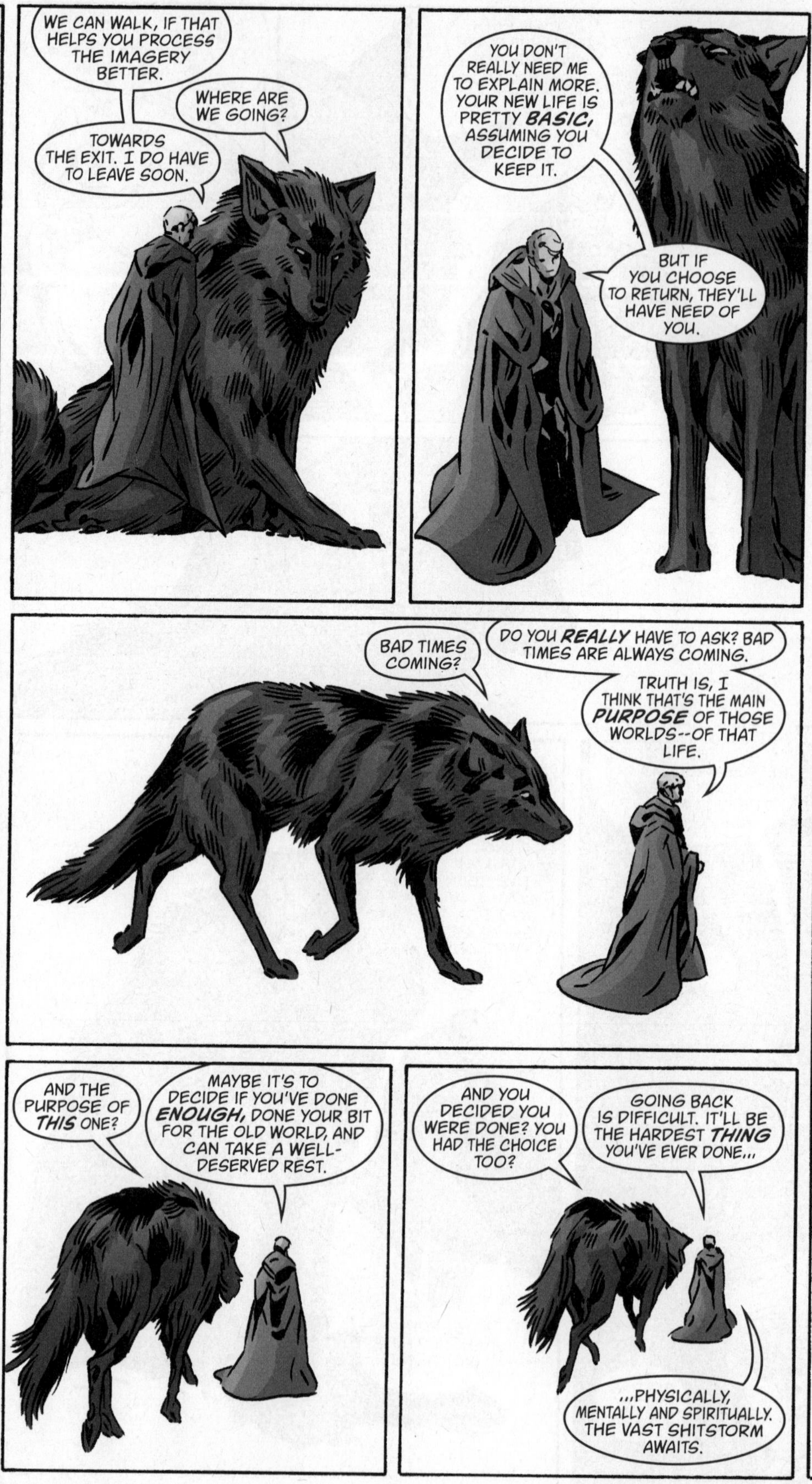

WE CAN WALK, IF THAT HELPS YOU PROCESS THE IMAGERY BETTER.
WHERE ARE WE GOING?
TOWARDS THE EXIT. I DO HAVE TO LEAVE SOON.
YOU DON'T REALLY NEED ME TO EXPLAIN MORE. YOUR NEW LIFE IS PRETTY BASIC, ASSUMING YOU DECIDE TO KEEP IT.
BUT IF YOU CHOOSE TO RETURN, THEY'LL HAVE NEED OF YOU.
BAD TIMES COMING?
DO YOU REALLY HAVE TO ASK? BAD TIMES ARE ALWAYS COMING.
TRUTH IS, I THINK THAT'S THE MAIN PURPOSE OF THOSE WORLDS--OF THAT LIFE.
AND THE PURPOSE OF THIS ONE?
MAYBE IT'S TO DECIDE IF YOU'VE DONE ENOUGH, DONE YOUR BIT FOR THE OLD WORLD, AND CAN TAKE A WELL-DESERVED REST.
AND YOU DECIDED YOU WERE DONE? YOU HAD THE CHOICE TOO?
GOING BACK IS DIFFICULT. IT'LL BE THE HARDEST THING YOU'VE EVER DONE...
...PHYSICALLY, MENTALLY AND SPIRITUALLY. THE VAST SHITSTORM AWAITS.

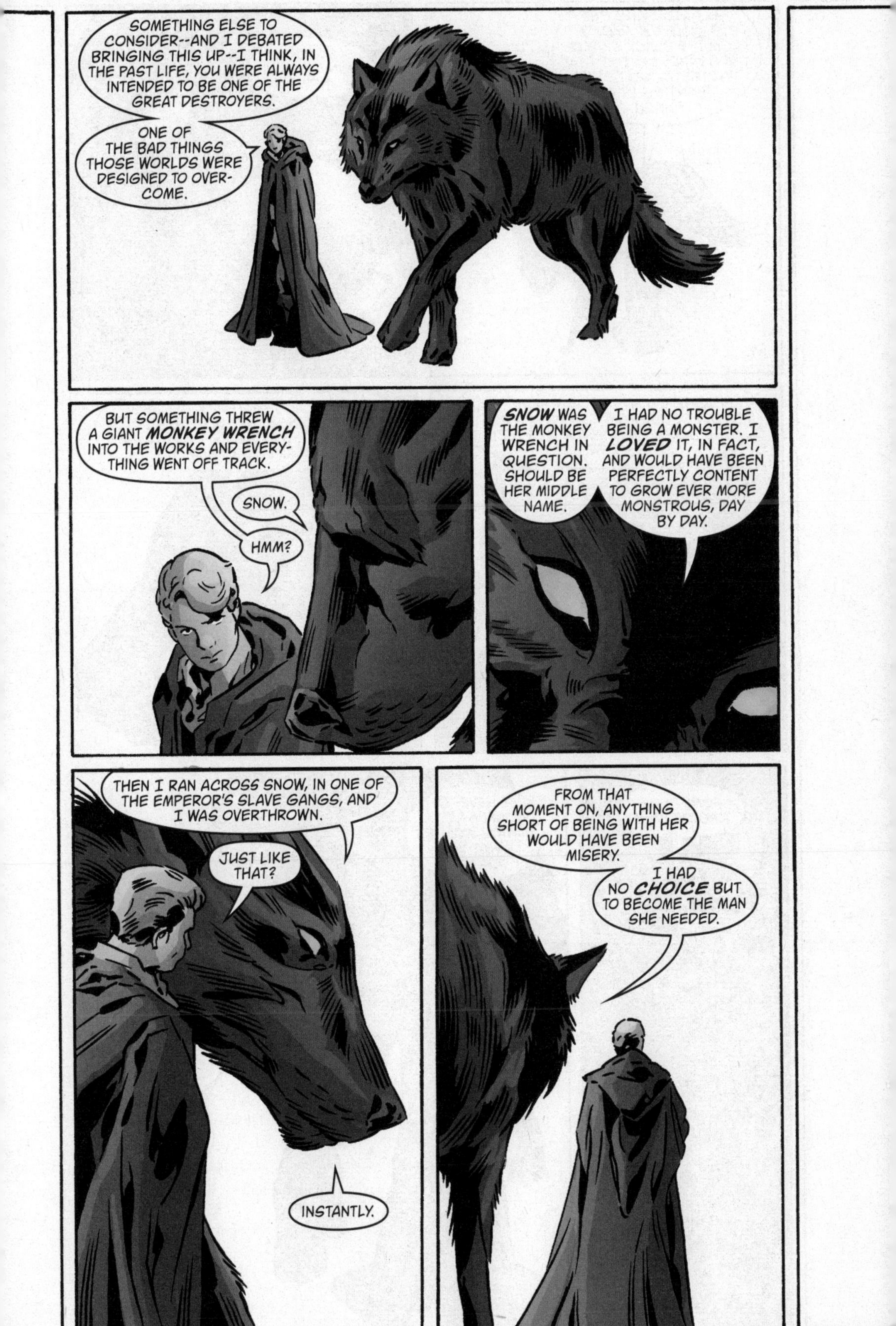
SOMETHING ELSE TO CONSIDER--AND I DEBATED BRINGING THIS UP--I THINK, IN THE PAST LIFE, YOU WERE ALWAYS INTENDED TO BE ONE OF THE GREAT DESTROYERS.
ONE OF THE BAD THINGS THOSE WORLDS WERE DESIGNED TO OVER-COME.
BUT SOMETHING THREW A GIANT MONKEY WRENCH INTO THE WORKS AND EVERY-THING WENT OFF TRACK.
SNOW.
HMM?
SNOW WAS THE MONKEY WRENCH IN QUESTION. SHOULD BE HER MIDDLE NAME.
I HAD NO TROUBLE BEING A MONSTER. I LOVED IT, IN FACT, AND WOULD HAVE BEEN PERFECTLY CONTENT TO GROW EVER MORE MONSTROUS, DAY BY DAY.
THEN I RAN ACROSS SNOW, IN ONE OF THE EMPEROR'S SLAVE GANGS, AND I WAS OVERTHROWN.
JUST LIKE THAT?
INSTANTLY.
FROM THAT MOMENT ON, ANYTHING SHORT OF BEING WITH HER WOULD HAVE BEEN MISERY.
I HAD NO CHOICE BUT TO BECOME THE MAN SHE NEEDED.

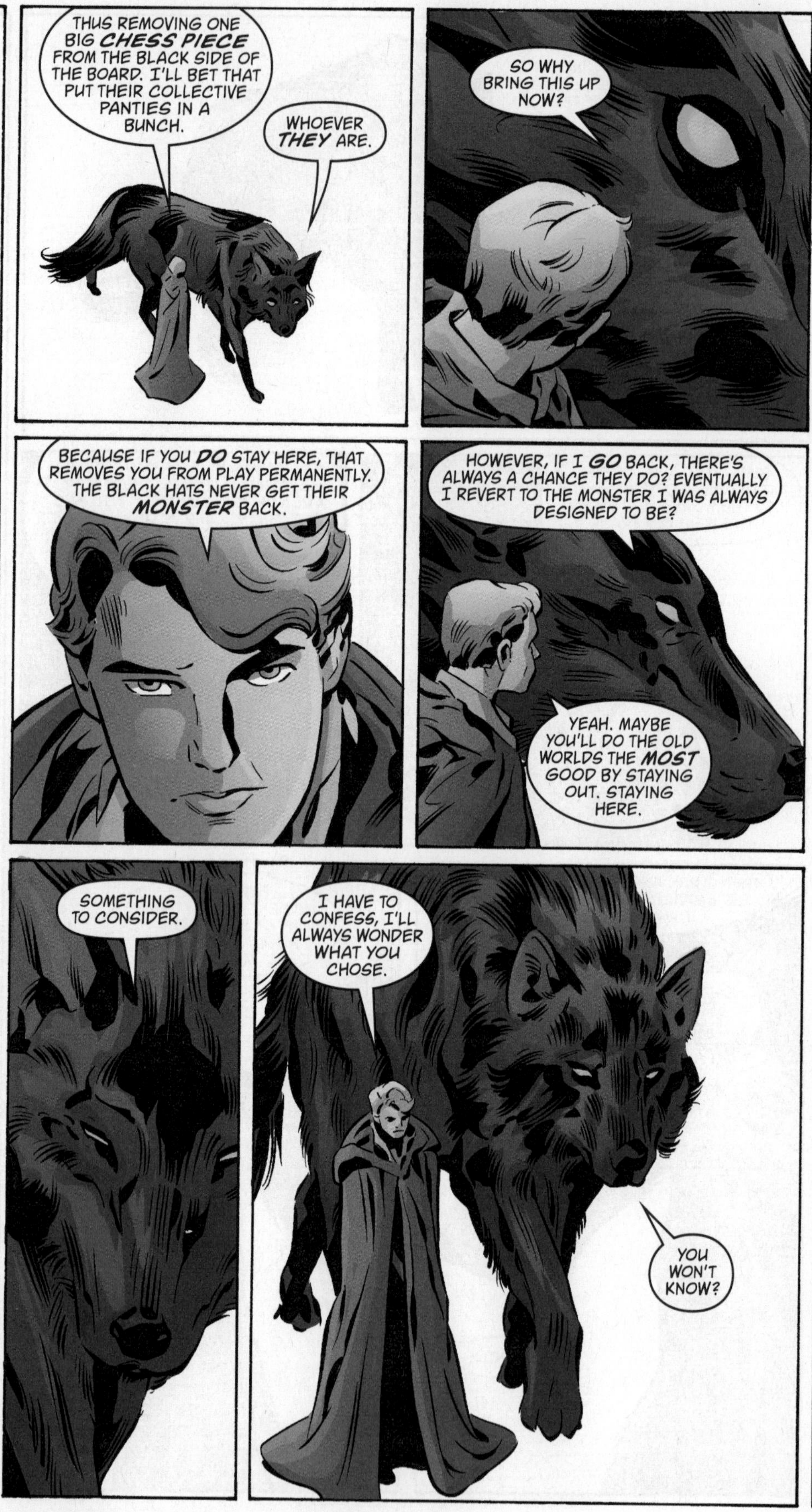

THUS REMOVING ONE BIG CHESS PIECE FROM THE BLACK SIDE OF THE BOARD. I'LL BET THAT PUT THEIR COLLECTIVE PANTIES IN A BUNCH.
WHOEVER THEY ARE.
SO WHY BRING THIS UP NOW?
BECAUSE IF YOU DO STAY HERE, THAT REMOVES YOU FROM PLAY PERMANENTLY. THE BLACK HATS NEVER GET THEIR MONSTER BACK.
HOWEVER, IF I GO BACK, THERE'S ALWAYS A CHANCE THEY DO? EVENTUALLY I REVERT TO THE MONSTER I WAS ALWAYS DESIGNED TO BE?
YEAH. MAYBE YOU'LL DO THE OLD WORLDS THE MOST GOOD BY STAYING OUT. STAYING HERE.
SOMETHING TO CONSIDER.
I HAVE TO CONFESS, I'LL ALWAYS WONDER WHAT YOU CHOSE.
YOU WON'T KNOW?

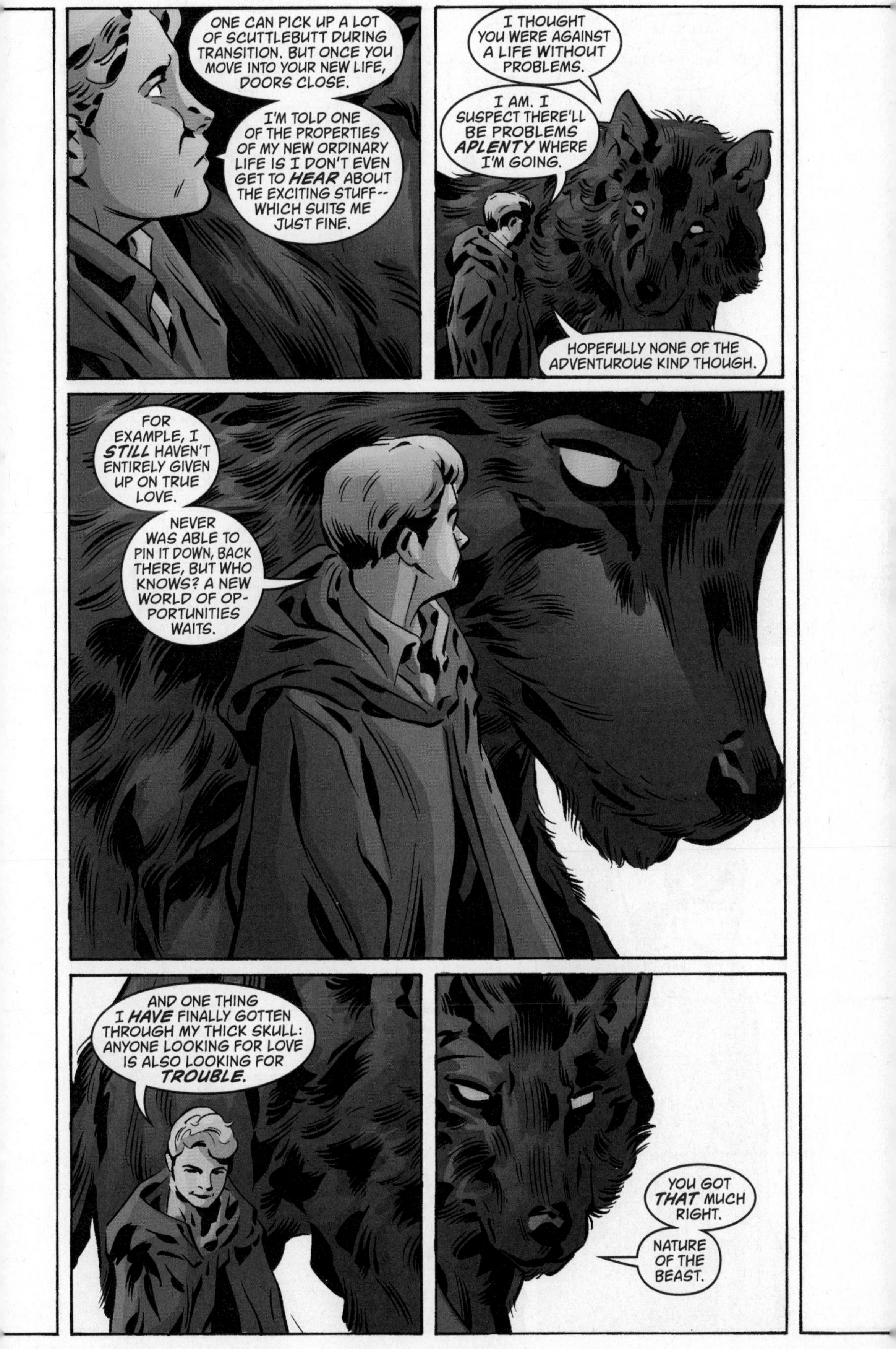
ONE CAN PICK UP A LOT OF SCUTTLEBUTT DURING TRANSITION. BUT ONCE YOU MOVE INTO YOUR NEW LIFE, DOORS CLOSE.
I'M TOLD ONE OF THE PROPERTIES OF MY NEW ORDINARY LIFE IS I DON'T EVEN GET TO HEAR ABOUT THE EXCITING STUFF-- WHICH SUITS ME JUST FINE.
I THOUGHT YOU WERE AGAINST A LIFE WITHOUT PROBLEMS.
I AM. I SUSPECT THERE'LL BE PROBLEMS APLENTY WHERE I'M GOING.
HOPEFULLY NONE OF THE ADVENTUROUS KIND THOUGH.
FOR EXAMPLE, I STILL HAVEN'T ENTIRELY GIVEN UP ON TRUE LOVE.
NEVER WAS ABLE TO PIN IT DOWN, BACK THERE, BUT WHO KNOWS? A NEW WORLD OF OP-PORTUNITIES WAITS.
AND ONE THING I HAVE FINALLY GOTTEN THROUGH MY THICK SKULL: ANYONE LOOKING FOR LOVE IS ALSO LOOKING FOR TROUBLE.
YOU GOT THAT MUCH RIGHT.
NATURE OF THE BEAST.

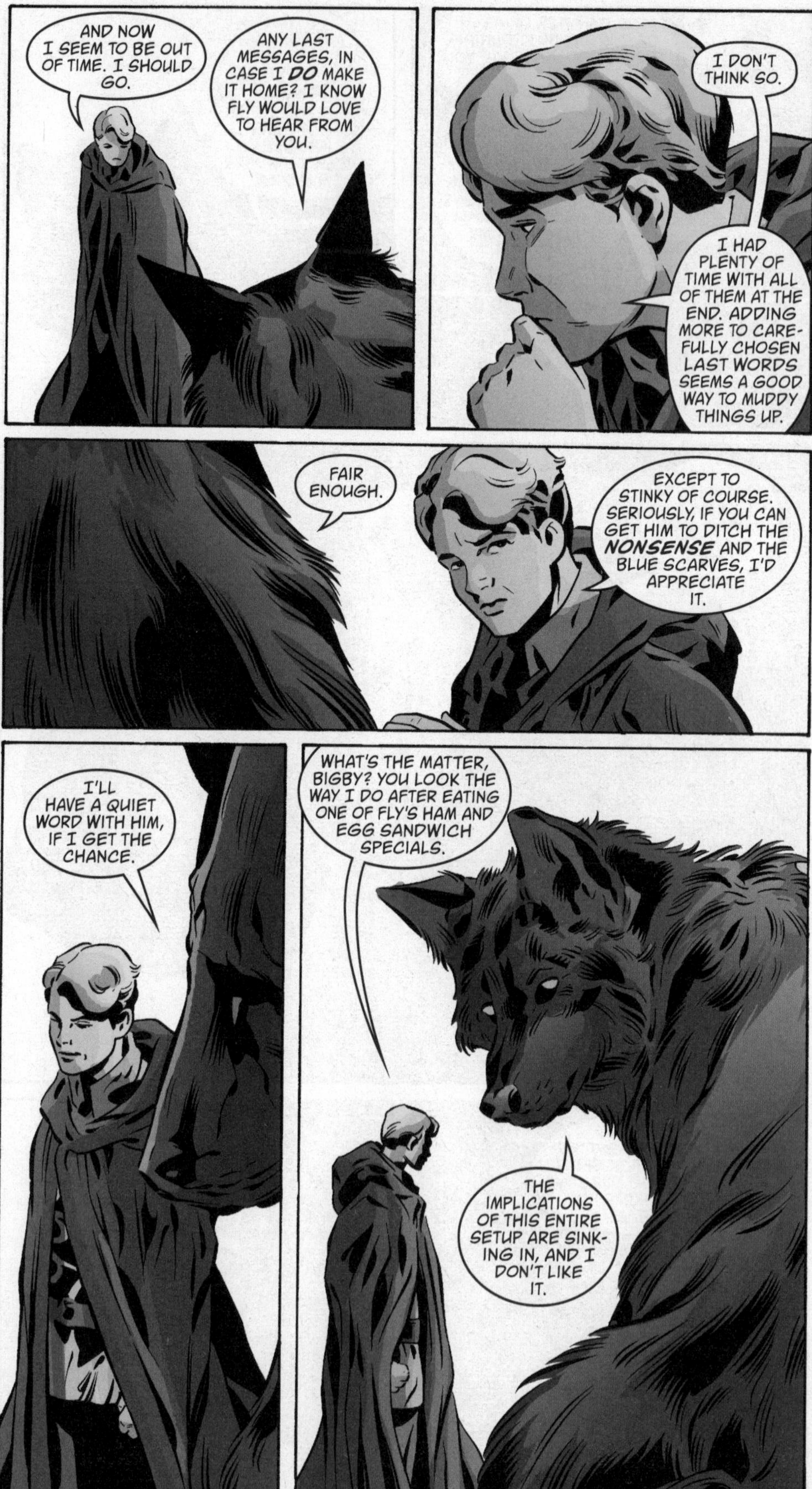
AND NOW I SEEM TO BE OUT OF TIME. I SHOULD GO.
ANY LAST MESSAGES, IN CASE I DO MAKE IT HOME? I KNOW FLY WOULD LOVE TO HEAR FROM YOU.
I DON'T THINK SO.
I HAD PLENTY OF TIME WITH ALL OF THEM AT THE END. ADDING MORE TO CARE-FULLY CHOSEN LAST WORDS SEEMS A GOOD WAY TO MUDDY THINGS UP.
FAIR ENOUGH.
EXCEPT TO STINKY OF COURSE. SERIOUSLY, IF YOU CAN GET HIM TO DITCH THE NONSENSE AND THE BLUE SCARVES, I'D APPRECIATE IT.
I'LL HAVE A QUIET WORD WITH HIM, IF I GET THE CHANCE.
WHAT'S THE MATTER, BIGBY? YOU LOOK THE WAY I DO AFTER EATING ONE OF FLY'S HAM AND EGG SANDWICH SPECIALS.
THE IMPLICATIONS OF THIS ENTIRE SETUP ARE SINK-ING IN, AND I DON'T LIKE IT.

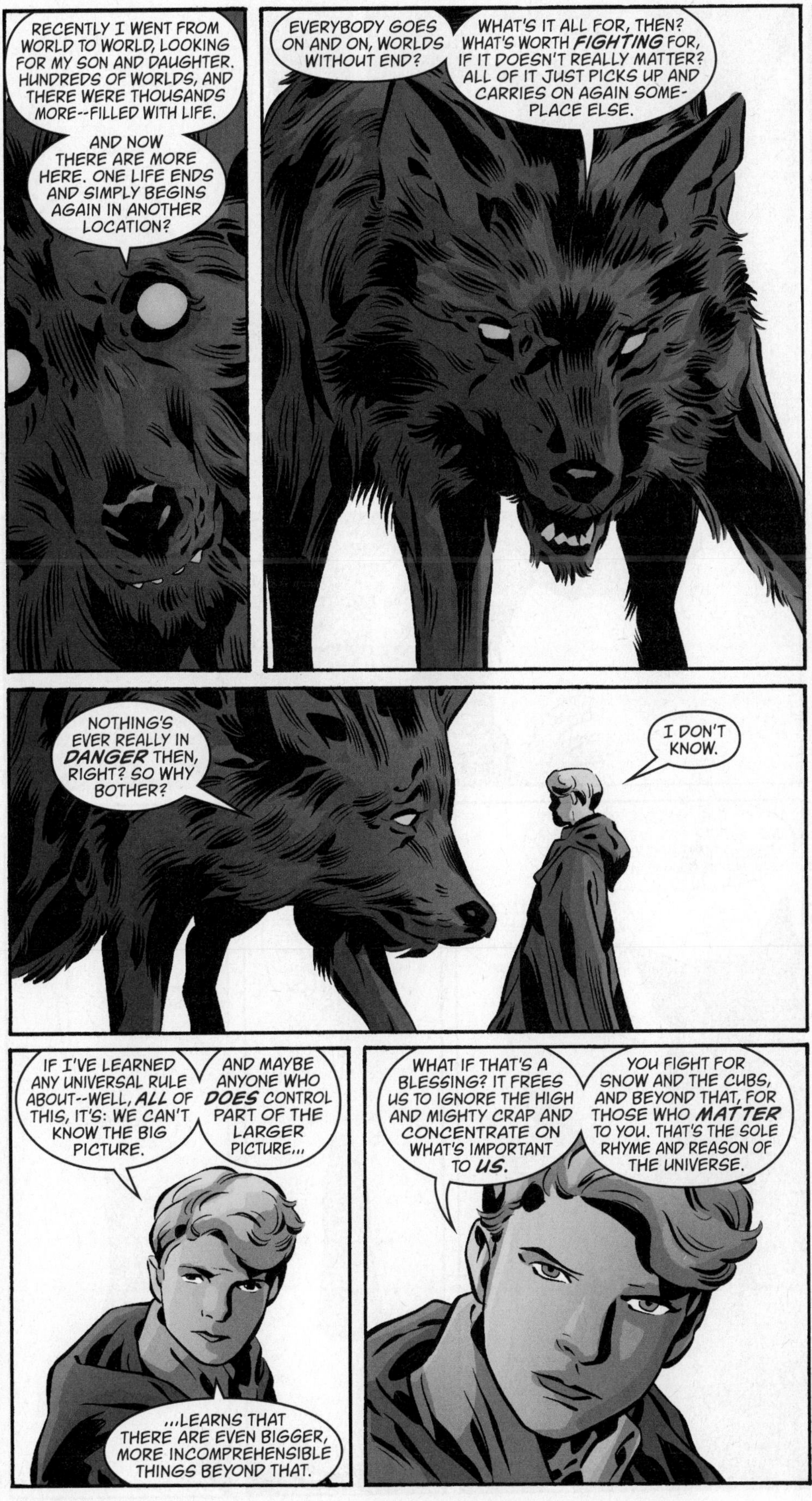
RECENTLY I WENT FROM WORLD TO WORLD, LOOKING FOR MY SON AND DAUGHTER. HUNDREDS OF WORLDS, AND THERE WERE THOUSANDS MORE--FILLED WITH LIFE.
AND NOW THERE ARE MORE HERE. ONE LIFE ENDS AND SIMPLY BEGINS AGAIN IN ANOTHER LOCATION?
EVERYBODY GOES ON AND ON, WORLDS WITHOUT END?
WHAT'S IT ALL FOR, THEN? WHAT'S WORTH FIGHTING FOR, IF IT DOESN'T REALLY MATTER? ALL OF IT JUST PICKS UP AND CARRIES ON AGAIN SOME-PLACE ELSE.
NOTHING'S EVER REALLY IN DANGER THEN, RIGHT? SO WHY BOTHER?
I DON'T KNOW.
IF I'VE LEARNED ANY UNIVERSAL RULE ABOUT--WELL, ALL OF THIS, IT'S: WE CAN'T KNOW THE BIG PICTURE.
AND MAYBE ANYONE WHO DOES CONTROL PART OF THE LARGER PICTURE...
...LEARNS THAT THERE ARE EVEN BIGGER, MORE INCOMPREHENSIBLE THINGS BEYOND THAT.
WHAT IF THAT'S A BLESSING? IT FREES US TO IGNORE THE HIGH AND MIGHTY CRAP AND CONCENTRATE ON WHAT'S IMPORTANT TO US.
YOU FIGHT FOR SNOW AND THE CUBS, AND BEYOND THAT, FOR THOSE WHO MATTER TO YOU. THAT'S THE SOLE RHYME AND REASON OF THE UNIVERSE.

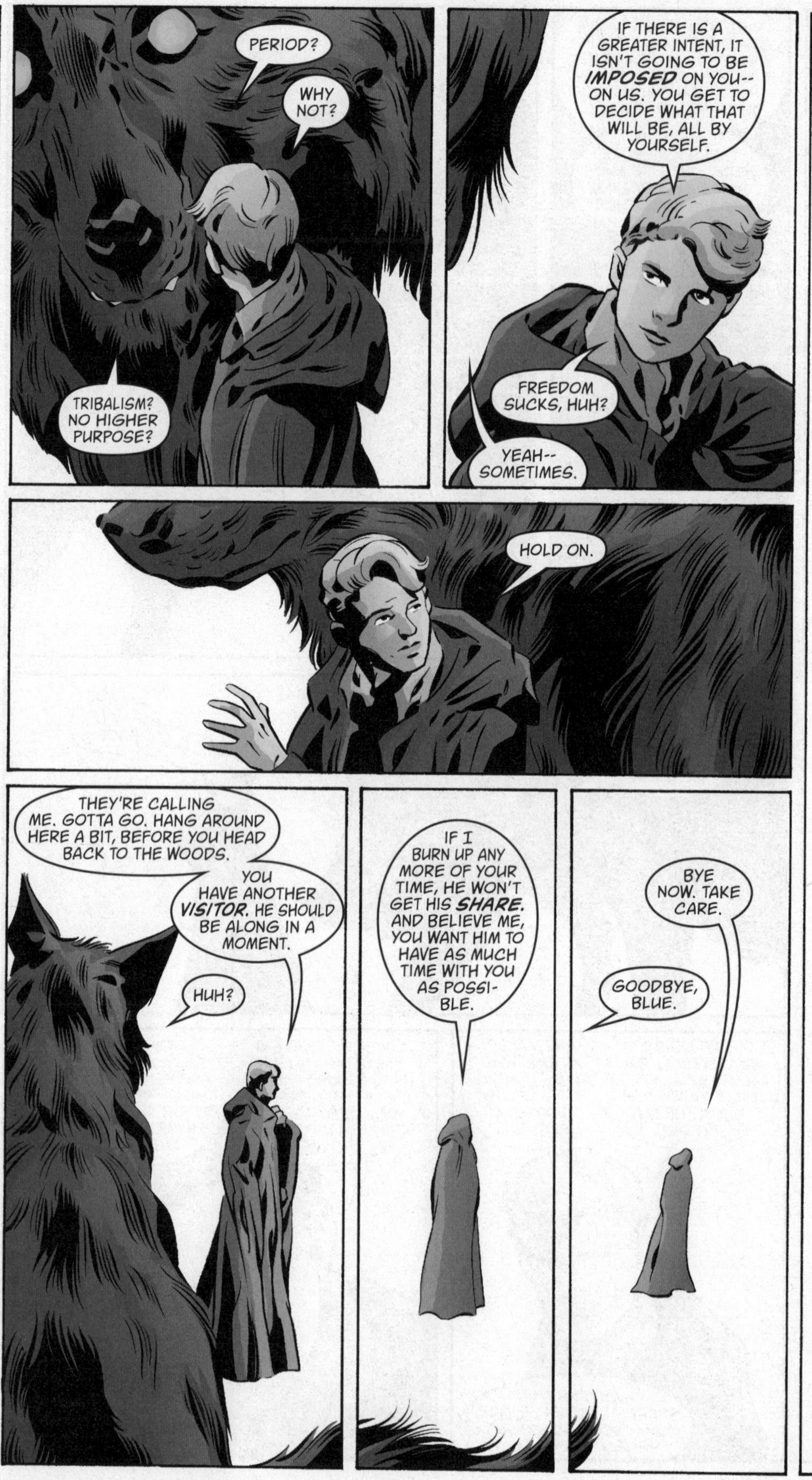
PERIOD?
WHY NOT?
TRIBALISM? NO HIGHER PURPOSE?
IF THERE IS A GREATER INTENT, IT ISN'T GOING TO BE IMPOSED ON YOU-- ON US. YOU GET TO DECIDE WHAT THAT WILL BE, ALL BY YOURSELF.
FREEDOM SUCKS, HUH?
YEAH-- SOMETIMES.
HOLD ON.
THEY'RE CALLING ME. GOTTA GO. HANG AROUND HERE A BIT, BEFORE YOU HEAD BACK TO THE WOODS.
YOU HAVE ANOTHER VISITOR. HE SHOULD BE ALONG IN A MOMENT.
HUH?
IF I BURN UP ANY MORE OF YOUR TIME, HE WON'T GET HIS SHARE. AND BELIEVE ME, YOU WANT HIM TO HAVE AS MUCH TIME WITH YOU AS POSSI-BLE.
BYE NOW. TAKE CARE.
GOODBYE, BLUE.

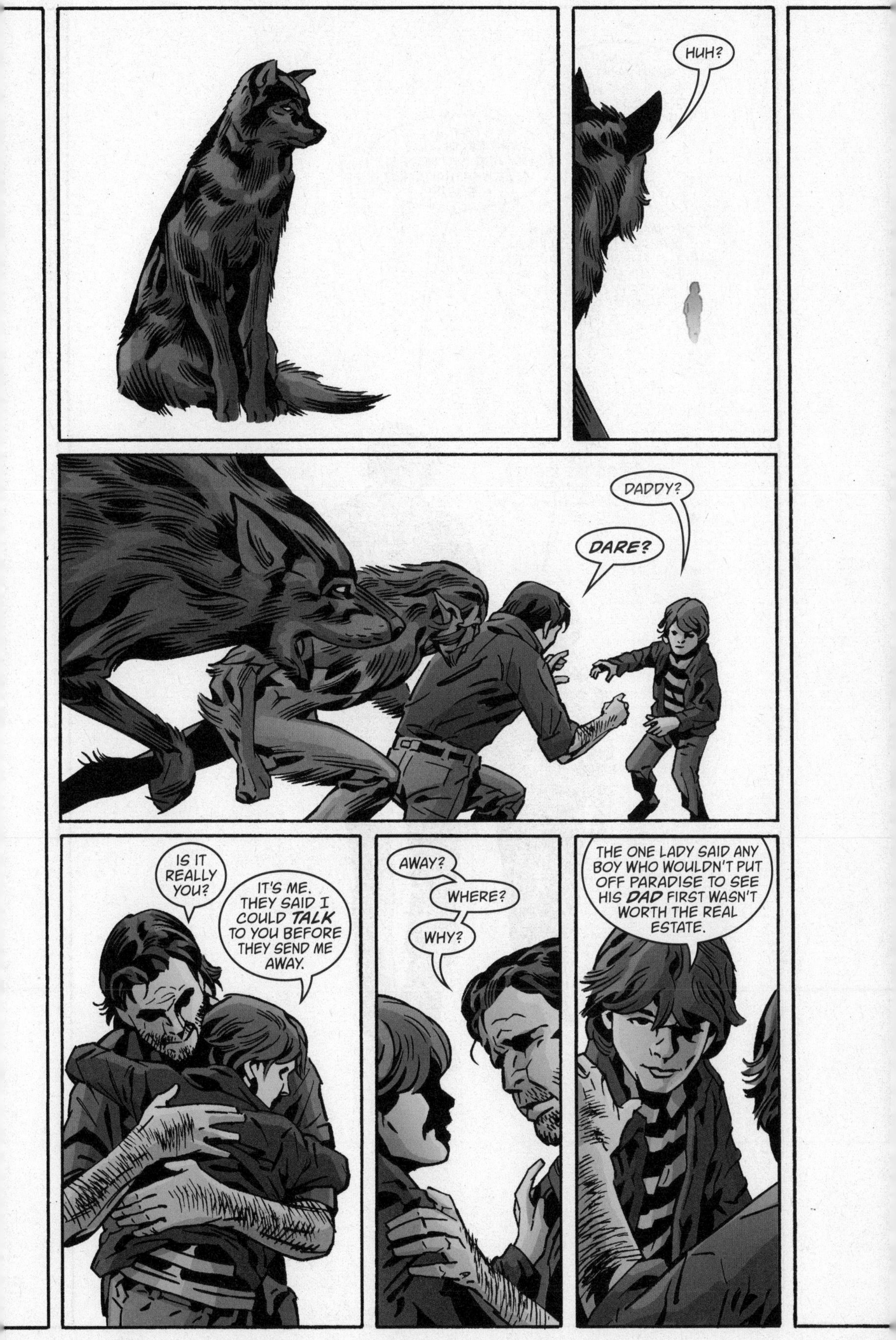
HUH?
DADDY?
DARE?
IS IT REALLY YOU?
IT'S ME. THEY SAID I COULD TALK TO YOU BEFORE THEY SEND ME AWAY.
AWAY?
WHERE?
WHY?
THE ONE LADY SAID ANY BOY WHO WOULDN'T PUT OFF PARADISE TO SEE HIS DAD FIRST WASN'T WORTH THE REAL ESTATE.

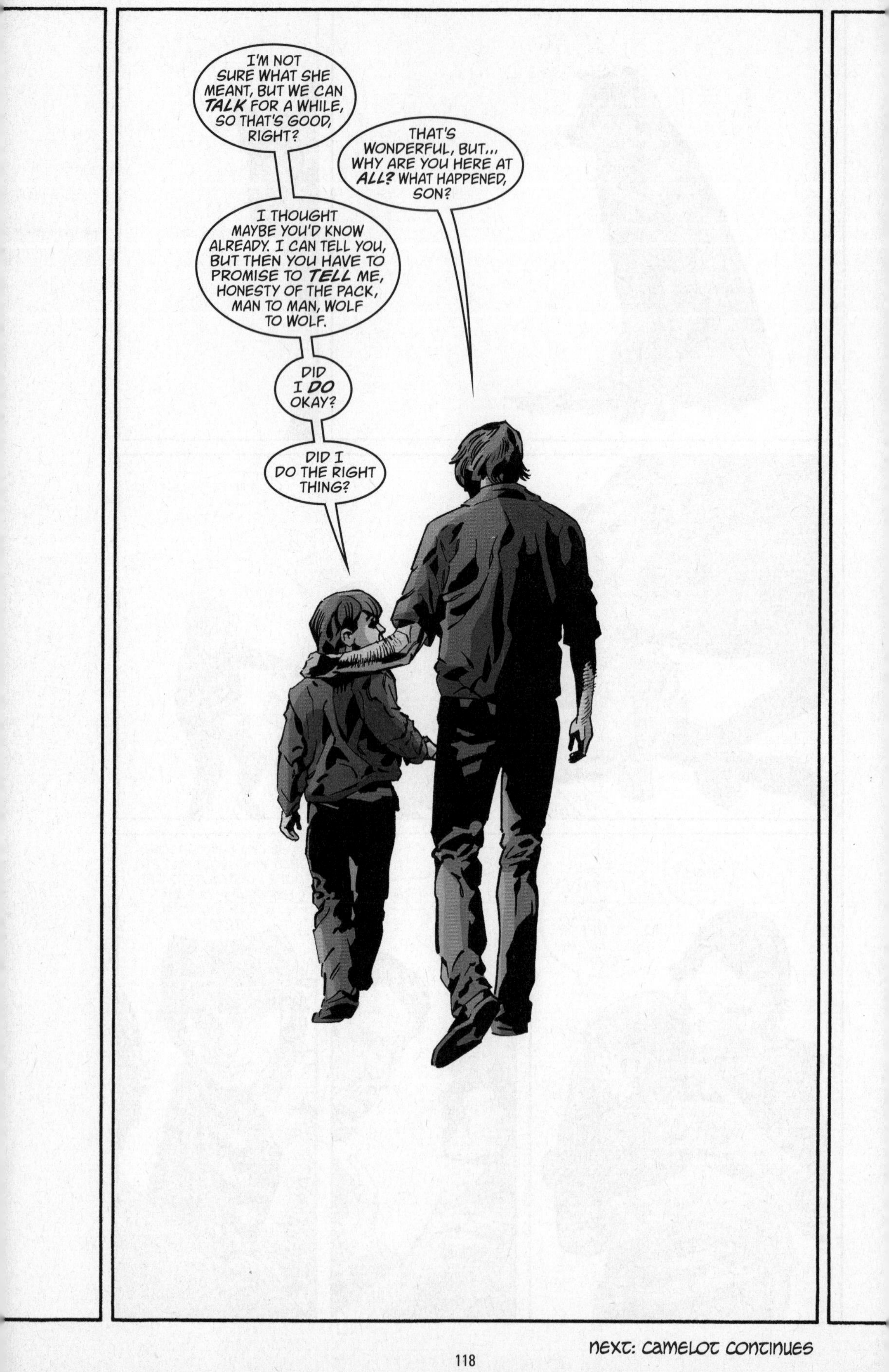
I'M NOT SURE WHAT SHE MEANT, BUT WE CAN TALK FOR A WHILE, SO THAT'S GOOD, RIGHT?
THAT'S WONDERFUL, BUT... WHY ARE YOU HERE AT ALL? WHAT HAPPENED, SON?
I THOUGHT MAYBE YOU'D KNOW ALREADY. I CAN TELL YOU, BUT THEN YOU HAVE TO PROMISE TO TELL ME, HONESTY OF THE PACK, MAN TO MAN, WOLF TO WOLF.
DID I DO OKAY?
DID I DO THE RIGHT THING?

NEXT: CAMELOT CONTINUES

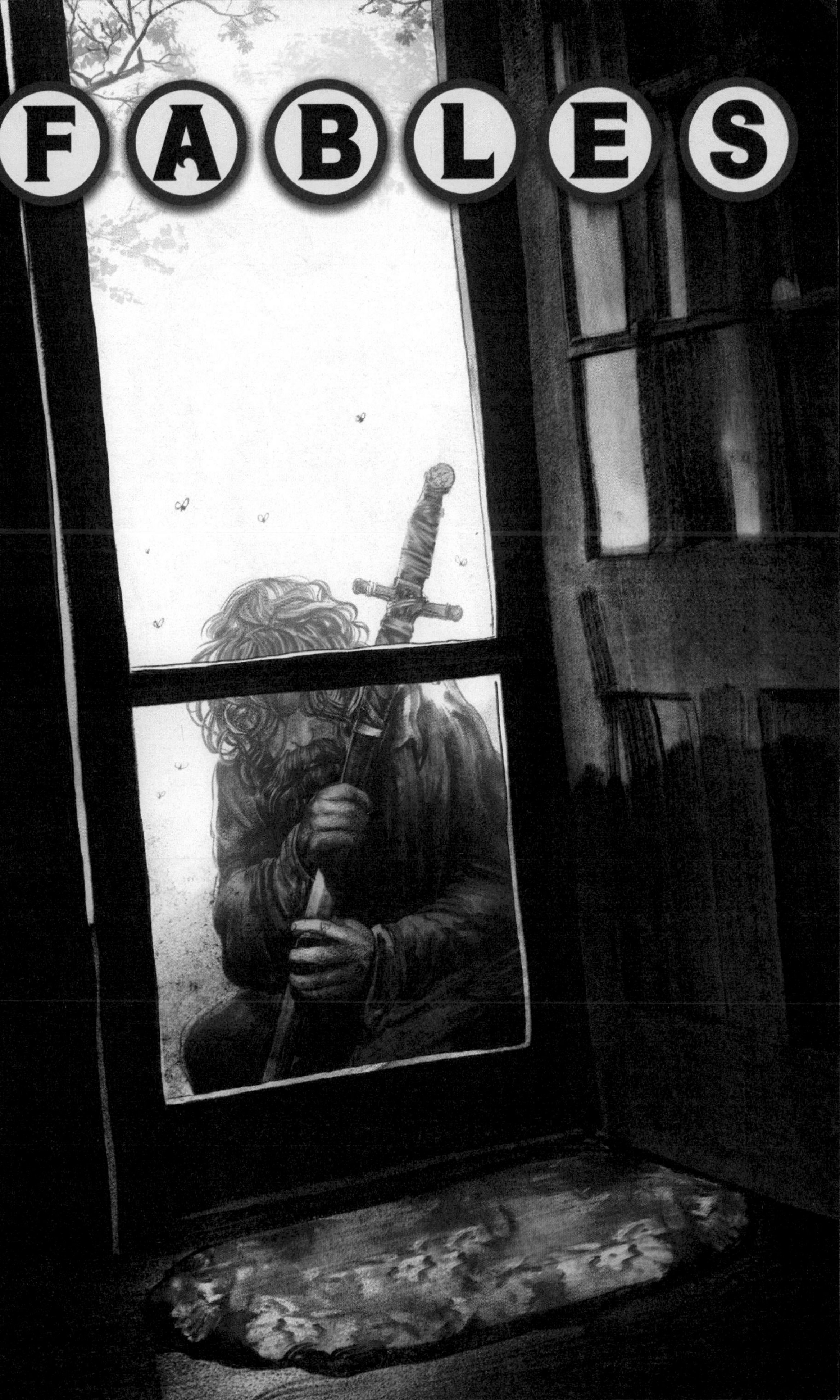
FABLES

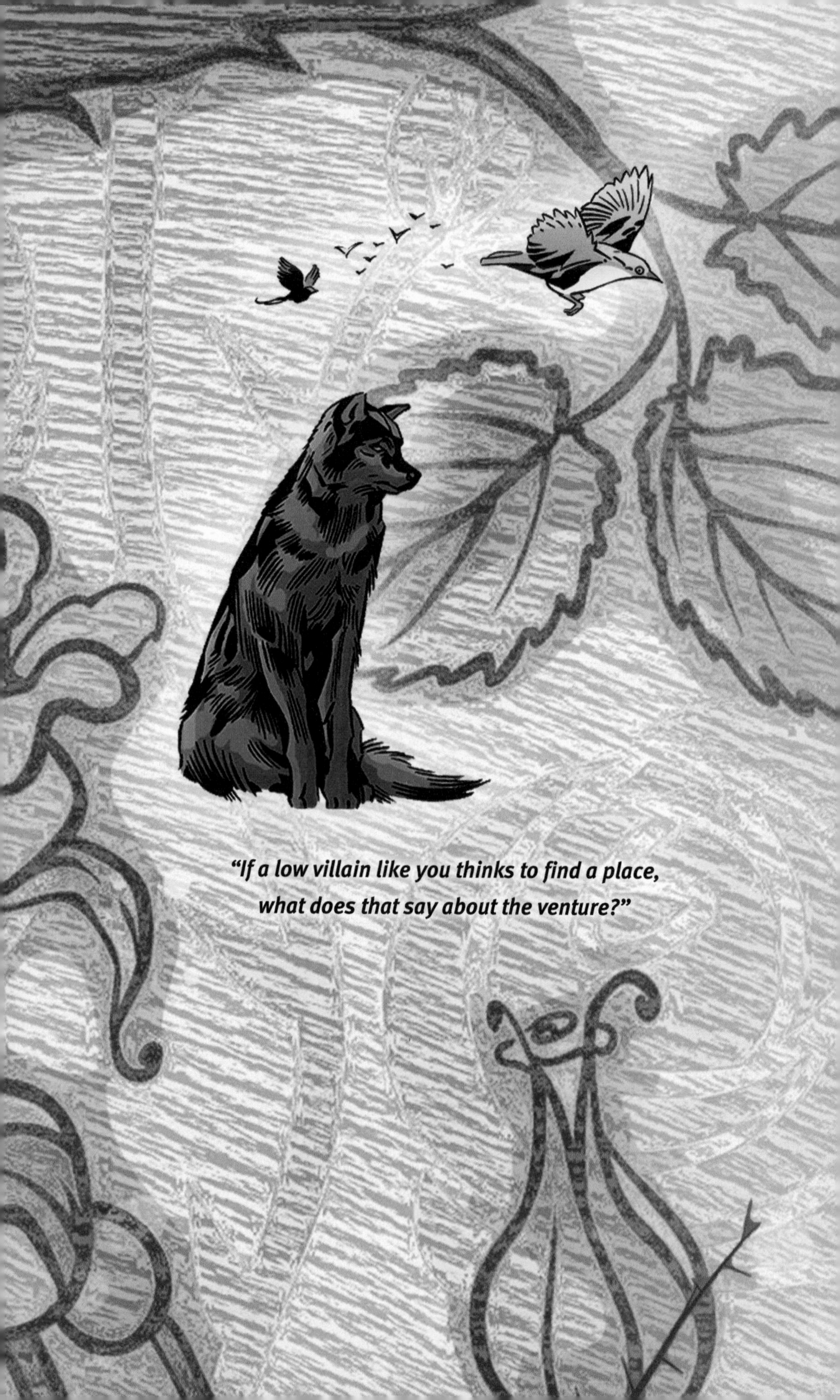

"If a low villain like you thinks to find a place, what does that say about the venture?"

HELLO?

DO YOU RECOGNIZE MY VOICE?

GOOD. I DON'T WANT TO USE OUR NAMES OVER AN OPEN LINE.

YOU OWE ME A *DEBT,* AND IT'S FINALLY TIME TO PAY IT.

YOU'VE HEARD ABOUT MY SISTER'S NEW CAMELOT PROJECT?

YOU'RE GOING TO INTERCEPT ONE OF HER *KNIGHTS* THE FIRST TIME HE'S SENT ON A QUEST.

IT CAN NEVER GET BACK TO ME.

NOW, HERE ARE THE DETAILS.

FIRST, YOU'RE GOING TO NEED TO DIG A VERY DEEP *PIT.*

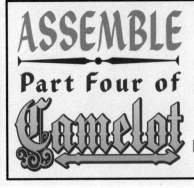

ASSEMBLE

Part Four of

Camelot

Bill Willingham
plot & script, creator

Russ Braun
finishes 1, 6-20

Lee Loughridge
colors

Todd Klein
letters

Mark Buckingham
layouts & script, pencils 2-5

Steve Leialoha
inks 2-3

Andrew Pepoy
inks 4-5

Greg Ruth
cover

Sara Miller
asst. ed.

Shelly Bond
editor

THANK YOU FOR COMING DOWN TO SEE ME, ROSE RED.

NO PROBLEM. UNLESS THERE *IS* A PROBLEM?

I'M SAD TO SAY IT'S ABOUT *MONEY* AGAIN. I KNOW I SOUND LIKE A BROKEN RECORD, BUT IT'S *ALWAYS* ABOUT MONEY.

EVEN WITH THE RECENT *GOLD* INFUSION, AND THE *FREE* LABOR FROM WEYLAND SMITH, I CAN'T SEE HOW WE'RE ABLE TO AFFORD AN ENTIRELY *NEW* CASTLE UP AT THE FARM.

WE *NEED* ONE. THE FARM POPULATION COULD *DOUBLE* IN SIZE OVER THE NEXT MONTHS, AND...

AND THAT'S THE OTHER THING, ROSE RED. YOU TOOK IT UPON YOURSELF TO INVITE A *HOST* OF NEW FABLES TO THE FARM WITHOUT *CONSULTING* ANYONE?

I'M THE *MAYOR* OF FABLETOWN, AND YOU DIDN'T THINK TO *ASK* ME?

AND I *RUN* THE FARM, YOUR HONOR. AREN'T OUR RELATIVE POSITIONS SUPPOSED TO BE ABOUT *EQUAL?* DO YOU CONSULT ME ABOUT EVERY DECISION *YOU* MAKE?

NO, AND THAT'S OKAY. I DON'T *EXPECT* YOU TO. WE SHOULD EACH RUN OUR OWN SHOP.

NODS

LEWIS ANTIQUE

COMIC MAGS

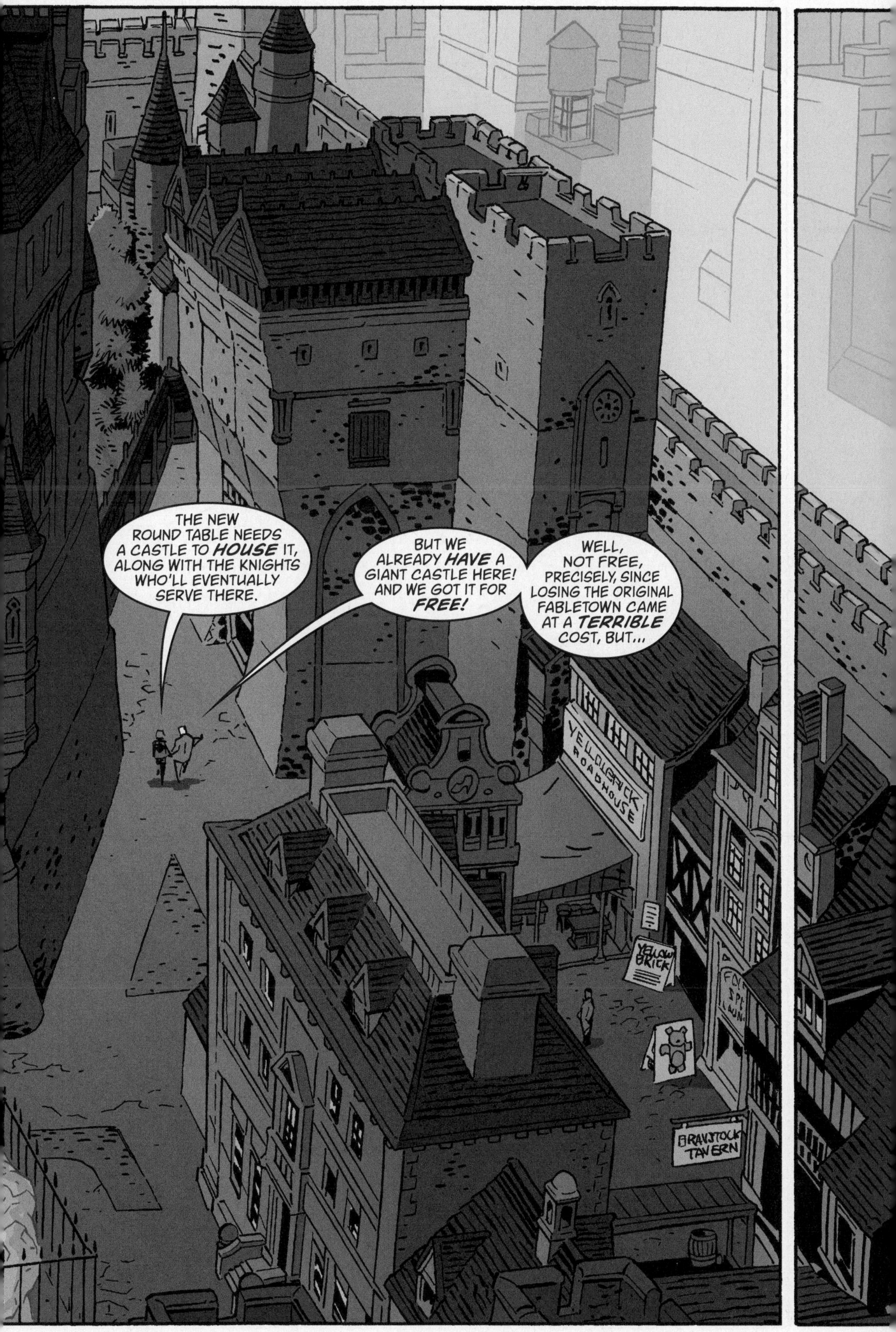
THE NEW ROUND TABLE NEEDS A CASTLE TO HOUSE IT, ALONG WITH THE KNIGHTS WHO'LL EVENTUALLY SERVE THERE.
BUT WE ALREADY HAVE A GIANT CASTLE HERE! AND WE GOT IT FOR FREE!
WELL, NOT FREE, PRECISELY, SINCE LOSING THE ORIGINAL FABLETOWN CAME AT A TERRIBLE COST, BUT...
YELLOWBRICK ROADHOUSE
YELLOW BRICK
BRAYSTOCK TAVERN

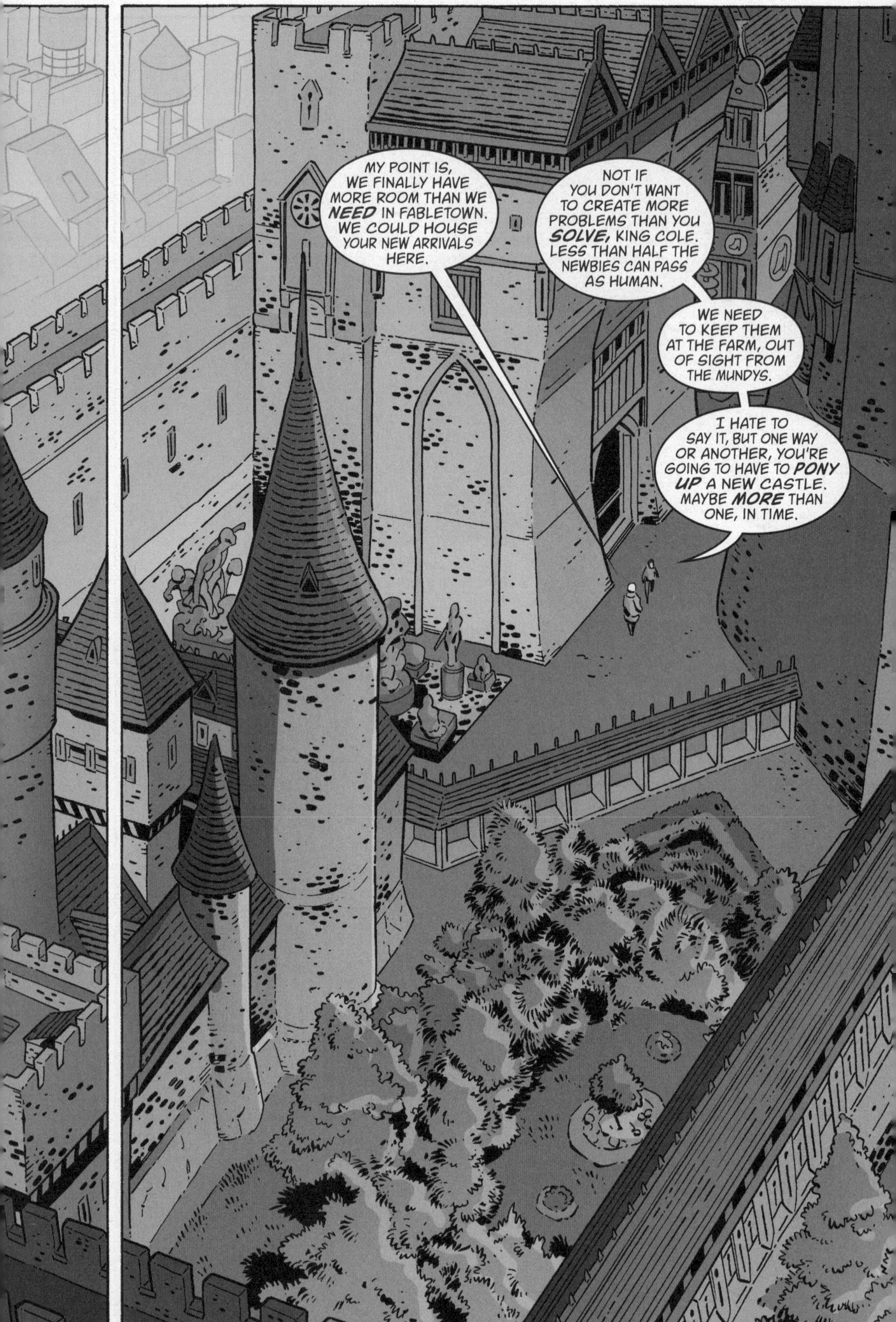
MY POINT IS, WE FINALLY HAVE MORE ROOM THAN WE NEED IN FABLETOWN. WE COULD HOUSE YOUR NEW ARRIVALS HERE.
NOT IF YOU DON'T WANT TO CREATE MORE PROBLEMS THAN YOU SOLVE, KING COLE. LESS THAN HALF THE NEWBIES CAN PASS AS HUMAN.
WE NEED TO KEEP THEM AT THE FARM, OUT OF SIGHT FROM THE MUNDYS.
I HATE TO SAY IT, BUT ONE WAY OR ANOTHER, YOU'RE GOING TO HAVE TO PONY UP A NEW CASTLE. MAYBE MORE THAN ONE, IN TIME.

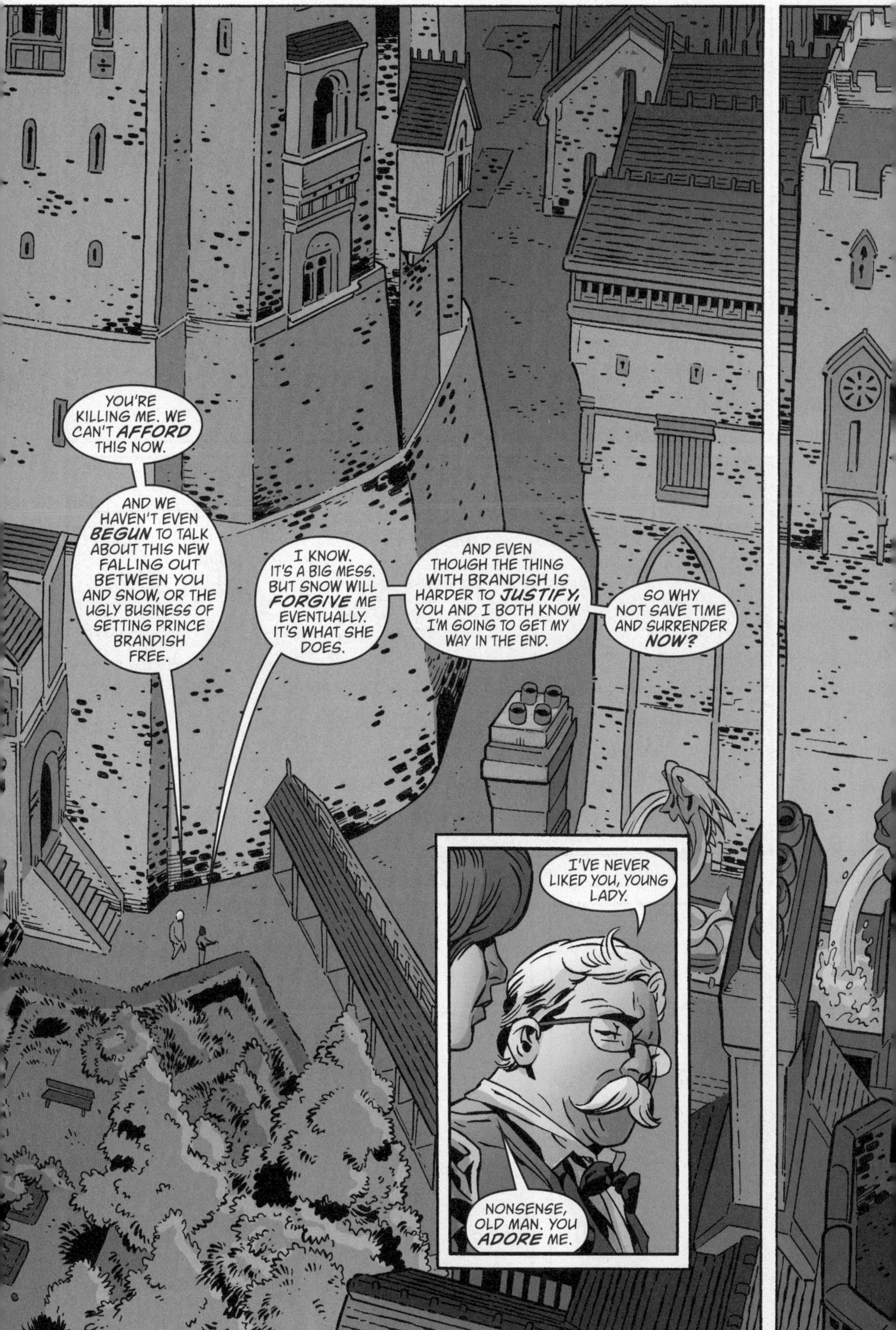

YOU'RE KILLING ME. WE CAN'T AFFORD THIS NOW.
AND WE HAVEN'T EVEN BEGUN TO TALK ABOUT THIS NEW FALLING OUT BETWEEN YOU AND SNOW, OR THE UGLY BUSINESS OF SETTING PRINCE BRANDISH FREE.
I KNOW. IT'S A BIG MESS. BUT SNOW WILL FORGIVE ME EVENTUALLY. IT'S WHAT SHE DOES.
AND EVEN THOUGH THE THING WITH BRANDISH IS HARDER TO JUSTIFY, YOU AND I BOTH KNOW I'M GOING TO GET MY WAY IN THE END.
SO WHY NOT SAVE TIME AND SURRENDER NOW?
I'VE NEVER LIKED YOU, YOUNG LADY.
NONSENSE, OLD MAN. YOU ADORE ME.

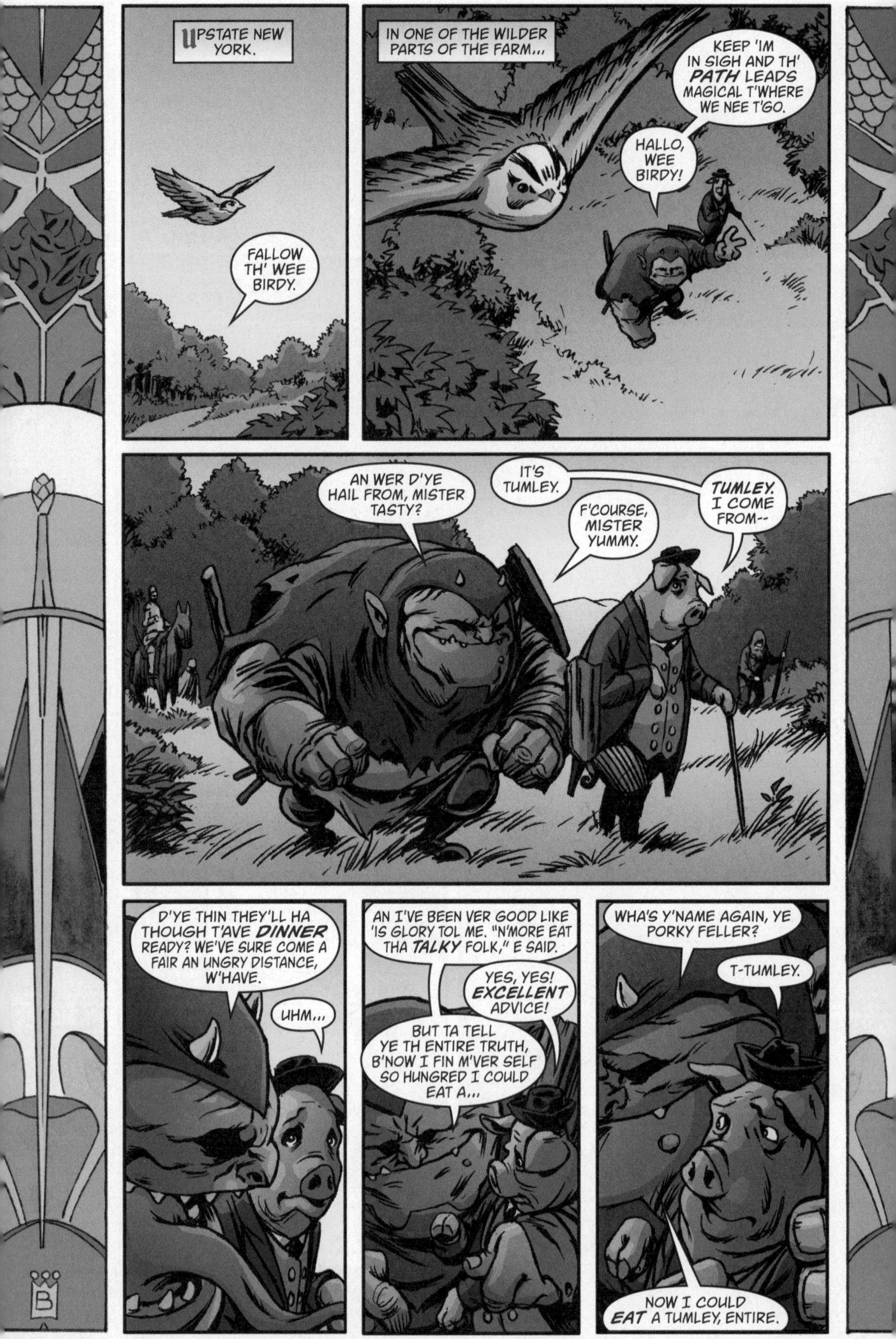
UPSTATE NEW YORK.
FALLOW TH' WEE BIRDY.
IN ONE OF THE WILDER PARTS OF THE FARM...
KEEP 'IM IN SIGH AND TH' PATH LEADS MAGICAL T'WHERE WE NEE T'GO.
HALLO, WEE BIRDY!
AN WER D'YE HAIL FROM, MISTER TASTY?
IT'S TUMLEY.
F'COURSE, MISTER YUMMY.
TUMLEY. I COME FROM--
D'YE THIN THEY'LL HA THOUGH T'AVE DINNER READY? WE'VE SURE COME A FAIR AN UNGRY DISTANCE, W'HAVE.
UHM...
AN I'VE BEEN VER GOOD LIKE 'IS GLORY TOL ME. "N'MORE EAT THA TALKY FOLK," E SAID.
YES, YES! EXCELLENT ADVICE!
BUT TA TELL YE TH ENTIRE TRUTH, B'NOW I FIN M'VER SELF SO HUNGRED I COULD EAT A...
WHA'S Y'NAME AGAIN, YE PORKY FELLER?
T-TUMLEY.
NOW I COULD EAT A TUMLEY, ENTIRE.

GRUBBY GOBLINS AND TALKING BEASTS? *REALLY?*

IF *THAT* IS THE CALIBER OF APPLICANTS FOR THIS NEW CAMELOT, I FEAR FOR ITS PUISSANCE AND PURPOSE, YOUNG SQUELCH.

YES, SIRE.

WHAT ABOUT *YOU*, THERE?

IF A LOW VILLAIN LIKE YOU THINKS TO FIND A PLACE, WHAT DOES THAT SAY ABOUT THE *VENTURE?*

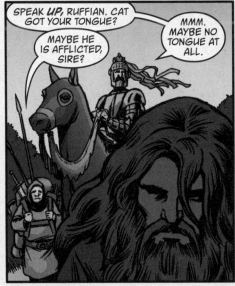

SPEAK *UP*, RUFFIAN. CAT GOT YOUR TONGUE?

MAYBE HE IS AFFLICTED, SIRE?

MMM. MAYBE NO TONGUE AT ALL.

AT LEAST THE LOW CHARACTERS ON OUR ROAD WILL HAVE THE HONOR OF WATCHING A *TRUE* KNIGHT WIN HIS PLACE.

MAYBE UNDER ALL THAT MUCK AND MUD THERE'S THE RAW METAL OF *ANOTHER* KNIGHT'S SQUIRE. *CRUDE* AT FIRST, BUT TRAINABLE. LIKE YOU, EH, SQUELCH?

YES, SIRE. THANKING YOU, SIRE.

I RATHER THINK WE'RE NOT THE FIRST TO ARRIVE.

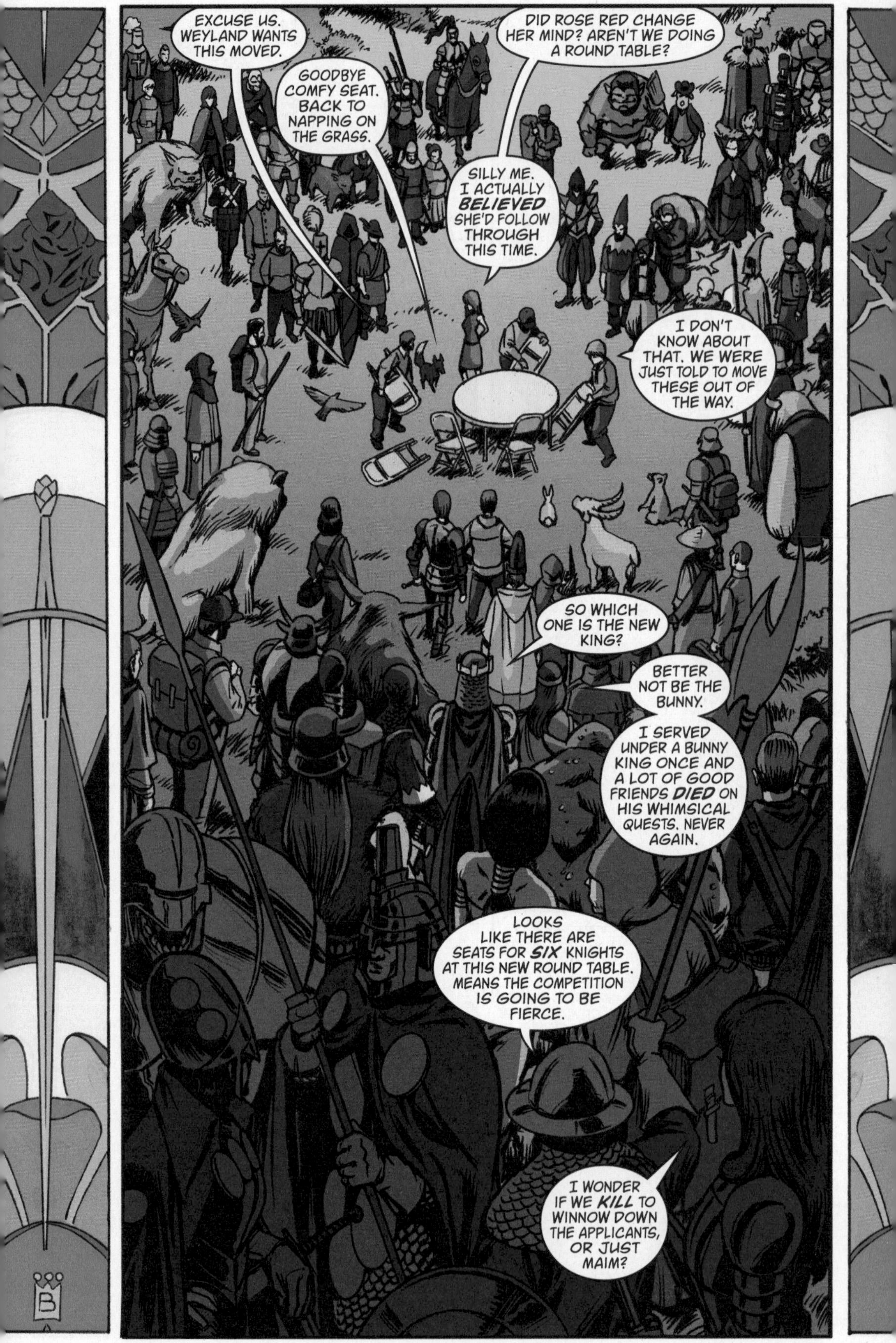
EXCUSE US. WEYLAND WANTS THIS MOVED.
GOODBYE COMFY SEAT. BACK TO NAPPING ON THE GRASS.
DID ROSE RED CHANGE HER MIND? AREN'T WE DOING A ROUND TABLE?
SILLY ME. I ACTUALLY BELIEVED SHE'D FOLLOW THROUGH THIS TIME.
I DON'T KNOW ABOUT THAT. WE WERE JUST TOLD TO MOVE THESE OUT OF THE WAY.
SO WHICH ONE IS THE NEW KING?
BETTER NOT BE THE BUNNY.
I SERVED UNDER A BUNNY KING ONCE AND A LOT OF GOOD FRIENDS DIED ON HIS WHIMSICAL QUESTS. NEVER AGAIN.
LOOKS LIKE THERE ARE SEATS FOR SIX KNIGHTS AT THIS NEW ROUND TABLE. MEANS THE COMPETITION IS GOING TO BE FIERCE.
I WONDER IF WE KILL TO WINNOW DOWN THE APPLICANTS, OR JUST MAIM?

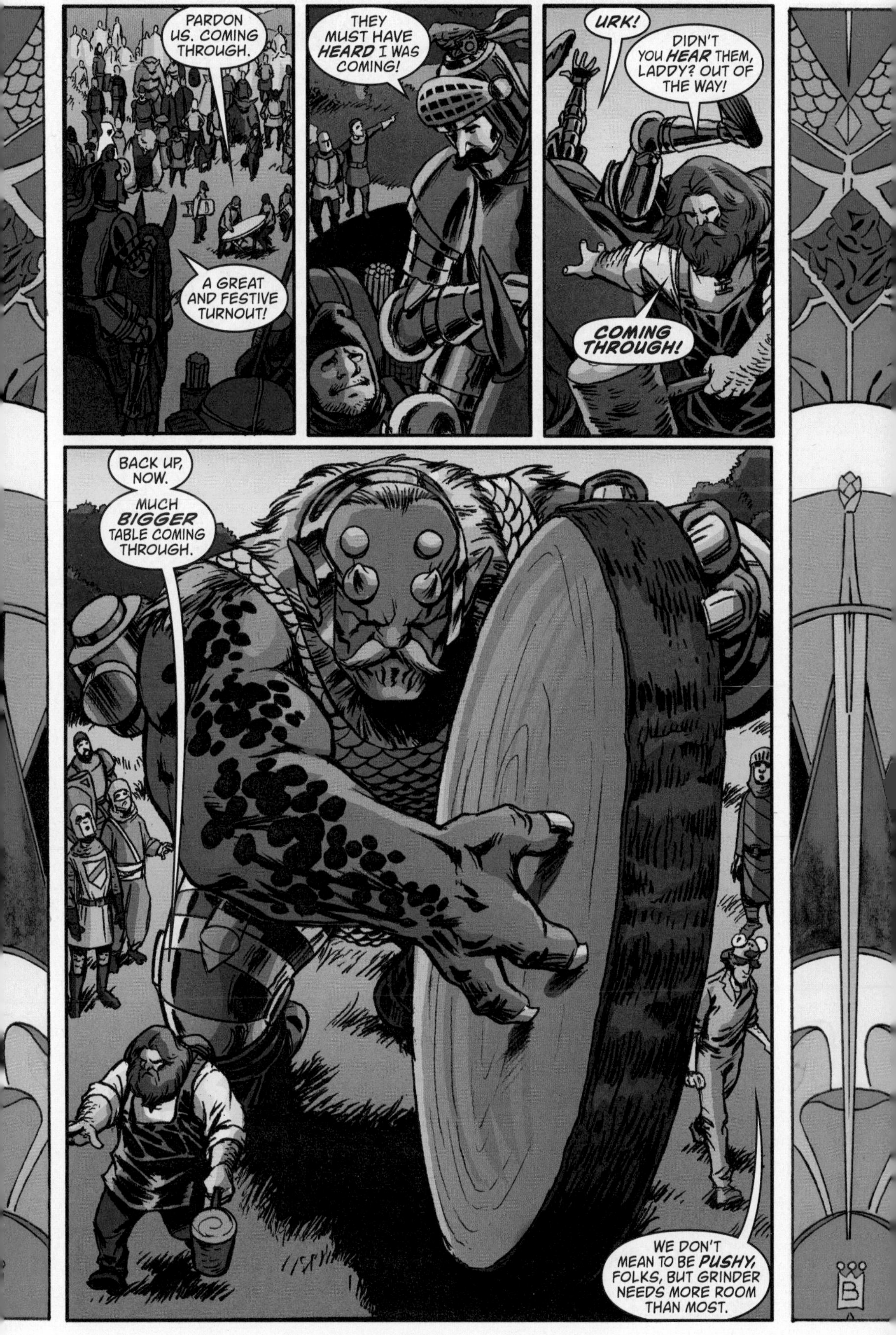

PARDON US. COMING THROUGH.
A GREAT AND FESTIVE TURNOUT!
THEY MUST HAVE HEARD I WAS COMING!
URK!
DIDN'T YOU HEAR THEM, LADDY? OUT OF THE WAY!
COMING THROUGH!
BACK UP, NOW.
MUCH BIGGER TABLE COMING THROUGH.
WE DON'T MEAN TO BE PUSHY, FOLKS, BUT GRINDER NEEDS MORE ROOM THAN MOST.

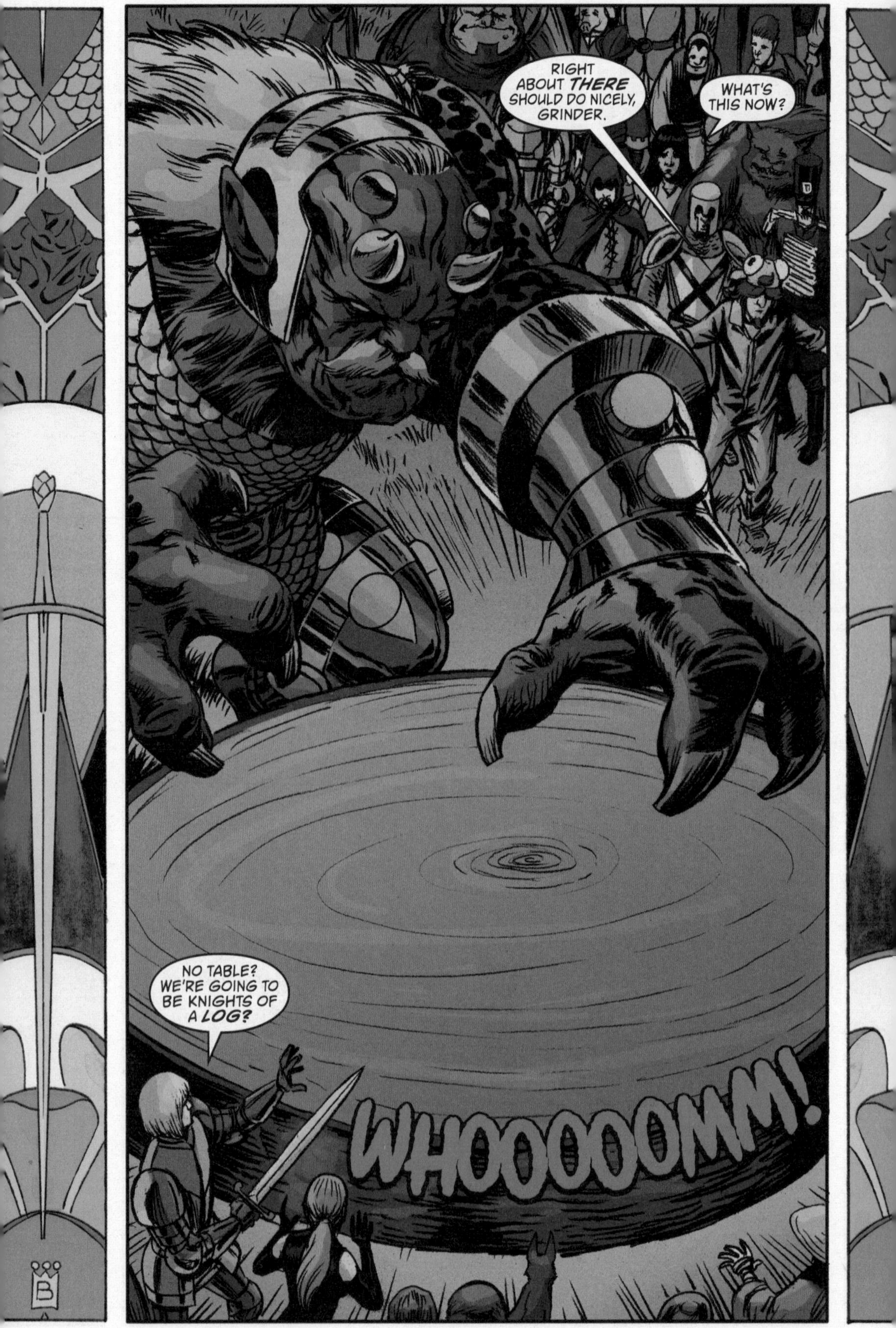

RIGHT ABOUT THERE SHOULD DO NICELY, GRINDER.
WHAT'S THIS NOW?
NO TABLE? WE'RE GOING TO BE KNIGHTS OF A LOG?
WHOOOOOMM!

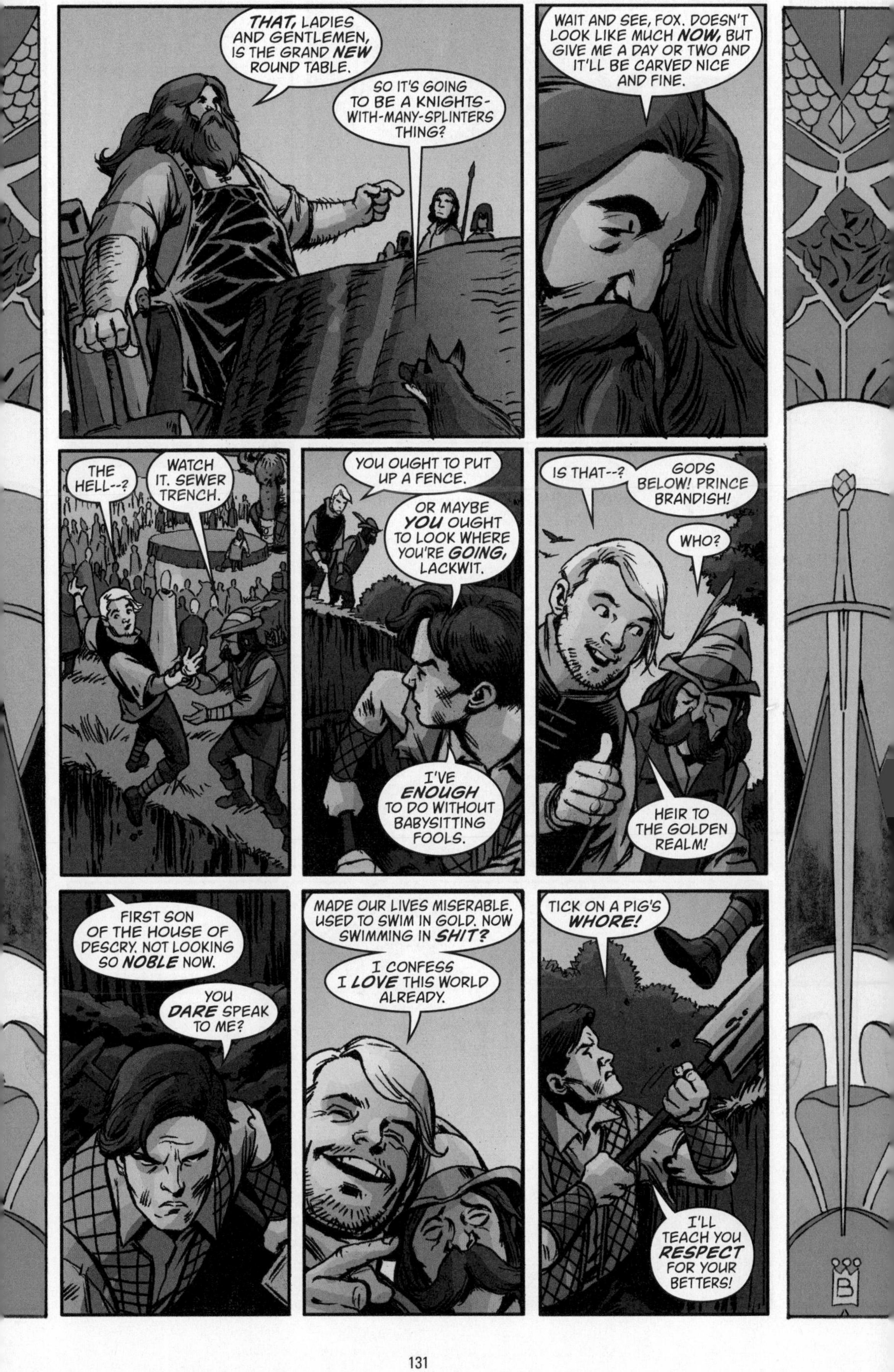
THAT, LADIES AND GENTLEMEN, IS THE GRAND NEW ROUND TABLE.
SO IT'S GOING TO BE A KNIGHTS-WITH-MANY-SPLINTERS THING?
WAIT AND SEE, FOX. DOESN'T LOOK LIKE MUCH NOW, BUT GIVE ME A DAY OR TWO AND IT'LL BE CARVED NICE AND FINE.
THE HELL--?
WATCH IT. SEWER TRENCH.
YOU OUGHT TO PUT UP A FENCE.
OR MAYBE YOU OUGHT TO LOOK WHERE YOU'RE GOING, LACKWIT.
I'VE ENOUGH TO DO WITHOUT BABYSITTING FOOLS.
IS THAT--?
GODS BELOW! PRINCE BRANDISH!
WHO?
HEIR TO THE GOLDEN REALM!
FIRST SON OF THE HOUSE OF DESCRY. NOT LOOKING SO NOBLE NOW.
YOU DARE SPEAK TO ME?
MADE OUR LIVES MISERABLE. USED TO SWIM IN GOLD. NOW SWIMMING IN SHIT?
I CONFESS I LOVE THIS WORLD ALREADY.
TICK ON A PIG'S WHORE!
I'LL TEACH YOU RESPECT FOR YOUR BETTERS!

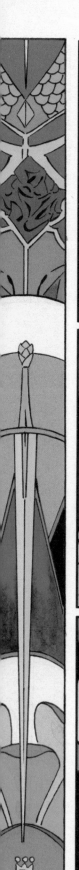

DO WE HAVE A **PROBLEM** HERE?

IF YOU'VE TIME TO STOP AND **CHAT,** YOU'VE TIME FOR MORE DUTIES.

MY APOLOGIES FOR NOT **PROVIDING** YOU ENOUGH TO DO. LET ME CORRECT THAT IMMEDIATELY.

WHAT DID I GIVE YOU, **TWO** DAYS TO FINISH THESE FOUNDATION TRENCHES? NOW YOU HAVE UNTIL **NIGHTFALL.**

YOU'RE... TOO... KIND.

ROSE IS HERE!

HMM?

TOO KIND BY HALF.

I'LL HAVE TO BE **EXTRA** CREATIVE IN THINKING OF THE BEST WAY TO REWARD YOU SOMEDAY.

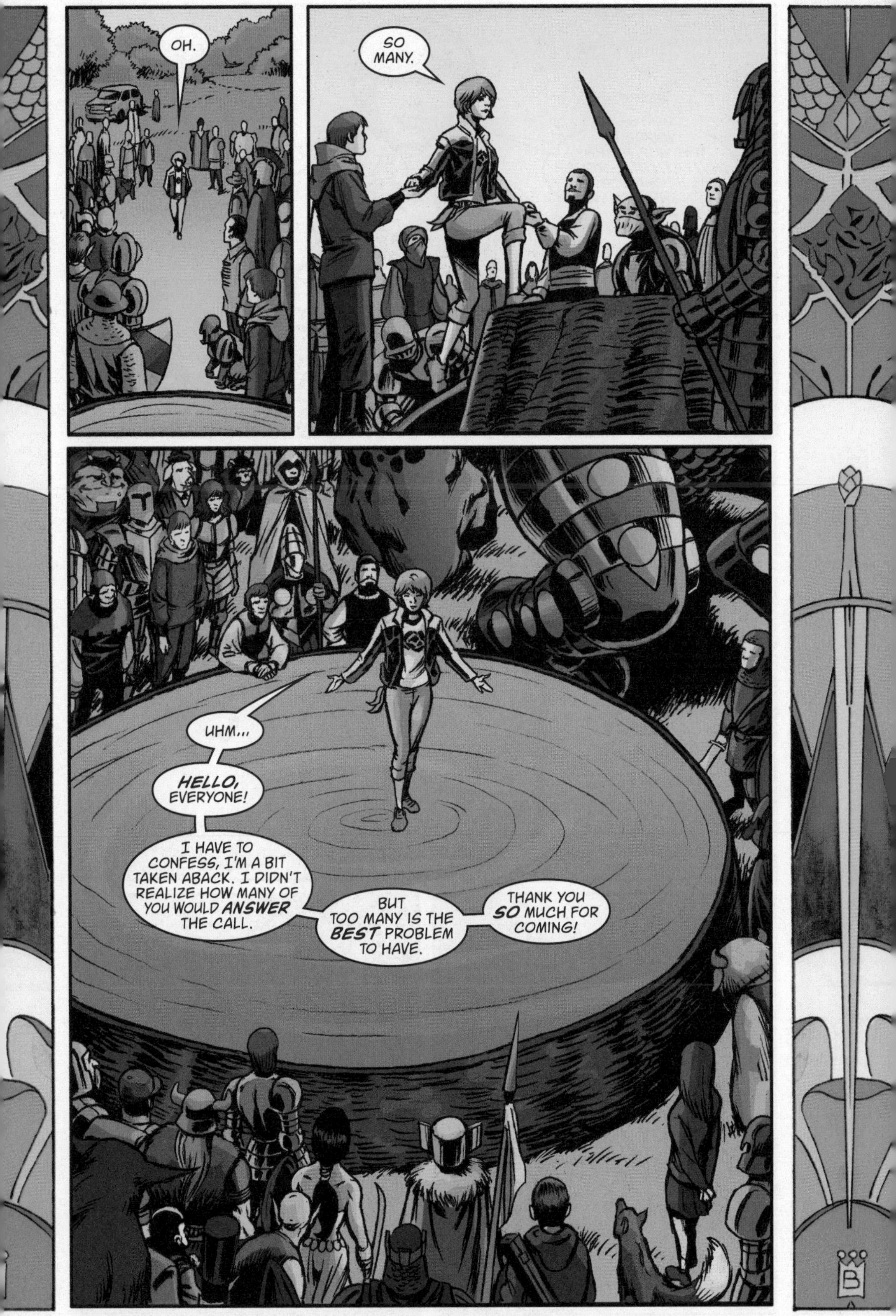
OH.
SO MANY.
UHM...
HELLO, EVERYONE!
I HAVE TO CONFESS, I'M A BIT TAKEN ABACK. I DIDN'T REALIZE HOW MANY OF YOU WOULD ANSWER THE CALL.
BUT TOO MANY IS THE BEST PROBLEM TO HAVE.
THANK YOU SO MUCH FOR COMING!

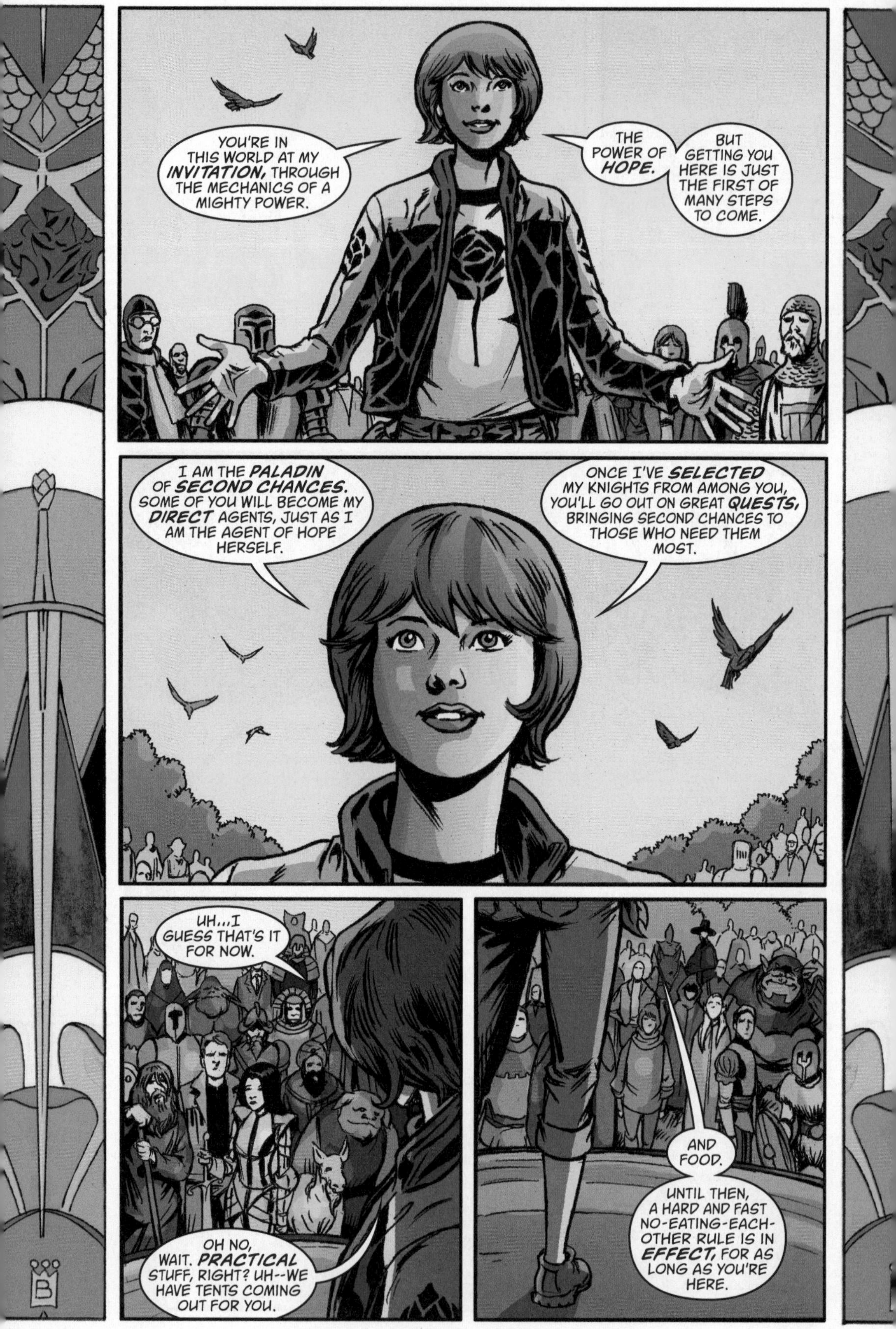
YOU'RE IN THIS WORLD AT MY INVITATION, THROUGH THE MECHANICS OF A MIGHTY POWER.
THE POWER OF HOPE.
BUT GETTING YOU HERE IS JUST THE FIRST OF MANY STEPS TO COME.
I AM THE PALADIN OF SECOND CHANCES. SOME OF YOU WILL BECOME MY DIRECT AGENTS, JUST AS I AM THE AGENT OF HOPE HERSELF.
ONCE I'VE SELECTED MY KNIGHTS FROM AMONG YOU, YOU'LL GO OUT ON GREAT QUESTS, BRINGING SECOND CHANCES TO THOSE WHO NEED THEM MOST.
UH...I GUESS THAT'S IT FOR NOW.
OH NO, WAIT. PRACTICAL STUFF, RIGHT? UH--WE HAVE TENTS COMING OUT FOR YOU.
AND FOOD.
UNTIL THEN, A HARD AND FAST NO-EATING-EACH-OTHER RULE IS IN EFFECT, FOR AS LONG AS YOU'RE HERE.

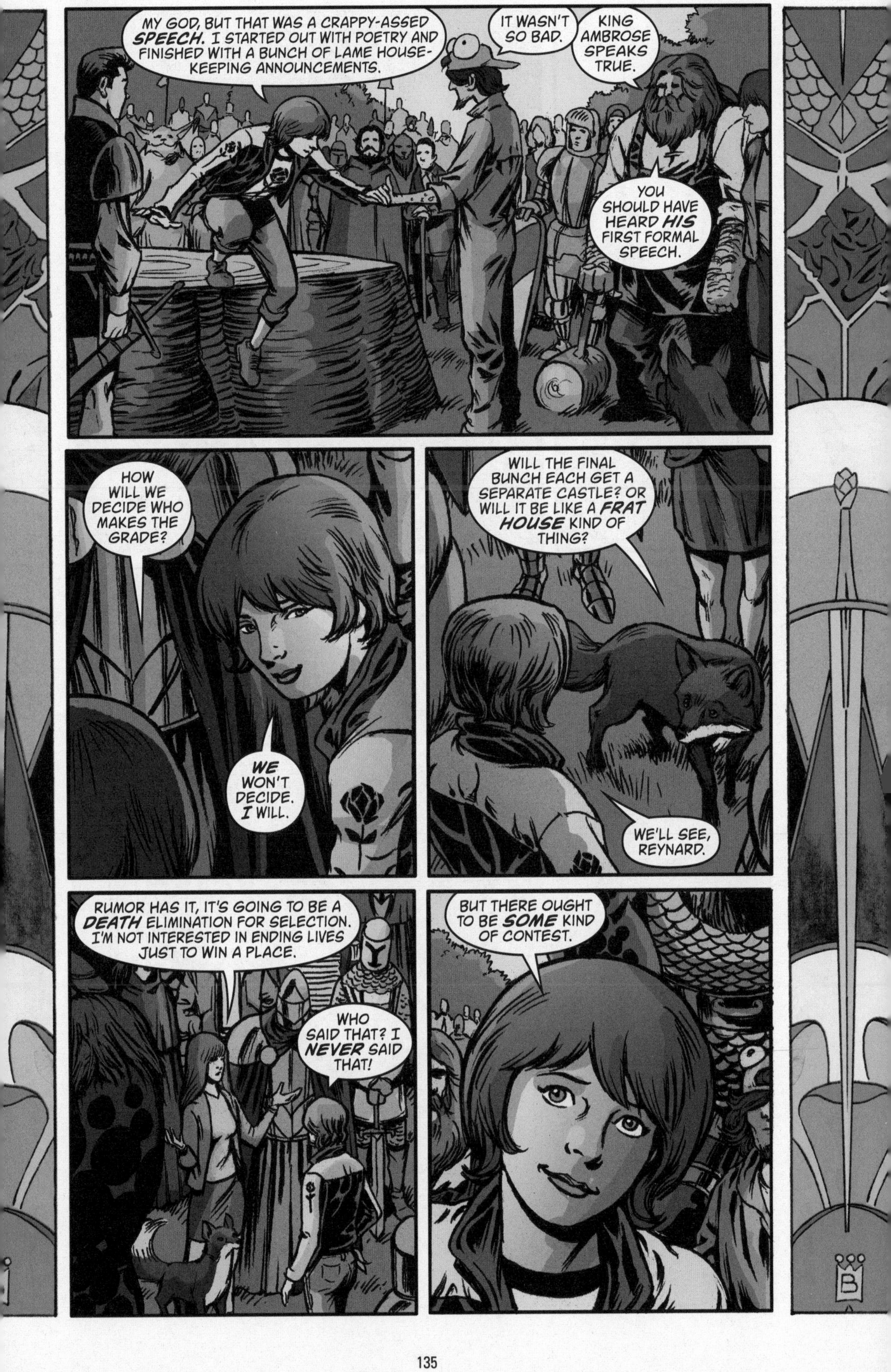
MY GOD, BUT THAT WAS A CRAPPY-ASSED SPEECH. I STARTED OUT WITH POETRY AND FINISHED WITH A BUNCH OF LAME HOUSE-KEEPING ANNOUNCEMENTS.
IT WASN'T SO BAD.
KING AMBROSE SPEAKS TRUE.
YOU SHOULD HAVE HEARD HIS FIRST FORMAL SPEECH.
HOW WILL WE DECIDE WHO MAKES THE GRADE?
WE WON'T DECIDE. I WILL.
WILL THE FINAL BUNCH EACH GET A SEPARATE CASTLE? OR WILL IT BE LIKE A FRAT HOUSE KIND OF THING?
WE'LL SEE, REYNARD.
RUMOR HAS IT, IT'S GOING TO BE A DEATH ELIMINATION FOR SELECTION. I'M NOT INTERESTED IN ENDING LIVES JUST TO WIN A PLACE.
WHO SAID THAT? I NEVER SAID THAT!
BUT THERE OUGHT TO BE SOME KIND OF CONTEST.

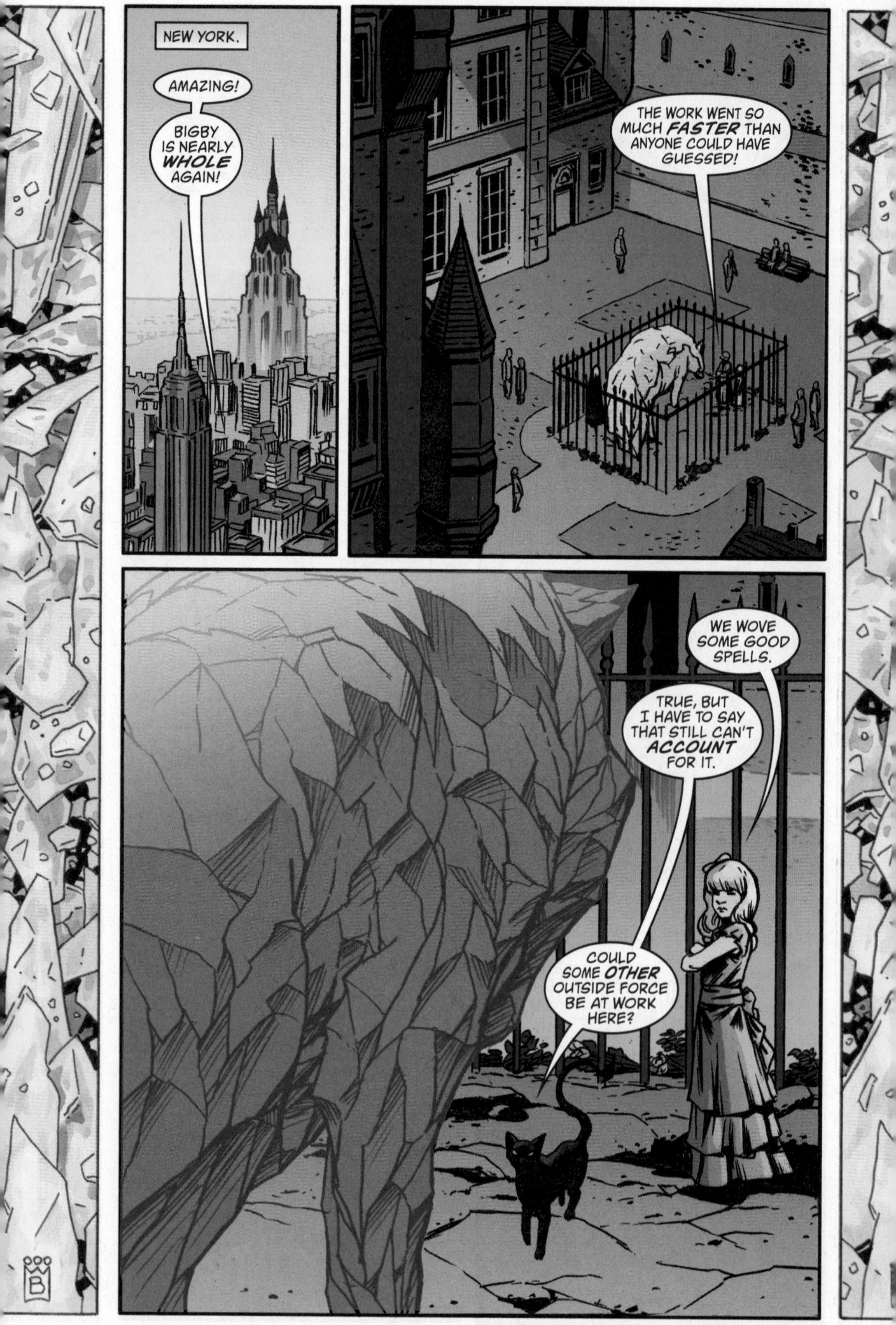
NEW YORK.
AMAZING!
BIGBY IS NEARLY WHOLE AGAIN!
THE WORK WENT SO MUCH FASTER THAN ANYONE COULD HAVE GUESSED!
WE WOVE SOME GOOD SPELLS.
TRUE, BUT I HAVE TO SAY THAT STILL CAN'T ACCOUNT FOR IT.
COULD SOME OTHER OUTSIDE FORCE BE AT WORK HERE?

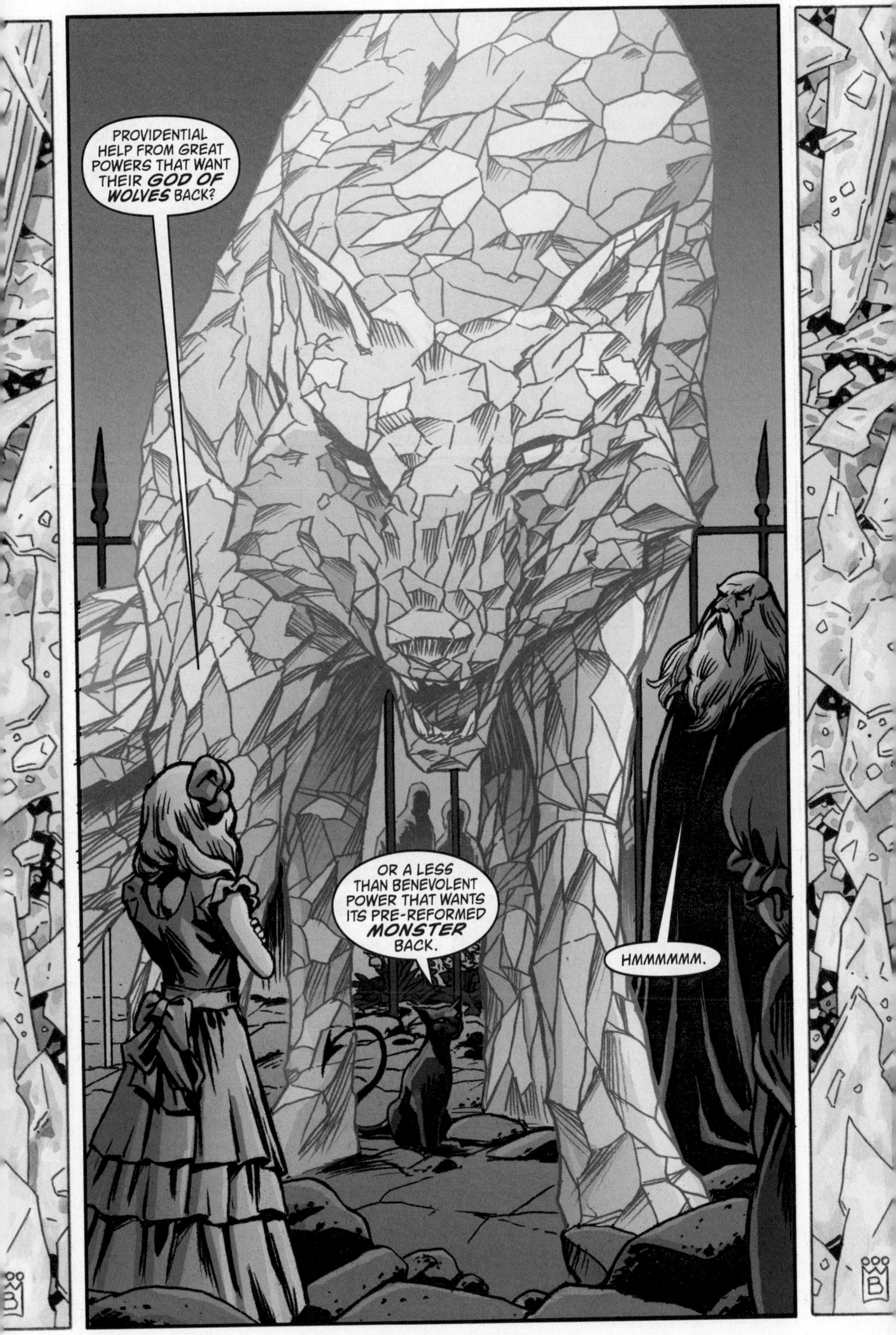
PROVIDENTIAL HELP FROM GREAT POWERS THAT WANT THEIR **GOD OF WOLVES** BACK?
OR A LESS THAN BENEVOLENT POWER THAT WANTS ITS PRE-REFORMED **MONSTER** BACK.
HMMMMMM.

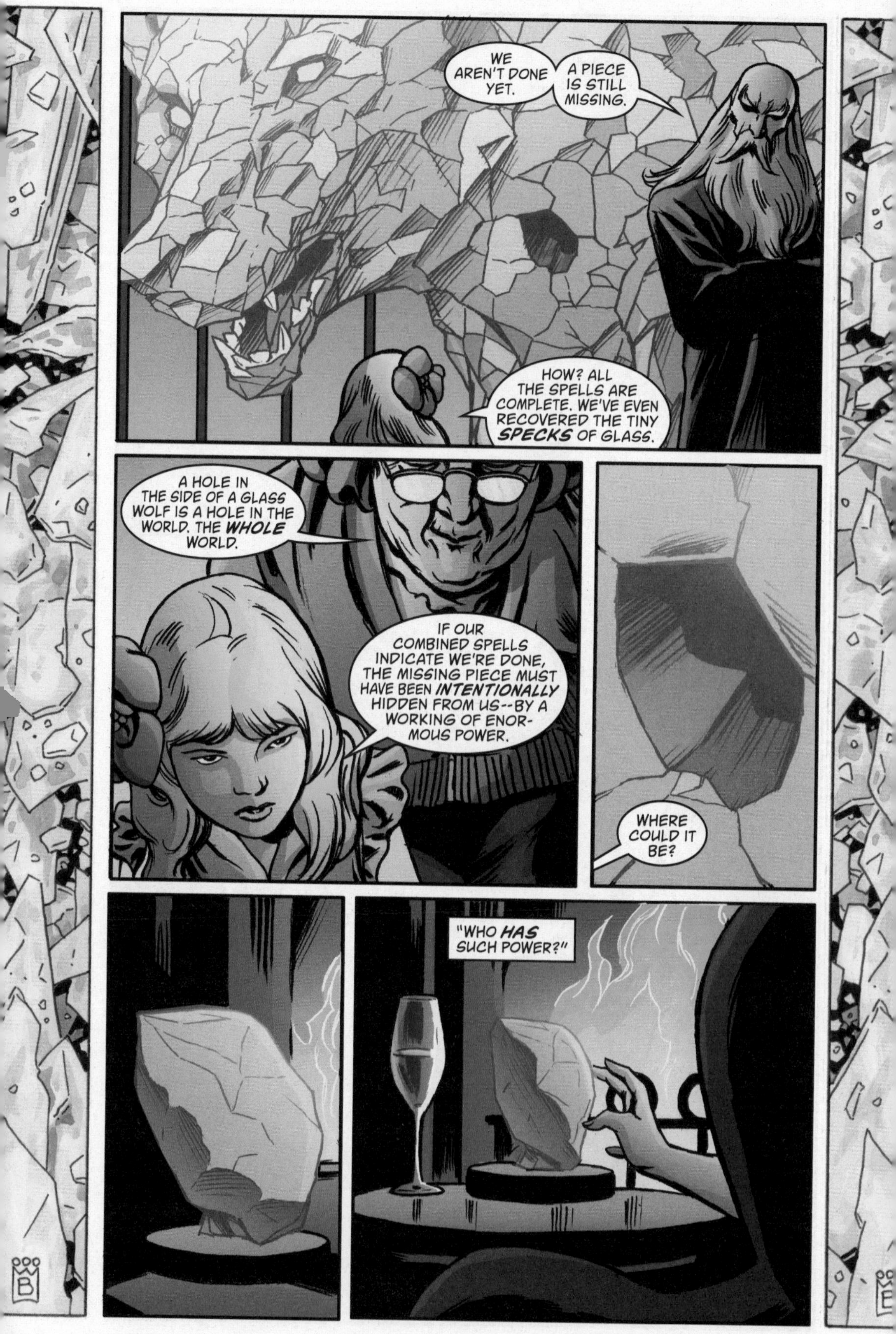
WE AREN'T DONE YET.
A PIECE IS STILL MISSING.
HOW? ALL THE SPELLS ARE COMPLETE. WE'VE EVEN RECOVERED THE TINY SPECKS OF GLASS.
A HOLE IN THE SIDE OF A GLASS WOLF IS A HOLE IN THE WORLD. THE WHOLE WORLD.
IF OUR COMBINED SPELLS INDICATE WE'RE DONE, THE MISSING PIECE MUST HAVE BEEN INTENTIONALLY HIDDEN FROM US--BY A WORKING OF ENOR-MOUS POWER.
WHERE COULD IT BE?
"WHO HAS SUCH POWER?"

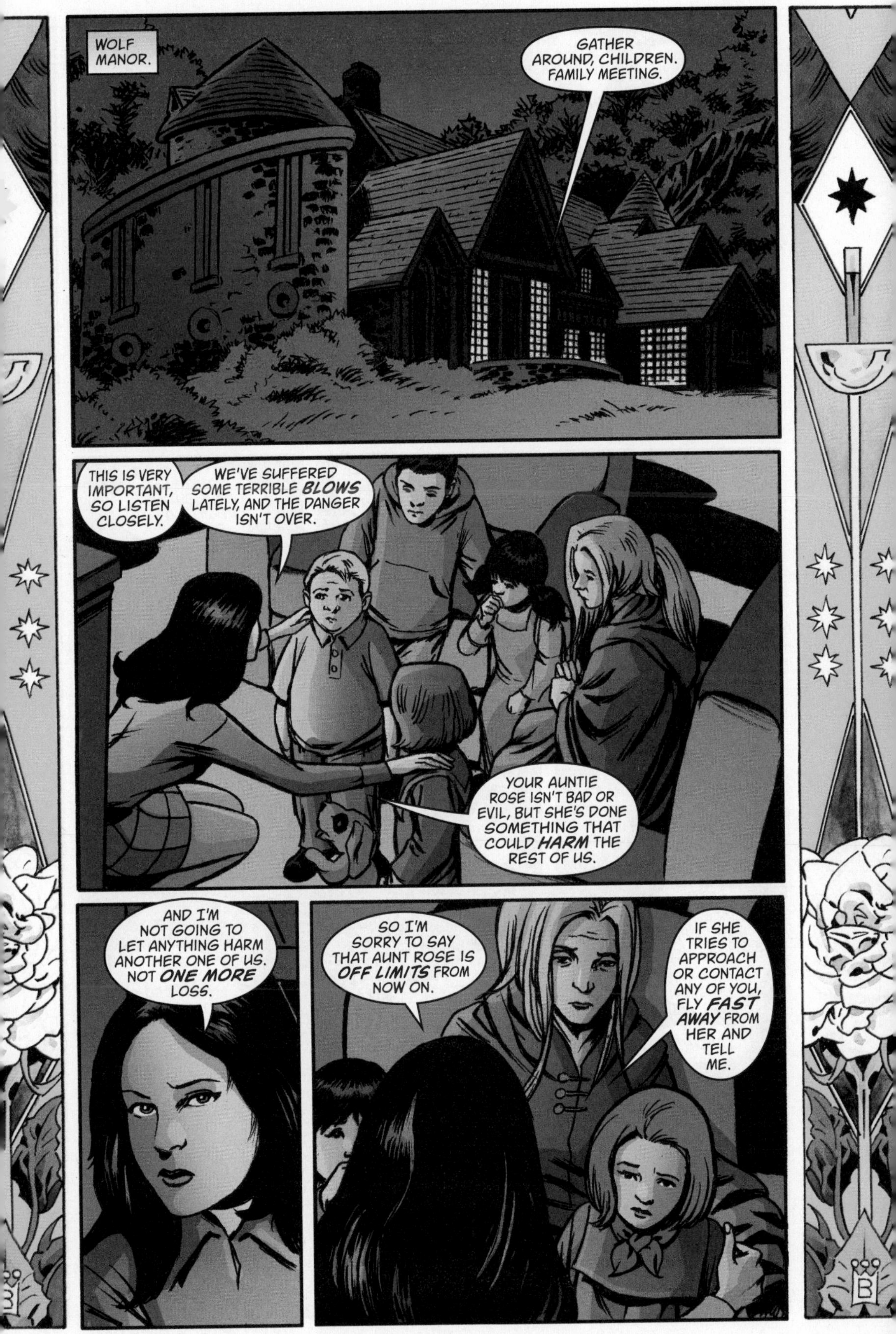
WOLF MANOR.
GATHER AROUND, CHILDREN. FAMILY MEETING.
THIS IS VERY IMPORTANT, SO LISTEN CLOSELY.
WE'VE SUFFERED SOME TERRIBLE BLOWS LATELY, AND THE DANGER ISN'T OVER.
YOUR AUNTIE ROSE ISN'T BAD OR EVIL, BUT SHE'S DONE SOMETHING THAT COULD HARM THE REST OF US.
AND I'M NOT GOING TO LET ANYTHING HARM ANOTHER ONE OF US. NOT ONE MORE LOSS.
SO I'M SORRY TO SAY THAT AUNT ROSE IS OFF LIMITS FROM NOW ON.
IF SHE TRIES TO APPROACH OR CONTACT ANY OF YOU, FLY FAST AWAY FROM HER AND TELL ME.

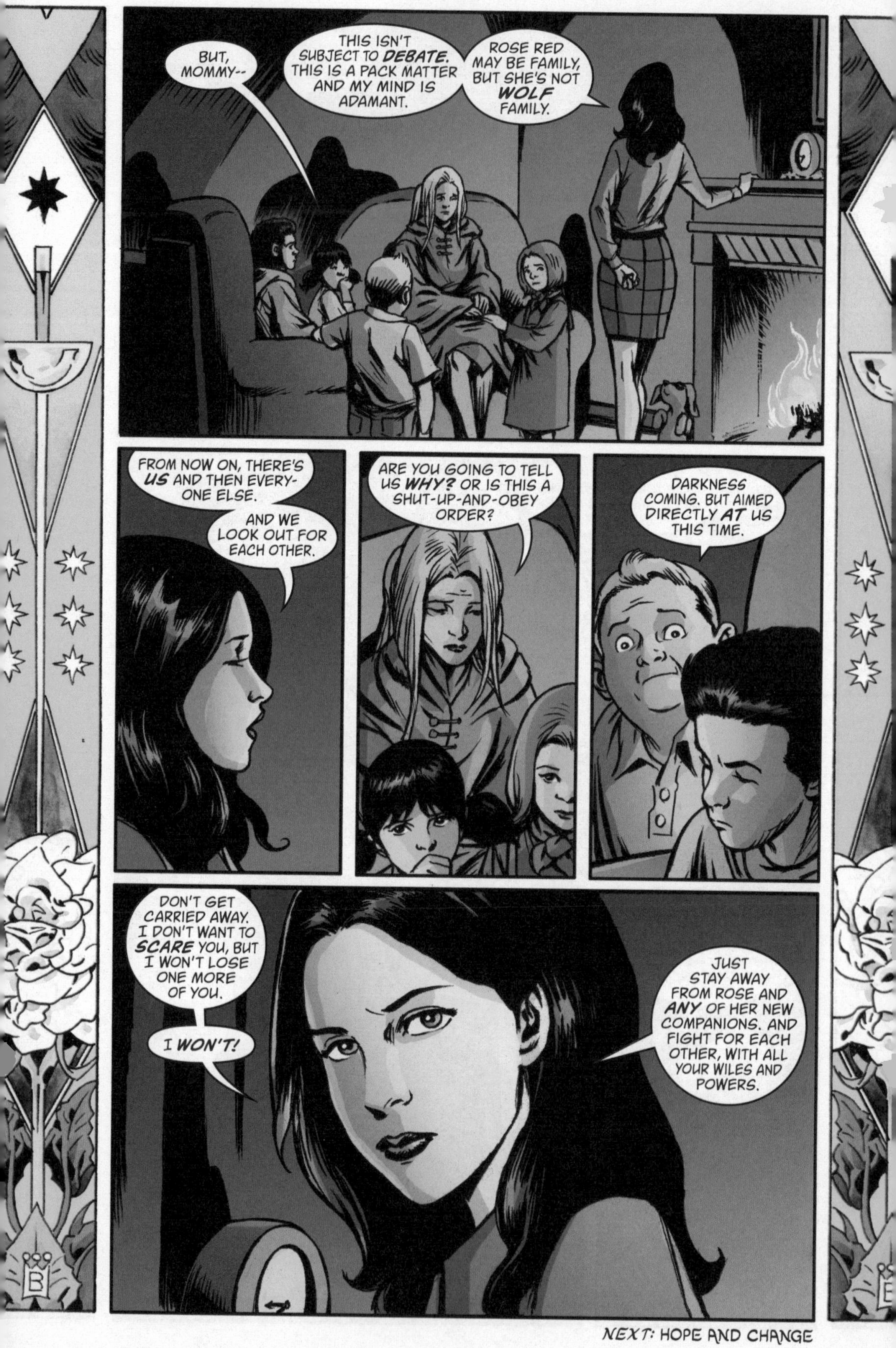
BUT, MOMMY--
THIS ISN'T SUBJECT TO DEBATE. THIS IS A PACK MATTER AND MY MIND IS ADAMANT.
ROSE RED MAY BE FAMILY, BUT SHE'S NOT WOLF FAMILY.
FROM NOW ON, THERE'S US AND THEN EVERYONE ELSE.
AND WE LOOK OUT FOR EACH OTHER.
ARE YOU GOING TO TELL US WHY? OR IS THIS A SHUT-UP-AND-OBEY ORDER?
DARKNESS COMING. BUT AIMED DIRECTLY AT US THIS TIME.
DON'T GET CARRIED AWAY. I DON'T WANT TO SCARE YOU, BUT I WON'T LOSE ONE MORE OF YOU.
I WON'T!
JUST STAY AWAY FROM ROSE AND ANY OF HER NEW COMPANIONS. AND FIGHT FOR EACH OTHER, WITH ALL YOUR WILES AND POWERS.

NEXT: HOPE AND CHANGE

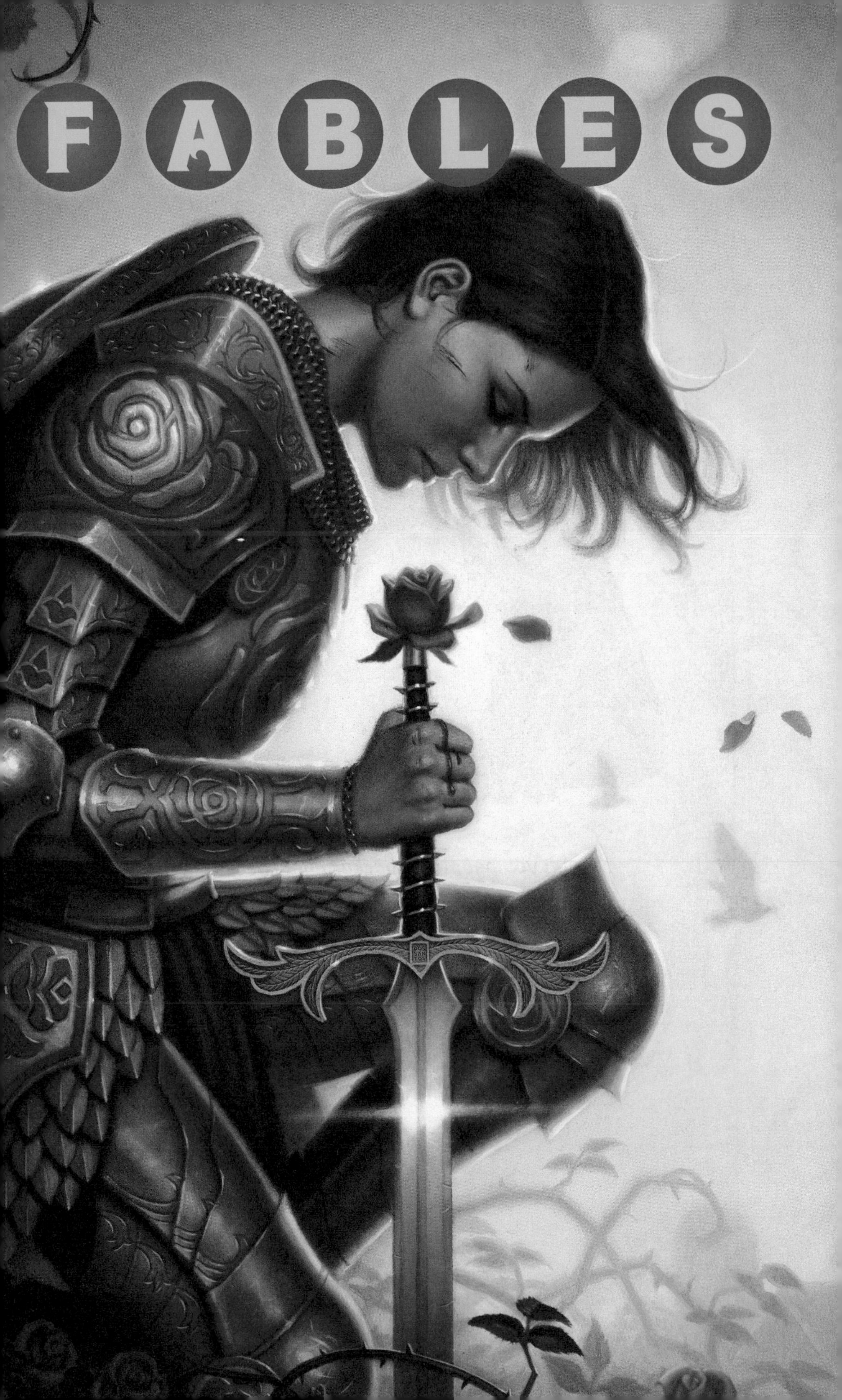
FABLES

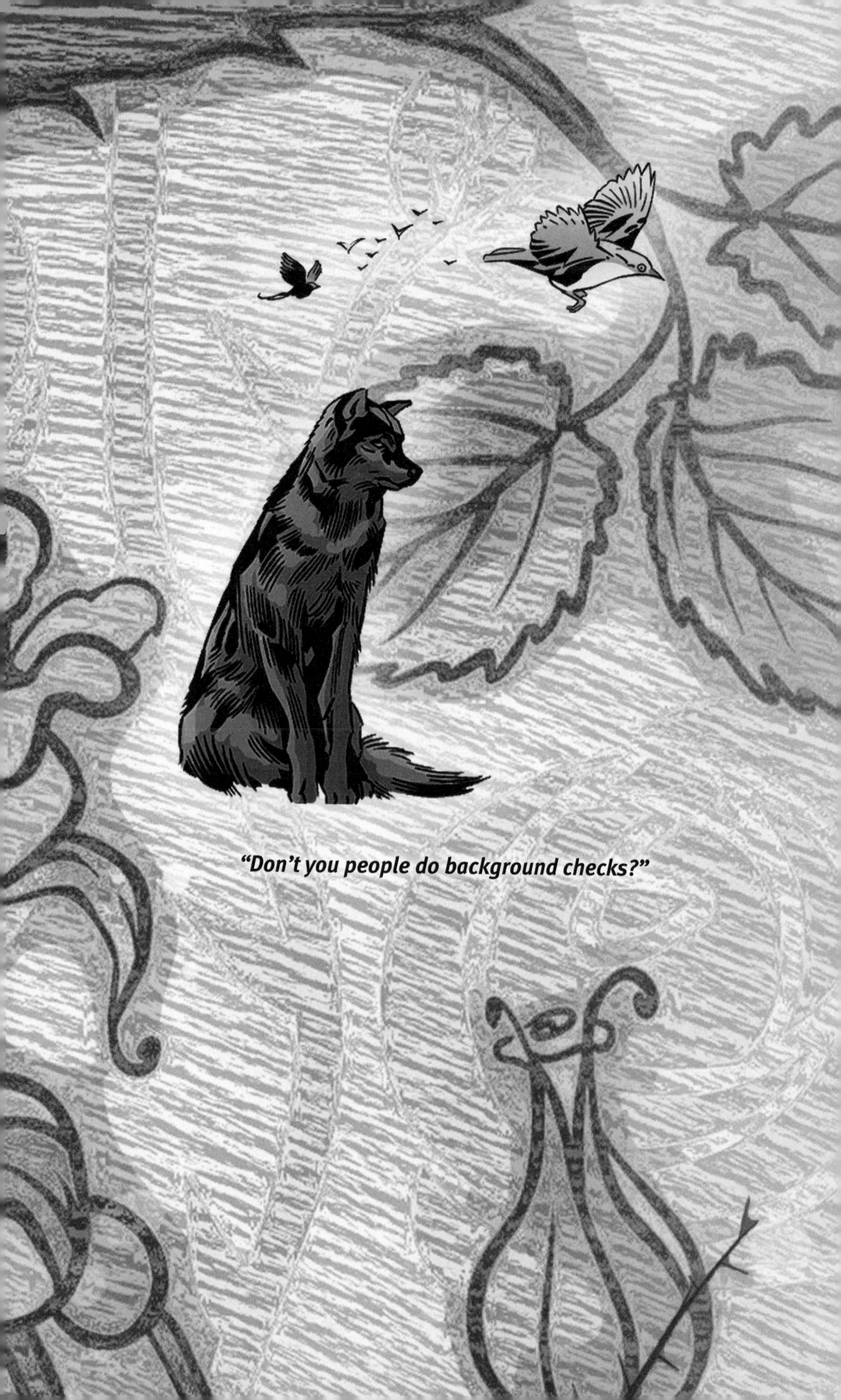

"Don't you people do background checks?"

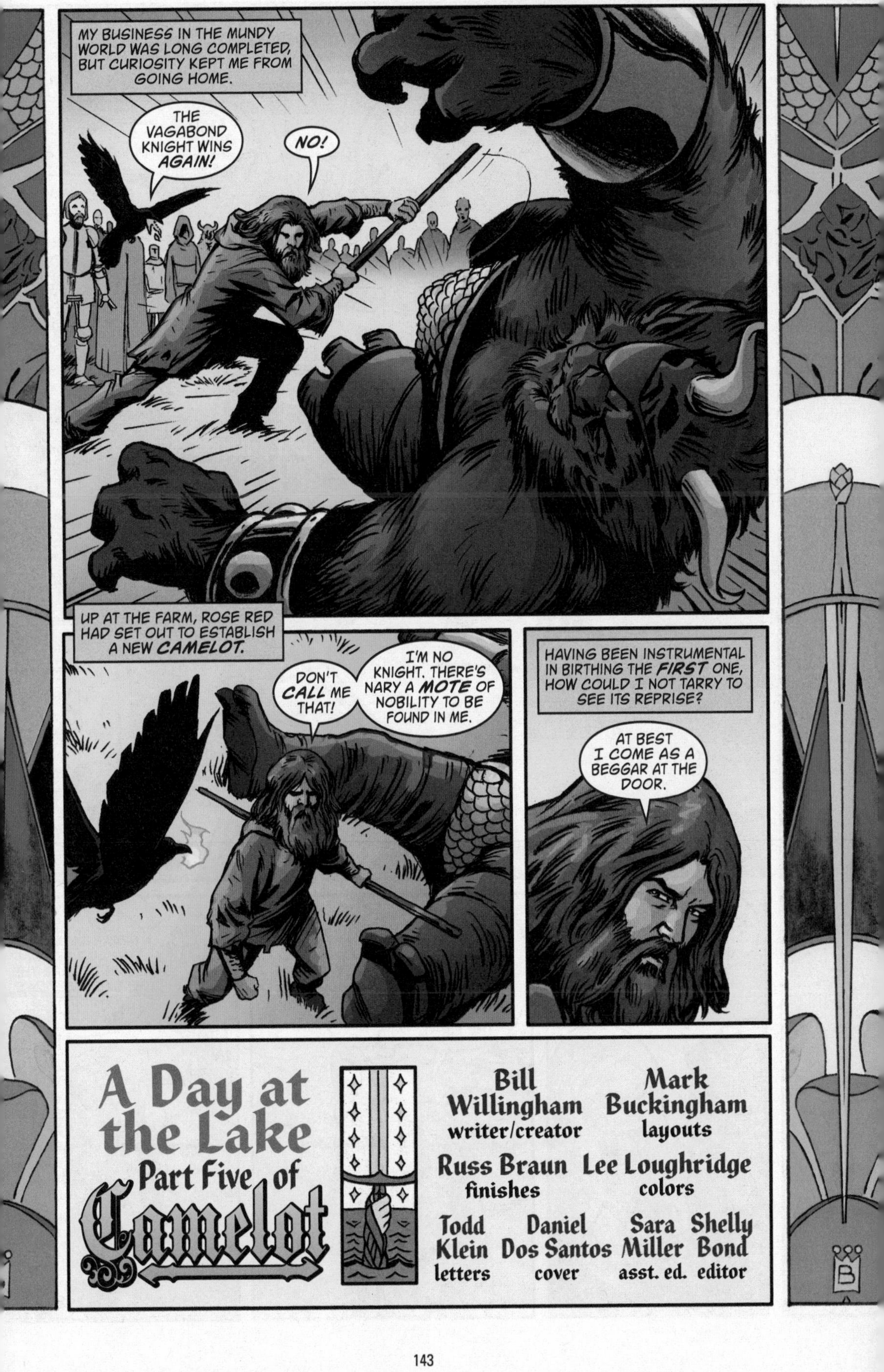
MY BUSINESS IN THE MUNDY WORLD WAS LONG COMPLETED, BUT CURIOSITY KEPT ME FROM GOING HOME.
THE VAGABOND KNIGHT WINS AGAIN!
NO!
UP AT THE FARM, ROSE RED HAD SET OUT TO ESTABLISH A NEW CAMELOT.
DON'T CALL ME THAT!
I'M NO KNIGHT. THERE'S NARY A MOTE OF NOBILITY TO BE FOUND IN ME.
HAVING BEEN INSTRUMENTAL IN BIRTHING THE FIRST ONE, HOW COULD I NOT TARRY TO SEE ITS REPRISE?
AT BEST I COME AS A BEGGAR AT THE DOOR.

A Day at the Lake
Part Five of Camelot

Bill Willingham writer/creator
Mark Buckingham layouts
Russ Braun finishes
Lee Loughridge colors
Todd Klein letters
Daniel Dos Santos cover
Sara Miller asst. ed.
Shelly Bond editor

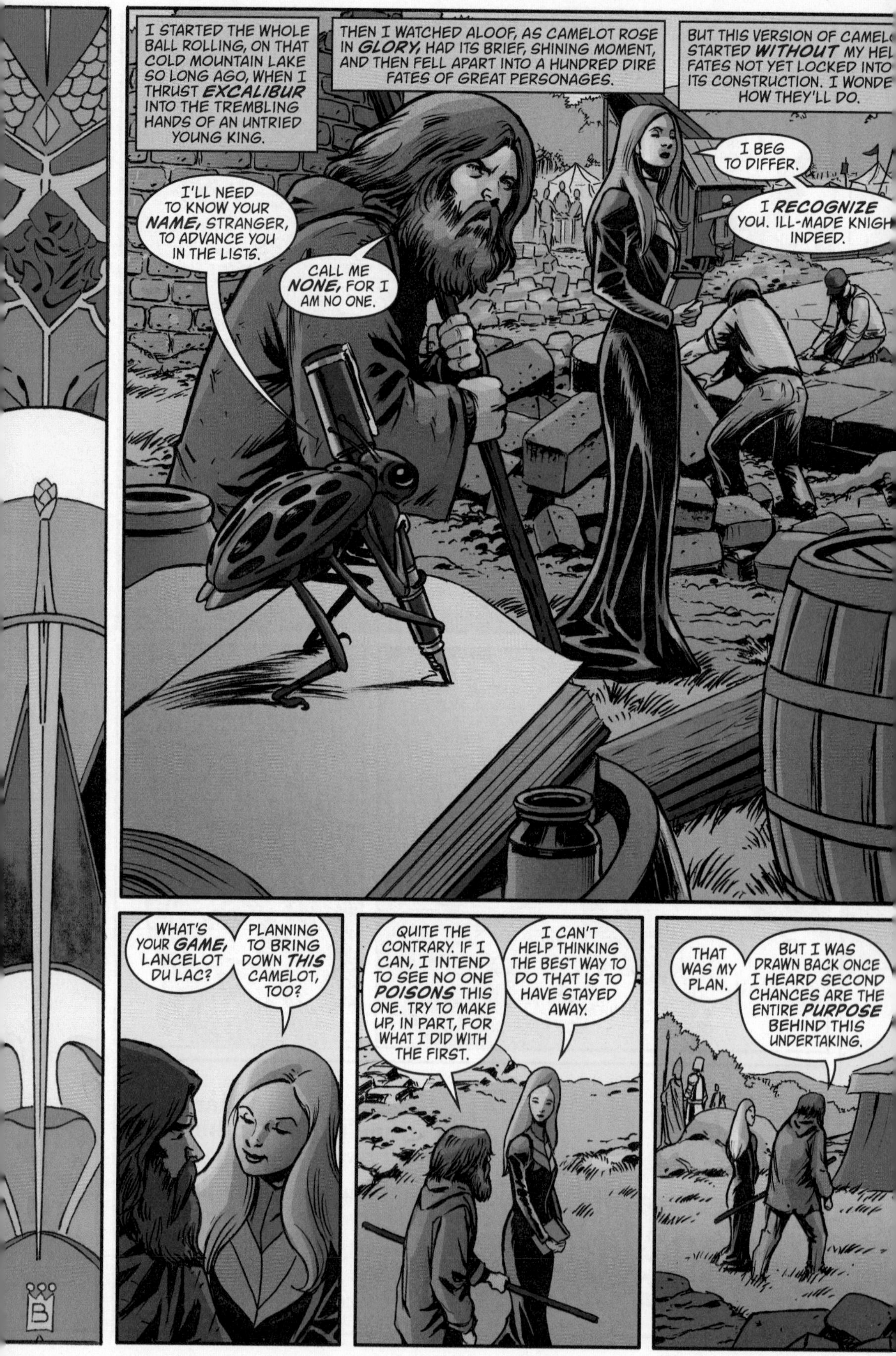
I STARTED THE WHOLE BALL ROLLING, ON THAT COLD MOUNTAIN LAKE SO LONG AGO, WHEN I THRUST EXCALIBUR INTO THE TREMBLING HANDS OF AN UNTRIED YOUNG KING.
THEN I WATCHED ALOOF, AS CAMELOT ROSE IN GLORY, HAD ITS BRIEF, SHINING MOMENT, AND THEN FELL APART INTO A HUNDRED DIRE FATES OF GREAT PERSONAGES.
BUT THIS VERSION OF CAMEL STARTED WITHOUT MY HEL FATES NOT YET LOCKED INTO ITS CONSTRUCTION. I WONDE HOW THEY'LL DO.
I'LL NEED TO KNOW YOUR NAME, STRANGER, TO ADVANCE YOU IN THE LISTS.
CALL ME NONE, FOR I AM NO ONE.
I BEG TO DIFFER.
I RECOGNIZE YOU. ILL-MADE KNIGH INDEED.
WHAT'S YOUR GAME, LANCELOT DU LAC?
PLANNING TO BRING DOWN THIS CAMELOT, TOO?
QUITE THE CONTRARY. IF I CAN, I INTEND TO SEE NO ONE POISONS THIS ONE. TRY TO MAKE UP, IN PART, FOR WHAT I DID WITH THE FIRST.
I CAN'T HELP THINKING THE BEST WAY TO DO THAT IS TO HAVE STAYED AWAY.
THAT WAS MY PLAN.
BUT I WAS DRAWN BACK ONCE I HEARD SECOND CHANCES ARE THE ENTIRE PURPOSE BEHIND THIS UNDERTAKING.

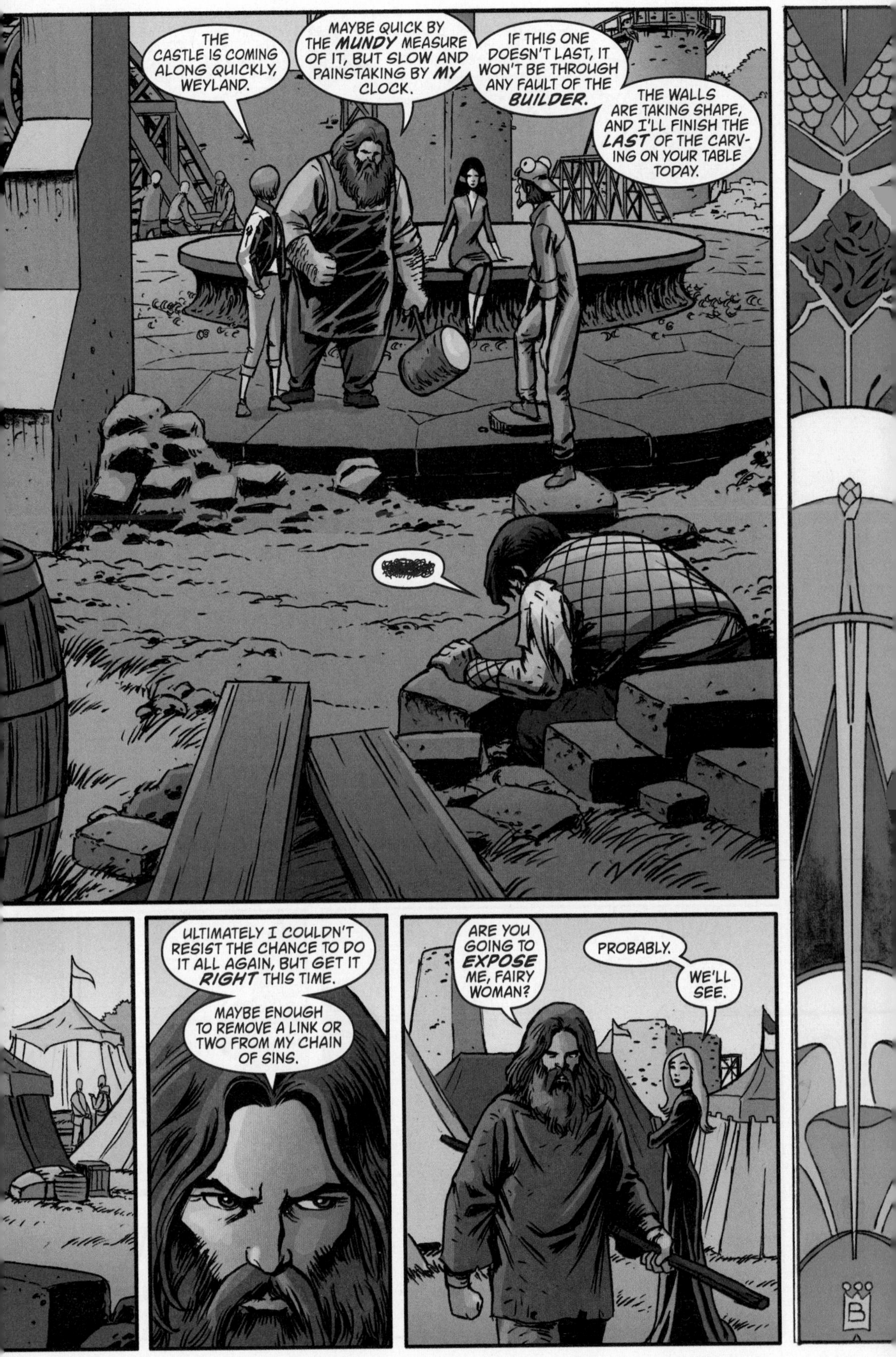
THE CASTLE IS COMING ALONG QUICKLY, WEYLAND.
MAYBE QUICK BY THE MUNDY MEASURE OF IT, BUT SLOW AND PAINSTAKING BY MY CLOCK.
IF THIS ONE DOESN'T LAST, IT WON'T BE THROUGH ANY FAULT OF THE BUILDER.
THE WALLS ARE TAKING SHAPE, AND I'LL FINISH THE LAST OF THE CARVING ON YOUR TABLE TODAY.
ULTIMATELY I COULDN'T RESIST THE CHANCE TO DO IT ALL AGAIN, BUT GET IT RIGHT THIS TIME.
MAYBE ENOUGH TO REMOVE A LINK OR TWO FROM MY CHAIN OF SINS.
ARE YOU GOING TO EXPOSE ME, FAIRY WOMAN?
PROBABLY.
WE'LL SEE.

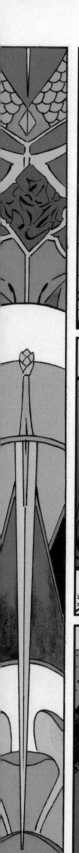

MEAN-WHILE... *THANK* YOU, ALL.

YOU EACH FOUGHT BRAVELY AND COMPETED WITH A VIGOR THAT BRINGS YOU HONOR.

BUT, SADLY, YOU DIDN'T MAKE THE CUT.

YOU WON'T BECOME *KNIGHTS* IN MY NEW ORDER.

HOWEVER, I TRUST YOU'LL CONTINUE TO LIVE AND ACT IN A MANNER *CONSISTENT* WITH OUR GOALS.

FOR NOW, THOUGH, YOU'RE FREE TO RETURN HOME.

UH...

WHO *DID* THAT?

I THINK MAYBE *YOU* DID.

HOW?

146

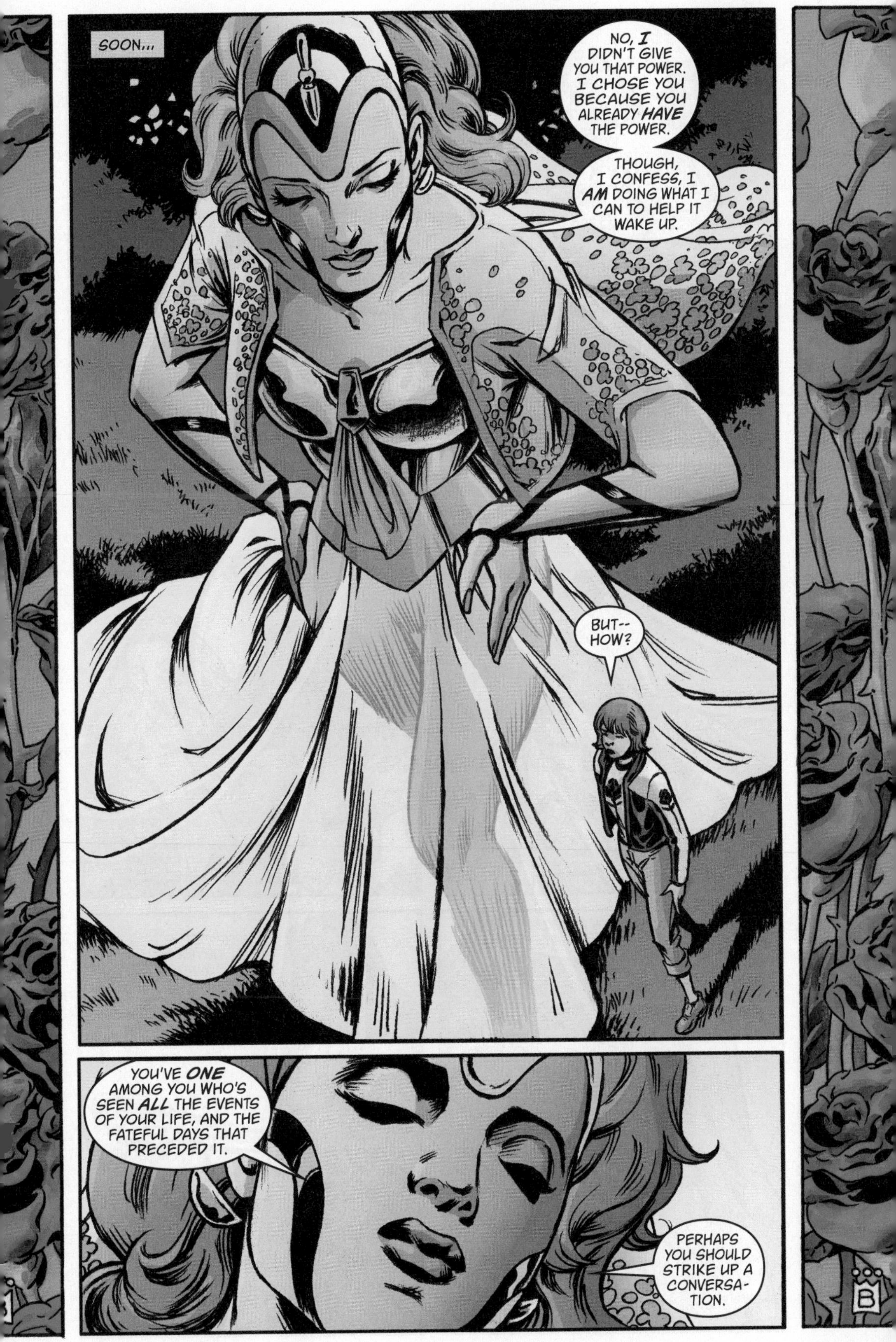

SOON...
NO, I DIDN'T GIVE YOU THAT POWER. I CHOSE YOU BECAUSE YOU ALREADY HAVE THE POWER.
THOUGH, I CONFESS, I AM DOING WHAT I CAN TO HELP IT WAKE UP.
BUT-- HOW?
YOU'VE ONE AMONG YOU WHO'S SEEN ALL THE EVENTS OF YOUR LIFE, AND THE FATEFUL DAYS THAT PRECEDED IT.
PERHAPS YOU SHOULD STRIKE UP A CONVERSA-TION.

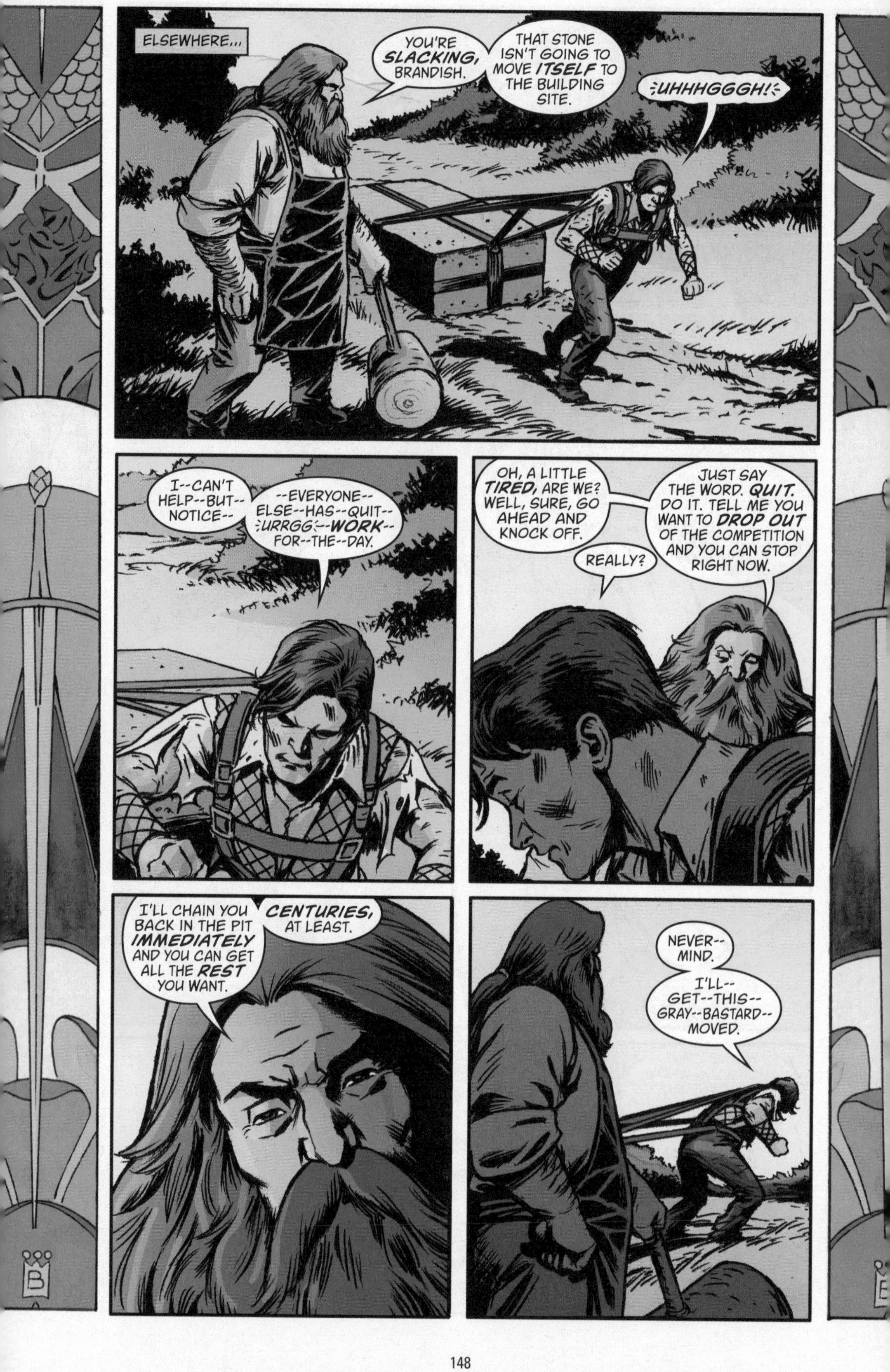
ELSEWHERE...
YOU'RE SLACKING, BRANDISH.
THAT STONE ISN'T GOING TO MOVE ITSELF TO THE BUILDING SITE.
UHHHGGGH!
I--CAN'T HELP--BUT--NOTICE--
--EVERYONE--ELSE--HAS--QUIT--URRGG--WORK--FOR--THE--DAY.
OH, A LITTLE TIRED, ARE WE? WELL, SURE, GO AHEAD AND KNOCK OFF.
REALLY?
JUST SAY THE WORD. QUIT. DO IT. TELL ME YOU WANT TO DROP OUT OF THE COMPETITION AND YOU CAN STOP RIGHT NOW.
I'LL CHAIN YOU BACK IN THE PIT IMMEDIATELY AND YOU CAN GET ALL THE REST YOU WANT.
CENTURIES, AT LEAST.
NEVER--MIND.
I'LL--GET--THIS--GRAY--BASTARD--MOVED.

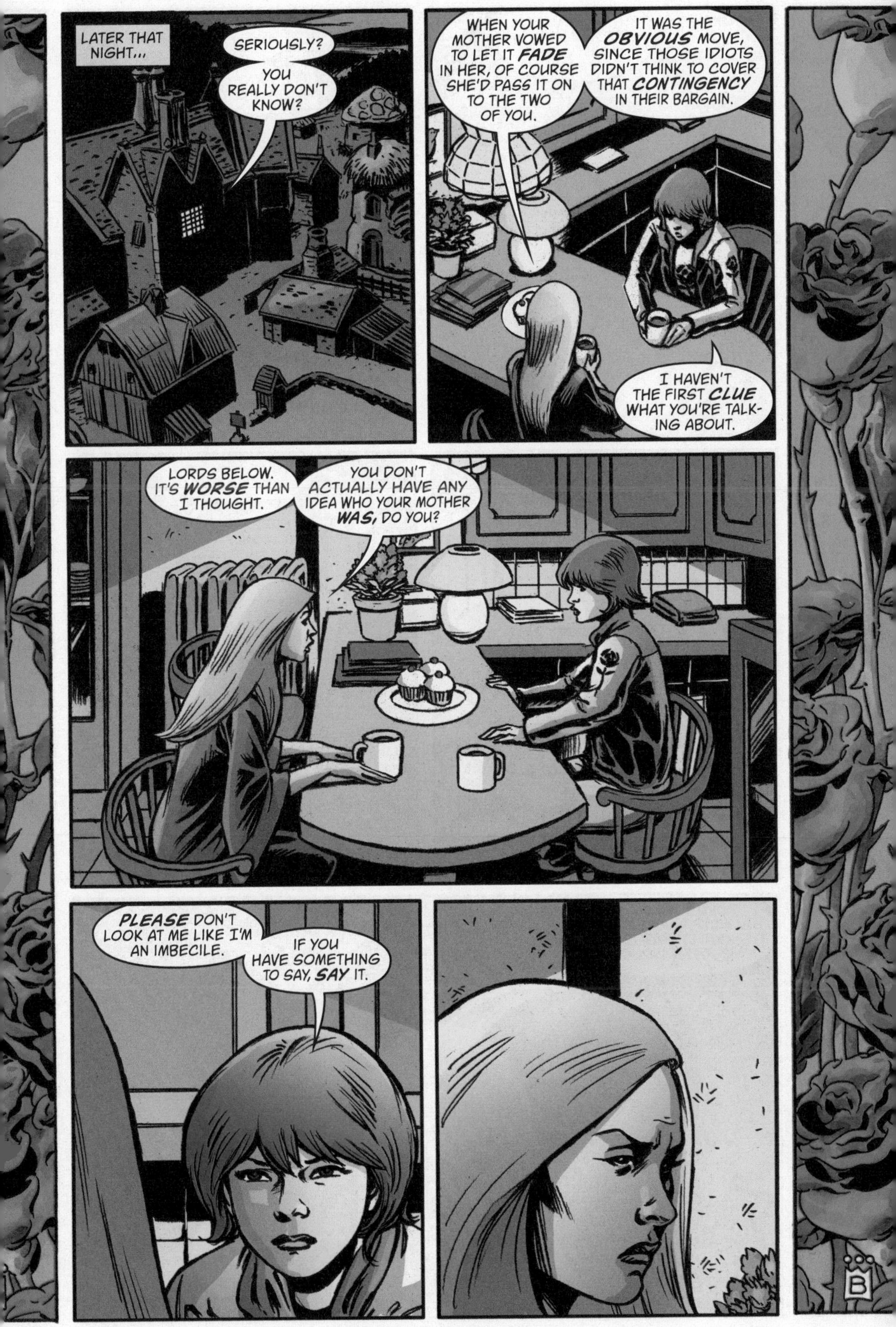
LATER THAT NIGHT...
SERIOUSLY?
YOU REALLY DON'T KNOW?
WHEN YOUR MOTHER VOWED TO LET IT FADE IN HER, OF COURSE SHE'D PASS IT ON TO THE TWO OF YOU.
IT WAS THE OBVIOUS MOVE, SINCE THOSE IDIOTS DIDN'T THINK TO COVER THAT CONTINGENCY IN THEIR BARGAIN.
I HAVEN'T THE FIRST CLUE WHAT YOU'RE TALKING ABOUT.
LORDS BELOW. IT'S WORSE THAN I THOUGHT.
YOU DON'T ACTUALLY HAVE ANY IDEA WHO YOUR MOTHER WAS, DO YOU?
PLEASE DON'T LOOK AT ME LIKE I'M AN IMBECILE.
IF YOU HAVE SOMETHING TO SAY, SAY IT.

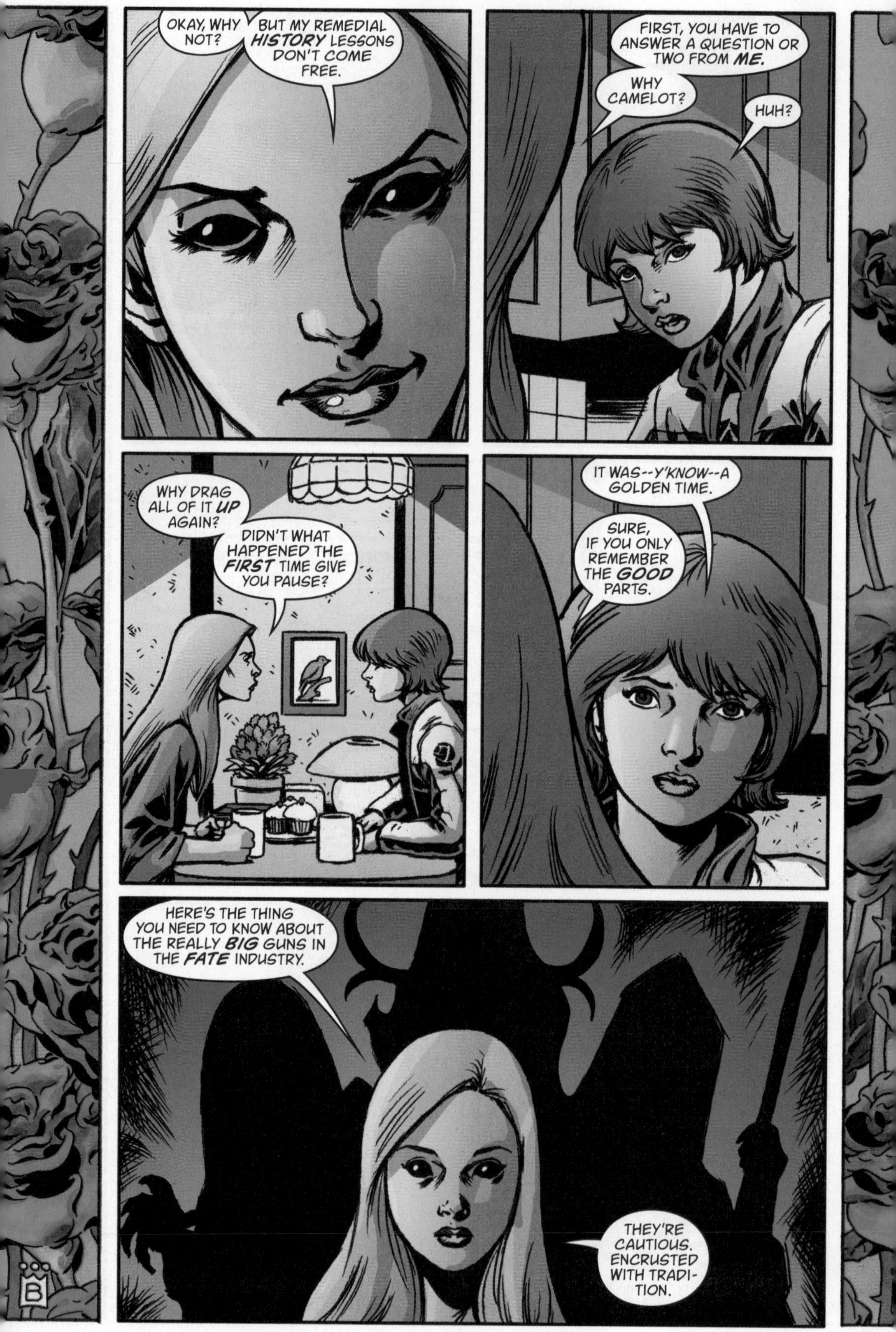

OKAY, WHY NOT?
BUT MY REMEDIAL *HISTORY* LESSONS DON'T COME FREE.
FIRST, YOU HAVE TO ANSWER A QUESTION OR TWO FROM *ME.*
WHY CAMELOT?
HUH?
WHY DRAG ALL OF IT *UP* AGAIN?
DIDN'T WHAT HAPPENED THE *FIRST* TIME GIVE YOU PAUSE?
IT WAS--Y'KNOW--A GOLDEN TIME.
SURE, IF YOU ONLY REMEMBER THE *GOOD* PARTS.
HERE'S THE THING YOU NEED TO KNOW ABOUT THE REALLY *BIG* GUNS IN THE *FATE* INDUSTRY.
THEY'RE CAUTIOUS. ENCRUSTED WITH TRADI-TION.

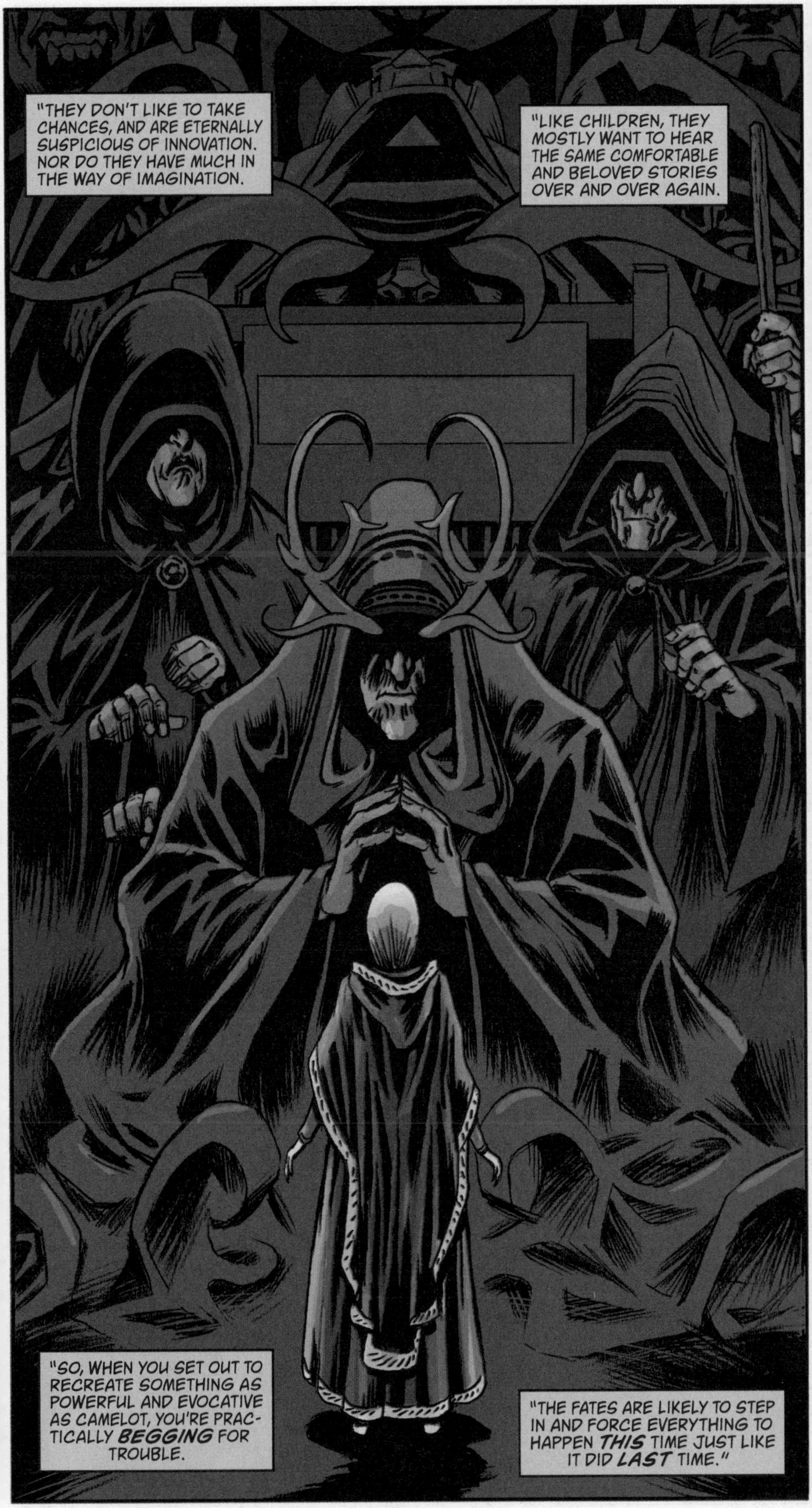
"THEY DON'T LIKE TO TAKE CHANCES, AND ARE ETERNALLY SUSPICIOUS OF INNOVATION. NOR DO THEY HAVE MUCH IN THE WAY OF IMAGINATION.
"LIKE CHILDREN, THEY MOSTLY WANT TO HEAR THE SAME COMFORTABLE AND BELOVED STORIES OVER AND OVER AGAIN.
"SO, WHEN YOU SET OUT TO RECREATE SOMETHING AS POWERFUL AND EVOCATIVE AS CAMELOT, YOU'RE PRACTICALLY BEGGING FOR TROUBLE.
"THE FATES ARE LIKELY TO STEP IN AND FORCE EVERYTHING TO HAPPEN THIS TIME JUST LIKE IT DID LAST TIME."

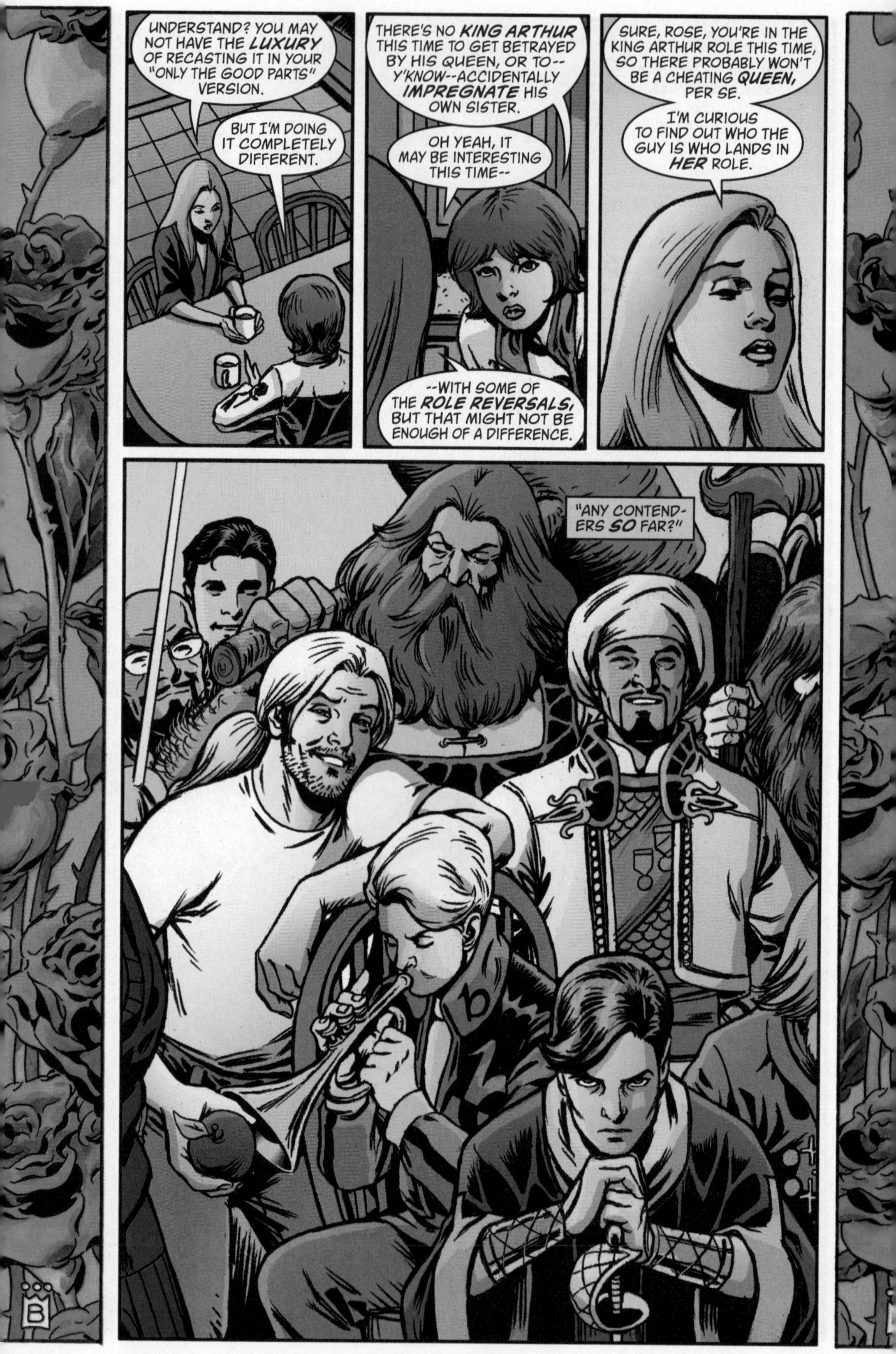

UNDERSTAND? YOU MAY NOT HAVE THE LUXURY OF RECASTING IT IN YOUR "ONLY THE GOOD PARTS" VERSION.
BUT I'M DOING IT COMPLETELY DIFFERENT.
THERE'S NO KING ARTHUR THIS TIME TO GET BETRAYED BY HIS QUEEN, OR TO-- Y'KNOW--ACCIDENTALLY IMPREGNATE HIS OWN SISTER.
OH YEAH, IT MAY BE INTERESTING THIS TIME--
--WITH SOME OF THE ROLE REVERSALS, BUT THAT MIGHT NOT BE ENOUGH OF A DIFFERENCE.
SURE, ROSE, YOU'RE IN THE KING ARTHUR ROLE THIS TIME, SO THERE PROBABLY WON'T BE A CHEATING QUEEN, PER SE.
I'M CURIOUS TO FIND OUT WHO THE GUY IS WHO LANDS IN HER ROLE.
"ANY CONTENDERS SO FAR?"

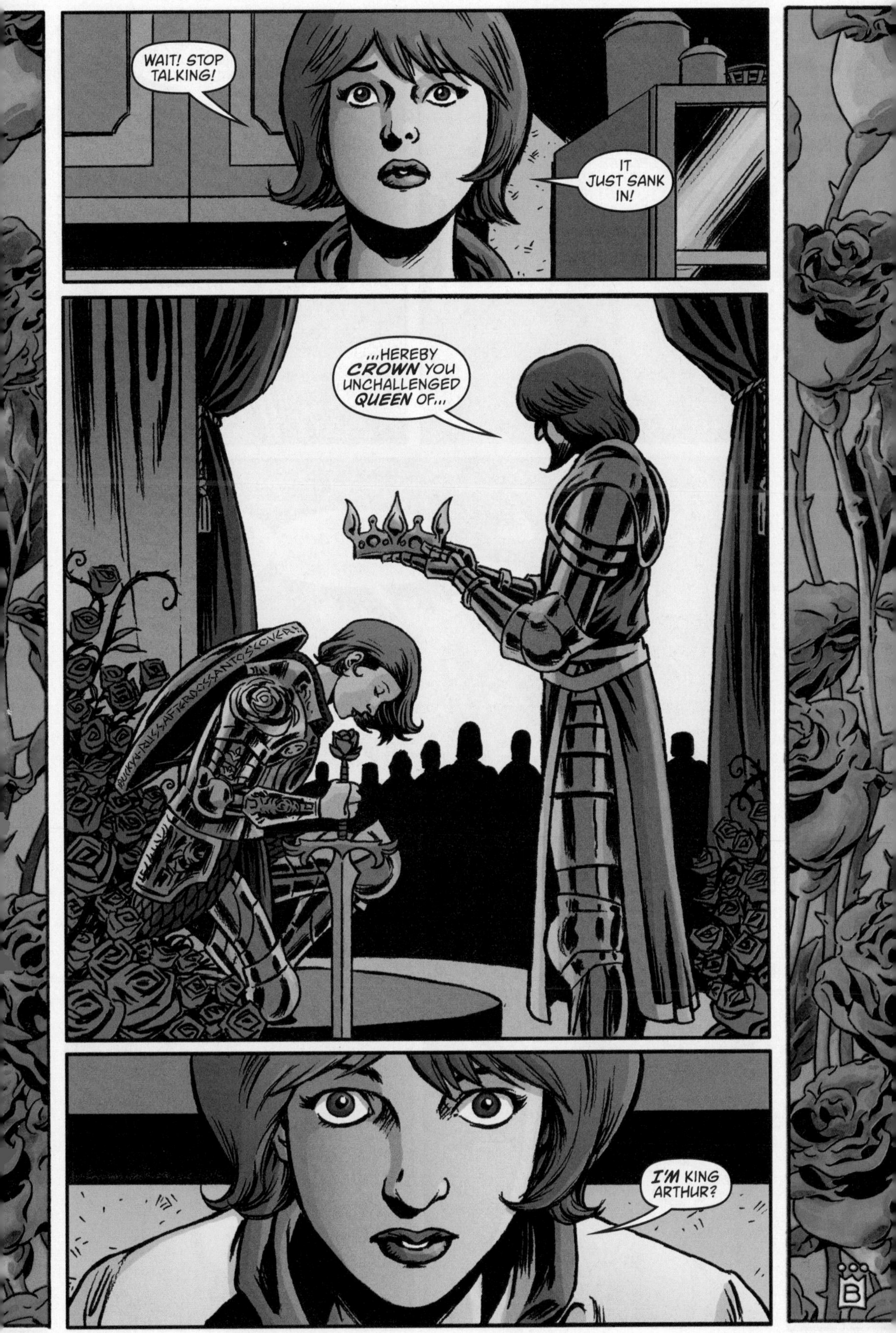
WAIT! STOP TALKING!
IT JUST SANK IN!
...HEREBY **CROWN** YOU UNCHALLENGED **QUEEN** OF...
I'M KING ARTHUR?

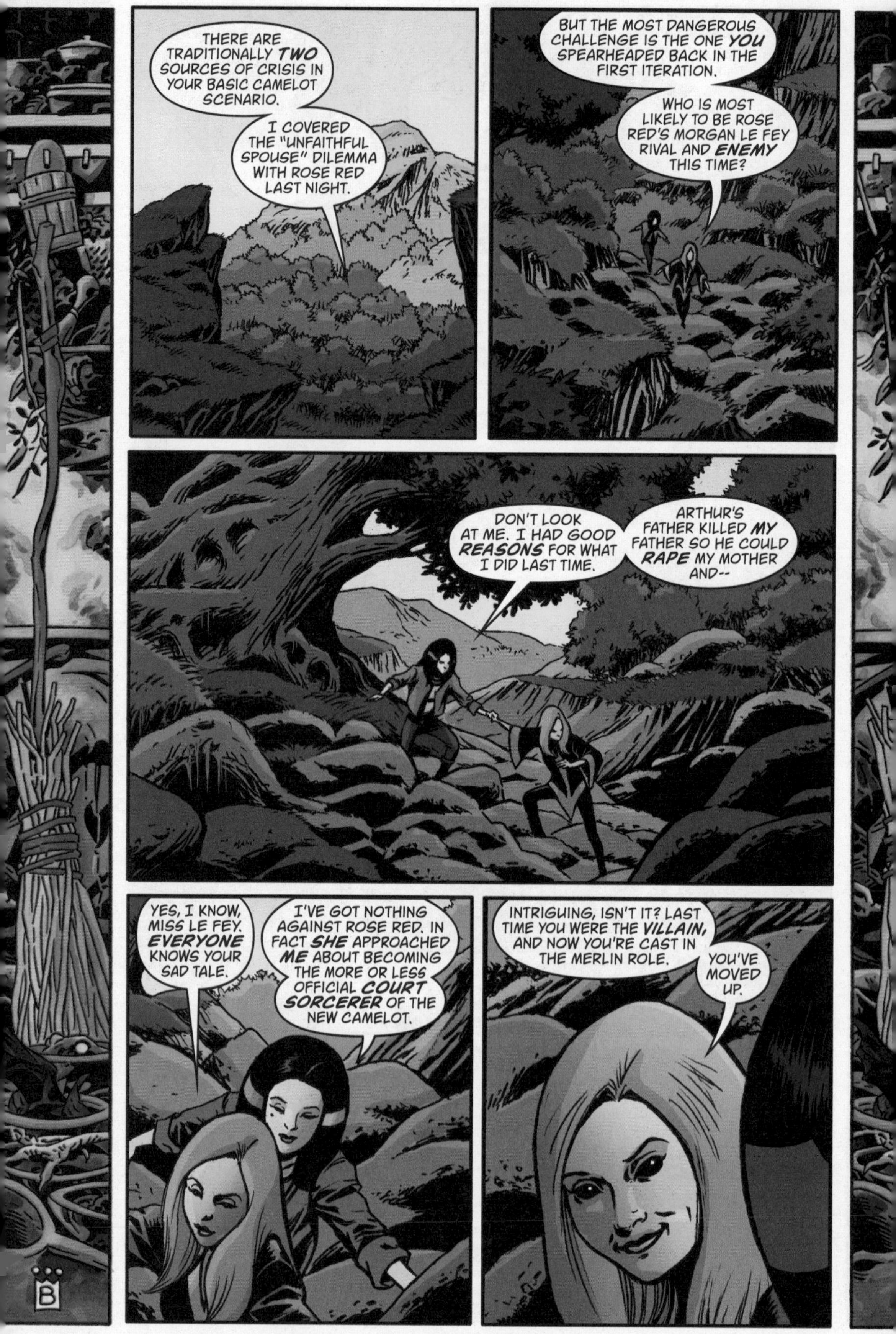

THERE ARE TRADITIONALLY TWO SOURCES OF CRISIS IN YOUR BASIC CAMELOT SCENARIO.
I COVERED THE "UNFAITHFUL SPOUSE" DILEMMA WITH ROSE RED LAST NIGHT.
BUT THE MOST DANGEROUS CHALLENGE IS THE ONE YOU SPEARHEADED BACK IN THE FIRST ITERATION.
WHO IS MOST LIKELY TO BE ROSE RED'S MORGAN LE FEY RIVAL AND ENEMY THIS TIME?
DON'T LOOK AT ME. I HAD GOOD REASONS FOR WHAT I DID LAST TIME.
ARTHUR'S FATHER KILLED MY FATHER SO HE COULD RAPE MY MOTHER AND--
YES, I KNOW, MISS LE FEY. EVERYONE KNOWS YOUR SAD TALE.
I'VE GOT NOTHING AGAINST ROSE RED. IN FACT SHE APPROACHED ME ABOUT BECOMING THE MORE OR LESS OFFICIAL COURT SORCERER OF THE NEW CAMELOT.
INTRIGUING, ISN'T IT? LAST TIME YOU WERE THE VILLAIN, AND NOW YOU'RE CAST IN THE MERLIN ROLE.
YOU'VE MOVED UP.

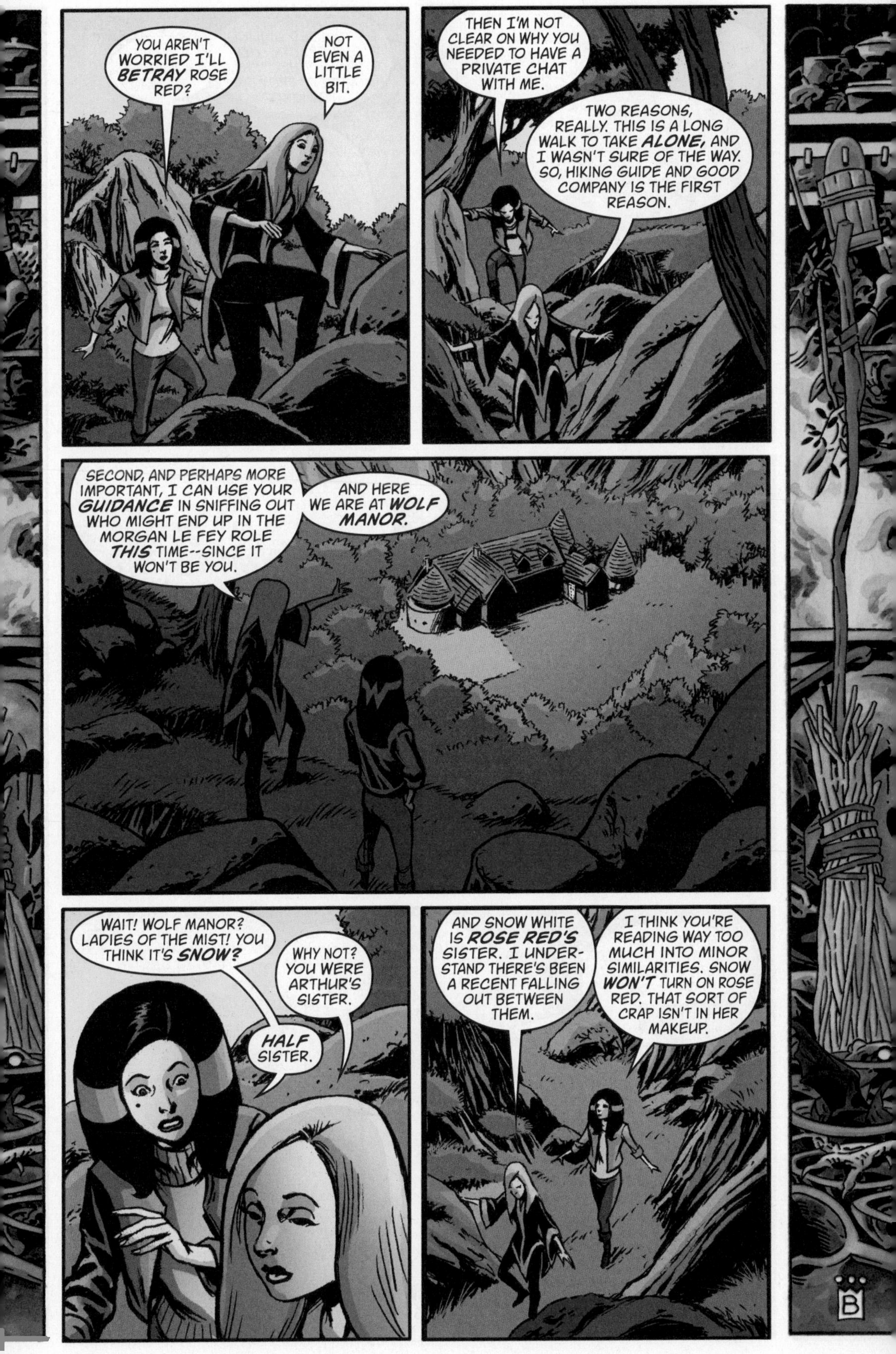
YOU AREN'T WORRIED I'LL BETRAY ROSE RED?
NOT EVEN A LITTLE BIT.
THEN I'M NOT CLEAR ON WHY YOU NEEDED TO HAVE A PRIVATE CHAT WITH ME.
TWO REASONS, REALLY. THIS IS A LONG WALK TO TAKE ALONE, AND I WASN'T SURE OF THE WAY. SO, HIKING GUIDE AND GOOD COMPANY IS THE FIRST REASON.
SECOND, AND PERHAPS MORE IMPORTANT, I CAN USE YOUR GUIDANCE IN SNIFFING OUT WHO MIGHT END UP IN THE MORGAN LE FEY ROLE THIS TIME--SINCE IT WON'T BE YOU.
AND HERE WE ARE AT WOLF MANOR.
WAIT! WOLF MANOR? LADIES OF THE MIST! YOU THINK IT'S SNOW?
WHY NOT? YOU WERE ARTHUR'S SISTER.
HALF SISTER.
AND SNOW WHITE IS ROSE RED'S SISTER. I UNDERSTAND THERE'S BEEN A RECENT FALLING OUT BETWEEN THEM.
I THINK YOU'RE READING WAY TOO MUCH INTO MINOR SIMILARITIES. SNOW WON'T TURN ON ROSE RED. THAT SORT OF CRAP ISN'T IN HER MAKEUP.

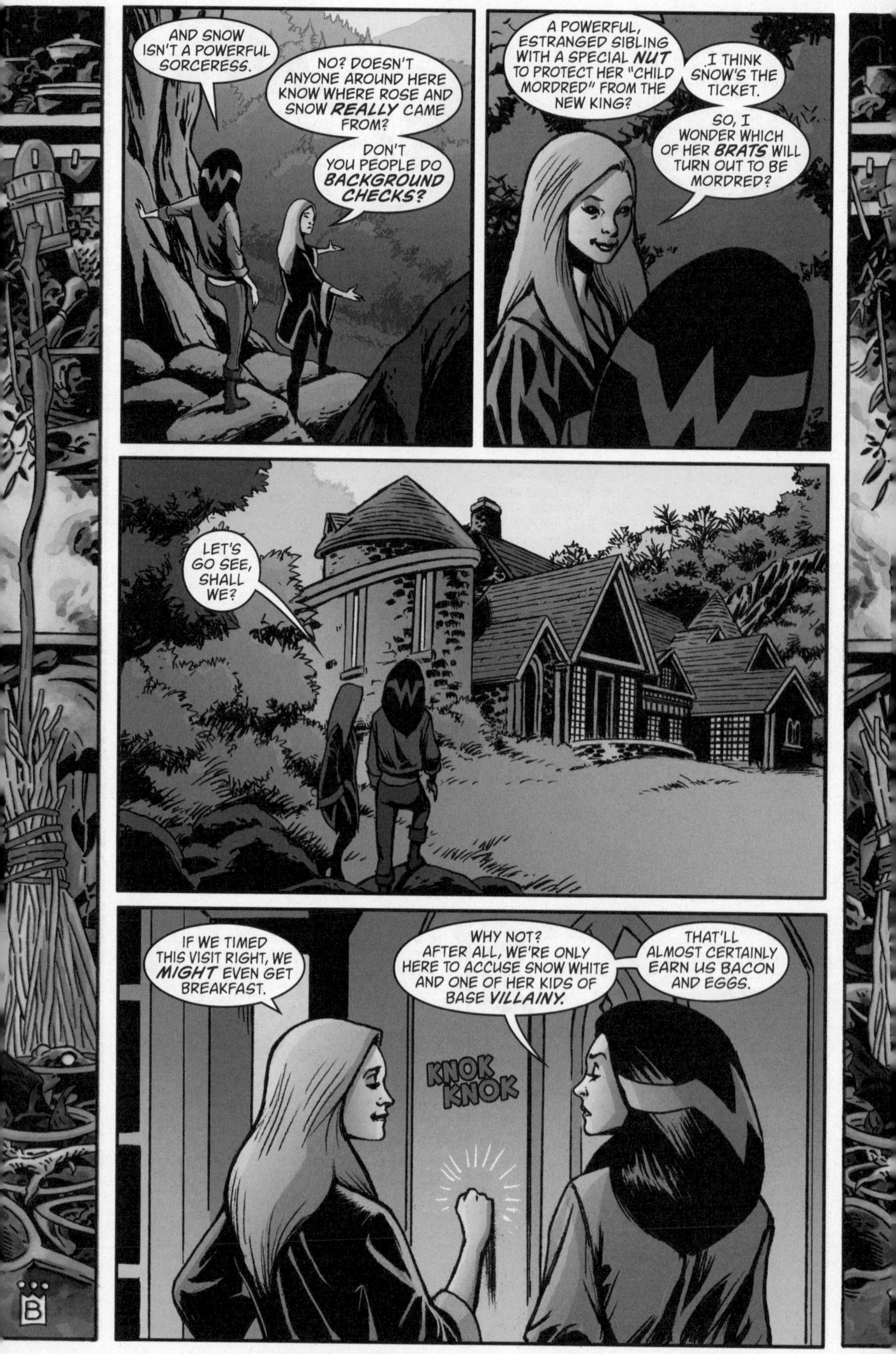
AND SNOW ISN'T A POWERFUL SORCERESS.
NO? DOESN'T ANYONE AROUND HERE KNOW WHERE ROSE AND SNOW REALLY CAME FROM?
DON'T YOU PEOPLE DO BACKGROUND CHECKS?
A POWERFUL, ESTRANGED SIBLING WITH A SPECIAL NUT TO PROTECT HER "CHILD MORDRED" FROM THE NEW KING?
I THINK SNOW'S THE TICKET.
SO, I WONDER WHICH OF HER BRATS WILL TURN OUT TO BE MORDRED?
LET'S GO SEE, SHALL WE?
IF WE TIMED THIS VISIT RIGHT, WE MIGHT EVEN GET BREAKFAST.
WHY NOT? AFTER ALL, WE'RE ONLY HERE TO ACCUSE SNOW WHITE AND ONE OF HER KIDS OF BASE VILLAINY.
THAT'LL ALMOST CERTAINLY EARN US BACON AND EGGS.
KNOK KNOK

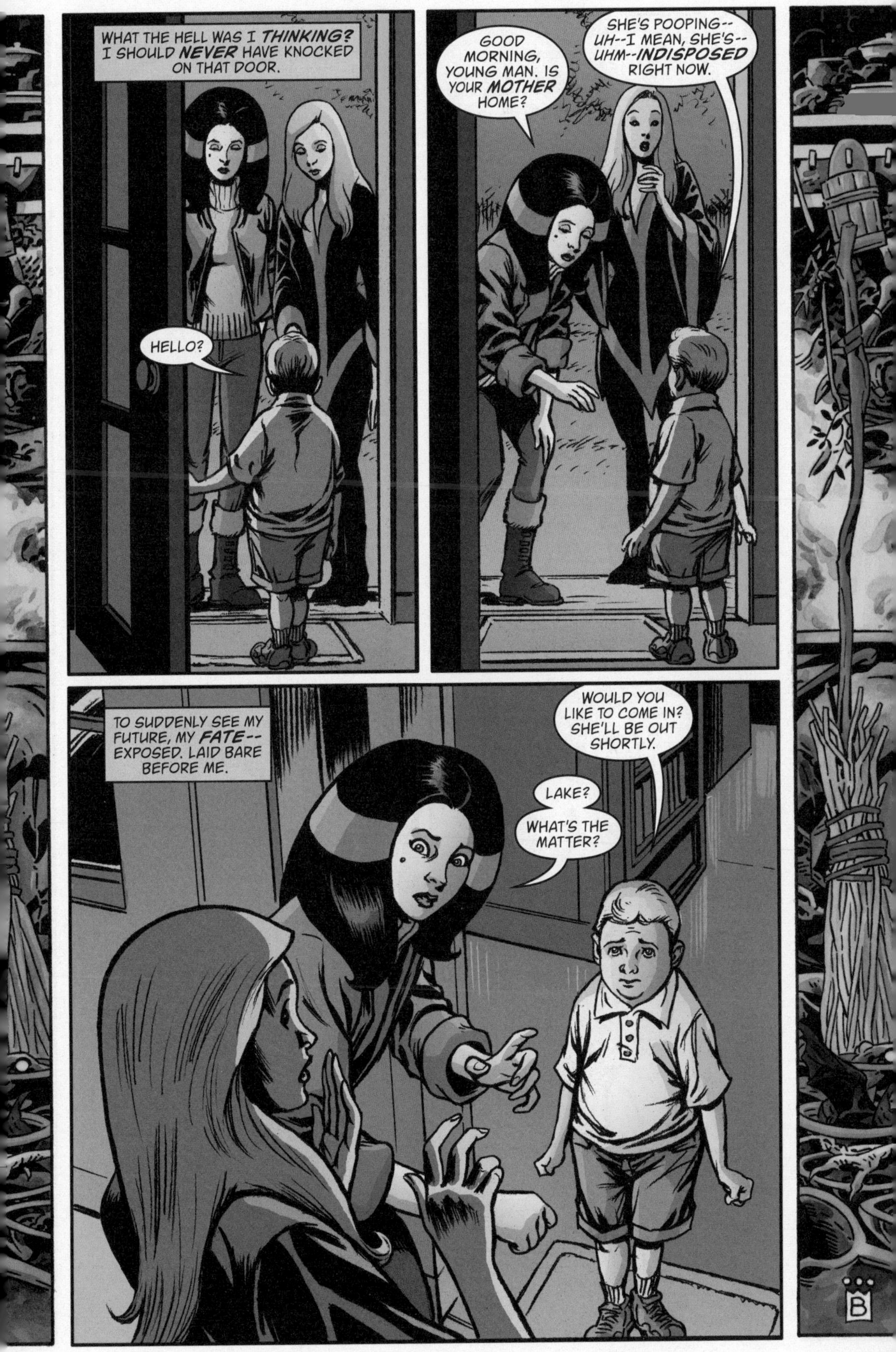
WHAT THE HELL WAS I THINKING? I SHOULD NEVER HAVE KNOCKED ON THAT DOOR.
HELLO?
GOOD MORNING, YOUNG MAN. IS YOUR MOTHER HOME?
SHE'S POOPING-- UH--I MEAN, SHE'S-- UHM--INDISPOSED RIGHT NOW.
TO SUDDENLY SEE MY FUTURE, MY FATE-- EXPOSED. LAID BARE BEFORE ME.
WOULD YOU LIKE TO COME IN? SHE'LL BE OUT SHORTLY.
LAKE?
WHAT'S THE MATTER?

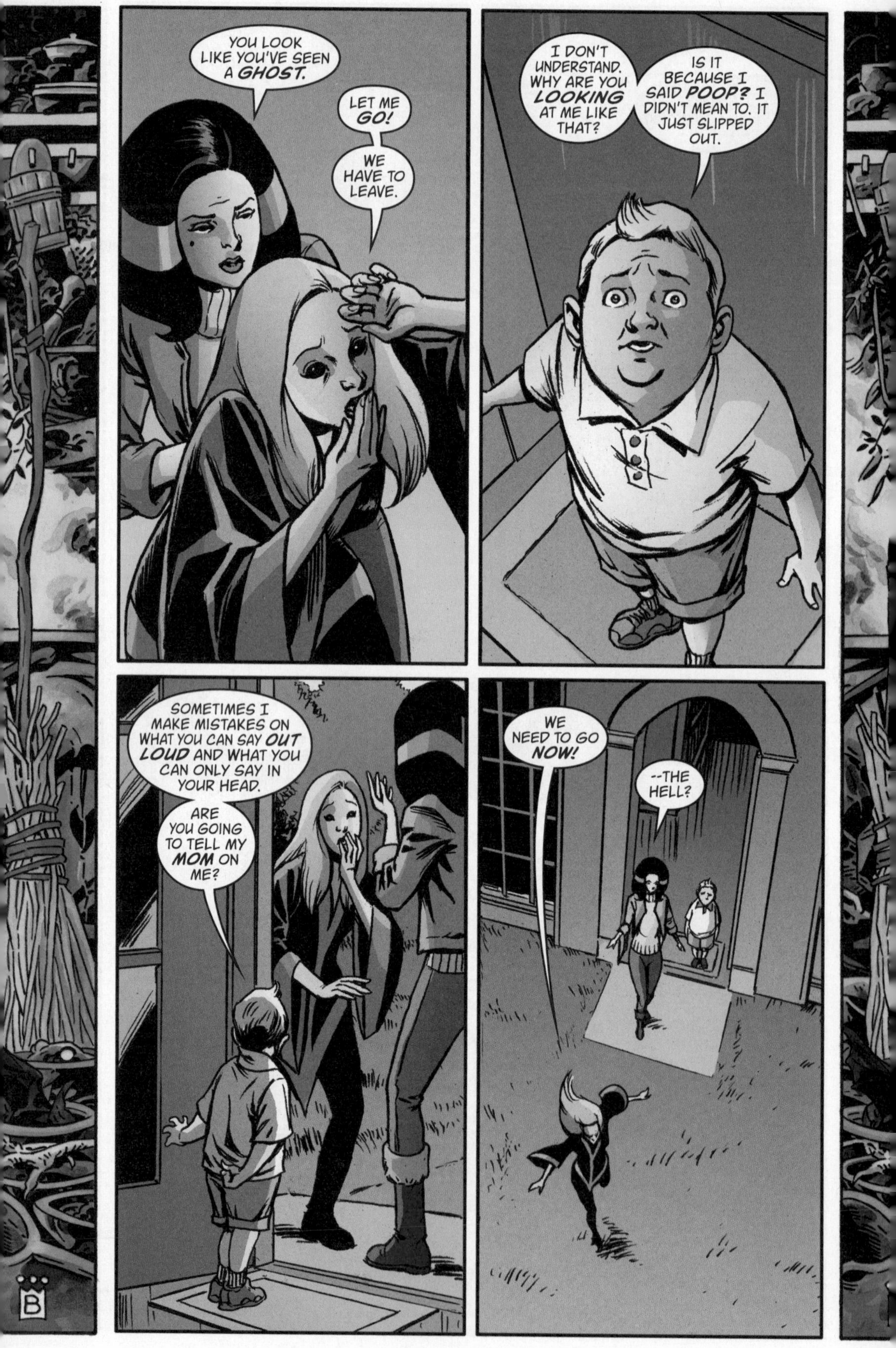
YOU LOOK LIKE YOU'VE SEEN A GHOST.
LET ME GO!
WE HAVE TO LEAVE.
I DON'T UNDERSTAND. WHY ARE YOU LOOKING AT ME LIKE THAT?
IS IT BECAUSE I SAID POOP? I DIDN'T MEAN TO. IT JUST SLIPPED OUT.
SOMETIMES I MAKE MISTAKES ON WHAT YOU CAN SAY OUT LOUD AND WHAT YOU CAN ONLY SAY IN YOUR HEAD.
ARE YOU GOING TO TELL MY MOM ON ME?
WE NEED TO GO NOW!
--THE HELL?

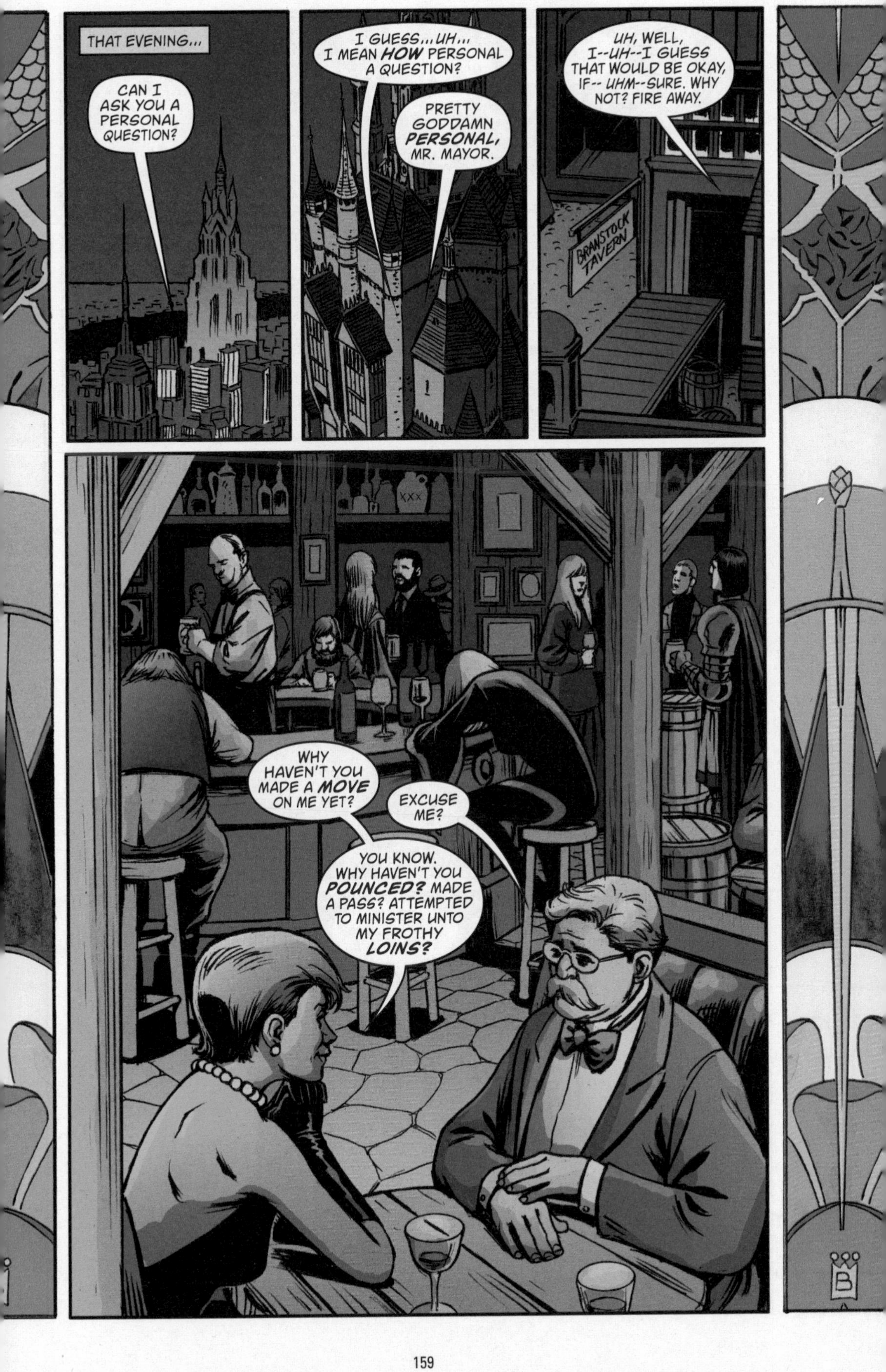

THAT EVENING...
CAN I ASK YOU A PERSONAL QUESTION?
I GUESS... UH... I MEAN HOW PERSONAL A QUESTION?
PRETTY GODDAMN PERSONAL, MR. MAYOR.
UH, WELL, I--UH--I GUESS THAT WOULD BE OKAY, IF-- UHM--SURE. WHY NOT? FIRE AWAY.
BRANSTOCK TAVERN
WHY HAVEN'T YOU MADE A MOVE ON ME YET?
EXCUSE ME?
YOU KNOW. WHY HAVEN'T YOU POUNCED? MADE A PASS? ATTEMPTED TO MINISTER UNTO MY FROTHY LOINS?

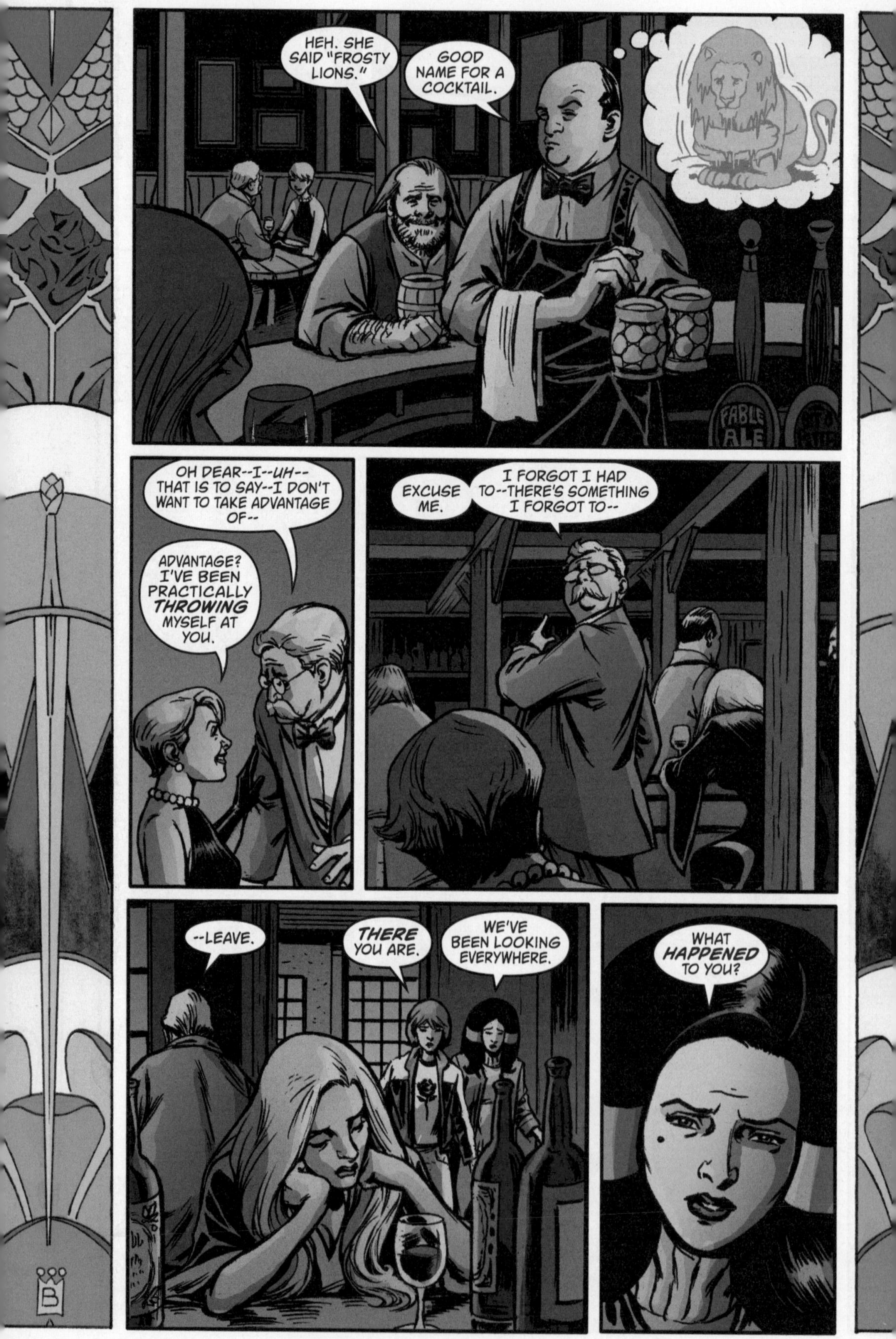
HEH. SHE SAID "FROSTY LIONS."
GOOD NAME FOR A COCKTAIL.
FABLE ALE
OH DEAR--I--UH--THAT IS TO SAY--I DON'T WANT TO TAKE ADVANTAGE OF--
ADVANTAGE? I'VE BEEN PRACTICALLY THROWING MYSELF AT YOU.
EXCUSE ME.
I FORGOT I HAD TO--THERE'S SOMETHING I FORGOT TO--
--LEAVE.
THERE YOU ARE.
WE'VE BEEN LOOKING EVERYWHERE.
WHAT HAPPENED TO YOU?

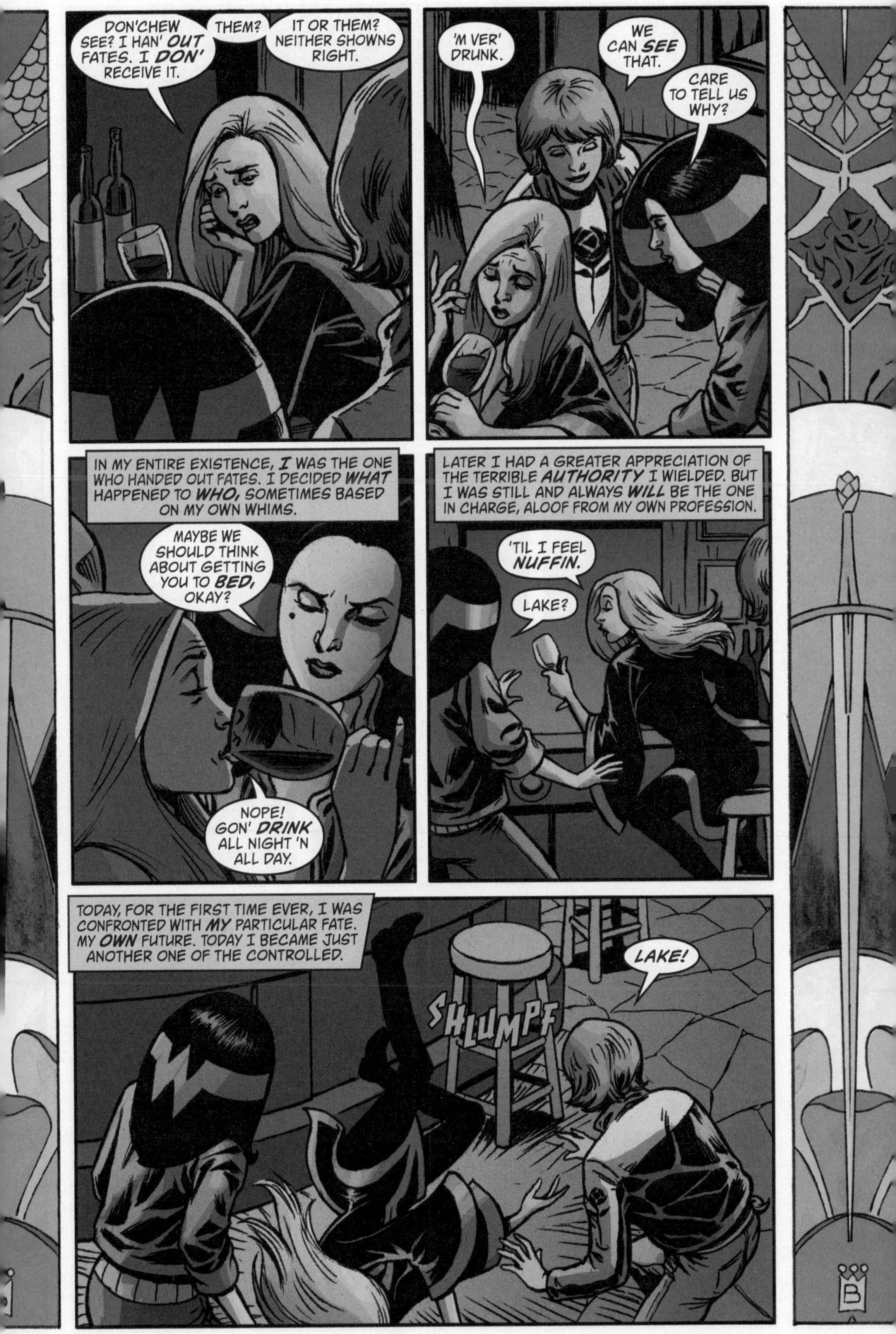

DON'CHEW SEE? I HAN' OUT FATES. I DON' RECEIVE IT.
THEM?
IT OR THEM? NEITHER SHOWNS RIGHT.
'M VER' DRUNK.
WE CAN SEE THAT.
CARE TO TELL US WHY?
IN MY ENTIRE EXISTENCE, I WAS THE ONE WHO HANDED OUT FATES. I DECIDED WHAT HAPPENED TO WHO, SOMETIMES BASED ON MY OWN WHIMS.
MAYBE WE SHOULD THINK ABOUT GETTING YOU TO BED, OKAY?
NOPE! GON' DRINK ALL NIGHT 'N ALL DAY.
LATER I HAD A GREATER APPRECIATION OF THE TERRIBLE AUTHORITY I WIELDED. BUT I WAS STILL AND ALWAYS WILL BE THE ONE IN CHARGE, ALOOF FROM MY OWN PROFESSION.
'TIL I FEEL NUFFIN.
LAKE?
TODAY, FOR THE FIRST TIME EVER, I WAS CONFRONTED WITH MY PARTICULAR FATE. MY OWN FUTURE. TODAY I BECAME JUST ANOTHER ONE OF THE CONTROLLED.
LAKE!
SHLUMPF

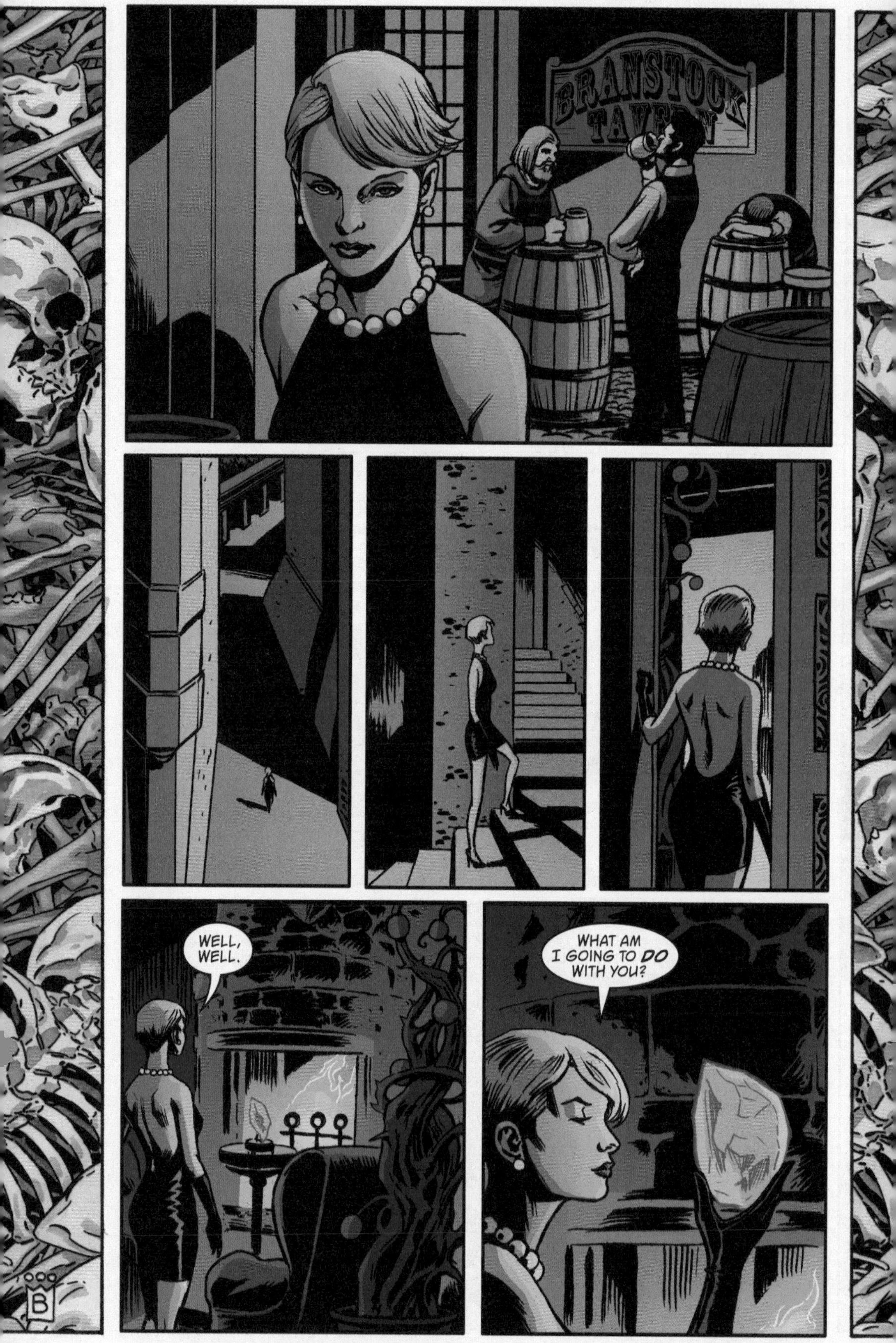
BRANSTOCK TAVERN
WELL, WELL.
WHAT AM I GOING TO *DO* WITH YOU?

NEXT: WHAT SHE DOES.

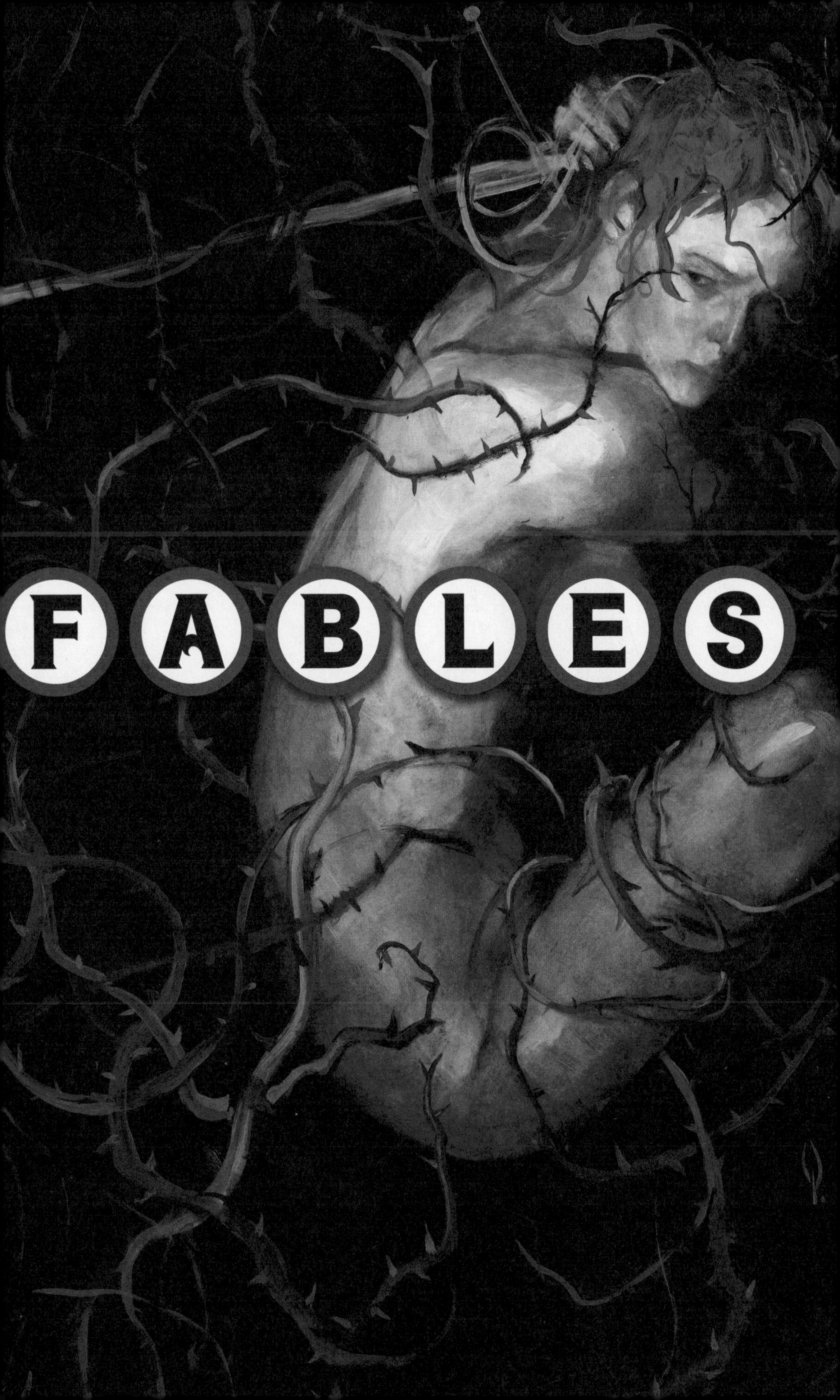
FABLES

"Magic isn't really alive. Not exactly. But it yearns."

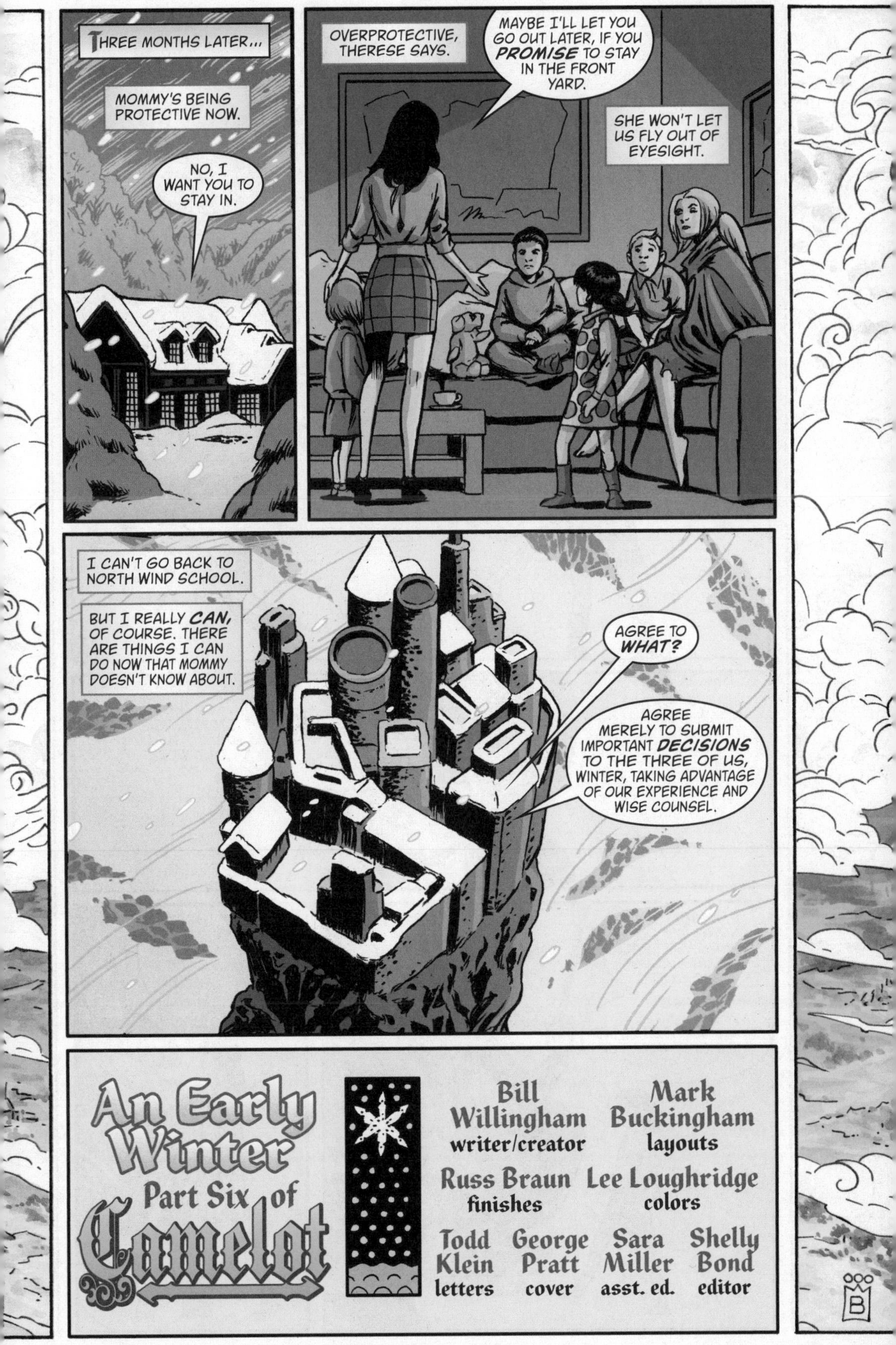
THREE MONTHS LATER...
MOMMY'S BEING PROTECTIVE NOW.
NO, I WANT YOU TO STAY IN.
OVERPROTECTIVE, THERESE SAYS.
MAYBE I'LL LET YOU GO OUT LATER, IF YOU PROMISE TO STAY IN THE FRONT YARD.
SHE WON'T LET US FLY OUT OF EYESIGHT.
I CAN'T GO BACK TO NORTH WIND SCHOOL.
BUT I REALLY CAN, OF COURSE. THERE ARE THINGS I CAN DO NOW THAT MOMMY DOESN'T KNOW ABOUT.
AGREE TO WHAT?
AGREE MERELY TO SUBMIT IMPORTANT DECISIONS TO THE THREE OF US, WINTER, TAKING ADVANTAGE OF OUR EXPERIENCE AND WISE COUNSEL.
An Early Winter
Part Six of Camelot
Bill Willingham writer/creator
Mark Buckingham layouts
Russ Braun finishes
Lee Loughridge colors
Todd Klein letters
George Pratt cover
Sara Miller asst. ed.
Shelly Bond editor

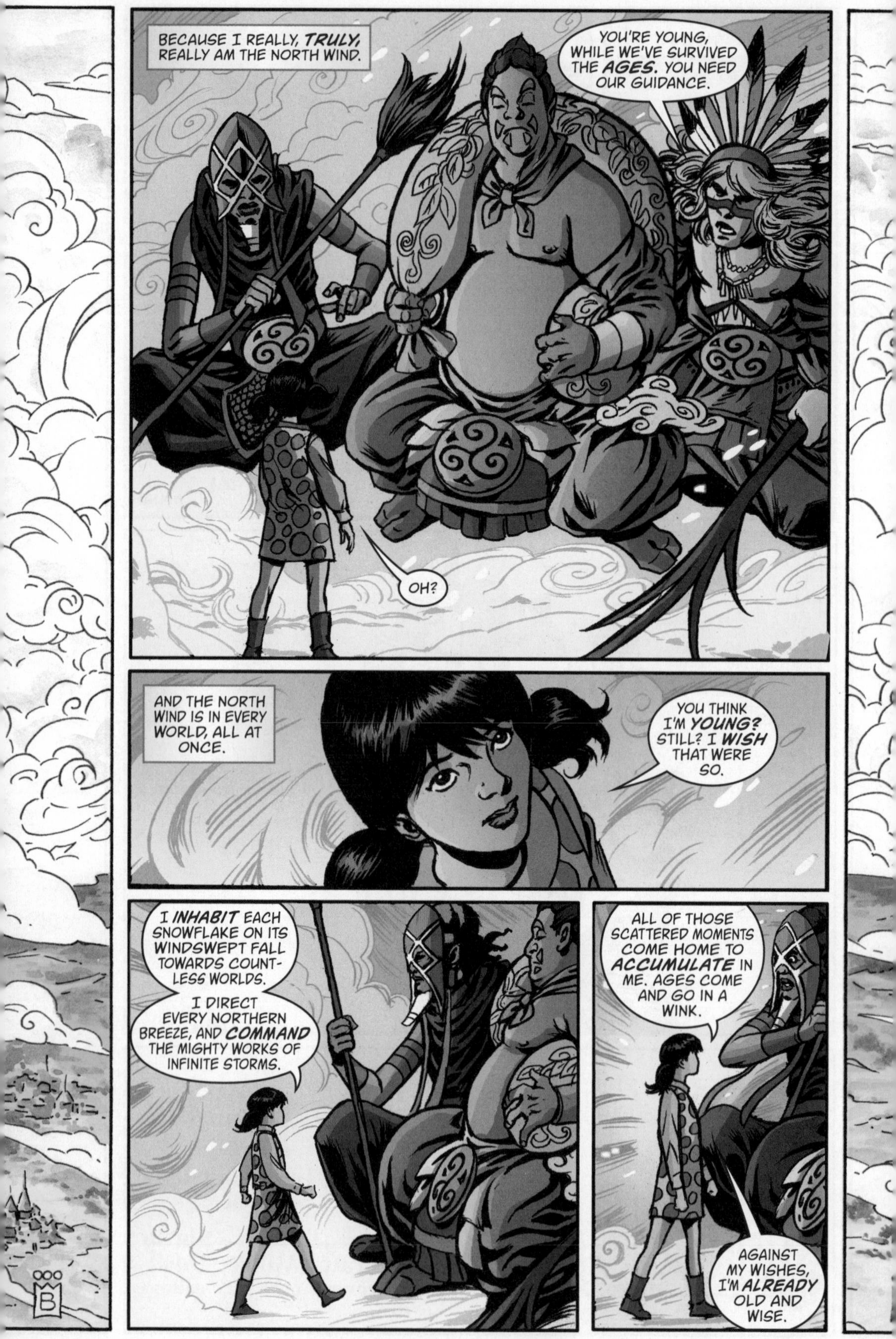

BECAUSE I REALLY, TRULY, REALLY AM THE NORTH WIND.
YOU'RE YOUNG, WHILE WE'VE SURVIVED THE AGES. YOU NEED OUR GUIDANCE.
OH?
AND THE NORTH WIND IS IN EVERY WORLD, ALL AT ONCE.
YOU THINK I'M YOUNG? STILL? I WISH THAT WERE SO.
I INHABIT EACH SNOWFLAKE ON ITS WINDSWEPT FALL TOWARDS COUNT-LESS WORLDS.
I DIRECT EVERY NORTHERN BREEZE, AND COMMAND THE MIGHTY WORKS OF INFINITE STORMS.
ALL OF THOSE SCATTERED MOMENTS COME HOME TO ACCUMULATE IN ME. AGES COME AND GO IN A WINK.
AGAINST MY WISHES, I'M ALREADY OLD AND WISE.

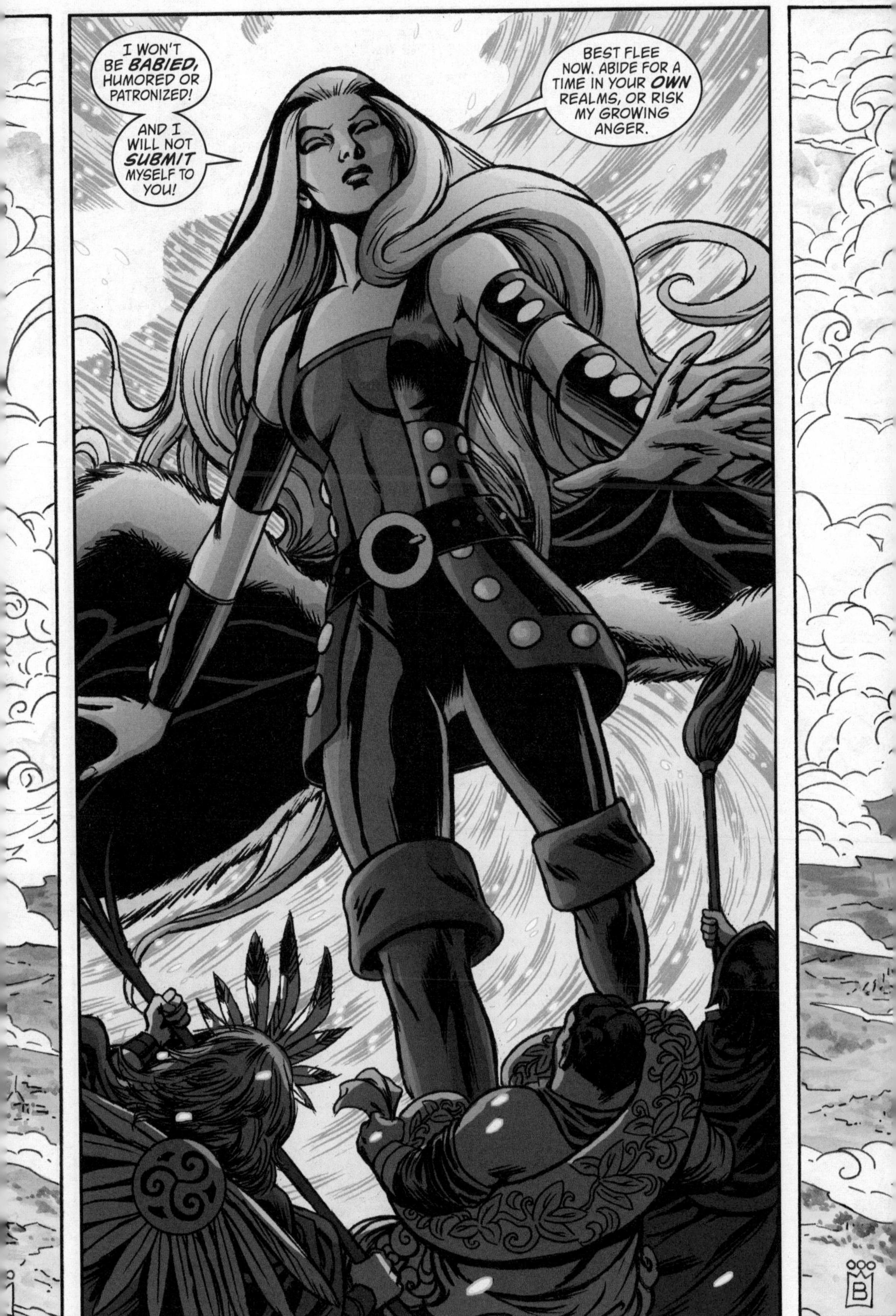
I WON'T BE BABIED, HUMORED OR PATRONIZED!
AND I WILL NOT SUBMIT MYSELF TO YOU!
BEST FLEE NOW. ABIDE FOR A TIME IN YOUR OWN REALMS, OR RISK MY GROWING ANGER.

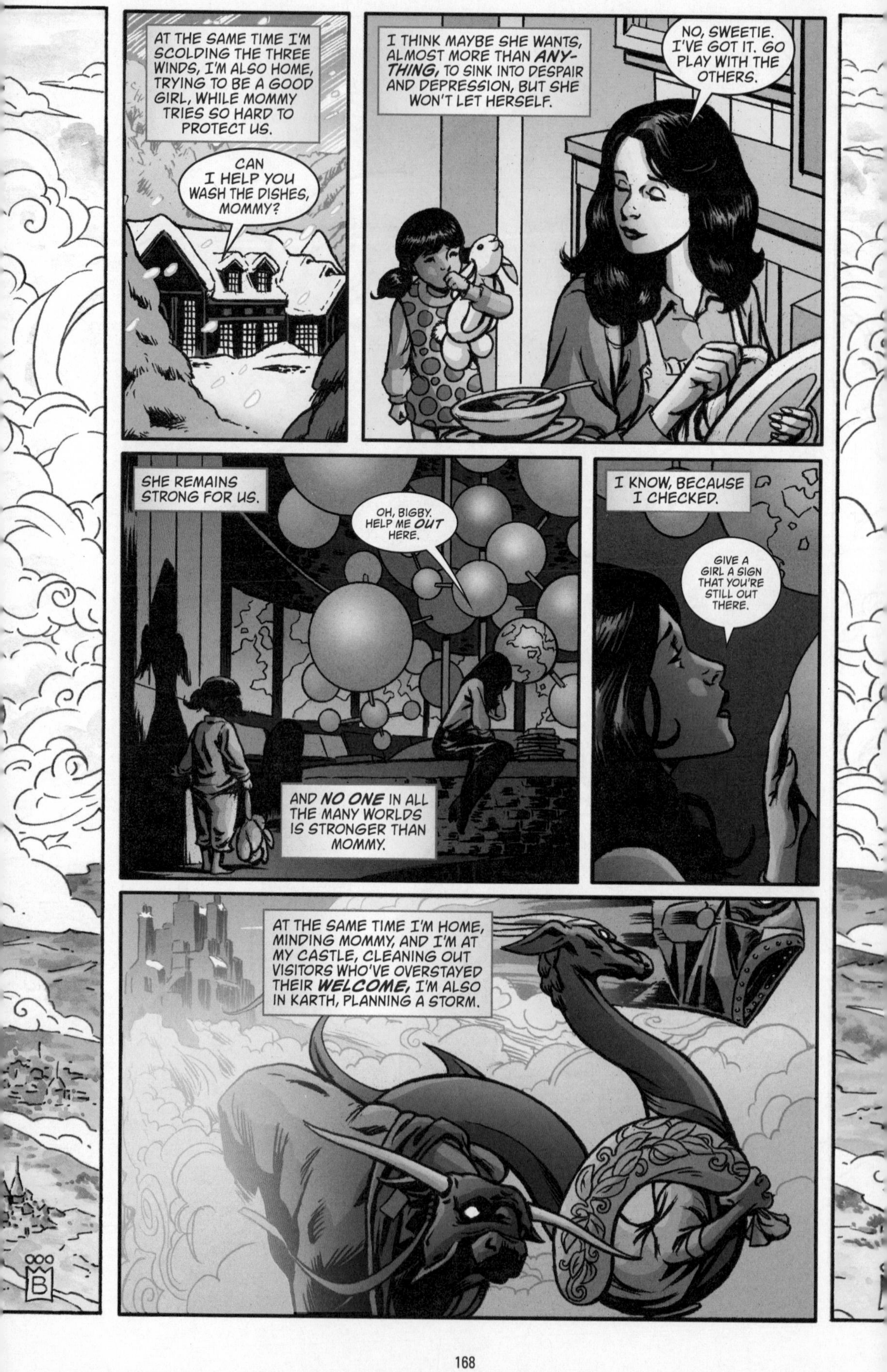
AT THE SAME TIME I'M SCOLDING THE THREE WINDS, I'M ALSO HOME, TRYING TO BE A GOOD GIRL, WHILE MOMMY TRIES SO HARD TO PROTECT US.
CAN I HELP YOU WASH THE DISHES, MOMMY?
I THINK MAYBE SHE WANTS, ALMOST MORE THAN ANY-THING, TO SINK INTO DESPAIR AND DEPRESSION, BUT SHE WON'T LET HERSELF.
NO, SWEETIE. I'VE GOT IT. GO PLAY WITH THE OTHERS.
SHE REMAINS STRONG FOR US.
OH, BIGBY. HELP ME OUT HERE.
AND NO ONE IN ALL THE MANY WORLDS IS STRONGER THAN MOMMY.
I KNOW, BECAUSE I CHECKED.
GIVE A GIRL A SIGN THAT YOU'RE STILL OUT THERE.
AT THE SAME TIME I'M HOME, MINDING MOMMY, AND I'M AT MY CASTLE, CLEANING OUT VISITORS WHO'VE OVERSTAYED THEIR WELCOME, I'M ALSO IN KARTH, PLANNING A STORM.

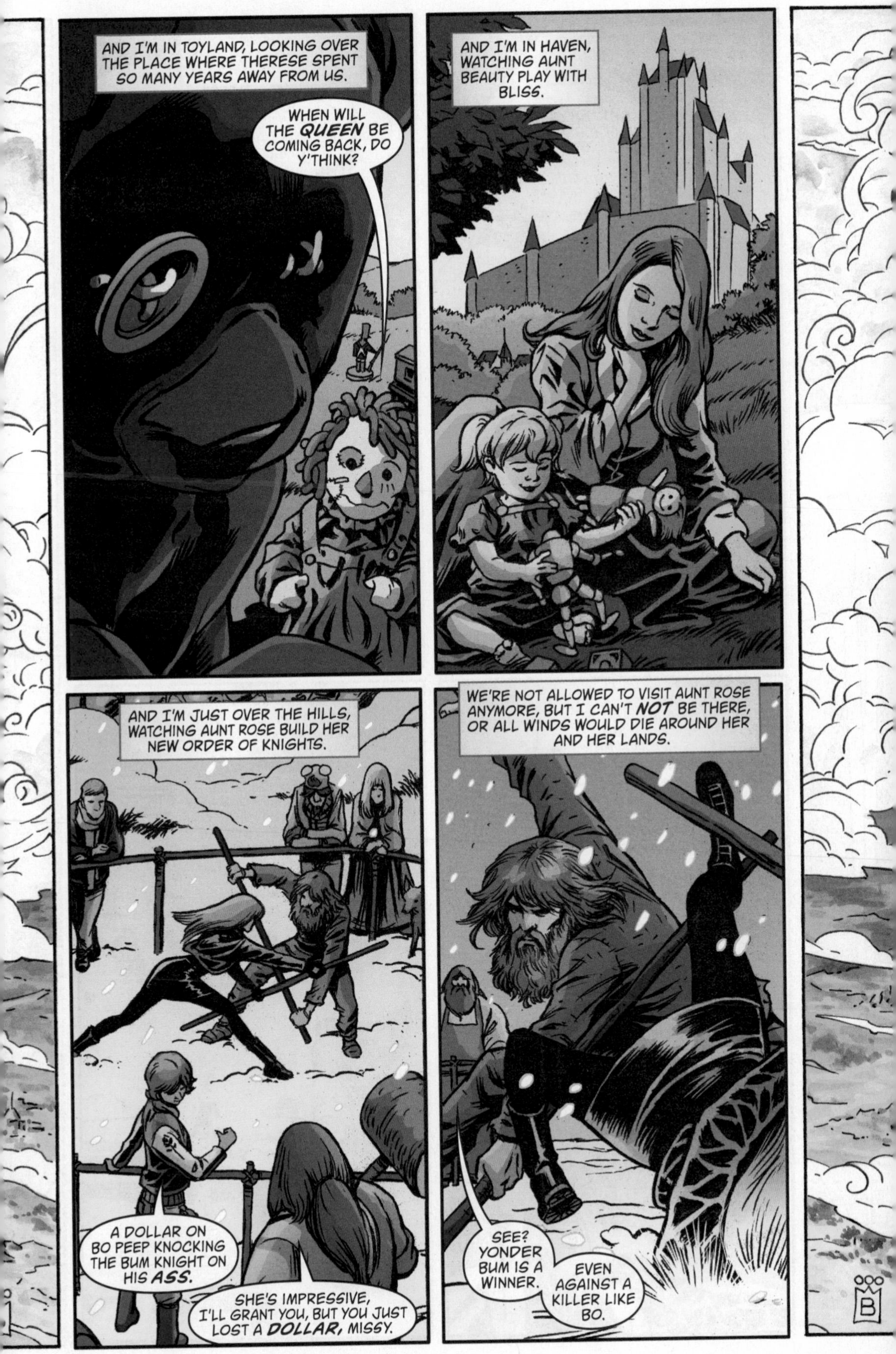
AND I'M IN TOYLAND, LOOKING OVER THE PLACE WHERE THERESE SPENT SO MANY YEARS AWAY FROM US.
WHEN WILL THE QUEEN BE COMING BACK, DO Y'THINK?
AND I'M IN HAVEN, WATCHING AUNT BEAUTY PLAY WITH BLISS.
AND I'M JUST OVER THE HILLS, WATCHING AUNT ROSE BUILD HER NEW ORDER OF KNIGHTS.
A DOLLAR ON BO PEEP KNOCKING THE BUM KNIGHT ON HIS ASS.
SHE'S IMPRESSIVE, I'LL GRANT YOU, BUT YOU JUST LOST A DOLLAR, MISSY.
WE'RE NOT ALLOWED TO VISIT AUNT ROSE ANYMORE, BUT I CAN'T NOT BE THERE, OR ALL WINDS WOULD DIE AROUND HER AND HER LANDS.
SEE? YONDER BUM IS A WINNER.
EVEN AGAINST A KILLER LIKE BO.

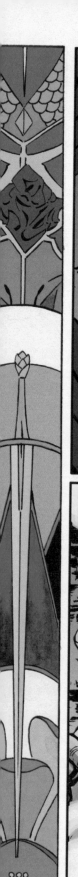

SO I DON'T LET HER SEE ME WHEN I WATCH HER.

FINE. LET'S GET OUT OF THE WEATHER AND FIND WHEREVER IT IS I'VE LEFT MY *WALLET* TODAY. GET YOU YOUR DOLLAR.

'TIS A FAIR MAN OR WOMAN WHO PAYS HER GAMBLING DEBTS IMMEDIATELY.

IT'S NOT CHEATING IF I STAY INVISIBLE AND DON'T ACTUALLY *TALK* TO HER, RIGHT?

YOU'VE DONE A *MAGNIFICENT* JOB WITH THE NEW CASTLE, WEYLAND. I COULDN'T ASK FOR MORE.

EXCEPT THAT YOU ALREADY *HAVE.*

I CAN SEE SOMETHING I DON'T THINK EVEN *AUNT ROSE* REALIZES. SHE'S GATHERING HER POWER.

A SPRAWL OF *ADDITIONAL* KEEPS AND CASTLES HUDDLING AROUND THIS ONE.

WELL, TRUE.

EVENTUALLY.

NO, I WAS WRONG. *NOT* JUST HERS. FOREIGN ENERGIES, TOO.

SIX KNIGHTS TO KICK OFF OUR NEW ORDER, AND THEY CAN EASILY BE HOUSED HERE, IN THE MAIN PALACE.

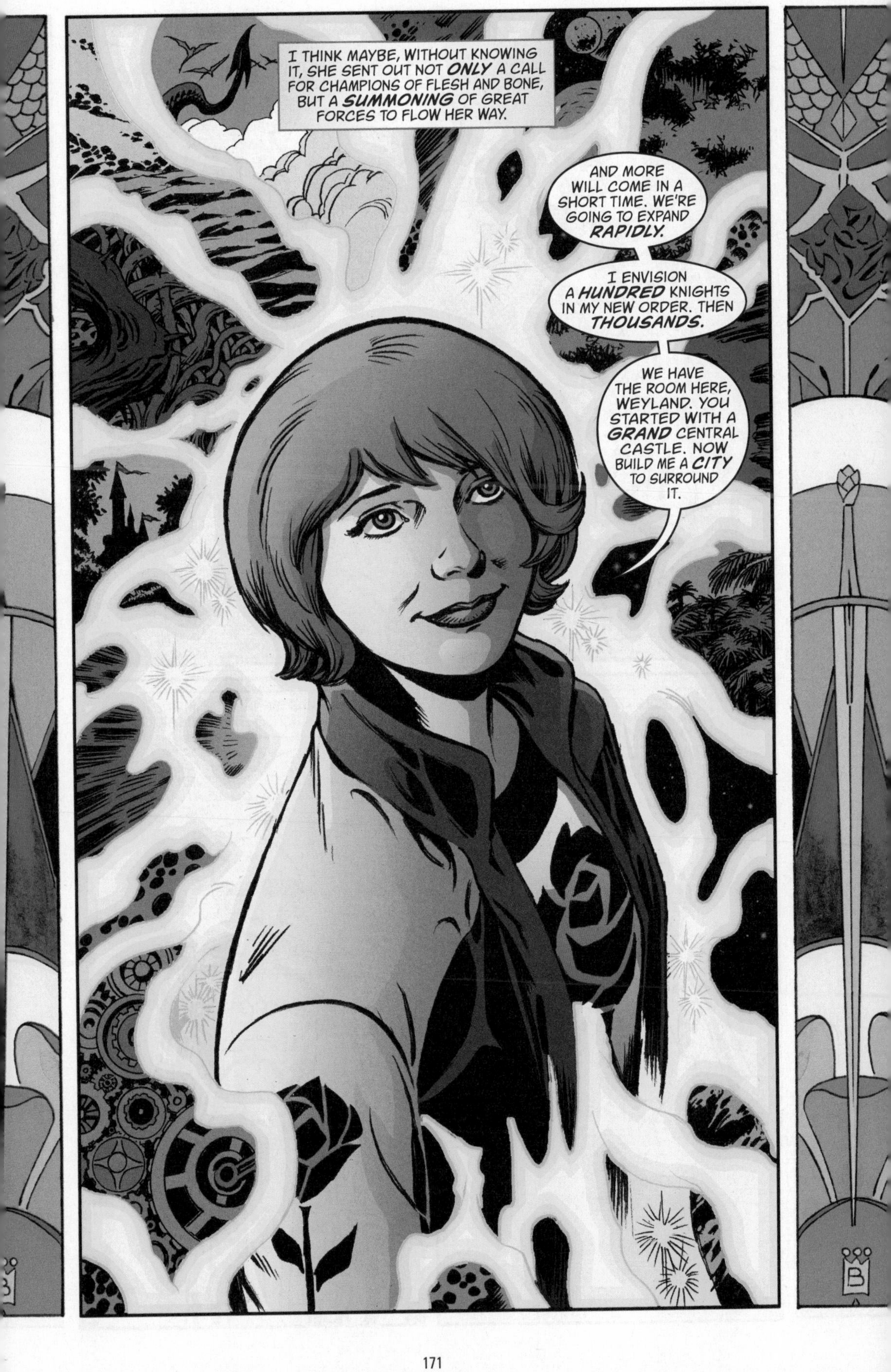
I THINK MAYBE, WITHOUT KNOWING IT, SHE SENT OUT NOT ONLY A CALL FOR CHAMPIONS OF FLESH AND BONE, BUT A SUMMONING OF GREAT FORCES TO FLOW HER WAY.
AND MORE WILL COME IN A SHORT TIME. WE'RE GOING TO EXPAND RAPIDLY.
I ENVISION A HUNDRED KNIGHTS IN MY NEW ORDER. THEN THOUSANDS.
WE HAVE THE ROOM HERE, WEYLAND. YOU STARTED WITH A GRAND CENTRAL CASTLE. NOW BUILD ME A CITY TO SURROUND IT.

TO **PLEDGE** THEMSELVES TO HER.

EXCELLENT WORK! YOU DID YOURSELVES PROUD!

I WANT YOU TO KNOW **EACH ONE** OF YOU HAS PROVED HIMSELF CAPABLE OF BECOMING A KNIGHT OF THE ROUND TABLE-- **SOMEDAY!**

MAGIC ISN'T REALLY ALIVE. NOT EXACTLY. BUT IT **YEARNS.**

SO I'M SENDING YOU **HOME,** FOR NOW.

LIKE BAD MEN, SOME MAGIC LONGS TO DO **BAD** THINGS.

BUT HOLD YOURSELVES READY!

THE CALL TO RETURN MAY COME AT **ANY TIME!**

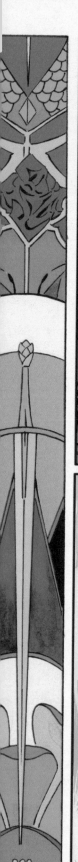

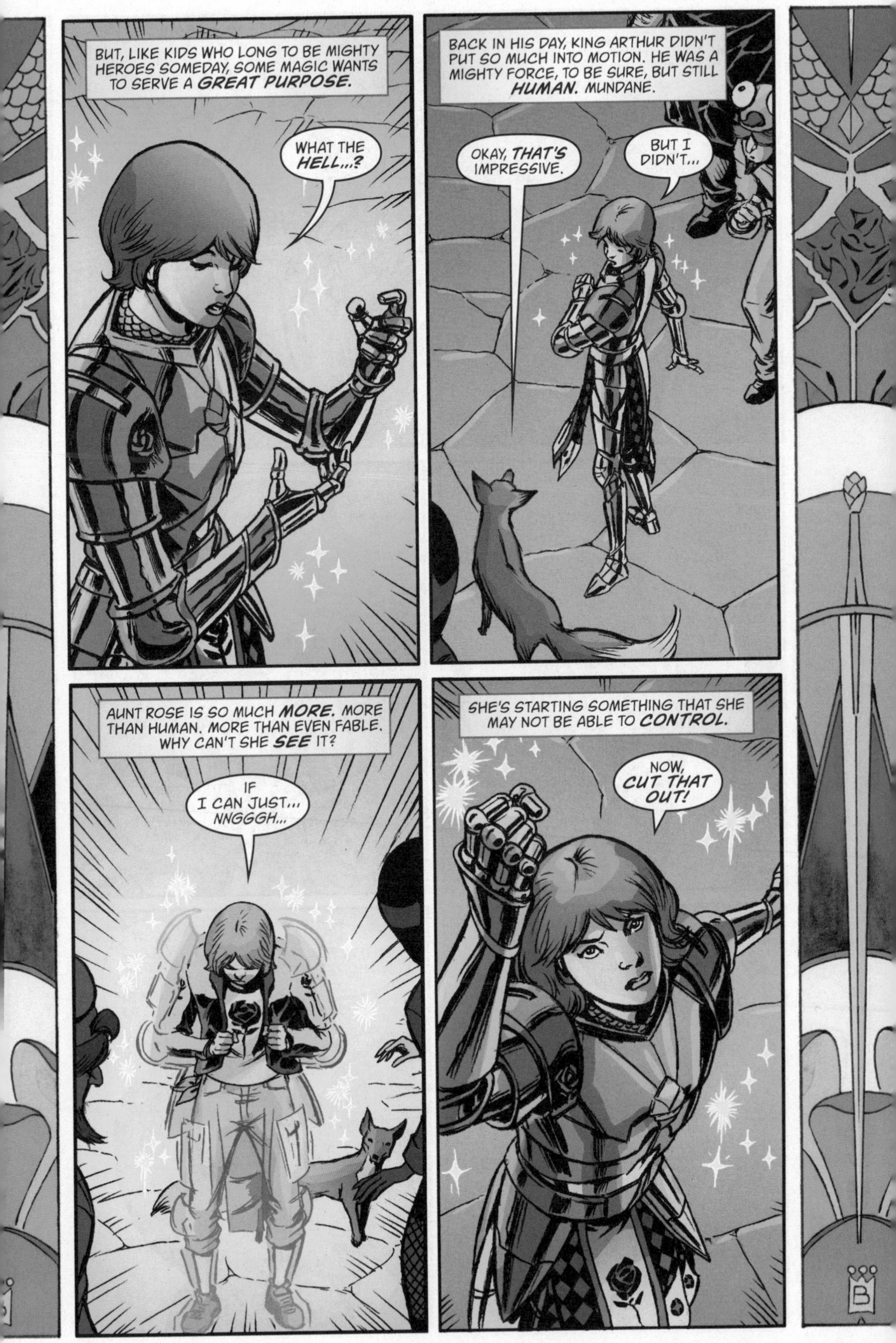
BUT, LIKE KIDS WHO LONG TO BE MIGHTY HEROES SOMEDAY, SOME MAGIC WANTS TO SERVE A GREAT PURPOSE.
WHAT THE HELL...?
BACK IN HIS DAY, KING ARTHUR DIDN'T PUT SO MUCH INTO MOTION. HE WAS A MIGHTY FORCE, TO BE SURE, BUT STILL HUMAN. MUNDANE.
OKAY, THAT'S IMPRESSIVE.
BUT I DIDN'T...
AUNT ROSE IS SO MUCH MORE. MORE THAN HUMAN. MORE THAN EVEN FABLE. WHY CAN'T SHE SEE IT?
IF I CAN JUST... NNGGGH...
SHE'S STARTING SOMETHING THAT SHE MAY NOT BE ABLE TO CONTROL.
NOW, CUT THAT OUT!

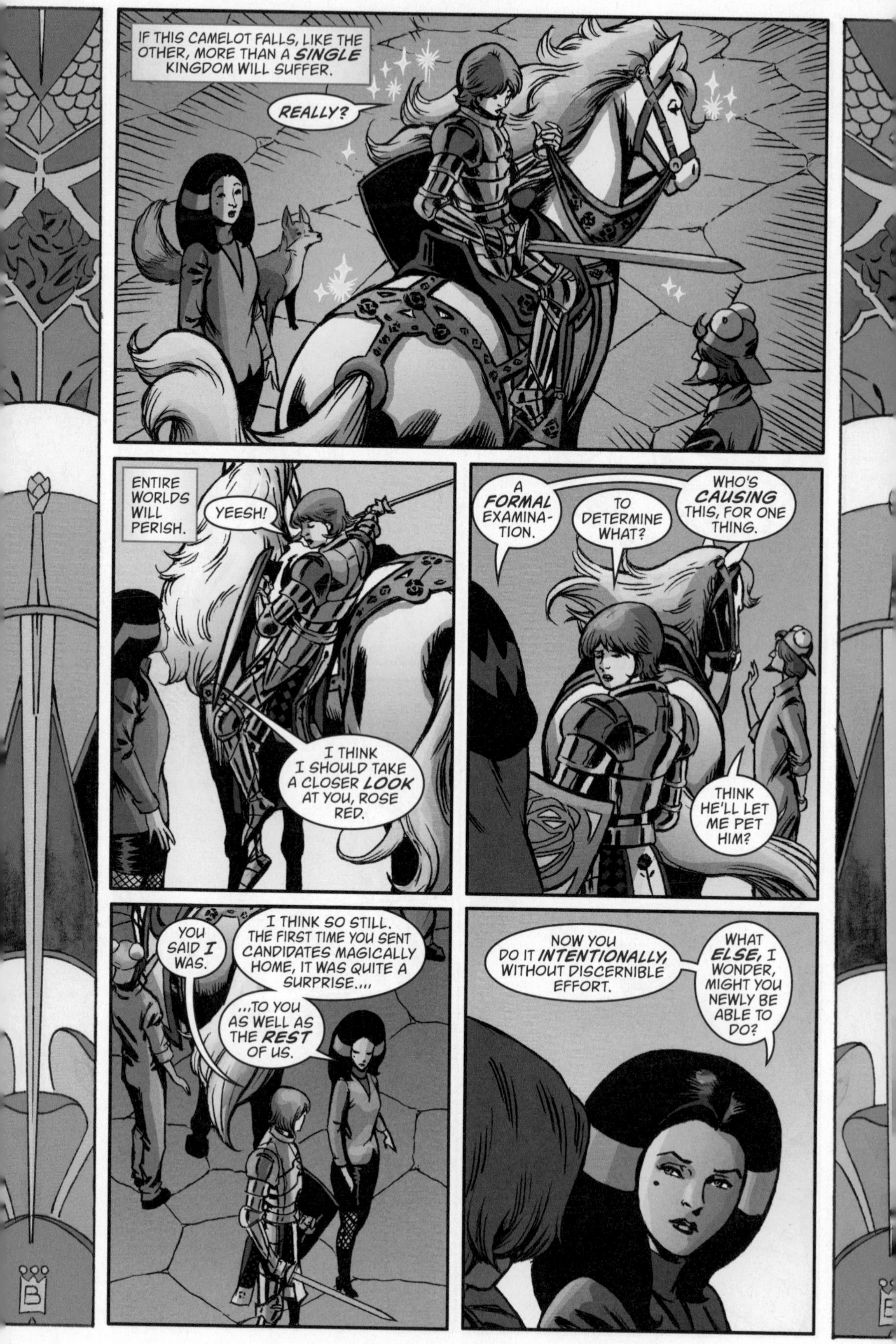
IF THIS CAMELOT FALLS, LIKE THE OTHER, MORE THAN A SINGLE KINGDOM WILL SUFFER.
REALLY?
ENTIRE WORLDS WILL PERISH.
YEESH!
I THINK I SHOULD TAKE A CLOSER LOOK AT YOU, ROSE RED.
A FORMAL EXAMINATION.
TO DETERMINE WHAT?
WHO'S CAUSING THIS, FOR ONE THING.
THINK HE'LL LET ME PET HIM?
YOU SAID I WAS.
I THINK SO STILL. THE FIRST TIME YOU SENT CANDIDATES MAGICALLY HOME, IT WAS QUITE A SURPRISE....
...TO YOU AS WELL AS THE REST OF US.
NOW YOU DO IT INTENTIONALLY, WITHOUT DISCERNIBLE EFFORT.
WHAT ELSE, I WONDER, MIGHT YOU NEWLY BE ABLE TO DO?

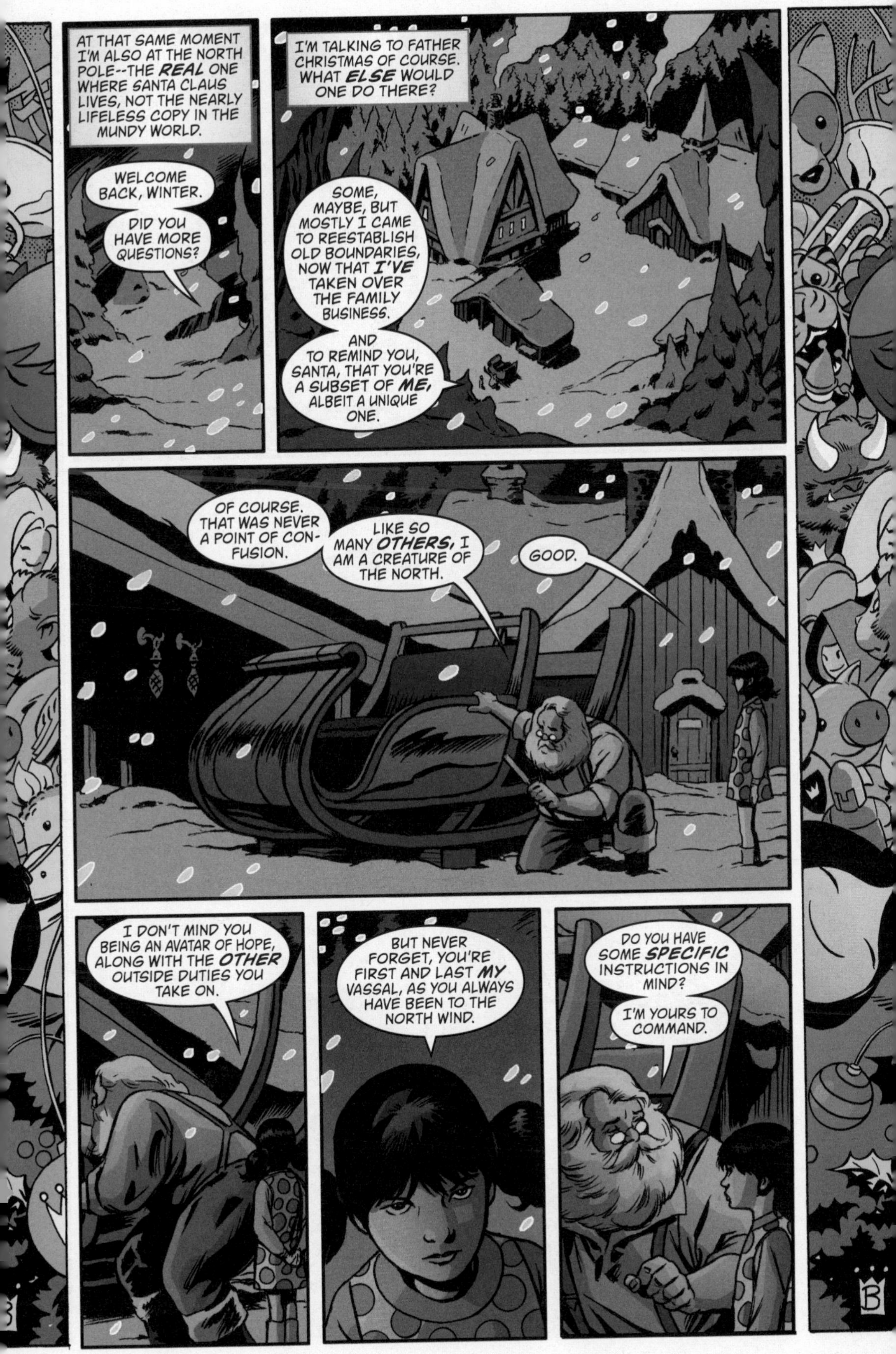
AT THAT SAME MOMENT I'M ALSO AT THE NORTH POLE--THE REAL ONE WHERE SANTA CLAUS LIVES, NOT THE NEARLY LIFELESS COPY IN THE MUNDY WORLD.
WELCOME BACK, WINTER.
DID YOU HAVE MORE QUESTIONS?
I'M TALKING TO FATHER CHRISTMAS OF COURSE. WHAT ELSE WOULD ONE DO THERE?
SOME, MAYBE, BUT MOSTLY I CAME TO REESTABLISH OLD BOUNDARIES, NOW THAT I'VE TAKEN OVER THE FAMILY BUSINESS.
AND TO REMIND YOU, SANTA, THAT YOU'RE A SUBSET OF ME, ALBEIT A UNIQUE ONE.
OF COURSE. THAT WAS NEVER A POINT OF CON-FUSION.
LIKE SO MANY OTHERS, I AM A CREATURE OF THE NORTH.
GOOD.
I DON'T MIND YOU BEING AN AVATAR OF HOPE, ALONG WITH THE OTHER OUTSIDE DUTIES YOU TAKE ON.
BUT NEVER FORGET, YOU'RE FIRST AND LAST MY VASSAL, AS YOU ALWAYS HAVE BEEN TO THE NORTH WIND.
DO YOU HAVE SOME SPECIFIC INSTRUCTIONS IN MIND?
I'M YOURS TO COMMAND.

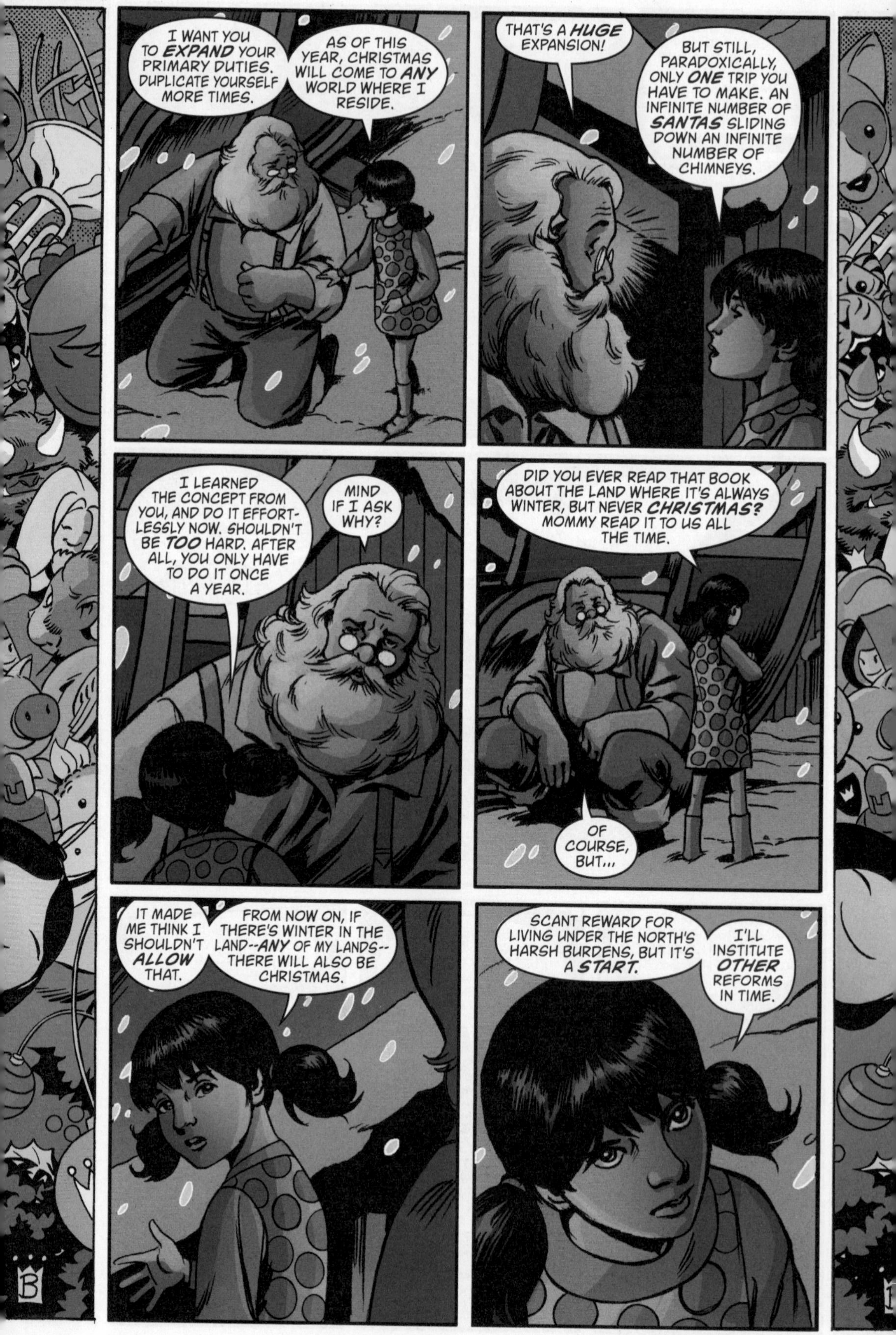
I WANT YOU TO EXPAND YOUR PRIMARY DUTIES. DUPLICATE YOURSELF MORE TIMES.
AS OF THIS YEAR, CHRISTMAS WILL COME TO ANY WORLD WHERE I RESIDE.
THAT'S A HUGE EXPANSION!
BUT STILL, PARADOXICALLY, ONLY ONE TRIP YOU HAVE TO MAKE. AN INFINITE NUMBER OF SANTAS SLIDING DOWN AN INFINITE NUMBER OF CHIMNEYS.
I LEARNED THE CONCEPT FROM YOU, AND DO IT EFFORTLESSLY NOW. SHOULDN'T BE TOO HARD. AFTER ALL, YOU ONLY HAVE TO DO IT ONCE A YEAR.
MIND IF I ASK WHY?
DID YOU EVER READ THAT BOOK ABOUT THE LAND WHERE IT'S ALWAYS WINTER, BUT NEVER CHRISTMAS? MOMMY READ IT TO US ALL THE TIME.
OF COURSE, BUT...
IT MADE ME THINK I SHOULDN'T ALLOW THAT.
FROM NOW ON, IF THERE'S WINTER IN THE LAND--ANY OF MY LANDS--THERE WILL ALSO BE CHRISTMAS.
SCANT REWARD FOR LIVING UNDER THE NORTH'S HARSH BURDENS, BUT IT'S A START.
I'LL INSTITUTE OTHER REFORMS IN TIME.

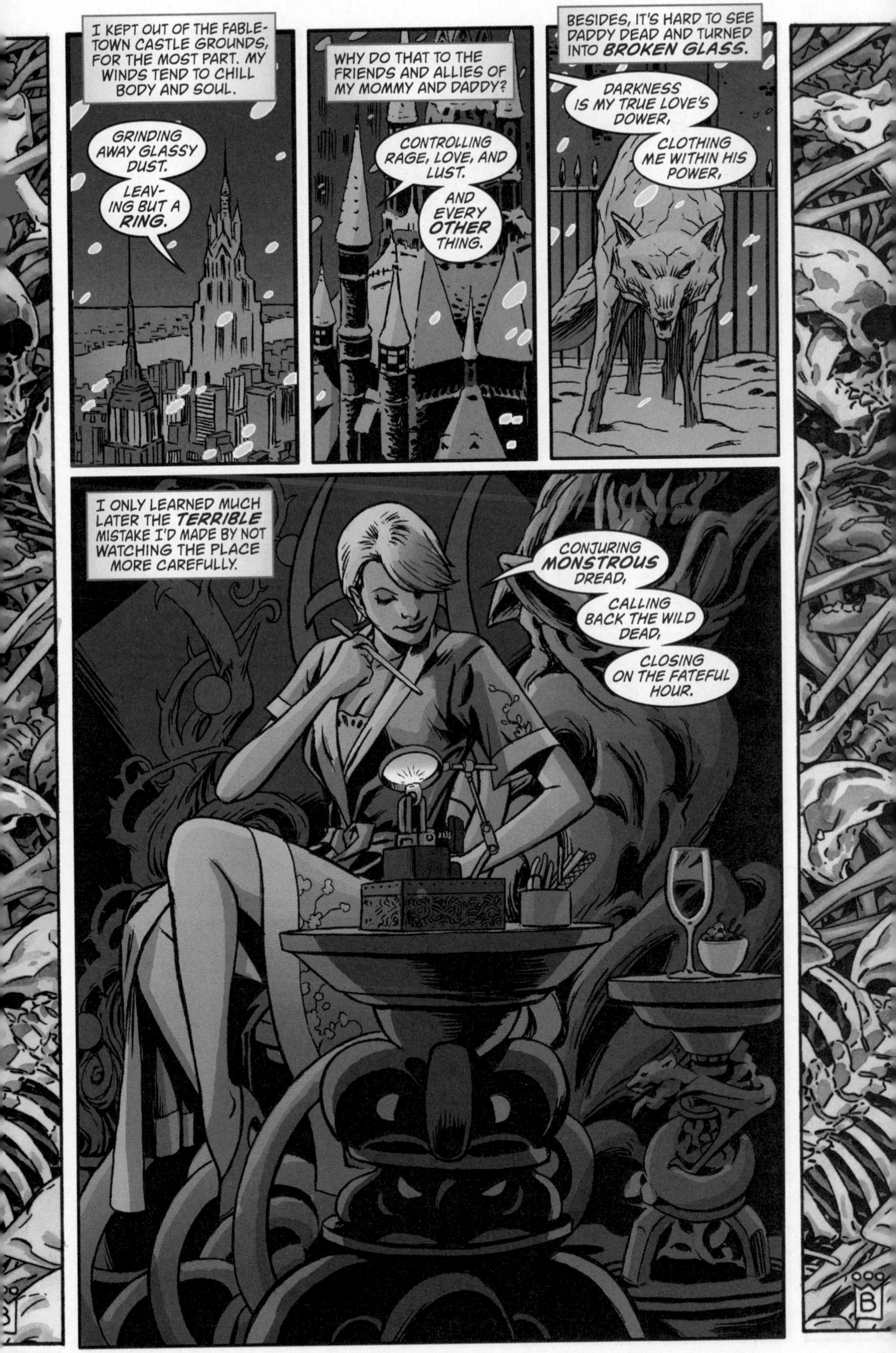
I KEPT OUT OF THE FABLE-TOWN CASTLE GROUNDS, FOR THE MOST PART. MY WINDS TEND TO CHILL BODY AND SOUL.
GRINDING AWAY GLASSY DUST.
LEAV-ING BUT A RING.
WHY DO THAT TO THE FRIENDS AND ALLIES OF MY MOMMY AND DADDY?
CONTROLLING RAGE, LOVE, AND LUST.
AND EVERY OTHER THING.
BESIDES, IT'S HARD TO SEE DADDY DEAD AND TURNED INTO BROKEN GLASS.
DARKNESS IS MY TRUE LOVE'S DOWER,
CLOTHING ME WITHIN HIS POWER,
I ONLY LEARNED MUCH LATER THE TERRIBLE MISTAKE I'D MADE BY NOT WATCHING THE PLACE MORE CAREFULLY.
CONJURING MONSTROUS DREAD,
CALLING BACK THE WILD DEAD,
CLOSING ON THE FATEFUL HOUR.

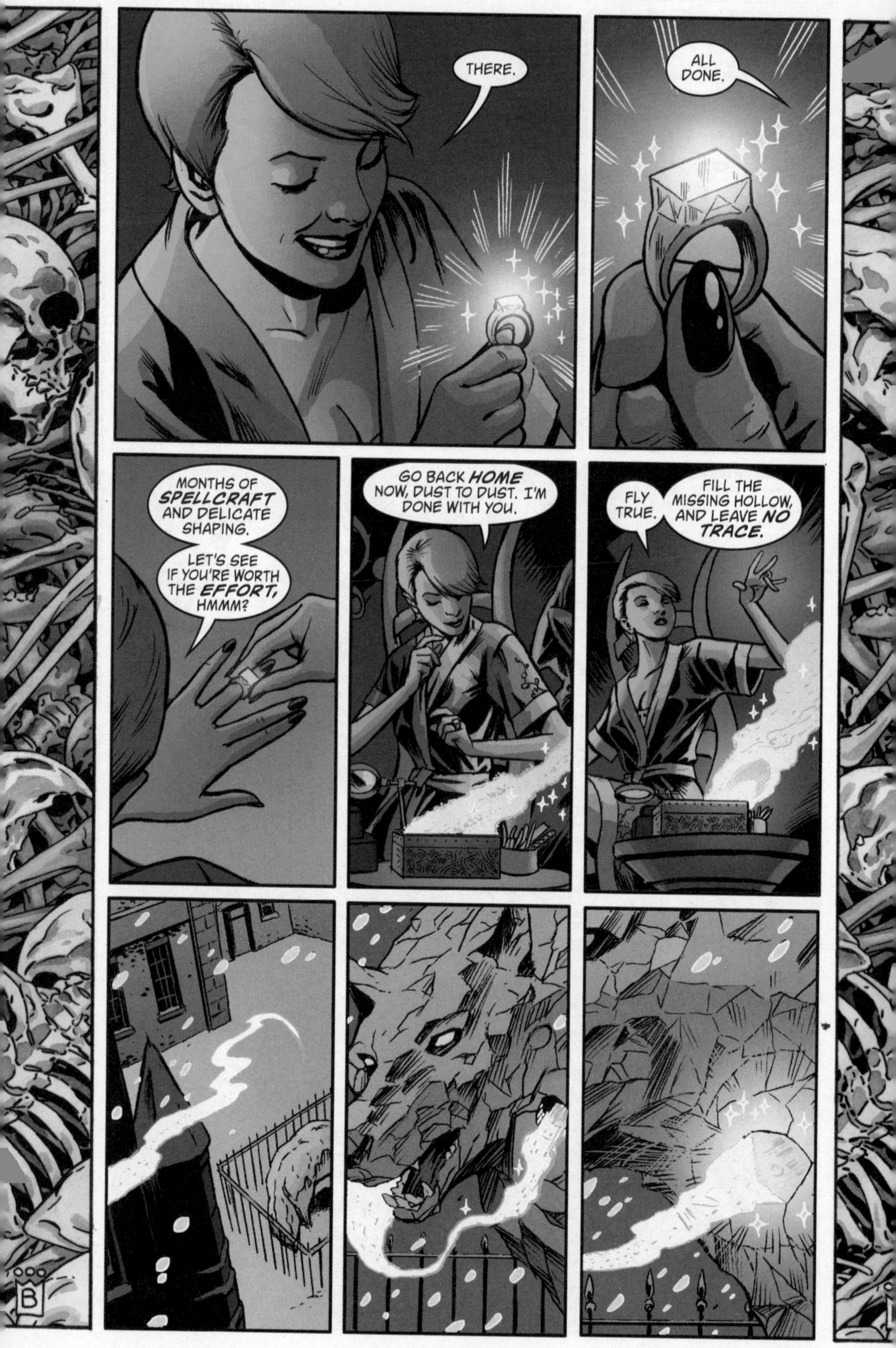
THERE.
ALL DONE.
MONTHS OF SPELLCRAFT AND DELICATE SHAPING.
LET'S SEE IF YOU'RE WORTH THE EFFORT, HMMM?
GO BACK HOME NOW, DUST TO DUST. I'M DONE WITH YOU.
FLY TRUE.
FILL THE MISSING HOLLOW, AND LEAVE NO TRACE.

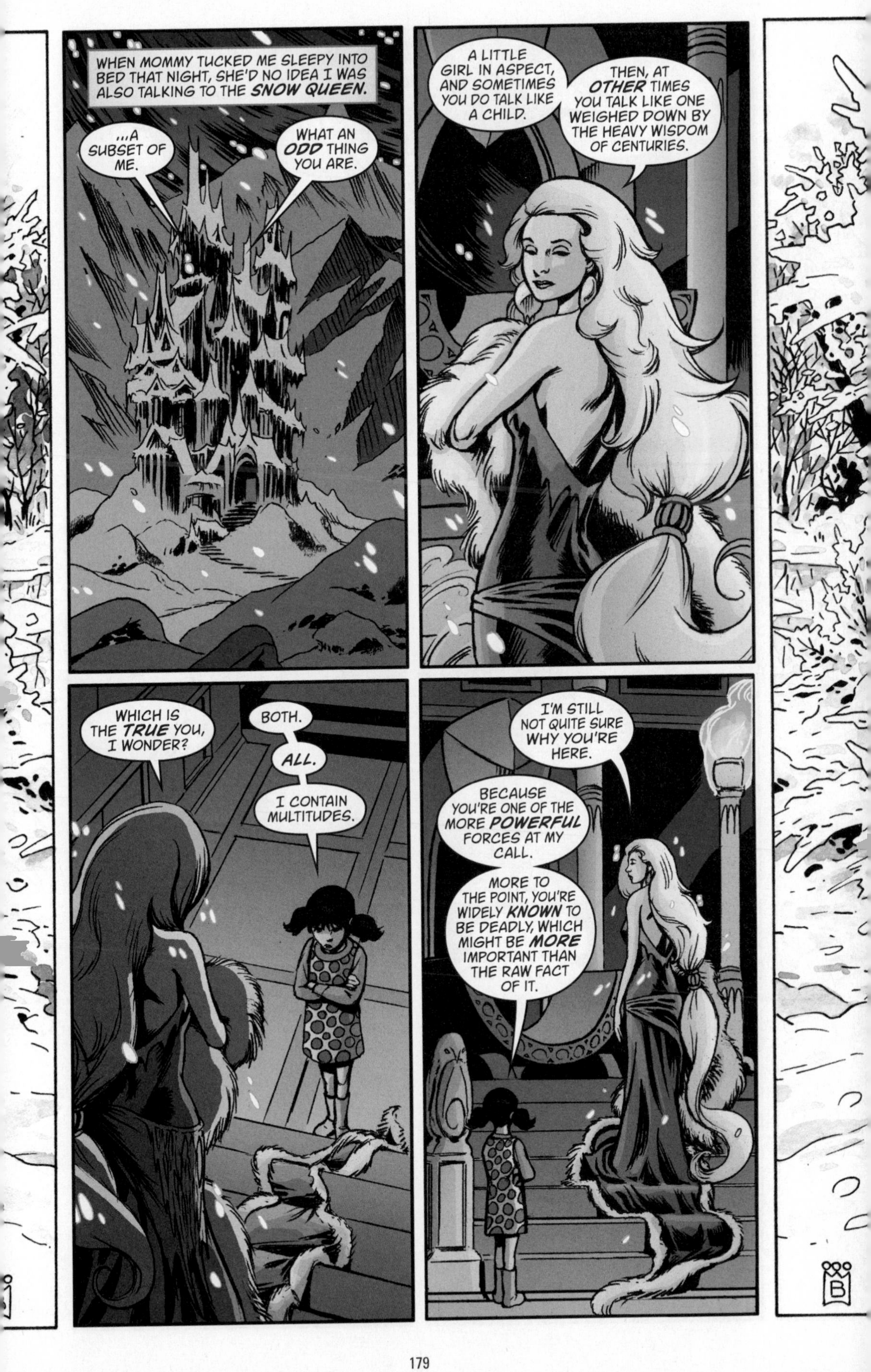

WHEN MOMMY TUCKED ME SLEEPY INTO BED THAT NIGHT, SHE'D NO IDEA I WAS ALSO TALKING TO THE SNOW QUEEN.
...A SUBSET OF ME.
WHAT AN ODD THING YOU ARE.
A LITTLE GIRL IN ASPECT, AND SOMETIMES YOU DO TALK LIKE A CHILD.
THEN, AT OTHER TIMES YOU TALK LIKE ONE WEIGHED DOWN BY THE HEAVY WISDOM OF CENTURIES.
WHICH IS THE TRUE YOU, I WONDER?
BOTH.
ALL.
I CONTAIN MULTITUDES.
I'M STILL NOT QUITE SURE WHY YOU'RE HERE.
BECAUSE YOU'RE ONE OF THE MORE POWERFUL FORCES AT MY CALL.
MORE TO THE POINT, YOU'RE WIDELY KNOWN TO BE DEADLY, WHICH MIGHT BE MORE IMPORTANT THAN THE RAW FACT OF IT.

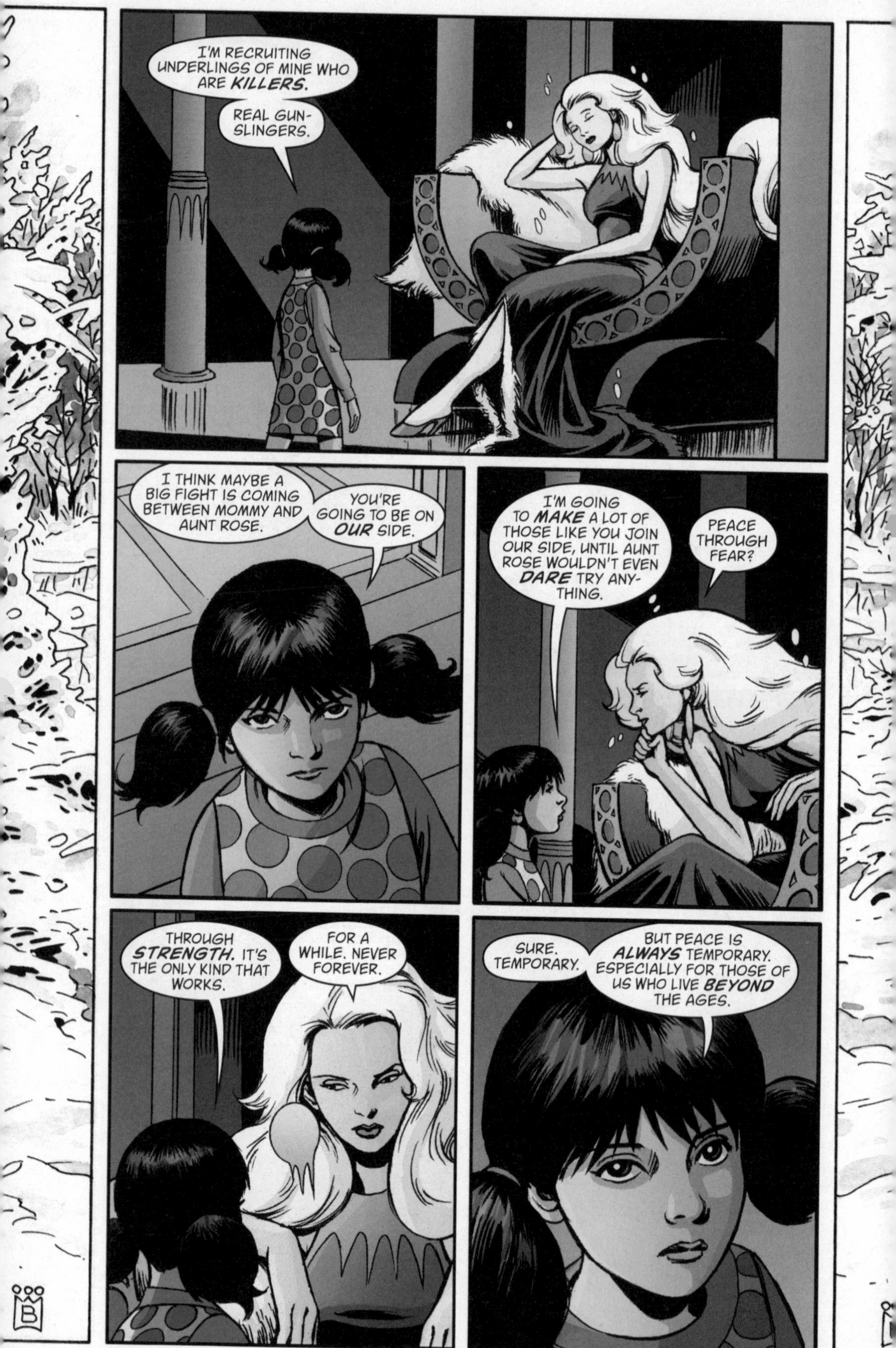
I'M RECRUITING UNDERLINGS OF MINE WHO ARE KILLERS.
REAL GUN-SLINGERS.
I THINK MAYBE A BIG FIGHT IS COMING BETWEEN MOMMY AND AUNT ROSE.
YOU'RE GOING TO BE ON OUR SIDE.
I'M GOING TO MAKE A LOT OF THOSE LIKE YOU JOIN OUR SIDE, UNTIL AUNT ROSE WOULDN'T EVEN DARE TRY ANY-THING.
PEACE THROUGH FEAR?
THROUGH STRENGTH. IT'S THE ONLY KIND THAT WORKS.
FOR A WHILE. NEVER FOREVER.
SURE. TEMPORARY.
BUT PEACE IS ALWAYS TEMPORARY. ESPECIALLY FOR THOSE OF US WHO LIVE BEYOND THE AGES.

DAYS MOVED ALONG...

...ARE THE DAYS OF *ROSE RED*, WHERE WE SHALL *REACH* FOR THE *STARS*.

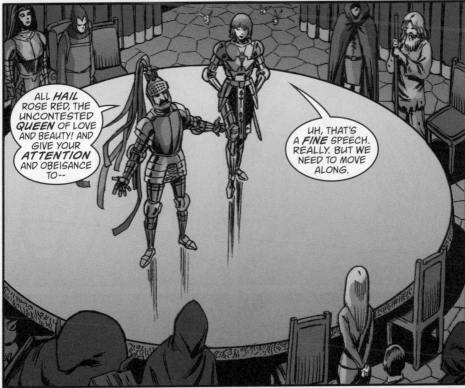

ALL *HAIL* ROSE RED, THE UNCONTESTED *QUEEN* OF LOVE AND BEAUTY! AND GIVE YOUR *ATTENTION* AND OBEISANCE TO--

UH, THAT'S A *FINE* SPEECH. REALLY. BUT WE NEED TO MOVE ALONG.

YOU'VE WAITED AND WONDERED LONG ENOUGH. SIX *KNIGHTS* WILL TAKE THEIR PLACE HERE IN *NEW CAMELOT*, AND BEGIN OUR WORK IN THE ORDER OF THE RED ROSE.

IN TIME, *HUNDREDS*, BUT FOR NOW, THE *SIX* KNIGHTS ARE...

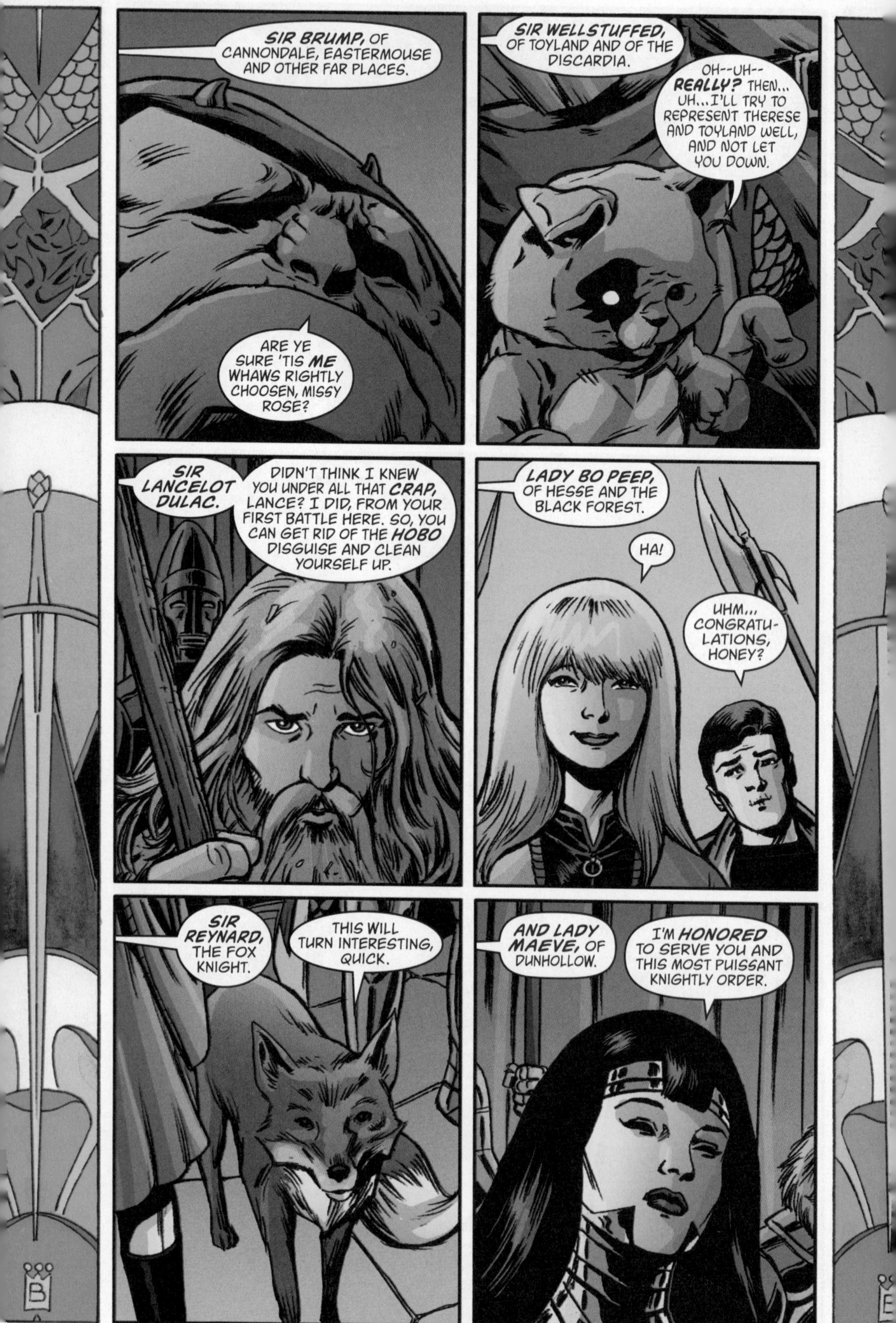

SIR BRUMP, OF CANNONDALE, EASTERMOUSE AND OTHER FAR PLACES.
ARE YE SURE 'TIS ME WHAWS RIGHTLY CHOOSEN, MISSY ROSE?
SIR WELLSTUFFED, OF TOYLAND AND OF THE DISCARDIA.
OH--UH-- REALLY? THEN... UH...I'LL TRY TO REPRESENT THERESE AND TOYLAND WELL, AND NOT LET YOU DOWN.
SIR LANCELOT DULAC.
DIDN'T THINK I KNEW YOU UNDER ALL THAT CRAP, LANCE? I DID, FROM YOUR FIRST BATTLE HERE. SO, YOU CAN GET RID OF THE HOBO DISGUISE AND CLEAN YOURSELF UP.
LADY BO PEEP, OF HESSE AND THE BLACK FOREST.
HA!
UHM... CONGRATU-LATIONS, HONEY?
SIR REYNARD, THE FOX KNIGHT.
THIS WILL TURN INTERESTING, QUICK.
AND LADY MAEVE, OF DUNHOLLOW.
I'M HONORED TO SERVE YOU AND THIS MOST PUISSANT KNIGHTLY ORDER.

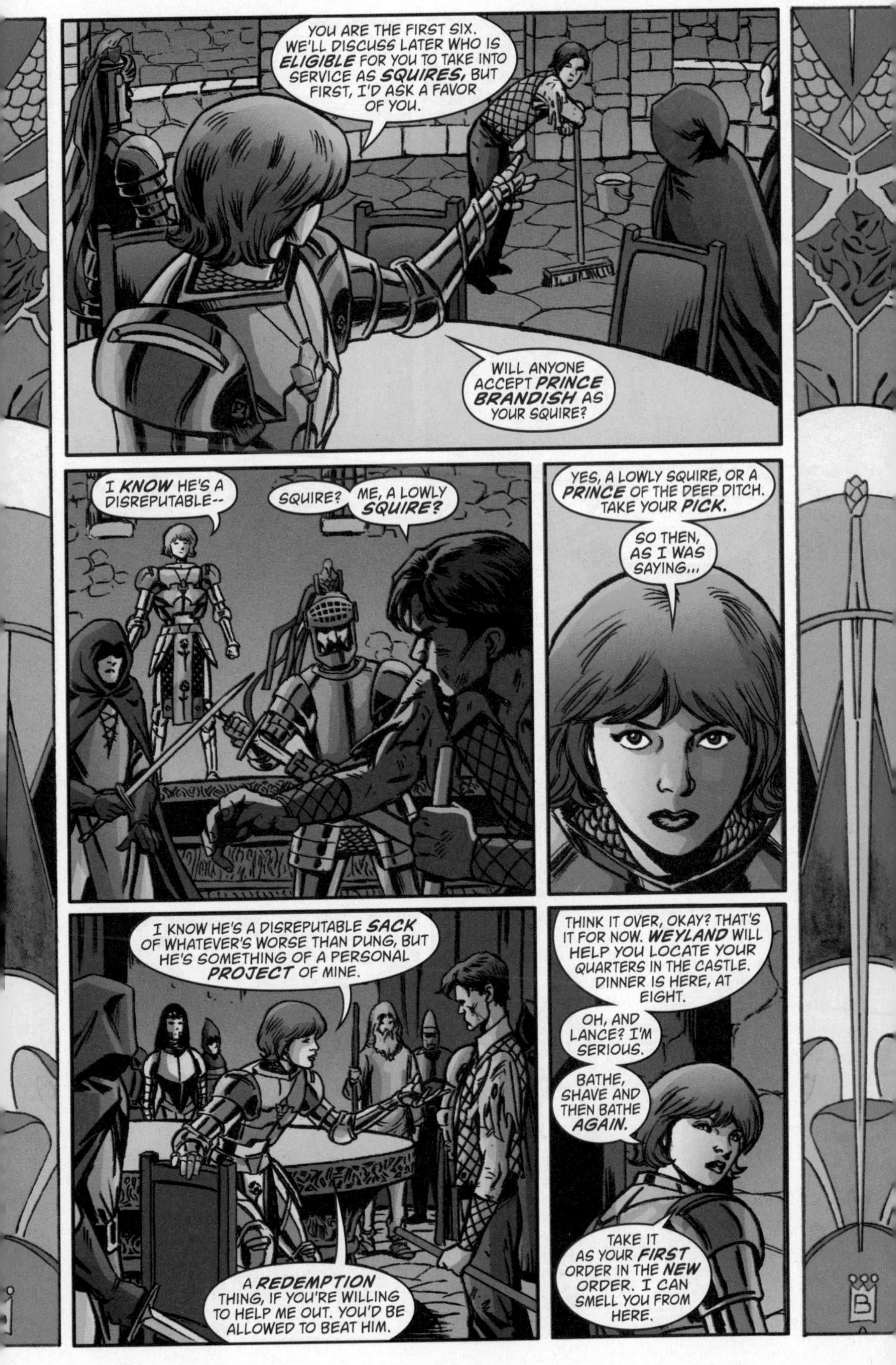
YOU ARE THE FIRST SIX. WE'LL DISCUSS LATER WHO IS ELIGIBLE FOR YOU TO TAKE INTO SERVICE AS SQUIRES, BUT FIRST, I'D ASK A FAVOR OF YOU.
WILL ANYONE ACCEPT PRINCE BRANDISH AS YOUR SQUIRE?
I KNOW HE'S A DISREPUTABLE--
SQUIRE?
ME, A LOWLY SQUIRE?
YES, A LOWLY SQUIRE, OR A PRINCE OF THE DEEP DITCH. TAKE YOUR PICK.
SO THEN, AS I WAS SAYING...
I KNOW HE'S A DISREPUTABLE SACK OF WHATEVER'S WORSE THAN DUNG, BUT HE'S SOMETHING OF A PERSONAL PROJECT OF MINE.
A REDEMPTION THING, IF YOU'RE WILLING TO HELP ME OUT. YOU'D BE ALLOWED TO BEAT HIM.
THINK IT OVER, OKAY? THAT'S IT FOR NOW. WEYLAND WILL HELP YOU LOCATE YOUR QUARTERS IN THE CASTLE. DINNER IS HERE, AT EIGHT.
OH, AND LANCE? I'M SERIOUS.
BATHE, SHAVE AND THEN BATHE AGAIN.
TAKE IT AS YOUR FIRST ORDER IN THE NEW ORDER. I CAN SMELL YOU FROM HERE.

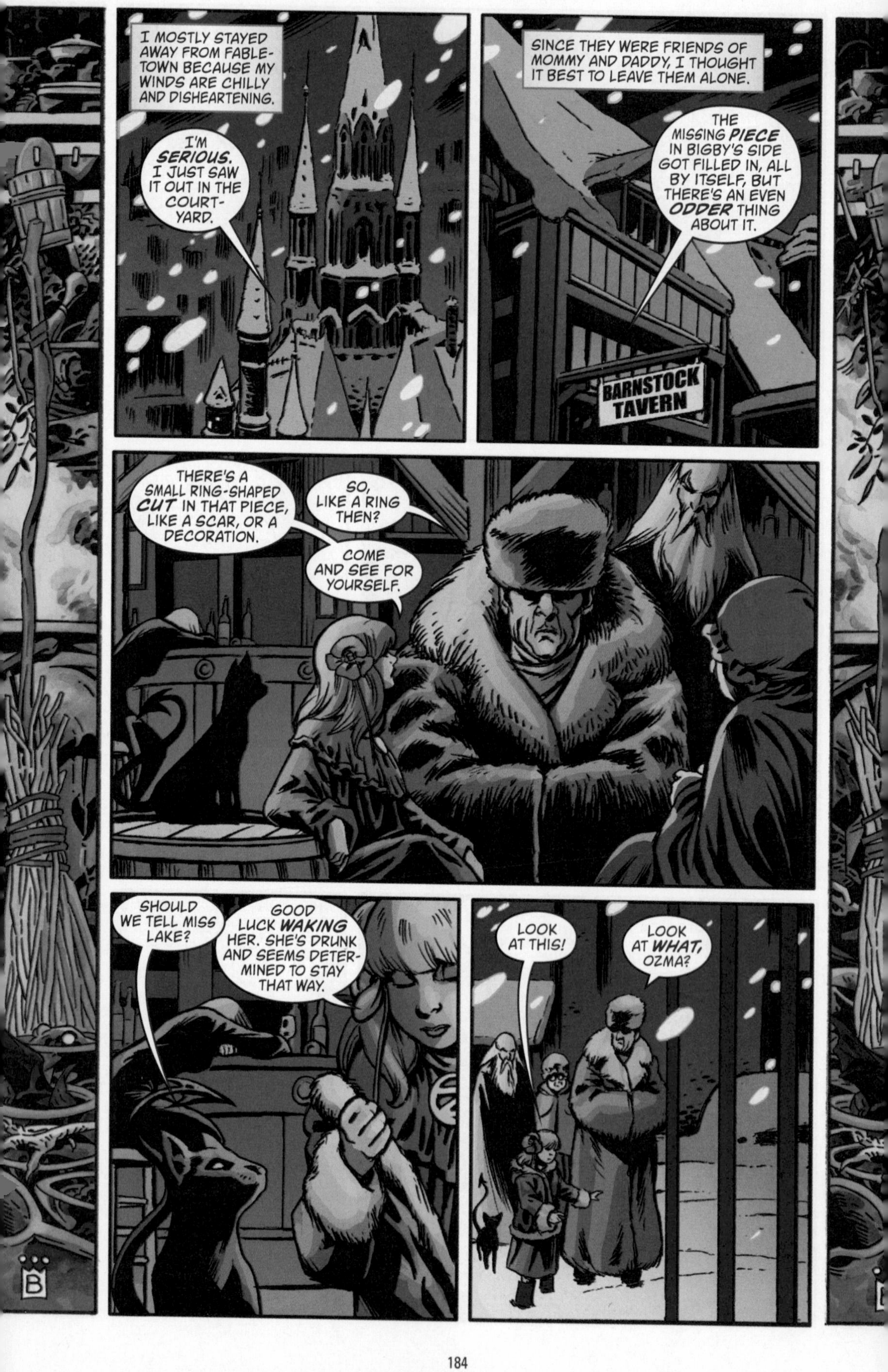
I MOSTLY STAYED AWAY FROM FABLETOWN BECAUSE MY WINDS ARE CHILLY AND DISHEARTENING.
I'M SERIOUS. I JUST SAW IT OUT IN THE COURTYARD.
SINCE THEY WERE FRIENDS OF MOMMY AND DADDY, I THOUGHT IT BEST TO LEAVE THEM ALONE.
THE MISSING PIECE IN BIGBY'S SIDE GOT FILLED IN, ALL BY ITSELF, BUT THERE'S AN EVEN ODDER THING ABOUT IT.
BARNSTOCK TAVERN
THERE'S A SMALL RING-SHAPED CUT IN THAT PIECE, LIKE A SCAR, OR A DECORATION.
SO, LIKE A RING THEN?
COME AND SEE FOR YOURSELF.
SHOULD WE TELL MISS LAKE?
GOOD LUCK WAKING HER. SHE'S DRUNK AND SEEMS DETERMINED TO STAY THAT WAY.
LOOK AT THIS!
LOOK AT WHAT, OZMA?

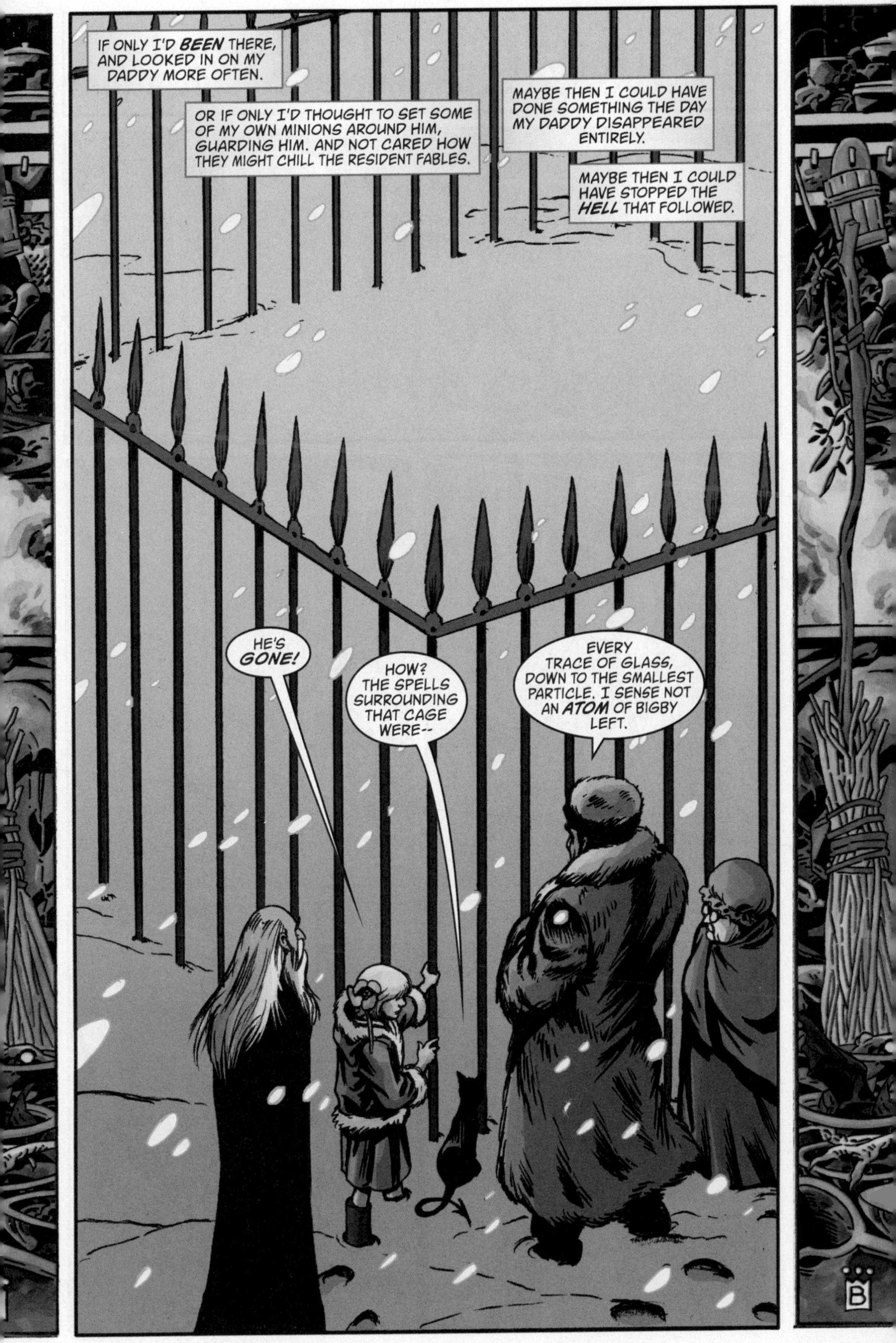
IF ONLY I'D BEEN THERE, AND LOOKED IN ON MY DADDY MORE OFTEN.
OR IF ONLY I'D THOUGHT TO SET SOME OF MY OWN MINIONS AROUND HIM, GUARDING HIM. AND NOT CARED HOW THEY MIGHT CHILL THE RESIDENT FABLES.
MAYBE THEN I COULD HAVE DONE SOMETHING THE DAY MY DADDY DISAPPEARED ENTIRELY.
MAYBE THEN I COULD HAVE STOPPED THE HELL THAT FOLLOWED.
HE'S GONE!
HOW? THE SPELLS SURROUNDING THAT CAGE WERE--
EVERY TRACE OF GLASS, DOWN TO THE SMALLEST PARTICLE. I SENSE NOT AN ATOM OF BIGBY LEFT.

EPILOGUE: The Shave and a Haircut Complication

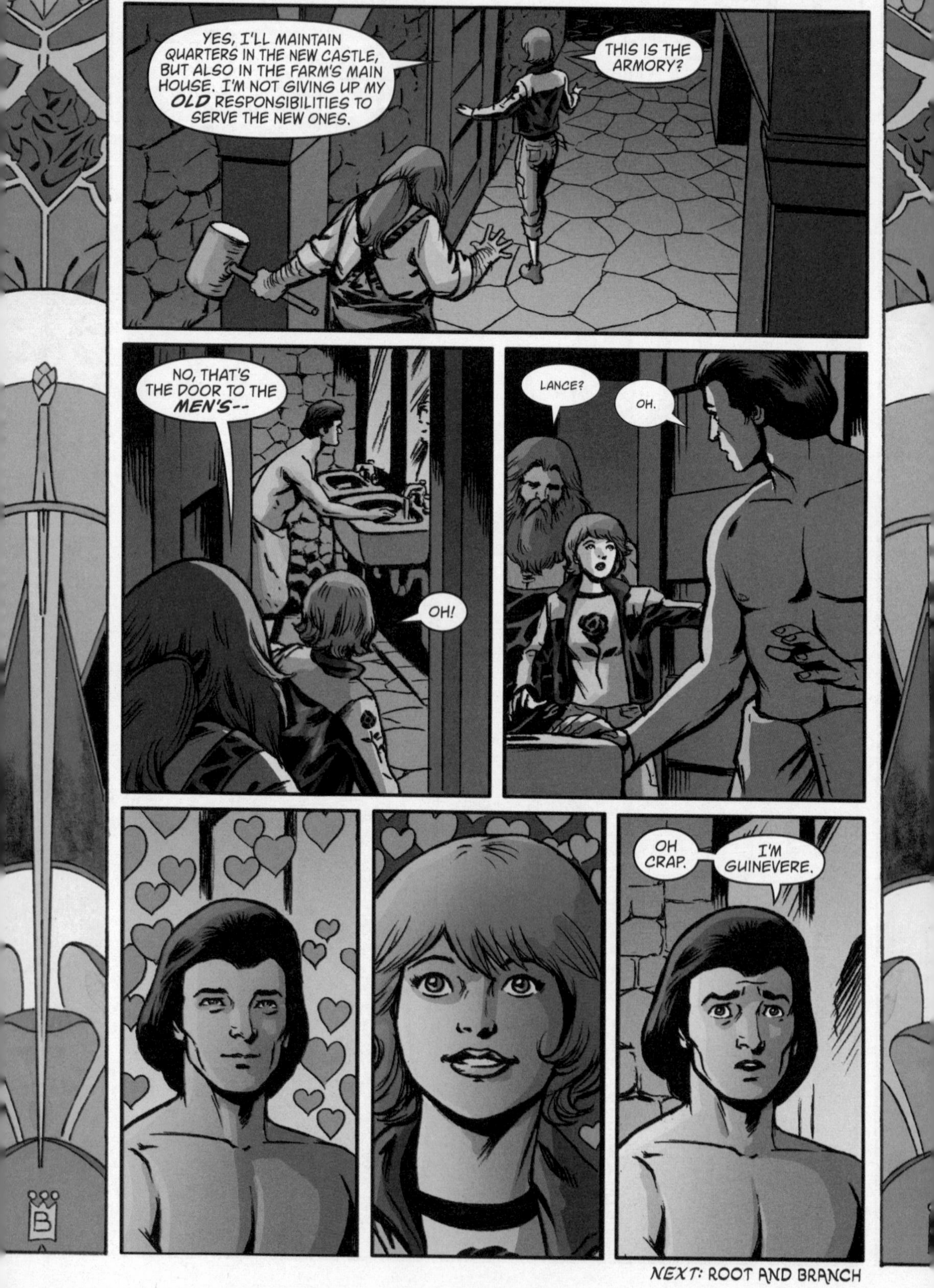
YES, I'LL MAINTAIN QUARTERS IN THE NEW CASTLE, BUT ALSO IN THE FARM'S MAIN HOUSE. I'M NOT GIVING UP MY OLD RESPONSIBILITIES TO SERVE THE NEW ONES.
THIS IS THE ARMORY?
NO, THAT'S THE DOOR TO THE MEN'S--
OH!
LANCE?
OH.
OH CRAP.
I'M GUINEVERE.

NEXT: ROOT AND BRANCH

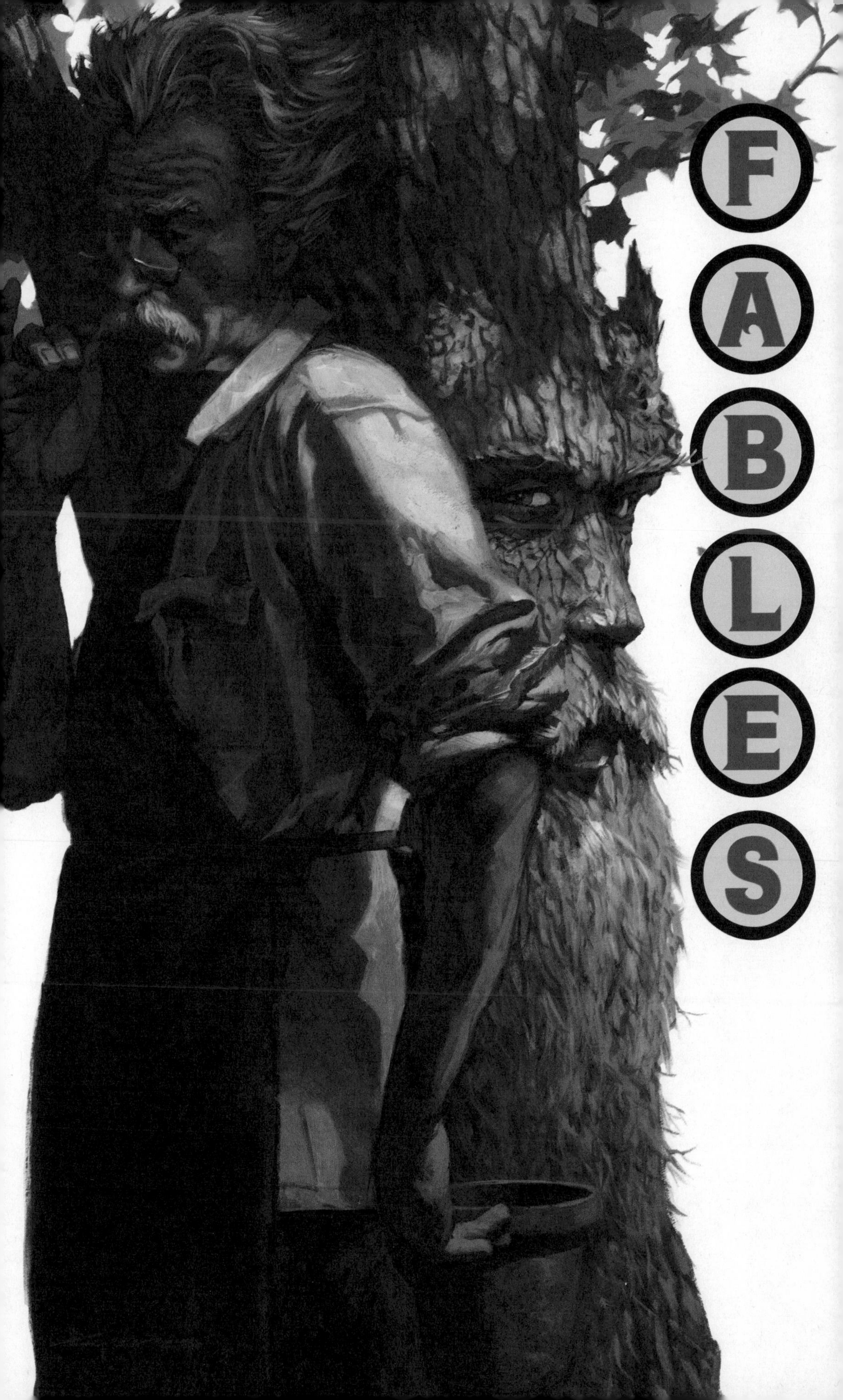
FABLES

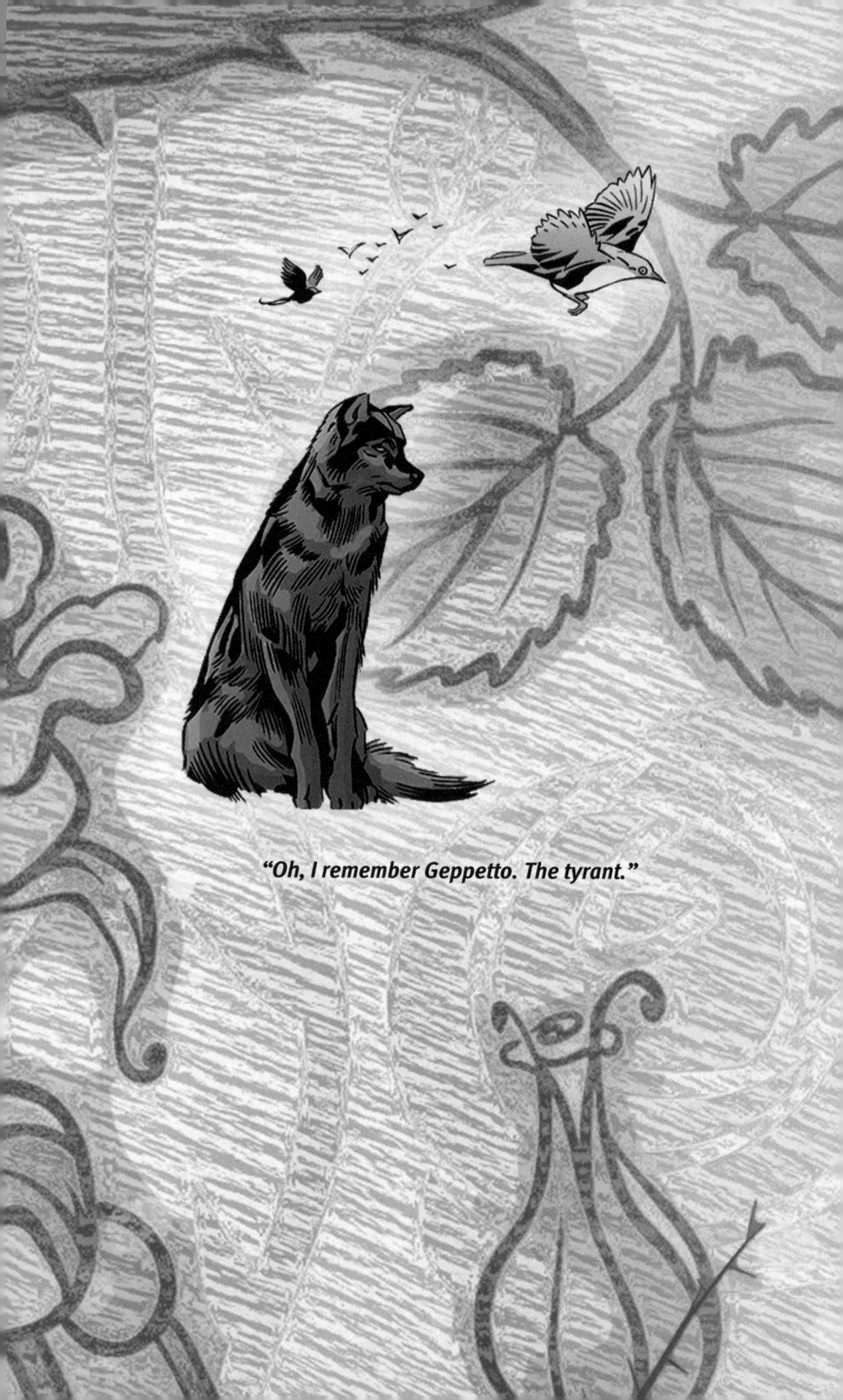

"Oh, I remember Geppetto. The tyrant."

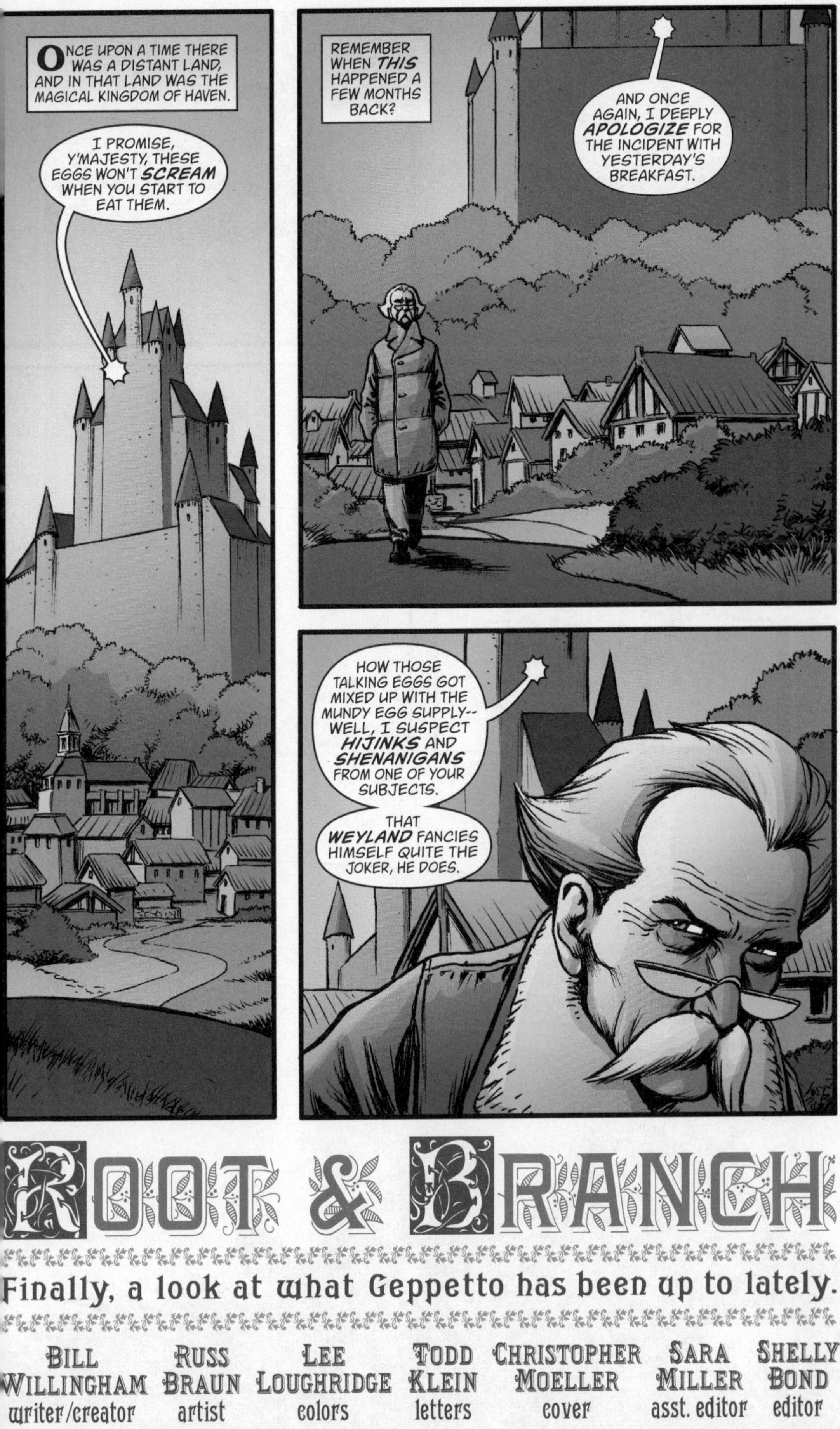
ONCE UPON A TIME THERE WAS A DISTANT LAND, AND IN THAT LAND WAS THE MAGICAL KINGDOM OF HAVEN.
I PROMISE, Y'MAJESTY, THESE EGGS WON'T SCREAM WHEN YOU START TO EAT THEM.
REMEMBER WHEN THIS HAPPENED A FEW MONTHS BACK?
AND ONCE AGAIN, I DEEPLY APOLOGIZE FOR THE INCIDENT WITH YESTERDAY'S BREAKFAST.
HOW THOSE TALKING EGGS GOT MIXED UP WITH THE MUNDY EGG SUPPLY--WELL, I SUSPECT HIJINKS AND SHENANIGANS FROM ONE OF YOUR SUBJECTS.
THAT WEYLAND FANCIES HIMSELF QUITE THE JOKER, HE DOES.

ROOT & BRANCH

Finally, a look at what Geppetto has been up to lately.

BILL WILLINGHAM writer/creator
RUSS BRAUN artist
LEE LOUGHRIDGE colors
TODD KLEIN letters
CHRISTOPHER MOELLER cover
SARA MILLER asst. editor
SHELLY BOND editor

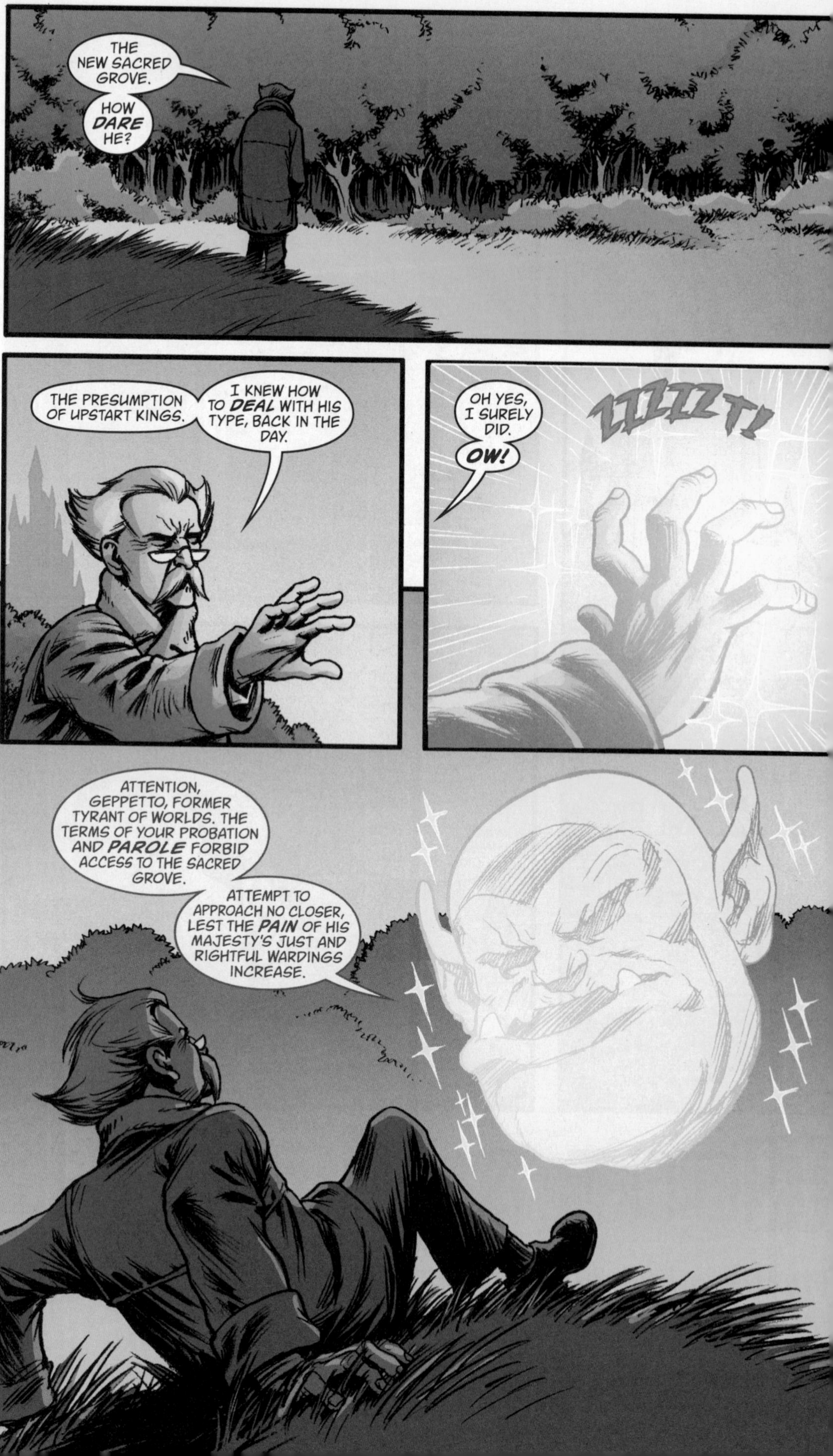
THE NEW SACRED GROVE.
HOW *DARE* HE?
THE PRESUMPTION OF UPSTART KINGS.
I KNEW HOW TO *DEAL* WITH HIS TYPE, BACK IN THE DAY.
OH YES, I SURELY DID.
OW!
ZZZZZT!
ATTENTION, GEPPETTO, FORMER TYRANT OF WORLDS. THE TERMS OF YOUR PROBATION AND *PAROLE* FORBID ACCESS TO THE SACRED GROVE.
ATTEMPT TO APPROACH NO CLOSER, LEST THE *PAIN* OF HIS MAJESTY'S JUST AND RIGHTFUL WARDINGS INCREASE.

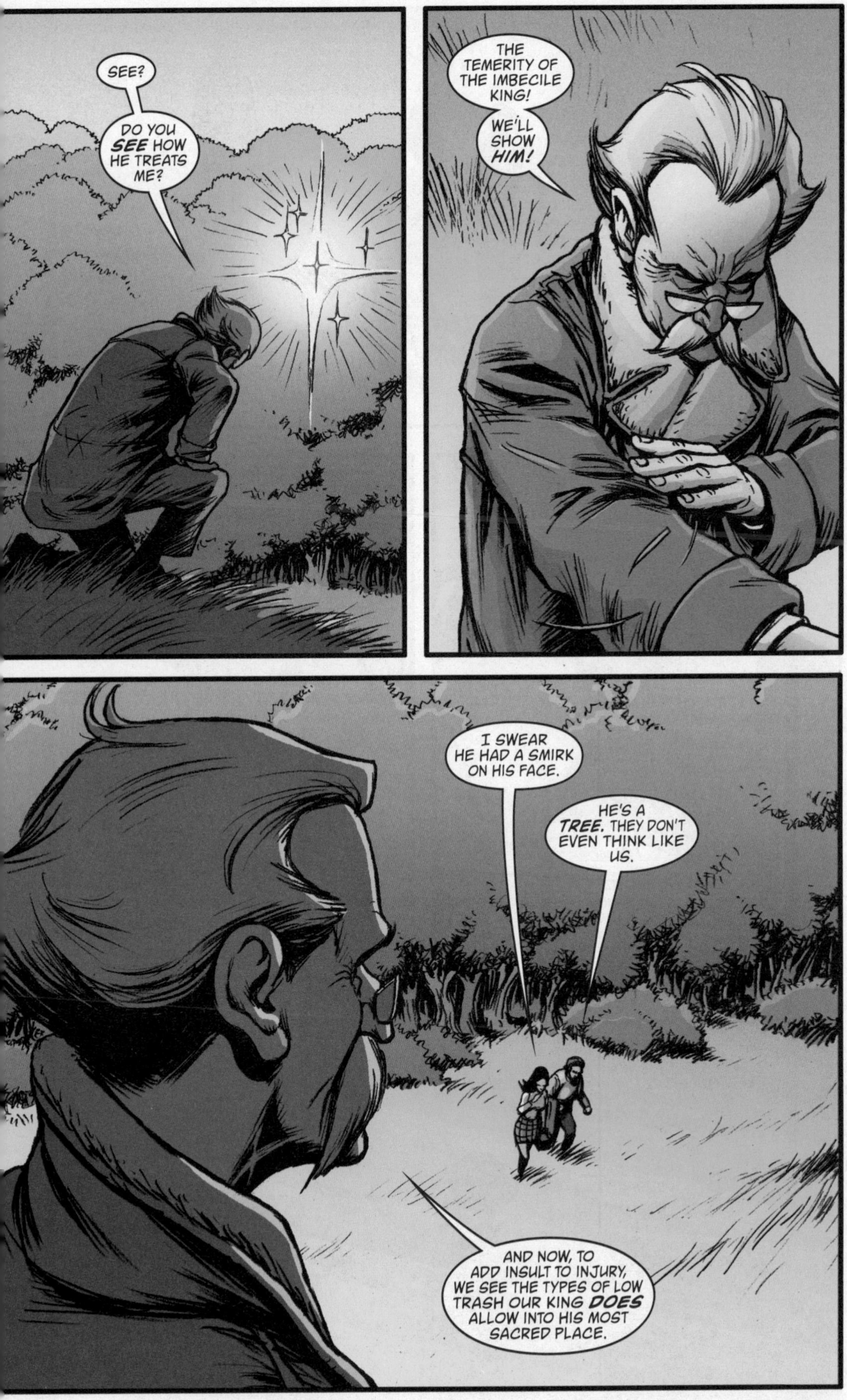
SEE?
DO YOU SEE HOW HE TREATS ME?
THE TEMERITY OF THE IMBECILE KING!
WE'LL SHOW HIM!
I SWEAR HE HAD A SMIRK ON HIS FACE.
HE'S A TREE. THEY DON'T EVEN THINK LIKE US.
AND NOW, TO ADD INSULT TO INJURY, WE SEE THE TYPES OF LOW TRASH OUR KING DOES ALLOW INTO HIS MOST SACRED PLACE.

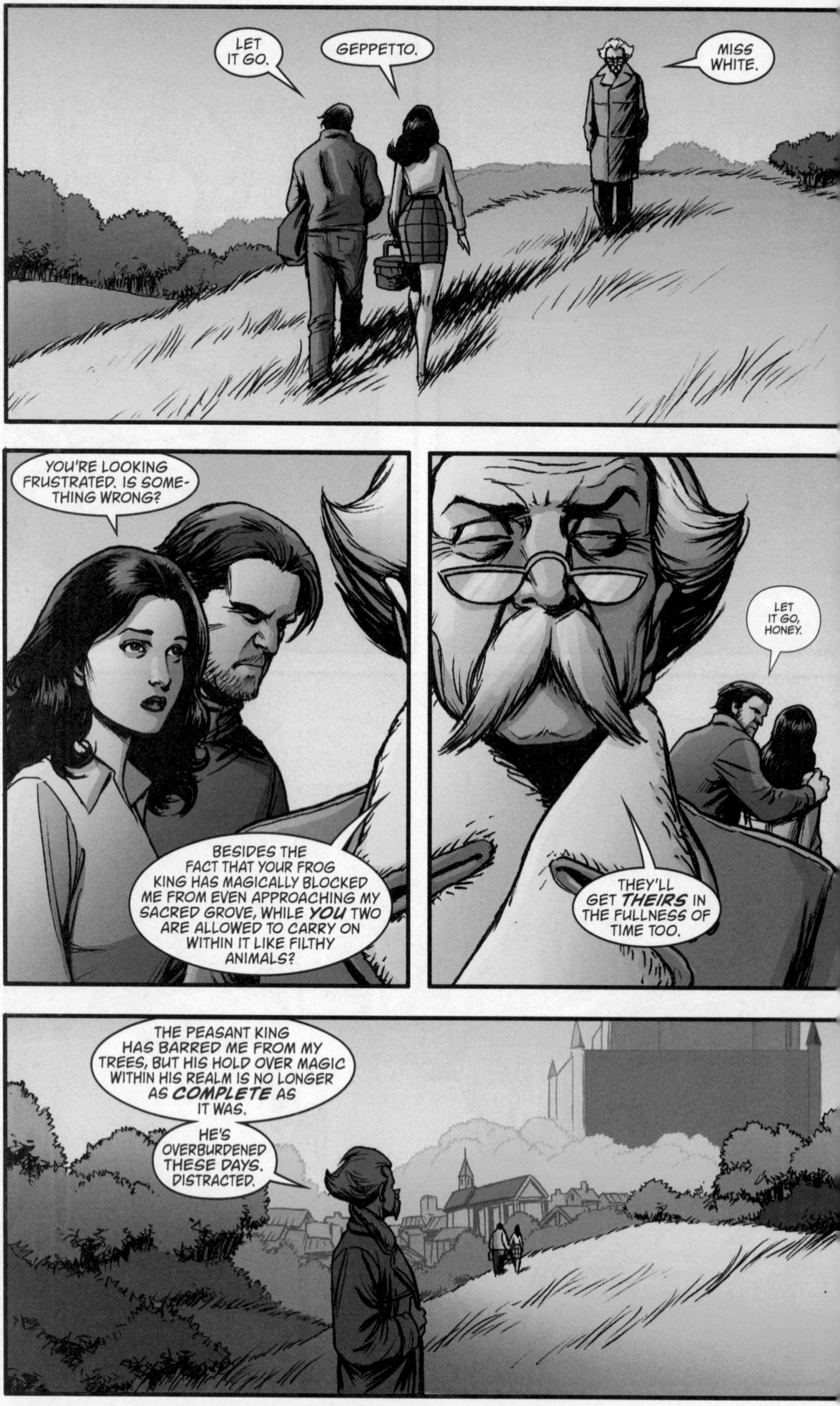
LET IT GO.
GEPPETTO.
MISS WHITE.
YOU'RE LOOKING FRUSTRATED. IS SOME-THING WRONG?
BESIDES THE FACT THAT YOUR FROG KING HAS MAGICALLY BLOCKED ME FROM EVEN APPROACHING MY SACRED GROVE, WHILE YOU TWO ARE ALLOWED TO CARRY ON WITHIN IT LIKE FILTHY ANIMALS?
LET IT GO, HONEY.
THEY'LL GET THEIRS IN THE FULLNESS OF TIME TOO.
THE PEASANT KING HAS BARRED ME FROM MY TREES, BUT HIS HOLD OVER MAGIC WITHIN HIS REALM IS NO LONGER AS COMPLETE AS IT WAS.
HE'S OVERBURDENED THESE DAYS. DISTRACTED.

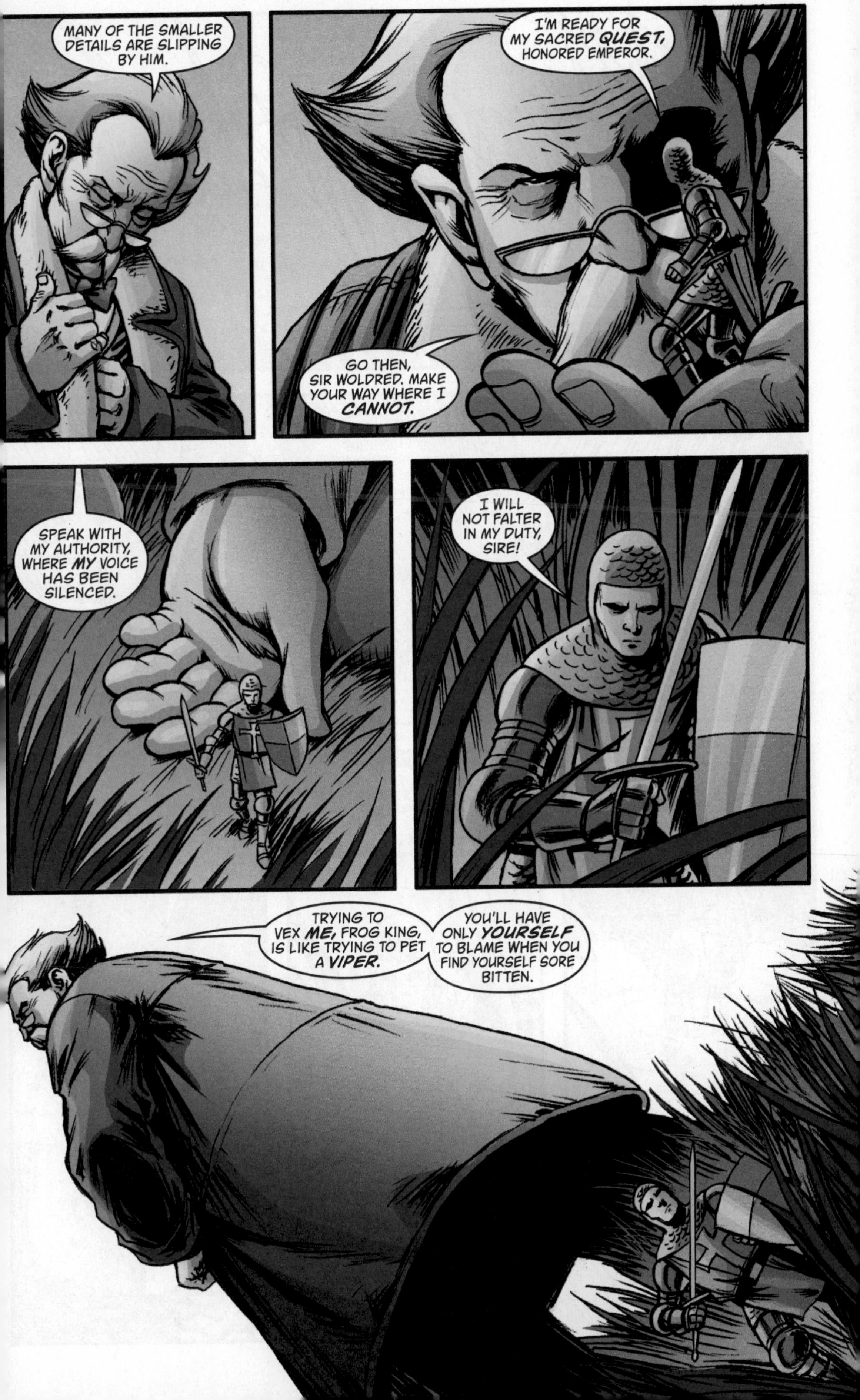
MANY OF THE SMALLER DETAILS ARE SLIPPING BY HIM.
I'M READY FOR MY SACRED QUEST, HONORED EMPEROR.
GO THEN, SIR WOLDRED. MAKE YOUR WAY WHERE I CANNOT.
SPEAK WITH MY AUTHORITY, WHERE MY VOICE HAS BEEN SILENCED.
I WILL NOT FALTER IN MY DUTY, SIRE!
TRYING TO VEX ME, FROG KING, IS LIKE TRYING TO PET A VIPER.
YOU'LL HAVE ONLY YOURSELF TO BLAME WHEN YOU FIND YOURSELF SORE BITTEN.

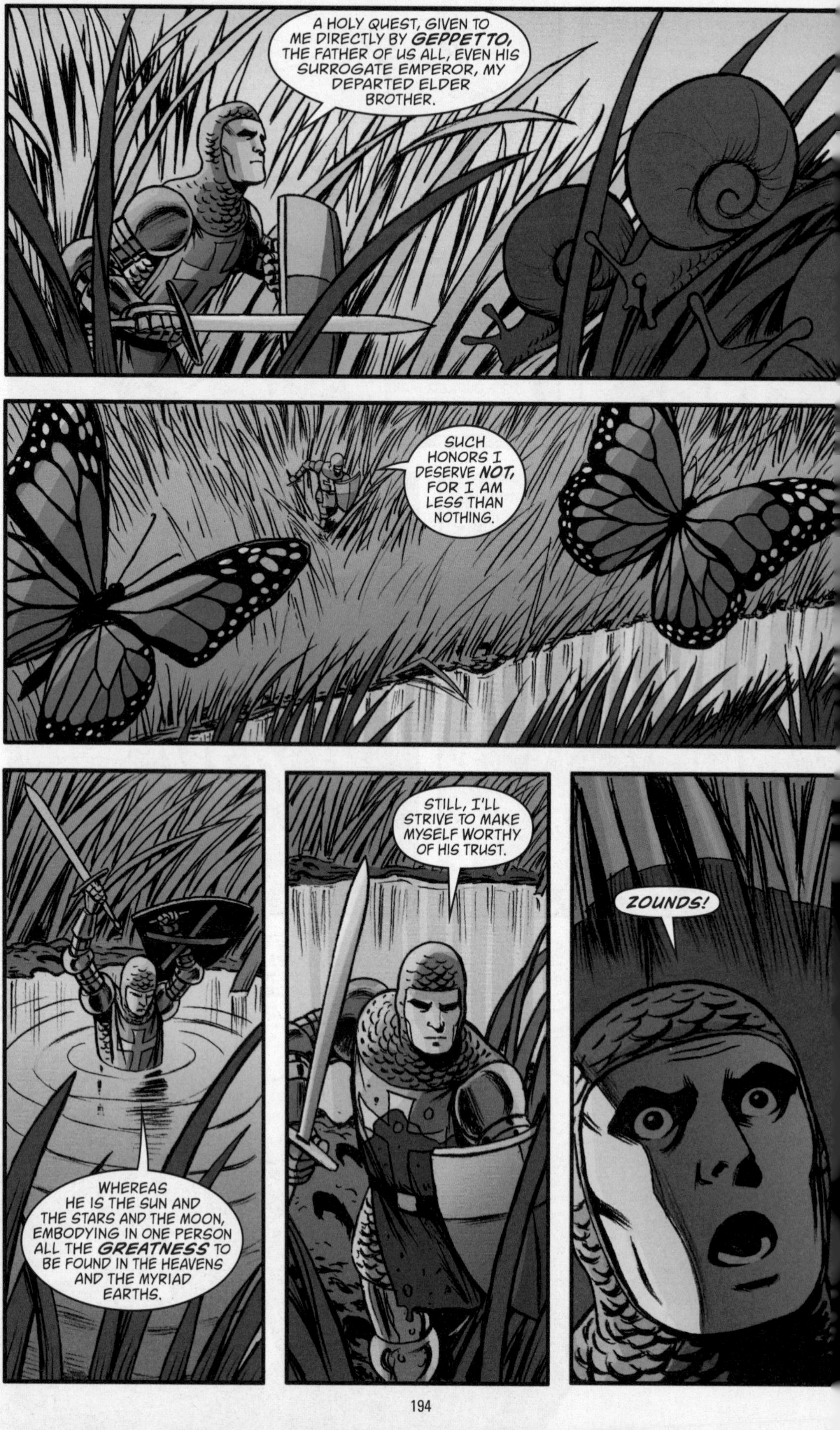
A HOLY QUEST, GIVEN TO ME DIRECTLY BY GEPPETTO, THE FATHER OF US ALL, EVEN HIS SURROGATE EMPEROR, MY DEPARTED ELDER BROTHER.
SUCH HONORS I DESERVE NOT, FOR I AM LESS THAN NOTHING.
WHEREAS HE IS THE SUN AND THE STARS AND THE MOON, EMBODYING IN ONE PERSON ALL THE GREATNESS TO BE FOUND IN THE HEAVENS AND THE MYRIAD EARTHS.
STILL, I'LL STRIVE TO MAKE MYSELF WORTHY OF HIS TRUST.
ZOUNDS!

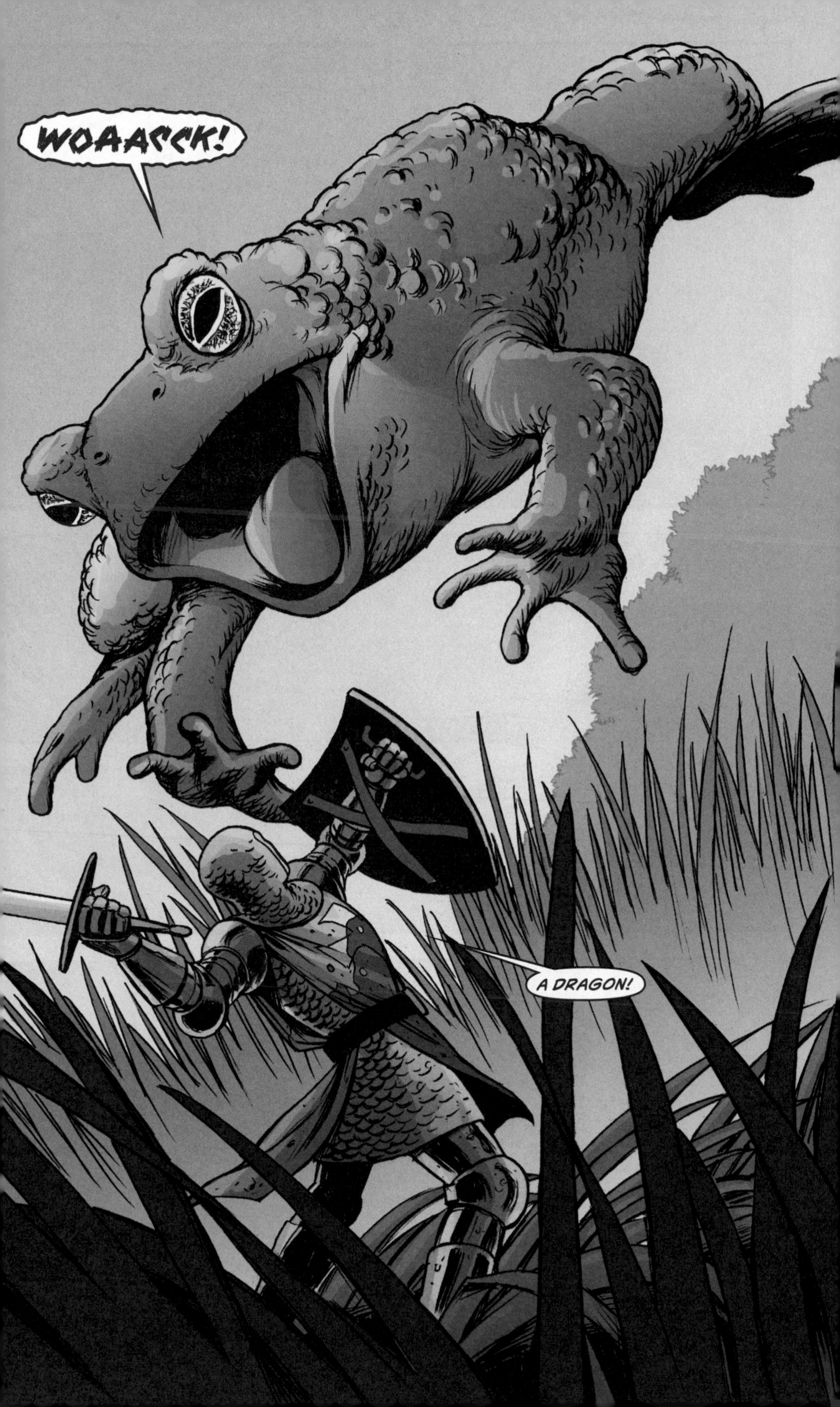
WOAACCK!
A DRAGON!

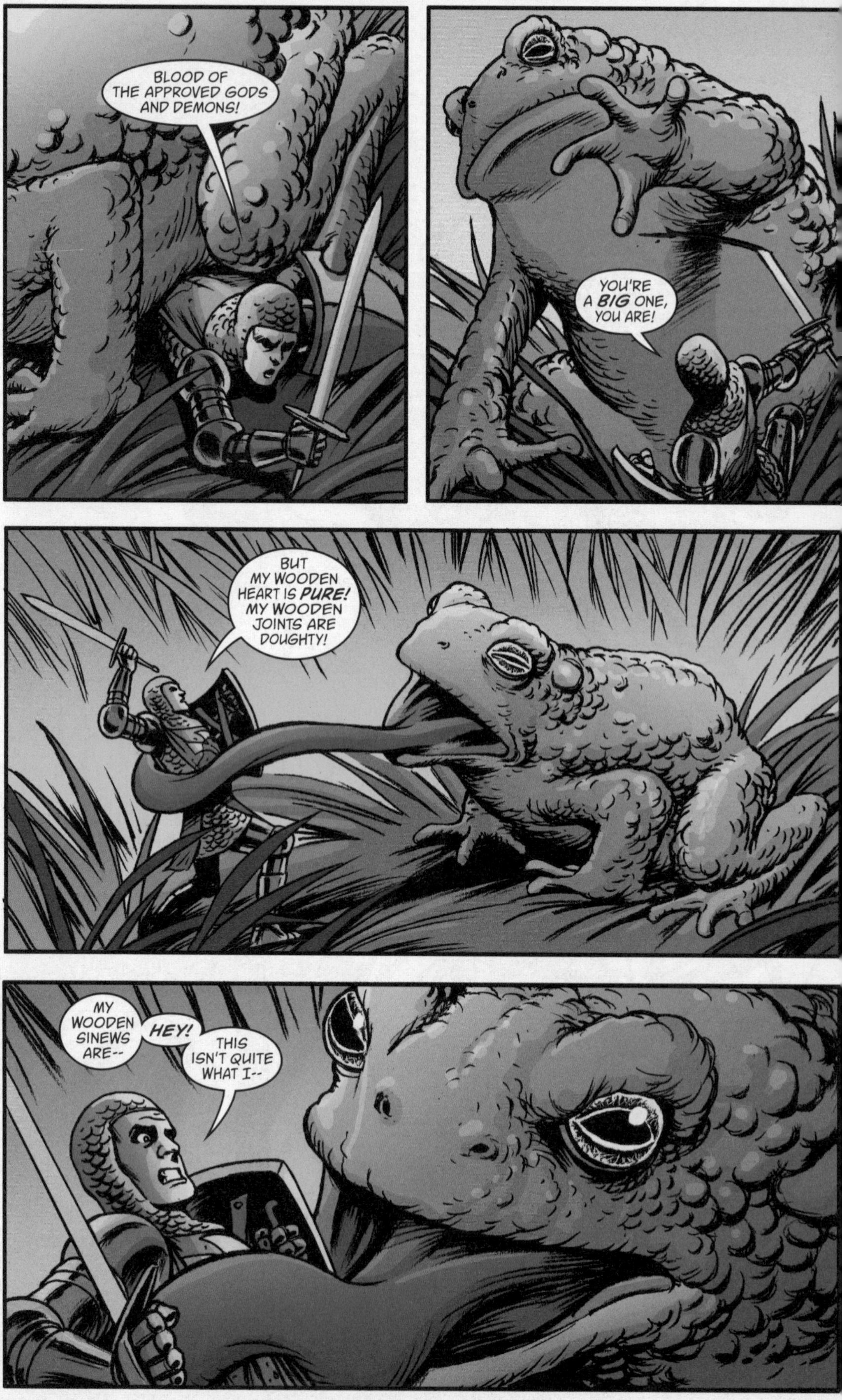
BLOOD OF THE APPROVED GODS AND DEMONS!
YOU'RE A *BIG* ONE, YOU ARE!
BUT MY WOODEN HEART IS *PURE!* MY WOODEN JOINTS ARE DOUGHTY!
MY WOODEN SINEWS ARE--
HEY!
THIS ISN'T QUITE WHAT I--

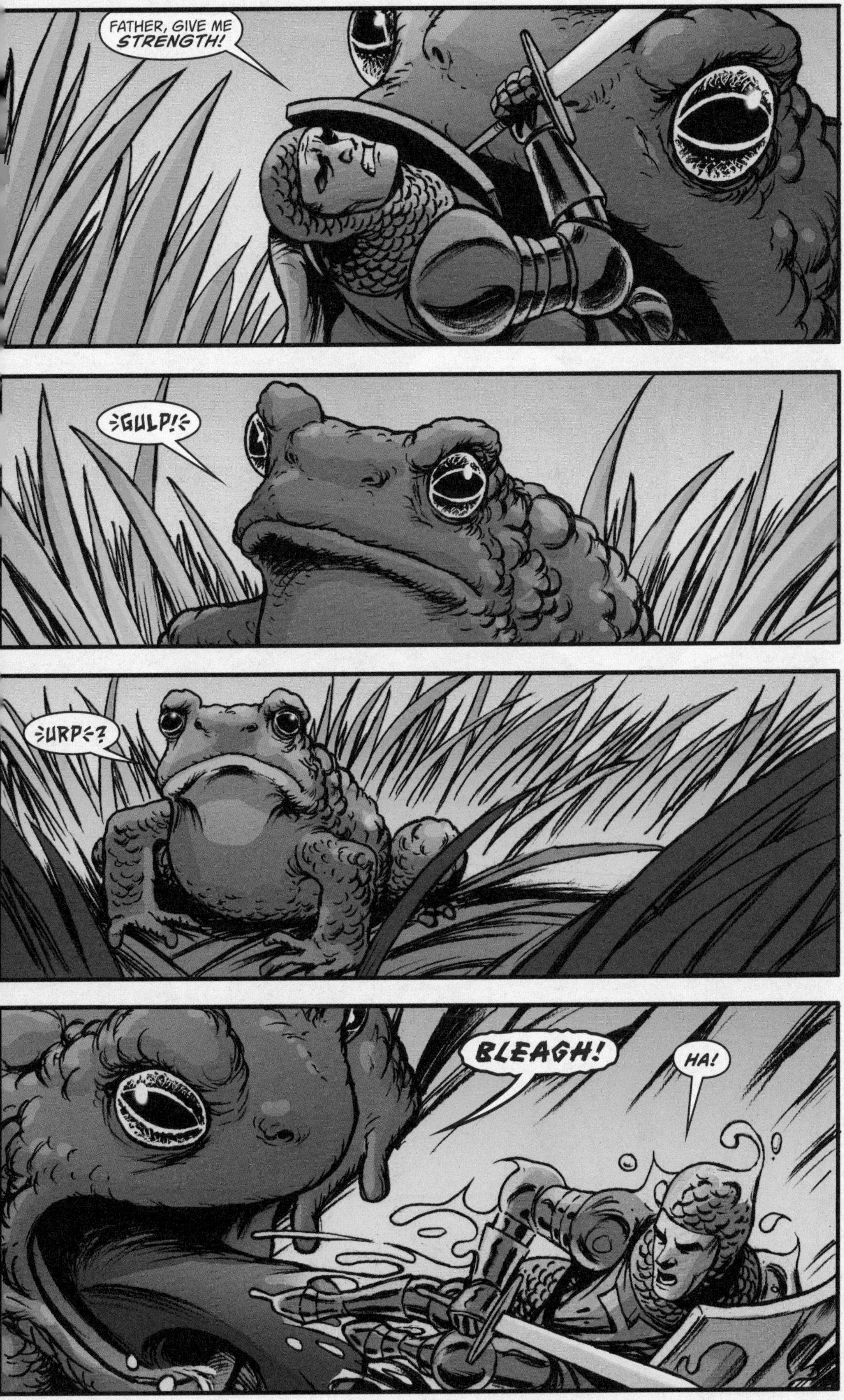
FATHER, GIVE ME STRENGTH!
GULP!
URP?
BLEAGH!
HA!

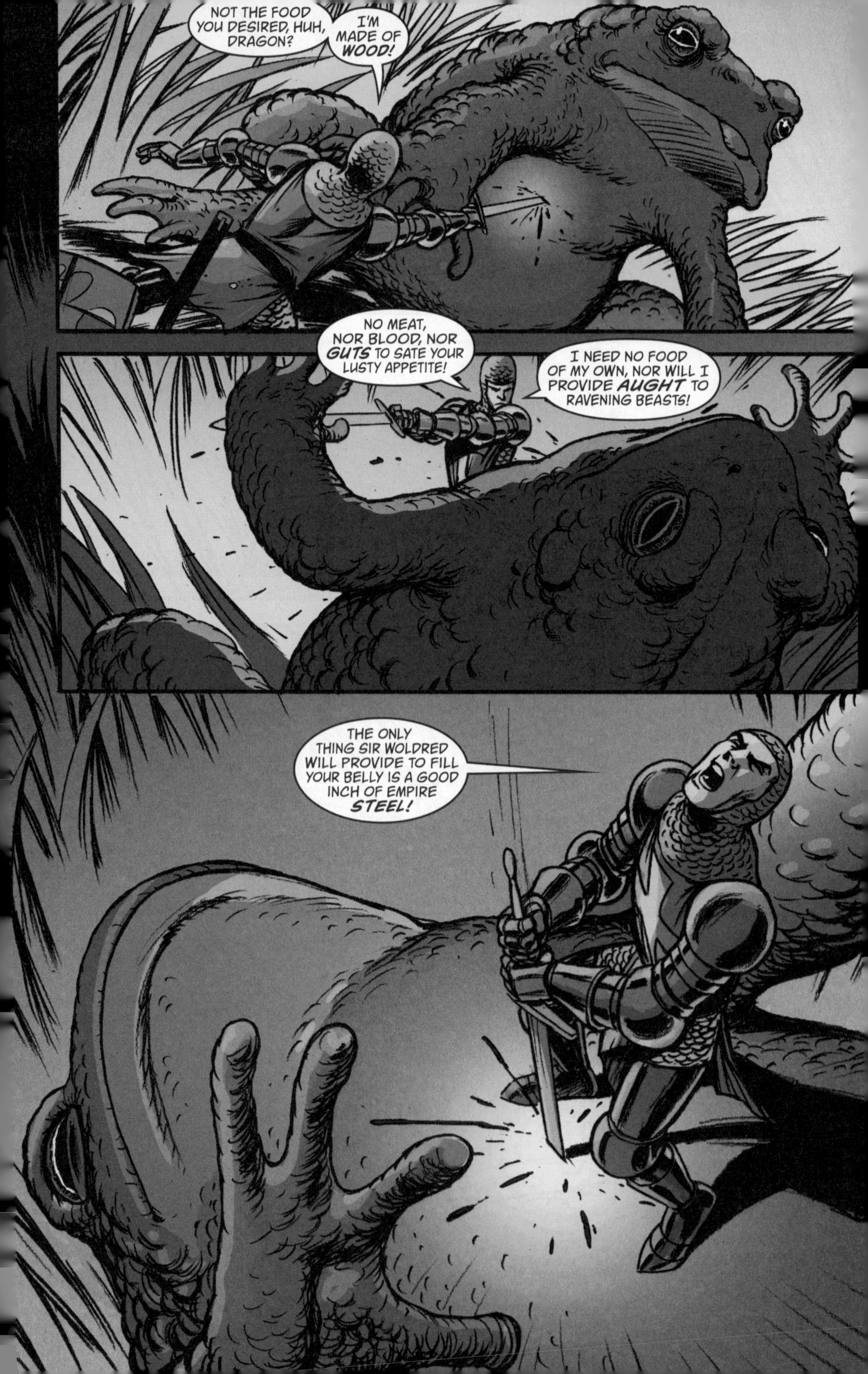
NOT THE FOOD YOU DESIRED, HUH, DRAGON?
I'M MADE OF WOOD!
NO MEAT, NOR BLOOD, NOR GUTS TO SATE YOUR LUSTY APPETITE!
I NEED NO FOOD OF MY OWN, NOR WILL I PROVIDE AUGHT TO RAVENING BEASTS!
THE ONLY THING SIR WOLDRED WILL PROVIDE TO FILL YOUR BELLY IS A GOOD INCH OF EMPIRE STEEL!

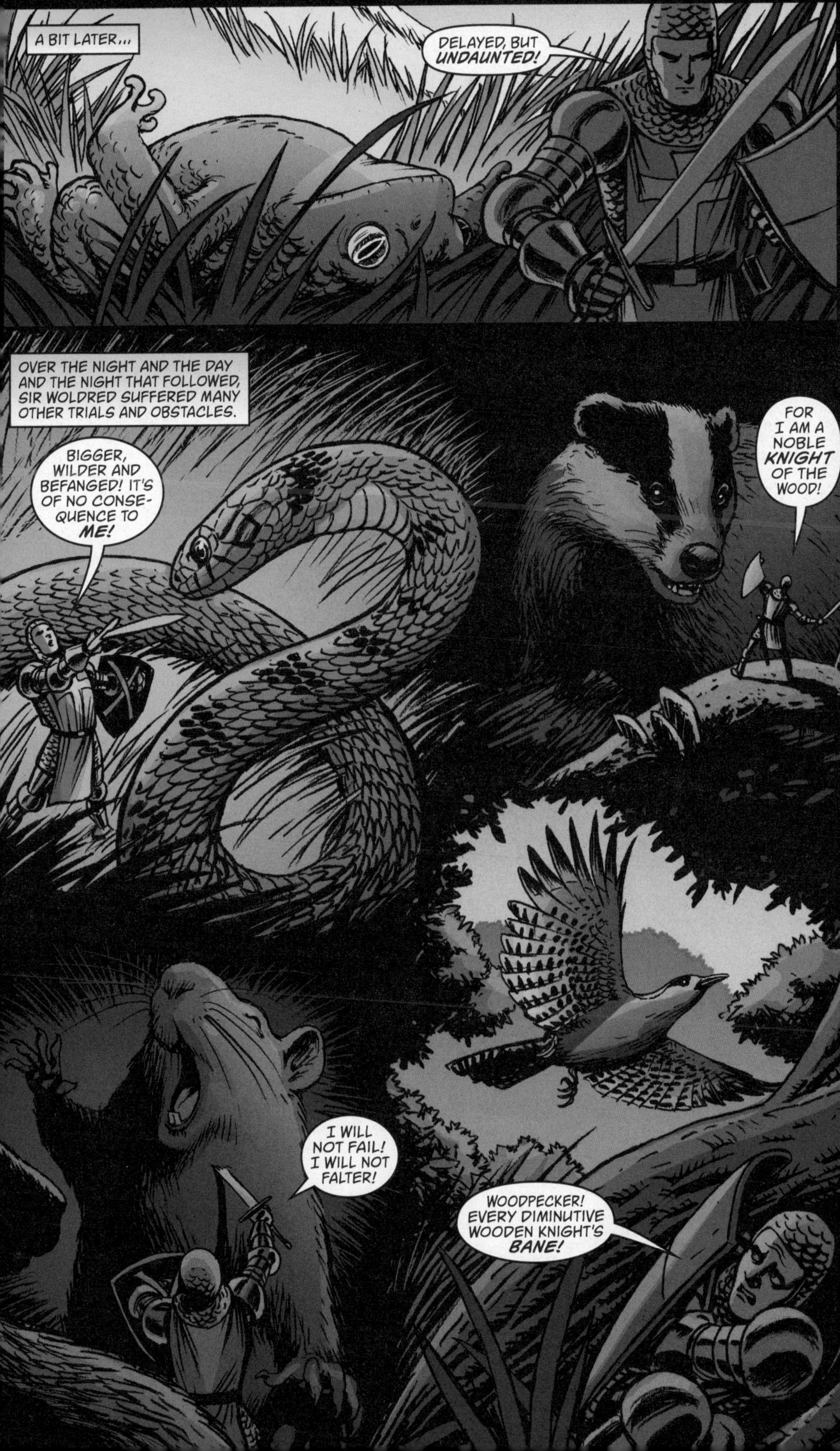
A BIT LATER...
DELAYED, BUT UNDAUNTED!
OVER THE NIGHT AND THE DAY AND THE NIGHT THAT FOLLOWED, SIR WOLDRED SUFFERED MANY OTHER TRIALS AND OBSTACLES.
BIGGER, WILDER AND BEFANGED! IT'S OF NO CONSEQUENCE TO ME!
FOR I AM A NOBLE KNIGHT OF THE WOOD!
I WILL NOT FAIL! I WILL NOT FALTER!
WOODPECKER! EVERY DIMINUTIVE WOODEN KNIGHT'S BANE!

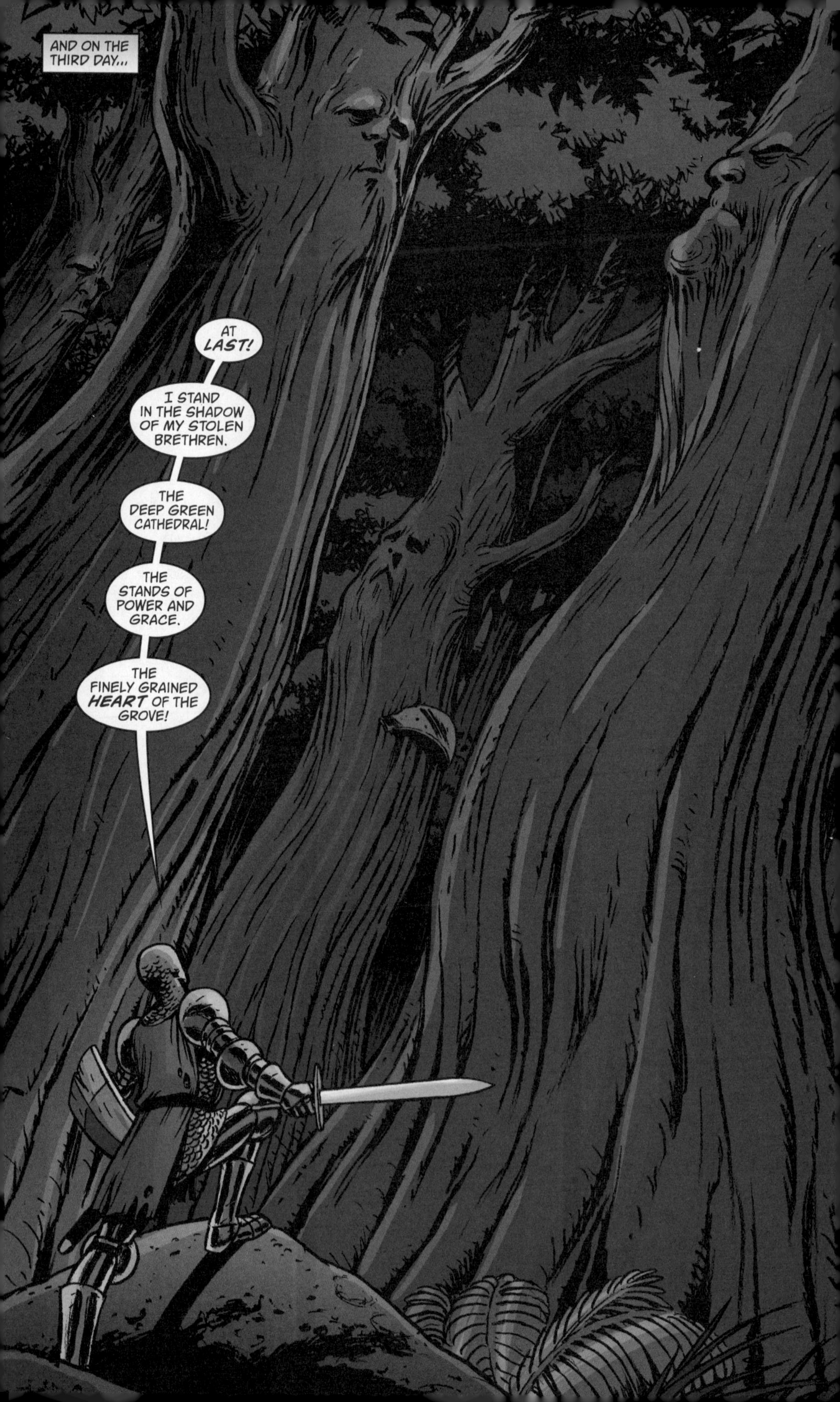
AND ON THE THIRD DAY...
AT LAST!
I STAND IN THE SHADOW OF MY STOLEN BRETHREN.
THE DEEP GREEN CATHEDRAL!
THE STANDS OF POWER AND GRACE.
THE FINELY GRAINED HEART OF THE GROVE!

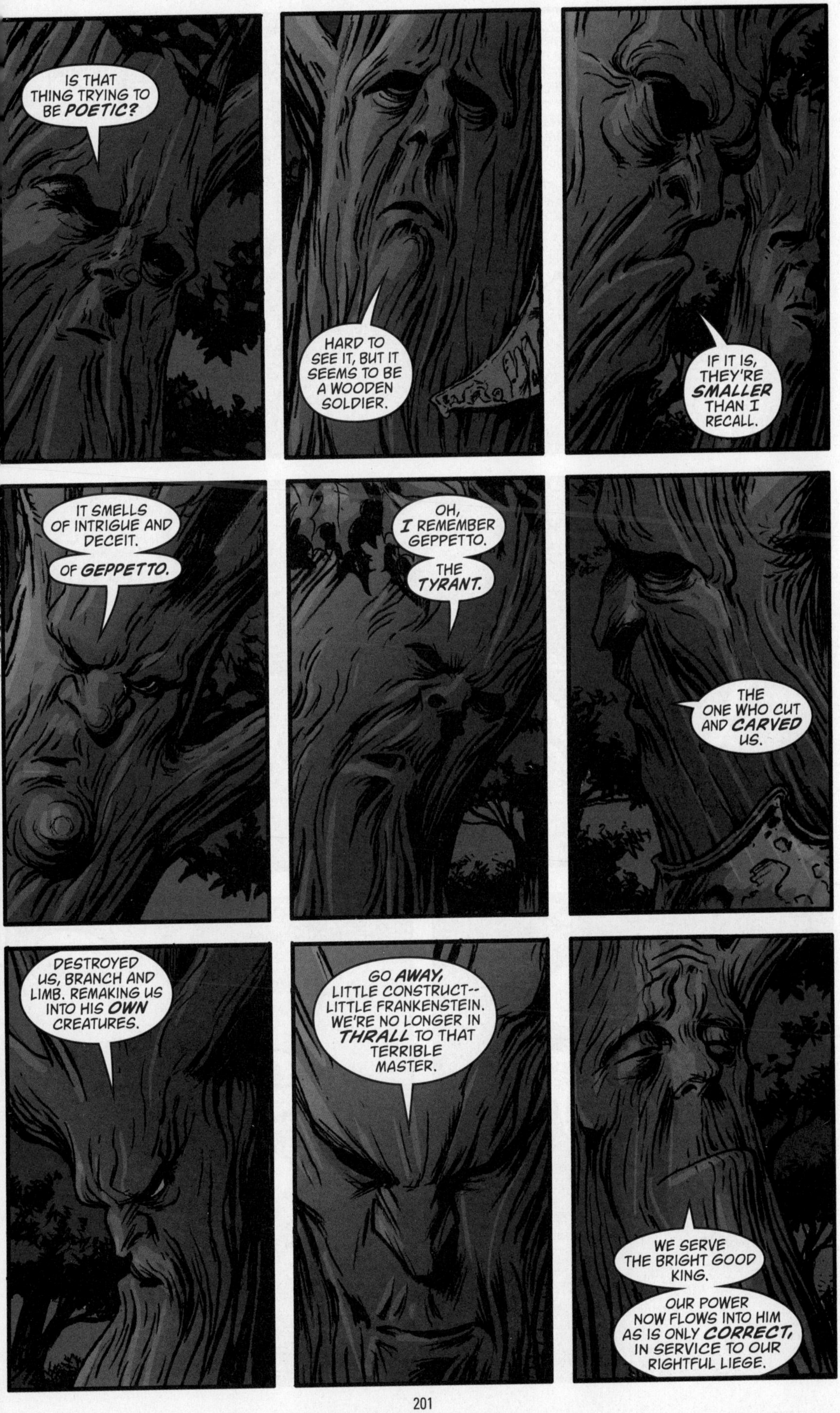
IS THAT THING TRYING TO BE POETIC?
HARD TO SEE IT, BUT IT SEEMS TO BE A WOODEN SOLDIER.
IF IT IS, THEY'RE SMALLER THAN I RECALL.
IT SMELLS OF INTRIGUE AND DECEIT.
OF GEPPETTO.
OH, I REMEMBER GEPPETTO.
THE TYRANT.
THE ONE WHO CUT AND CARVED US.
DESTROYED US, BRANCH AND LIMB. REMAKING US INTO HIS OWN CREATURES.
GO AWAY, LITTLE CONSTRUCT-- LITTLE FRANKENSTEIN. WE'RE NO LONGER IN THRALL TO THAT TERRIBLE MASTER.
WE SERVE THE BRIGHT GOOD KING.
OUR POWER NOW FLOWS INTO HIM AS IS ONLY CORRECT, IN SERVICE TO OUR RIGHTFUL LIEGE.

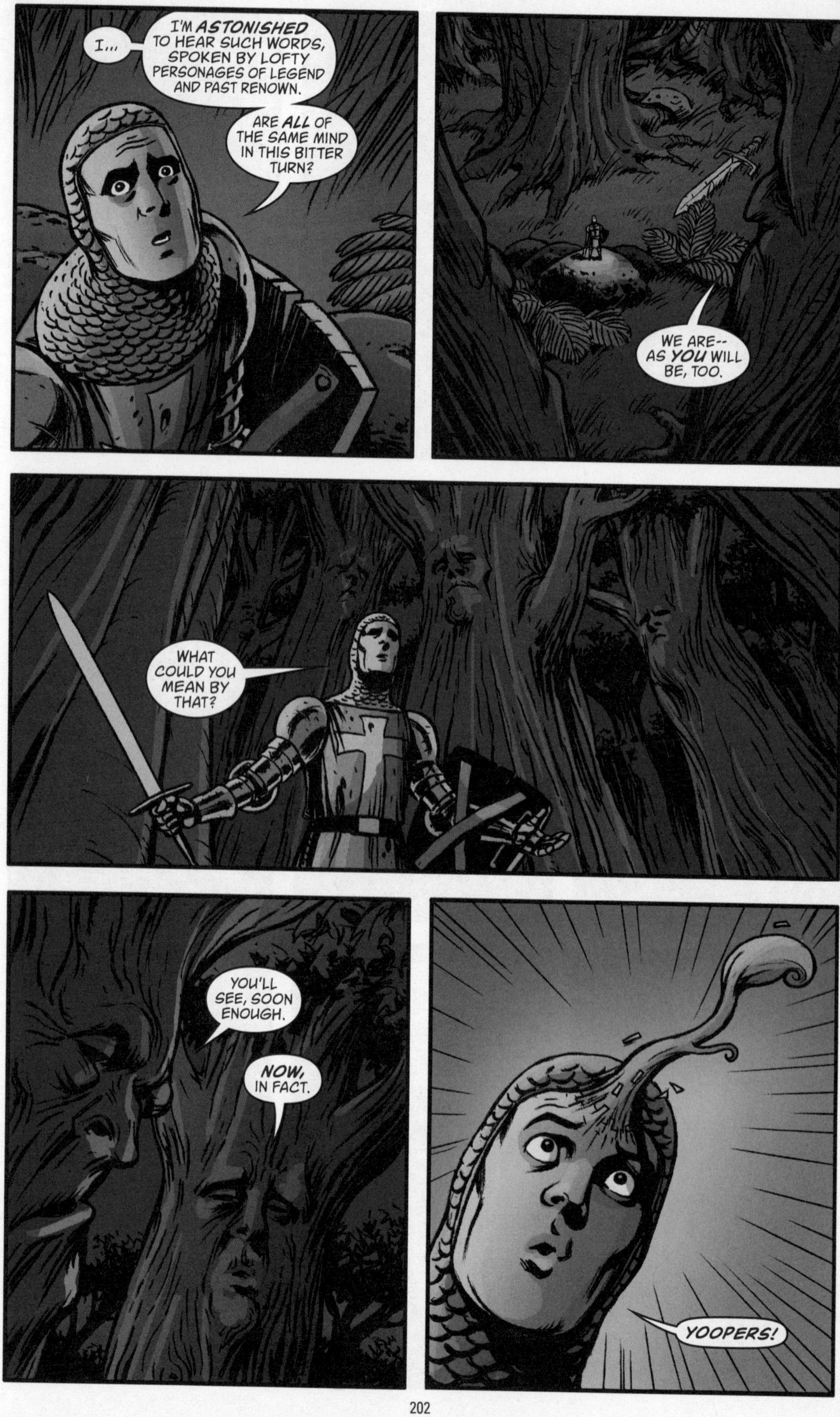
I...
I'M ASTONISHED TO HEAR SUCH WORDS, SPOKEN BY LOFTY PERSONAGES OF LEGEND AND PAST RENOWN.
ARE ALL OF THE SAME MIND IN THIS BITTER TURN?
WE ARE-- AS YOU WILL BE, TOO.
WHAT COULD YOU MEAN BY THAT?
YOU'LL SEE, SOON ENOUGH.
NOW, IN FACT.
YOOPERS!

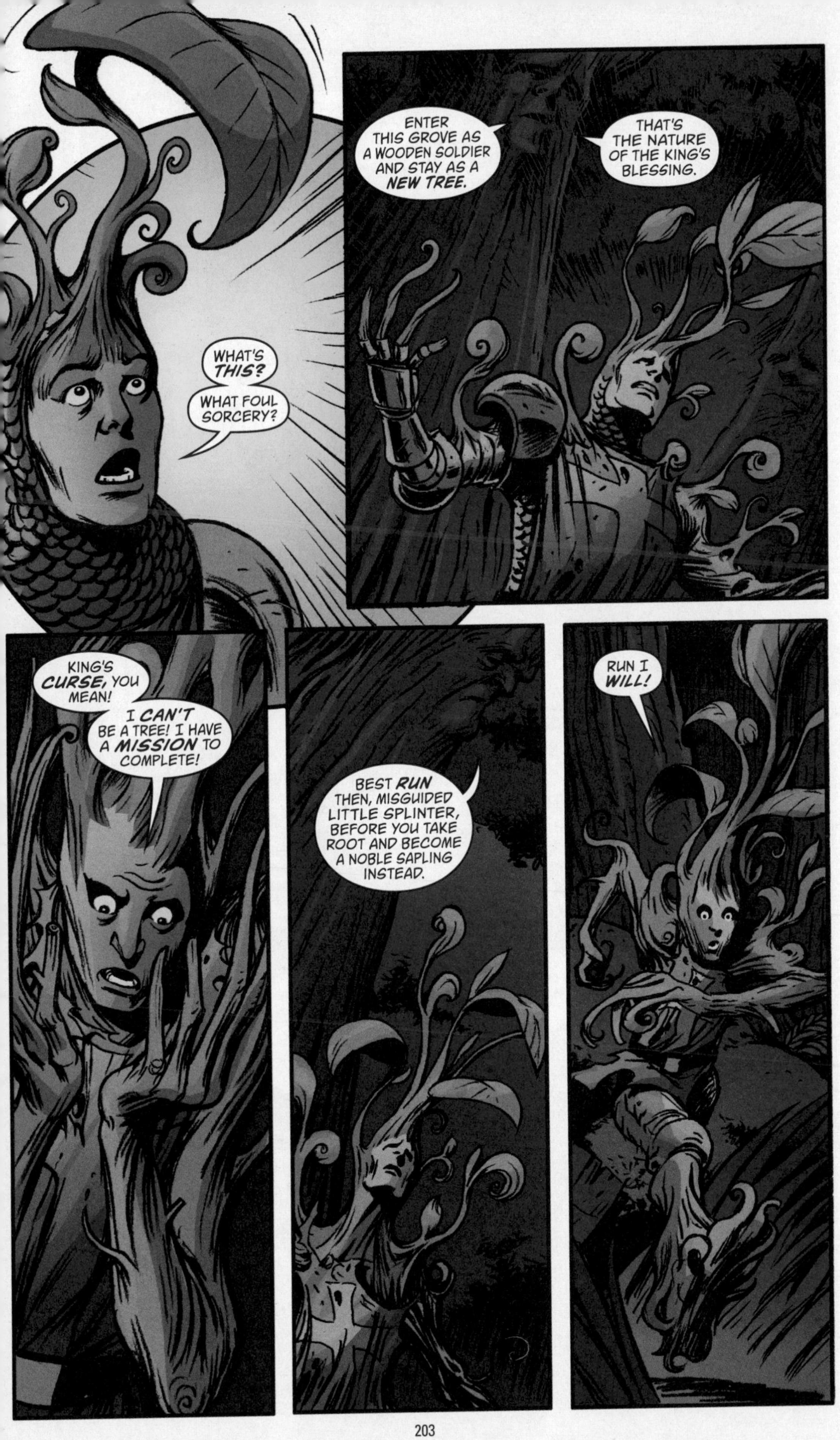
WHAT'S THIS? WHAT FOUL SORCERY?
ENTER THIS GROVE AS A WOODEN SOLDIER AND STAY AS A NEW TREE.
THAT'S THE NATURE OF THE KING'S BLESSING.
KING'S CURSE, YOU MEAN!
I CAN'T BE A TREE! I HAVE A MISSION TO COMPLETE!
BEST RUN THEN, MISGUIDED LITTLE SPLINTER, BEFORE YOU TAKE ROOT AND BECOME A NOBLE SAPLING INSTEAD.
RUN I WILL!

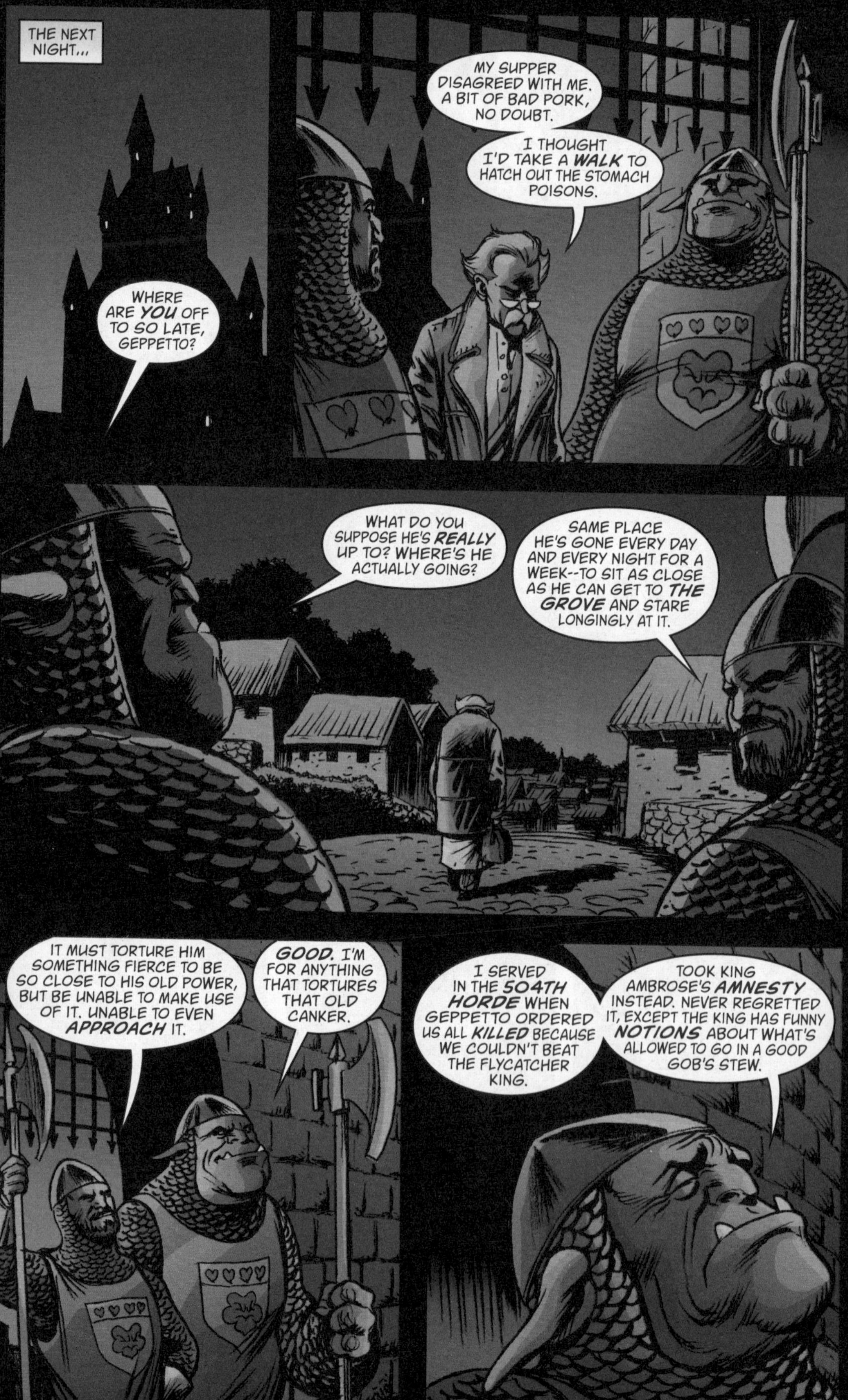
THE NEXT NIGHT...
WHERE ARE YOU OFF TO SO LATE, GEPPETTO?
MY SUPPER DISAGREED WITH ME. A BIT OF BAD PORK, NO DOUBT.
I THOUGHT I'D TAKE A WALK TO HATCH OUT THE STOMACH POISONS.
WHAT DO YOU SUPPOSE HE'S REALLY UP TO? WHERE'S HE ACTUALLY GOING?
SAME PLACE HE'S GONE EVERY DAY AND EVERY NIGHT FOR A WEEK--TO SIT AS CLOSE AS HE CAN GET TO THE GROVE AND STARE LONGINGLY AT IT.
IT MUST TORTURE HIM SOMETHING FIERCE TO BE SO CLOSE TO HIS OLD POWER, BUT BE UNABLE TO MAKE USE OF IT. UNABLE TO EVEN APPROACH IT.
GOOD. I'M FOR ANYTHING THAT TORTURES THAT OLD CANKER.
I SERVED IN THE 504TH HORDE WHEN GEPPETTO ORDERED US ALL KILLED BECAUSE WE COULDN'T BEAT THE FLYCATCHER KING.
TOOK KING AMBROSE'S AMNESTY INSTEAD. NEVER REGRETTED IT, EXCEPT THE KING HAS FUNNY NOTIONS ABOUT WHAT'S ALLOWED TO GO IN A GOOD GOB'S STEW.

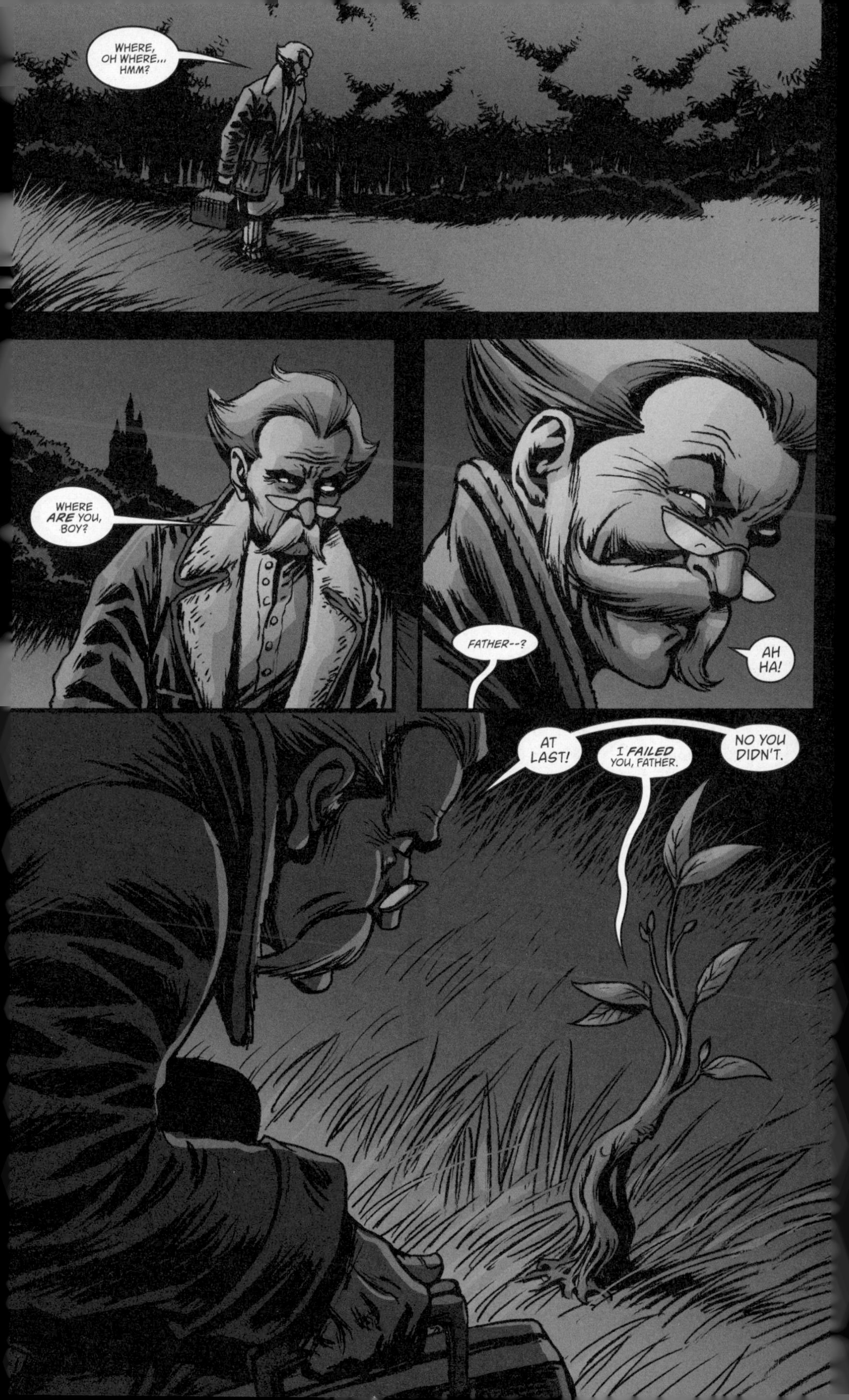
WHERE, OH WHERE... HMM?
WHERE ARE YOU, BOY?
FATHER--?
AH HA!
AT LAST!
I FAILED YOU, FATHER.
NO YOU DIDN'T.

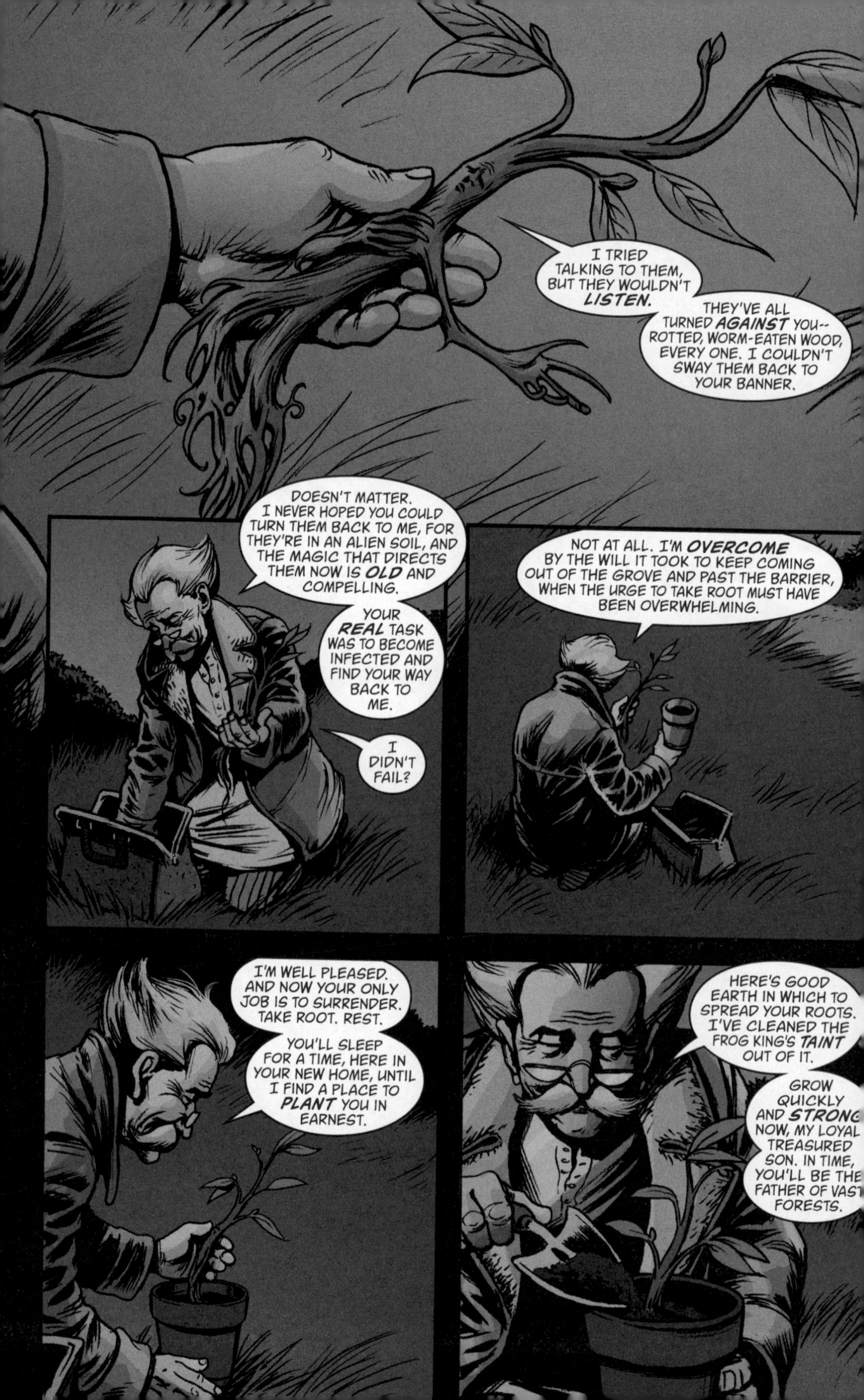
I TRIED TALKING TO THEM, BUT THEY WOULDN'T LISTEN.
THEY'VE ALL TURNED AGAINST YOU-- ROTTED, WORM-EATEN WOOD, EVERY ONE. I COULDN'T SWAY THEM BACK TO YOUR BANNER.
DOESN'T MATTER. I NEVER HOPED YOU COULD TURN THEM BACK TO ME, FOR THEY'RE IN AN ALIEN SOIL, AND THE MAGIC THAT DIRECTS THEM NOW IS OLD AND COMPELLING.
YOUR REAL TASK WAS TO BECOME INFECTED AND FIND YOUR WAY BACK TO ME.
I DIDN'T FAIL?
NOT AT ALL. I'M OVERCOME BY THE WILL IT TOOK TO KEEP COMING OUT OF THE GROVE AND PAST THE BARRIER, WHEN THE URGE TO TAKE ROOT MUST HAVE BEEN OVERWHELMING.
I'M WELL PLEASED. AND NOW YOUR ONLY JOB IS TO SURRENDER. TAKE ROOT. REST.
YOU'LL SLEEP FOR A TIME, HERE IN YOUR NEW HOME, UNTIL I FIND A PLACE TO PLANT YOU IN EARNEST.
HERE'S GOOD EARTH IN WHICH TO SPREAD YOUR ROOTS. I'VE CLEANED THE FROG KING'S TAINT OUT OF IT.
GROW QUICKLY AND STRONG NOW, MY LOYAL TREASURED SON. IN TIME, YOU'LL BE THE FATHER OF VAST FORESTS.

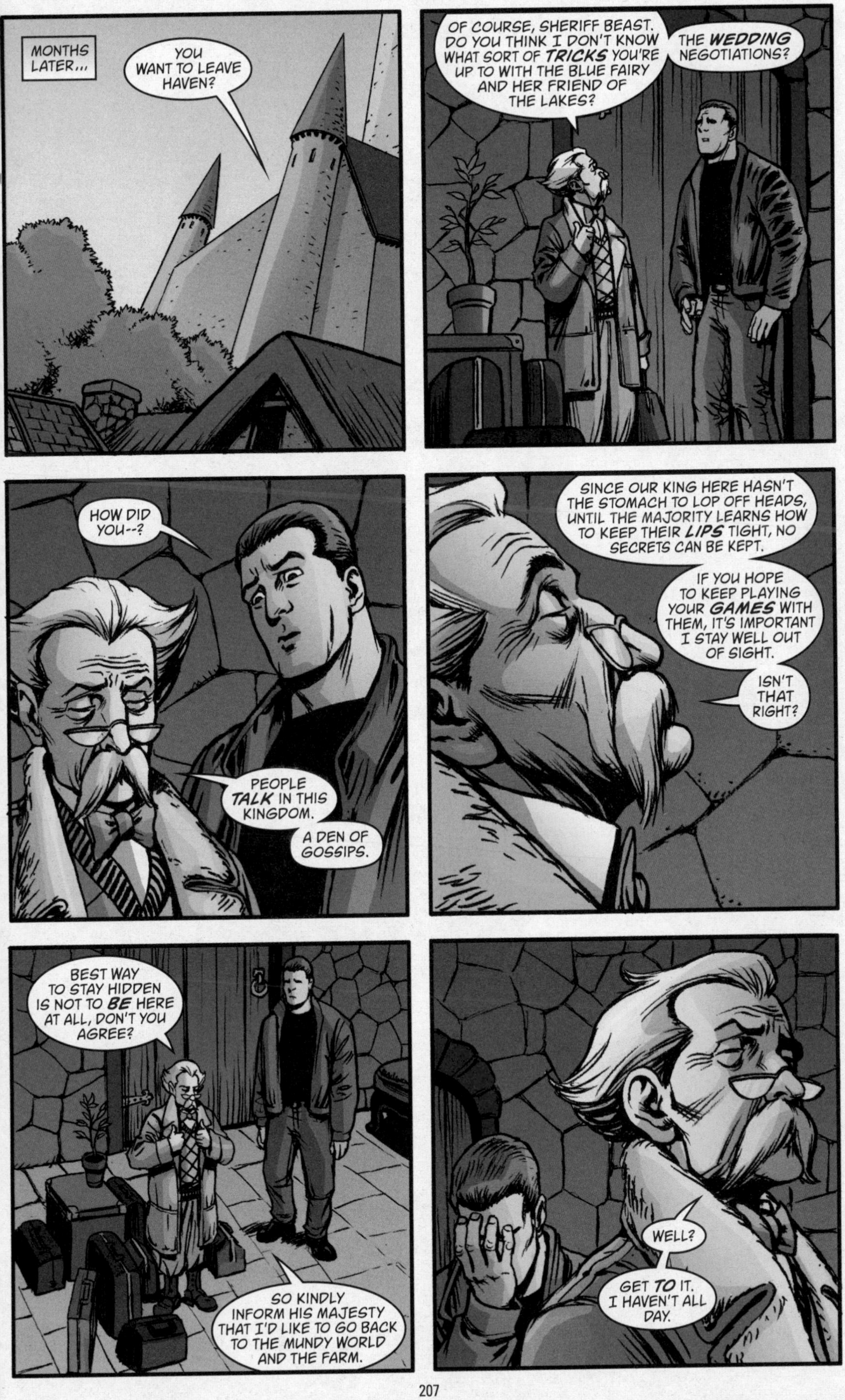
MONTHS LATER...
YOU WANT TO LEAVE HAVEN?
OF COURSE, SHERIFF BEAST. DO YOU THINK I DON'T KNOW WHAT SORT OF TRICKS YOU'RE UP TO WITH THE BLUE FAIRY AND HER FRIEND OF THE LAKES?
THE WEDDING NEGOTIATIONS?
HOW DID YOU--?
PEOPLE TALK IN THIS KINGDOM.
A DEN OF GOSSIPS.
SINCE OUR KING HERE HASN'T THE STOMACH TO LOP OFF HEADS, UNTIL THE MAJORITY LEARNS HOW TO KEEP THEIR LIPS TIGHT, NO SECRETS CAN BE KEPT.
IF YOU HOPE TO KEEP PLAYING YOUR GAMES WITH THEM, IT'S IMPORTANT I STAY WELL OUT OF SIGHT.
ISN'T THAT RIGHT?
BEST WAY TO STAY HIDDEN IS NOT TO BE HERE AT ALL, DON'T YOU AGREE?
SO KINDLY INFORM HIS MAJESTY THAT I'D LIKE TO GO BACK TO THE MUNDY WORLD AND THE FARM.
WELL?
GET TO IT. I HAVEN'T ALL DAY.

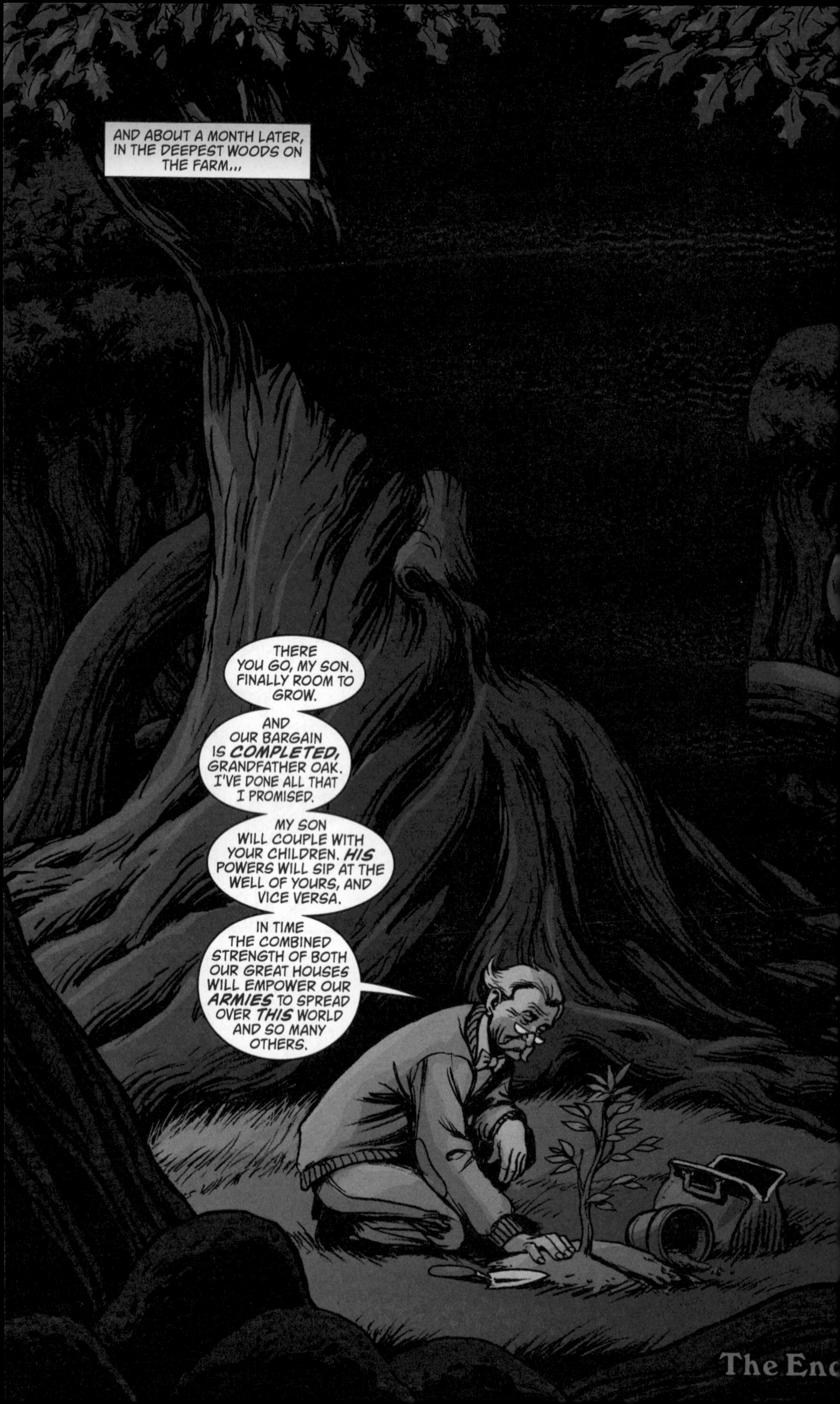
AND ABOUT A MONTH LATER, IN THE DEEPEST WOODS ON THE FARM...
THERE YOU GO, MY SON. FINALLY ROOM TO GROW.
AND OUR BARGAIN IS *COMPLETED,* GRANDFATHER OAK. I'VE DONE ALL THAT I PROMISED.
MY SON WILL COUPLE WITH YOUR CHILDREN. *HIS* POWERS WILL SIP AT THE WELL OF YOURS, AND VICE VERSA.
IN TIME THE COMBINED STRENGTH OF BOTH OUR GREAT HOUSES WILL EMPOWER OUR *ARMIES* TO SPREAD OVER *THIS* WORLD AND SO MANY OTHERS.
The End

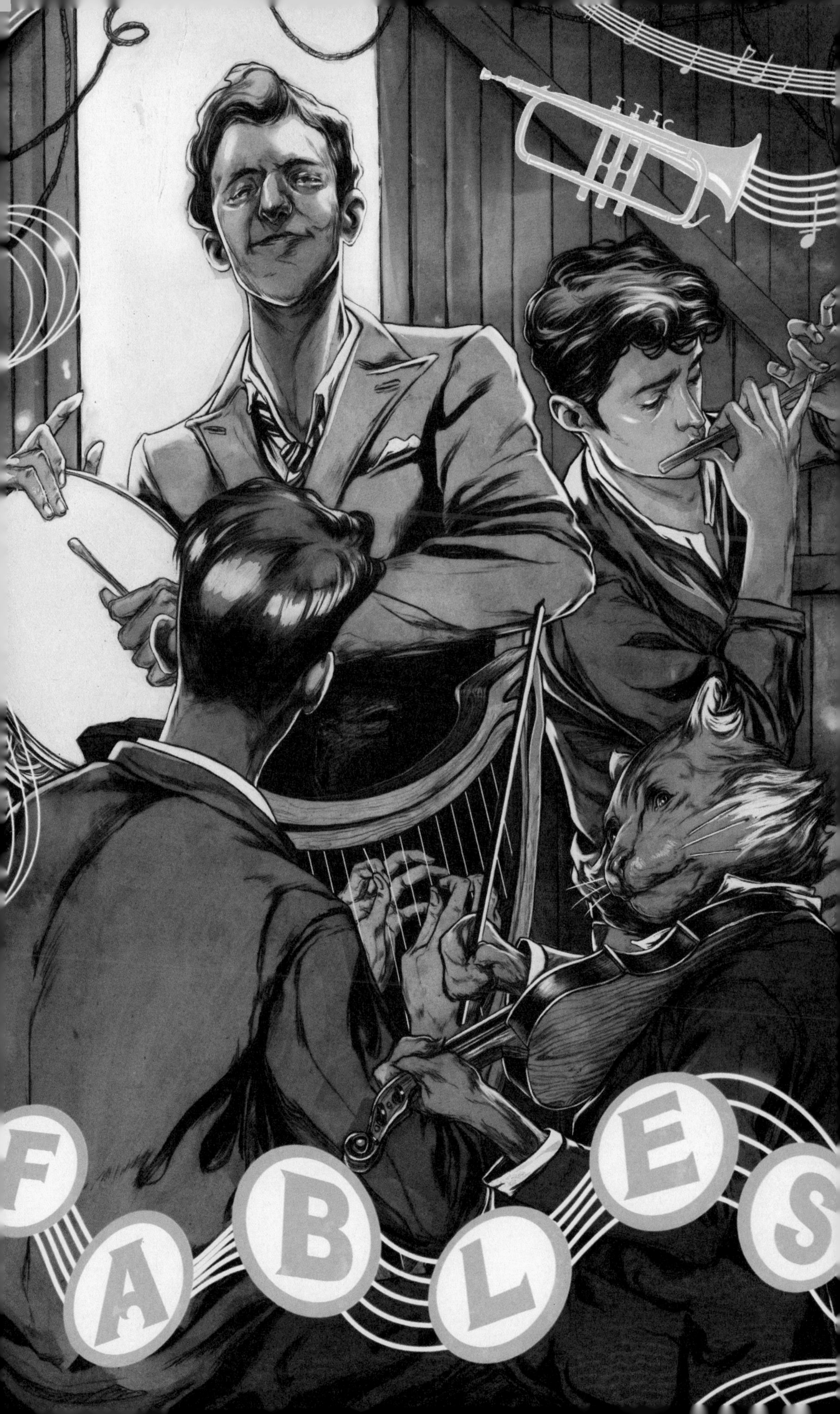
FABLES

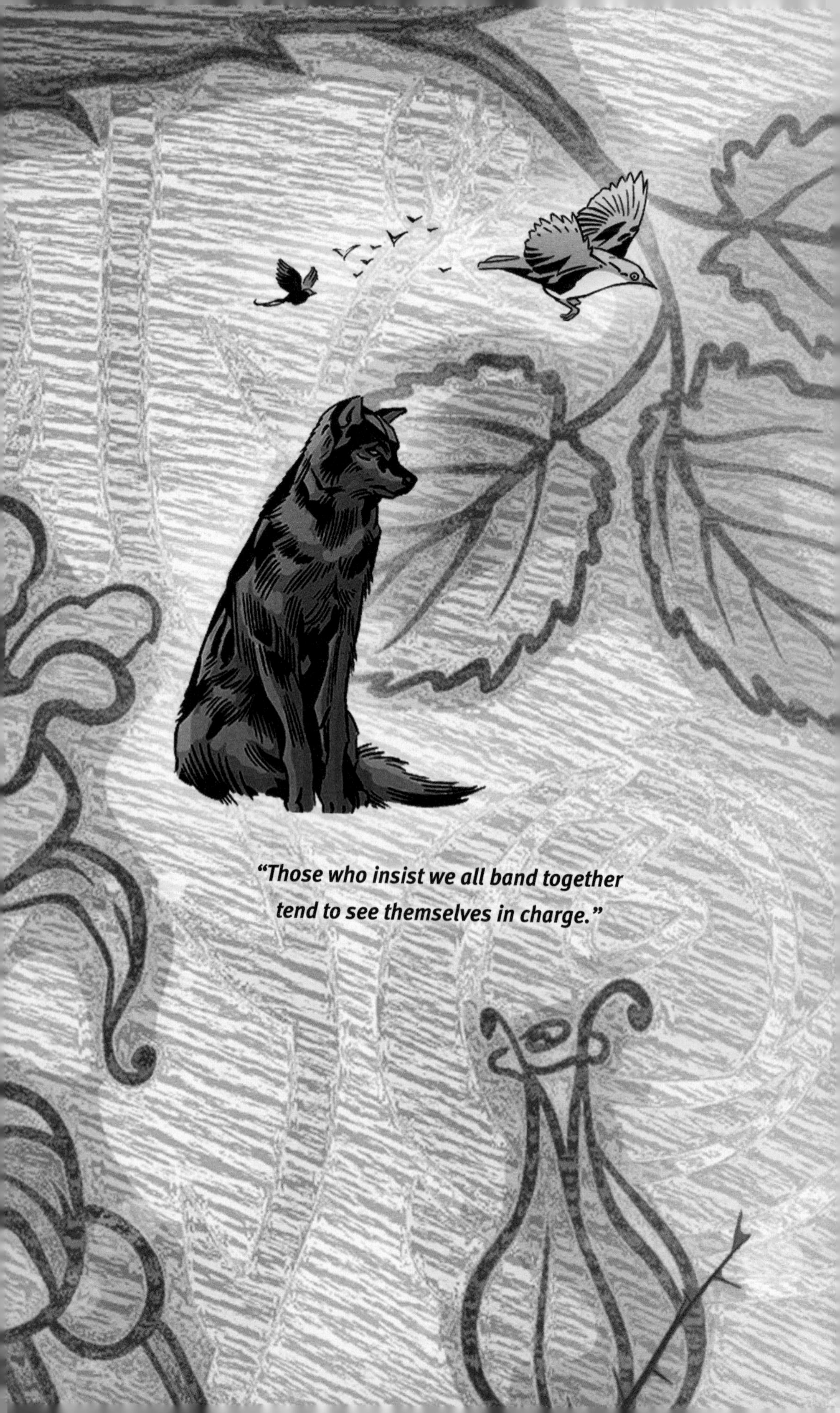
"Those who insist we all band together
tend to see themselves in charge."

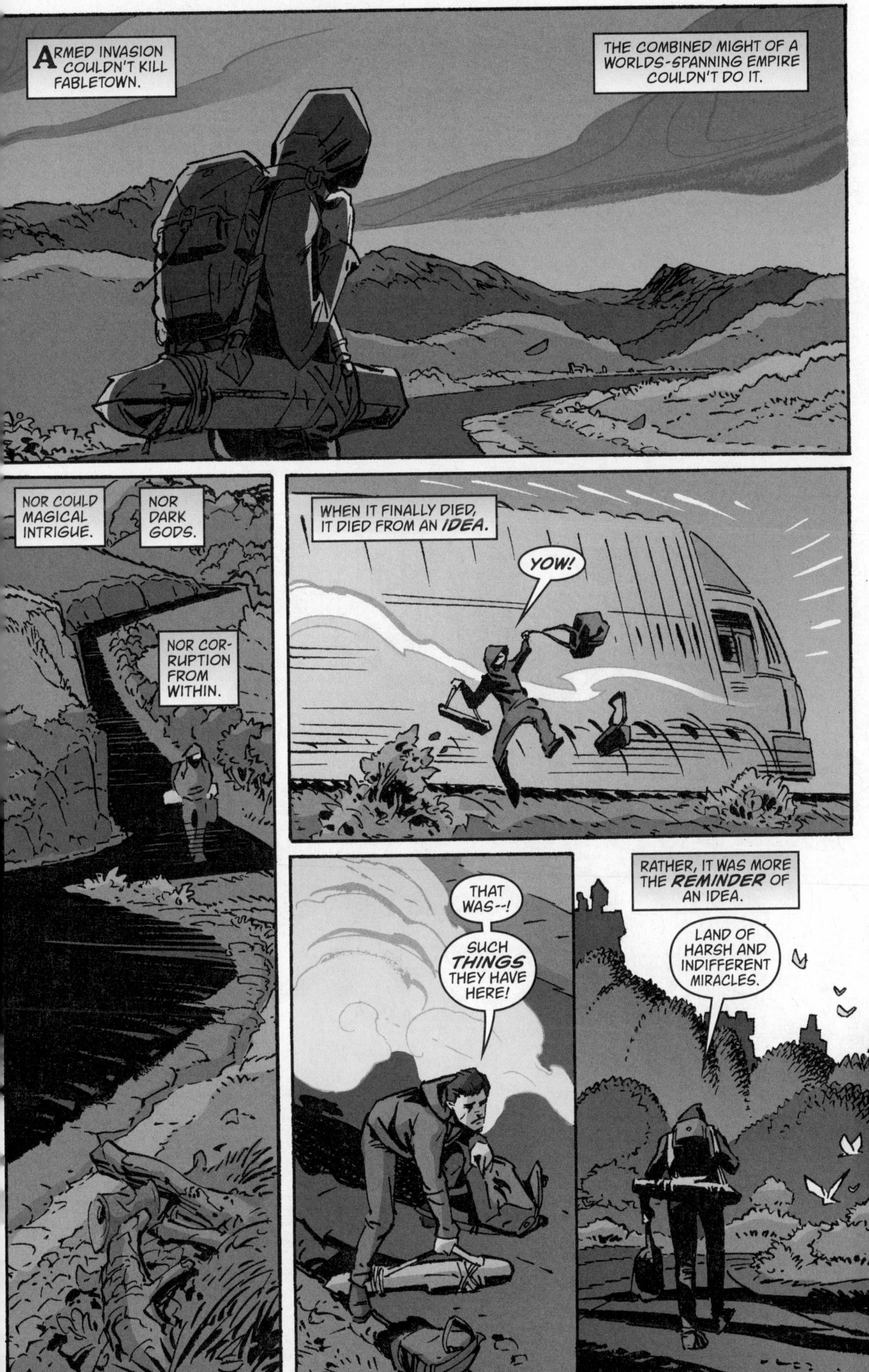
ARMED INVASION COULDN'T KILL FABLETOWN.
THE COMBINED MIGHT OF A WORLDS-SPANNING EMPIRE COULDN'T DO IT.
NOR COULD MAGICAL INTRIGUE.
NOR DARK GODS.
NOR COR-RUPTION FROM WITHIN.
WHEN IT FINALLY DIED, IT DIED FROM AN *IDEA*.
YOW!
THAT WAS--!
SUCH *THINGS* THEY HAVE HERE!
RATHER, IT WAS MORE THE *REMINDER* OF AN IDEA.
LAND OF HARSH AND INDIFFERENT MIRACLES.

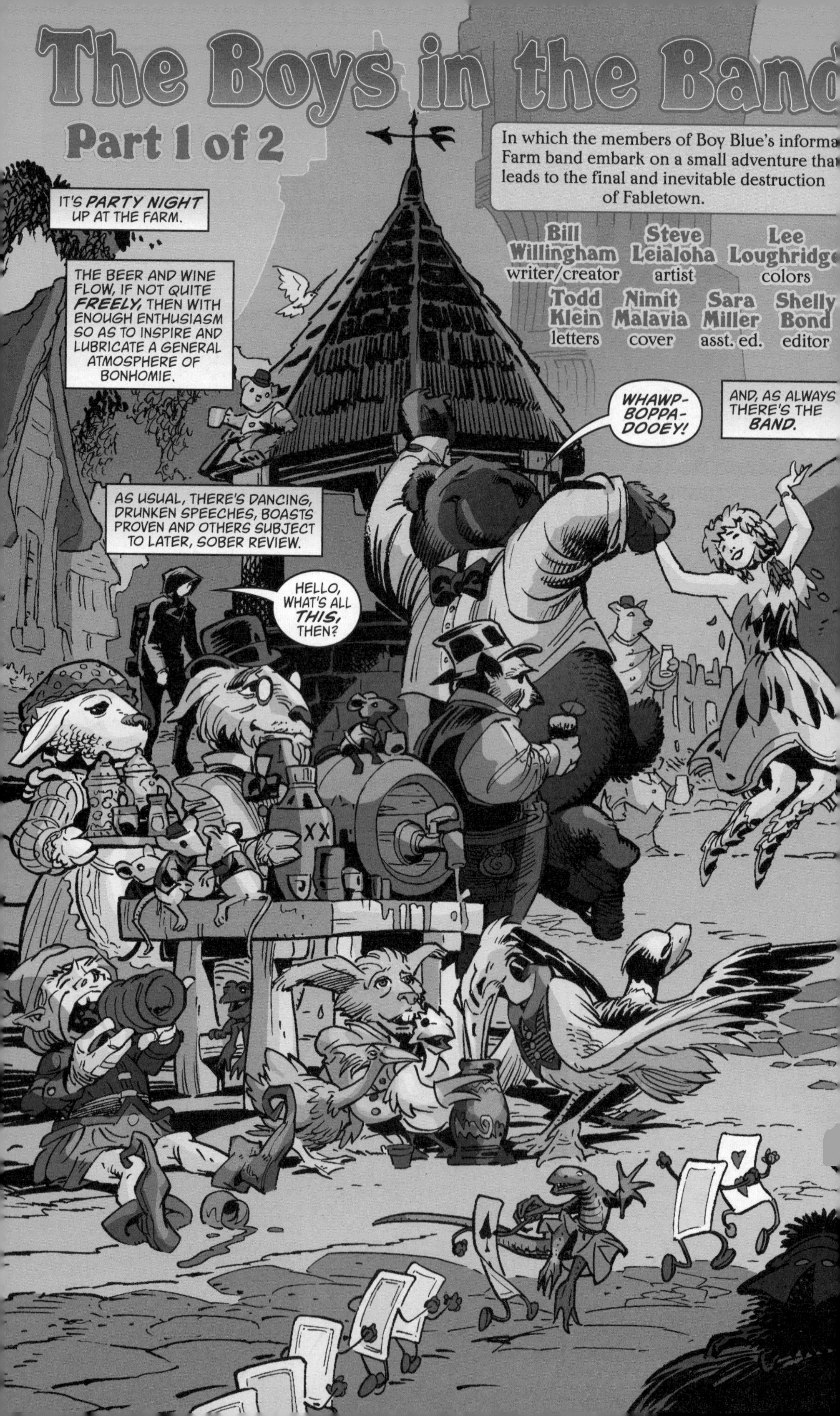
The Boys in the Band
Part 1 of 2
In which the members of Boy Blue's informa
Farm band embark on a small adventure tha
leads to the final and inevitable destruction
of Fabletown.
Bill Willingham writer/creator
Steve Leialoha artist
Lee Loughridge colors
Todd Klein letters
Nimit Malavia cover
Sara Miller asst. ed.
Shelly Bond editor
IT'S PARTY NIGHT UP AT THE FARM.
THE BEER AND WINE FLOW, IF NOT QUITE FREELY, THEN WITH ENOUGH ENTHUSIASM SO AS TO INSPIRE AND LUBRICATE A GENERAL ATMOSPHERE OF BONHOMIE.
AS USUAL, THERE'S DANCING, DRUNKEN SPEECHES, BOASTS PROVEN AND OTHERS SUBJECT TO LATER, SOBER REVIEW.
WHAWP-BOPPA-DOOEY!
AND, AS ALWAYS THERE'S THE BAND.
HELLO, WHAT'S ALL THIS, THEN?
XX

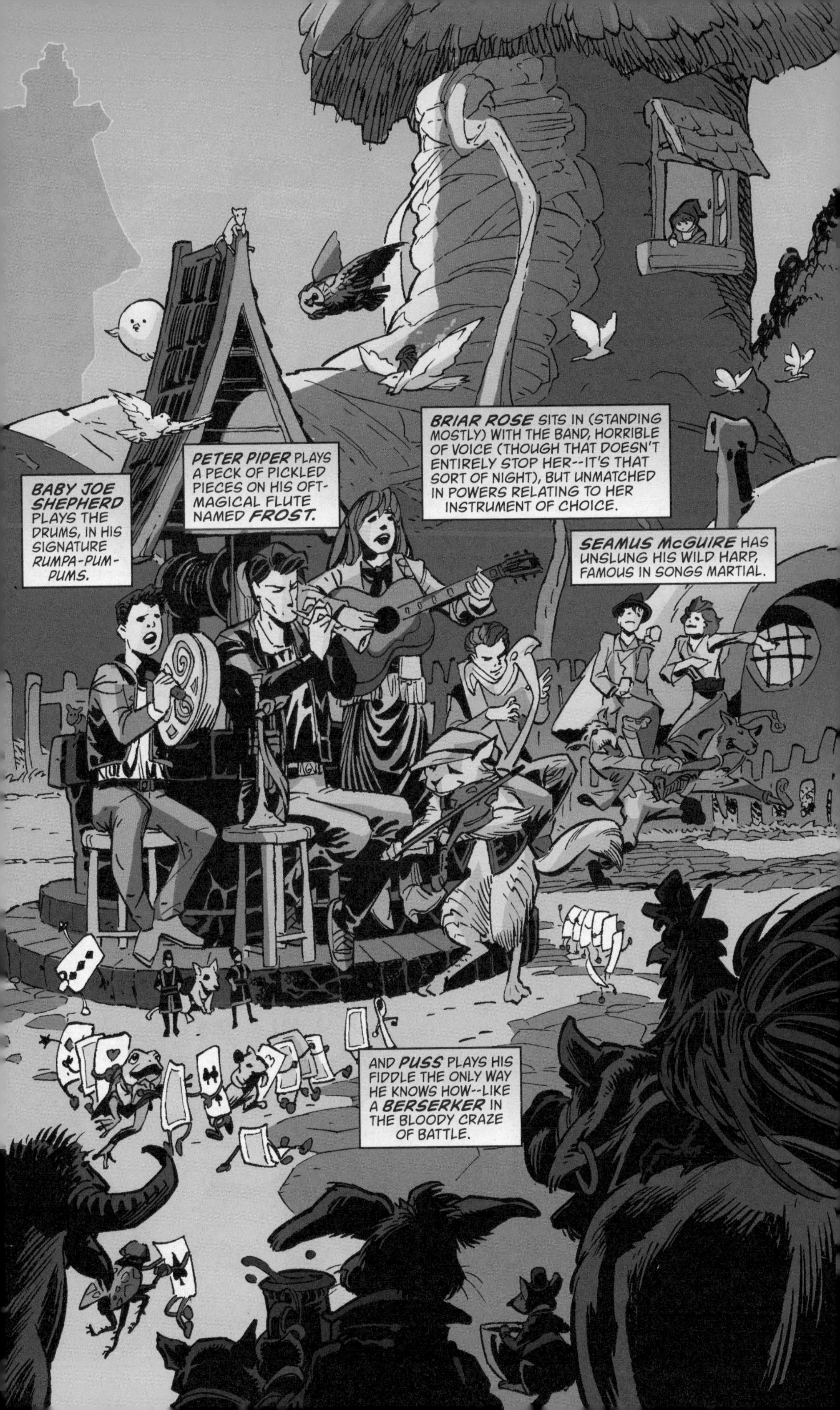
BABY JOE SHEPHERD PLAYS THE DRUMS, IN HIS SIGNATURE RUMPA-PUM-PUMS.
PETER PIPER PLAYS A PECK OF PICKLED PIECES ON HIS OFT-MAGICAL FLUTE NAMED FROST.
BRIAR ROSE SITS IN (STANDING MOSTLY) WITH THE BAND, HORRIBLE OF VOICE (THOUGH THAT DOESN'T ENTIRELY STOP HER--IT'S THAT SORT OF NIGHT), BUT UNMATCHED IN POWERS RELATING TO HER INSTRUMENT OF CHOICE.
SEAMUS McGUIRE HAS UNSLUNG HIS WILD HARP, FAMOUS IN SONGS MARTIAL.
AND PUSS PLAYS HIS FIDDLE THE ONLY WAY HE KNOWS HOW--LIKE A BERSERKER IN THE BLOODY CRAZE OF BATTLE.

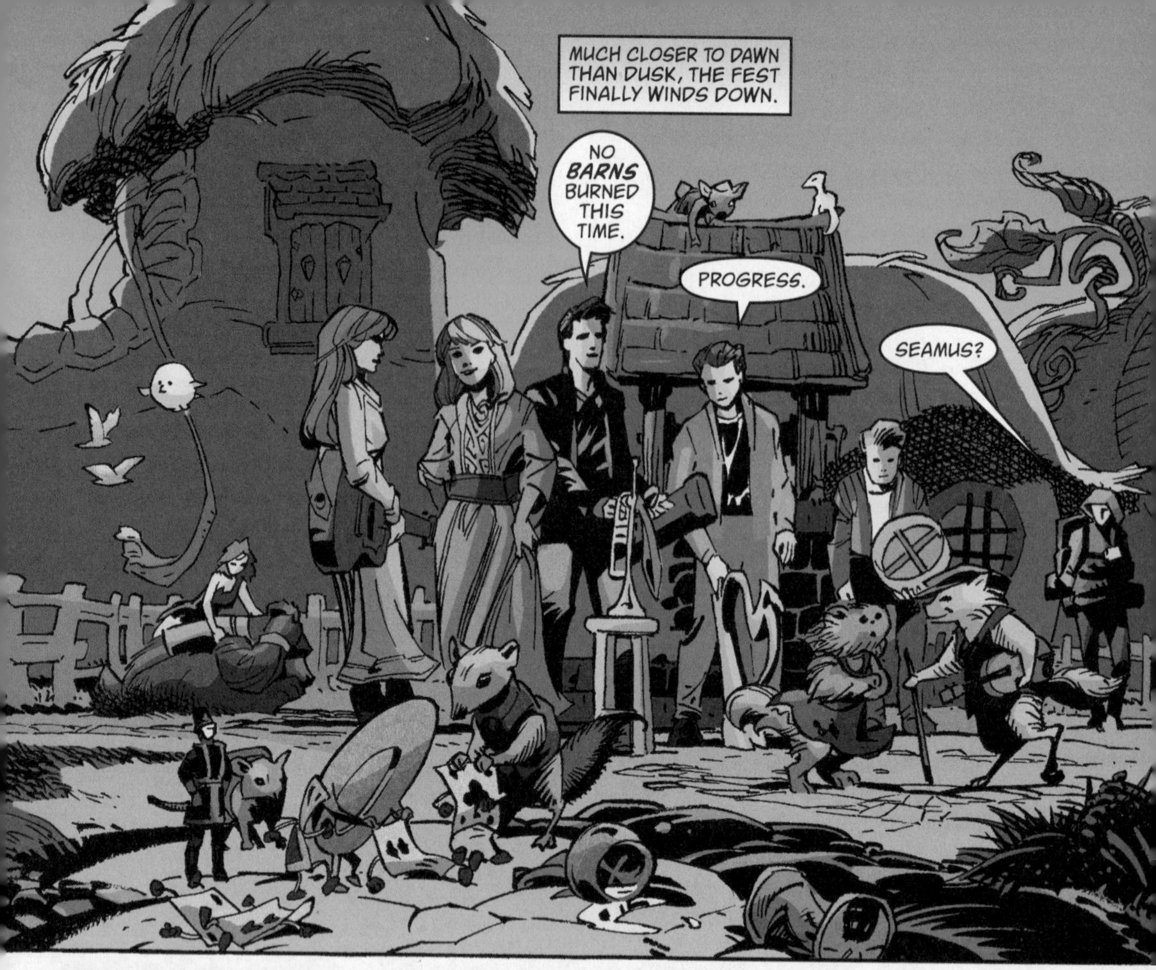
MUCH CLOSER TO DAWN THAN DUSK, THE FEST FINALLY WINDS DOWN.
NO BARNS BURNED THIS TIME.
PROGRESS.
SEAMUS?

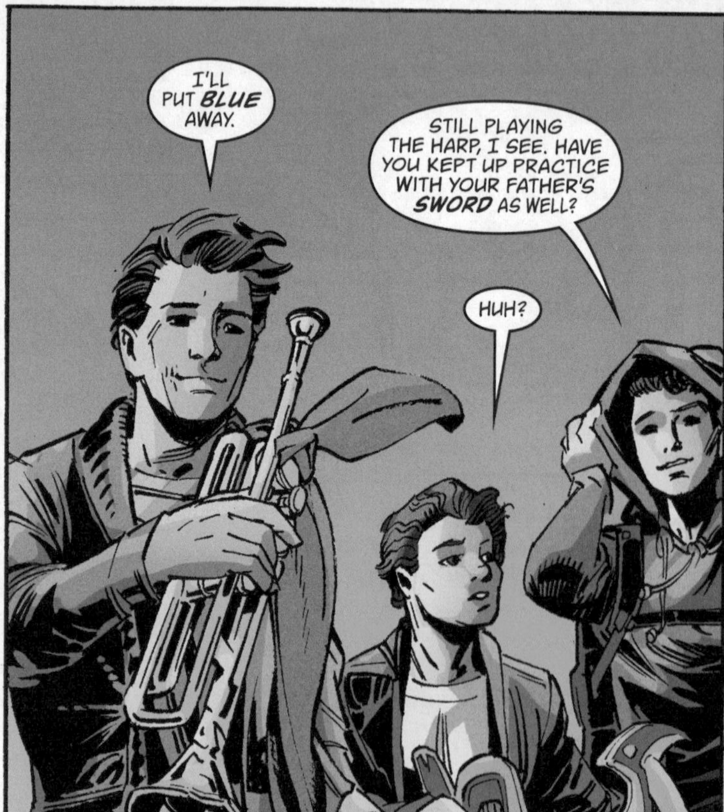
I'LL PUT BLUE AWAY.
STILL PLAYING THE HARP, I SEE. HAVE YOU KEPT UP PRACTICE WITH YOUR FATHER'S SWORD AS WELL?
HUH?

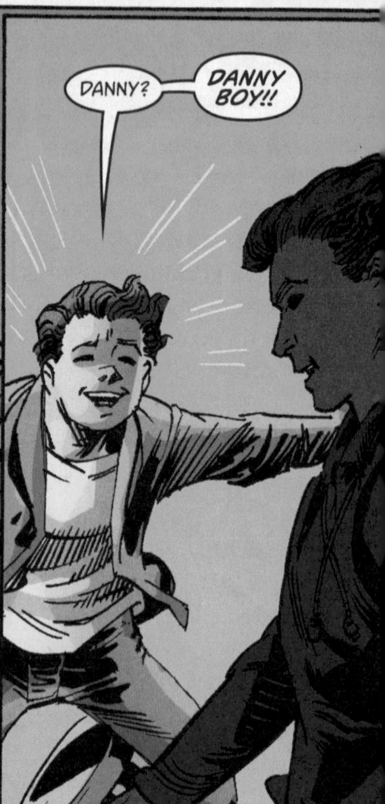
DANNY?
DANNY BOY!!

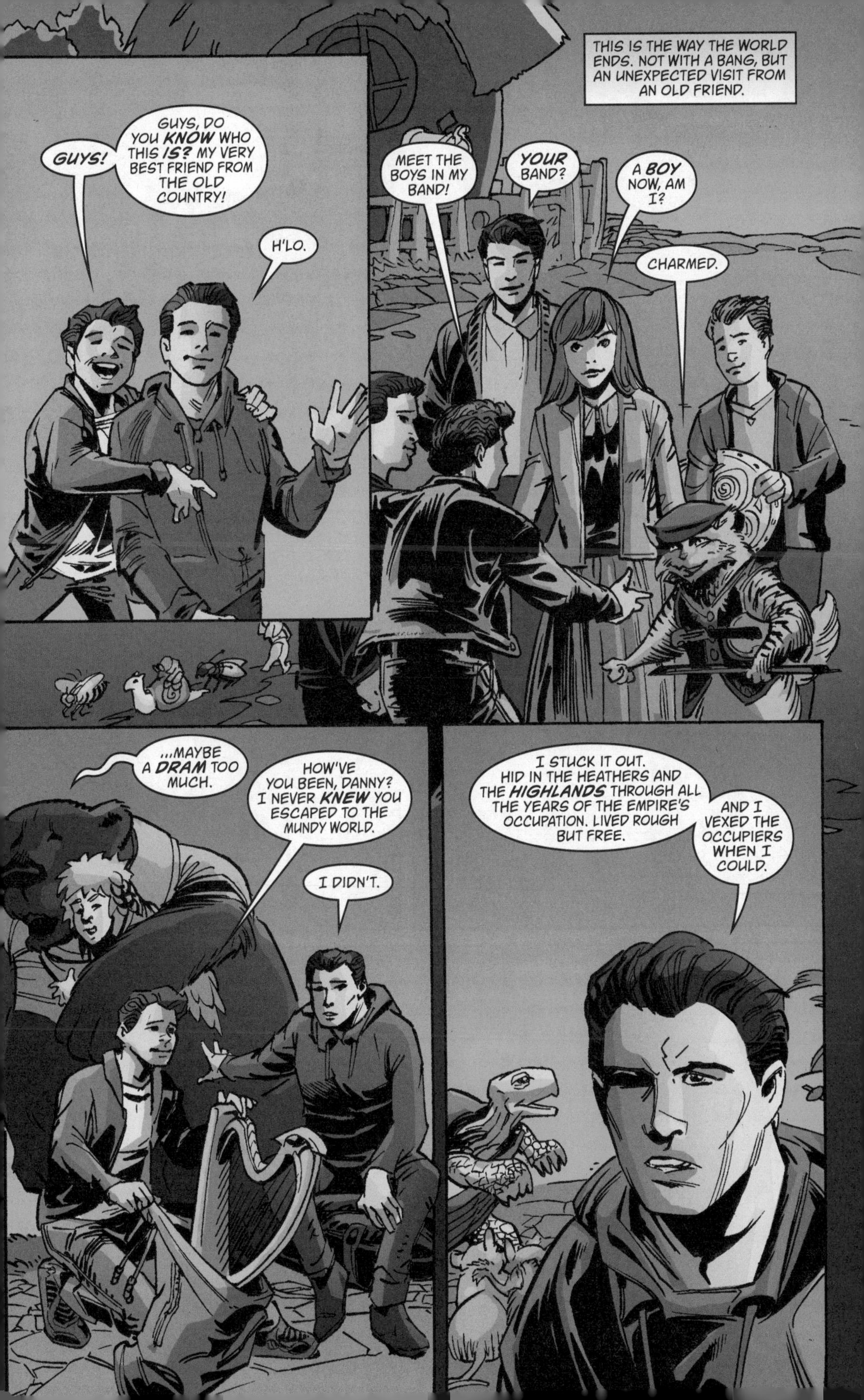
THIS IS THE WAY THE WORLD ENDS. NOT WITH A BANG, BUT AN UNEXPECTED VISIT FROM AN OLD FRIEND.
GUYS!
GUYS, DO YOU KNOW WHO THIS IS? MY VERY BEST FRIEND FROM THE OLD COUNTRY!
H'LO.
MEET THE BOYS IN MY BAND!
YOUR BAND?
A BOY NOW, AM I?
CHARMED.
...MAYBE A DRAM TOO MUCH.
HOW'VE YOU BEEN, DANNY? I NEVER KNEW YOU ESCAPED TO THE MUNDY WORLD.
I DIDN'T.
I STUCK IT OUT. HID IN THE HEATHERS AND THE HIGHLANDS THROUGH ALL THE YEARS OF THE EMPIRE'S OCCUPATION. LIVED ROUGH BUT FREE.
AND I VEXED THE OCCUPIERS WHEN I COULD.

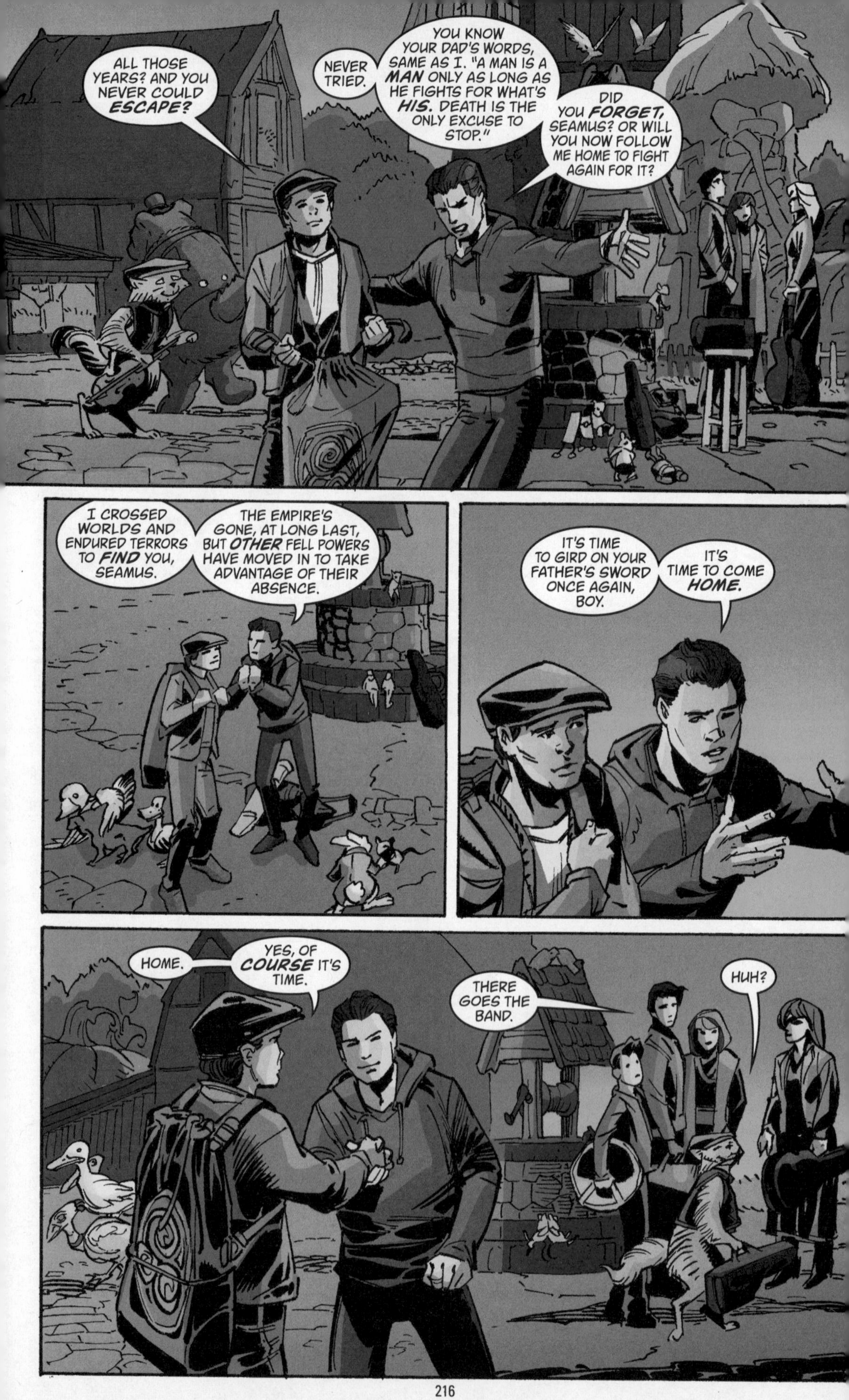
ALL THOSE YEARS? AND YOU NEVER COULD ESCAPE?
NEVER TRIED.
YOU KNOW YOUR DAD'S WORDS, SAME AS I. "A MAN IS A MAN ONLY AS LONG AS HE FIGHTS FOR WHAT'S HIS. DEATH IS THE ONLY EXCUSE TO STOP."
DID YOU FORGET, SEAMUS? OR WILL YOU NOW FOLLOW ME HOME TO FIGHT AGAIN FOR IT?
I CROSSED WORLDS AND ENDURED TERRORS TO FIND YOU, SEAMUS.
THE EMPIRE'S GONE, AT LONG LAST, BUT OTHER FELL POWERS HAVE MOVED IN TO TAKE ADVANTAGE OF THEIR ABSENCE.
IT'S TIME TO GIRD ON YOUR FATHER'S SWORD ONCE AGAIN, BOY.
IT'S TIME TO COME HOME.
HOME.
YES, OF COURSE IT'S TIME.
THERE GOES THE BAND.
HUH?

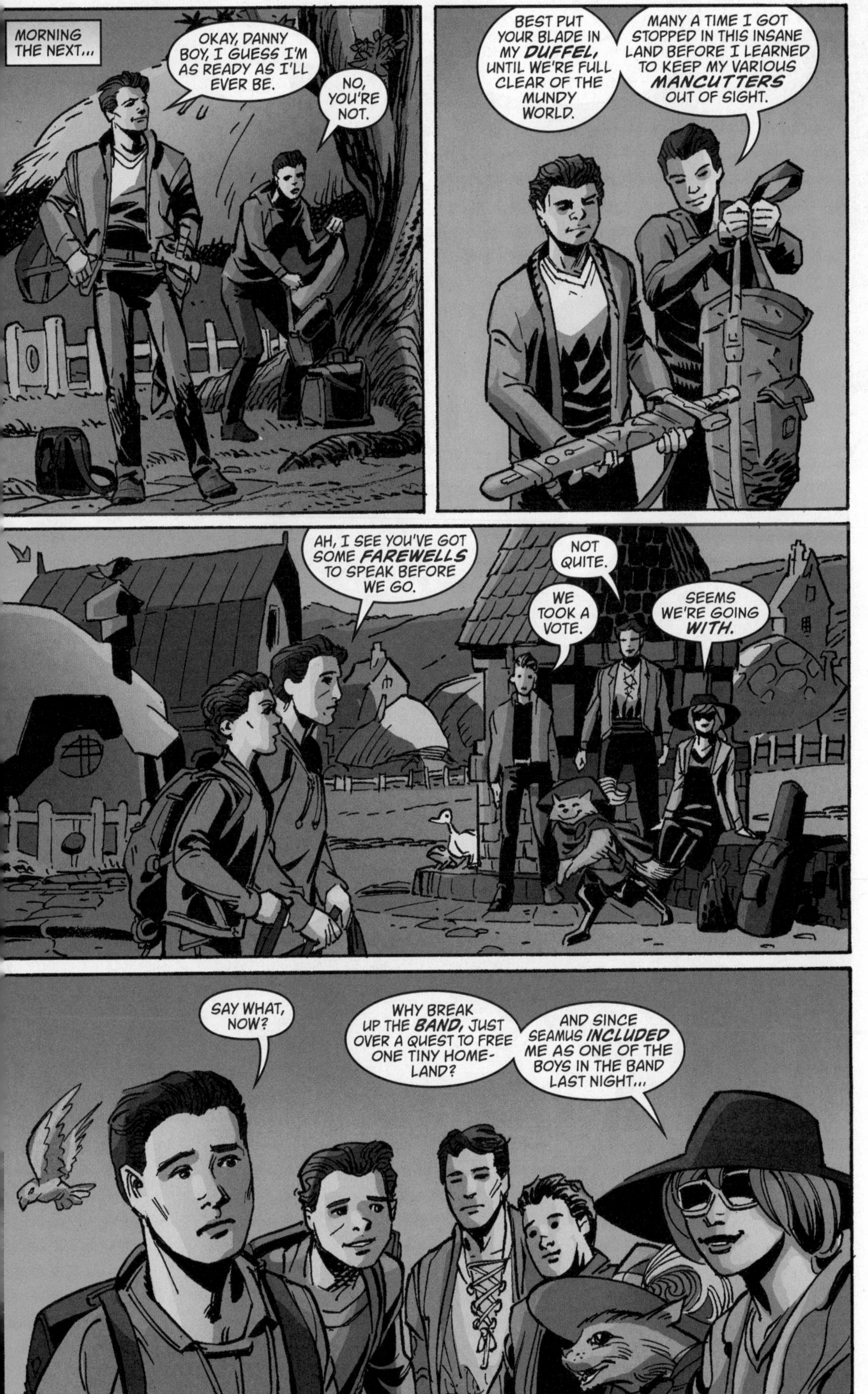
MORNING THE NEXT...
OKAY, DANNY BOY, I GUESS I'M AS READY AS I'LL EVER BE.
NO, YOU'RE NOT.
BEST PUT YOUR BLADE IN MY DUFFEL, UNTIL WE'RE FULL CLEAR OF THE MUNDY WORLD.
MANY A TIME I GOT STOPPED IN THIS INSANE LAND BEFORE I LEARNED TO KEEP MY VARIOUS MANCUTTERS OUT OF SIGHT.
AH, I SEE YOU'VE GOT SOME FAREWELLS TO SPEAK BEFORE WE GO.
NOT QUITE.
WE TOOK A VOTE.
SEEMS WE'RE GOING WITH.
SAY WHAT, NOW?
WHY BREAK UP THE BAND, JUST OVER A QUEST TO FREE ONE TINY HOME-LAND?
AND SINCE SEAMUS INCLUDED ME AS ONE OF THE BOYS IN THE BAND LAST NIGHT...

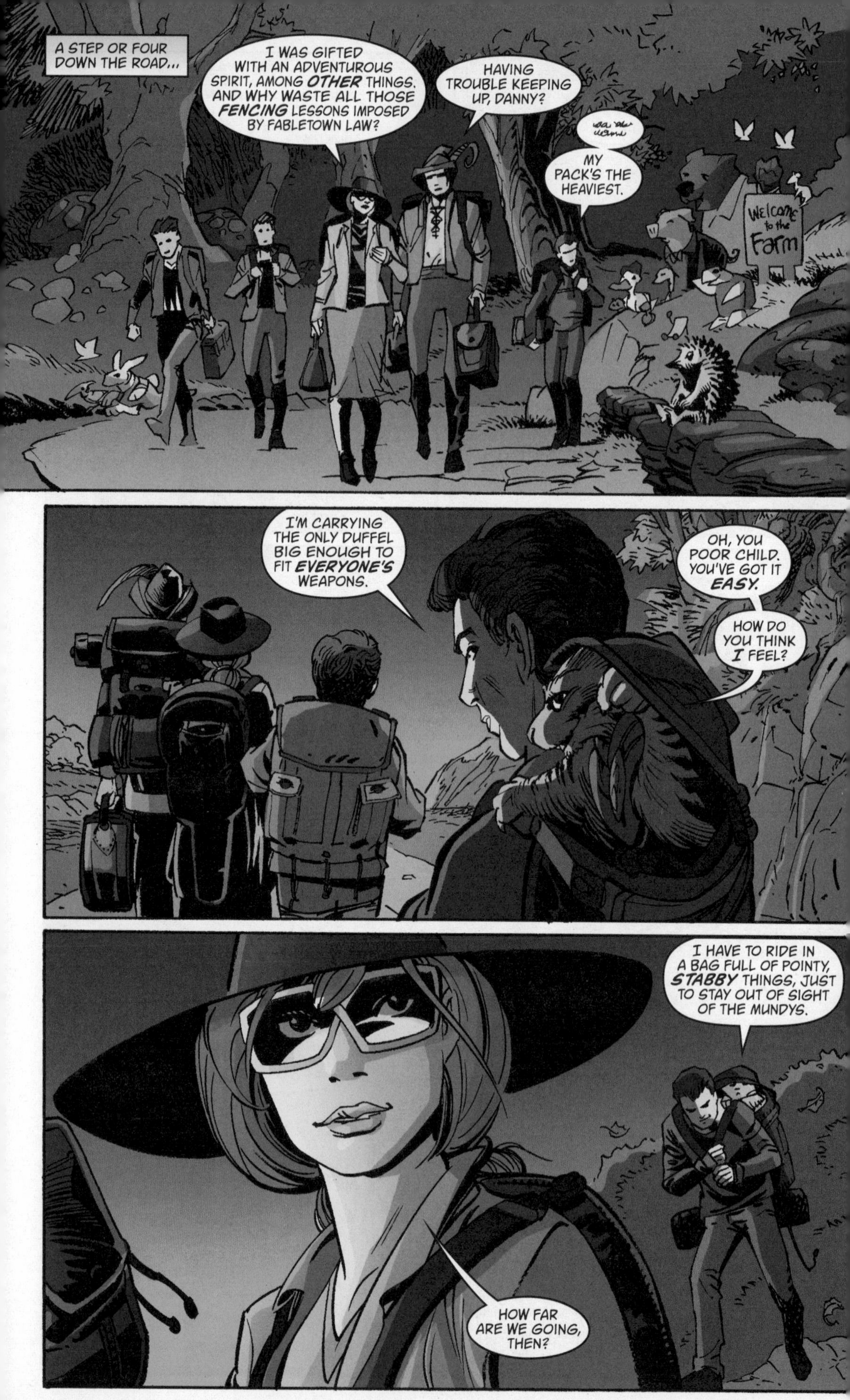
A STEP OR FOUR DOWN THE ROAD...
I WAS GIFTED WITH AN ADVENTUROUS SPIRIT, AMONG OTHER THINGS. AND WHY WASTE ALL THOSE FENCING LESSONS IMPOSED BY FABLETOWN LAW?
HAVING TROUBLE KEEPING UP, DANNY?
MY PACK'S THE HEAVIEST.
Welcome to the Farm
I'M CARRYING THE ONLY DUFFEL BIG ENOUGH TO FIT EVERYONE'S WEAPONS.
OH, YOU POOR CHILD. YOU'VE GOT IT EASY.
HOW DO YOU THINK I FEEL?
I HAVE TO RIDE IN A BAG FULL OF POINTY, STABBY THINGS, JUST TO STAY OUT OF SIGHT OF THE MUNDYS.
HOW FAR ARE WE GOING, THEN?

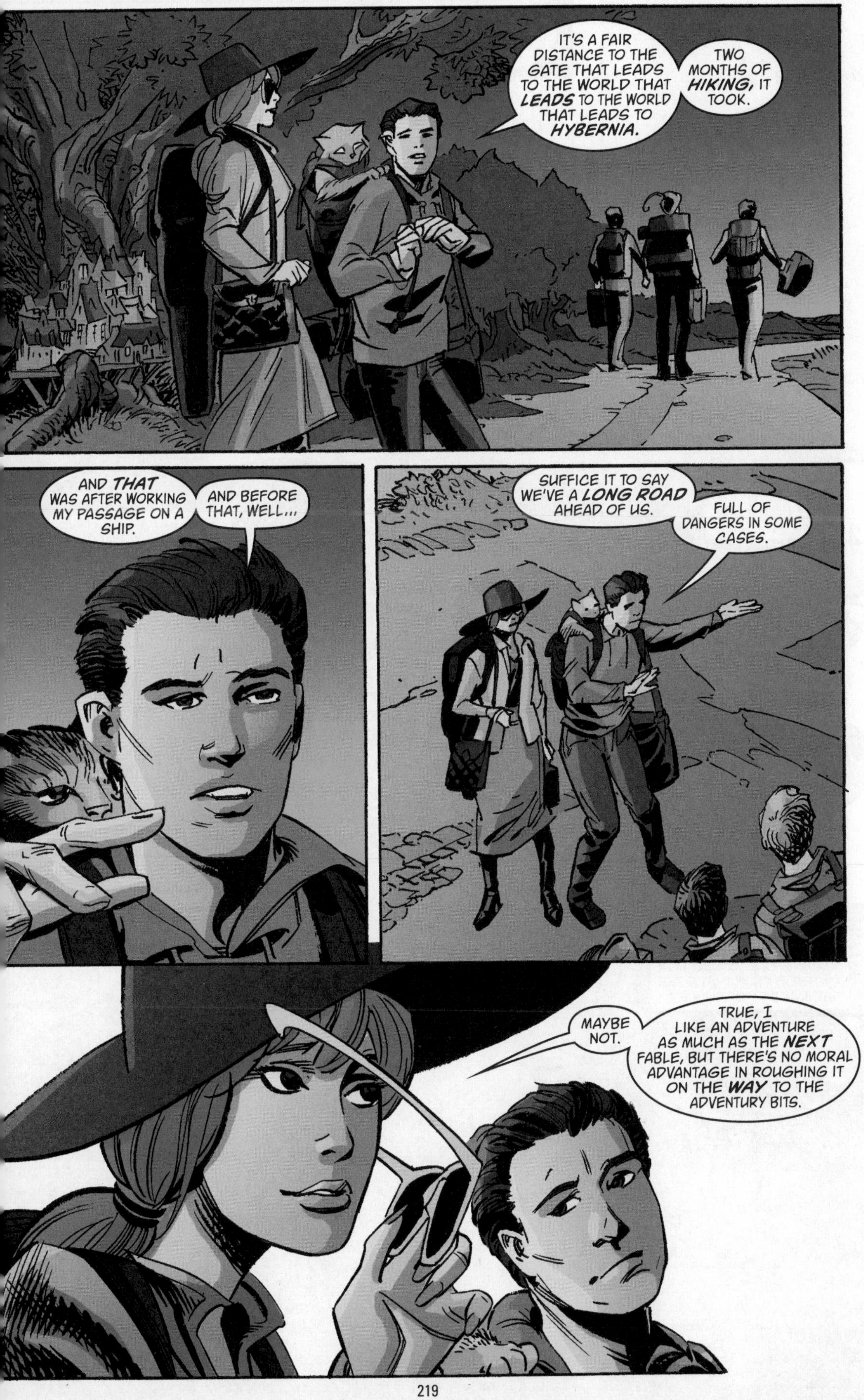
IT'S A FAIR DISTANCE TO THE GATE THAT LEADS TO THE WORLD THAT *LEADS* TO THE WORLD THAT LEADS TO *HYBERNIA.*
TWO MONTHS OF *HIKING,* IT TOOK.
AND *THAT* WAS AFTER WORKING MY PASSAGE ON A SHIP.
AND BEFORE THAT, WELL...
SUFFICE IT TO SAY WE'VE A *LONG ROAD* AHEAD OF US.
FULL OF DANGERS IN SOME CASES.
MAYBE NOT.
TRUE, I LIKE AN ADVENTURE AS MUCH AS THE *NEXT* FABLE, BUT THERE'S NO MORAL ADVANTAGE IN ROUGHING IT ON THE *WAY* TO THE ADVENTURY BITS.

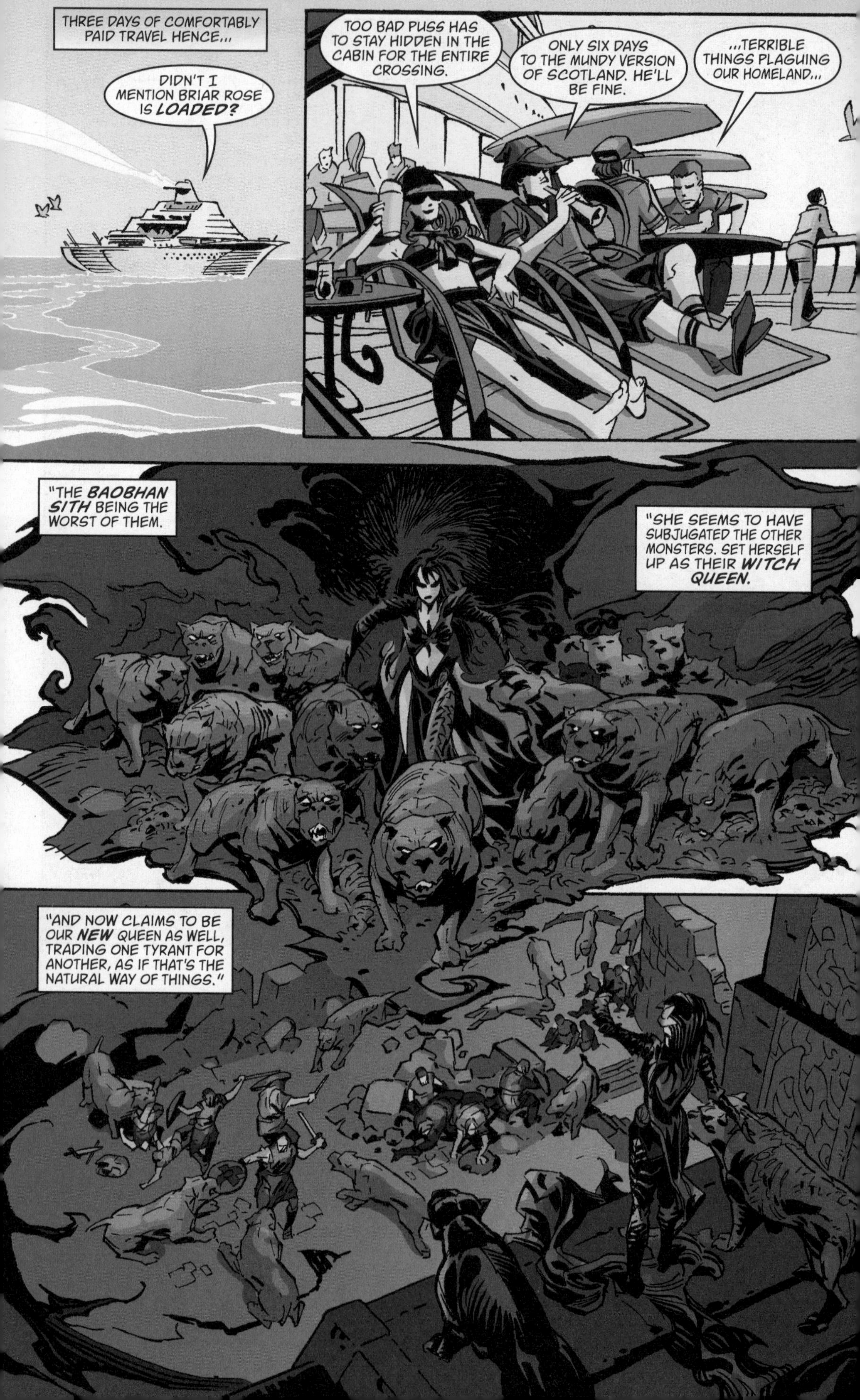
THREE DAYS OF COMFORTABLY PAID TRAVEL HENCE...
DIDN'T I MENTION BRIAR ROSE IS LOADED?
TOO BAD PUSS HAS TO STAY HIDDEN IN THE CABIN FOR THE ENTIRE CROSSING.
ONLY SIX DAYS TO THE MUNDY VERSION OF SCOTLAND. HE'LL BE FINE.
...TERRIBLE THINGS PLAGUING OUR HOMELAND...
"THE BAOBHAN SITH BEING THE WORST OF THEM.
"SHE SEEMS TO HAVE SUBJUGATED THE OTHER MONSTERS. SET HERSELF UP AS THEIR WITCH QUEEN.
"AND NOW CLAIMS TO BE OUR NEW QUEEN AS WELL, TRADING ONE TYRANT FOR ANOTHER, AS IF THAT'S THE NATURAL WAY OF THINGS."

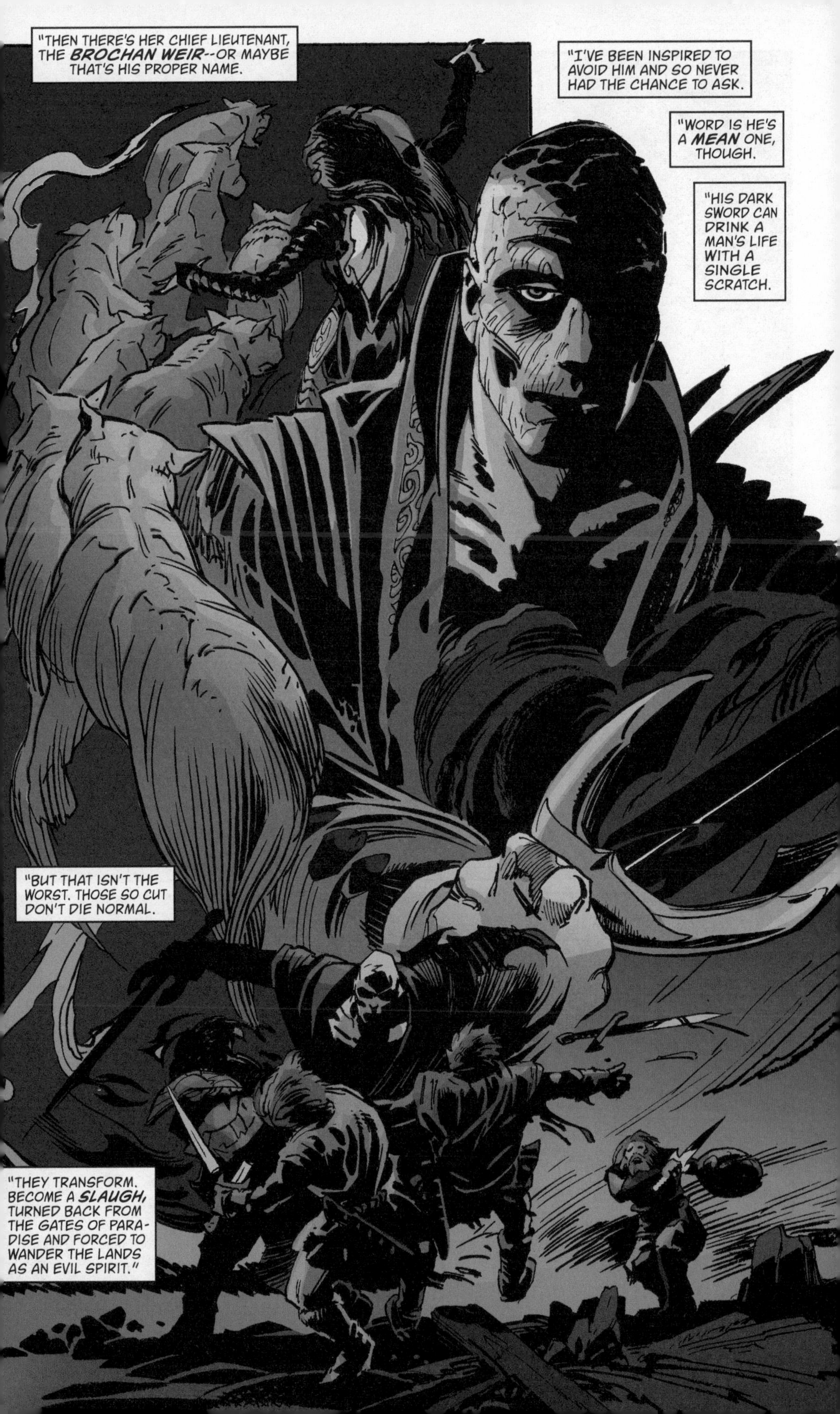
"THEN THERE'S HER CHIEF LIEUTENANT, THE BROCHAN WEIR--OR MAYBE THAT'S HIS PROPER NAME.
"I'VE BEEN INSPIRED TO AVOID HIM AND SO NEVER HAD THE CHANCE TO ASK.
"WORD IS HE'S A MEAN ONE, THOUGH.
"HIS DARK SWORD CAN DRINK A MAN'S LIFE WITH A SINGLE SCRATCH.
"BUT THAT ISN'T THE WORST. THOSE SO CUT DON'T DIE NORMAL.
"THEY TRANSFORM. BECOME A SLAUGH, TURNED BACK FROM THE GATES OF PARA-DISE AND FORCED TO WANDER THE LANDS AS AN EVIL SPIRIT."

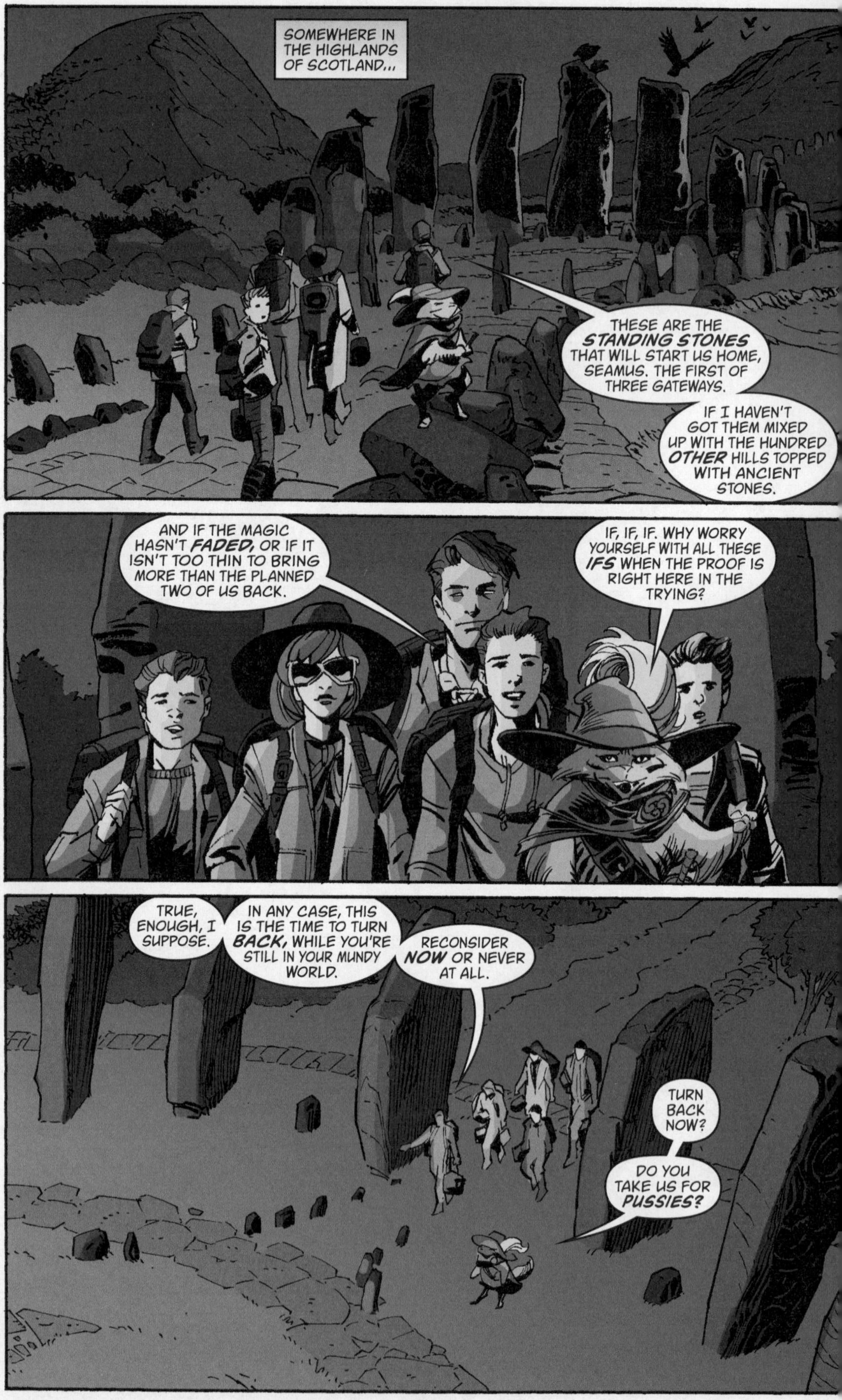
SOMEWHERE IN THE HIGHLANDS OF SCOTLAND...
THESE ARE THE STANDING STONES THAT WILL START US HOME, SEAMUS. THE FIRST OF THREE GATEWAYS.
IF I HAVEN'T GOT THEM MIXED UP WITH THE HUNDRED OTHER HILLS TOPPED WITH ANCIENT STONES.
AND IF THE MAGIC HASN'T FADED, OR IF IT ISN'T TOO THIN TO BRING MORE THAN THE PLANNED TWO OF US BACK.
IF, IF, IF. WHY WORRY YOURSELF WITH ALL THESE IFS WHEN THE PROOF IS RIGHT HERE IN THE TRYING?
TRUE, ENOUGH, I SUPPOSE.
IN ANY CASE, THIS IS THE TIME TO TURN BACK, WHILE YOU'RE STILL IN YOUR MUNDY WORLD.
RECONSIDER NOW OR NEVER AT ALL.
TURN BACK NOW?
DO YOU TAKE US FOR PUSSIES?

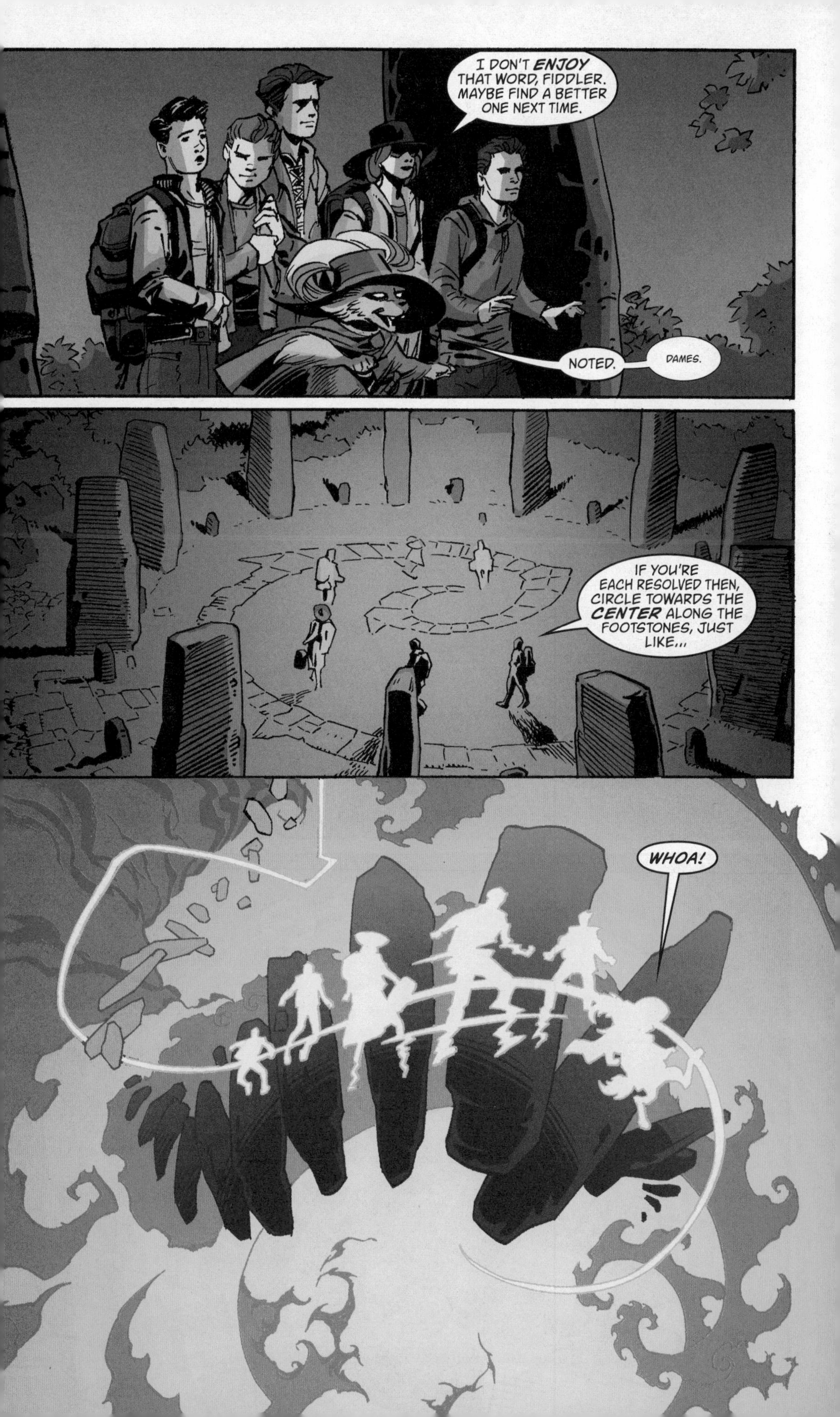
I DON'T ENJOY THAT WORD, FIDDLER. MAYBE FIND A BETTER ONE NEXT TIME.
NOTED.
DAMES.
IF YOU'RE EACH RESOLVED THEN, CIRCLE TOWARDS THE CENTER ALONG THE FOOTSTONES, JUST LIKE...
WHOA!

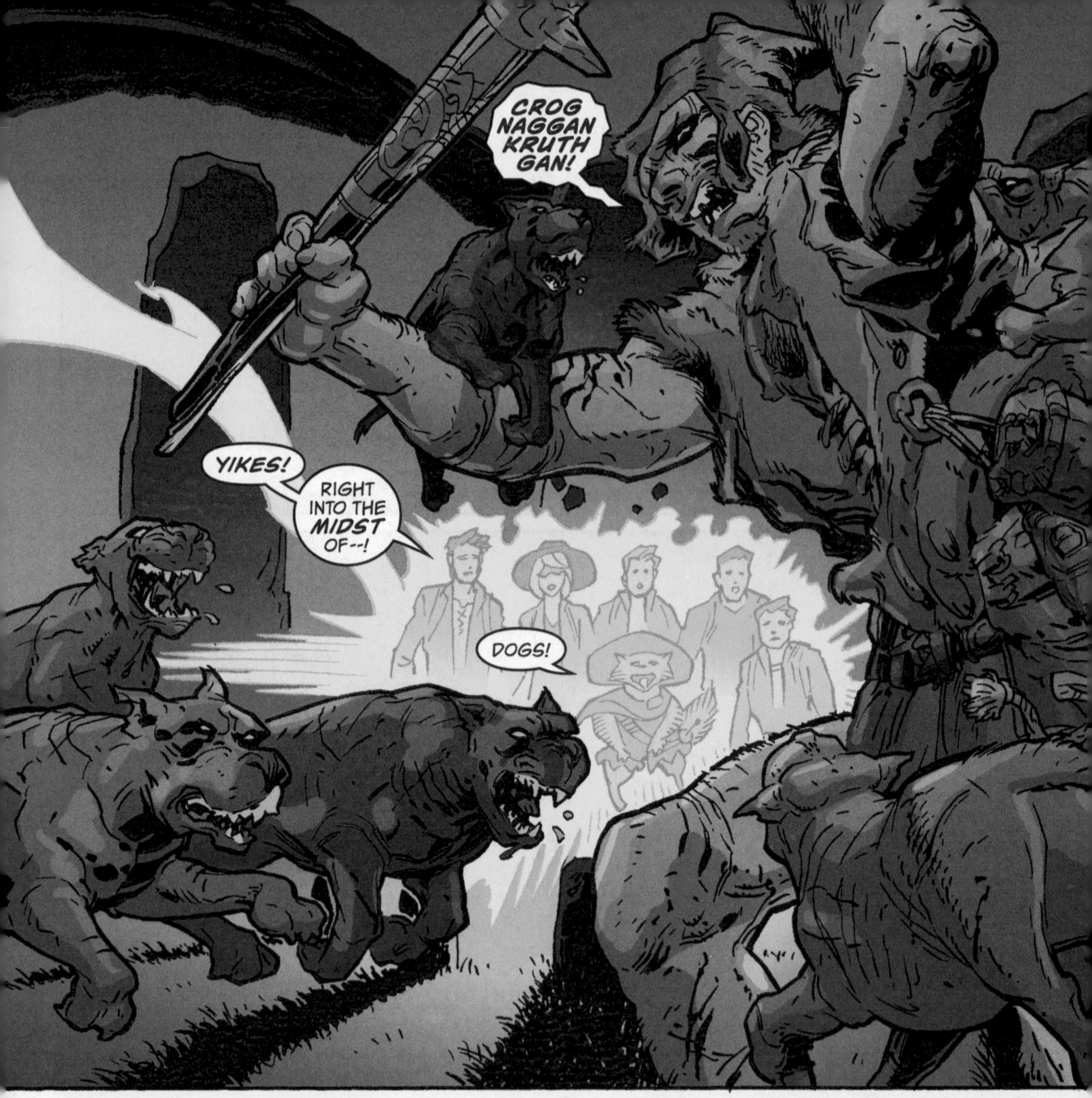
CROG NAGGAN KRUTH GAN!
YIKES!
RIGHT INTO THE MIDST OF--!
DOGS!

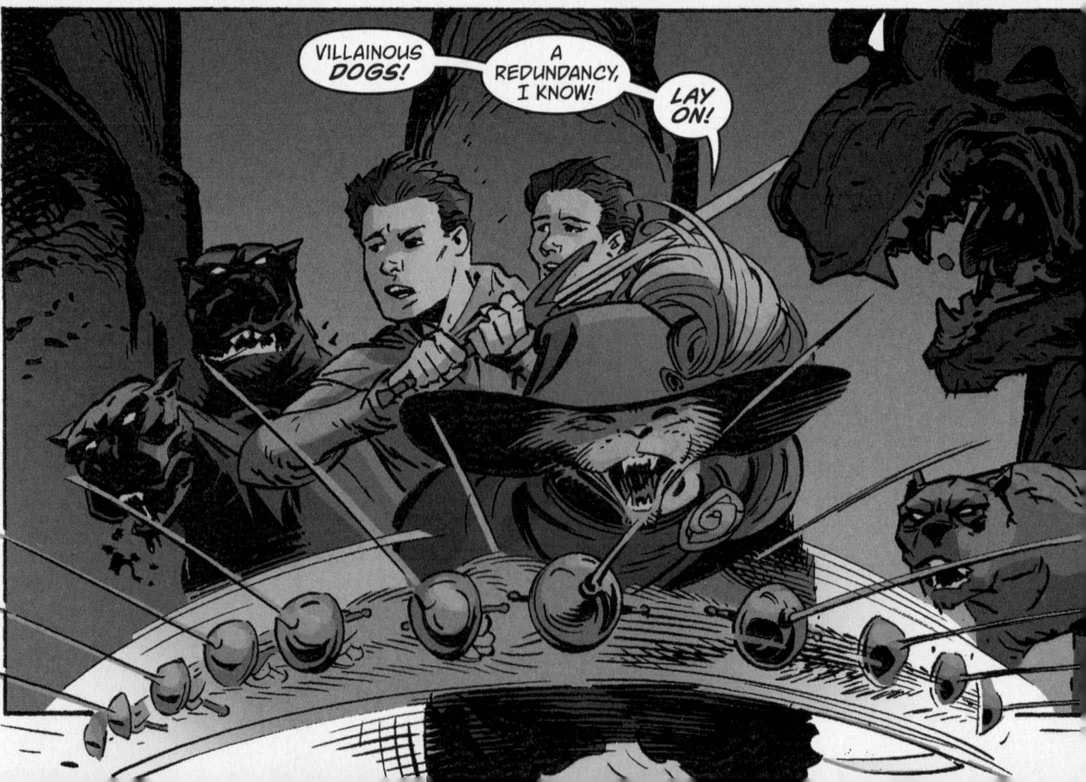
VILLAINOUS DOGS!
A REDUNDANCY, I KNOW!
LAY ON!

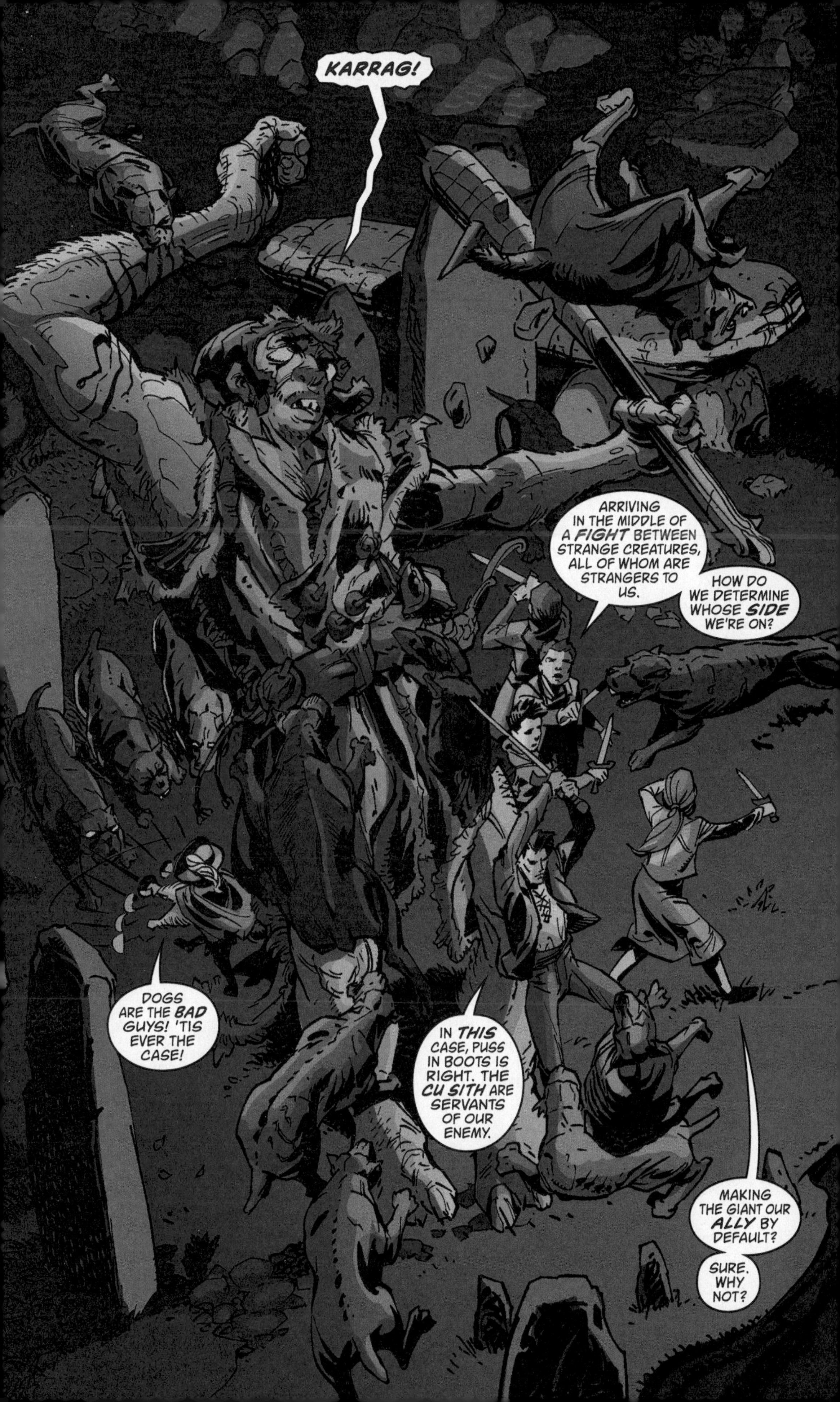
KARRAG!
ARRIVING IN THE MIDDLE OF A FIGHT BETWEEN STRANGE CREATURES, ALL OF WHOM ARE STRANGERS TO US.
HOW DO WE DETERMINE WHOSE SIDE WE'RE ON?
DOGS ARE THE BAD GUYS! 'TIS EVER THE CASE!
IN THIS CASE, PUSS IN BOOTS IS RIGHT. THE CU SITH ARE SERVANTS OF OUR ENEMY.
MAKING THE GIANT OUR ALLY BY DEFAULT?
SURE. WHY NOT?

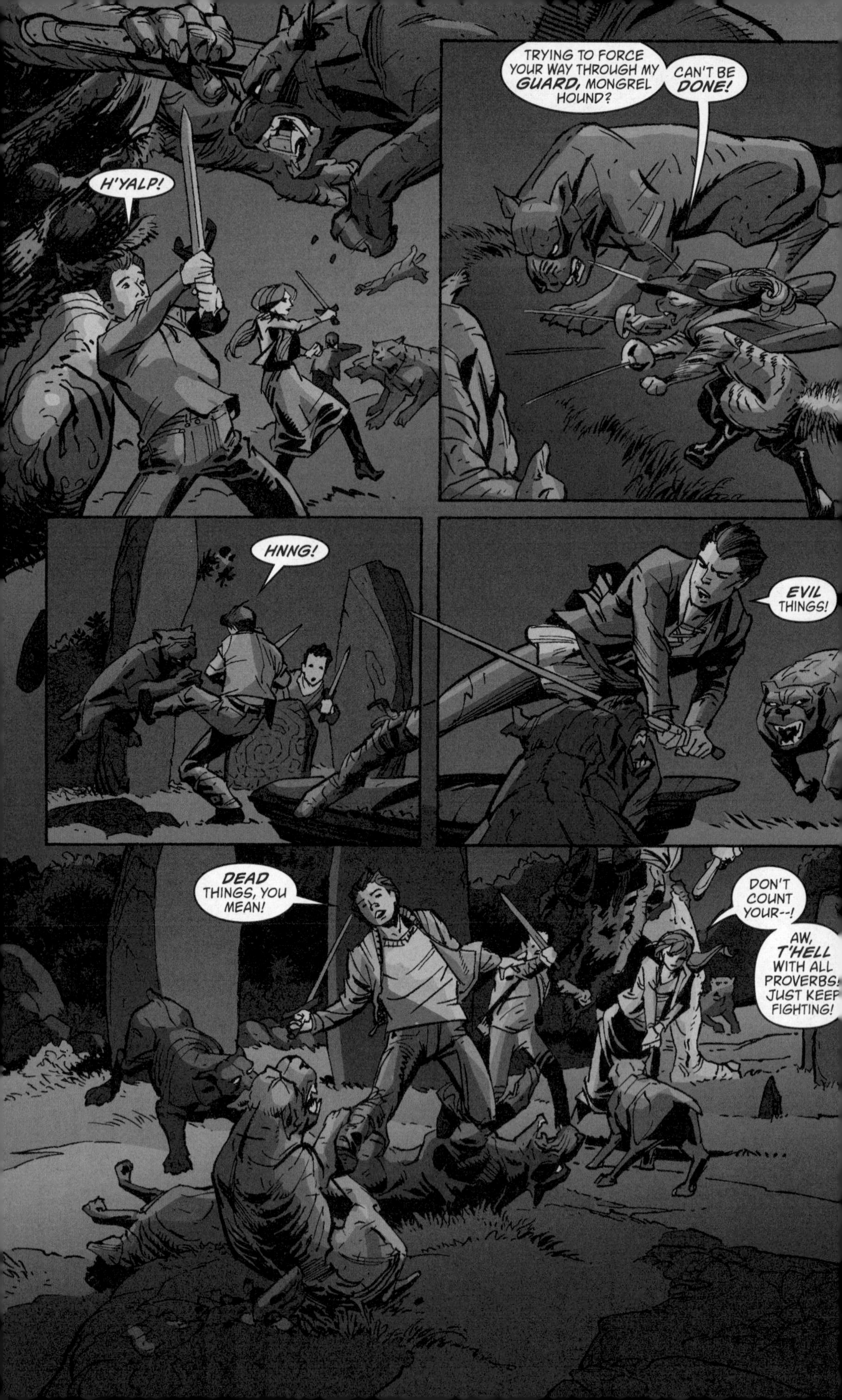
H'YALP!
TRYING TO FORCE YOUR WAY THROUGH MY GUARD, MONGREL HOUND?
CAN'T BE DONE!
HNNG!
EVIL THINGS!
DEAD THINGS, YOU MEAN!
DON'T COUNT YOUR--!
AW, T'HELL WITH ALL PROVERBS! JUST KEEP FIGHTING!

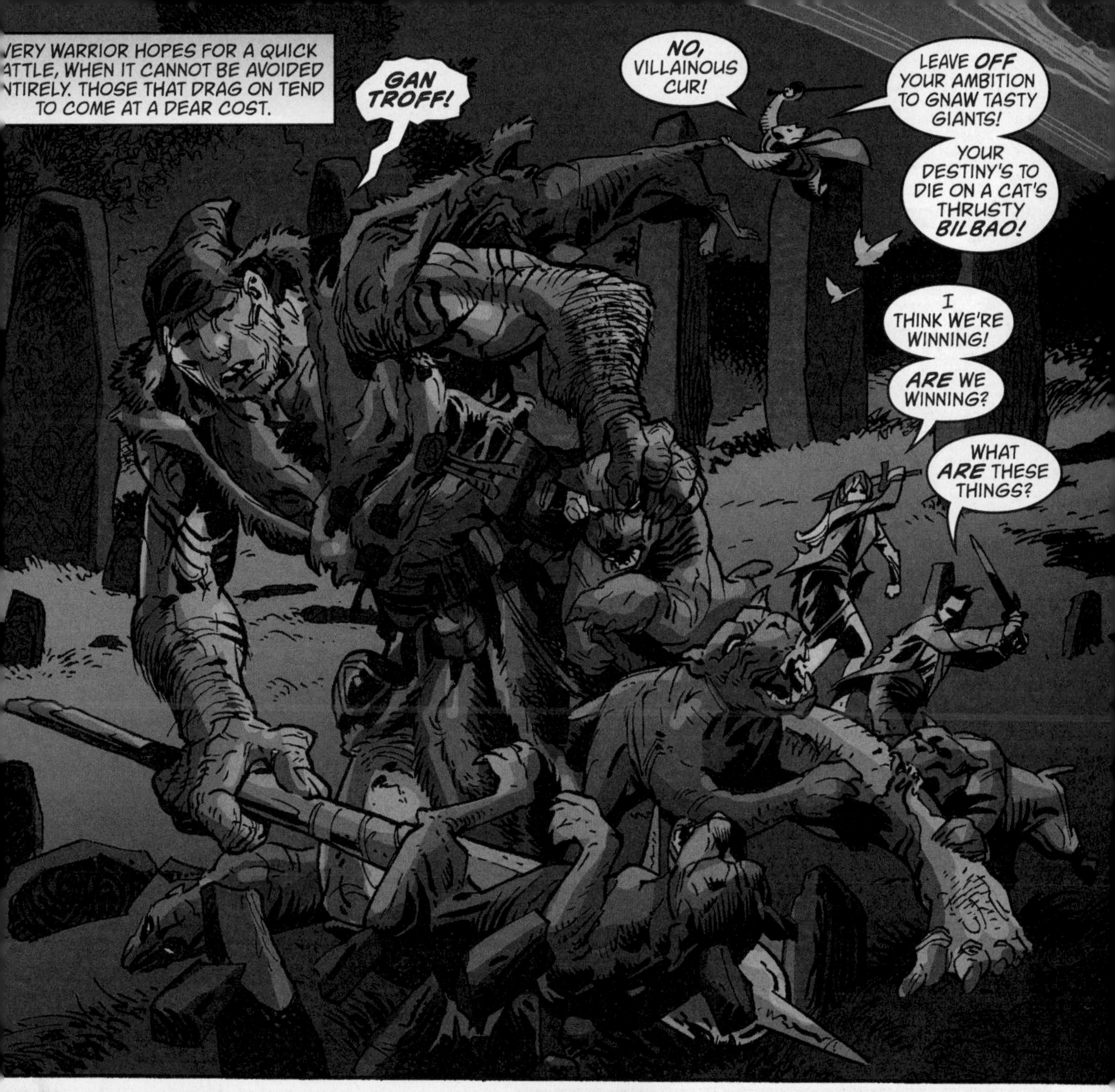
VERY WARRIOR HOPES FOR A QUICK ATTLE, WHEN IT CANNOT BE AVOIDED NTIRELY. THOSE THAT DRAG ON TEND TO COME AT A DEAR COST.
GAN TROFF!
NO, VILLAINOUS CUR!
LEAVE OFF YOUR AMBITION TO GNAW TASTY GIANTS!
YOUR DESTINY'S TO DIE ON A CAT'S THRUSTY BILBAO!
I THINK WE'RE WINNING!
ARE WE WINNING?
WHAT ARE THESE THINGS?

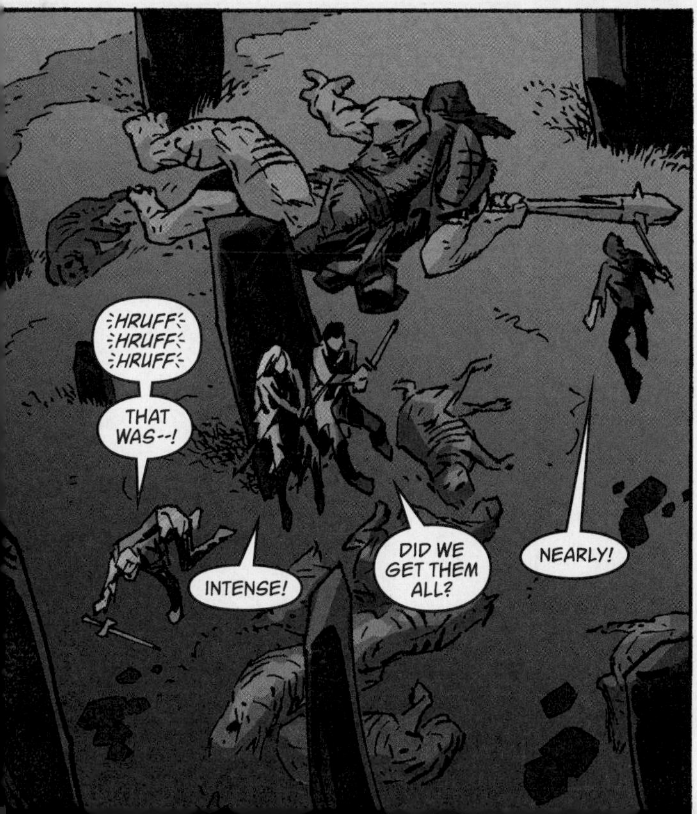
HRUFF HRUFF HRUFF
THAT WAS--!
INTENSE!
DID WE GET THEM ALL?
NEARLY!

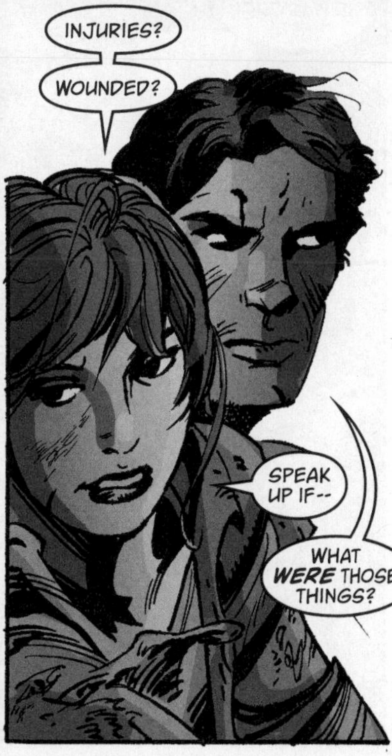
INJURIES?
WOUNDED?
SPEAK UP IF--
WHAT WERE THOSE THINGS?

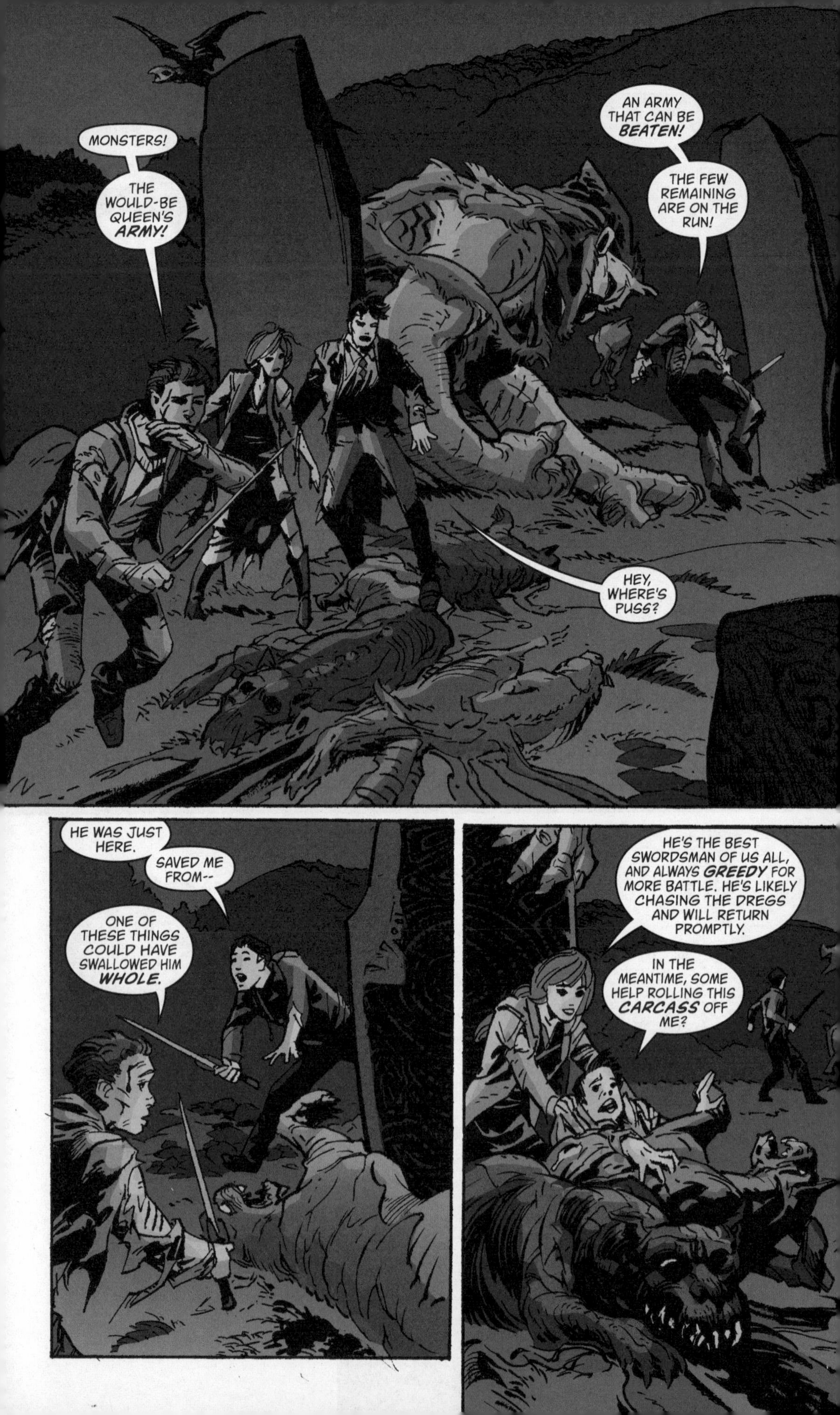
MONSTERS!
THE WOULD-BE QUEEN'S ARMY!
AN ARMY THAT CAN BE BEATEN!
THE FEW REMAINING ARE ON THE RUN!
HEY, WHERE'S PUSS?
HE WAS JUST HERE.
SAVED ME FROM--
ONE OF THESE THINGS COULD HAVE SWALLOWED HIM WHOLE.
HE'S THE BEST SWORDSMAN OF US ALL, AND ALWAYS GREEDY FOR MORE BATTLE. HE'S LIKELY CHASING THE DREGS AND WILL RETURN PROMPTLY.
IN THE MEANTIME, SOME HELP ROLLING THIS CARCASS OFF ME?

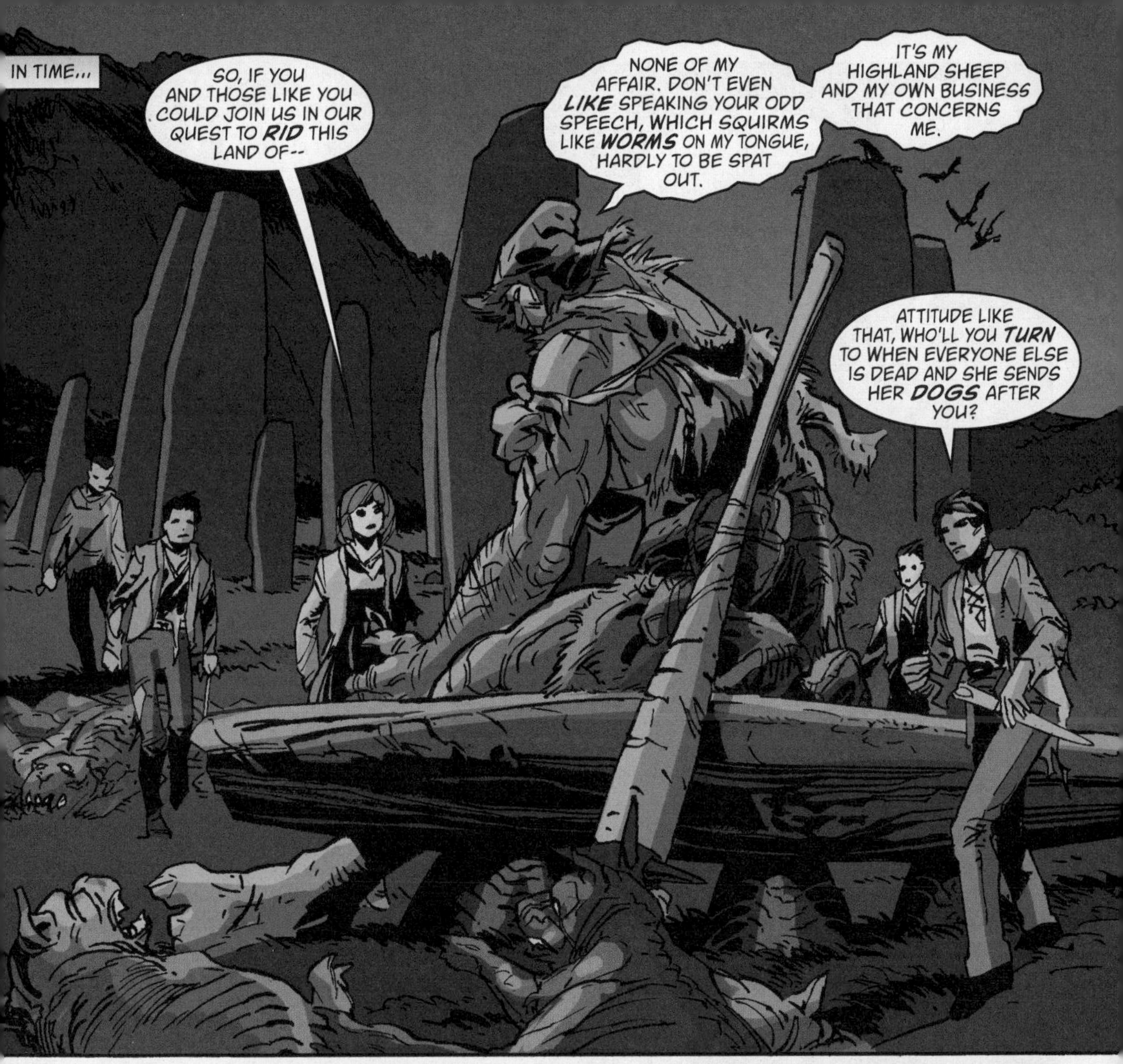
IN TIME...
SO, IF YOU AND THOSE LIKE YOU COULD JOIN US IN OUR QUEST TO RID THIS LAND OF--
NONE OF MY AFFAIR. DON'T EVEN LIKE SPEAKING YOUR ODD SPEECH, WHICH SQUIRMS LIKE WORMS ON MY TONGUE, HARDLY TO BE SPAT OUT.
IT'S MY HIGHLAND SHEEP AND MY OWN BUSINESS THAT CONCERNS ME.
ATTITUDE LIKE THAT, WHO'LL YOU TURN TO WHEN EVERYONE ELSE IS DEAD AND SHE SENDS HER DOGS AFTER YOU?

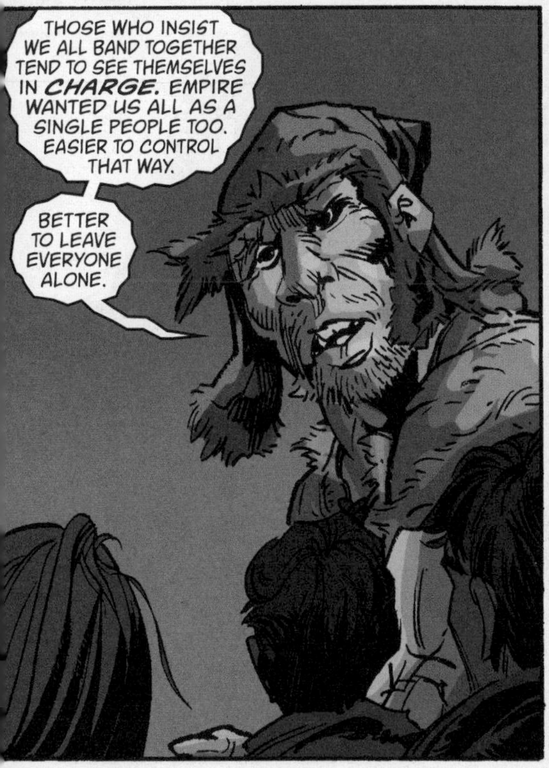
THOSE WHO INSIST WE ALL BAND TOGETHER TEND TO SEE THEMSELVES IN CHARGE. EMPIRE WANTED US ALL AS A SINGLE PEOPLE TOO. EASIER TO CONTROL THAT WAY.
BETTER TO LEAVE EVERYONE ALONE.

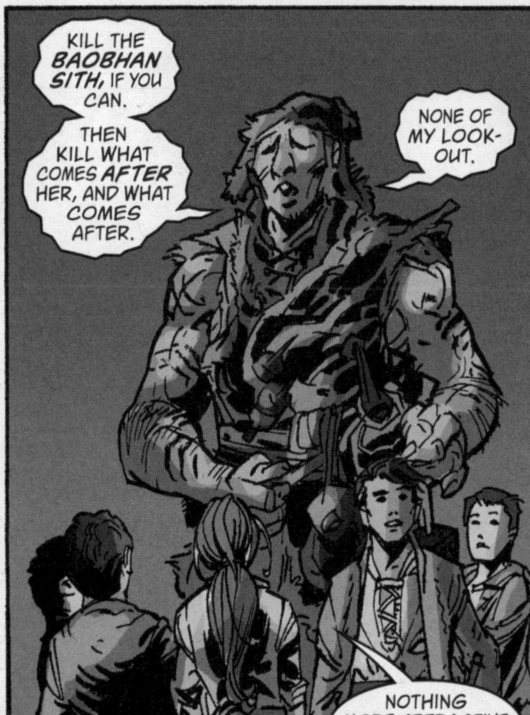
KILL THE BAOBHAN SITH, IF YOU CAN.
THEN KILL WHAT COMES AFTER HER, AND WHAT COMES AFTER.
NONE OF MY LOOK-OUT.
NOTHING MORE ATTRACTIVE THAN GRATITUDE.

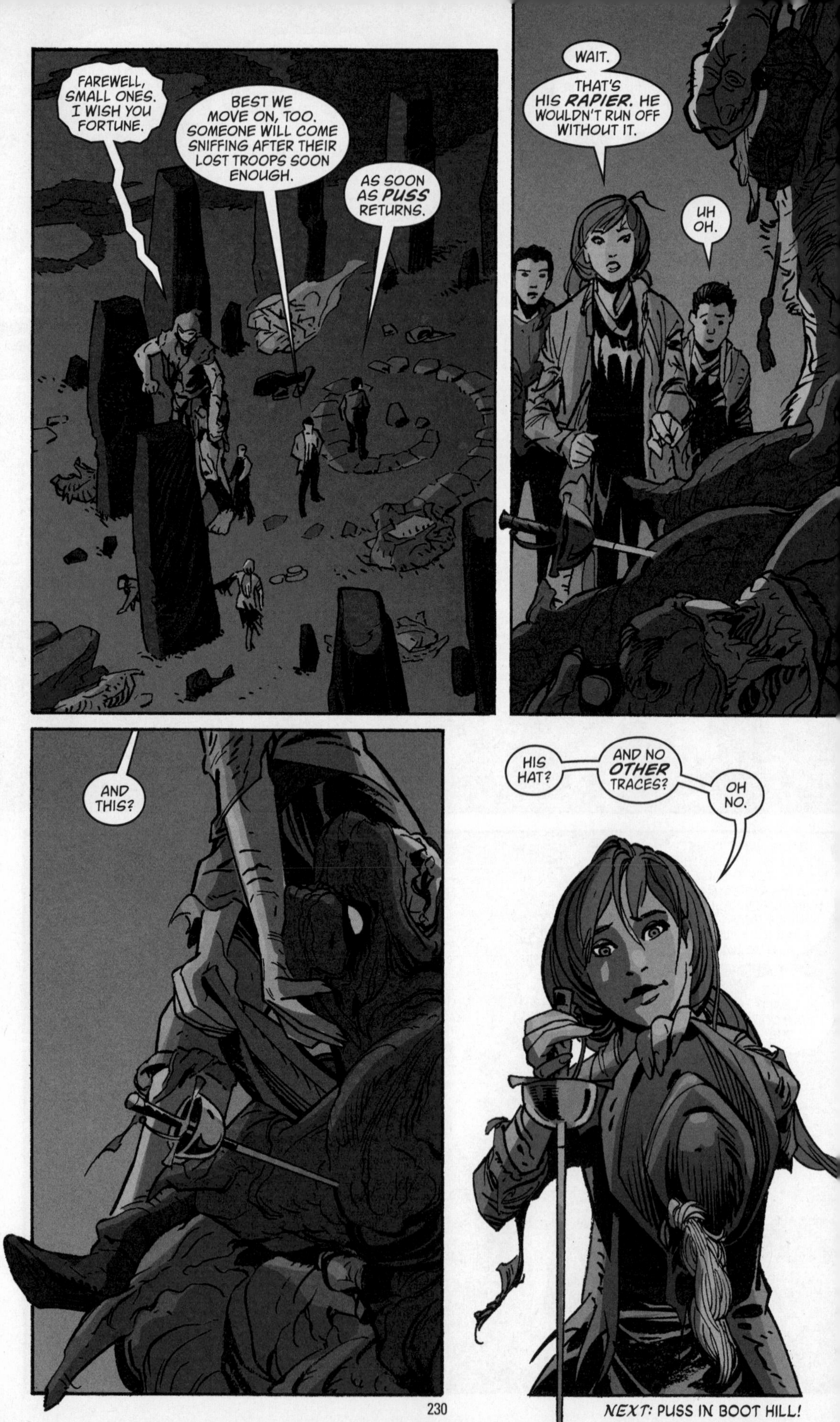

FAREWELL, SMALL ONES. I WISH YOU FORTUNE.
BEST WE MOVE ON, TOO. SOMEONE WILL COME SNIFFING AFTER THEIR LOST TROOPS SOON ENOUGH.
AS SOON AS PUSS RETURNS.
WAIT.
THAT'S HIS RAPIER. HE WOULDN'T RUN OFF WITHOUT IT.
UH OH.
AND THIS?
HIS HAT?
AND NO OTHER TRACES?
OH NO.

NEXT: PUSS IN BOOT HILL!

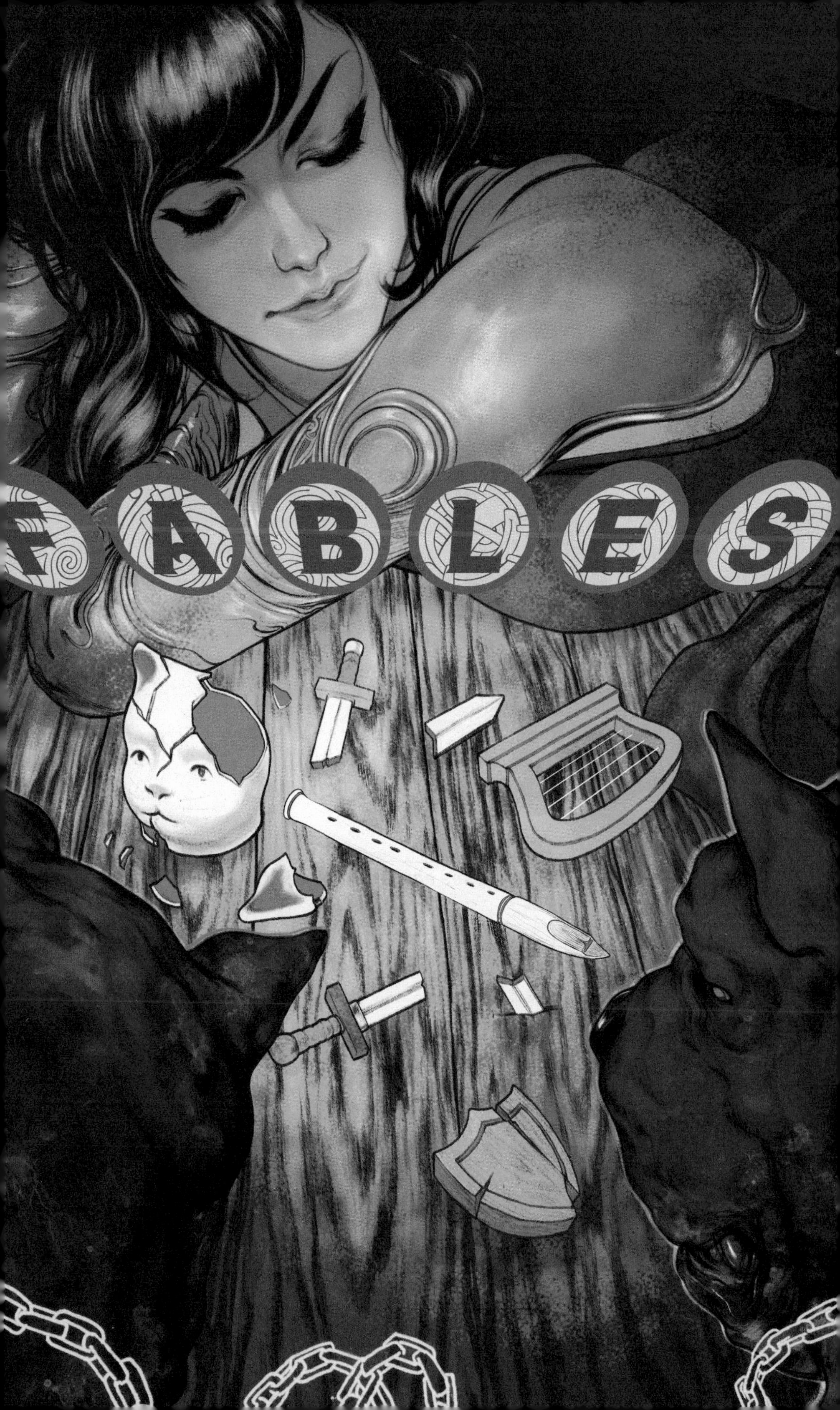
FABLES

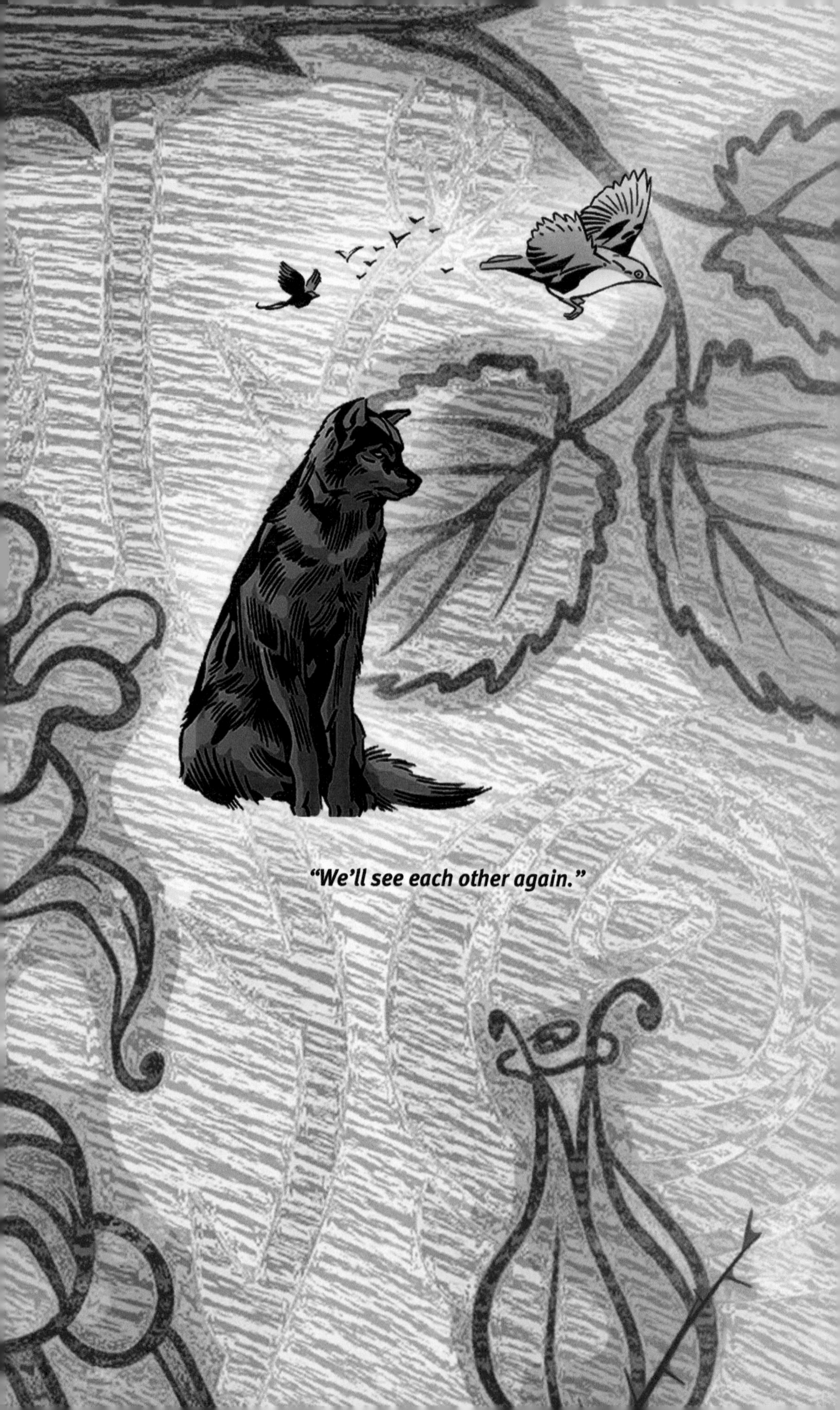
"We'll see each other again."

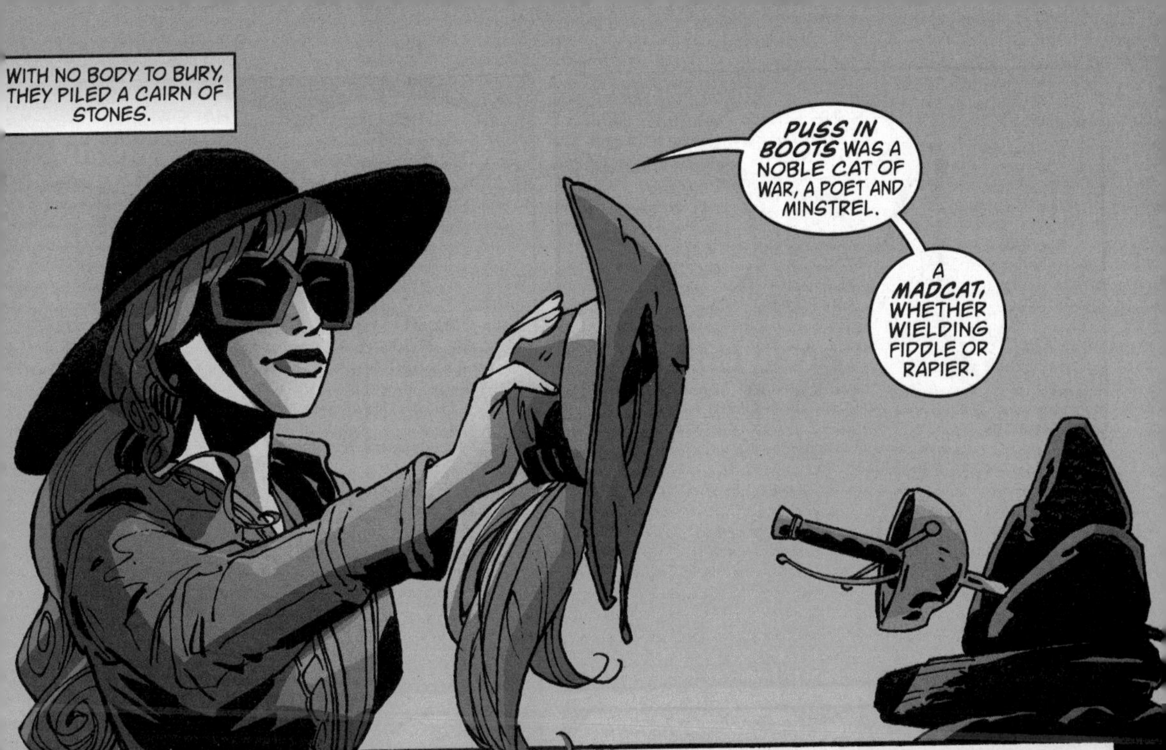
WITH NO BODY TO BURY, THEY PILED A CAIRN OF STONES.
PUSS IN BOOTS WAS A NOBLE CAT OF WAR, A POET AND MINSTREL.
A MADCAT, WHETHER WIELDING FIDDLE OR RAPIER.

The Boys in the Band

In which our tale of bladed adventure and tartan noir continues.

Part 2 of 2

Bill Willingham writer/creator · **Steve Leialoha** artist · **Lee Loughridge** colors · **Todd Klein** letters · **Nimit Malavia** cover · **Sara Miller** asst. ed. · **Shelly Bond** editor

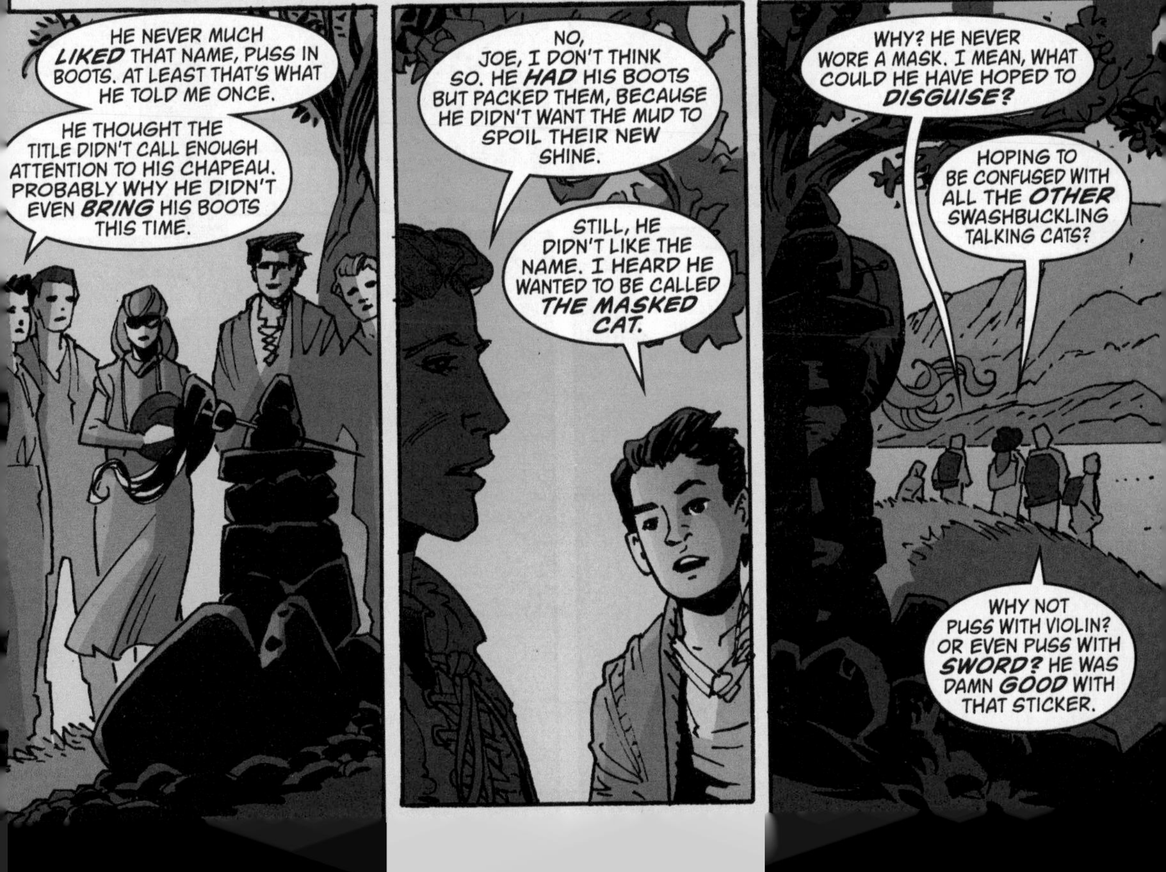
HE NEVER MUCH LIKED THAT NAME, PUSS IN BOOTS. AT LEAST THAT'S WHAT HE TOLD ME ONCE.
HE THOUGHT THE TITLE DIDN'T CALL ENOUGH ATTENTION TO HIS CHAPEAU. PROBABLY WHY HE DIDN'T EVEN BRING HIS BOOTS THIS TIME.
NO, JOE, I DON'T THINK SO. HE HAD HIS BOOTS BUT PACKED THEM, BECAUSE HE DIDN'T WANT THE MUD TO SPOIL THEIR NEW SHINE.
STILL, HE DIDN'T LIKE THE NAME. I HEARD HE WANTED TO BE CALLED THE MASKED CAT.
WHY? HE NEVER WORE A MASK. I MEAN, WHAT COULD HE HAVE HOPED TO DISGUISE?
HOPING TO BE CONFUSED WITH ALL THE OTHER SWASHBUCKLING TALKING CATS?
WHY NOT PUSS WITH VIOLIN? OR EVEN PUSS WITH SWORD? HE WAS DAMN GOOD WITH THAT STICKER.

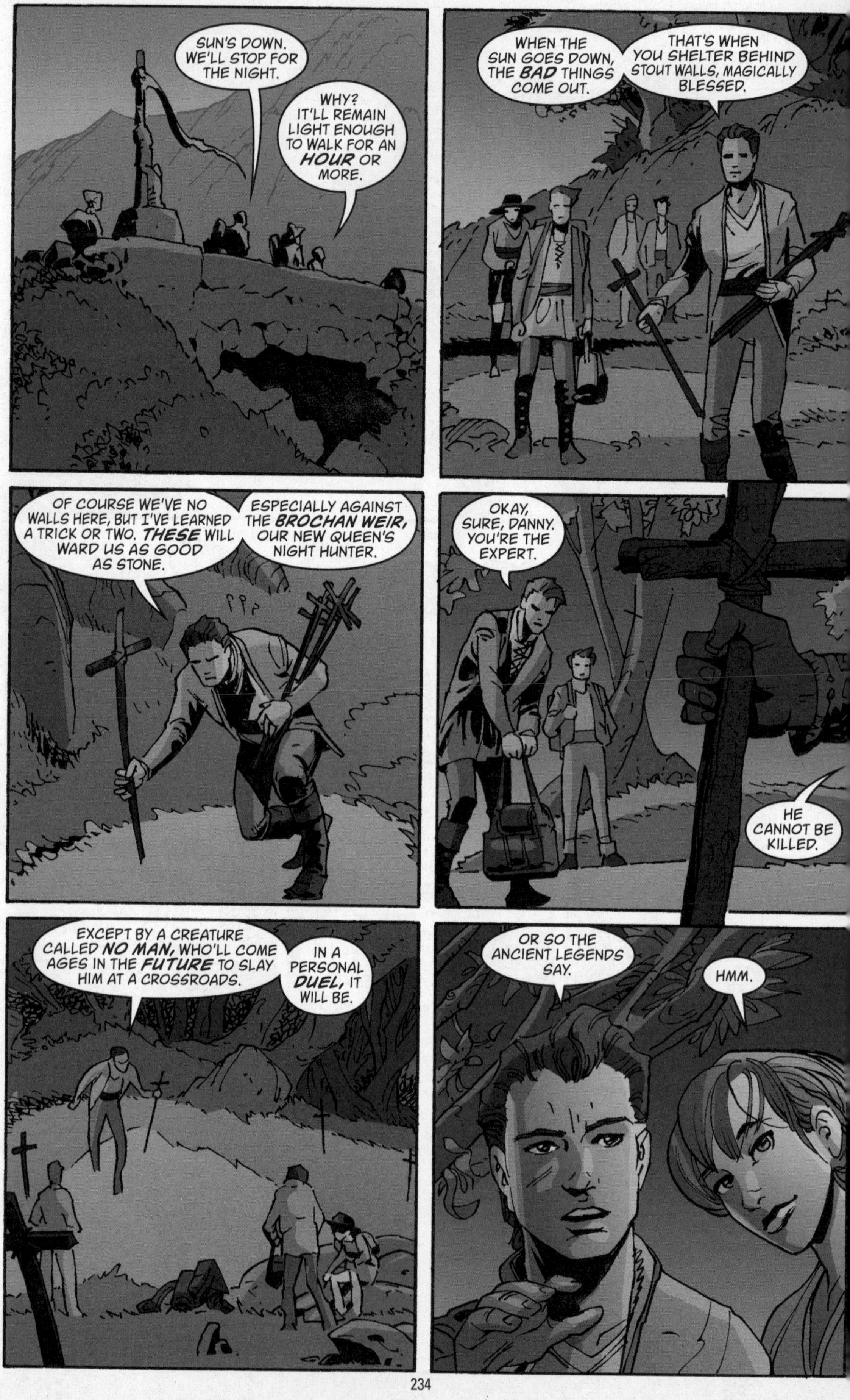
SUN'S DOWN. WE'LL STOP FOR THE NIGHT.
WHY? IT'LL REMAIN LIGHT ENOUGH TO WALK FOR AN HOUR OR MORE.
WHEN THE SUN GOES DOWN, THE BAD THINGS COME OUT.
THAT'S WHEN YOU SHELTER BEHIND STOUT WALLS, MAGICALLY BLESSED.
OF COURSE WE'VE NO WALLS HERE, BUT I'VE LEARNED A TRICK OR TWO. THESE WILL WARD US AS GOOD AS STONE.
ESPECIALLY AGAINST THE BROCHAN WEIR, OUR NEW QUEEN'S NIGHT HUNTER.
OKAY, SURE, DANNY. YOU'RE THE EXPERT.
HE CANNOT BE KILLED.
EXCEPT BY A CREATURE CALLED NO MAN, WHO'LL COME AGES IN THE FUTURE TO SLAY HIM AT A CROSSROADS.
IN A PERSONAL DUEL, IT WILL BE.
OR SO THE ANCIENT LEGENDS SAY.
HMM.

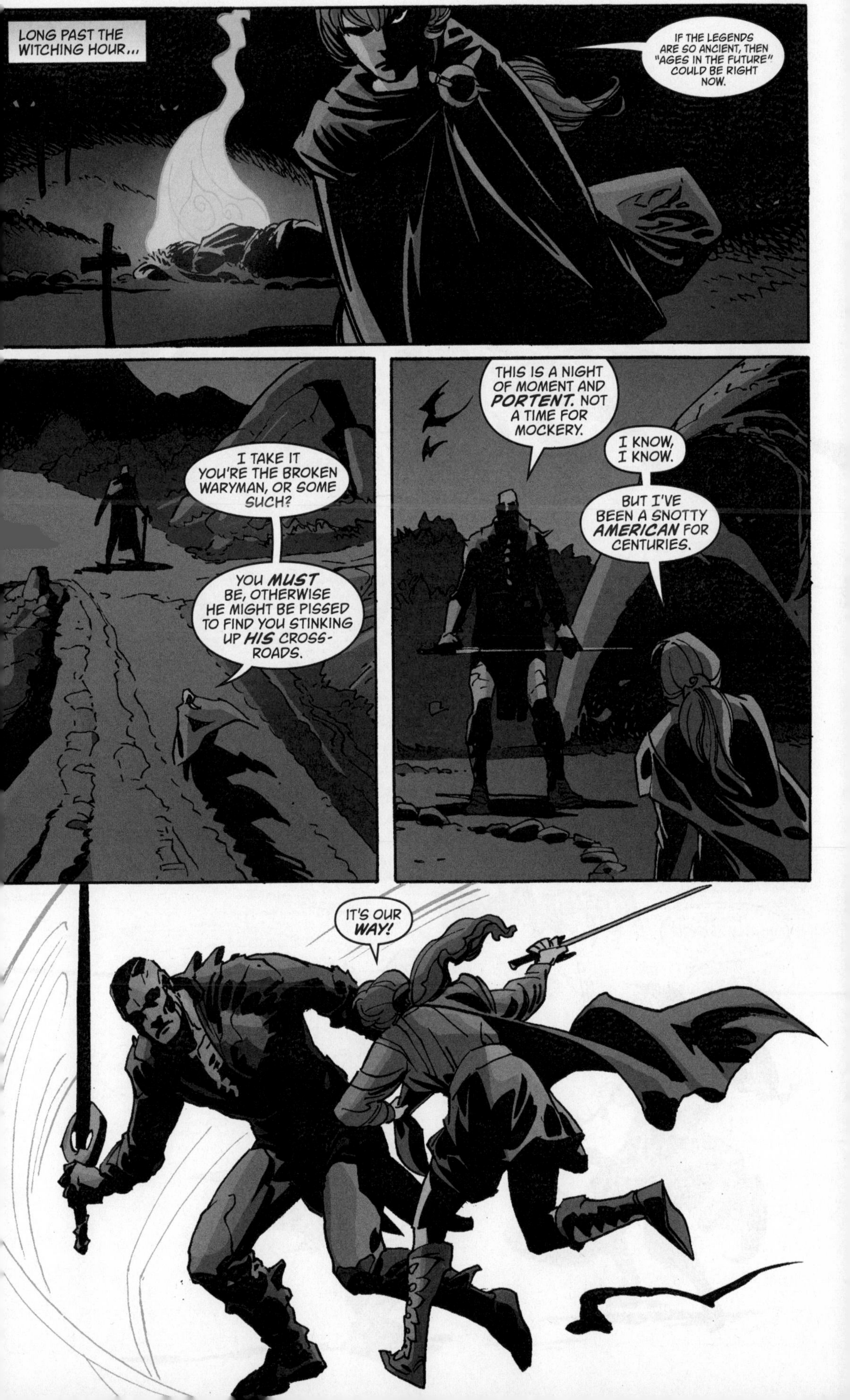

LONG PAST THE WITCHING HOUR...
IF THE LEGENDS ARE SO ANCIENT, THEN "AGES IN THE FUTURE" COULD BE RIGHT NOW.
I TAKE IT YOU'RE THE BROKEN WARYMAN, OR SOME SUCH?
YOU MUST BE, OTHERWISE HE MIGHT BE PISSED TO FIND YOU STINKING UP HIS CROSS-ROADS.
THIS IS A NIGHT OF MOMENT AND PORTENT. NOT A TIME FOR MOCKERY.
I KNOW, I KNOW.
BUT I'VE BEEN A SNOTTY AMERICAN FOR CENTURIES.
IT'S OUR WAY!

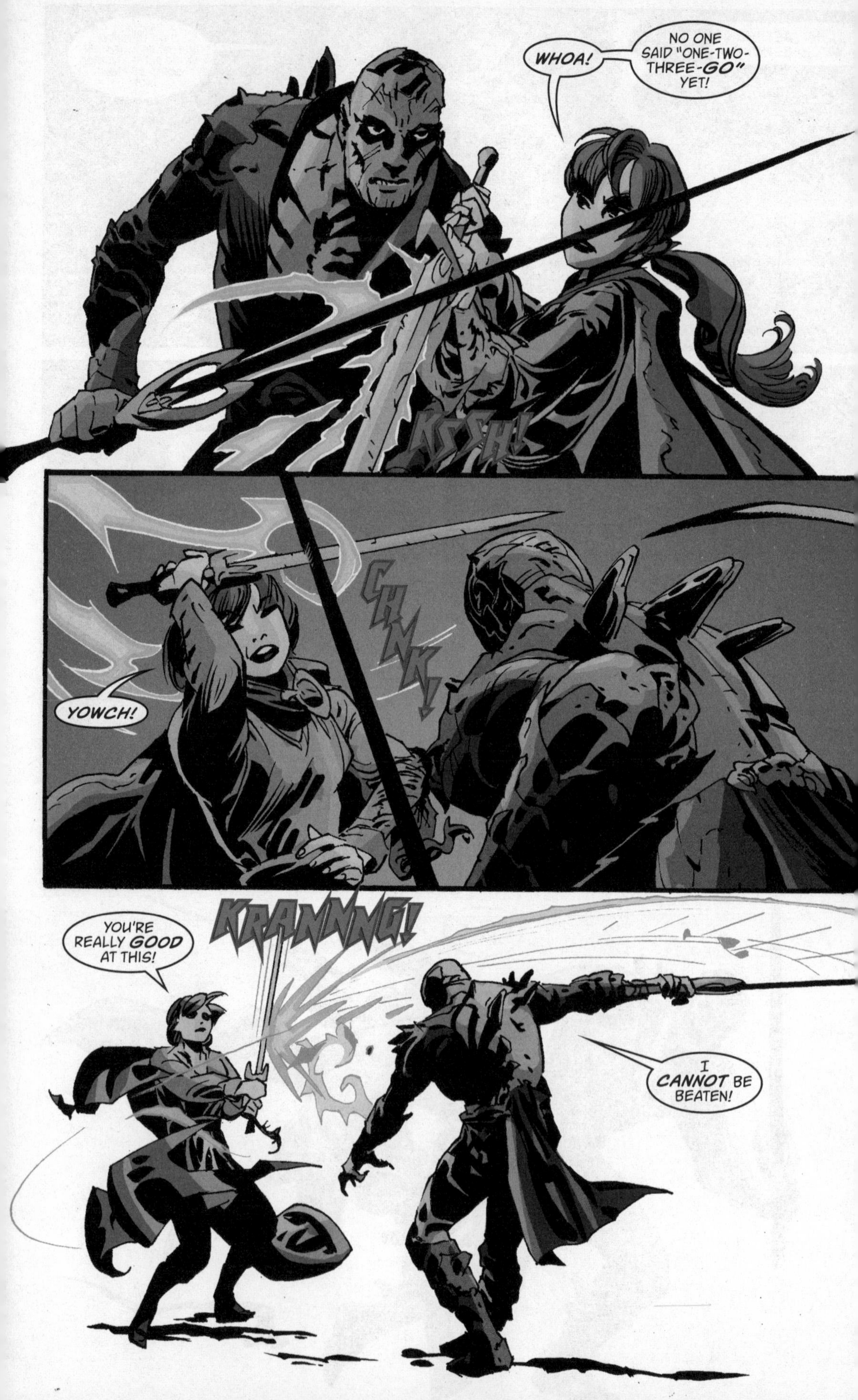
WHOA!
NO ONE SAID "ONE-TWO-THREE-GO" YET!
KSSH!
CHINK!
YOWCH!
KRANNNG!
YOU'RE REALLY GOOD AT THIS!
I CANNOT BE BEATEN!

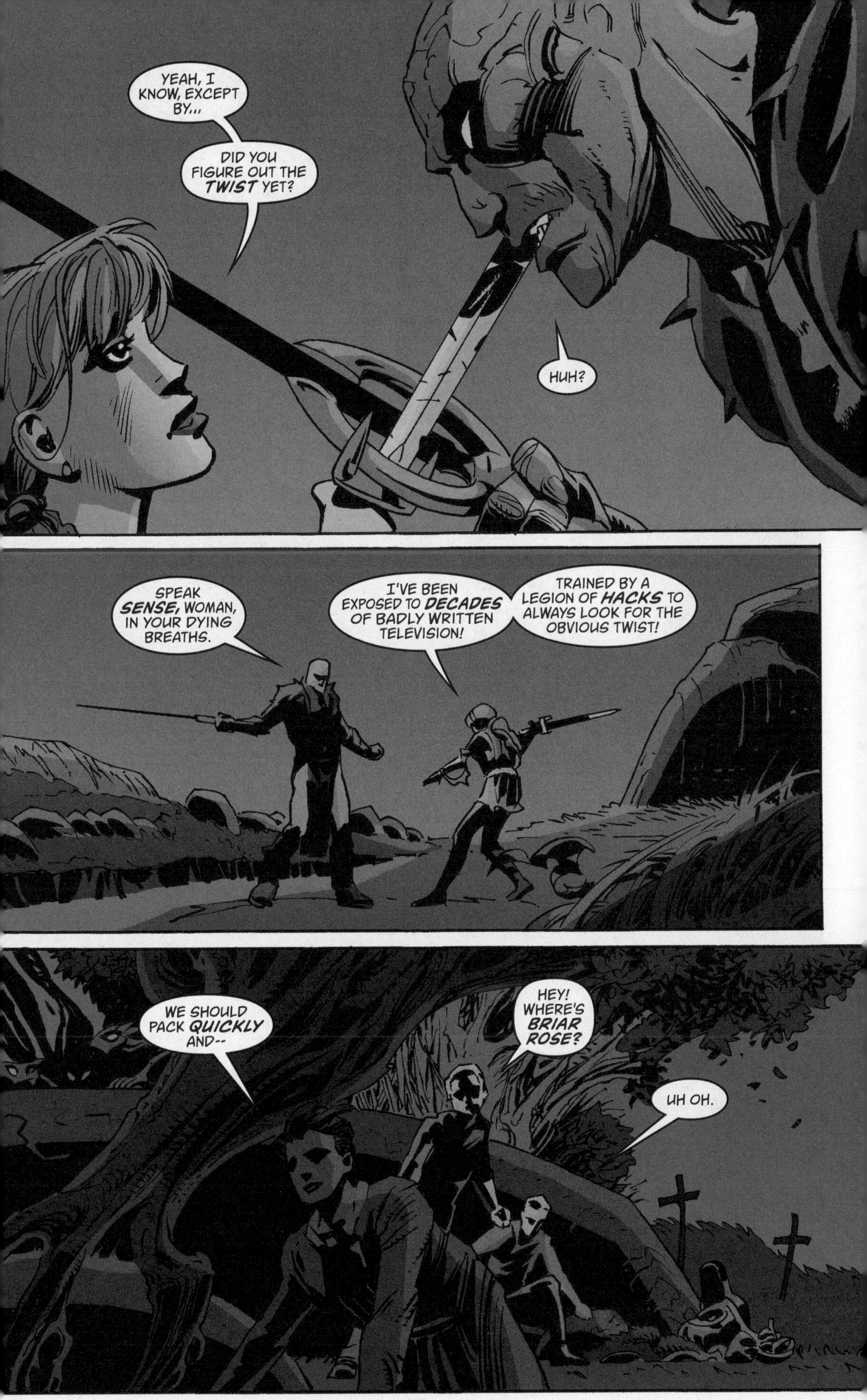

YEAH, I KNOW, EXCEPT BY...
DID YOU FIGURE OUT THE TWIST YET?
HUH?
SPEAK SENSE, WOMAN, IN YOUR DYING BREATHS.
I'VE BEEN EXPOSED TO DECADES OF BADLY WRITTEN TELEVISION!
TRAINED BY A LEGION OF HACKS TO ALWAYS LOOK FOR THE OBVIOUS TWIST!
WE SHOULD PACK QUICKLY AND--
HEY! WHERE'S BRIAR ROSE?
UH OH.

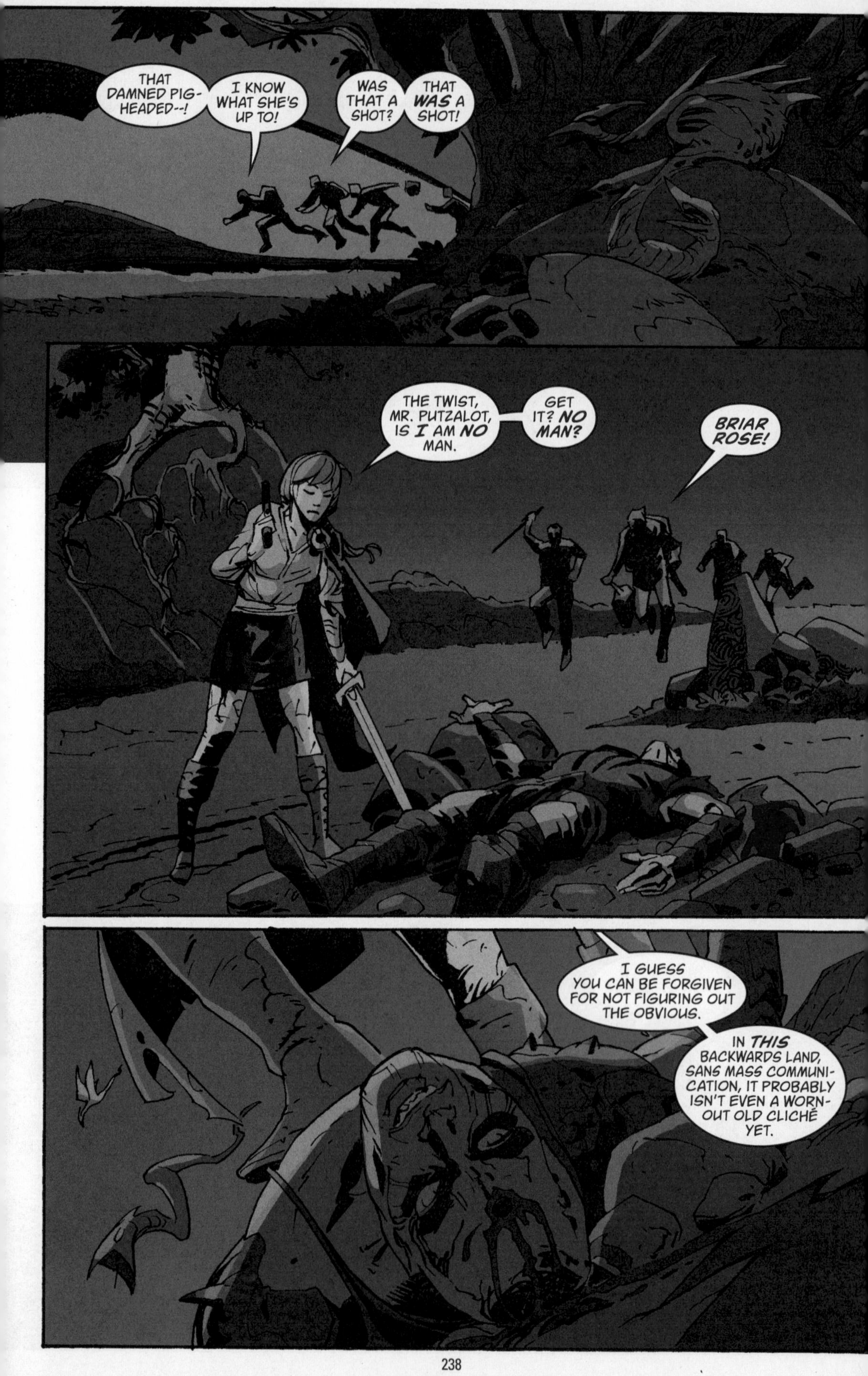
THAT DAMNED PIG-HEADED--!
I KNOW WHAT SHE'S UP TO!
WAS THAT A SHOT?
THAT WAS A SHOT!
THE TWIST, MR. PUTZALOT, IS I AM NO MAN.
GET IT? NO MAN?
BRIAR ROSE!
I GUESS YOU CAN BE FORGIVEN FOR NOT FIGURING OUT THE OBVIOUS.
IN THIS BACKWARDS LAND, SANS MASS COMMUNICATION, IT PROBABLY ISN'T EVEN A WORN-OUT OLD CLICHÉ YET.

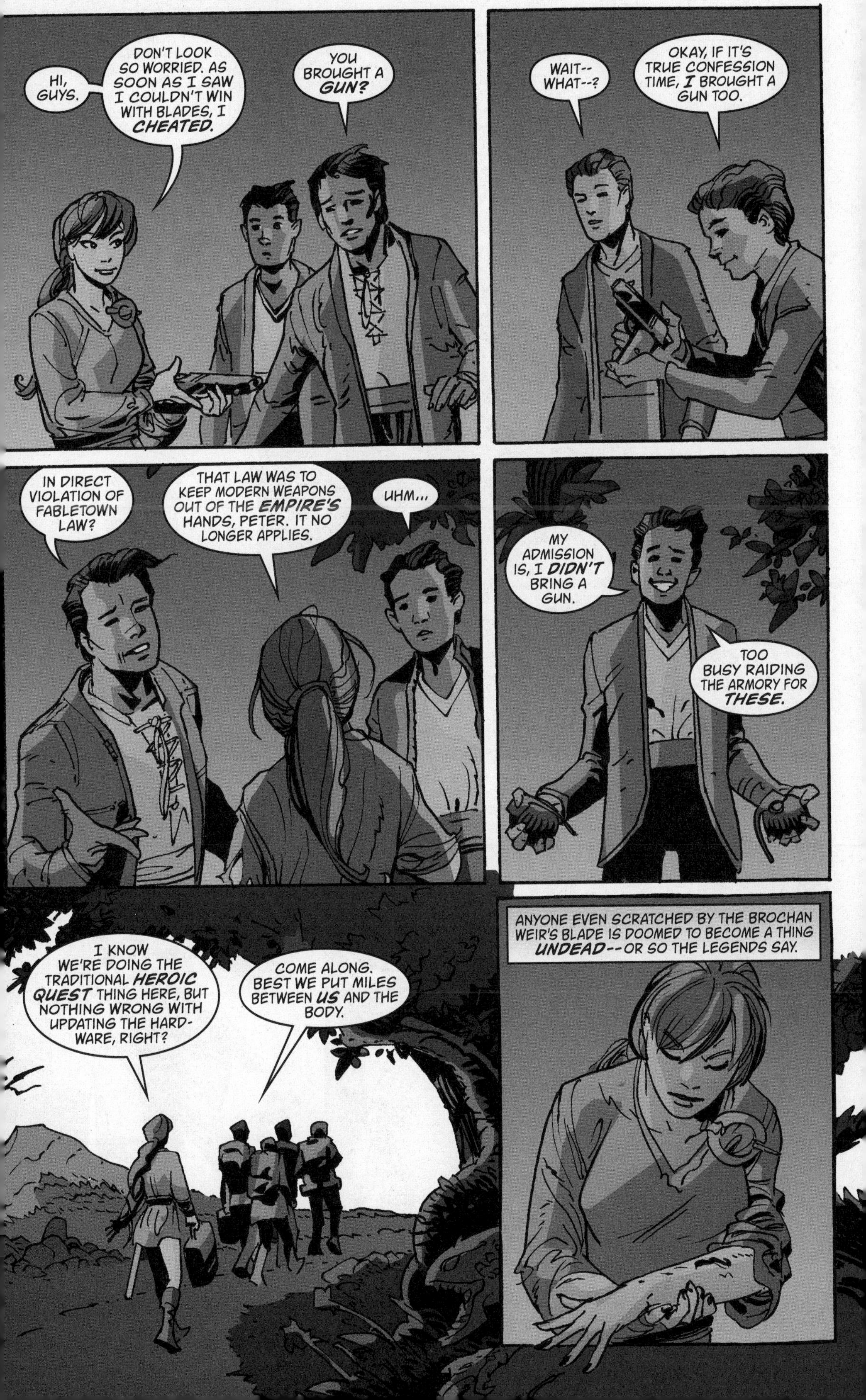
HI, GUYS.
DON'T LOOK SO WORRIED. AS SOON AS I SAW I COULDN'T WIN WITH BLADES, I CHEATED.
YOU BROUGHT A GUN?
WAIT-- WHAT--?
OKAY, IF IT'S TRUE CONFESSION TIME, I BROUGHT A GUN TOO.
IN DIRECT VIOLATION OF FABLETOWN LAW?
THAT LAW WAS TO KEEP MODERN WEAPONS OUT OF THE EMPIRE'S HANDS, PETER. IT NO LONGER APPLIES.
UHM...
MY ADMISSION IS, I DIDN'T BRING A GUN.
TOO BUSY RAIDING THE ARMORY FOR THESE.
I KNOW WE'RE DOING THE TRADITIONAL HEROIC QUEST THING HERE, BUT NOTHING WRONG WITH UPDATING THE HARD-WARE, RIGHT?
COME ALONG. BEST WE PUT MILES BETWEEN US AND THE BODY.
ANYONE EVEN SCRATCHED BY THE BROCHAN WEIR'S BLADE IS DOOMED TO BECOME A THING UNDEAD--OR SO THE LEGENDS SAY.

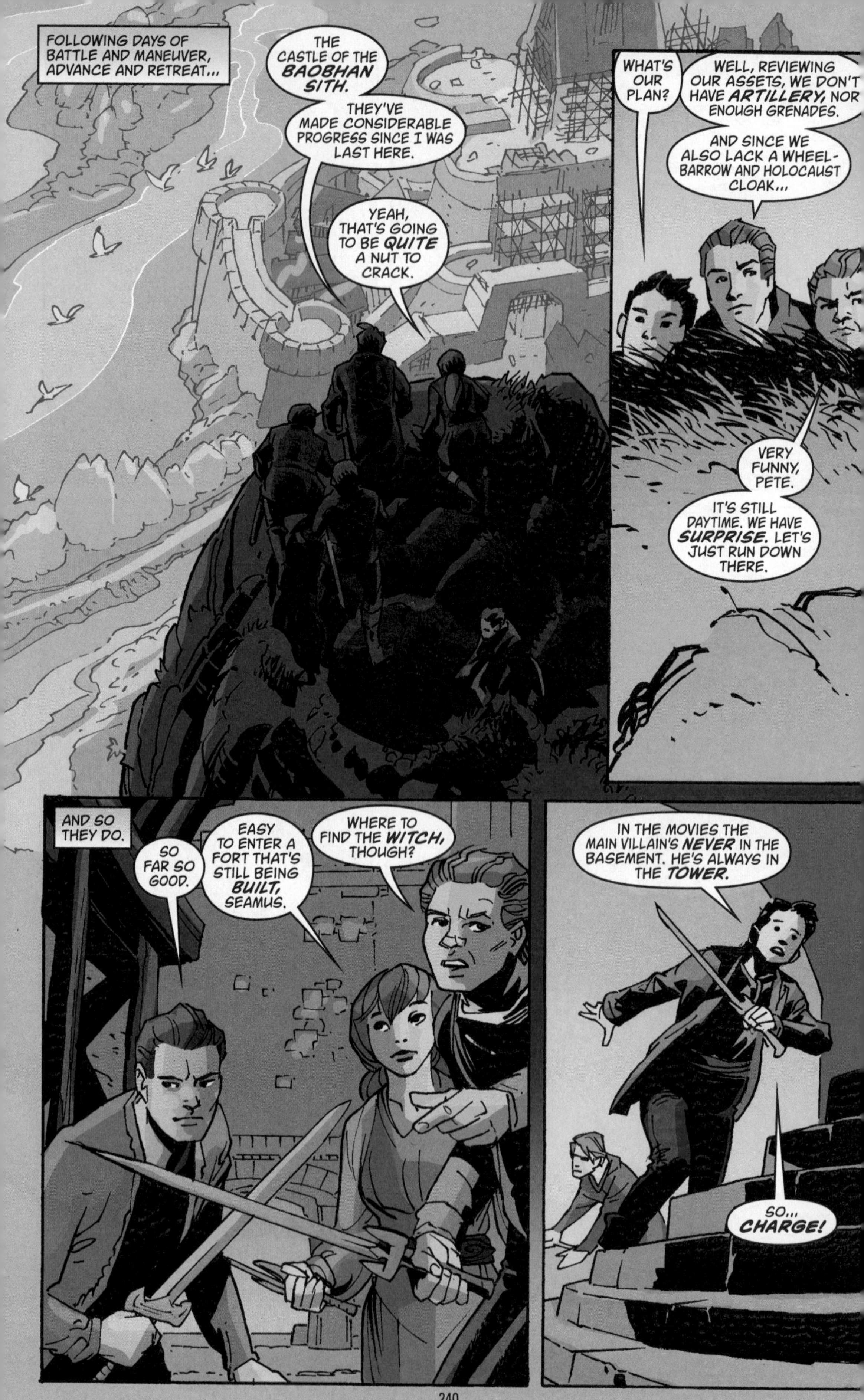
FOLLOWING DAYS OF BATTLE AND MANEUVER, ADVANCE AND RETREAT...
THE CASTLE OF THE BAOBHAN SITH.
THEY'VE MADE CONSIDERABLE PROGRESS SINCE I WAS LAST HERE.
YEAH, THAT'S GOING TO BE QUITE A NUT TO CRACK.
WHAT'S OUR PLAN?
WELL, REVIEWING OUR ASSETS, WE DON'T HAVE ARTILLERY, NOR ENOUGH GRENADES.
AND SINCE WE ALSO LACK A WHEEL-BARROW AND HOLOCAUST CLOAK...
VERY FUNNY, PETE.
IT'S STILL DAYTIME. WE HAVE SURPRISE. LET'S JUST RUN DOWN THERE.
AND SO THEY DO.
SO FAR SO GOOD.
EASY TO ENTER A FORT THAT'S STILL BEING BUILT, SEAMUS.
WHERE TO FIND THE WITCH, THOUGH?
IN THE MOVIES THE MAIN VILLAIN'S NEVER IN THE BASEMENT. HE'S ALWAYS IN THE TOWER.
SO... CHARGE!

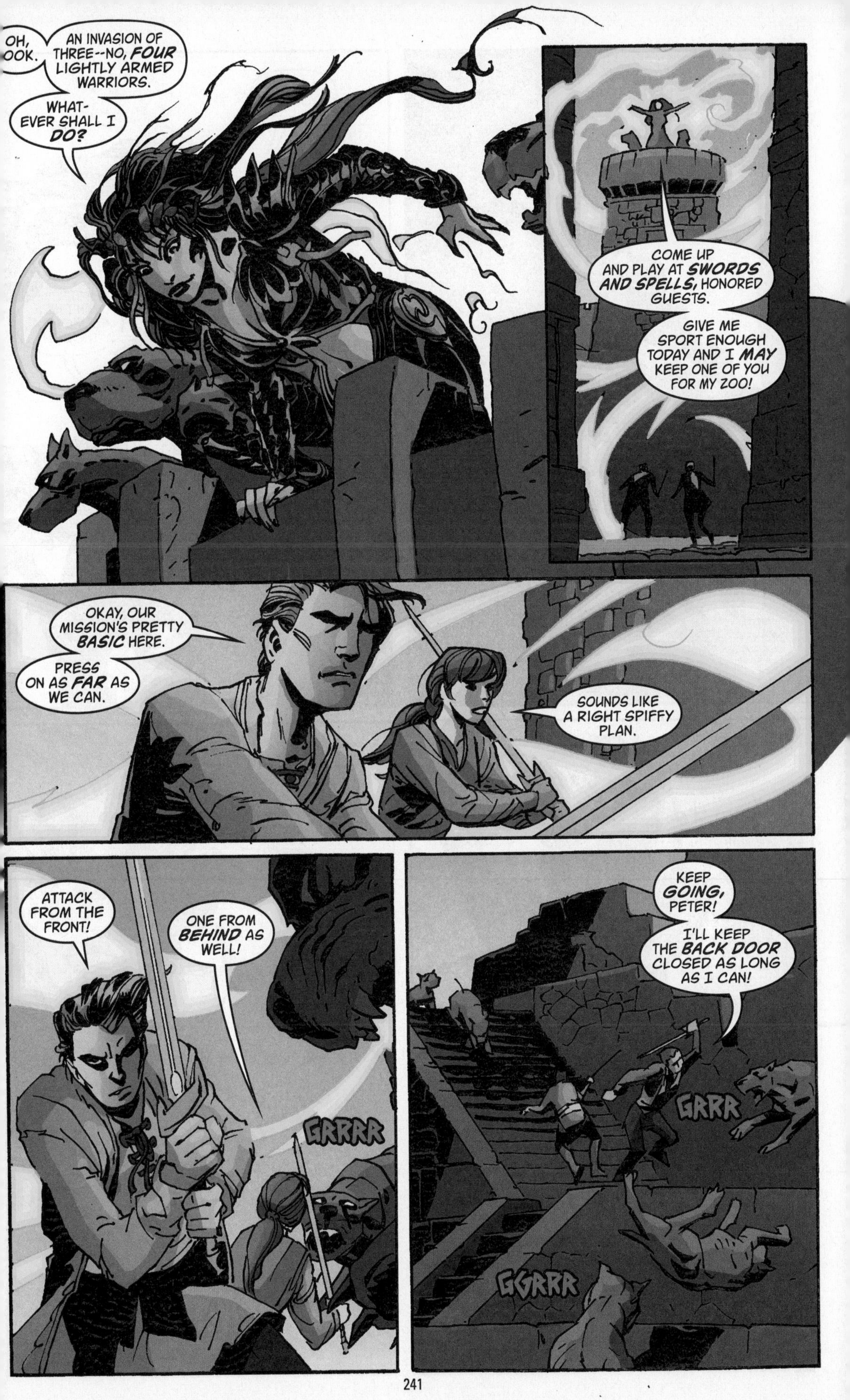

OH, LOOK.
AN INVASION OF THREE--NO, FOUR LIGHTLY ARMED WARRIORS.
WHAT-EVER SHALL I DO?
COME UP AND PLAY AT SWORDS AND SPELLS, HONORED GUESTS.
GIVE ME SPORT ENOUGH TODAY AND I MAY KEEP ONE OF YOU FOR MY ZOO!
OKAY, OUR MISSION'S PRETTY BASIC HERE.
PRESS ON AS FAR AS WE CAN.
SOUNDS LIKE A RIGHT SPIFFY PLAN.
ATTACK FROM THE FRONT!
ONE FROM BEHIND AS WELL!
GRRRR
KEEP GOING, PETER!
I'LL KEEP THE BACK DOOR CLOSED AS LONG AS I CAN!
GRRR
GGRRR

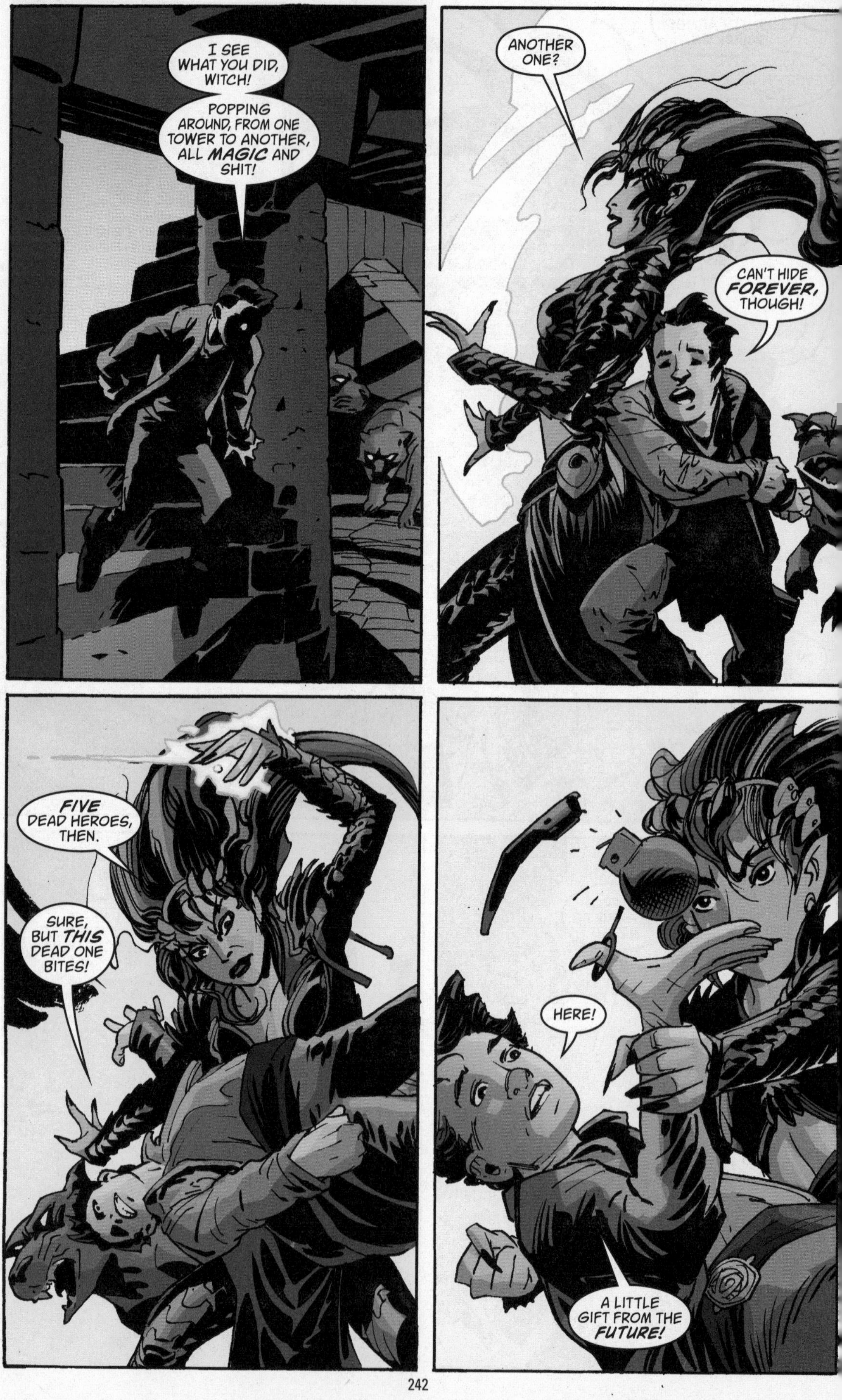
I SEE WHAT YOU DID, WITCH!
POPPING AROUND, FROM ONE TOWER TO ANOTHER, ALL *MAGIC* AND SHIT!
ANOTHER ONE?
CAN'T HIDE *FOREVER,* THOUGH!
FIVE DEAD HEROES, THEN.
SURE, BUT *THIS* DEAD ONE BITES!
HERE!
A LITTLE GIFT FROM THE *FUTURE!*

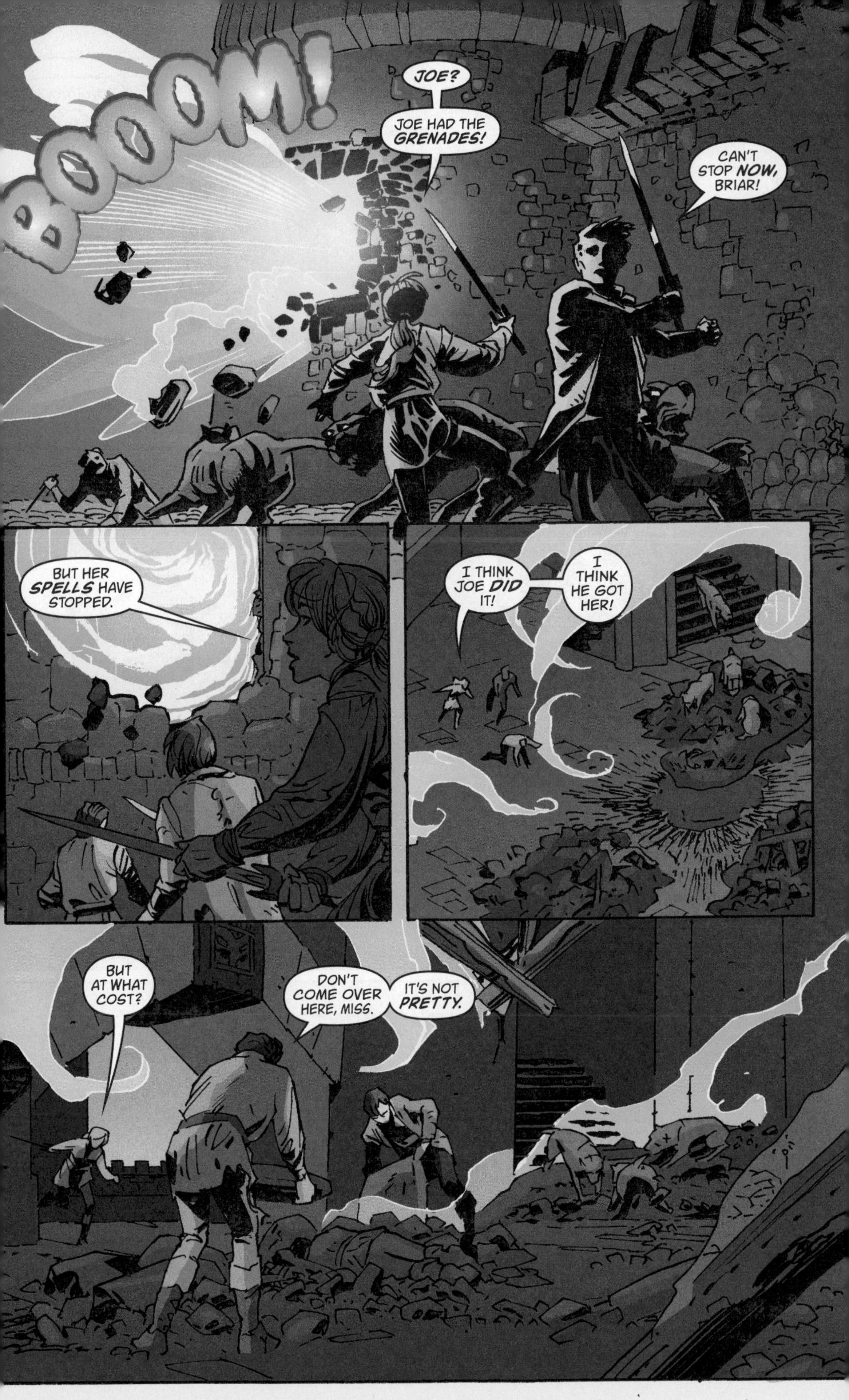
BOOOOM!
JOE?
JOE HAD THE GRENADES!
CAN'T STOP NOW, BRIAR!
BUT HER SPELLS HAVE STOPPED.
I THINK JOE DID IT!
I THINK HE GOT HER!
BUT AT WHAT COST?
DON'T COME OVER HERE, MISS.
IT'S NOT PRETTY.

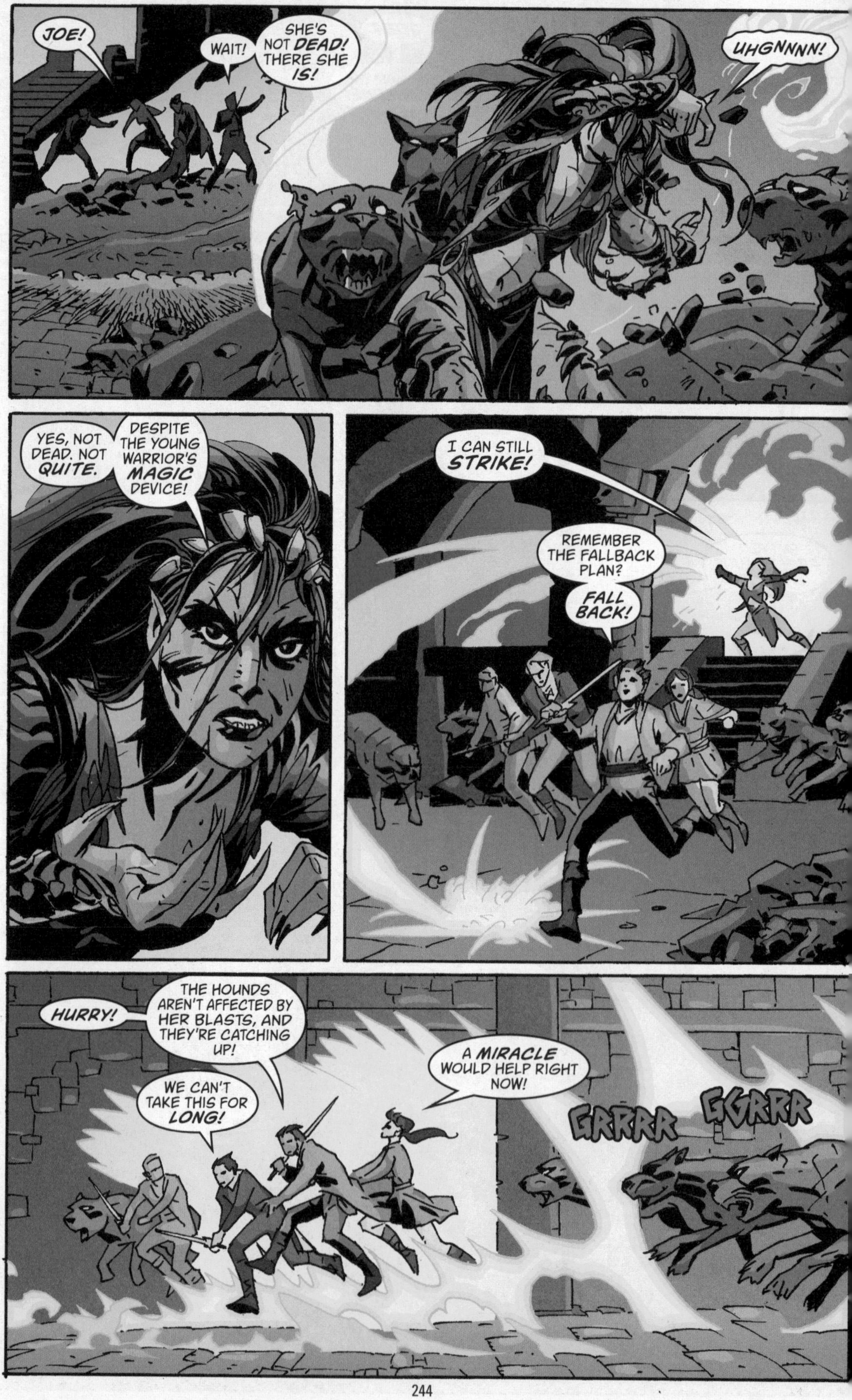
JOE!
WAIT!
SHE'S NOT DEAD! THERE SHE IS!
UHGNNNN!
YES, NOT DEAD. NOT QUITE.
DESPITE THE YOUNG WARRIOR'S MAGIC DEVICE!
I CAN STILL STRIKE!
REMEMBER THE FALLBACK PLAN?
FALL BACK!
HURRY!
THE HOUNDS AREN'T AFFECTED BY HER BLASTS, AND THEY'RE CATCHING UP!
WE CAN'T TAKE THIS FOR LONG!
A MIRACLE WOULD HELP RIGHT NOW!
GRRRR
GGRRR

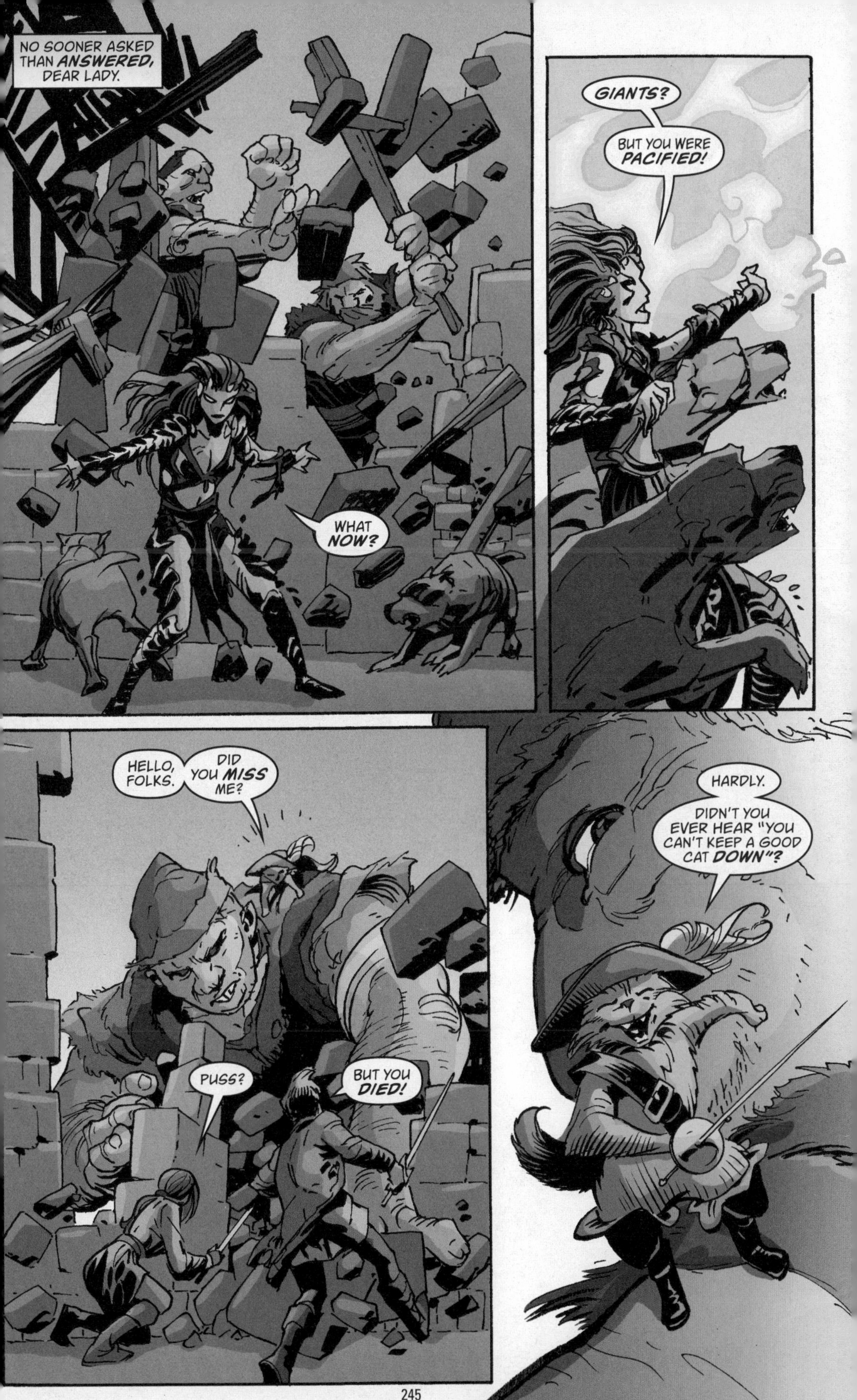

NO SOONER ASKED THAN ANSWERED, DEAR LADY.
WHAT NOW?
GIANTS?
BUT YOU WERE PACIFIED!
HELLO, FOLKS.
DID YOU MISS ME?
PUSS?
BUT YOU DIED!
HARDLY.
DIDN'T YOU EVER HEAR "YOU CAN'T KEEP A GOOD CAT DOWN"?

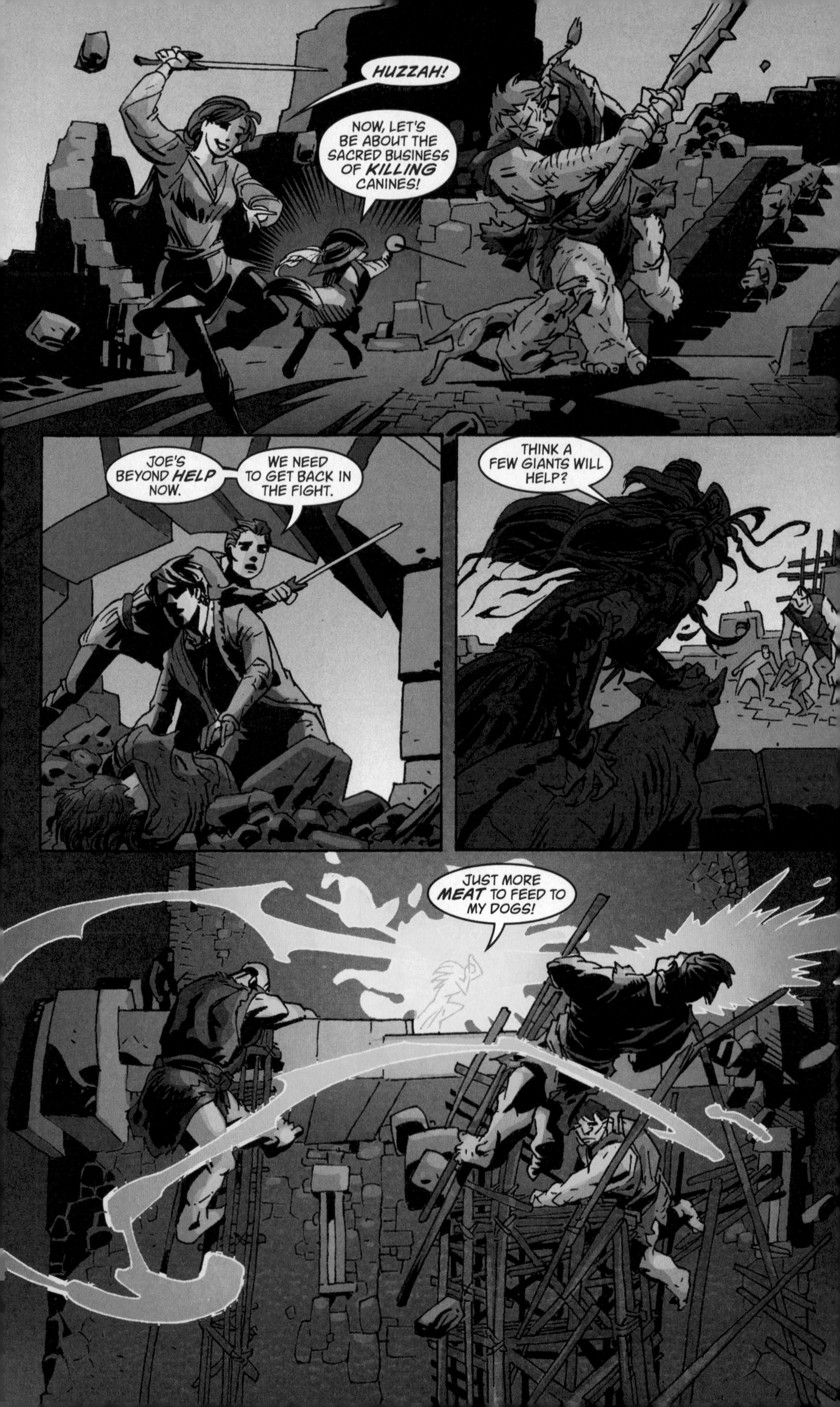
HUZZAH!
NOW, LET'S BE ABOUT THE SACRED BUSINESS OF KILLING CANINES!
JOE'S BEYOND HELP NOW.
WE NEED TO GET BACK IN THE FIGHT.
THINK A FEW GIANTS WILL HELP?
JUST MORE MEAT TO FEED TO MY DOGS!

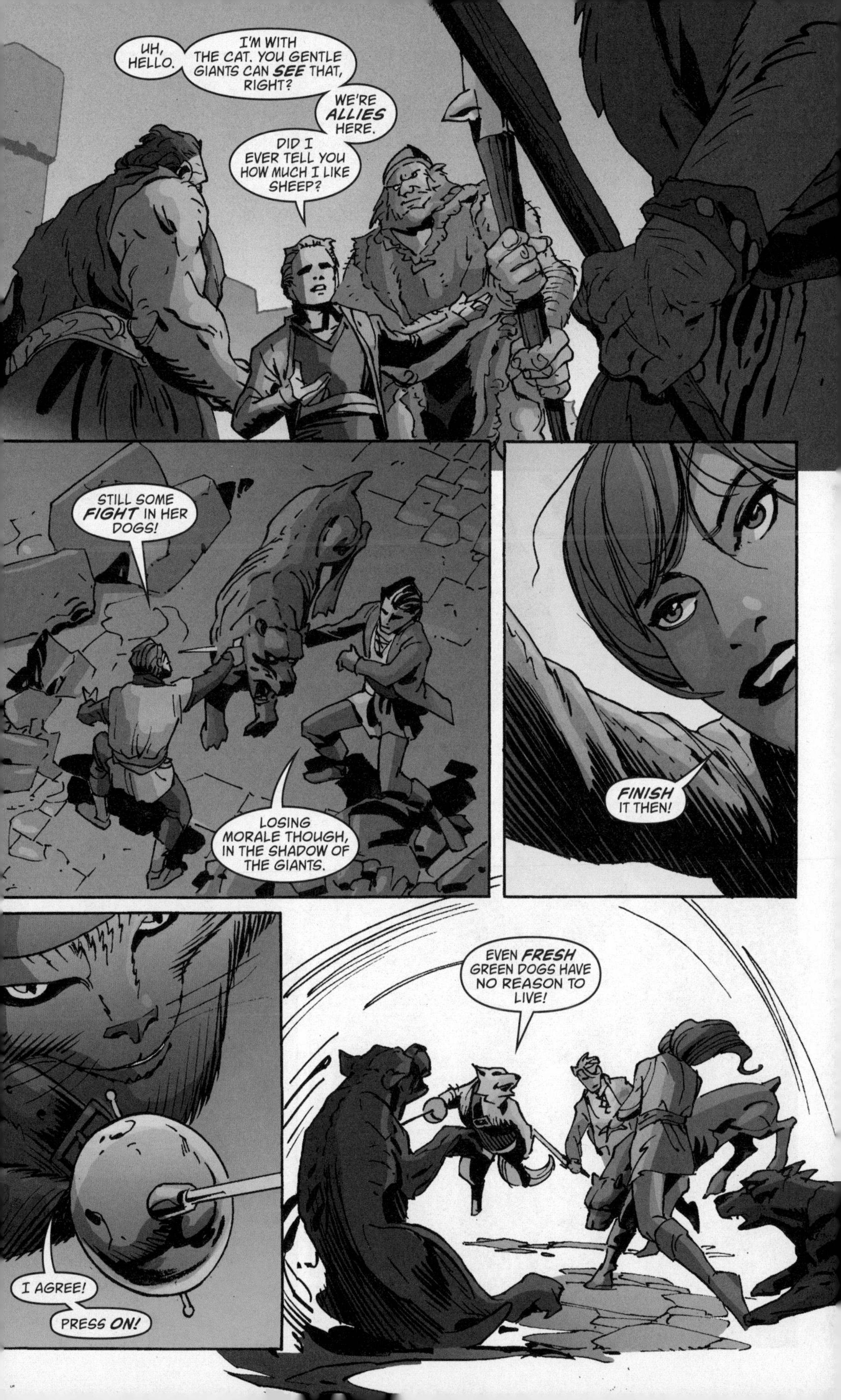
UH, HELLO.
I'M WITH THE CAT. YOU GENTLE GIANTS CAN SEE THAT, RIGHT?
WE'RE ALLIES HERE.
DID I EVER TELL YOU HOW MUCH I LIKE SHEEP?
STILL SOME FIGHT IN HER DOGS!
LOSING MORALE THOUGH, IN THE SHADOW OF THE GIANTS.
FINISH IT THEN!
I AGREE!
PRESS ON!
EVEN FRESH GREEN DOGS HAVE NO REASON TO LIVE!

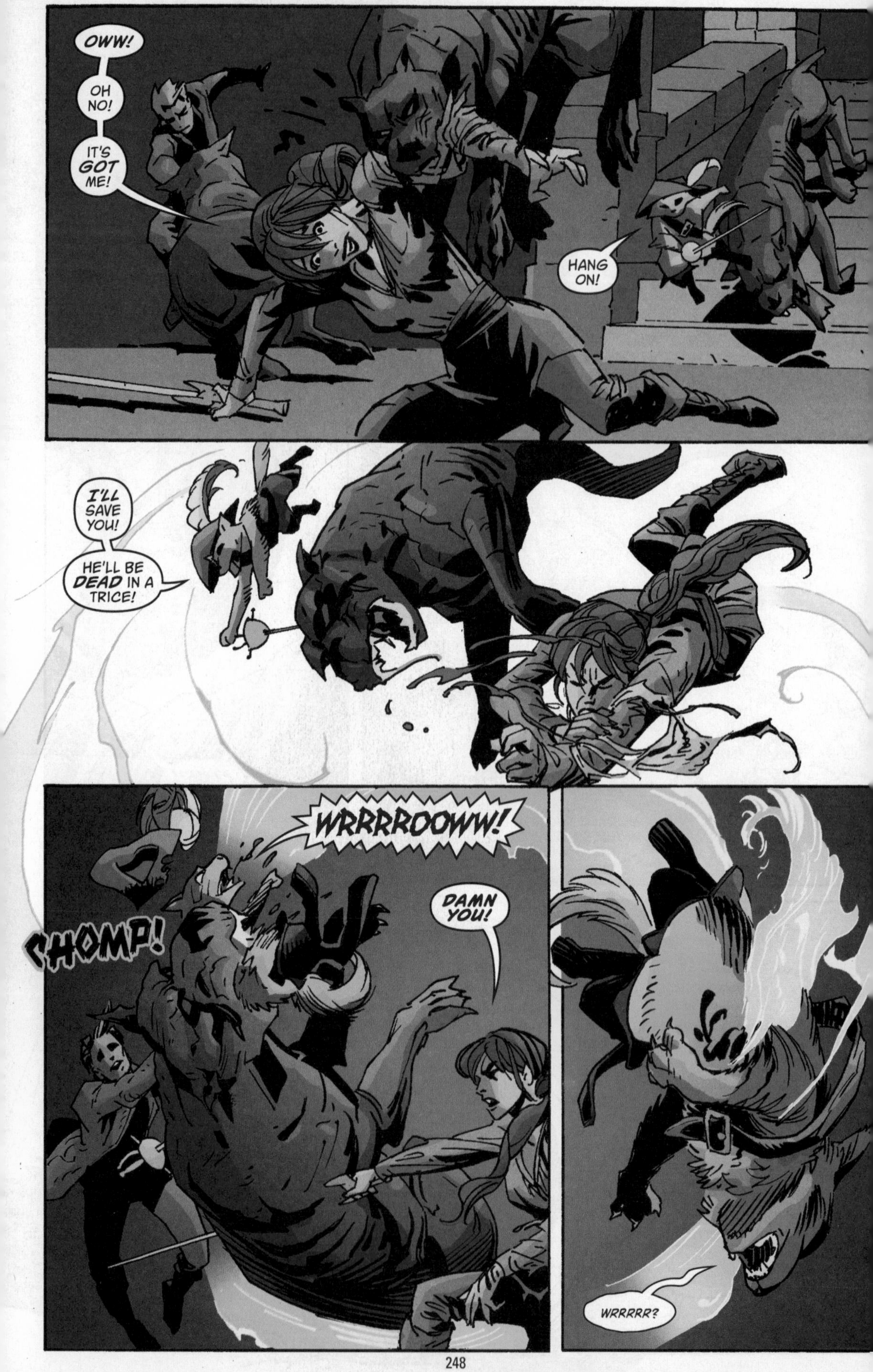
OWW!
OH NO!
IT'S GOT ME!
HANG ON!
I'LL SAVE YOU!
HE'LL BE DEAD IN A TRICE!
WRRRROOWW!
CHOMP!
DAMN YOU!
WRRRRR?

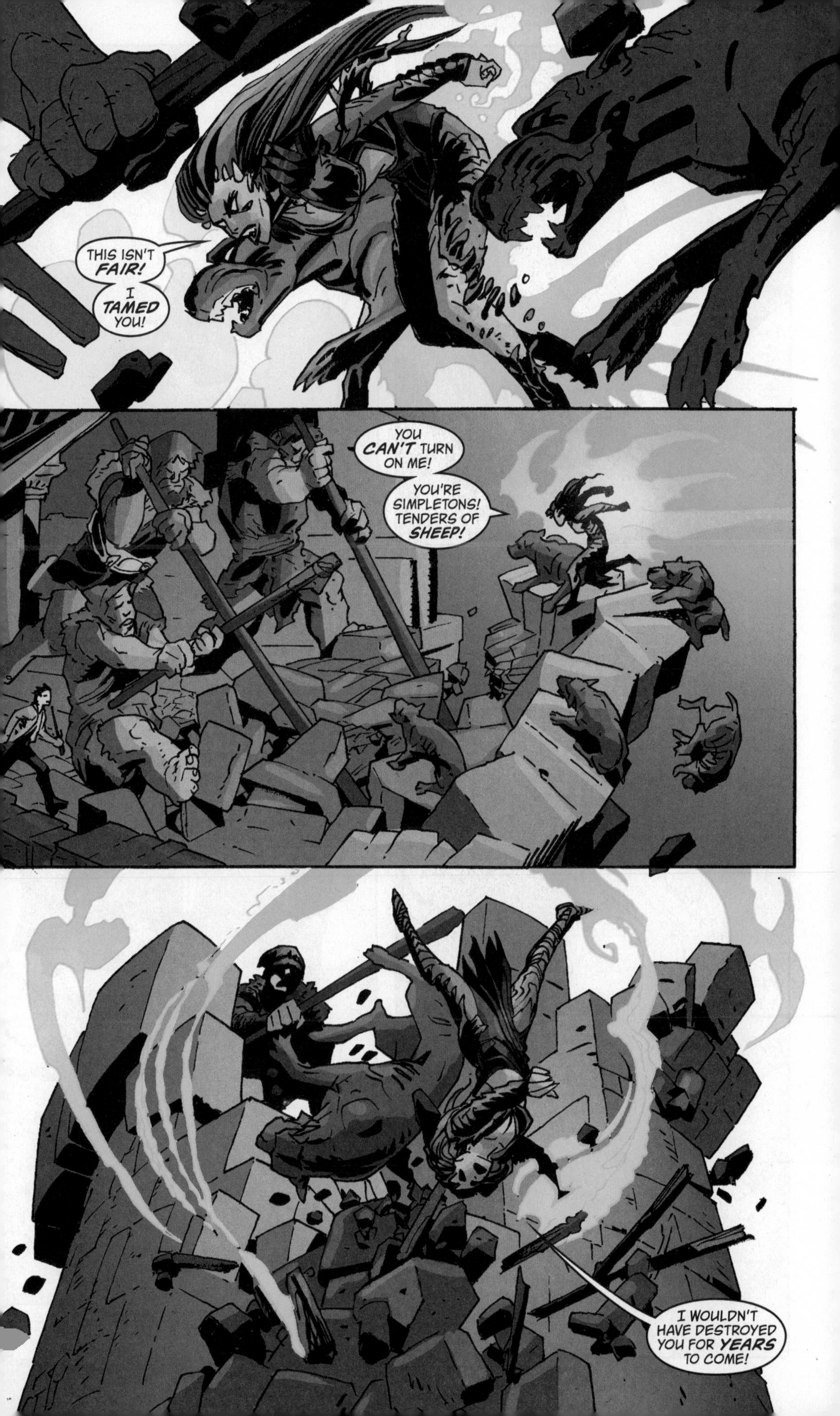
THIS ISN'T *FAIR!*
I *TAMED* YOU!
YOU *CAN'T* TURN ON ME!
YOU'RE SIMPLETONS! TENDERS OF *SHEEP!*
I WOULDN'T HAVE DESTROYED YOU FOR *YEARS* TO COME!

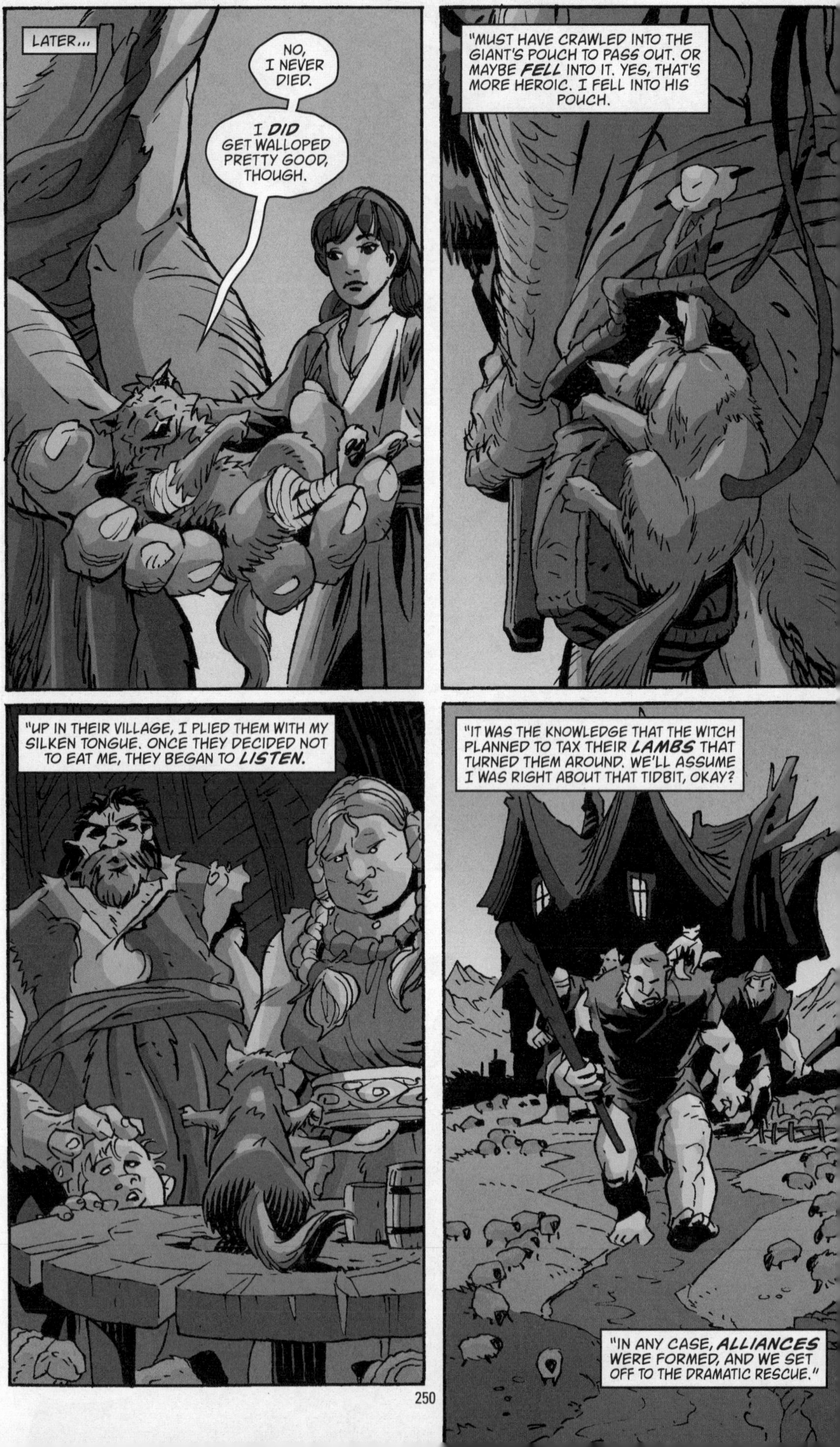

LATER...
NO, I NEVER DIED.
I DID GET WALLOPED PRETTY GOOD, THOUGH.
"MUST HAVE CRAWLED INTO THE GIANT'S POUCH TO PASS OUT. OR MAYBE FELL INTO IT. YES, THAT'S MORE HEROIC. I FELL INTO HIS POUCH.
"UP IN THEIR VILLAGE, I PLIED THEM WITH MY SILKEN TONGUE. ONCE THEY DECIDED NOT TO EAT ME, THEY BEGAN TO LISTEN.
"IT WAS THE KNOWLEDGE THAT THE WITCH PLANNED TO TAX THEIR LAMBS THAT TURNED THEM AROUND. WE'LL ASSUME I WAS RIGHT ABOUT THAT TIDBIT, OKAY?
"IN ANY CASE, ALLIANCES WERE FORMED, AND WE SET OFF TO THE DRAMATIC RESCUE."

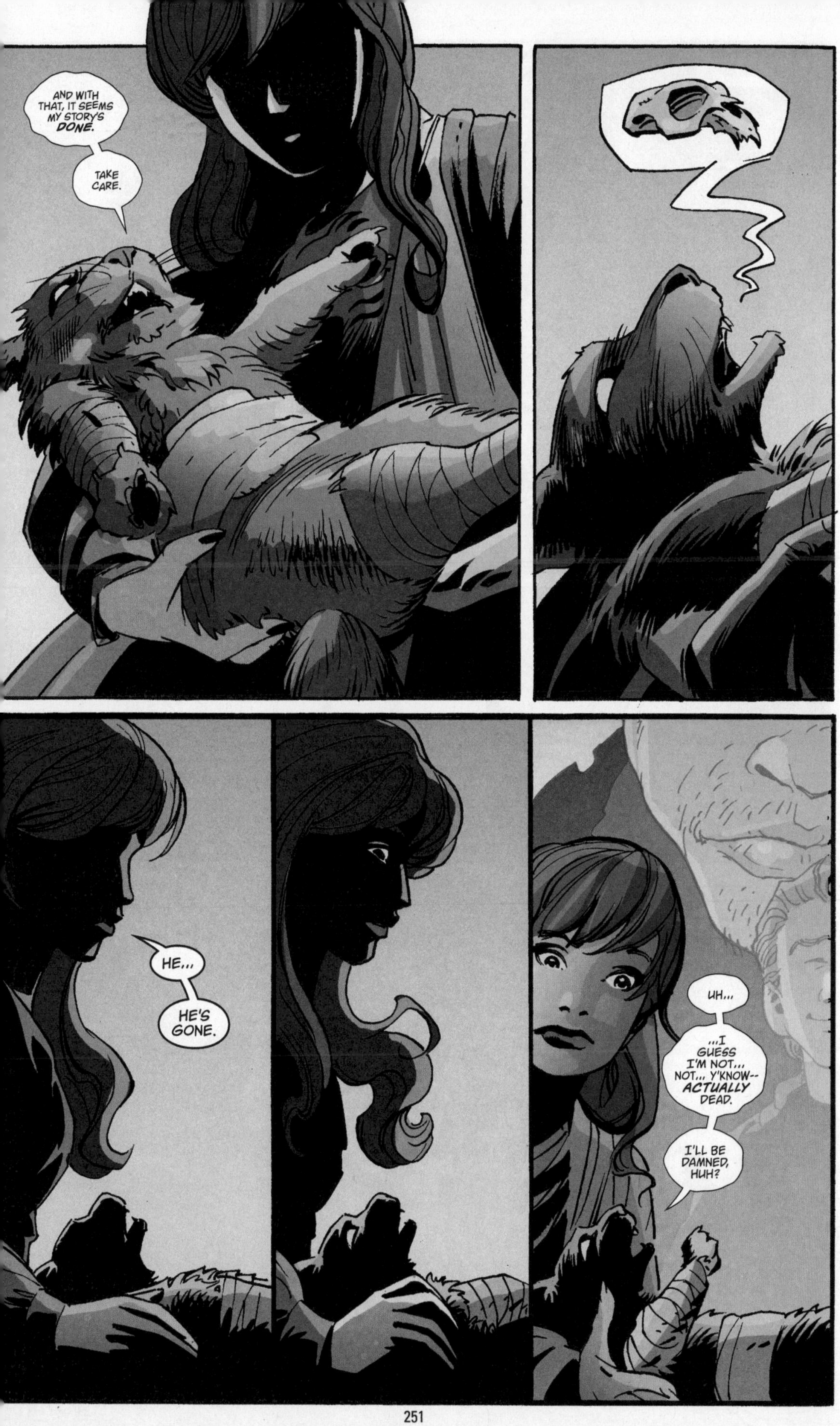

AND WITH THAT, IT SEEMS MY STORY'S DONE.
TAKE CARE.
HE...
HE'S GONE.
UH...
...I GUESS I'M NOT... NOT... Y'KNOW-- ACTUALLY DEAD.
I'LL BE DAMNED, HUH?

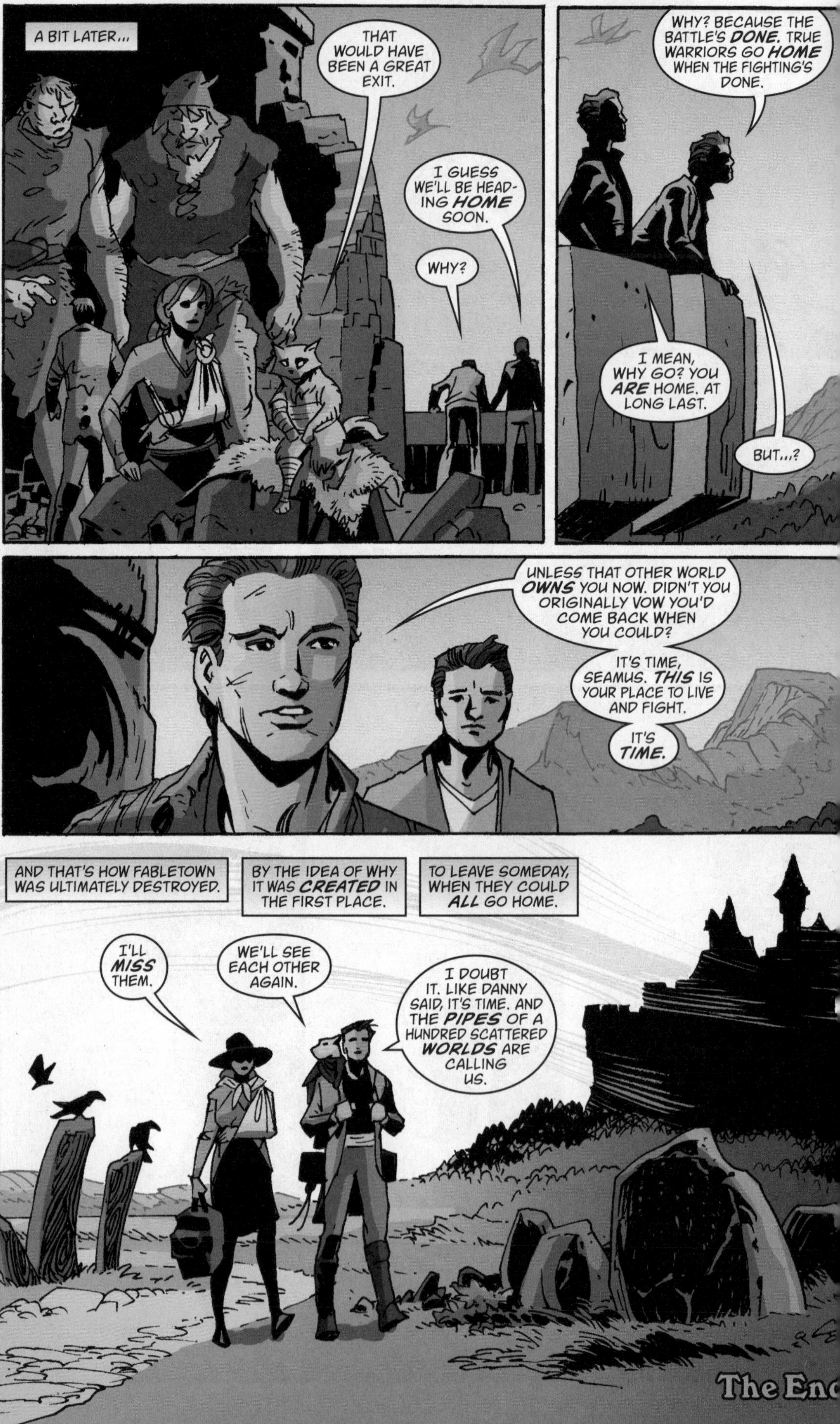
A BIT LATER...
THAT WOULD HAVE BEEN A GREAT EXIT.
I GUESS WE'LL BE HEADING HOME SOON.
WHY?
WHY? BECAUSE THE BATTLE'S DONE. TRUE WARRIORS GO HOME WHEN THE FIGHTING'S DONE.
I MEAN, WHY GO? YOU ARE HOME. AT LONG LAST.
BUT...?
UNLESS THAT OTHER WORLD OWNS YOU NOW. DIDN'T YOU ORIGINALLY VOW YOU'D COME BACK WHEN YOU COULD?
IT'S TIME, SEAMUS. THIS IS YOUR PLACE TO LIVE AND FIGHT.
IT'S TIME.
AND THAT'S HOW FABLETOWN WAS ULTIMATELY DESTROYED.
BY THE IDEA OF WHY IT WAS CREATED IN THE FIRST PLACE.
TO LEAVE SOMEDAY, WHEN THEY COULD ALL GO HOME.
I'LL MISS THEM.
WE'LL SEE EACH OTHER AGAIN.
I DOUBT IT. LIKE DANNY SAID, IT'S TIME. AND THE PIPES OF A HUNDRED SCATTERED WORLDS ARE CALLING US.
The End

KNIGHTHOOD IN FLOWER

COVER DESIGNS AND PRELIMINARY ART BY MARK BUCKINGHAM

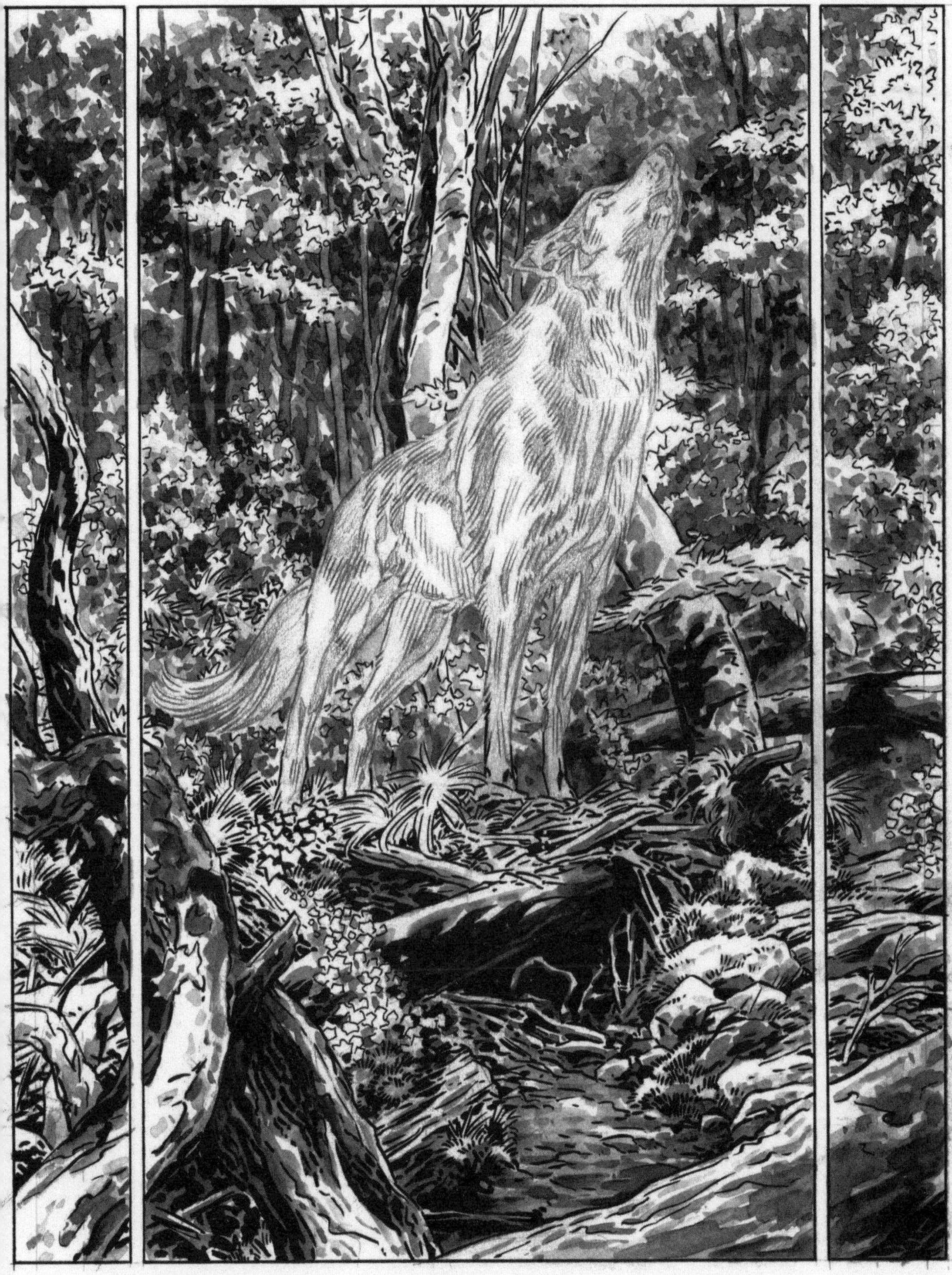

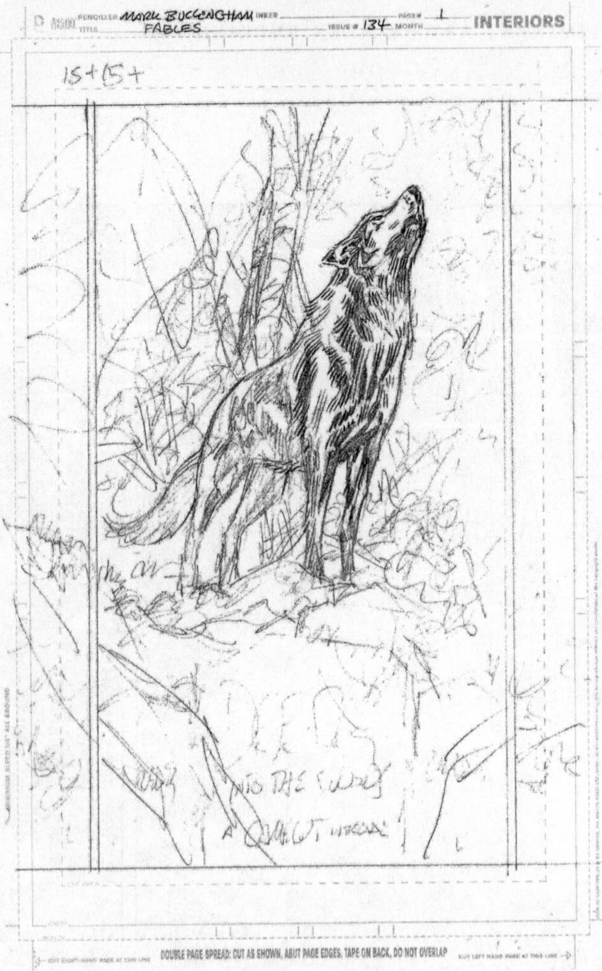
PENCILLER MARK BUCKINGHAM INKER PAGE# 1
TITLE FABLES ISSUE # 134 MONTH
INTERIORS
15+15+
DOUBLE PAGE SPREAD: CUT AS SHOWN, ABUT PAGE EDGES, TAPE ON BACK, DO NOT OVERLAP

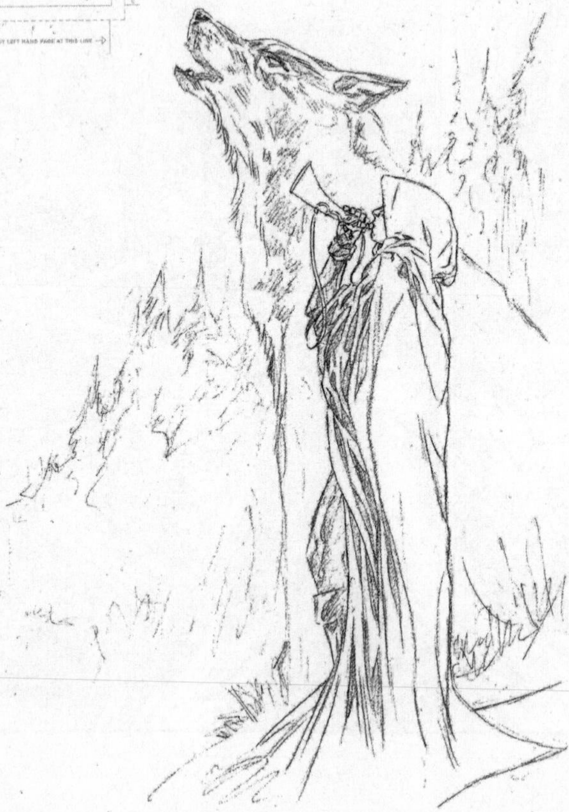

FABLES # 134

COVER SKETCHES —

⑤

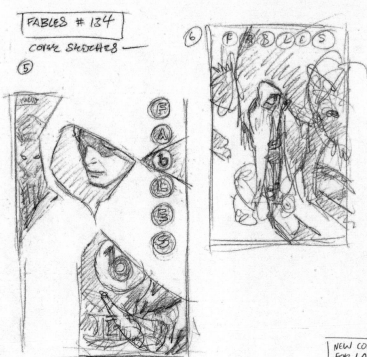

F
A
b
L
E
S

⑥

F A B L E S

NEW COSTUME FOR LAKE

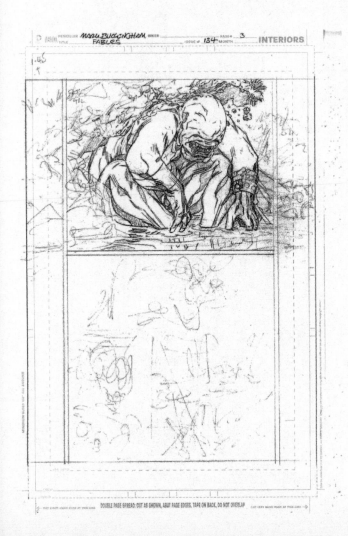

PENCILLER MARK BUCKINGHAM INKER
TITLE FABLES ISSUE # 134 MONTH
PAGE # 3
INTERIORS
DOUBLE PAGE SPREAD: CUT AS SHOWN, ABUT PAGE EDGES, TAPE ON BACK, DO NOT OVERLAP

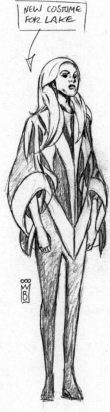

FABLES #134

COVER SKETCHES

1

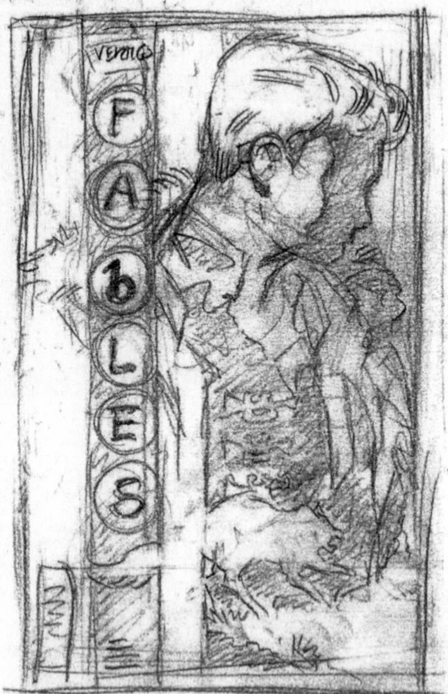
FABLES

2

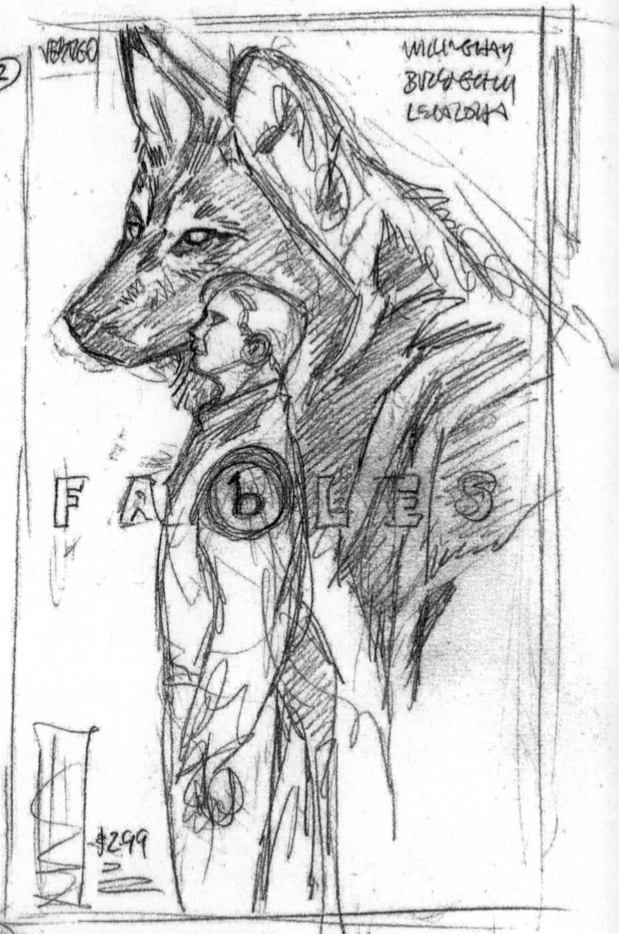
VERTIGO
FABLES
$2.99

3

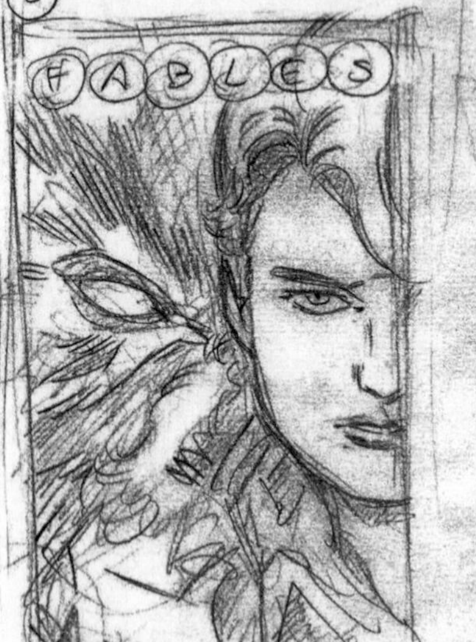
FABLES

4

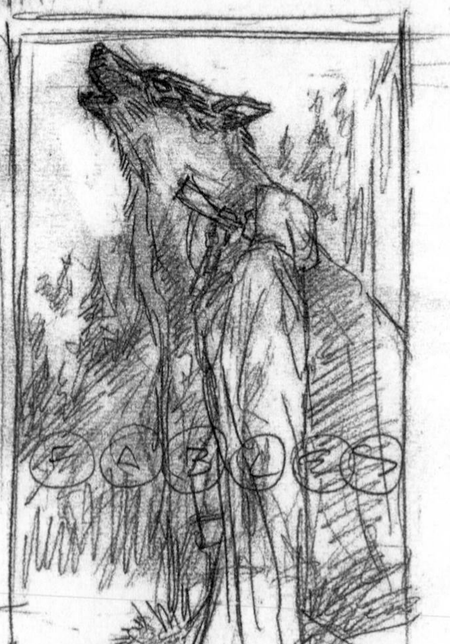
VERTIGO
FABLES